Feminist Theory

BLACKWELL PHILOSOPHY ANTHOLOGIES

Each volume in this outstanding series provides an authoritative and comprehensive collection of the essential primary readings from philosophy's main fields of study. Designed to complement the *Blackwell Companions to Philosophy* series, each volume represents an unparalleled resource in its own right, and will provide the ideal platform for course use.

1 Cottingham: *Western Philosophy: An Anthology*
2 Cahoone: *From Modernism to Postmodernism: An Anthology* (expanded second edition)
3 LaFollette: *Ethics in Practice: An Anthology* (second edition)
4 Goodin and Pettit: *Contemporary Political Philosophy: An Anthology*
5 Eze: *African Philosophy: An Anthology*
6 McNeill and Feldman: *Continental Philosophy: An Anthology*
7 Kim and Sosa: *Metaphysics: An Anthology*
8 Lycan: *Mind and Cognition: An Anthology* (second edition)
9 Kuhse and Singer: *Bioethics: An Anthology*
10 Cummins and Cummins: *Minds, Brains, and Computers – The Foundations of Cognitive Science: An Anthology*
11 Sosa and Kim: *Epistemology: An Anthology*
12 Kearney and Rasmussen: *Continental Aesthetics – Romanticism to Postmodernism: An Anthology*
13 Martinich and Sosa: *Analytic Philosophy: An Anthology*
14 Jacquette: *Philosophy of Logic: An Anthology*
15 Jacquette: *Philosophy of Mathematics: An Anthology*
16 Harris, Pratt, and Waters: *American Philosophies: An Anthology*
17 Emmanuel and Goold: *Modern Philosophy – From Descartes to Nietzsche: An Anthology*
18 Scharff and Dusek: *Philosophy of Technology – The Technological Condition: An Anthology*
19 Light and Rolston: *Environmental Ethics: An Anthology*
20 Taliaferro and Griffiths: *Philosophy of Religion: An Anthology*
21 Lamarque and Olsen: *Aesthetics and the Philosophy of Art – The Analytic Tradition: An Anthology*
22 John and Lopes: *Philosophy of Literature – Contemporary and Classic Readings: An Anthology*
23 Cudd and Andreasen: *Feminist Theory: A Philosophical Anthology*

Feminist Theory: A Philosophical Anthology

Edited by

Ann E. Cudd and Robin O. Andreasen

Blackwell Publishing

BLACKWELL PUBLISHING
350 Main Street, Malden, MA 02148–5020, USA
108 Cowley Road, Oxford OX4 1JF, UK
550 Swanston Street, Carlton, Victoria 3053, Australia

First published 2005 by Blackwell Publishing Ltd

Library of Congress Cataloging-in-Publication Data

Feminist theory : a philosophical anthology/edited by Ann E. Cudd and Robin O. Andreasen.
p. cm. — (Blackwell philosophy anthologies ; 23)
Includes bibliographical references and index.
ISBN 1–4051–1660–9 (hardcover : alk. paper) — ISBN 1–4051–1661–7 (pbk. : alk. paper)
1. Feminism. 2. Feminist theory. I. Cudd, Ann E., 1959– II. Andreasen, Robin O. III. Series.

B2424.F45F46 2004
305.42′01—dc22

2004009495

A catalogue record for this title is available from the British Library

Set in 9/11 pt Ehrhardt
by Integra Software Services Pvt. Ltd, Pondicherry, India
Printed and bound in the United Kingdom
by MPG Books Ltd, Bodmin, Cornwall

The publisher's policy is to use permanent paper from mills that operate a sustainable forestry policy, and which has been manufactured from pulp processed using acid-free and elementary chlorine-free practices. Furthermore, the publisher ensures that the text paper and cover board used have met acceptable environmental accreditation standards.

For further information on Blackwell Publishing, visit our website:
www.blackwellpublishing.com

Contents

Acknowledgments

Ann Cudd would like to thank her teachers and mentors in feminist theory, Tamara Horowitz and Jean Hampton, who are sadly no longer able to receive that thanks, and Annette Baier and Marcia Homiak. She also acknowledges the assistance of Jan Emerson of the Women's Studies Program at the University of Kansas.

Robin Andreasen would like to thank her friends and colleagues in the Philosophy Department and Women's Studies programs at the University of Delaware and the University of Wisconsin–Madison. Special thanks are due to Fred Adams and Elliott Sober for their ongoing guidance and mentorship. She would also like to acknowledge the University of Delaware General University Research Fund for financial support at an early stage of this project.

We would both like to thank Jeff Dean and Nirit Simon at Blackwell Publishing for their helpful and informative assistance. Finally, we would like to thank our families for their loving support and encouragement.

Text acknowledgments

The editors and publisher gratefully acknowledge the permission granted to reproduce the copyright material in this book:

1 Mary Wollstonecraft, "Of the Pernicious Effects which arise from the Unnatural Distinctions Established in Society," *A Vindication of the Rights of Woman*, originally published in 1792.

2 John Stuart Mill, from *The Subjection of Women*, originally published in 1869.

3 Simone de Beauvoir, pp. xv–xxxiv and 301 from *The Second Sex*, translated by H. M. Parshley. New York: Vintage Books, 1952. © 1952 and renewed 1980 by Alfred A. Knopf, a division of Random House, Inc. Used by permission of Alfred A. Knopf, a division of Random House, Inc. and The Random House Group Ltd.

4 Kate Millett, "Theory of Sexual Politics," pp. 23–58 from *Sexual Politics*. Chicago, IL: University of Illinois Press, 2000. © 1969, 1970, 1990, 2000 by Kate Millett. Reprinted by permission of Georges Borchardt, Inc., Literary Agency.

5 bell hooks, "Black Women: Shaping Feminist Theory," pp. 1–15 and 165 from *Feminist Theory: From Margin to Center*. Boston, MA: South End Press, 1984. Reprinted by permission of South End Press.

6 Ann E. Cudd and Leslie E. Jones, "Sexism," pp. 102–17 from R. G. Frey and C. H. Wellman (eds), *A Companion to Applied Ethics*. Oxford: Blackwell, 2003. Reprinted by permission of Blackwell Publishing Ltd.

7 Marilyn Frye, "Oppression," pp. 1–16 from *The Politics of Reality*. Freedom, CA: The Crossing Press, 1983. © 1983 by Marilyn Frye, Ten Speed Press, Berkeley, CA. Available at Ten Speed Press by calling 1-800-841-2665, or online at www.tenspeed.com.

8 Iris Marion Young, "Five Faces of Oppression," pp. 270–90 from *Philosophical Forum* 19(4), 1998. Reprinted by permission of Blackwell Publishing Ltd.

9 Sandra Bartky, "On Psychological Oppression," pp. 22–32 and 121–4 (notes) from *Femininity and Domination: Studies in the Phenomenology of Oppression*. New York: Routledge, 1990. Reproduced by permission of Routledge/Taylor & Francis Books, Inc.

10 Elisabeth A. Lloyd, "Pre-Theoretical Assumptions in Evolutionary Explanations of Female Sexuality," pp. 139–53 from *Philosophical Studies* 69, 1993. Reproduced with kind permission from Kluwer Academic Publishers.

11 Louise M. Antony, "Natures and Norms," pp. 8–36 from *Ethics* 111(1), 2000. Reprinted by permission of the University of Chicago Press and the author.

12 Judith Butler, "Subjects of Sex/Gender/Desire," pp. 3–14, 18–22 and 193–7 (notes) from *Gender Trouble*, 2nd edn. New York: Routledge, 1999. Reproduced by permission of Routledge/Taylor & Francis Books, Inc. and the author.

13 Sally Haslanger, "Gender and Race: (What) Are They? (What) Do We Want Them to Be?," pp. 31–55 from *Noûs* 34(1), 2000. Reprinted by permission of Blackwell Publishing Ltd.

14 Genevieve Lloyd, "The Man of Reason," pp. 18–37 from *Metaphilosophy* 10(1), 1979. Reprinted by permission of Blackwell Publishing Ltd.

15 Elizabeth Anderson, "Feminist Epistemology: An Interpretation and a Defense," pp. 50–84 from *Hypatia* 10(3), 1995. Reprinted by permission of Indiana University Press, as the publisher.

16 Helen E. Longino, "Can there be a Feminist Science?," pp. 51–64 from *Hypatia* 2(3), 1987. Reprinted by permission of Indiana University Press, as the publisher.

17 Sandra Harding, "Rethinking Standpoint Epistemology: What is Strong Objectivity?," pp. 49–82 from Linda Alcoff and Elizabeth Potter (eds), *Feminist Epistemologies*. New York: Routledge, 1993. Reproduced by permission of Routledge/Taylor & Francis Books, Inc. and the author.

18 Annette C. Baier, "The Need for More than Justice," from *Canadian Journal of Philosophy*, supp. Vol. 13 (1987). Reprinted by the University of Calgary Press, Calgary, Alberta.

19 Joan Tronto, "An Ethic of Care," pp. 125–37, 141–52 and 208–13 (notes) from *Moral Boundaries*. New York, Routledge, 1993. Reproduced by permission of Routledge/Taylor & Francis Books, Inc. and the author.

20 Eva Feder Kittay, "Vulnerability and the Moral Nature of Dependency Relations," pp. 51–73 and 198–202 (notes) from *Love's Labor: Essays on Women, Equality, and Dependency*. New York: Routledge, 1999. Reproduced by permission of Routledge/Taylor & Francis Books, Inc. and the author.

21 Jean Hampton, "Feminist Contractarianism," pp. 337–68 from Louise M. Antony and Charlotte E. Witt (eds.), *A Mind of One's Own: Feminist Essays on Reason and Objectivity*, 2nd edn. Boulder, CO: Westview Press, 2002. © 1992 by Westview Press. Reprinted by permission of Westview Press, a member of Perseus Books, L.L.C.

22 Martha C. Nussbaum, "Women and Cultural Universals," pp. 29–54 and 377–84 (notes) from *Sex and Social Justice*, Oxford: Oxford University Press, 1999. © 1999 by Martha Nussbaum. Used by permission of Oxford University Press, Inc.

23 Jean Grimshaw, "Autonomy and Identity in Feminist Thinking," pp. 90–108 from Morwenna Griffiths and Margaret Whitford (eds.), *Feminist Perspectives in Philosophy*. Indianapolis, IN: Indiana University Press, 1988. Reproduced with permission of Palgrave Macmillan.

24 Marilyn Friedman, "Autonomy, Social Disruption, and Women," pp. 35–51 from Catriona Mackenzie and Natalie Stoljar (eds.), *Relational Autonomy: Feminist Perspectives on Autonomy, Agency, and the Self*. New York: Oxford University Press, 2000. © 2000 by Oxford University Press, Inc. Used by permission of Oxford University Press, Inc.

25 Anita L. Allen, "Forgetting Yourself," pp. 104–23 from Diana Tietjens Meyers (ed.), *Feminists Rethink the Self*. Boulder, CO: Westview Press, 1997. © 1997 by Westview

Press. Reprinted by permission of Westview Press, a member of Perseus Books, L.L.C.

26 Susan Brison, "Outliving Oneself," pp. 38–50, 53–5, 57–66 and 133–8 from *Aftermath: Violence and the Remaking of the Self*. Princeton, NJ: Princeton University Press, 2002. © 2002 by Princeton University Press. Reprinted by permission of Princeton University Press.

27 Simone de Beauvoir, "Conclusion," pp. 716–32 from *The Second Sex*, translated and edited by H. M. Parshley. New York: Alfred A. Knopf, 1953. © 1952 and renewed 1980 by Alfred A. Knopf, a division of Random House, Inc. Used by permission of Alfred A. Knopf, a division of Random House, Inc. and The Random House Group Ltd.

28 Catharine A. MacKinnon, "Difference and Dominance: On Sex Discrimination," pp. 32–45 and 240–5 (notes) from *Feminism Unmodified: Discourses on Life and Law*. Cambridge, MA: Harvard University Press, 1987. © 1987 by the President and Fellows of Harvard College.

29 Susan Moller Okin, "Toward a Humanist Justice," pp. 170–86 and 209–10 (notes) from *Justice, Gender, and the Family*. New York: Basic Books, 1989. © 1989 by Basic Books, Inc. Reprinted by permission of Basic Books, a member of Perseus Books, L.L.C.

30 Drucilla Cornell, "Feminism, Utopianism, and the Role of the Ideal in Political Philosophy," pp. 174–86 and 229–32 (notes) from *At the Heart of Freedom: Feminism, Sex, and Equality*. Princeton, NJ: Princeton University Press, 1998. © 1998 by Princeton University Press. Reprinted by permission of Princeton University Press.

Every effort has been made to trace copyright holders and to obtain their permission for the use of copyright material. The publisher apologizes for any errors or omissions in the above list and would be grateful if notified of any corrections that should be incorporated in future reprints or editions of this book.

Introduction

I Feminist Theory and its Relation to Philosophy

Feminist theory is the attempt to make intellectual sense of, and then to critique, the subordination of women to men. As such it has a relatively short history, for the history of seeing subordination as something that needs to be understood, rather than simply accommodated or perhaps given a rationale, is relatively short. This history begins with the Enlightenment, which brought forward the idea that legitimate authority requires the consent (in some sense) of those who are asked to submit to it. Of course, the thinkers that one immediately connects with the Enlightenment did not think that this applied to women (or many other groups, for that matter). But ideas have a way of getting loose and taking root in places not originally intended for them, and this was the case for liberalism. Thus, early feminist theory took root in the imaginations of women and men such as Mary Astell, Olympe de Gouges, Mary Wollstonecraft and Poulain de Le Barre, and later, Harriet Taylor and John Stuart Mill, and the suffragists in England and the United States. Feminist theory, though, begins as a self-consciously distinct field only in the latter part of the twentieth century, with the publication of Simone de Beauvoir's *The Second Sex*.

Making intellectual sense of the subordination of women to men has turned out to be a more encompassing project than political analyses of it might suggest. For women are dominated not only politically and economically, but also sexually, physically, and in nearly every field of artistic or intellectual endeavor and philosophical thought. Women are not only under represented in the history of ideas, they are also largely denigrated by many of these theories and ideas. Since the end of the Second World War, however, women have come in ever larger numbers to the academy and are now a significant minority of intellectuals and theorists in many fields. This has slowly but assuredly led to the recognition of the male bias of the history of ideas and of society. This bias has resulted in several distinct kinds of mistakes that feminist theorists have revealed. One mistake is sexism, that is, taking men to be of greater value than women. This anthology includes an entire part of chapters that characterize and criticize sexism. Another is androcentrism, which is taking maleness or masculinity to be the norm for humanness or humanity. Many of the chapters explicitly or implicitly reveal this sort of mistake in the history of ideas. A third is the illegitimate cognitive authority that males and androcentric theories have been accorded. This kind of mistake is perhaps the most difficult to recognize. In dispassionate intellectual discourse ideas are supposed to stand or fall on their own merits. When they do fall to criticism, it is considered awkward or indelicate to diagnose the previous acceptance of the theory as due to something other than the (ultimately mistaken) persuasiveness of the idea itself. Sometimes, though, the idea seems so implausible on examination that the only explanation of its previous acceptance is a misplaced authority lent to the author of it. Each of these mistakes has been revealed through feminist analysis, and no doubt more discoveries are to come.

Many of the early feminist theorists are philosophers by training and affiliation. Philosophers are trained to conceptualize and theorize, to question assumptions and to deduce principles from the assumptions that they have justified. Thus it was logical that feminist theory would begin philosophically. Much important work in feminist theory has been done in the past three decades by historians, literary theorists, anthropologists, sociologists, political scientists, and economists. Philosophers, however, provide a uniquely foundational and general perspective from which to understand women's subordination. This anthology aims to capture and characterize the unique perspective of philosophers on feminist theory.

This is not to say that philosophy has an easy relation to feminism, any more than the other disciplines just mentioned. Indeed, it must be admitted that perhaps more than the others, philosophy fears feminism. Feminist theory has quickly come to challenge much of what has been said by the long history of philosophy as itself deeply biased by sexism and androcentrism. Such challenges have not always been welcomed by influential philosophers. Feminism is thus not yet a part of the mainstream of philosophical thought. When one does epistemology from a feminist perspective, for example, it is called feminist epistemology, not epistemology *tout court*. Feminist philosophers have had to choose sides – either they will be considered feminist philosophers, and thus not completely philosophers, or they will couch their feminist ideas in carefully worded phrases so as not to be written off by the mainstream philosophers of their chosen field. This unfortunate state of affairs forced many women in philosophy who wished to be part of the mainstream dialogue among philosophers to avoid feminist theory, or at least to avoid calling themselves or being called "feminists". Particularly among analytic philosophers, the dominant strain of philosophy in the Anglo-American world, this dilemma has been powerful. However, in the past decade, many female (and some male) analytic philosophers have overcome their fear of feminism and joined in the project of feminist theorizing. The result has been a flowering of philosophical thought that has come to be known as the analytic feminism movement in philosophy. This anthology draws heavily, though not exclusively, on this burgeoning literature, in the hope that by doing so more productive dialogue will arise between and among feminist theorists of all stripes and philosophers who have not dared to call themselves feminists.

II The Value of Feminist Theory

Feminist theory affords several intellectual and practical values. First, it sustains social criticism, by revealing subordination and the moral and political implications of that subordination. Since there are by definition those who benefit from others' subordination, it is essential that there be a way of proving that subordination exists and that it is morally unsupportable. Secondly, it provides a lens through which ideas and social practices can be analyzed. Feminist theory has proven to be applicable across a wide variety of human thought and action, for it has shown that much of what we do, and how we conceptualize what we do, is affected by gender. Thirdly, feminist theory offers visions of liberation, of what life, persons, and society would be like without the subordination of women.

For philosophy specifically feminist theory has unique value. Critical analysis of past philosophers through the lens of feminist theory allows us to see how their theories are infected by sexism. Although this sort of critical analysis can take the form of simply pointing out sexism as a kind of meanness, at a deeper level it can allow us to see how theories and ideas can be simply false or skewed by taking it for granted that the subordination of women is justifiable or natural. Theories of justice are the most obvious examples of theories shown to be false by revealing them as sexist, since sexism is a form of injustice, after all. Ethical theory, as is shown by the chapters in Part V of this anthology, are good examples of theories that have been simply skewed by the sexist assumption that the activities performed by women are not rational activities to be judged by the standards of right and wrong.

Finally, through feminist theorizing philosophers can reclaim women's writings from the past as a part of the dialogue of philosophy. Feminist theory has expanded the domain of what counts as ethical or political theory, of what sorts of questions epistemology should entertain, of what counts as a theory of the self. Once this domain has been expanded and shown to be a proper part of philosophy, it is possible to look back at the history of ideas and see that women who discussed such issues and questions were in fact philosophizing. Feminist theory also has encouraged historians to look again at the writings of women to see whether they have been forgotten more because of their inferior gender than for the inferior quality of their ideas. This anthology does not include chapters pursuing this specifically historical project, worthy though it is, but rather focuses on the work of specifically feminist theorists. Not surprisingly, many of the women who have been rediscovered by this project play no part in the history of feminist theory, but rather engaged their contemporaries in the philosophical questions of the day, which only rarely directly considered the subordination of women.

III Aims of this Book

The chapters in this anthology have been selected and arranged to address the major questions of feminist theory in philosophical way. The editors have attempted to choose chapters that are well argued and well representative of major views among feminist theorists, although at times we have had to choose sides. In almost all such cases we have sided with what we consider to be the most well-argued position from the perspective of analytic feminist philosophers. Thus we have attempted to provide a book that is analytic in orientation, though not exclusive, to expand the dialogue among philosophers and feminists from different fields and orientations. One justification for our choice is that philosophically oriented feminist theory has been dominated in other disciplines by continental feminists. We believe that is at least in part because analytic feminist theory is a latecomer for reasons explained above. There are few collections of analytic feminist work, the hallmark exception being the excellent volume, *A Mind of One's Own*, edited by Louise Antony and Charlotte Witt, now in its second edition. This anthology is intended to present another philosophical perspective on feminism, both for philosophers and for those working in other fields, as well as for students of philosophy and of feminism.

IV The Questions

This book is divided into parts, each of which address what we consider to be the most significant questions of feminism. These questions (and part titles) are: (1) What is feminism? (2) What is sexism? (3) What is gender? (4) Is knowledge gendered? (5) Is value gendered? (6) What is a self? (7) What would liberation be? Some of these questions map into some of the major fields of philosophy, such as question 4, which is properly a part of epistemology, question 5, which is a question in ethics, and question 6, which is both an issue of metaphysics and of ethics. But the other questions reveal the unique contributions of feminism to philosophy.

We begin the book quite logically with the question of what feminism is. The chapters in this first part are included to develop an understanding of the central developments in the history of feminist thought, including pieces from the three recognized "waves" of feminist theory and activism. These chapters seek to elucidate the situation of women and the need for a theoretical understanding of it. Since feminism begins as a movement for freedom from oppression, the second part of the book addresses the question of what sexist oppression is. This questions deals with the central claim of feminism: that women are oppressed. The chapters in this part theorize the nature of sexism and of oppression, and the unique aspects of the oppression of women as distinct from other oppressed groups. The third part takes up what we consider to be the single greatest contribution of feminist theory to thought: the sex/gender distinction. The chapters of this part consider the alleged scientific understandings of sex, and the ways that these have been confused with socially constructed differences of gender, and the nature of the claim that some difference is socially constructed. In the fourth part of the book we include chapters in the sub-field that has come to be known as feminist epistemology. These readings address the ways in which conceptions of gender and gender-based norms influence conceptions of rationality, knowledge, and scientific objectivity. The fifth part includes chapters on feminist ethics, including two authors' takes on the ethics of care, a chapter on contractarianism as a feminist ethic, and finally a chapter on the universality of moral and political principles. The sixth part takes up the question of the self as feminist philosophers have addressed it. A great deal of feminist work has been done on this in the past decade because of the importance of defining the self for moral and social theory. The chapters there include chapters on identity and autonomy. In the last part we ask what liberation would look like and include some chapters that address the question of whether liberation would require the elimination of gender. We also include a chapter that argues that freedom, not equality, is the important value for feminists to strive for.

V The Future of Feminist Theory and Philosophy

We hope that this anthology shows the rich interaction between feminist theory and philosophy, and encourages philosophers and feminists to continue devising new and better feminist theories. One might wonder whether feminist theory will some day come to be a mainstream branch of philosophy. There are good reasons to think that this will not be the case, nor that it is desirable. First there are institutional obstacles to this, since much feminist theory is developed as criticism of philosophy or the main currents of philosophy. Thus, it often seems not to fit within those main currents but to be talking about something that is beside the point. Second, although criticism is the main line of work that philosophers are in, the discipline sometimes balks at the depth of criticism that feminist theory offers. There are also good intellectual reasons for why feminist theory cannot be subsumed by philosophy. Feminist theory often advances through interdisciplinary work. Feminist theory will always need to connect to empirical social and natural sciences for observation of and evidence for subordination. Indeed the hallmark of feminist theory is its insistence on a connection to actual women's and men's lives. Philosophy regards itself as more foundational and prior to empirical observation, and this keeps those more empirically infused branches farther out from the main trunk of the philosophical tree.

It is sometimes asked of feminist theorists what would happen to their branch of intellectual endeavor if the day came when there was no sexism or no gender. To a feminist this is something like asking whether there would be a need for political philosophy if there were no need for government. It is perhaps a hopeful idea to consider, if somewhat difficult to imagine how that state might come about. If we consider the hypothetical philosophically, though, as philosophers are wont to consider the logically possible as if it were actual, we could say this: At that point feminist theory would be relegated to the collection of outmoded theories, not as Ptolemaic astronomy has been, or as craniometry was, but rather as the science of constructing mud huts no longer has a use, yet could be put to use should human needs, conditions, or desires change. That we have not reached beyond the pioneer days of conquering sexist oppression is clear, however. It is our hope that this anthology aids in clarifying our vision of both the present and the possibilities for an enlightened future.

Part I

What is Feminism?

Introduction to Part I

"Feminism" is a term that has acquired a number of different meanings, many of which indicate key turning points in the history of feminist thought. Feminist thought is sometimes characterized as occurring in waves. The first wave is often dated to the publication of Mary Wollstonecraft's *A Vindication of the Rights of Woman* (1792). Under the influence of nineteenth century liberal political philosophy, first wave feminism concerned itself largely with gaining equal political rights and economic opportunities for women. Since at this time the possession of rationality was taken to be the appropriate basis for the attribution of rights, liberal feminists argued for women's equality on the grounds that women have the same capacity to reason as men. Liberal feminist political action brought about many important changes in the situation of women. Not only did it result in women's suffrage in the 1920s, liberal feminists also won property rights for women, more reproductive freedoms, and greater access to education and the professional realm.

Soon after the ratification of the Nineteenth Amendment, there was a period of relative inactivity in feminist theory and politics. The second wave of feminism can most easily be dated to 1949 with the publication of Simone de Beauvoir's *The Second Sex*. This movement is sometimes characterized by its efforts to move beyond the first wave and its focus on the political and legal sources of women's inequality. Second wave feminists maintain that, although important, political and legal equality is not enough to end women's oppression. On their view, sexist oppression is not simply rooted in legal and political arrangements; its causes are all pervasive and deeply embedded in every aspect of human social life – including economic, political, and social arrangements as well as unquestioned norms, habits, everyday interactions, and personal relationships. Moreover, second wave feminists criticized first wave feminism for not going far enough in its economic reforms. They argued that feminism must demand full economic equality for women, rather than simple economic survival. Third, second wave feminists challenged the public/private dichotomy by scrutinizing areas of human social life that were previously seen as political – such as the institution of marriage, motherhood, heterosexual relationships, women's sexuality, and so forth. Thus, rather than trying to reform existing political structures, second wave feminists aim to radically transform almost every aspect of personal and political life.

Third wave feminism began in the late 1980s by feminists who wanted to make women's diversity – or diversity in general – more central to feminist theory and politics. For example, women of color maintained that their experiences, interests, and concerns were not fully represented by second wave feminism. Part of the reason is that, historically, second wave feminism was largely represented by middle-class white women who tended to focus on the commonalities among women and their experiences of oppression without taking social circumstance into account. In response to this trend, feminists of color argued that women from different social groups – racial, economic, sexual, and so forth – experience different types of oppression. They also questioned whether it makes sense to talk about "woman"as a single unified category – or about "women's oppression" as single unified phenomenon. Other third wave feminists have also questioned the category "woman." They challenge its very basis – namely, the division of people into sexes and genders – and argue that feminism should no longer be viewed as a cohesive political and theoretical movement with common liberatory aims for all women (see also Butler, Part 3). Rather, they maintain that we need a feminism that accepts diversity and allows for a multiplicity of feminist goals.

The readings in this part aim to represent some of the central developments in the history of feminist thought. We begin with a chapter from Mary Wollstonecraft's *A Vindication of the Rights of Woman*, which is widely acknowledged as one of the first sustained works in feminist philosophy. In the selection included here, Wollstonecraft describes the psychological and economic damage that is done to women as a result of their economic dependence on men and their exclusion from the public sphere. It is important to note, however, that Wollstonecraft does not defend full political equality for women. Rather, she defends differential gender roles but argues that women would be more virtuous and better able to fulfill their roles, if there were more economic and political equality between the sexes.

Nearly a century later, John Stuart Mill argues on liberal grounds that "the legal subordination of one sex to another is wrong in itself, and is one of the chief hindrances to human improvement." Although Mill agrees with Wollstonecraft that a system of inequality is unjust and harmful to society, he goes further by defending women's full political and legal equality. He argues that there is no rational justification for a system of inequality of rights. It was not adopted as the best result of a conscientious comparison among various modes of social organization. Rather, it rests on custom alone. He adds that over the course of history, many European social institutions have gradually abandoned systems of inequality – such as slavery and feudalism – and asks why the same has not been done for women. Mill also addresses the then commonly held assumption that men's and women's natures adapt them to differential social roles. He maintains that to the extent that gender-based differences exist, they are differences only in averages. Hence, even if the average man is better than the average woman at something, some women might be better than some men at that that very same thing. Moreover, he argues that what is referred to as "the nature of the two sexes" is an artificial construct. On his view it is not possible to know whether men and women are different by nature, since women have always been in a subordinate position relative to men. Finally, he argues that even if women are, by nature, poorly suited for some task or social role, this does not justify legalized inequality. After all, "[w]hat women by nature cannot do, it is quite superfluous to forbid them from doing. What they can do, but not so well as the men who are their competitors, competition suffices to exclude them from."

As mentioned above, second wave feminism is often dated to the publication of Simone de Beauvoir's *The Second Sex*. One cannot overstate the importance of this work, for it raises a number of important themes that are still under discussion in current feminist discourse. In the selection included here, Beauvoir argues that gender differences are not rooted in biology. Rather they are artificial constructs that work to reinforce women's oppression. This theme is reflected in her classic statement: "[o]ne is not born, but rather becomes a woman...; it is civilization as a whole that produces this creature... which is described as feminine." It is also reflected in her argument that historical and contemporary constructions of gender treat masculinity as a positive norm and femininity as a deviation from the masculine ideal – thus making women the "other," or the "second sex." Of course, feminists today are still discussing these ideas by developing gender constructivism and by arguing that that andocentric bias is an all-pervasive feature of our social, political, and economic structures.

Kate Millett's *Sexual Politics* (1970) is another early and influential example of second wave feminism. In "Theory of Sexual Politics," Millett provides an overarching account patriarchy – male control of nearly all aspects of public and private life – and women's oppression. Along with Beauvoir and a few others, she was one of the first feminists to argue that the causes of women's subordination run much deeper than political and economic inequality. She was also among to first to defend an expanded conception of politics – namely, one that sees the personal life, including the everyday relations between the sexes, as political. She maintains that patriarchy is all pervasive and deeply entrenched in nearly every aspect of human social life. Indeed, some of the most powerful mechanisms of women's oppression are those that exercise their power on a daily basis. For example, gender differences (masculinity and femininity) are, on her view, ideological constructs that were fabricated so as to ensure women's subordination to men. Other examples include the perpetuation of patriarchy through everyday institutions such as religious and educational institutions, family structures, the institution of marriage, heterosexual relationships, and so forth. She concludes that patriarchal ideology is so ubiquitous and its power is so great that women often unknowingly consent to their own oppression.

In "Black Women: Shaping Feminist Theory," bell hooks argues that earlier forms of feminism have been biased in the issues that they address and the perspectives that they represent. She maintains that many feminists have traditionally assumed that all women are oppressed in the same way. In addition, due to an overrepresentation of middle-class white feminists, earlier forms of feminism have tended to overlooked many of the issues and concerns specific to women of color. Hooks challenges both the pattern and the assumption, first by arguing that although women everywhere suffer oppression, different groups experience different forms of oppression due to the ways in which different types of oppression (racial, economic, sexual, etc.) interact. For example, the oppression experienced by middle-class white women differs significantly from the oppression experienced by middle-class African American women. Likewise, the oppression experienced by heterosexual women differs from the oppression experienced by lesbian women, and so forth. Second, hooks maintains that white women have been complicit in the perpetuation of racism – in part by overlooking women of color and partly by implicitly or explicitly silencing them in feminist discourse. She adds that women of color need to assert their perspectives and experiences so that they can play a more central role in shaping feminist theory.

1

Of the Pernicious Effects which Arise from the Unnatural Distinctions Established in Society

Mary Wollstonecraft

From the respect paid to property flow, as from a poisoned fountain, most of the evils and vices which render this world such a dreary scene to the contemplative mind. For it is in the most polished society that noisome reptiles and venomous serpents lurk under the rank herbage; and there is voluptuousness pampered by the still sultry air, which relaxes every good disposition before it ripens into virtue.

One class presses on another, for all are aiming to procure respect on account of their property; and property once gained will procure the respect due only to talents and virtue. Men neglect the duties incumbent on man, yet are treated like demigods. Religion is also separated from morality by a ceremonial veil, yet men wonder that the world is almost, literally speaking, a den of sharpers or oppressors.

There is a homely proverb, which speaks a shrewd truth, that whoever the devil finds idle he will employ. And what but habitual idleness can hereditary wealth and titles produce? For man is so constituted that he can only attain a proper use of his faculties by exercising them, and will not exercise them unless necessity of some kind first set the wheels in motion. Virtue likewise can only be acquired by the discharge of relative duties; but the importance of these sacred duties will scarcely be felt by the being who is cajoled out of his humanity by the flattery of sycophants. There must be more equality established in society, or morality will never gain ground, and this virtuous equality will not rest firmly even when founded on a rock, if one-half of mankind be chained to its bottom by fate, for they will be continually undermining it through ignorance or pride.

It is vain to expect virtue from women till they are in some degree independent of men; nay, it is vain to expect that strength of natural affection which would make them good wives and mothers. Whilst they are absolutely dependent on their husbands they will be cunning, mean, and selfish; and the men who can be gratified by the fawning fondness of spaniel-like affection have not much delicacy, for love is not to be bought; in any sense of the words, its silken wings are instantly shrivelled up when anything beside a return in kind is sought. Yet whilst wealth enervates men, and women live, as it were, by their personal charms, how can we expect them to discharge those ennobling duties which equally require exertion and self-denial? Hereditary property sophisticates the mind, and the unfortunate victims to it – if I may so express myself – swathed from their birth, seldom exert the locomotive faculty of body or mind, and thus

Mary Wollstonecraft, "Of the Pernicious Effects which arise from the Unnatural Distinctions Established in Society," *A Vindication of the Rights of Woman*, originally published in 1792.

viewing everything through one medium, and that a false one, they are unable to discern in what true merit and happiness consist. False, indeed, must be the light when the drapery of situation hides the man, and makes him stalk in masquerade, dragging from one scene of dissipation to another the nerveless limbs that hang with stupid listlessness, and rolling round the vacant eye, which plainly tells us that there is no mind at home.

I mean therefore to infer that the society is not properly organised which does not compel men and women to discharge their respective duties by making it the only way to acquire that countenance from their fellow-creatures, which every human being wishes some way to attain. The respect consequently which is paid to wealth and mere personal charms is a true north-east blast that blights the tender blossoms of affection and virtue. Nature has wisely attached affections to duties to sweeten toil, and to give that vigour to the exertions of reason which only the heart can give. But the affections which is put on merely because it is the appropriated insignia of a certain character, when its duties are not fulfilled, is one of the empty compliments which vice and folly are obliged to pay to virtue and the real nature of things.

To illustrate my opinion, I need only observe that when a woman is admired for her beauty, and suffers herself to be so far intoxicated by the admiration she receives as to neglect to discharge the indispensable duty of a mother, she sins against herself by neglecting to cultivate an affection that would equally tend to make her useful and happy. True happiness – I mean all the contentment and virtuous satisfaction that can be snatched in this imperfect state – must arise from well-regulated affections, and an affection includes a duty. Men are not aware of the misery they cause, and the vicious weakness they cherish, by only inciting women to render themselves pleasing; they do not consider that they thus make natural and artificial duties clash by sacrificing the comfort and respectability of a woman's life to voluptuous notions of beauty, when in nature they all harmonise.

Cold would be the heart of a husband, were he not rendered unnatural by early debauchery, who did not feel more delight at seeing his child suckled by its mother than the most artful wanton tricks could ever raise, yet this natural way of cementing the matrimonial tie, and twisting esteem with fonder recollections, wealth leads women to spurn. To preserve their beauty, and wear the flowery crown of the day, which gives them a kind of right to reign for a short time over the sex, they neglect to stamp impressions on their husbands' hearts that would be remembered with more tenderness when the snow on the head began to chill the bosom than even their virgin charms. The maternal solicitude of a reasonable affectionate woman is very interesting, and the chastened dignity with which a mother returns the caresses that she and her child receive from a father who has been fulfilling the serious duties of his station is not only a respectable, but a beautiful sight. So singular, indeed, are my feelings – and I have endeavoured not to catch factitious ones – that after having been fatigued with the sight of insipid grandeur and the slavish ceremonies that with cumbrous pomp supplied the place of domestic affections, I have turned to some other scene to relieve my eye by resting it on the refreshing green everywhere scattered by Nature. I have then viewed with pleasure a woman nursing her children, and discharging the duties of her station with perhaps merely a servant-maid to take off her hands the servile part of the household business. I have seen her prepare herself and children, with only the luxury of cleanliness, to receive her husband, who, returning weary home in the evening, found smiling babes and a clean hearth. My heart has loitered in the midst of the group, and has even throbbed with sympathetic emotion when the scraping of the well-known foot has raised a pleasing tumult.

Whilst my benevolence has been gratified by contemplating this artless picture, I have thought that a couple of this description, equally necessary and independent of each other, because each fulfilled the respective duties of their station, possessed all that life could give. Raised sufficiently above abject poverty not to be obliged to weigh the consequence of every farthing they spend, and having sufficient to prevent their attending to a frigid system of economy which narrows both heart and mind, I declare, so vulgar are my conceptions, that I know not what is wanted to render this the happiest as well as the most respectable situation in the world, but a taste for literature, to throw a little variety and interest into social converse, and some superfluous money to give to the needy and to buy books. For it is not pleasant when the heart is opened by compassion, and the head active in arranging plans of usefulness, to have a prim urchin continually twitching back the elbow to prevent the hand from drawing out an almost empty purse, whispering at the same time some prudential maxim about the priority of justice.

Destructive, however, as riches and inherited honours are to the human character, women are more debased and cramped, if possible, by them than men, because men may still in some degree unfold their faculties by becoming soldiers and statesmen.

As soldiers, I grant they can now only gather for the most part vain-glorious laurels, whilst they adjust to a hair the European balance, taking especial care that no bleak northern nook or sound incline the beam. But the days of true heroism are over, when a citizen fought for his country like a Fabricius or a Washington, and then returned to his farm to let his virtuous fervour run in a more placid, but not a less salutary, stream. No, our British heroes are oftener sent from the gaming-table than from the plough; and their passions have been rather inflamed by hanging with dumb suspense on the turn of a die, than sublimated by panting after the adventurous march of virtue in the historic page.

The statesman, it is true, might with more propriety quit the faro bank, or card-table, to guide the helm, for he has still but to shuffle and trick – the whole system of British politics, if system it may courteously be called, consisting in multiplying dependents and contriving taxes which grind the poor to pamper the rich. Thus a war, or any wild-goose chase, is, as the vulgar use the phrase, a lucky turn-up of patronage for the minister, whose chief merit is the art of keeping himself in place. It is not necessary then that he should have bowels for the poor, so he can secure for his family the odd trick. Or should some show of respect, for what is termed with ignorant ostentation an Englishman's birthright, be expedient to bubble the gruff mastiff that he has to lead by the nose, he can make an empty show, very safely, by giving his single voice, and suffering his light squadron to file off to the other side. And when a question of humanity is agitated, he may dip a sop in the milk of human kindness to silence Cerberus, and talk of the interest which his heart takes in an attempt to make the earth no longer cry for vengeance as it sucks in its children's blood, though his cold hand may at the very moment rivet their chains, by sanctioning the abominable traffic. A minister is no longer a minister, than while he can carry a point, which he is determined to carry. Yet it is not necessary that a minister should feel like a man, when a bold push might shake his seat.

But, to have done with these episodical observations, let me return to the more specious slavery which chains the very soul of woman, keeping her for ever under the bondage of ignorance.

The preposterous distinctions of rank, which render civilisation a curse, by dividing the world between voluptuous tyrants and cunning envious dependents, corrupt, almost equally, every class of people, because respectability is not attached to the discharge of the relative duties of life, but to the station, and when the duties are not fulfilled the affections cannot gain sufficient strength to fortify the virtue of which they are the natural reward. Still there are some loop-holes out of which a man may creep, and dare to think and act for himself; but for a woman it is an herculean task, because she has difficulties peculiar to her sex to overcome, which require almost superhuman powers.

A truly benevolent legislator always endeavours to make it the interest of each individual to be virtuous; and thus private virtue becoming the cement of public happiness, an orderly whole is consolidated by the tendency of all the parts towards a common centre. But the private or public virtue of woman is very problematical, for Rousseau, and a numerous list of male writers, insist that she should all her life be subjected to a severe restraint, that of propriety. Why subject her to propriety – blind propriety – if she be capable of acting from a nobler spring, if she be an heir of immortality? Is sugar always to be produced by vital blood? Is one half of the human species, like the poor African slaves, to be subject to prejudices that brutalise them, when principles would be a surer guard, only to sweeten the cup of man? Is not this indirectly to deny woman reason? for a gift is a mockery, if it be unfit for use.

Women are, in common with men, rendered weak and luxurious by the relaxing pleasures which wealth procures; but added to this they are made slaves to their persons, and must render them alluring that man may lend them his reason to guide their tottering steps aright. Or should they be ambitious, they must govern their tyrants by sinister tricks, for without right there cannot be any incumbent duties. The laws respecting woman, which I mean to discuss in a future part, make an absurd unit of a man and his wife; and then, by the easy transition of only considering him as responsible, she is reduced to a mere cipher.

The being who discharges the duties of its station is independent; and, speaking of women at large, their first duty is to themselves as rational creatures, and the next, in point of importance, as citizens, is that, which includes so many, of a mother. The rank in life which dispenses with their fulfilling this duty, necessarily degrades them by making them mere dolls. Or should they turn to something more important than merely fitting drapery upon a smooth block, their minds are only occupied by some soft platonic attachment; or the actual management of an intrigue may keep their thoughts in motion; for when they neglect domestic duties, they have it not in their power to take the field and march and counter-march like soldiers, or wrangle in the senate to keep their faculties from rusting.

I know that, as a proof of the inferiority of the sex, Rousseau has exultingly exclaimed, How can they leave the nursery for the camp! And the camp has by some moralists been proved the school of the most heroic virtues; though I think it would puzzle a keen casuist to prove the reasonableness of the greater number of wars that have dubbed heroes. I do not mean to consider this question critically; because, having frequently viewed these freaks of ambition as the first natural mode of civilisation, when the ground must be torn up, and the woods cleared by fire and sword, I do not choose to call them pests; but surely the present system of war has little connection with virtue of any denomination, being rather the school of *finesse* and effeminacy than of fortitude.

Yet, if defensive war, the only justifiable war, in the present advanced state of society, where virtue can show its face and ripen amidst the rigours which purify the air on the mountain's top, were alone to be adopted as just and glorious, the true heroism of antiquity might again animate female bosoms. But fair and softly, gentle reader, male or female, do not alarm thyself, for though I have compared the character of a modern soldier with that of a civilised woman, I am not going to advise them to turn their distaff into a musket, though I sincerely wish to see the bayonet converted into a pruning-hook. I only re-created an imagination, fatigued by contemplating the vices and follies which all proceed from a feculent stream of wealth that has muddied the pure rills of natural affection, by supposing that society will some time or other be so constituted, that man must necessarily fulfil the duties of a citizen, or be despised, and that while he was employed in any of the departments of civil life, his wife, also an active citizen, should be equally intent to manage her family, educate her children, and assist her neighbours.

But to render her really virtuous and useful, she must not, if she discharge her civil duties, want individually the protection of civil laws; she must not be dependent on her husband's bounty for her subsistence during his life, or support after his death; for how can a being be generous who has nothing of its own? or virtuous who is not free? The wife, in the present state of things, who is faithful to her husband, and neither suckles nor educates her children, scarcely deserves the name of a wife, and has no right to that of a citizen. But take away natural rights, and duties become null.

Women then must be considered as only the wanton solace of men, when they become so weak in mind and body that they cannot exert themselves unless to pursue some frothy pleasure, or to invent some frivolous fashion. What can be a more melancholy sight to a thinking mind, than to look into the numerous carriages that drive helter-skelter about this metropolis in a morning full of pale-faced creatures who are flying from themselves! I have often wished, with Dr Johnson, to place some of them in a little shop with half a dozen children looking up to their languid countenances for support. I am much mistaken, if some latent vigour would not soon give health and spirit to their eyes, and some lines drawn by the exercise of reason on the blank cheeks, which before were only undulated by dimples, might restore lost dignity to the character, or rather enable it to attain the true dignity of its nature. Virtue is not to be acquired even by speculation, much less by the negative supineness that wealth naturally generates.

Besides, when poverty is more disgraceful than even vice, is not morality cut to the quick? Still to avoid misconstruction, though I consider that women in the common walks of life are called to fulfil the duties of wives and mothers, by religion and reason, I cannot help lamenting that women of a superior cast have not a road open by which they can pursue more extensive plans of usefulness and independence. I may excite laughter, by dropping an hint, which I mean to pursue, some future time, for I really think that women ought to have representatives, instead of being arbitrarily governed without having any direct share allowed them in the deliberations of government.

But, as the whole system of representation is now, in this country, only a convenient handle for despotism, they need not complain, for they are as well represented as a numerous class of hard-working mechanics, who pay for the support of royalty when they can scarcely stop their children's mouths with bread. How are they represented whose very sweat supports the splendid stud of an heir-apparent, or varnishes the chariot of some female favourite who looks down on shame? Taxes on the very necessaries of life, enable an endless tribe of idle princes and princesses to pass with stupid pomp before a gaping crowd, who almost worship the very parade which costs them so dear. This is mere gothic grandeur, something like the barbarous useless parade of having sentinels on horseback at Whitehall, which I could never view without a mixture of contempt and indignation.

How strangely must the mind be sophisticated when this sort of state impresses it! But, till these monuments of folly are levelled by virtue, similar follies will leaven the whole mass. For the same character, in some degree, will prevail in the aggregate of society; and the refinements of luxury, or the vicious repinings of envious poverty, will equally banish virtue from society, considered as the characteristic of that society, or only allow it to appear as one of the stripes of the harlequin coat, worn by the civilised man.

In the superior ranks of life, every duty is done by deputies, as if duties could ever be waived, and the vain pleasures which consequent idleness forces the rich to pursue, appear so enticing to the next rank, that the numerous scramblers for wealth sacrifice everything to tread on their heels. The most sacred trusts are then considered as sinecures, because they were procured by interest, and only sought to enable a man to keep *good company*. Women, in particular, all want to be ladies. Which is simply to have nothing to do, but listlessly to go they scarcely care where, for they cannot tell what.

But what have women to do in society? I may be asked, but to loiter with easy grace; surely you would not condemn them all to suckle fools and chronicle small beer! No. Women might certainly study the art of healing, and be physicians as well as nurses. And midwifery, decency seems to allot to them, though I am afraid, the word midwife, in our dictionaries, will soon give place to *accoucheur*, and one proof of the former delicacy of the sex be effaced from the language.

They might also study politics, and settle their benevolence on the broadest basis; for the reading of history will scarcely be more useful than the perusal of romances, if read as mere biography; if the character of the times, the political improvements, arts, etc., be not observed. In short, if it be not considered as the history of man; and not of particular men, who filled a niche in the temple of fame, and dropped into the black rolling stream of time, that silently sweeps all before it into the shapeless void called – eternity. – For shape, can it be called, "that shape hath none"?

Business of various kinds, they might likewise pursue, if they were educated in a more orderly manner, which might save many from common and legal prostitution. Women would not then marry for a support, as men accept of places under Government, and neglect the implied duties; nor would an attempt to earn their own subsistence, a most laudable one! sink them almost to the level of those poor abandoned creatures who live by prostitution. For are not milliners and mantuamakers reckoned the next class? The few employments open to women, so far, from being liberal, are menial; and when a superior education enables them to take charge of the education of children as governesses, they are not treated like the tutors of sons, though even clerical tutors are not always treated in a manner calculated to render them respectable in the eyes of their pupils, to say nothing of the private comfort of the individual. But as women educated like gentlewomen, are never designed for the humiliating situation which necessity sometimes forces them to fill; these situations are considered in the light of a degradation; and they know little of the human heart, who need to be told, that nothing so painfully sharpens sensibility as such a fall in life.

Some of these women might be restrained from marrying by a proper spirit of delicacy, and others may not have had it in their power to escape in this pitiful way from servitude; is not that Government then very defective, and very unmindful of the happiness of one-half of its members, that does not provide for honest, independent women, by encouraging them to fill respectable stations? But in order to render their private virtue a public benefit, they must have a civil existence in the State, married or single; else we shall continually see some worthy woman, whose sensibility has been rendered painfully acute by undeserved contempt, droop like "the lily broken down by a plowshare."

It is a melancholy truth; yet such is the blessed effect of civilisation! the most respectable women are the most oppressed; and, unless they have understandings far superior to the common run of understandings, taking in both sexes, they must, from being treated like contemptible beings, become contemptible. How many women thus waste life away the prey of discontent, who might have practised as physicians, regulated a farm, managed a shop, and stood erect, supported by their own industry, instead of hanging their heads surcharged with the dew of sensibility, that consumes the beauty to which it at first gave lustre; nay, I doubt whether pity and love are so near akin as poets feign, for I have seldom seen much compassion excited by the helplessness of females, unless they were fair; then, perhaps, pity was the soft handmaid of love, or the harbinger of lust.

How much more respectable is the woman who earns her own bread by fulfilling any duty, than the most accomplished beauty! – beauty did I say! – so sensible am I of the beauty of moral loveliness, or the harmonious propriety that attunes the passions of a well-regulated mind, that I blush at making the comparison; yet I sigh to think how few women aim at attaining this respectability by withdrawing from the giddy whirl of pleasure, or the indolent calm that stupefies the good sort of women it sucks in.

Proud of their weakness, however, they must always be protected, guarded from care, and all the rough toils that dignify the mind. If this be the fiat of fate, if they will make themselves insignificant and contemptible, sweetly to waste "life away," let them not expect to be valued when their beauty fades, for it is the fate of the fairest flowers to be admired and pulled to pieces by the careless hand that plucked them. In how many ways do I wish, from the purest benevolence, to impress this truth on my sex; yet I fear that they will not listen to a truth that dear bought experience has brought home to many an agitated bosom, nor willingly resign the privileges of rank and sex for the privileges of humanity, to which those have no claim who do not discharge its duties.

Those writers are particularly useful, in my opinion, who make man feel for man, independent of the station he fills, or the drapery of factitious sentiments. I then would fain convince reasonable men of the importance of some of my remarks; and prevail on them to weigh dispassionately the whole tenor of my observations. I appeal to their understandings; and, as a fellow-creature, claim, in the name of my sex, some interest in their hearts. I entreat them to assist to emancipate their companion, to make her a *helpmeet* for them.

Would men but generously snap our chains, and be content with rational fellowship instead of slavish obedience, they would find us more observant daughters, more affectionate sisters, more faithful wives, more reasonable mothers – in a word, better citizens. We should then love them with true affection, because we should learn to respect ourselves; and the peace of mind of a worthy man would not be interrupted by the idle vanity of his wife, nor the babes sent to nestle in a strange bosom, having never found a home in their mother's.

2

The Subjection of Women

John Stuart Mill

The object of this essay is to explain as clearly as I am able, the grounds of an opinion which I have held from the very earliest period when I had formed any opinions at all on social or political matters, and which, instead of being weakened or modified, has been constantly growing stronger by the progress of reflection and the experience of life. That the principle which regulates the existing social relations between the two sexes – the legal subordination of one sex to the other – is wrong in itself, and now one of the chief hindrances to human improvement; and that it ought to be replaced by a principle of perfect equality, admitting no power or privilege on the one side, nor disability on the other.

The very words necessary to express the task I have undertaken, show how arduous it is. But it would be a mistake to suppose that the difficulty of the case must lie in the insufficiency or obscurity of the grounds of reason on which my conviction rests. The difficulty is that which exists in all cases in which there is a mass of feeling to be contended against. So long as an opinion is strongly rooted in the feelings, it gains rather than loses in stability by having a preponderating weight of argument against it. For if it were accepted as a result of argument, the refutation of the argument might shake the solidity of the conviction; but when it rests solely on feeling, the worse it fares in argumentative contest, the more persuaded its adherents are that their feeling must have some deeper ground, which the arguments do not reach; and while the feeling remains, it is always throwing up fresh intrenchments of argument to repair any breach made in the old. And there are so many causes tending to make the feelings connected with this subject the most intense and most deeply-rooted of all those which gather round and protect old institutions and customs, that we need not wonder to find them as yet less undermined and loosened than any of the rest by the progress of the great modern spiritual and social transition; nor suppose that the barbarisms to which men cling longest must be less barbarisms than those which they earlier shake off.

[...] In practical matters, the burthen of proof is supposed to be with those who are against liberty; who contend for any restriction or prohibition; either any limitation of the general freedom of human action, or any disqualification or disparity of privilege affecting one person or kind of persons, as compared with others. The *à priori* presumption is in favour of freedom and impartiality. It is held that there should be no restraint not required by the general good, and that the law should be no respecter of persons, but should treat all alike, save

John Stuart Mill, from *The Subjection of Woman*, originally published in 1869.

where dissimilarity of treatment is required by positive reasons, either of justice or of policy. But of none of these rules of evidence will the benefit be allowed to those who maintain the opinion I profess. It is useless for me to say that those who maintain the doctrine that men have a right to command and women are under an obligation to obey, or that men are fit for government and women unfit, are on the affirmative side of the question, and that they are bound to show positive evidence for the assertions, or submit to their rejection. It is equally unavailing for me to say that those who deny to women any freedom or privilege rightly allowed to men, having the double presumption against them that they are opposing freedom and recommending partiality, must be held to the strictest proof of their case, and unless their success be such as to exclude all doubt, the judgment ought to go against them. These would be thought good pleas in any common case; but they will not be thought so in this instance. Before I could hope to make any impression, I should be expected not only to answer all that has ever been said by those who take the other side of the question, but to imagine all that could be said by them – to find them in reasons, as well as answer all I find: and besides refuting all arguments for the affirmative, I shall be called upon for invincible positive arguments to prove a negative. And even if I could do all this, and leave the opposite party with a host of unanswered arguments against them, and not a single unrefuted one on their side, I should be thought to have done little; for a cause supported on the one hand by universal usage, and on the other by so great a preponderance of popular sentiment, is supposed to have a presumption in its favour, superior to any conviction which an appeal to reason has power to produce in any intellects but those of a high class.

I do not mention these difficulties to complain of them; first, because it would be useless; they are inseparable from having to contend through people's understandings against the hostility of their feelings and practical tendencies: and truly the understandings of the majority of mankind would need to be much better cultivated than has ever yet been the case, before they can be asked to place such reliance in their own power of estimating arguments, as to give up practical principles in which they have been born and bred and which are the basis of much of the existing order of the world, at the first argumentative attack which they are not capable of logically resisting. I do not therefore quarrel with them for having too little faith in argument, but for having too much faith in custom and the general feeling. [. . .] As regards the present question, I am willing to accept the unfavourable conditions which the prejudice assigns to me. I consent that established custom, and the general feeling, should be deemed conclusive against me, unless that custom and feeling from age to age can be shown to have owed their existence to other causes than their soundness, and to have derived their power from the worse rather than the better parts of human nature. I am willing that judgment should go against me, unless I can show that my judge has been tampered with. The concession is not so great as it might appear; for to prove this, is by far the easiest portion of my task.

The generality of a practice is in some cases a strong presumption that it is, or at all events once was, conducive to laudable ends. This is the case, when the practice was first adopted, or afterwards kept up, as a means to such ends, and was grounded on experience of the mode in which they could be most effectually attained. If the authority of men over women, when first established, had been the result of a conscientious comparison between different modes of constituting the government of society; if, after trying various other modes of social organisation – the government of women over men, equality between the two, and such mixed and divided modes of government as might be invented – it had been decided, on the testimony of experience, that the mode in which women are wholly under the rule of men, having no share at all in public concerns, and each in private being under the legal obligation of obedience to the man with whom she has associated her destiny, was the arrangement most conducive to the happiness and well-being of both; its general adoption might then be fairly thought to be some evidence that, at the time when it was adopted, it was the best: though even then the considerations which recommended it may, like so many other primeval social facts of the greatest importance, have subsequently, in the course of ages, ceased to exist. But the state of the case is in every respect the reverse of this. In the first place, the opinion in favour of the present system, which entirely subordinates the weaker sex to the stronger, rests upon theory only; for there never has been trial made of any other: so that experience, in the sense in which it is vulgarly opposed to theory, cannot be pretended to have pronounced any verdict. And in the second place, the adoption of this system of inequality never was the result of deliberation, or forethought, or any social ideas, or any notion whatever of what conduced to the benefit of humanity or the good order of society. It arose simply from the fact that from the very earliest twilight of human society, every woman (owing to the value attached to her by men, combined with her inferiority in muscular strength), was found in a state of bondage to some man. Laws and systems of polity always begin by recognising the relations they find already existing between individuals. They convert what was a mere physical fact into a legal right, give it the sanction of society, and principally aim at the substitution of public and organised means of asserting and protecting these rights, instead of the irregular and lawless conflict of physical strength. Those who had already been compelled to obedience became in this manner legally bound to it. Slavery, from being a mere affair of force between the master and the slave, became regularised and a matter of compact among the masters, who, binding themselves to one another for common protection, guaranteed by their collective strength the private possessions of each, including his slaves. In early times, the great majority of the male sex were slaves, as well as the whole of the female. And many ages elapsed, some of them ages of high cultivation, before any thinker was bold enough to question the rightfulness, and the absolute social necessity, either of the one slavery or of the other. [...]

If people are mostly so little aware how completely, during the greater part of the duration of our species, the law of force was the avowed rule of general conduct, any other being only a special and exceptional consequence of peculiar ties – and from how very recent a date it is that the affairs of society in general have been even pretended to be regulated according to any moral law; as little do people remember or consider, how institutions and customs which never had any ground but the law of force, last on into ages and states of general opinion which never would have permitted their first establishment. Less than forty years ago, Englishmen might still by law hold human beings in bondage as saleable property: within the present century they might kidnap them and carry them off, and work them literally to death. This absolutely extreme case of the law of force, condemned by those who can tolerate almost every other form of arbitrary power, and which, of all others presents features the most revolting to the feelings of all who look at it from an impartial position, was the law of civilised and Christian England within the memory of persons now living: and in one half of Anglo-Saxon America three or four years ago, not only did slavery exist, but the slave-trade, and the breeding of slaves expressly for it, was a general practice between slave-states. Yet not only was there a greater strength of sentiment against it, but, in England at least, a less amount either of feeling or of interest in favour of it, than of any other of the customary abuses of force: for its motive was the love of gain, unmixed and undisguised; and those who profited by it were a very small numerical fraction of the country, while the natural feeling of all who were not personally interested in it, was unmitigated abhorrence. So extreme an instance makes it almost superfluous to refer to any other: but consider the long duration of absolute monarchy. In England at present it is the almost universal conviction that military despotism is a case of the law of force, having no other origin or justification. Yet in all the great nations of Europe except England it either still exists, or has only just ceased to exist, and has even now a strong party favourable to it in all ranks of the people, especially among persons of station and consequence. Such is the power of an established system, even when far from universal; when not only in almost every period of history there have been great and well-known examples of the contrary system, but these have almost invariably been afforded by the most illustrious and most prosperous communities. In this case, too, the possessor of the undue power, the person directly interested in it, is only one person, while those who are subject to it and suffer from it are literally all the rest. The yoke is naturally and necessarily humiliating to all persons, except the one who is on the throne, together with, at most, the one who expects to succeed to it. How different are these cases from that of the power of men over women! I am not now prejudging the question of its justifiableness. I am showing how vastly more permanent it could not but be, even if not justifiable, than these other dominations which have nevertheless lasted down to our own time. Whatever gratification of pride there is in the possession of power, and whatever personal interest in its exercise, is in this case not confined to a limited class, but common to the whole male sex. Instead of being, to most of its supporters, a thing desirable chiefly in the abstract, or, like the political ends usually contended for by factions, of little private importance to any but the leaders; it comes home to the person and hearth of every male head of a family, and of everyone who looks forward to being so. The clodhopper exercises, or is to exercise, his share of the power equally with the highest nobleman. And the case is that in which the desire of power is the strongest: for everyone who desires power, desires it most over those who are nearest to him, with whom his life is passed, with whom he has most concerns in common, and in whom any independence of his authority is oftenest likely to interfere with his individual preferences. If, in the other cases specified, powers manifestly grounded only on force, and having so much less to support them, are so slowly and with so much difficulty got rid of, much more must it be so with this, even if it rests on no better foundation than those. We must consider, too, that the possessors of the power have facilities in this case, greater than in any other, to prevent any uprising against it. Every one of the subjects lives under the very eye, and almost, it may be said, in the hands, of one of the masters – in closer intimacy with him than with any of her fellow-subjects; with no means of combining against him, no power of even locally overmastering him, and, on the other hand, with the strongest motives for seeking his favour and avoiding to give him offence. In struggles for political emancipation, everybody knows how often its champions are bought off by bribes, or daunted by terrors. In the case of women, each individual of the subject-class is in a chronic state of bribery and intimidation combined. In setting up the standard of resistance, a large number of the leaders, and still more of the followers, must make an almost complete sacrifice of the pleasures or the alleviations of their own individual lot. If ever any system of privilege and enforced subjection had its yoke tightly riveted on the necks of those who are kept down by it, this has. [. . .]

Some will object, that a comparison cannot fairly be made between the government of the male sex and the forms of unjust power which I have adduced in illustration of it, since these are arbitrary, and the effect of mere usurpation, while it on the contrary is natural. But was there ever any domination which did not appear natural to those who possessed it? There was a time when the division of mankind into two classes, a small one of masters and a numerous one of slaves, appeared, even to the most cultivated minds, to be natural, and the only natural, condition of the human race. No less an intellect, and one which contributed no less to the progress of human thought, than Aristotle, held this opinion without doubt or misgiving; and rested it on the same premises on which the same assertion in regard to the dominion of men over women is usually based, namely that there are different natures among mankind, free natures, and slave natures; that the Greeks were of a free nature, the barbarian races of Thracians and Asiatics of a slave nature. But why need I go back to Aristotle? Did not the slave-owners of the Southern United States maintain the same doctrine, with all the fanaticism with which men cling to the theories that justify their passions and legitimate their personal interests? Did they not call heaven and earth to witness that the dominion of the white man over the black is natural, that the black race is by nature incapable of freedom, and marked out for slavery? some even going so far as to say that the freedom of manual labourers is an unnatural order of things anywhere. Again, the theorists of absolute monarchy have always affirmed it to be the only natural form of government; issuing from the patriarchal, which was the primitive and spontaneous form of society, framed on the model of the paternal, which is anterior to society itself, and, as they contend, the most natural authority of all. [. . .] So true is it that unnatural generally means only uncustomary, and that everything which is usual appears natural. The subjection of women to men being a universal custom, any departure from it quite naturally appears unnatural. But how entirely, even in this case, the feeling is dependent on custom, appears by ample experience. Nothing so much astonishes the people of distant parts of the world, when they first learn anything about England, as to be told that it is under a queen; the thing seems to them so unnatural as to be almost incredible. To Englishmen this does not seem in the least degree unnatural, because they are used to it; but they do feel it unnatural that women should be soldiers or Members of Parliament. In the feudal ages, on the contrary, war and politics were not thought unnatural to women, because not unusual; it seemed natural that women of the privileged classes should be of manly character, inferior in nothing but bodily strength to their husbands and fathers. The independence of women seemed rather less unnatural to the Greeks than to other ancients, on account of the fabulous Amazons (whom they believed to be historical), and the partial example afforded by the Spartan women; who, though no less subordinate by law than in other Greek states, were more free in fact, and being trained to bodily exercises in the same manner with men, gave ample proof that they were not naturally disqualified for them. There can be little doubt that Spartan experience suggested to Plato, among many other of his doctrines, that of the social and political equality of the two sexes.

But, it will be said, the rule of men over women differs from all these others in not being a rule of force: it is accepted voluntarily; women make no complaint, and are consenting parties to it. In the first place, a great number of women do not accept it. Ever since there have been women able to make their sentiments known by their writings (the only mode of publicity which society permits to them), an increasing number of them have recorded protests against their present social condition: and recently many thousands of them, headed by the most eminent women known to the public, have petitioned Parliament for their admission to the Parliamentary Suffrage. The claim of women to be educated as solidly, and in the same branches of knowledge, as men, is urged with growing intensity, and with a great prospect of success; while the demand for their admission into professions and occupations hitherto closed against them, becomes every year more urgent. [...] It is a political law of nature that those who are under any power of ancient origin, never begin by complaining of the power itself, but only of its oppressive exercise. There is never any want of women who complain of ill-usage by their husbands. There would be infinitely more, if complaint were not the greatest of all provocatives to a repetition and increase of the ill-usage. It is this which frustrates all attempts to maintain the power but protect the woman against its abuses. In no other case (except that of a child) is the person who has been proved judicially to have suffered an injury, replaced under the physical power of the culprit who inflicted it. Accordingly wives, even in the most extreme and protracted cases of bodily ill-usage, hardly ever dare avail themselves of the laws made for their protection: and if, in a moment of irrepressible indignation, or by the interference of neighbours, they are induced to do so, their whole effort afterwards is to disclose as little as they can, and to beg off their tyrant from his merited chastisement.

All causes, social and natural, combine to make it unlikely that women should be collectively rebellious to the power of men. They are so far in a position different from all other subject classes, that their masters require something more from them than actual service. Men do not want solely the obedience of women, they want their sentiments. All men, except the most brutish, desire to have, in the woman most nearly connected with them, not a forced slave but a willing one, not a slave merely, but a favourite. They have therefore put everything in practice to enslave their minds. The masters of all other slaves rely, for maintaining obedience, on fear; either fear of themselves, or religious fears. The masters of women wanted more than simple obedience, and they turned the whole force of education to effect their purpose. All women are brought up from the very earliest years in the belief that their ideal of character is the very opposite to that of men; not self-will, and government by self-control, but submission, and yielding to the control of others. All the moralities tell them that it is the duty of women, and all the current sentimentalities that it is their nature, to live for others; to make complete abnegation of themselves, and to have no life but in their affections. And by their affections are meant the only ones they are allowed to have – those to the men with whom they are connected, or to the children who constitute an additional and indefeasible tie between them and a man. When we put together these three things – first, the natural attraction between opposite sexes; secondly, the wife's entire dependence on the husband, every privilege or pleasure she has being either his gift, or depending entirely on his will; and lastly, that the principal object of human pursuit, consideration, and all objects of social ambition, can in general be sought or obtained by her only through him, it would be a miracle if the object of being attractive to men had not become the polar star of feminine education and formation of character. And, this great means of influence over the minds of women having been acquired, an instinct of selfishness made men avail themselves of it to the utmost as a means of holding women in subjection, by representing to them meekness, submissiveness, and resignation of all individual will into the hands of a man, as an essential part of sexual attractiveness. Can it be doubted that any of the other yokes which mankind have succeeded in breaking, would have subsisted till now if the same means had existed, and had been so sedulously used, to bow down their minds to it? If it had been made the object of the life of every young plebeian to find personal favour in the eyes of some patrician, of every young serf with some seigneur; if domestication with him, and a share of his personal affections, had been held out as the prize which they all should look out for, the most gifted and aspiring being able to reckon on the most desirable prizes; and if, when this prize had been obtained, they had been shut out by a wall of brass from all interests not centring in him, all feelings and desires but those which he shared or inculcated; would not serfs and seigneurs, plebeians and patricians, have been as broadly distinguished at this day as men and women are? and would not all but a thinker here and there, have believed the distinction to be a fundamental and unalterable fact in human nature?

The preceding considerations are amply sufficient to show that custom, however universal it may be, affords in this case no presumption, and ought not to create any prejudice, in favour of the arrangements which place women in social and political subjection to men. But I may go farther, and maintain that the course of history, and the tendencies of progressive human society, afford not only no presumption in favour of this system of inequality of rights, but a strong one against it; and that, so far as the whole course of human improvement up to the time, the whole stream of modern tendencies, warrants any inference on the subject, it is, that this relic of the past is discordant with the future, and must necessarily disappear.

For, what is the peculiar character of the modern world – the difference which chiefly distinguishes modern institutions, modern social ideas, modern life itself, from those of times long past? It is, that human beings are no longer born to their place in life, and chained down by an inexorable bond to the place they are born to, but are free to employ their faculties, and such favourable chances as offer, to achieve the lot which may appear to them most desirable. Human society of old was constituted on a very different principle. All were born to a fixed social position, and were mostly kept in it by law, or interdicted from any means by which they could emerge from it. As some men are born white and others black, so some were born slaves and others freemen and citizens; some were born patricians, others plebeians; some were born feudal nobles, others commoners and *roturiers*. A slave or serf could never make himself free, nor, except by the will of his master, become so. In most European countries it was not till towards the close of the middle ages, and as a consequence of the growth of regal power, that commoners could be ennobled. Even among nobles, the eldest son was born the exclusive heir to the paternal possessions, and a long time elapsed before it was fully established that the father could disinherit him. Among the industrious classes, only those who were born members of a guild, or were admitted into it by its members, could lawfully practise their calling within its local limits; and nobody could practise any calling deemed important, in any but the legal manner – by processes authoritatively prescribed. Manufacturers have stood in the pillory for presuming to carry on their business by new and improved methods. In modern Europe, and most in those parts of it which have participated most largely in all other modern improvements, diametrically opposite doctrines now prevail. Law and government do not undertake to prescribe by whom any social or industrial operation shall or shall not be conducted, or what modes of conducting them shall be lawful. These things are left to the unfettered choice of individuals. Even the laws which required that workmen should serve an apprenticeship, have in this country been repealed: there being ample assurance that in all cases in which an apprenticeship is necessary, its necessity will suffice to enforce it. The old theory was, that the least possible should be left to the choice of the individual agent; that all he had to do should, as far as practicable, be laid down for him by superior wisdom. Left to himself he was sure to go wrong. The modern conviction, the fruit of a thousand years of experience, is, that things in which the individual is the person directly interested, never go right but as they are left to his own discretion; and that any regulation of them by authority, except to protect the rights of others, is sure to be mischievous. This conclusion, slowly arrived at, and not adopted until almost every possible application of the contrary theory had been made with disastrous result, now (in the industrial department) prevails universally in the most advanced countries, almost universally in all that have pretensions to any sort of advancement. It is not that all processes are supposed to be equally good, or all persons to be equally qualified for everything; but that freedom of individual choice is now known to be the only thing which procures the adoption of the best processes, and throws each operation into the hands of those who are best qualified for it. Nobody thinks it necessary to make a law that only a strong-armed man shall be a blacksmith. Freedom and competition suffice to make blacksmiths strong-armed men, because the weak-armed can earn more by engaging in occupations for which they are more fit. In consonance with this doctrine, it is felt to be an overstepping of the proper bounds of authority to fix beforehand, on some general presumption, that certain persons are not fit to do certain things. It is now thoroughly known and admitted that if some such presumptions exist, no such presumption is infallible. Even if it be well grounded in a majority of cases, which it is very likely not to be, there will be a minority of exceptional cases in which it does not hold: and in those it is both an injustice to the individuals, and a detriment to society, to place barriers in the way of their using their faculties for their own benefit and for that of others. In the cases, on the other hand, in which the unfitness is real, the ordinary motives of human conduct will on the whole suffice to prevent the incompetent person from making, or from persisting in, the attempt.

If this general principle of social and economical science is not true; if individuals, with such help as they can derive from the opinion of those who know them, are not better judges than the law and the government, of their own capacities and vocation; the world cannot too soon abandon this principle, and return to the old system of regulations and disabilities. But if the principle is true, we ought to act as if we believed it, and not to ordain that to be born a girl instead of a boy, any more than to be born black instead of white, or a commoner instead of a nobleman, shall decide the person's position through all life – shall interdict people from all the more elevated social positions, and from all, except a few, respectable occupations. Even were we to admit the utmost that is ever pretended as to the superior fitness of men for all the functions now reserved to them, the same argument applies which forbids a legal qualification for Members of Parliament. If only once in a dozen years the conditions of eligibility exclude a fit person, there is a real loss, while the exclusion of thousands of unfit persons is no gain; for if the constitution of the electoral body disposes them to choose unfit persons, there are always plenty of such persons to choose from. In all things of any difficulty and importance, those who can do them well are fewer than the need, even with the most unrestricted latitude of choice: and any limitation of the field of selection deprives society of some chances of being served by the competent, without ever saving it from the incompetent.

At present, in the more improved countries, the disabilities of women are the only case, save one, in which laws and institutions take persons at their birth, and ordain that they shall never in all their lives be allowed to compete for certain things. [. . .] All other dignities and social advantages are open to the whole male sex: many indeed are only attainable by wealth, but wealth may be striven for by anyone, and is actually obtained by many men of the very humblest origin. The difficulties, to the majority, are indeed insuperable without the aid of fortunate accidents; but no male human being is under any legal ban: neither law nor opinion superadd artificial obstacles to the natural ones. [. . .]

The social subordination of women thus stands out an isolated fact in modern social institutions; a solitary breach of what has become their fundamental law; a single relic of an old world of thought and practice exploded in everything else, but retained in the one thing of most universal interest; as if a gigantic dolmen, or a vast temple of Jupiter Olympius, occupied the site of St Paul's and received daily worship, while the surrounding Christian churches were only resorted to on fasts and festivals. This entire discrepancy between one social fact and all those which accompany it, and the radical opposition between its nature and the progressive movement which is the boast of the modern world, and which has successively swept away everything else of an analogous character, surely affords, to a conscientious observer of human tendencies, serious matter for reflection. It raises a prima facie presumption on the unfavourable side, far outweighing any which custom and usage could in such circumstances create on the favourable; and should at least suffice to make this, like the choice between republicanism and royalty, a balanced question.

The least that can be demanded is, that the question should not be considered as prejudged by existing fact and existing opinion, but open to discussion on its merits, as a question of justice and expediency: the decision on this, as on any of the other social arrangements of mankind, depending on what an enlightened estimate of tendencies and consequences may show to be most advantageous to humanity in general, without distinction of sex. And the discussion must be a real discussion, descending to foundations, and not resting satisfied with vague and general assertions. It will not do, for instance, to assert in general terms, that the experience of mankind has pronounced in favour of the existing system. Experience cannot possibly have decided between two courses, so long as there has only been experience of one. If it be said that the doctrine of the equality of the sexes rests only on theory, it must be remembered that the contrary doctrine also has only theory to rest upon. All that is proved in its favour by direct experience, is that mankind have been able to exist under it, and to attain the degree of improvement and prosperity which we now see; but whether that prosperity has been attained sooner, or is now greater, than it would have been under the other system, experience does not say. On the other hand, experience does say, that every step in improvement has been so invariably accompanied by a step made in raising the social position of women, that historians and philosophers have been led to adopt their elevation or debasement as on the whole the surest test and most correct measure of the civilisation of a people or an age. Through all the progressive period of human history, the condition of women has been approaching nearer to equality with men. This does not of itself prove that the assimilation must go on to complete equality; but it assuredly affords some presumption that such is the case.

Neither does it avail anything to say that the *nature* of the two sexes adapts them to their present functions and position, and renders these appropriate to them. Standing on the ground of common sense and the constitution of the human mind, I deny that anyone knows, or can know, the nature of the two sexes, as long as they have only been seen in their present relation to one another. If men had ever been found in society without women, or women without men, or if there had been a society of men and women in which the women were not under the control of the men, something might have been positively known about the mental and moral differences which may be inherent in the nature of each. What is now called the nature of women is an eminently artificial thing – the result of forced repression in some directions, unnatural stimulation in others. It may be asserted without scruple, that no other class of dependents have had their character so entirely distorted from its natural proportions by their relation with their masters; for, if conquered and slave races have been, in some respects, more forcibly repressed, whatever in them has not been crushed down by an iron heel has generally been let alone, and if left with any liberty of development, it has developed itself according to its own laws; but in the case of women, a hot-house and stove cultivation has always been carried on of some of the capabilities of their nature, for the benefit and pleasure of their masters. [. . .]

Hence, in regard to that most difficult question, what are the natural differences between the two sexes – a subject on which it is impossible in the present state of society to obtain complete and correct knowledge – while almost everybody dogmatises upon it, almost all neglect and make light of the only means by which any partial insight can be obtained into it. This is, an analytic study of the most important department of psychology, the laws of the influence of circumstances on character. For, however great and apparently ineradicable the moral and intellectual differences between men and women might be, the evidence of there being natural differences could only be negative. Those only could be inferred to be natural which could not possibly be artificial – the residuum, after deducting every characteristic of either sex which can admit of being explained from education or external circumstances. The profoundest knowledge of the laws of the formation of character is indispensable to entitle anyone to affirm even that there is any difference, much more what the difference is, between the two sexes considered as moral and rational beings; and since no one, as yet, has that knowledge (for there is hardly any subject which, in proportion to its importance, has been so little studied), no one is thus far entitled to any positive opinion on the subject. Conjectures are all that can at present be made; conjectures more or less probable, according as more or less authorised by such knowledge as we yet have of the laws of psychology, as applied to the formation of character.

Even the preliminary knowledge, what the differences between the sexes now are, apart from all question as to how they are made what they are, is still in the crudest and most incomplete state. [. . .]

I have dwelt so much on the difficulties which at present obstruct any real knowledge by men of the true nature of women, because in this as in so many other things "opinio copiæ inter maximas causas inopiæ est";[1] and there is little chance of reasonable thinking on the matter, while people flatter themselves that they perfectly understand a subject of which most men know absolutely nothing, and of which it is at present impossible that any man, or all men taken together, should have knowledge which can qualify them to lay down the law to women as to what is, or is not, their vocation. Happily, no such knowledge is necessary for any practical purpose connected with the position of women in relation to society and life. For, according to all the principles involved in modern society, the question rests with women themselves – to be decided by their own experience, and by the use of their own faculties. There are no means of finding what either one person or many can do, but by trying – and no means by which anyone else can discover for them what it is for their happiness to do or leave undone.

One thing we may be certain of – that what is contrary to women's nature to do, they never will be made to do by simply giving their nature free play. The anxiety of mankind to interfere in behalf of nature, for fear lest nature should not succeed in effecting its purpose, is an altogether unnecessary solicitude. What women by nature cannot do, it is quite superfluous to forbid them from doing. What they can do, but not so well as the men who are their competitors, competition suffices to exclude them from; since nobody asks for protective duties and bounties in favour of women; it is only asked that the present bounties and protective duties in favour of men should be recalled. If women have a greater natural inclination for some things than for others, there is no need of laws or social inculcation to make the majority of them do the former in preference to the latter. Whatever women's services are most wanted for, the free play of competition will hold out the strongest inducements to them to undertake. And, as the words imply, they are most wanted for the things for which they are most fit; by the apportionment of which to them, the collective faculties of the two sexes can be applied on the whole with the greatest sum of valuable result.

The general opinion of men is supposed to be, that the natural vocation of a woman is that of a wife and mother. I say, is supposed to be, because, judging from acts – from the whole of the present constitution of society – one might infer that their opinion was the direct contrary. They might be supposed to think that the alleged natural vocation of women was of all things the most repugnant to their nature; insomuch that if they are free to do anything else – if any other means of living or occupation of their time and faculties, is open, which has any chance of appearing desirable to them – there will not be enough of them who will be willing to accept the condition said to be natural to them. If this is the real opinion of men in general, it would be well that it should be spoken out. I should like to hear somebody openly enunciating the doctrine (it is already implied in much that is written on the subject) – "It is necessary to society that women should marry and produce children. They will not do so unless they are compelled. Therefore it is necessary to compel them." The merits of the case would then be clearly defined. It would be exactly that of the slave-holders of South Carolina and Louisiana. "It is necessary that cotton and sugar should be grown. White men cannot produce them. Negroes will not, for any wages which we choose to give. *Ergo* they must be compelled." An illustration still closer to the point is that of impressment. Sailors must absolutely be had to defend the country. It often happens that they will not voluntarily enlist. Therefore there must be the power of forcing them. How often has this logic been used! and, but for one flaw in it, without doubt it would have been successful up to this day. But it is open to the retort – First pay the sailors the honest value of their labour. When you have made it as well worth their while to serve you, as to work for other employers, you will have no more difficulty than others have in obtaining their services. To this there is no logical answer except "I will not": and as people are now not only ashamed, but are not desirous, to rob the labourer of his hire, impressment is no longer advocated. Those who attempt to force women into marriage by closing all other doors against them, lay themselves open to a similar retort. If they mean what they say, their opinion must evidently be, that men do not render the married condition so desirable to women, as to induce them to accept it for its own recommendations. It is not a sign of one's thinking the boon one offers very attractive, when one allows only Hobson's choice, "that or none." And here, I believe, is the clue to the feelings of those men, who have a real antipathy to the equal freedom of women. I believe they are afraid, not lest women should be unwilling to marry, for I do not think that anyone in reality has that apprehension; but lest they should insist that marriage should be on equal conditions; lest all women of spirit and capacity should prefer doing almost anything else, not in their own eyes degrading, rather than marry, when marrying is giving themselves a master, and a master too of all their earthly possessions. And truly, if this consequence were necessarily incident to marriage, I think that the apprehension would be very well founded. I agree in thinking it probable that few women, capable of anything else, would, unless under an irresistible *entraînement*, rendering them for the time insensible to anything but itself, choose such a lot, when any other means were open to them of filling a conventionally honourable place in life: and if men are determined that the law of marriage shall be a law of despotism, they are quite right, in point of mere policy, in leaving to women only Hobson's choice. But, in that case, all that has been done in the modern world to relax the chain on the minds of women, has been a mistake. They never should have been allowed to receive a literary education. Women who read, much more women who write, are, in the existing constitution of things, a contradiction and à disturbing element: and it was wrong to bring women up with any acquirements but those of an odalisque, or of a domestic servant.

Note

1 "General opinion is inadequate on most matters."

3

Introduction from *The Second Sex*

Simone de Beauvoir

Introduction

For a long time I have hesitated to write a book on woman. The subject is irritating, especially to women; and it is not new. Enough ink has been spilled in the quarreling over feminism, now practically over, and perhaps we should say no more about it. It is still talked about, however, for the voluminous nonsense uttered during the last century seems to have done little to illuminate the problem. After all, is there a problem? And if so, what is it? Are there women, really? Most assuredly the theory of the eternal feminine still has its adherents who will whisper in your ear: "Even in Russia women still are *women*"; and other erudite persons – sometimes the very same – say with a sigh: "Woman is losing her way, woman is lost." One wonders if women still exist, if they will always exist, whether or not it is desirable that they should, what place they occupy in this world, what their place should be. "What has become of women?" was asked recently in an ephemeral magazine.[1]

But first we must ask: what is a woman? "*Tota mulier in utero*," says one, "woman is a womb." But in speaking of certain women, connoisseurs declare that they are not women, although they are equipped with a uterus like the rest. All agree in recognizing the fact that females exist in the human species; today as always they make up about one half of humanity. And yet we are told that femininity is in danger; we are exhorted to be women, remain women, become women. It would appear, then, that every female human being is not necessarily a woman; to be so considered she must share in that mysterious and threatened reality known as femininity. Is this attribute something secreted by the ovaries? Or is it a Platonic essence, a product of the philosophic imagination? Is a rustling petticoat enough to bring it down to earth? Although some women try zealously to incarnate this essence, it is hardly patentable. It is frequently described in vague and dazzling terms that seem to have been borrowed from the vocabulary of the seers, and indeed in the times of St Thomas it was considered an essence as certainly defined as the somniferous virtue of the poppy.

But conceptualism has lost ground. The biological and social sciences no longer admit the existence of unchangeably fixed entities that determine

Simone de Beauvoir, pp. xv–xxxiv and 301 from *The Second Sex*, translated and edited by H. M. Parshley. New York: Vintage Books, 1952.

given characteristics, such as those ascribed to woman, the Jew, or the Negro. Science regards any characteristic as a reaction dependent in part upon a *situation*. If today femininity no longer exists, then it never existed. But does the word *woman*, then, have no specific content? This is stoutly affirmed by those who hold to the philosophy of the enlightenment, of rationalism, of nominalism; women, to them, are merely the human beings arbitrarily designated by the word *woman*. Many American women particularly are prepared to think that there is no longer any place for woman as such; if a backward individual still takes herself for a woman, her friends advise her to be psychoanalyzed and thus get rid of this obsession. In regard to a work, *Modern Woman: The Lost Sex*, which in other respects has its irritating features, Dorothy Parker has written: "I cannot be just to books which treat of woman as woman.... My idea is that all of us, men as well as women, should be regarded as human beings." But nominalism is a rather inadequate doctrine, and the antifemininists have had no trouble in showing that women simply *are not* men. Surely woman is, like man, a human being; but such a declaration is abstract. The fact is that every concrete human being is always a singular, separate individual. To decline to accept such notions as the eternal feminine, the black soul, the Jewish character, is not to deny that Jews, Negroes, women exist today – this denial does not represent a liberation for those concerned, but rather a flight from reality. Some years ago a well-known woman writer refused to permit her portrait to appear in a series of photographs especially devoted to women writers; she wished to be counted among the men. But in order to gain this privilege she made use of her husband's influence! Women who assert that they are men lay claim none the less to masculine consideration and respect. I recall also a young Trotskyite standing on a platform at a boisterous meeting and getting ready to use her fists, in spite of her evident fragility. She was denying her feminine weakness; but it was for love of a militant male whose equal she wished to be. The attitude of defiance of many American women proves that they are haunted by a sense of their femininity. In truth, to go for a walk with one's eyes open is enough to demonstrate that humanity is divided into two classes of individuals whose clothes, faces, bodies, smiles, gaits, interests, and occupations are manifestly different. Perhaps these differences are superficial, perhaps they are destined to disappear. What is certain is that right now they do most obviously exist.

If her functioning as a female is not enough to define woman, if we decline also to explain her through "the eternal feminine," and if nevertheless we admit, provisionally, that women do exist, then we must face the question: what is a woman?

To state the question is, to me, to suggest, at once, a preliminary answer. The fact that I ask it is in itself significant. A man would never get the notion of writing a book on the peculiar situation of the human male.[2] But if I wish to define myself, I must first of all say: "I am a woman"; on this truth must be based all further discussion. A man never begins by presenting himself as an individual of a certain sex; it goes without saying that he is a man. The terms *masculine* and *feminine* are used symmetrically only as a matter of form, as on legal papers. In actuality the relation of the two sexes is not quite like that of two electrical poles, for man represents both the positive and the neutral, as is indicated by the common use of *man* to designate human beings in general; whereas woman represents only the negative, defined by limiting criteria, without reciprocity. In the midst of an abstract discussion it is vexing to hear a man say: "You think thus and so because you are a woman"; but I know that my only defense is to reply: "I think thus and so because it is true," thereby removing my subjective self from the argument. It would be out of the question to reply: "And you think the contrary because you are a man," for it is understood that the fact of being a man is no peculiarity. A man is in the right in being a man; it is the woman who is in the wrong. It amounts to this: just as for the ancients there was an absolute vertical with reference to which the oblique was defined, so there is an absolute human type, the masculine. Woman has ovaries, a uterus; these peculiarities imprison her in her subjectivity, circumscribe her within the limits of her own nature. It is often said that she thinks with her glands. Man superbly ignores the fact that his anatomy also includes glands, such as the testicles, and that they secrete hormones. He thinks of his body as a direct and normal connection with the world, which he believes he apprehends objectively, whereas he regards the body of woman as a hindrance, a prison, weighed down by everything peculiar to it. "The female is a female by virtue of a certain *lack* of qualities," said Aristotle; "we should regard the female nature as afflicted with a natural defectiveness." And St Thomas for his part pronounced woman to be an "imperfect man," an "incidental" being. This is symbolized in Genesis where Eve is depicted as made from what Bossuet called "a supernumerary bone" of Adam.

Thus humanity is male and man defines woman not in herself but as relative to him; she is not regarded as an autonomous being. Michelet writes: "Woman, the relative being...." And Benda is most positive in his *Rapport d'Uriel*: "The body of man makes sense in itself quite apart from that of woman, whereas the latter seems wanting in significance by itself.... Man can think of himself without woman. She cannot think of herself without man." And she is simply what man decrees; thus she is called "the sex," by which is meant that she appears essentially to the male as a sexual being. For him she is sex – absolute sex, no less. She is defined and differentiated with reference to man and not he with reference to her; she is the incidental, the inessential as opposed to the essential. He is the Subject, he is the Absolute – she is the Other.[3]

The category of the *Other* is as primordial as consciousness itself. In the most primitive societies, in the most ancient mythologies, one finds the expression of a duality – that of the Self and the Other. This duality was not originally attached to the division of the sexes; it was not dependent upon any empirical facts. It is revealed in such works as that of Granet on Chinese thought and those of Dumézil on the East Indies and Rome. The feminine element was at first no more involved in such pairs as Varuna-Mitra, Uranus-Zeus, Sun-Moon, and Day-Night than it was in the contrasts between Good and Evil, lucky and unlucky auspices, right and left, God and Lucifer. Otherness is a fundamental category of human thought.

Thus it is that no group ever sets itself up as the One without at once setting up the Other over against itself. If three travelers chance to occupy the same compartment, that is enough to make vaguely hostile "others" out of all the rest of the passengers on the train. In small-town eyes all persons not belonging to the village are "strangers" and suspect; to the native of a country all who inhabit other countries are "foreigners"; Jews are "different" for the anti-Semite, Negroes are "inferior" for American racists, aborigines are "natives" for colonists, proletarians are the "lower class" for the privileged.

Lévi-Strauss, at the end of a profound work on the various forms of primitive societies, reaches the following conclusion: "Passage from the state of Nature to the state of Culture is marked by man's ability to view biological relations as a series of contrasts; duality, alternation, opposition, and symmetry, whether under definite or vague forms, constitute not so much phenomena to be explained as fundamental and immediately given data of social reality."[4] These phenomena would be incomprehensible if in fact human society were simply a *Mitsein* or fellowship based on solidarity and friendliness. Things become clear, on the contrary, if, following Hegel, we find in consciousness itself a fundamental hostility toward every other consciousness; the subject can be posed only in being opposed – he sets himself up as the essential, as opposed to the other, the inessential, the object.

But the other consciousness, the other ego, sets up a reciprocal claim. The native traveling abroad is shocked to find himself in turn regarded as a "stranger" by the natives of neighboring countries. As a matter of fact, wars, festivals, trading, treaties, and contests among tribes, nations, and classes tend to deprive the concept *Other* of its absolute sense and to make manifest its relativity; willy-nilly, individuals and groups are forced to realize the reciprocity of their relations. How is it, then, that this reciprocity has not been recognized between the sexes, that one of the contrasting terms is set up as the sole essential, denying any relativity in regard to its correlative and defining the latter as pure otherness? Why is it that women do not dispute male sovereignty? No subject will readily volunteer to become the object, the inessential; it is not the Other who, in defining himself as the Other, establishes the One. The Other is posed as such by the One in defining himself as the One. But if the Other is not to regain the status of being the One, he must be submissive enough to accept this alien point of view. Whence comes this submission in the case of woman?

There are, to be sure, other cases in which a certain category has been able to dominate another completely for a time. Very often this privilege depends upon inequality of numbers – the majority imposes its rule upon the minority or persecutes it. But women are not a minority, like the American Negroes or the Jews; there are as many women as men on earth. Again, the two groups concerned have often been originally independent; they may have been formerly unaware of each other's existence, or perhaps they recognized each other's autonomy. But a historical event has resulted in the subjugation of the weaker by the stronger. The scattering of the Jews, the introduction of slavery into America, the conquests of imperialism are examples in point. In these cases the oppressed retained at least the memory of former days; they possessed in common a past, a tradition, sometimes a religion or a culture.

The parallel drawn by Bebel between women and the proletariat is valid in that neither ever formed a minority or a separate collective unit of mankind. And instead of a single historical event it is in both cases a historical development that explains their status as a class and accounts for the membership of *particular individuals* in that class. But proletarians have not always existed, whereas there have always been women. They are women in virtue of their anatomy and physiology. Throughout history they have always been subordinated to men,[5] and hence their dependency is not the result of a historical event or a social change – it was not something that *occurred*. The reason why otherness in this case seems to be an absolute is in part that it lacks the contingent or incidental nature of historical facts. A condition brought about at a certain time can be abolished at some other time, as the Negroes of Haiti and others have proved; but it might seem that a natural condition is beyond the possibility of change. In truth, however, the nature of things is no more immutably given, once for all, than is historical reality. If woman seems to be the inessential which never becomes the essential, it is because she herself fails to bring about this change. Proletarians say "We"; Negroes also. Regarding themselves as subjects, they transform the bourgeois, the whites, into "others." But women do not say "We," except at some congress of feminists or similar formal demonstration; men say "women," and women use the same word in referring to themselves. They do not authentically assume a subjective attitude. The proletarians have accomplished the revolution in Russia, the Negroes in Haiti, the Indo-Chinese are battling for it in Indo-China; but the women's effort has never been anything more than a symbolic agitation. They have gained only what men have been willing to grant; they have taken nothing, they have only received.

The reason for this is that women lack concrete means for organizing themselves into a unit which can stand face to face with the correlative unit. They have no past, no history, no religion of their own; and they have no such solidarity of work and interest as that of the proletariat. They are not even promiscuously herded together in the way that creates community feeling among the American Negroes, the ghetto Jews, the workers of Saint-Denis, or the factory hands of Renault. They live dispersed among the males, attached through residence, housework, economic condition, and social standing to certain men – fathers or husbands – more firmly than they are to other women. If they belong to the bourgeoisie, they feel solidarity with men of that class, not with proletarian women; if they are white, their allegiance is to white men, not to Negro women. The proletariat can propose to massacre the ruling class, and a sufficiently fanatical Jew or Negro might dream of getting sole possession of the atomic bomb and making humanity wholly Jewish or black; but woman cannot even dream of exterminating the males. The bond that unites her to her oppressors is not comparable to any other. The division of the sexes is a biological fact, not an event in human history. Male and female stand opposed within a primordial *Mitsein*, and woman has not broken it. The couple is a fundamental unity with its two halves riveted together, and the cleavage of society along the line of sex is impossible. Here is to be found the basic trait of woman: she is the Other in a totality of which the two components are necessary to one another.

One could suppose that this reciprocity might have facilitated the liberation of woman. When Hercules sat at the feet of Omphale and helped with her spinning, his desire for her held him captive; but why did she fail to gain a lasting power? To revenge herself on Jason, Medea killed their children; and this grim legend would seem to suggest that she might have obtained a formidable influence over him through his love for his offspring. In *Lysistrata* Aristophanes gaily depicts a band of women who joined forces to gain social ends through the sexual needs of their men; but this is only a play. In the legend of the Sabine women, the latter soon abandoned their plan of remaining sterile to punish their ravishers. In truth woman has not been socially emancipated through man's need – sexual desire and the desire for offspring – which makes the male dependent for satisfaction upon the female.

Master and slave, also, are united by a reciprocal need, in this case economic, which does not liberate the slave. In the relation of master to slave the master does not make a point of the need that he has for the other; he has in his grasp the power of satisfying this need through his own action; whereas the slave, in his dependent condition, his hope and fear, is quite conscious of the need he has for his master. Even if the need is at bottom equally urgent for both, it always works in favor of the oppressor and against the oppressed. That is why the liberation of the working class, for example, has been slow.

Now, woman has always been man's dependent, if not his slave; the two sexes have never shared the world in equality. And even today woman is heavily handicapped, though her situation is beginning to change. Almost nowhere is her legal status the same as man's,[6] and frequently it is much to her disadvantage. Even when her rights are legally recognized in the abstract, long-standing custom prevents their full expression in the mores. In the economic sphere men and women can almost be said to make up two castes; other things being equal, the former hold the better jobs, get higher wages, and have more opportunity for success than their new competitors. In industry and politics men have a great many more positions and they monopolize the most important posts. In addition to all this, they enjoy a traditional prestige that the education of children tends in every way to support, for the present enshrines the past – and in the past all history has been made by men. At the present time, when women are beginning to take part in the affairs of the world, it is still a world that belongs to men – they have no doubt of it at all and women have scarcely any. To decline to be the Other, to refuse to be a party to the deal – this would be for women to renounce all the advantages conferred upon them by their alliance with the superior caste. Man-the-sovereign will provide woman-the-liege with material protection and will undertake the moral justification of her existence; thus she can evade at once both economic risk and the metaphysical risk of a liberty in which ends and aims must be contrived without assistance. Indeed, along with the ethical urge of each individual to affirm his subjective existence, there is also the temptation to forgo liberty and become a thing. This is an inauspicious road, for he who takes it – passive, lost, ruined – becomes henceforth the creature of another's will, frustrated in his transcendence and deprived of every value. But it is an easy road; on it one avoids the strain involved in undertaking an authentic existence. When man makes of woman the *Other*, he may, then, expect her to manifest deep-seated tendencies toward complicity. Thus, woman may fail to lay claim to the status of subject because she lacks definite resources, because she feels the necessary bond that ties her to man regardless of reciprocity, and because she is often very well pleased with her role as the *Other*.

But it will be asked at once: how did all this begin? It is easy to see that the duality of the sexes, like any duality, gives rise to conflict. And doubtless the winner will assume the status of absolute. But why should man have won from the start? It seems possible that women could have won the victory; or that the outcome of the conflict might never have been decided. How is it that this world has always belonged to the men and that things have begun to change only recently? Is this change a good thing? Will it bring about an equal sharing of the world between men and women?

These questions are not new, and they have often been answered. But the very fact that woman *is the Other* tends to cast suspicion upon all the justifications that men have ever been able to provide for it. These have all too evidently been dictated by men's interest. A little-known feminist of the seventeenth century, Poulain de la Barre, put it this way: "All that has been written about women by men should be suspect, for the men are at once judge and party to the lawsuit." Everywhere, at all times, the males have displayed their satisfaction in feeling that they are the lords of creation. "Blessed be God . . . that He did not make me a woman," say the Jews in their morning prayers, while their wives pray on a note of resignation: "Blessed be the Lord, who created me according to His will." The first among the blessings for which Plato thanked the gods was that he had been created free, not enslaved; the second, a man, not a woman. But the males could not enjoy this privilege fully unless they believed it to be founded on the absolute and the eternal; they sought to make the fact of their supremacy into a right. "Being men, those who have made and compiled the laws have favored their own sex, and jurists have elevated these laws into principles," to quote Poulain de la Barre once more.

Legislators, priests, philosophers, writers, and scientists have striven to show that the subordinate position of woman is willed in heaven and advantageous on earth. The religions invented by men reflect this wish for domination. In the legends of Eve and Pandora men have taken up arms against women. They have made use of philosophy and theology, as the quotations from Aristotle and St Thomas have shown. Since ancient times satirists and moralists have delighted in showing up the weaknesses of women. We are familiar with the savage indictments hurled against women throughout French literature. Montherlant, for example, follows the tradition of Jean de Meung, though with less gusto. This hostility may at times be well founded, often it is gratuitous; but in truth it more or less successfully conceals a desire for self-justification. As Montaigne says, "It is easier to accuse one sex than to excuse the other." Sometimes what is going on is clear enough. For instance, the Roman law limiting the rights of woman cited "the imbecility, the instability of the sex" just when the weakening of family ties seemed to threaten the interests of male heirs. And in the effort to keep the married woman under guardianship, appeal was made in the sixteenth century to the authority of St Augustine, who declared that "woman is a creature neither decisive nor constant," at a time when the single woman was thought capable of managing her property. Montaigne understood clearly how arbitrary and unjust was woman's appointed lot: "Women are not in the wrong when they decline to accept the rules laid down for them, since the men make these rules without consulting them. No wonder intrigue and strife abound." But he did not go so far as to champion their cause.

It was only later, in the eighteenth century, that genuinely democratic men began to view the matter objectively. Diderot, among others, strove to show that woman is, like man, a human being. Later John Stuart Mill came fervently to her defense. But these philosophers displayed unusual impartiality. In the nineteenth century the feminist quarrel became again a quarrel of partisans. One of the consequences of the industrial revolution was the entrance of women into productive labor, and it was just here that the claims of the feminists emerged from the realm of theory and acquired an economic basis, while their opponents became the more aggressive. Although landed property lost power to some extent, the bourgeoisie clung to the old morality that found the guarantee of private property in the solidity of the family. Woman was ordered back into the home the more harshly as her emancipation became a real menace. Even within the working class the men endeavored to restrain woman's liberation, because they began to see the women as dangerous competitors – the more so because they were accustomed to work for lower wages.

In proving woman's inferiority, the antifeminists then began to draw not only upon religion, philosophy, and theology, as before, but also upon science – biology, experimental psychology, etc. At most they were willing to grant "equality in difference" to the *other* sex. That profitable formula is most significant; it is precisely like the "equal but separate" formula of the Jim Crow laws aimed at the North American Negroes. As is well known, this so-called equalitarian segregation has resulted only in the most extreme discrimination. The similarity just noted is in no way due to chance, for whether it is a race, a caste, a class, or a sex that is reduced to a position of inferiority, the methods of justification are the same. "The eternal feminine" corresponds to "the black soul" and to "the Jewish character." True, the Jewish problem is on the whole very different from the other two – to the anti-Semite the Jew is not so much an inferior as he is an enemy for whom there is to be granted no place on earth, for whom annihilation is the fate desired. But there are deep similarities between the situation of woman and that of the Negro. Both are being emancipated today from a like paternalism, and the former master class wishes to "keep them in their place" – that is, the place chosen for them. In both cases the former masters lavish more or less sincere eulogies, either on the virtues of "the good Negro" with his dormant, childish, merry soul – the submissive Negro – or on the merits of the woman who is "truly feminine" – that is, frivolous, infantile, irresponsible – the submissive woman. In both cases the dominant class bases its argument on a state of affairs that it has itself created. As George Bernard Shaw puts it, in substance, "The American white relegates the black to the rank of shoeshine boy; and he concludes from this that the black is good for nothing but shining shoes." This vicious circle is met with in all analogous circumstances; when an individual (or a group of individuals) is kept in a situation of inferiority, the fact is that he *is* inferior. But the significance of the verb *to be* must be rightly understood here; it is in bad faith to give it a static value when it really has the dynamic Hegelian sense of "to have become." Yes, women on the whole *are* today inferior to men; that is, their situation affords them fewer possibilities. The question is: should that state of affairs continue?

Many men hope that it will continue; not all have given up the battle. The conservative bourgeoisie still see in the emancipation of women a menace to their morality and their interests. Some men dread feminine competition. Recently a male student wrote in the *Hebdo-Latin*: "Every woman student who goes into medicine or law robs us of a job." He never questioned his rights in this world. And economic interests are not the only ones concerned. One of the benefits that oppression confers upon the oppressors is that the most humble among them is made to *feel* superior; thus, a "poor white" in the South can console himself with the thought that he is not a "dirty nigger" – and the more prosperous whites cleverly exploit this pride.

Similarly, the most mediocre of males feels himself a demigod as compared with women. It was much easier for M. de Montherlant to think himself a hero when he faced women (and women chosen for his purpose) than when he was obliged to act the man among men – something many women have done better than he, for that matter. And in September 1948, in one of his articles in the *Figaro littéraire*, Claude Mauriac – whose great originality is admired by all – could[7] write regarding woman: "*We* listen on a tone [*sic*!] of polite indifference... to the most brilliant among them, well knowing that her wit reflects more or less luminously ideas that come from *us*." Evidently the speaker referred to is not reflecting the ideas of Mauriac himself, for no one knows of his having any. It may be that she reflects ideas originating with men, but then, even among men there are those who have been known to appropriate ideas not their own; and one can well ask whether Claude Mauriac might not find more interesting a conversation reflecting Descartes, Marx, or Gide rather than himself. What is really remarkable is that by using the questionable *we* he identifies himself with St Paul, Hegel, Lenin, and Nietzsche, and from the lofty eminence of their grandeur looks down disdainfully upon the bevy of women who make bold to converse with him on a footing of equality. In truth, I know of more than one woman who would refuse to suffer with patience Mauriac's "tone of polite indifference."

I have lingered on this example because the masculine attitude is here displayed with disarming ingenuousness. But men profit in many more subtle ways from the otherness, the alterity of woman. Here is miraculous balm for those afflicted with an inferiority complex, and indeed no one is more arrogant toward women, more aggressive or scornful, than the man who is anxious about his virility. Those who are not fear-ridden in the presence of their fellow men are much more disposed to recognize a fellow creature in woman; but even to these the myth of woman, the Other, is precious for many reasons.[8] They cannot be blamed for not cheerfully relinquishing all the benefits they derive from the myth, for they realize what they would lose in relinquishing woman as they fancy her to be, while they fail to realize what they have to gain from the woman of tomorrow. Refusal to pose oneself as the Subject, unique and absolute, requires great self-denial. Furthermore, the vast majority of men make no such claim explicitly. They do not *postulate* woman as inferior, for today they are too thoroughly imbued with the ideal of democracy not to recognize all human beings as equals.

In the bosom of the family, woman seems in the eyes of childhood and youth to be clothed in the same social dignity as the adult males. Later on, the young man, desiring and loving, experiences the resistance, the independence of the woman desired and loved; in marriage, he respects woman as wife and mother, and in the concrete events of conjugal life she stands there before him as a free being. He can therefore feel that social subordination as between the sexes no longer exists and that on the whole, in spite of differences, woman is an equal. As, however, he observes some points of inferiority – the most important being unfitness for the professions – he attributes these to natural causes. When he is in a co-operative and benevolent relation with woman, his theme is the principle of abstract equality, and he does not base his attitude upon such inequality as may exist. But when he is in conflict with her, the situation is reversed: his theme will be the existing inequality, and he will even take it as justification for denying abstract equality.[9]

So it is that many men will affirm as if in good faith that women *are* the equals of man and that they have nothing to clamor for, while *at the same time* they will say that women can never be the equals of man and that their demands are in vain. It is, in point of fact, a difficult matter for man to realize the extreme importance of social discriminations which seem outwardly insignificant but which produce in woman moral and intellectual effects so profound that they appear to spring from her original nature. The most sympathetic of men never fully comprehend woman's concrete situation. And there is no reason to put much trust in the men when they rush to the defense of privileges whose full extent they can hardly measure. We shall not, then, permit ourselves to be intimidated by the number and violence of the attacks launched against women, nor to be entrapped by the self-seeking eulogies bestowed on the "true woman," nor to profit by the enthusiasm for woman's destiny manifested by men who would not for the world have any part of it.

We should consider the arguments of the feminists with no less suspicion, however, for very often their controversial aim deprives them of all real value. If the "woman question" seems trivial, it is because masculine arrogance has made of it a "quarrel"; and when quarreling, one no longer reasons well. People have tirelessly sought to prove that woman is superior, inferior, or equal to man. Some say that, having been created after Adam, she is evidently a secondary being; others say on the contrary that Adam was only a rough draft and that God succeeded in producing the human being in perfection when He created Eve. Woman's brain is smaller; yes, but it is relatively larger. Christ was made a man; yes, but perhaps for his greater humility. Each argument at once suggests its opposite, and both are often fallacious. If we are to gain understanding, we must get out of these ruts; we must discard the vague notions of superiority, inferiority, equality which have hitherto corrupted every discussion of the subject and start afresh.

Very well, but just how shall we pose the question? And, to begin with, who are we to propound it at all? Man is at once judge and party to the case; but so is woman. What we need is an angel – neither man nor woman – but where shall we find one? Still, the angel would be poorly qualified to speak, for an angel is ignorant of all the basic facts involved in the problem. With a hermaphrodite we should be no better off, for here the situation is most peculiar; the hermaphrodite is not really the combination of a whole man and a whole woman, but consists of parts of each and thus is neither. It looks to me as if there are, after all, certain women who are best qualified to elucidate the situation of woman. Let us not be misled by the sophism that because Epimenides was a Cretan he was necessarily a liar; it is not a mysterious essence that compels men and women to act in good or in bad faith, it is their situation that inclines them more or less toward the search for truth. Many of today's women, fortunate in the restoration of all the privileges pertaining to the estate of the human being, can afford the luxury of impartiality – we even recognize its necessity. We are no longer like our partisan elders; by and large we have won the game. In recent debates on the status of women the United Nations has persistently maintained that the equality of the sexes is now becoming a reality, and already some of us have never had to sense in our femininity an inconvenience or an obstacle. Many problems appear to us to be more pressing than those which concern us in particular, and this detachment even allows us to hope that our attitude will be objective. Still, we know the feminine world more intimately than do the men because we have our roots in it, we grasp more immediately than do men what it means to a human being to be feminine; and we are more concerned with such knowledge. I have said that there are more pressing problems, but this does not prevent us from seeing some importance in asking how the fact of being women will affect our lives. What opportunities precisely have been given us and what withheld? What fate awaits our younger sisters, and what directions should they take? It is significant that books by women on women are in general animated in our day less by a wish to demand our rights than by an effort toward clarity and understanding. As we emerge from an era of excessive controversy, this book is offered as one attempt among others to confirm that statement.

But it is doubtless impossible to approach any human problem with a mind free from bias. The way in which questions are put, the points of view assumed, presuppose a relativity of interest; all characteristics imply values, and every objective description, so called, implies an ethical background. Rather than attempt to conceal principles more or less definitely implied, it is better to state them openly at the beginning. This will make it unnecessary to specify on every page in just what sense one uses such words as *superior*, *inferior*, *better*, *worse*, *progress*, *reaction*, and the like. If we survey some of the works on woman, we note that one of the points of view most frequently adopted is that of the public good, the general interest; and one always means by this the benefit of society as one wishes it to be maintained or established. For our part, we hold that the only public good is that which assures the private good of the citizens; we shall pass judgment on institutions according to their effectiveness in giving concrete opportunities to individuals. But we do not confuse the idea of private interest with that of happiness, although that is another common point of view. Are not women of the harem more happy than women voters? Is not the housekeeper happier than the workingwoman? It is not too clear just what the word *happy* really means and still less what true values it may mask. There is no possibility of measuring the happiness of others, and it is always easy to describe as happy the situation in which one wishes to place them.

In particular those who are condemned to stagnation are often pronounced happy on the pretext that happiness consists in being at rest. This notion we reject, for our perspective is that of existentialist ethics. Every subject plays his part as such specifically through exploits or projects that serve as a mode of transcendence; he achieves liberty only through a continual reaching out toward other liberties. There is no justification for present existence other than its expansion into an indefinitely open future. Every time transcendence falls back into immanence, stagnation, there is a degradation of existence into the "*en-soi*" – the brutish life of subjection to given conditions – and of liberty into constraint and contingence. This downfall represents a moral fault if the subject consents to it; if it is inflicted upon him, it spells frustration and oppression. In both cases it is an absolute evil. Every individual concerned to justify his existence feels that his existence involves an undefined need to transcend himself, to engage in freely chosen projects.

Now, what peculiarly signalizes the situation of woman is that she – a free and autonomous being like all human creatures – nevertheless finds herself living in a world where men compel her to assume the status of the Other. They propose to stabilize her as object and to doom her to immanence since her transcendence is to be overshadowed and forever transcended by another ego (*conscience*) which is essential and sovereign. The drama of woman lies in this conflict between the fundamental aspirations of every subject (ego) – who always regards the self as the essential – and the compulsions of a situation in which she is the inessential. How can a human being in woman's situation attain fulfillment? What roads are open to her? Which are blocked? How can independence be recovered in a state of dependency? What circumstances limit woman's liberty and how can they be overcome? These are the fundamental questions on which I would fain throw some light. This means that I am interested in the fortunes of the individual as defined not in terms of happiness but in terms of liberty.

Quite evidently this problem would be without significance if we were to believe that woman's destiny is inevitably determined by physiological, psychological, or economic forces. Hence I shall discuss first of all the light in which woman is viewed by biology, psychoanalysis, and historical materialism. Next I shall try to show exactly how the concept of the "truly feminine" has been fashioned – why woman has been defined as the Other – and what have been the consequences from man's point of view. Then from woman's point of view I shall describe the world in which women must live; and thus we shall be able to envisage the difficulties in their way as, endeavoring to make their escape from the sphere hitherto assigned them, they aspire to full membership in the human race. . . .

One is not born, but rather becomes, a woman. No biological, psychological, or economic fate determines the figure that the human female presents in society; it is civilization as a whole that produces this creature, intermediate between male and eunuch, which is described as feminine. Only the intervention of someone else can establish an individual as an *Other*.

Notes

1 *Franchise*, dead today.

2 The Kinsey Report [Alfred C. Kinsey and others: *Sexual Behavior in the Human Male* (W. B. Saunders Co., 1948)] is no exception, for it is limited to describing the sexual characteristics of American men, which is quite a different matter.

3 E. Levinas expresses this idea most explicitly in his essay *Temps et l'Autre*. "Is there not a case in which otherness, alterity [*altérité*], unquestionably marks the nature of a being, as its essence, an instance of otherness not consisting purely and simply in the opposition of two species of the same genus? I think that the feminine represents the contrary in its absolute sense, this contrariness being in no wise affected by any relation between it and its correlative and thus remaining absolutely other. Sex is not a certain specific difference . . . no more is the sexual difference a mere contradiction. . . . Nor does this difference lie in the duality of two complementary terms, for two complementary terms imply a pre-existing whole. . . . Otherness reaches its full flowering in the feminine, a term of the same rank as consciousness but of opposite meaning."

I suppose that Levinas does not forget that woman, too, is aware of her own consciousness, or ego. But it is striking that he deliberately takes a man's point of view, disregarding the reciprocity of subject and object. When he writes that woman is mystery, he implies that she is mystery for man. Thus his description, which is intended to be objective, is in fact an assertion of masculine privilege.

4 See C. Lévi-Strauss: *Les Structures élémentaires de la parenté*. My thanks are due to C. Lévi-Strauss for his kindness in furnishing me with the proofs of his work, which, among others, I have used liberally in Part II.

5 With rare exceptions, perhaps, like certain matriarchal rulers, queens, and the like – Tr.

6 At the moment in "equal rights" amendment to the Constitution of the United States is before Congress. – Tr.

7 Or at least he thought he could.

8 A significant article on this theme by Michel Carrouges appeared in No. 292 of the *Cahiers du Sud*. He writes indignantly: "Would that there were no woman-myth at all but only a cohort of cooks, matrons, prostitutes, and bluestockings serving functions of pleasure or usefulness!" That is to say, in his view woman has no existence in and for herself; he thinks only of her *function* in the male world. Her reason for existence lies in man. But then, in fact, her poetic "function" as a myth might be more valued than any other. The real problem is precisely to find out why woman should be defined with relation to man.

9 For example, a man will say that he considers his wife in no wise degraded because she has no gainful occupation. The profession of housewife is just as lofty, and so on. But when the first quarrel comes he will exclaim: "Why, you couldn't make your living without me!"

4

Theory of Sexual Politics

Kate Millett

[. . .] In introducing the term "sexual politics," one must first answer the inevitable question "Can the relationship between the sexes be viewed in a political light at all?" The answer depends on how one defines politics.[1] This essay does not define the political as that relatively narrow and exclusive world of meetings, chairmen, and parties. The term "politics" shall refer to power-structured relationships, arrangements whereby one group of persons is controlled by another. By way of parenthesis one might add that although an ideal politics might simply be conceived of as the arrangement of human life on agreeable and rational principles from whence the entire notion of power *over* others should be banished, one must confess that this is not what constitutes the political as we know it, and it is to this that we must address ourselves.

The following sketch, which might be described as "notes toward a theory of patriarchy," will attempt to prove that sex is a status category with political implications. Something of a pioneering effort, it must perforce be both tentative and imperfect. Because the intention is to provide an overall description, statements must be generalized, exceptions neglected, and subheadings overlapping and, to some degree, arbitrary as well.

The word "politics" is enlisted here when speaking of the sexes primarily because such a word is eminently useful in outlining the real nature of their relative status, historically and at the present. It is opportune, perhaps today even mandatory, that we develop a more relevant psychology and philosophy of power relationships beyond the simple conceptual framework provided by our traditional formal politics. Indeed, it may be imperative that we give some attention to defining a theory of politics which treats of power relationships on grounds less conventional than those to which we are accustomed.[2] I have therefore found it pertinent to define them on grounds of personal contact and interaction between members of well-defined and coherent groups: races, castes, classes, and sexes. For it is precisely because certain groups have no representation in a number of recognized political structures that their position tends to be so stable, their oppression so continuous.

In America, recent events have forced us to acknowledge at last that the relationship between the races is indeed a political one which involves the general control of one collectivity, defined by birth, over another collectivity, also defined by birth. Groups who rule by birthright are fast disappearing,

Kate Millett, "Theory of Sexual Politics," pp. 23–58 from *Sexual Politics*. Chicago, IL: University of Illinois Press, 2000.

yet there remains one ancient and universal scheme for the domination of one birth group by another – the scheme that prevails in the area of sex. The study of racism has convinced us that a truly political state of affairs operates between the races to perpetuate a series of oppressive circumstances. The subordinated group has inadequate redress through existing political institutions, and is deterred thereby from organizing into conventional political struggle and opposition.

Quite in the same manner, a disinterested examination of our system of sexual relationship must point out that the situation between the sexes now, and throughout history, is a case of that phenomenon Max Weber defined as *herrschaft*, a relationship of dominance and subordinance.[3] What goes largely unexamined, often even unacknowledged (yet is institutionalized nonetheless) in our social order, is the birthright priority whereby males rule females. Through this system a most ingenious form of "interior colonization" has been achieved. It is one which tends moreover to be sturdier than any form of segregation, and more rigorous than class stratification, more uniform, certainly more enduring. However muted its present appearance may be, sexual dominion obtains nevertheless as perhaps the most pervasive ideology of our culture and provides its most fundamental concept of power.

This is so because our society, like all other historical civilizations, is a patriarchy.[4] The fact is evident at once if one recalls that the military, industry, technology, universities, science, political office, and finance – in short, every avenue of power within the society, including the coercive force of the police, is entirely in male hands. As the essence of politics is power, such realization cannot fail to carry impact. What lingers of supernatural authority, the Deity, "His" ministry, together with the ethics and values, the philosophy and art of our culture – its very civilization – as T. S. Eliot once observed, is of male manufacture.

If one takes patriarchal government to be the institution whereby that half of the populace which is female is controlled by that half which is male, the principles of patriarchy appear to be two fold: male shall dominate female, elder male shall dominate younger. However, just as with any human institution, there is frequently a distance between the real and the ideal; contradictions and exceptions do exist within the system. While patriarchy as an institution is a social constant so deeply entrenched as to run through all other political, social, or economic forms, whether of caste or class, feudality or bureaucracy, just as it pervades all major religions, it also exhibits great variety in history and locale. In democracies,[5] for example, females have often held no office or do so (as now) in such minuscule numbers as to be below even token representation. Aristocracy, on the other hand, with its emphasis upon the magic and dynastic properties of blood, may at times permit women to hold power. The principle of rule by elder males is violated even more frequently. Bearing in mind the variation and degree in patriarchy – as say between Saudi Arabia and Sweden, Indonesia and Red China – we also recognize our own form in the US and Europe to be much altered and attenuated by the reforms described in the next chapter.

I Ideological

Hannah Arendt[6] has observed that government is upheld by power supported either through consent or imposed through violence. Conditioning to an ideology amounts to the former. Sexual politics obtains consent through the "socialization" of both sexes to basic patriarchal polities with regard to temperament, role, and status. As to status, a pervasive assent to the prejudice of male superiority guarantees superior status in the male, inferior in the female. The first item, temperament, involves the formation of human personality along stereotyped lines of sex category ("masculine" and "feminine"), based on the needs and values of the dominant group and dictated by what its members cherish in themselves and find convenient in subordinates: aggression, intelligence, force, and efficacy in the male; passivity, ignorance, docility, "virtue," and ineffectuality in the female. This is complemented by a second factor, sex role, which decrees a consonant and highly elaborate code of conduct, gesture and attitude for each sex. In terms of activity, sex role assigns domestic service and attendance upon infants to the female, the rest of human achievement, interest, and ambition to the male. The limited role allotted the female tends to arrest her at the level of biological experience. Therefore, nearly all that can be described as distinctly human rather than animal activity (in their own way animals also give birth and care for their young) is largely reserved for the male. Of course, status again follows from such an assignment. Were one to analyze the three categories one might designate status as the political component, role as the sociological, and temperament as the psychological – yet their interdependence is unquestionable and they form a chain. Those awarded higher status tend to adopt roles of mastery, largely because they are first encouraged to develop temperaments of dominance. That this is true of caste and class as well is self-evident.

II Biological

Patriarchal religion, popular attitude, and to some degree, science as well[7] assumes these psycho-social distinctions to rest upon biological differences between the sexes, so that where culture is acknowledged as shaping behavior, it is said to do no more than cooperate with nature. Yet the temperamental distinctions created in patriarchy ("masculine" and "feminine" personality traits) do not appear to originate in human nature, those of role and status still less.

The heavier musculature of the male, a secondary sexual characteristic and common among mammals, is biological in origin but is also culturally encouraged through breeding, diet and exercise. Yet it is hardly an adequate category on which to base political relations *within civilization*.[8] Male supremacy, like other political creeds, does not finally reside in physical strength but in the acceptance of a value system which is not biological. Superior physical strength is not a factor in political relations – vide those of race and class. Civilization has always been able to substitute other methods (technic, weaponry, knowledge) for those of physical strength, and contemporary civilization has no further need of it. At present, as in the past, physical exertion is very generally a class factor, those at the bottom performing the most strenuous tasks, whether they be strong or not.

It is often assumed that patriarchy is endemic in human social life, explicable or even inevitable on the grounds of human physiology. Such a theory grants patriarchy logical as well as historical origin. Yet if as some anthropologists believe, patriarchy is not of primeval origin, but was preceded by some other social form we shall call pre-patriarchal, then the argument of physical strength as a theory of patriarchal *origins* would hardly constitute a sufficient explanation – unless the male's superior physical strength was released in accompaniment with some change in orientation through new values or new knowledge. Conjecture about origins is always frustrated by lack of certain evidence. Speculation about prehistory, which of necessity is what this must be, remains nothing but speculation. Were one to indulge in it, one might argue the likelihood of a hypothetical period preceding patriarchy.[9] What would be crucial to such a premise would be a state of mind in which the primary principle would be regarded as fertility or vitalist processes. In a primitive condition, before it developed civilization or any but the crudest technic, humanity would perhaps find the most impressive evidence of creative force in the visible birth of children, something of a miraculous event and linked analogically with the growth of the earth's vegetation.

It is possible that the circumstance which might drastically redirect such attitudes would be the discovery of paternity. There is some evidence that fertility cults in ancient society at some point took a turn toward patriarchy, displacing and downgrading female function in procreation and attributing the power of life to the phallus alone. Patriarchal religion could consolidate this position by the creation of a male God or gods, demoting, discrediting, or eliminating goddesses and constructing a theology whose basic postulates are male supremacist, and one of whose central functions is to uphold and validate the patriarchal structure.[10]

So much for the evanescent delights afforded by the game of origins. The question of the historical origins of patriarchy – whether patriarchy originated primordially in the male's superior strength, or upon a later mobilization of such strength under certain circumstances – appears at the moment to be unanswerable. It is also probably irrelevant to contemporary patriarchy, where we are left with the realities of sexual politics, still grounded, we are often assured, on nature. Unfortunately, as the psycho-social distinctions made between the two sex groups which are said to justify their present political relationship are not the clear, specific, measurable and neutral ones of the physical sciences, but are instead of an entirely different character – vague, amorphous, often even quasi-religious in phrasing – it must be admitted that many of the generally understood distinctions between the sexes in the more significant areas of role and temperament, not to mention status, have in fact, essentially cultural, rather than biological, bases. Attempts to prove that temperamental dominance is inherent in the male (which for its advocates, would be tantamount to validating, logically as well as historically, the patriarchal situation regarding role and status) have been notably unsuccessful. Sources in the field are in hopeless disagreement about the nature of sexual differences, but the most reasonable among them have despaired of the ambition of any definite equation between temperament and biological nature. It appears that we are not soon to be enlightened as to the existence of any significant inherent differences between male and female beyond the bio-genital ones we already know. Endocrinology and genetics afford no definite evidence of determining mental-emotional differences.[11]

Not only is there insufficient evidence for the thesis that the present social distinctions of patriarchy (status, role, temperament) are physical in origin, but we are hardly in a position to assess the existing differentiations, since distinctions which we know to be culturally induced at present so outweigh them. Whatever the "real" differences between the sexes may be, we are not likely to know them until the sexes are treated differently, that is alike. And this is very far from being the case at present. Important new research not only suggests that the possibilities of innate temperamental differences seem more remote than ever, but even raises questions as to the validity and permanence of psychosexual identity. In doing so it gives fairly concrete positive evidence of the overwhelmingly *cultural* character of gender, i.e. personality structure in terms of sexual category.

What Stoller and other experts define as "core gender identity" is now thought to be established in the young by the age of eighteen months. This is how Stoller differentiates between sex and gender:

> Dictionaries stress that the major connotation of *sex* is a biological one, as for example, in the phrases *sexual relations* or *the male sex*. In agreement with this, the word *sex*, in this work will refer to the male or female sex and the component biological parts that determine whether one is a male or a female; the word *sexual* will have connotations of anatomy and physiology. This obviously leaves tremendous areas of behavior, feelings, thoughts and fantasies that are related to the sexes and yet do not have primarily biological connotations. It is for some of these psychological phenomena that the term gender will be used: one can speak of the male sex or the female sex, but one can also talk about masculinity and femininity and not necessarily be implying anything about anatomy or physiology. Thus, while *sex* and *gender* seem to common sense inextricably bound together, one purpose of this study will be to confirm the fact that the two realms (sex and gender) are not inevitably bound in anything like a one-to-one relationship, but each may go into quite independent ways.[12]

In cases of genital malformation and consequent erroneous gender assignment at birth, studied at the California Gender Identity Center, the discovery was made that it is easier to change the sex of an adolescent male, whose biological identity turns out to be contrary to his gender assignment and conditioning – through surgery – than to undo the educational consequences of years, which have succeeded in making the subject temperamentally feminine in gesture, sense of self, personality and interests. Studies done in California under Stoller's direction offer proof that gender identity (I am a girl, I am a boy) is the primary identity any human being holds – the first as well as the most permanent and far-reaching. Stoller later makes emphatic the distinction that sex is biological, gender psychological, and therefore cultural: "*Gender* is a term that has psychological or cultural rather than biological connotations. If the proper terms for sex are "male" and "female," the corresponding terms for gender are "masculine" and "feminine"; these latter may be quite independent of (biological) sex."[13] Indeed, so arbitrary is gender, that it may even be contrary to physiology: "... although the external genitalia (penis, testes, scrotum) contribute to the sense of maleness, no one of them is essential for it, not even all of them together. In the absence of complete evidence, I agree in general with Money, and the Hampsons who show in their large series of intersexed patients that gender role is determined by postnatal forces, regardless of the anatomy and physiology of the external genitalia."[14]

It is now believed[15] that the human fetus is originally physically female until the operation of androgen at a certain stage of gestation causes those with Y chromosomes to develop into males. Psychosexually (e.g., in terms of masculine and feminine, and in contradistinction to male and female) there is no differentiation between the sexes at birth. Psychosexual personality is therefore postnatal and learned:

> the condition existing at birth and for several months thereafter is one of psychosexual undifferentiation. Just as in the embryo, morphologic sexual differentiation passes from a plastic stage to one of fixed immutability, so also does psychosexual differentiation become fixed and immutable – so much so, that mankind has traditionally assumed that so strong and fixed a feeling as personal sexual identity must stem from something innate, instinctive, and not subject to postnatal experience and learning. The error of this traditional assumption is that the power and permanence of something learned has been underestimated. The experiments of animal ethologists on imprinting have now corrected this misconception.[16]

John Money who is quoted above, believes that "the acquisition of a native language is a human counterpart to imprinting," and gender first established "with the establishment of a native language."[17] This would place the time of establishment at about eighteen months. Jerome Kagin's[18] studies in how children of pre-speech age are handled and touched, tickled and spoken to in terms of their sexual identity ("Is it a boy or a girl?" "Hello, little fellow," "Isn't she pretty," etc.) put the most considerable emphasis on purely tactile learning which would have much to do with the child's sense of self, even before speech is attained.

Because of our social circumstances, male and female are really two cultures and their life experiences are utterly different – and this is crucial. Implicit in all the gender identity development which takes place through childhood is the sum total of the parents', the peers', and the culture's notions of what is appropriate to each gender by way of temperament, character, interests, status, worth, gesture, and expression. Every moment of the child's life is a clue to how he or she must think and behave to attain or satisfy the demands which gender places upon one. In adolescence, the merciless task of conformity grows to crisis proportions, generally cooling and settling in maturity.

Since patriarchy's biological foundations appear to be so very insecure, one has some cause to admire the strength of a "socialization" which can continue a universal condition "on faith alone," as it were, or through an acquired value system exclusively. What does seem decisive in assuring the maintenance of the temperamental differences between the sexes is the conditioning of early childhood. Conditioning runs in a circle of self-perpetuation and self-fulfilling prophecy. To take a simple example: expectations the culture cherishes about his gender identity encourage the young male to develop aggressive impulses, and the female to thwart her own or turn them inward. The result is that the male tends to have aggression reinforced in his behavior, often with significant anti-social possibilities. Thereupon the culture consents to believe the possession of the male indicator, the testes, penis, and scrotum, in itself characterizes the aggressive impulse, and even vulgarly celebrates it in such encomiums as "that guy has balls." The same process of reinforcement is evident in producing the chief "feminine" virtue of passivity.

In contemporary terminology, the basic division of temperamental trait is marshaled along the line of "aggression is male" and "passivity is female." All other temperamental traits are somehow – often with the most dexterous ingenuity – aligned to correspond. If aggressiveness is the trait of the master class, docility must be the corresponding trait of a subject group. The usual hope of such line of reasoning is that "nature," by some impossible outside chance, might still be depended upon to rationalize the patriarchal system. An important consideration to be remembered here is that in patriarchy, the function of norm is unthinkingly delegated to the male – were it not, one might as plausibly speak of "feminine" behavior as active, and "masculine" behavior as hyperactive or hyperaggressive.

Here it might be added, by way of a coda, that data from physical sciences has recently been enlisted again to support sociological arguments, such as those of Lionel Tiger[19] who seeks a genetic justification of patriarchy by proposing a "bonding instinct" in males which assures their political and social control of human society. One sees the implication of such a theory by applying its premise to any ruling group. Tiger's thesis appears to be a misrepresentation of the work of Lorenz and other students of animal behavior. Since his evidence of inherent trait is patriarchal history and organization, his pretensions to physical evidence are both specious and circular. One can only advance genetic evidence when one has genetic (rather than historical) evidence to advance. As many authorities dismiss the possibility of instincts (complex inherent behavioral patterns) in humans altogether, admitting only reflexes and drives (far simpler neural responses),[20] the prospects of a "bonding instinct" appear particularly forlorn.

Should one regard sex in humans as a drive, it is still necessary to point out that the enormous area of our lives, both in early "socialization" and in adult experience, labeled "sexual behavior," is almost entirely the product of learning. So much is this the case that even the act of coitus itself is the product of a long series of learned responses – responses to the patterns and attitudes, even as to the object of sexual choice, which are set up for us by our social environment.

The arbitrary character of patriarchal ascriptions of temperament and role has little effect upon their power over us. Nor do the mutually exclusive, contradictory, and polar qualities of the categories "masculine" and "feminine" imposed upon human personality give rise to sufficiently serious question among us. Under their aegis each personality becomes little more, and often less than half, of its human potential. Politically, the fact that each group exhibits a circumscribed but complementary personality and range of activity is of secondary importance to the fact that each represents a status or power division. In the matter of conformity patriarchy is a governing ideology without peer; it is probable that no other system has ever exercised such a complete control over its subjects.

III Sociological

Patriarchy's chief institution is the family. It is both a mirror of and a connection with the larger society; a patriarchal unit within a patriarchal whole. Mediating between the individual and the social structure, the family effects control and conformity where political and other authorities are insufficient.[21] As the fundamental instrument and the foundation unit of patriarchal society the family and its roles are prototypical. Serving as an agent of the larger society, the family not only encourages its own members to adjust and conform, but acts as a unit in the government of the patriarchal state which rules its citizens through its family heads. Even in patriarchal societies where they are granted legal citizenship, women tend to be ruled through the family alone and have little or no formal relation to the state.[22]

As co-operation between the family and the larger society is essential, else both would fall apart, the fate of three patriarchal institutions, the family, society, and the state are interrelated. In most forms of patriarchy this has generally led to the granting of religious support in statements such as the Catholic precept that "the father is head of the family," or Judaism's delegation of quasi-priestly authority to the male parent. Secular governments today also confirm this, as in census practices of designating the male as head of household, taxation, passports, etc. Female heads of household tend to be regarded as undesirable; the phenomenon is a trait of poverty or misfortune. The Confucian prescription that the relationship between ruler and subject is parallel to that of father and children points to the essentially feudal character of the patriarchal family (and conversely, the familial character of feudalism) even in modern democracies.[23]

Traditionally, patriarchy granted the father nearly total ownership over wife or wives and children, including the powers of physical abuse and often even those of murder and sale. Classically, as head of the family the father is both begetter and owner in a system in which kinship is property.[24] Yet in strict patriarchy, kinship is acknowledged only through association with the male line. Agnation excludes the descendants of the female line from property right and often even from recognition.[25] The first formulation of the patriarchal family was made by Sir Henry Maine, a nineteenth-century historian of ancient jurisprudence. Maine argues that the patriarchal basis of kinship is put in terms of dominion rather than blood; wives, though outsiders, are assimilated into the line, while sister's sons are excluded. Basing his definition of the family upon the *patria potestes* of Rome, Maine defined it as follows: "The eldest male parent is absolutely supreme in his household. His dominion extends to life and death and is as unqualified over his children and their houses as over his slaves."[26] In the archaic patriarchal family "the group consists of animate and inanimate property, of wife, children, slaves, land and goods, all held together by subjection to the despotic authority of the eldest male."[27]

McLennon's rebuttal[28] to Maine argued that the Roman *patria potestes* was an extreme form of patriarchy and by no means, as Maine had imagined, universal. Evidence of matrilineal societies (preliterate societies in Africa and elsewhere) refute Maine's assumption of the universality of agnation. Certainly Maine's central argument, as to the primeval or state of nature character of patriarchy is but a rather naïf[29] rationalization of an institution Maine tended to exalt. The assumption of patriarchy's primeval character is contradicted by much evidence which points to the conclusion that full patriarchal authority, particularly that of the *patria potestes* is a late development and the total erosion of female status was likely to be gradual as has been its recovery.

In contemporary patriarchies the male's *de jure* priority has recently been modified through the granting of divorce[30] protection, citizenship, and property to women. Their chattel status continues in their loss of name, their obligation to adopt the husband's domicile, and the general legal assumption that marriage involves an exchange of the female's domestic service and (sexual) consortium in return for financial support.[31]

The chief contribution of the family in patriarchy is the socialization of the young (largely through the example and admonition of their parents) into patriarchal ideology's prescribed attitudes toward the categories of role, temperament, and status. Although slight differences of definition depend here upon the parents' grasp of cultural values, the general effect of uniformity is achieved, to be further reinforced through peers, schools, media, and other learning sources, formal and informal. While we may niggle over the balance of authority between the personalities of various households, one must remember that the entire culture supports masculine authority in all areas of life and – outside of the home – permits the female none at all.

To insure that its crucial functions of reproduction and socialization of the young take place only within its confines, the patriarchal family insists upon legitimacy. Bronislaw Malinowski describes this as "the principle of legitimacy" formulating it as an insistence that "no child should be brought into the world without a man – and one man at that – assuming the role of sociological father."[32] By this apparently consistent and universal prohibition (whose penalties vary by class and in accord with the expected operations of the double standard) patriarchy decrees that the status of both child and mother is primarily or ultimately dependent upon the male. And since it is not only his social status, but even his economic power upon which his dependents generally rely, the position of the masculine figure within the family – as without – is materially, as well as ideologically, extremely strong.

Although there is no biological reason why the two central functions of the family (socialization and reproduction) need be inseparable from or even take place within it, revolutionary or utopian efforts to remove these functions from the family have been so frustrated, so beset by difficulties, that most experiments so far have involved a gradual return to tradition. This is strong evidence of how basic a form patriarchy is within all societies, and of how pervasive its effects upon family members. It is perhaps also an admonition that change undertaken without a thorough understanding of the socio-political institution to be changed is hardly productive. And yet radical social change cannot take place without having an effect upon patriarchy. And not simply because it is the political form which subordinates such a large percentage of the population (women and youth) but because it serves as a citadel of property and traditional interests. Marriages are financial alliances, and each household operates as an economic entity much like a corporation. As one student of the family states it, "the family is the keystone of the stratification system, the social mechanism by which it is maintained."[33]

IV Class

It is in the area of class that the castelike status of the female within patriarchy is most liable to confusion, for sexual status often operates in a superficially confusing way within the variable of class. In a society where status is dependent upon the economic, social, and educational circumstances of class, it is possible for certain females to appear to stand higher than some males. Yet not when one looks more closely at the subject. This is perhaps easier to see by means of analogy: a black doctor or lawyer has higher social status than a poor white sharecropper. But race, itself a caste system which subsumes class, persuades the latter citizen that he belongs to a higher order of life, just as it oppresses the black professional in spirit, whatever his material success may be. In much the same manner, a truck driver or butcher has always his "manhood" to fall back upon. Should this final vanity be offended, he may contemplate more violent methods. The literature of the past thirty years provides a staggering number of incidents in which the caste of virility triumphs over the social status of wealthy or even educated women. In literary contexts one has to deal here with wish-fulfillment. Incidents from life (bullying, obscene, or hostile remarks) are probably another sort of psychological gesture of ascendancy. Both convey more hope than reality, for class divisions are generally quite impervious to the hostility of individuals. And yet while the existence of class division is not seriously threatened by such expressions of enmity, the existence of sexual hierarchy has been re-affirmed and mobilized to "punish" the female quite effectively.

The function of class or ethnic mores in patriarchy is largely a matter of how overtly displayed or how loudly enunciated the general ethic of masculine supremacy allows itself to become. Here one is confronted by what appears to be a paradox: while in the lower social strata, the male is more likely to claim authority on the strength of his sex rank alone, he is actually obliged more often to share power with the women of his class who are economically productive; whereas in the middle and upper classes, there is less tendency to assert a blunt patriarchal dominance, as men who enjoy such status have more power in any case.[34]

It is generally accepted that Western patriarchy has been much softened by the concepts of courtly and romantic love. While this is certainly true, such influence has also been vastly overestimated. In comparison with the candor of "machismo" or oriental behavior, one realizes how much of a concession traditional chivalrous behavior represents – a sporting kind of reparation to allow the subordinate female certain means of saving face. While a palliative to the injustice of woman's social position, chivalry is also a technique for disguising it. One must acknowledge that the chivalrous stance is a game the master group plays in elevating its subject to pedestal level. Historians of courtly love stress the fact that the raptures of the poets had no effect upon the legal or economic standing of women, and very little upon their social status.[35] As the sociologist Hugo Beigel has observed, both the courtly and the romantic versions of love are "grants" which the male concedes out of his total powers.[36] Both have had the effect of obscuring the patriarchal character of Western culture and in their general tendency to attribute impossible virtues to women, have ended by confining them in a narrow and often remarkably conscribing sphere of behavior. It was a Victorian habit, for example, to insist the female assume the function of serving as the male's conscience and living the life of goodness he found tedious but felt someone ought to do anyway.

The concept of romantic love affords a means of emotional manipulation which the male is free to exploit, since love is the only circumstance in which the female is (ideologically) pardoned for sexual activity. And convictions of romantic love are convenient to both parties since this is often the only condition in which the female can overcome the far more powerful conditioning she has received toward sexual inhibition. Romantic love also obscures the realities of female status and the burden of economic dependency. As to "chivalry," such gallant gesture as still resides in the middle classes has degenerated to a tired ritualism, which scarcely serves to mask the status situation of the present.

Within patriarchy one must often deal with contradictions which are simply a matter of class style. David Riesman has noted that as the working class has been assimilated into the middle class, so have its sexual mores and attitudes. The fairly blatant male chauvinism which was once a province of the lower class or immigrant male has been absorbed and taken on a certain glamour through a number of contemporary figures, who have made it, and a certain number of other working-class male attitudes, part of a new, and at the moment, fashionable life style. So influential is this working-class ideal of brute virility (or more accurately, a literary and therefore middle-class version of it) become in our time that it may replace more discreet and "gentlemanly" attitudes of the past.[37]

One of the chief effects of class within patriarchy is to set one woman against another, in the past creating a lively antagonism between whore and matron, and in the present between career woman and housewife. One envies the other her "security" and prestige, while the envied yearns beyond the confines of respectability for what she takes to be the other's freedom, adventure, and contact with the great world. Through the multiple advantages of the double standard, the male participates in both worlds, empowered by his superior social and economic resources to play the estranged women against each other as rivals. One might also recognize subsidiary status categories among women: not only is virtue class, but beauty and age as well.

Perhaps, in the final analysis, it is possible to argue that women tend to transcend the usual class stratifications in patriarchy, for whatever the class of her birth and education, the female has fewer permanent class associations than does the male.

Economic dependency renders her affiliations with any class a tangential, vicarious, and temporary matter. Aristotle observed that the only slave to whom a commoner might lay claim was his woman, and the service of an unpaid domestic still provides working-class males with a "cushion" against the buffets of the class system which incidentally provides them with some of the psychic luxuries of the leisure class. Thrown upon their own resources, few women rise above working class in personal prestige and economic power, and women as a group do not enjoy many of the interests and benefits any class may offer its male members. Women have therefore less of an investment in the class system. But it is important to understand that as with any group whose existence is parasitic to its rulers, women are a dependency class who live on surplus. And their marginal life frequently renders them conservative, for like all persons in their situation (slaves are a classic example here) they identify their own survival with the prosperity of those who feed them. The hope of seeking liberating radical solutions of their own seems too remote for the majority to dare contemplate and remains so until consciousness on the subject is raised.

As race is emerging as one of the final variables in sexual politics, it is pertinent, especially in a discussion of modern literature, to devote a few words to it as well. Traditionally, the white male has been accustomed to concede the female of his own race, in her capacity as "his woman" a higher status than that ascribed to the black male.[38] Yet as white racist ideology is exposed and begins to erode, racism's older protective attitudes toward (white) women also begin to give way. And the priorities of maintaining male supremacy might outweigh even those of white supremacy; sexism may be more endemic in our own society than racism. For example, one notes in authors whom we would now term overtly racist, such as D. H. Lawrence – whose contempt for what he so often designates as inferior breeds is unabashed – instances where the lower-caste male is brought on to master or humiliate the white man's own insubordinate mate. Needless to say, the female of the non-white races does not figure in such tales save as an exemplum of "true" womanhood's servility, worthy of imitation by other less carefully instructed females. Contemporary white sociology often operates under a similar patriarchal bias when its rhetoric inclines toward the assertion that the "matriarchal" (e.g. matrifocal) aspect of black society and the "castration" of the black male are the most deplorable symptoms of black oppression in white racist society, with the implication that racial inequity is capable of solution by a restoration of masculine authority. Whatever the facts of the matter may be, it can also be suggested that analysis of this kind presupposes patriarchal values without questioning them, and tends to obscure both the true character of and the responsibility for racist injustice toward black humanity of both sexes.

V Economic and Educational

One of the most efficient branches of patriarchal government lies in the agency of its economic hold over its female subjects. In traditional patriarchy, women, as non-persons without legal standing, were permitted no actual economic existence as they could neither own nor earn in their own right. Since women have always worked in patriarchal societies, often at the most routine or strenuous tasks, what is at issue here is not labor but economic reward. In modern reformed patriarchal societies, women have certain economic rights, yet the "woman's work" in which some two thirds of the female population in most developed countries are engaged is work that is not paid for.[39] In a money economy where autonomy and prestige depend upon currency, this is a fact of great importance. In general, the position of women in patriarchy is a continuous function of their economic dependence. Just as their social position is vicarious and achieved (often on a temporary or marginal basis) through males, their relation to the economy is also typically vicarious or tangential.

Of that third of women who are employed, their average wages represent only half of the average income enjoyed by men. These are the US Department of Labor statistics for average year-round income: white male, $6,704, non-white male $4,277, white female, $3,991, and non-white female $2,816.[40] The disparity is made somewhat more remarkable because the educational level of women is generally higher than that of men in comparable income brackets.[41] Further, the kinds of employment open to women in modern patriarchies are, with few exceptions, menial, ill paid and without status.[42]

In modern capitalist countries women also function as a reserve labor force, enlisted in times of war and expansion and discharged in times of peace and recession. In this role American women have replaced immigrant labor and now compete with the racial minorities. In socialist countries the female labor force is generally in the lower ranks as well, despite a high incidence of women in certain professions such as medicine. The status and rewards of such professions have declined as women enter them, and they are permitted to enter such areas under a rationale that society or the state (and socialist countries are also patriarchal) rather than woman is served by such activity.

Since woman's independence in economic life is viewed with distrust, prescriptive agencies of all kinds (religion, psychology, advertising, etc.) continuously admonish or even inveigh against the employment of middle-class women, particularly mothers. The toil of working-class women is more readily accepted as "need," if not always by the working-class itself, at least by the middle-class. And to be sure, it serves the purpose of making available cheap labor in factory and lower-grade service and clerical positions. Its wages and tasks are so unremunerative that, unlike more prestigious employment for women, it fails to threaten patriarchy financially or psychologically. Women who are employed have two jobs since the burden of domestic service and child care is unrelieved either by day care or other social agencies, or by the co-operation of husbands. The invention of labor-saving devices has had no appreciable effect on the duration, even if it has affected the quality of their drudgery.[43] Discrimination in matters of hiring, maternity, wages and hours is very great.[44] In the US a recent law forbidding discrimination in employment, the first and only federal legislative guarantee of rights granted to American women since the vote, is not enforced, has not been enforced since its passage, and was not enacted to be enforced.[45]

In terms of industry and production, the situation of women is in many ways comparable both to colonial and to pre-industrial peoples. Although they achieved their first economic autonomy in the industrial revolution and now constitute a large and underpaid factory population, women do not participate directly in technology or in production. What they customarily produce (domestic and personal service) has no market value and is, as it were, pre-capital. Nor, where they do participate in production of commodities through employment, do they own or control or even comprehend the process in which they participate. An example might make this clearer: the refrigerator is a machine all women use, some assemble it in factories, and a very few with scientific education understand its principles of operation. Yet the heavy industries which roll its steel and produce the dies for its parts are in male hands. The same is true of the typewriter, the auto, etc. Now, while knowledge is fragmented even among the male population, collectively they could reconstruct any technological device. But in the absence of males, women's distance from technology today is sufficiently great that it is doubtful that they could replace or repair such machines on any significant scale. Woman's distance from higher technology is even greater: large-scale building construction; the development of computers; the moon shot, occur as further examples. If knowledge is power, power is also knowledge, and a large factor in their subordinate position is the fairly systematic ignorance patriarchy imposes upon women.

Since education and economy are so closely related in the advanced nations, it is significant that the general level and style of higher education for women, particularly in their many remaining segregated institutions, is closer to that of Renaissance humanism than to the skills of mid-twentieth-century scientific and technological society. Traditionally patriarchy permitted occasional minimal literacy to women while higher education was closed to them. While modern patriarchies have, fairly recently, opened all educational levels to women,[46] the kind and quality of education is not the same for each sex. This difference is of course apparent in early socialization, but it persists and enters into higher education as well. Universities, once places of scholarship and the training of a few professionals, now also produce the personnel of a technocracy. This is not the case with regard to women. Their own colleges typically produce neither scholars nor professionals nor technocrats. Nor are they funded by government and corporations as are male colleges and those co-educational colleges and universities whose primary function is the education of males.

As patriarchy enforces a temperamental imbalance of personality traits between the sexes, its educational institutions, segregated or co-educational, accept a cultural programing toward the generally operative division between "masculine" and "feminine" subject matter, assigning the humanities and certain social sciences (at least in their lower or marginal branches) to the female – and science and technology, the professions, business and engineering to the male. Of course the balance of employment, prestige and reward at present lie with the latter. Control of these fields is very eminently a matter of political power. One might also point out how the exclusive dominance of males in the more prestigious fields directly serves the interests of patriarchal power in industry, government, and the military. And since patriarchy encourages an imbalance in human temperament along sex lines, both divisions of learning (science and the humanities) reflect this imbalance. The humanities, because not exclusively male, suffer in prestige: the sciences, technology, and business, because they are nearly exclusively male reflect the deformation of the "masculine" personality, e.g., a certain predatory or aggressive character.

In keeping with the inferior sphere of culture to which women in patriarchy have always been restricted, the present encouragement of their "artistic" interests through study of the humanities is hardly more than an extension of the "accomplishments" they once cultivated in preparation for the marriage market. Achievement in the arts and humanities is reserved, now, as it has been historically, for males. Token representation, be it Susan Sontag's or Lady Murasaki's, does not vitiate this rule.

VI Force

We are not accustomed to associate patriarchy with force. So perfect is its system of socialization, so complete the general assent to its values, so long and so universally has it prevailed in human society, that it scarcely seems to require violent implementation. Customarily, we view its brutalities in the past as exotic or "primitive" custom. Those of the present are regarded as the product of individual deviance, confined to pathological or exceptional behavior, and without general import. And yet, just as under other total ideologies (racism and colonialism are somewhat analogous in this respect) control in patriarchal society would be imperfect, even inoperable, unless it had the rule of force to rely upon, both in emergencies and as an ever-present instrument of intimidation.

Historically, most patriarchies have institutionalized force through their legal systems. For example, strict patriarchies such as that of Islam, have implemented the prohibition against illegitimacy or sexual autonomy with a death sentence. In Afghanistan and Saudi Arabia the adulteress is still stoned to death with a mullah presiding at the execution. Execution by stoning was once common practice through the Near East. It is still condoned in Sicily. Needless to say there was and is no penalty imposed upon the male corespondent. Save in recent times or exceptional cases, adultery was not generally recognized in males except as an offense one male might commit against another's property interest. In Tokugawa Japan, for example, an elaborate set of legal distinctions were made according to class. A samurai was entitled, and in the face of public knowledge, even obliged, to execute an adulterous wife, whereas a chōnin (common citizen) or peasant might respond as he pleased. In cases of cross-class adultery, the lower-class male convicted of sexual intimacy with his employer's wife would, because he had violated taboos of class and property, be beheaded together with her. Upperstrata males had, of course, the same license to seduce lower-class women as we are familiar with in Western societies.

Indirectly, one form of "death penalty" still obtains even in America today. Patriarchal legal systems in depriving women of control over their own bodies drive them to illegal abortions; it is estimated that between two and five thousand women die each year from this cause.[47]

Excepting a social license to physical abuse among certain class and ethnic groups, force is diffuse and generalized in most contemporary patriarchies. Significantly, force itself is restricted to the male who alone is psychologically and technically equipped to perpetrate physical violence.[48] Where differences in physical strength have become immaterial through the use of arms, the female is rendered innocuous by her socialization. Before assault she is almost universally defenseless both by her physical and emotional training. Needless to say, this has the most far-reaching effects on the social and psychological behavior of both sexes.

Patriarchal force also relies on a form of violence particularly sexual in character and realized most completely in the act of rape. The figures of rapes reported represent only a fraction of those which occur,[49] as the "shame" of the event is sufficient to deter women from the notion of civil prosecution under the public circumstances of a trial. Traditionally rape has been viewed as an offense one male commits upon another – a matter of abusing "his woman." Vendetta, such as occurs in the American South, is carried out for masculine satisfaction, the exhilarations of race hatred, and the interests of property and vanity (honor). In rape, the emotions of aggression, hatred, contempt, and the desire to break or violate personality, take a form consummately appropriate to sexual politics. In the passages analyzed at the outset of this study, such emotions were present at a barely sublimated level and were a key factor in explaining the attitude behind the author's use of language and tone.[50]

Patriarchal societies typically link feelings of cruelty with sexuality, the latter often equated both with evil and with power. This is apparent both in the sexual fantasy reported by psychoanalysis and that reported by pornography. The rule here associates sadism with the male ("the masculine role") and victimization with the female ("the feminine role").[51] Emotional response to violence against women in patriarchy is often curiously ambivalent; references to wife-beating, for example, invariably produce laughter and some embarrassment. Exemplary atrocity, such as the mass murders committed by Richard Speck, greeted at one level with a certain scandalized, possibly hypocritical indignation, is capable of eliciting a mass response of titillation at another level. At such times one even hears from men occasional expressions of envy or amusement. In view of the sadistic character of such public fantasy as caters to male audiences in pornography or semi-pornographic media, one might expect that a certain element of identification is by no means absent from the general response. Probably a similar collective *frisson* sweeps through racist society when its more "logical" members have perpetrated a lynching. Unconsciously, both crimes may serve the larger group as a ritual act, cathartic in effect.

Hostility is expressed in a number of ways. One is laughter. Misogynist literature, the primary vehicle of masculine hostility, is both an hortatory and comic genre. Of all artistic forms in patriarchy it is the most frankly propagandistic. Its aim is to reinforce both sexual factions in their status. Ancient, Medieval, and Renaissance literature in the West has each had a large element of misogyny.[52] Nor is the East without a strong tradition here, notably in the Confucian strain which held sway in Japan as well as China. The Western tradition was indeed moderated somewhat by the introduction of courtly love. But the old diatribes and attacks were coterminous with the new idealization of woman. In the case of Petrarch, Boccaccio, and some others, one can find both attitudes fully expressed, presumably as evidence of different moods, a courtly pose adopted for the ephemeral needs of the vernacular, a grave animosity for sober and eternal Latin.[53] As courtly love was transformed to romantic love, literary misogyny grew somewhat out of fashion. In some places in the eighteenth century it declined into ridicule and exhortative satire. In the nineteenth century its more acrimonious forms almost disappeared in English. Its resurrection in twentieth-century attitudes and literature is the result of a resentment over patriarchal reform, aided by the growing permissiveness in expression which has taken place at an increasing rate in the last fifty years.

Since the abatement of censorship, masculine hostility (psychological or physical) in specifically *sexual* contexts has become far more apparent. Yet as masculine hostility has been fairly continuous, one deals here probably less with a matter of increase than with a new frankness in expressing hostility in specifically sexual contexts. It is a matter of release and freedom to express what was once forbidden expression outside of pornography or other "underground" productions, such as those of De Sade. As one recalls both the euphemism and the idealism of descriptions of coitus in the Romantic poets (Keats's *Eve of St Agnes*), or the Victorian novelists (Hardy, for example) and contrasts it with Miller or William Burroughs, one has an idea of how contemporary literature has absorbed not only the truthful explicitness of pornography, but its anti-social character as well. Since this tendency to hurt or insult has been given free expression, it has become far easier to assess sexual antagonism in the male.

The history of patriarchy presents a variety of cruelties and barbarities: the suttee execution in India, the crippling deformity of footbinding in China, the lifelong ignominy of the veil in Islam, or the widespread persecution of sequestration, the gynacium, and purdah. Phenomenon such as clitoroidectomy, clitoral incision, the sale and enslavement of women under one guise or another, involuntary and child marriages, concubinage and prostitution, still take place – the first in Africa, the latter in the Near and Far East, the last generally. The rationale which accompanies that imposition of male authority euphemistically referred to as "the battle of the sexes" bears a certain resemblance to the formulas of nations at war, where any heinousness is justified on the grounds that the enemy is either an inferior species or really not human at all. The patriarchal mentality has concocted a whole series of rationales about women which accomplish this purpose tolerably well. And these traditional beliefs still invade our consciousness and affect our thinking to an extent few of us would be willing to admit.

VII Anthropological: Myth and Religion

Evidence from anthropology, religious and literary myth all attests to the politically expedient character of patriarchal convictions about women. One anthropologist refers to a consistent patriarchal strain of assumption that "woman's biological differences set her apart... she is essentially inferior," and since "human institutions grow from deep and primal anxieties and are shaped by irrational psychological mechanisms... socially organized attitudes toward women arise from basic tensions expressed by the male."[54] Under patriarchy the female did not herself develop the symbols by which she is described. As both the primitive and the civilized worlds are male worlds, the ideas which shaped culture in regard to the female were also of male design. The image of women as we know it is an image created by men and fashioned to suit their needs. These needs spring from a fear of the "otherness" of woman. Yet this notion itself presupposes that patriarchy has already been established and the male has already set himself as the human norm, the subject and referent to which the female is "other" or alien. Whatever its origin, the function of the male's sexual antipathy is to provide a means of control over a subordinate group and a rationale which justifies the inferior station of those in a lower order, "explaining" the oppression of their lives.

The feeling that woman's sexual functions are impure is both world-wide and persistent. One sees evidence of it everywhere in literature, in myth, in primitive and civilized life. It is striking how the notion persists today. The event of menstruation, for example, is a largely clandestine affair, and the psycho-social effect of the stigma attached must have great effect on the female ego. There is a large anthropological literature on menstrual taboo; the practice of isolating offenders in huts at the edge of the village occurs throughout the primitive world. Contemporary slang denominates menstruation as "the curse." There is considerable evidence that such discomfort as women suffer during their period is often likely to be psychosomatic, rather than physiological, cultural rather than biological, in origin. That this may also be true to some extent of labor and delivery is attested to by the recent experiment with "painless childbirth." Patriarchal circumstances and beliefs seem to have the effect of poisoning the female's own sense of physical self until it often truly becomes the burden it is said to be.

Primitive peoples explain the phenomenon of the female's genitals in terms of a wound, sometimes reasoning that she was visited by a bird or snake and mutilated into her present condition. Once she was wounded, now she bleeds. Contemporary slang for the vagina is "gash." The Freudian description of the female genitals is in terms of a "castrated" condition. The uneasiness and disgust female genitals arouse in patriarchal societies is attested to through religious, cultural, and literary proscription. In preliterate groups fear is also a factor, as in the belief in a castrating *vagina dentata*. The penis, badge of the male's superior status in both preliterate and civilized patriarchies, is given the most crucial significance, the subject both of endless boasting and endless anxiety.

Nearly all patriarchies enforce taboos against women touching ritual objects (those of war or religion) or food. In ancient and preliterate societies women are generally not permitted to eat with men. Women eat apart today in a great number of cultures, chiefly those of the Near and Far East. Some of the inspiration of such custom appears to lie in fears of contamination, probably sexual in origin. In their function of domestic servants, females are forced to prepare food, yet at the same time may be liable to spread their contagion through it. A similar situation obtains with blacks in the United States. They are considered filthy and infectious, yet as domestics they are forced to prepare food for their queasy superiors. In both cases the dilemma is generally solved in a deplorably illogical fashion by segregating the act of eating itself, while cooking is carried on out of sight by the very group who would infect the table. With an admirable consistency, some Hindu males do not permit their wives to touch their food at all. In nearly every patriarchal group it is expected that the dominant male will eat first or eat better, and even where the sexes feed together, the male shall be served by the female.[55]

All patriarchies have hedged virginity and defloration in elaborate rites and interdictions. Among preliterates virginity presents an interesting problem in ambivalence. On the one hand, it is, as in every patriarchy, a mysterious good because a sign of property received intact. On the other hand, it represents an unknown evil associated with the mana of blood and terrifyingly "other." So auspicious is the event of defloration that in many tribes the owner-groom is willing to relinquish breaking the seal of his new possession to a stronger or older personality who can neutralize the attendant dangers.[56] Fears of defloration appear to originate in a fear of the alien sexuality of the female. Although any physical suffering endured in defloration must be on the part of the female (and most societies cause her – bodily and mentally – to suffer anguish), the social interest, institutionalized in patriarchal ritual and custom, is exclusively on the side of the male's property interest, prestige, or (among preliterates) hazard.

Patriarchal myth typically posits a golden age before the arrival of women, while its social practices permit males to be relieved of female company. Sexual segregation is so prevalent in patriarchy that one encounters evidence of it everywhere. Nearly every powerful circle in contemporary patriarchy is a men's group. But men form groups of their own on every level. Women's groups are typically auxiliary in character, imitative of male efforts and methods on a generally trivial or ephemeral plane. They rarely operate without recourse to male authority, church or religious groups appealing to the superior authority of a cleric, political groups to male legislators, etc.

In sexually segregated situations the distinctive quality of culturally enforced temperament becomes very vivid. This is particularly true of those exclusively masculine organizations which anthropology generally refers to as men's house institutions. The men's house is a fortress of patriarchal association and emotion. Men's houses in preliterate society strengthen masculine communal experience through dances, gossip, hospitality, recreation, and religious ceremony. They are also the arsenals of male weaponry.

David Riesman has pointed out that sports and some other activities provide males with a supportive solidarity which society does not trouble to provide for females.[57] While hunting, politics, religion, and commerce may play a role, sport and warfare are consistently the chief cement of men's house comradery. Scholars of men's house culture from Hutton Webster and Heinrich Schurtz to Lionel Tiger tend to be sexual patriots whose aim is to justify the apartheid the institution represents.[58] Schurtz believes an innate gregariousness and a drive toward fraternal pleasure among peers urges the male away from the inferior and constricting company of women. Notwithstanding his conviction that a mystical "bonding instinct" exists in males, Tiger exhorts the public, by organized effort, to preserve the men's house tradition from its decline. The institution's less genial function as power center within a state of sexual antagonism is an aspect of the phenomenon which often goes unnoticed.

The men's houses of Melanesia fulfill a variety of purposes and are both armory and the site of masculine ritual initiation ceremony. Their atmosphere is not very remote from that of military institutions in the modern world; they reek of physical exertion, violence, the aura of the kill, and the throb of homosexual sentiment. They are the scenes of scarification, headhunting celebrations, and boasting sessions. Here young men are to be "hardened" into manhood. In the men's houses boys have such low status they are often called the "wives" of their initiators, the term "wife" implying both inferiority and the status of sexual object. Untried youths become the erotic interest of their elders and betters, a relationship also encountered in the Samurai order, in oriental priesthood, and in the Greek gymnasium. Preliterate wisdom decrees that while inculcating the young with the masculine ethos, it is necessary first to intimidate them with the tutelary status of the female. An anthropologist's comment on Melanesian men's houses is applicable equally to Genet's underworld, or Mailer's US Army: "It would seem that the sexual brutalizing of the young boy and the effort to turn him into a woman both enhances the older warrior's desire of power, gratifies his sense of hostility toward the maturing male competitor, and eventually, when he takes him into the male group, strengthens the male solidarity in its symbolic attempt to do without women."[59] The derogation of feminine status in lesser males is a consistent patriarchal trait. Like any hazing procedure, initiation once endured produces devotees who will ever after be ardent initiators, happily inflicting their own former sufferings on the newcomer.

The psychoanalytic term for the generalized adolescent tone of men's house culture is "phallic state." Citadels of virility, they reinforce the most saliently power-oriented characteristics of patriarchy. The Hungarian psychoanalytic anthropologist Géza Róheim stressed the patriarchal character of men's house organization in the preliterate tribes he studied, defining their communal and religious practices in terms of a "group of men united in the cult of an object that is a materialized penis and excluding the women from their society."[60] The tone and ethos of men's house culture is sadistic, power-oriented, and latently homosexual, frequently narcissistic in its energy and motives.[61] The men's house inference that the penis is a weapon, endlessly equated with other weapons, is also clear. The practice of castrating prisoners is itself a comment on the cultural confusion of anatomy and status with weaponry. Much of the glamorization of masculine comradery in warfare originates in what one might designate as "the men's house sensibility." Its sadistic and brutalizing aspects are disguised in military glory and a particularly cloying species of masculine sentimentality. A great deal of our culture partakes of this tradition, and one might locate its first statement in Western literature in the heroic intimacy of Patroclus and Achilles. Its development can be traced through the epic and the saga to the *chanson de geste*. The tradition still flourishes in war novel and movie, not to mention the comic book.

Considerable sexual activity does take place in the men's house, all of it, needless to say, homosexual. But the taboo against homosexual behavior (at least among equals) is almost universally of far stronger force than the impulse and tends to effect a rechanneling of the libido into violence. This association of sexuality and violence is a particularly militaristic habit of mind.[62] The negative and militaristic coloring of such men's house homosexuality as does exist, is of course by no means the whole character of homosexual sensibility. Indeed, the warrior caste of mind with its ultravirility, is more *incipiently* homosexual, in its exclusively male orientation, than it is *overtly* homosexual. (The Nazi experience is an extreme case in point here.) And the heterosexual role-playing indulged in, and still more persuasively, the contempt in which the younger, softer, or more "feminine" members are held, is proof that the actual ethos is misogynist, or perversely rather than positively heterosexual. The true inspiration of men's house association therefore comes from the patriarchal situation rather than from any circumstances inherent in the homo-amorous relationship.

If a positive attitude toward heterosexual love is not quite, in Seignebos' famous dictum, the invention of the twelfth century, it can still claim to be a novelty. Most patriarchies go to great length to exclude love as a basis of mate selection. Modern patriarchies tend to do so through class, ethnic, and religious factors. Western classical though was prone to see in heterosexual love either a fatal stroke of ill luck bound to end in tragedy, or a contemptible and brutish consorting with inferiors. Medieval opinion was firm in its conviction that love was sinful if sexual, and sex sinful if loving.

Primitive society practices its misogyny in terms of taboo and mana which evolve into explanatory myth. In historical cultures, this is transformed into ethical, then literary, and in the modern period, scientific rationalizations for the sexual politic. Myth is, of course, a felicitous advance in the level of propaganda, since it so often bases its arguments on ethics or theories of origins. The two leading myths of Western culture are the classical tale of Pandora's box and the Biblical story of the Fall. In both cases earlier mana concepts of feminine evil have passed through a final literary phase to become highly influential ethical justifications of things as they are.

Pandora appears to be a discredited version of a Mediterranean fertility goddess, for in Hesiod's *Theogony* she wears a wreath of flowers and a sculptured diadem in which are carved all the creatures of land and sea.[63] Hesiod ascribes to her the introduction of sexuality which puts an end to the golden age when "the races of men had been living on earth free from all evils, free from laborious work, and free from all wearing sickness."[64] Pandora was the origin of "the damnable race of women – a plague which men must live with."[65] The introduction of what are seen to be evils of the male human condition came through the introduction of the female and what is said to be her unique product, sexuality. In *Works and Days* Hesiod elaborates on Pandora and what she represents – a perilous temptation with "the mind of a bitch and a thievish nature," full of "the cruelty of desire and longings that wear out the body," "lies and cunning words and a deceitful soul," a snare sent by Zeus to be "the ruin of men."[66]

Patriarchy has God on its side. One of its most effective agents of control is the powerfully expeditious character of its doctrines as to the nature and origin of the female and the attribution to her alone of the dangers and evils it imputes to sexuality. The Greek example is interesting here: when it wishes to exalt sexuality it celebrates fertility through the phallus; when it wishes to denigrate sexuality, it cites Pandora. Patriarchal religion and ethics tend to lump the female and sex together as if the whole burden of the onus and stigma it attaches to sex were the fault of the female alone. Thereby sex, which is known to be unclean, sinful, and debilitating, pertains to the female, and the male identity is preserved as a human, rather than a sexual one.

The Pandora myth is one of two important Western archetypes which condemn the female through her sexuality and explain her position as her well-deserved punishment for the primal sin under whose unfortunate consequences the race yet labors. Ethics have entered the scene, replacing the simplicities of ritual, taboo, and mana. The more sophisticated vehicle of myth also provides official explanations of sexual history. In Hesiod's tale, Zeus, a rancorous and arbitrary father figure, in sending Epimetheus evil in the form of female genitalia, is actually chastising him for adult heterosexual knowledge and activity. In opening the vessel she brings (the vulva or hymen, Pandora's "box") the male satisfies his curiosity but sustains the discovery only by punishing himself at the hands of the father god with death and the assorted calamities of postlapsarian life. The patriarchal trait of male rivalry across age or status line, particularly those of powerful father and rival son, is present as well as the ubiquitous maligning of the female.

The myth of the Fall is a highly finished version of the same themes. As the central myth of the Judeo-Christian imagination and therefore of our immediate cultural heritage, it is well that we appraise and acknowledge the enormous power it still holds over us even in a rationalist era which has long ago given up literal belief in it while maintaining its emotional assent intact.[67] This mythic version of the female as the cause of human suffering, knowledge, and sin is still the foundation of sexual attitudes, for it represents the most crucial argument of the patriarchal tradition in the West.

The Israelites lived in a continual state of war with the fertility cults of their neighbors; these latter afforded sufficient attraction to be the source of constant defection, and the figure of Eve, like that of Pandora, has vestigial traces of a fertility goddess overthrown. There is some, probably unconscious, evidence of this in the Biblical account which announces, even before the narration of the fall has begun – "Adam called his wife's name Eve; because she was the mother of all living things." Due to the fact that the tale represents a compilation of different oral traditions, it provides two contradictory schemes for Eve's creation, one in which both sexes are created at the same time, and one in which Eve is fashioned later than Adam, an afterthought born from his rib, peremptory instance of the male's expropriation of the life force through a god who created the world without benefit of female assistance.

The tale of Adam and Eve is, among many other things, a narrative of how humanity invented sexual intercourse. Many such narratives exist in preliterate myth and folk tale. Most of them strike us now as delightfully funny stories of primal innocents who require a good deal of helpful instruction to figure it out. There are other major themes in the story: the loss of primeval simplicity, the arrival of death, and the first conscious experience of knowledge. All of them revolve about sex. Adam is forbidden to eat of the fruit of life or of the knowledge of good and evil, the warning states explicitly what should happen if he tastes of the latter: "in that day that thou eatest thereof thou shalt surely die." He eats but fails to die (at least in the story), from which one might infer that the serpent told the truth.

But at the moment when the pair eat of the forbidden tree they awake to their nakedness and feel shame. Sexuality is clearly involved, though the fable insists it is only tangential to a higher prohibition against disobeying orders in the matter of another and less controversial appetite – one for food. Róheim points out that the Hebrew verb for "eat" can also mean coitus. Everywhere in the Bible "knowing" is synonymous with sexuality, and clearly a product of contact with the phallus, here in the fable objectified as a snake. To blame the evils and sorrows of life – loss of Eden and the rest – on sexuality, would all too logically implicate the male, and such implication is hardly the purpose of the story, designed as it is expressly in order to blame all this world's discomfort on the female. Therefore it is the female who is tempted first and "beguiled" by the penis, transformed into something else, a snake. Thus Adam has "beaten the rap" of sexual guilt, which appears to be why the sexual motive is so repressed in the Biblical account. Yet the very transparency of the serpent's universal phallic value shows how uneasy the mythic mind can be about its shifts. Accordingly, in her inferiority and vulnerability the woman takes and eats, simple carnal thing that she is, affected by flattery even in a reptile. Only after this does the male fall, and with him, humanity – for the fable has made him the racial type, whereas Eve is a mere sexual type and, according to tradition, either expendable or replaceable. And as the myth records the original sexual adventure, Adam was seduced by woman, who was seduced by a penis. "The woman whom thou gavest to be with me, she gave me of the fruit and I did eat" is the first man's defense. Seduced by the phallic snake, Eve is convicted for Adam's participation in sex.

Adam's curse is to toil in the "sweat of his brow," namely the labor the male associates with civilization. Eden was a fantasy world without either effort or activity, which the entrance of the female, and with her sexuality, has destroyed. Eve's sentence is far more political in nature and a brilliant "explanation" of her inferior status. "In sorrow thou shalt bring forth children. And thy desire shall be to thy husband. And he shall rule over thee." Again, as in the Pandora myth, a proprietary father figure is punishing his subjects for adult heterosexuality. It is easy to agree with Róheim's comment on the negative attitude the myth adopts toward sexuality: "Sexual maturity is regarded as a misfortune, something that has robbed mankind of happiness . . . the explanation of how death came into the world."[68]

What requires further emphasis is the responsibility of the female, a marginal creature, in bringing on this plague, and the justice of her suborned condition as dependent on her primary role in this original sin. The connection of woman, sex, and sin constitutes the fundamental pattern of western patriarchal thought thereafter.

VIII Psychological

The aspects of patriarchy already described have each an effect upon the psychology of both sexes. Their principal result is the interiorization of patriarchal ideology. Status, temperament, and role are all value systems with endless psychological ramifications for each sex. Patriarchal marriage and the family with its ranks and division of labor play a large part in enforcing them. The male's superior economic position, the female's inferior one have also grave implications. The large quantity of guilt attached to sexuality in patriarchy is overwhelmingly placed upon the female, who is, culturally speaking, held to be the culpable or the more culpable party in nearly any sexual liaison, whatever the extenuating circumstances. A tendency toward the reification of the female makes her more often a sexual object than a person. This is particularly so when she is denied human rights through chattel status. Even where this has been partly amended the cumulative effect of religion and custom is still very powerful and has enormous psychological consequences. Woman is still denied sexual freedom and the biological control over her body through the cult of virginity, the double standard, the proscription against abortion, and in many places because contraception is physically or psychically unavailable to her.

The continual surveillance in which she is held tends to perpetuate the infantilization of women even in situations such as those of higher education. The female is continually obliged to seek survival or advancement through the approval of males as those who hold power. She may do this either through appeasement or through the exchange of her sexuality for support and status. As the history of patriarchal culture and the representations of herself within all levels of its cultural media, past and present, have a devastating effect upon her self image, she is customarily deprived of any but the most trivial sources of dignity or self-respect. In many patriarchies, language, as well as cultural tradition, reserve the human condition for the male. With the Indo-European languages this is a nearly inescapable habit of mind, for despite all the customary pretense that "man" and "humanity" are terms which apply equally to both sexes, the fact is hardly obscured that in practice, general application favors the male far more often than the female as referent, or even sole referent, for such designations.[69]

When in any group of persons, the ego is subjected to such invidious versions of itself through social beliefs, ideology, and tradition, the effect is bound to be pernicious. This coupled with the persistent though frequently subtle denigration women encounter daily through personal contacts, the impressions gathered from the images and media about them, and the discrimination in matters of behavior, employment, and education which they endure, should make it no very special cause for surprise that women develop group characteristics common to those who suffer minority status and a marginal existence. A witty experiment by Philip Goldberg proves what everyone knows, that having internalized the disesteem in which they are held, women despise both themselves and each other.[70] This simple test consisted of asking women undergraduates to respond to the scholarship in an essay signed alternately by one John McKay and one

Joan McKay. In making their assessments the students generally agreed that John was a remarkable thinker, Joan an unimpressive mind. Yet the articles were identical: the reaction was dependent on the sex of the supposed author.

As women in patriarchy are for the most part marginal citizens when they are citizens at all, their situation is like that of other minorities, here defined not as dependent upon numerical size of the group, but on its status. "A minority group is any group of people who because of their physical or cultural characteristics, are singled out from others in the society in which they live for differential and unequal treatment."[71] Only a handful of sociologists have ever addressed themselves in any meaningful way to the minority status of women.[72] And psychology has yet to produce relevant studies on the subject of ego damage to the female which might bear comparison to the excellent work done on the effects of racism on the minds of blacks and colonials. The remarkably small amount of modern research devoted to the psychological and social effects of masculine supremacy on the female and on the culture in general attests to the widespread ignorance or unconcern of a conservative social science which takes patriarchy to be both the status quo and the state of nature.

What little literature the social sciences afford us in this context confirms the presence in women of the expected traits of minority status: group self-hatred and self-rejection, a contempt both for herself and for her fellows – the result of that continual, however subtle, reiteration of her inferiority which she eventually accepts as a fact.[73] Another index of minority status is the fierceness with which all minority group members are judged. The double standard is applied not only in cases of sexual conduct but other contexts as well. In the relatively rare instances of female crime too: in many American states a woman convicted of crime is awarded a longer sentence.[74] Generally an accused woman acquires a notoriety out of proportion to her acts and due to sensational publicity she may be tried largely for her "sex life." But so effective is her conditioning toward passivity in patriarchy, woman is rarely extrovert enough in her maladjustment to enter upon criminality. Just as every minority member must either apologize for the excesses of a fellow or condemn him with a strident enthusiasm, women are characteristically harsh, ruthless and frightened in their censure of aberration among their numbers.

The gnawing suspicion which plagues any minority member, that the myths propagated about his inferiority might after all be true often reaches remarkable proportions in the personal insecurities of women. Some find their subordinate position so hard to bear that they repress and deny its existence. But a large number will recognize and admit their circumstances when they are properly phrased. Of two studies which asked women if they would have preferred to be born male, one found that one fourth of the sample admitted as much, and in another sample, one half.[75] When one inquires of children, who have not yet developed as serviceable techniques of evasion, what their choice might be, if they had one, the answers of female children in a large majority of cases clearly favor birth into the elite group, whereas boys overwhelmingly reject the option of being girls.[76] The phenomenon of parents' prenatal preference for male issue is too common to require much elaboration. In the light of the imminent possibility of parents actually choosing the sex of their child, such a tendency is becoming the cause of some concern in scientific circles.[77]

Comparisons such as Myrdal, Hacker, and Dixon draw between the ascribed attributes of blacks and women reveal that common opinion associates the same traits with both: inferior intelligence, an instinctual or sensual gratification, an emotional nature both primitive and childlike, an imagined prowess in or affinity for sexuality, a contentment with their own lot which is in accord with a proof of its appropriateness, a wily habit of deceit, and concealment of feeling. Both groups are forced to the same accommodational tactics: an ingratiating or supplicatory manner invented to please, a tendency to study those points at which the dominant group are subject to influence or corruption, and an assumed air of helplessness involving fraudulent appeals for direction through a show of ignorance.[78] It is ironic how misogynist literature has for centuries concentrated on just these traits, directing its fiercest enmity at feminine guile and corruption, and particularly that element of it which is sexual, or, as such sources would have it, "wanton."

As with other marginal groups a certain handful of women are accorded higher status that they may perform a species of cultural policing over the rest. Hughes speaks of marginality as a case of status dilemma experienced by women, blacks, or second-generation Americans who have "come up" in the world but are often refused the rewards of their efforts on the grounds of their origins.[79] This is particularly the case with "new" or educated women. Such exceptions are generally obliged to make ritual, and often comic, statements of deference to justify their elevation. These characteristically take the form of pledges of "femininity," namely a delight in docility and a large appetite for masculine dominance. Politically, the most useful persons for such a role are entertainers and public sex objects. It is a common trait of minority status that a small percentage of the fortunate are permitted to entertain their rulers. (That they may entertain their fellow subjects in the process is less to the point.) Women entertain, please, gratify, satisfy and flatter men with their sexuality. In most minority groups athletes or intellectuals are allowed to emerge as "stars," identification with whom should content their less fortunate fellows. In the case of women both such eventualities are discouraged on the reasonable grounds that the most popular explanations of the female's inferior status ascribe it to her physical weakness or intellectual inferiority. Logically, exhibitions of physical courage or agility are indecorous, just as any display of serious intelligence tends to be out of place.

Perhaps patriarchy's greatest psychological weapon is simply its universality and longevity. A referent scarcely exists with which it might be contrasted or by which it might be confuted. While the same might be said of class, patriarchy has a still more tenacious or powerful hold through its successful habit of passing itself off as nature. Religion is also universal in human society and slavery was once nearly so; advocates of each were fond of arguing in terms of fatality, or irrevocable human "instinct" – even "biological origins." When a system of power is thoroughly in command, it has scarcely need to speak itself aloud; when its workings are exposed and questioned, it becomes not only subject to discussion, but even to change. Such a period is the one next under discussion.

Notes

1 The American Heritage Dictionary's fourth definition is fairly approximate: "methods or tactics involved in managing a state or government." *American Heritage Dictionary* (New York: American Heritage and Houghton Mifflin, 1969). One might expand this to a set of stratagems designed to maintain a system. If one understands patriarchy to be an institution perpetuated by such techniques of control, one has a working definition of how politics is conceived in this essay.

2 I am indebted here to Ronald V. Samson's *The Psychology of Power* (New York: Random House, 1968) for his intelligent investigation of the connection between formal power structures and the family and for his analysis of how power corrupts basic human relationships.

3 "Domination in the quite general sense of power, i.e. the possibility of imposing one's will upon the behavior of other persons, can emerge in the most diverse forms." In this central passage of *Wirtschaft und Gesellschaft* Weber is particularly interested in two such forms: control through social authority ("patriarchal, magisterial, or princely") and control through economic force. In patriarchy as in other forms of domination "that control over economic goods, i.e. economic power, is a frequent, often purposively willed, consequence of domination as well as one of its most important instruments." Quoted from Max Rheinstein's and Edward Shils' translation of portions of *Wirtschaft und Gesellschaft* entitled *Max Weber on Law in Economy and Society* (New York: Simon and Schuster, 1967), pp. 323–4.

4 No matriarchal societies are known to exist at present. Matrilineality, which may be, as some anthropologists have held, a residue or a transitional stage of matriarchy, does not constitute an exception to patriarchal rule, it simply channels the power held by males through female descent –, e.g. the Avunculate.

5 Radical democracy would, of course, preclude patriarchy. One might find evidence of a general satisfaction with a less than perfect democracy in the fact that women have so rarely held power within modern "democracies."

6 Hannah Arendt, "Speculations on Violence," *The New York Review of Books*, Vol. XII No. 4, February 27, 1969, p. 24.

7 The social, rather than the physical sciences are referred to here. Traditionally, medical science had often subscribed to such beliefs. This is no longer the case today, when the best medical research points to the conclusion that sexual stereotypes have no bases in biology.

8 "The historians of Roman laws, having very justly remarked that neither birth nor affection was the foundation of the Roman family, have concluded that this foundation must be found in the power of the father or husband. They make a sort of primordial institution of this power; but they do not explain how this power was established, unless it was by the superiority of strength of the husband over the wife, and of the father over the children. Now, we deceive ourselves sadly when we thus place force as the origin of law. We shall see farther on that the authority of the father or husband, far from having been the first cause, was itself an effect; it was derived from religion,

and was established by religion. Superior strength, therefore, was not the principle that established the family." Numa Denis Fustel de Coulanges, *The Ancient City* (1864). English translation by Willard Small (1873), Doubleday Anchor Reprint, pp. 41–2. Unfortunately Fustel de Coulanges neglects to mention how religion came to uphold patriarchal authority, since patriarchal religion is also an effect, rather than an original cause.

9 One might also include the caveat that such a social order need not imply the domination of one sex which the term "matriarchy" would, by its semantic analogue to patriarchy, infer. Given the simpler scale of life and the fact that female-centered fertility religion might be offset by male physical strength, pre-patriarchy might have been fairly equalitarian.

10 Something like this appears to have taken place as the culture of Neolithic agricultural villages gave way to the culture of civilization and to patriarchy with the rise of cities. See Louis Mumford, *The City in History* (New York: Harcourt, Brace, 1961), Chapter One. A discovery such as paternity, a major acquisition of "scientific" knowledge might, hypothetically, have led to an expansion of population, surplus labor and strong-class stratification. There is good reason to suppose that the transformation of hunting into war also played a part.

11 No convincing evidence has so far been advanced in this area. Experimentation regarding the connection between hormones and animal behavior not only yields highly ambivalent results but brings with it the hazards of reasoning by analogy to human behavior. For a summary of the arguments see David C. Glass (editor), *Biology and Behavior* (New York: Rockefeller University and the Russell Sage Foundation, 1968).

12 Robert J. Stoller, *Sex and Gender* (New York, Science House, 1968), from the preface, pp. viii–ix.

13 Ibid., p. 9.

14 Ibid., p. 48.

15 See Mary Jane Sherfey, "The Evolution and Nature of Female Sexuality in Relation to Psychoanalytic Theory," *Journal of the American Psychoanalytic Association*, Vol. 14, January 1966, no. 1 (New York, International Universities Press Inc.), and John Money, "Psychosexual Differentiation," in *Sex Research, New Developments* (New York, Holt, 1965).

16 Ibid., p. 12.

17 Ibid., p. 13.

18 Jerome Kagin, "The Acquisition and Significance of Sex-Typing," in *Review of Child Development Research*, ed. M. Hoffman (New York, Russell Sage Foundation, 1964).

19 Lionel Tiger, *Men in Groups* (New York, Random House, 1968).

20 Through instinct subhuman species might undertake the activity of building a complex nest or hive; through reflex or drive a human being might simply blink, feel hunger, etc.

21 In some of my remarks on the family I am indebted to Goode's short and concise analysis. See William J. Goode, *The Family* (Englewood Cliffs, New Jersey, Prentice-Hall, 1964).

22 Family, society, and state are three separate but connected entities: women have a decreasing importance as one goes from the first to the third category. But as each of the three categories exists within or is influenced by the overall institution of patriarchy, I am concerned here less with differentiation than with pointing out a general similarity.

23 J. K. Folsom makes a convincing argument as to the anomalous character of patriarchal family systems within democratic society. See Joseph K. Folsom *The Family and Democratic Society* (New York: John Wiley, 1934, 1943).

24 Marital as well as consanguine relation to the head of the family made one his property.

25 Strict patriarchal descent is traced and recognized only though male heirs rather than through sister's sons etc. In a few generations descendants of female branches lose touch. Only those who "bear the name," who descend from male branches, may be regognized for kinship or inheritance.

26 Sir Henry Maine, *Ancient Law* (London, Murray, 1861), p. 122.

27 Sir Henry Maine, *The Early History of Institutions* (London), pp. 310–11.

28 John McLennon, *The Patriarchal Theory* (London, Macmillan, 1885).

29 Maine took the patriarchal family as the cell from which society evolved as gens, phratry, tribe, and nation grew, rather in the simplistic manner of Israel's twelve tribes descending from Jacob. Since Maine also dated the origin of patriarchy from the discovery of paternity, hardly a primeval condition, this too operates against the eternal character of patriarchal society.

30 Many patriarchies granted divorce to males only. It has been accessible to women on any scale only during this century. Goode states that divorce rates were as high in Japan during the 1880s as they are in the US today. Goode, *The Family*, p. 3.

31 Divorce is granted to a male for his wife's failure in domestic service and consortium: it is not granted him for his wife's failure to render him financial support. Divorce is granted to a woman if her husband fails to support her, but not for his failure at domestic service or consortium. But see Karczewski versus Baltimore and Ohio Railroad, 274 F. Supp. 169.175 N.D. Illinois, 1967, where a precedent was set and the common law that decrees a wife might not sue for loss of consortium overturned.

32 Bronislaw Malinowski, *Sex, Culture and Myth* (New York, Harcourt, 1962), p. 63. An earlier statement is even more sweeping: "In all human societies

moral tradition and the law decree that the group consisting of a woman and her offspring is not a sociologically complete unit." *Sex and Repression in Savage Society* (London, Humanities, 1927), p. 213.

33 Goode, *The Family*, p. 80.

34 Ibid., p. 74.

35 This is the gist of Valency's summary of the situation before the troubadours, acknowledging that courtly love is an utter anomaly: "With regard to the social background, all that can be stated with confidence is that we know nothing of the objective relationships of men and women in the Middle Ages which might conceivably motivate the strain of love-poetry which the troubadours developed." Maurice Valency, *In Praise of Love* (Macmillan, New York, 1958), p. 5.

36 Hugo Beigel, "Romantic Love," *The American Sociological Review*, Vol. 16, 1951, p. 331.

37 Mailer and Miller occur to one in this connection, and Lawrence as well. One might trace Rojack's very existence as a fictional figure to the virility symbol of Jack London's Ernest Everhard or Tennessee Williams' Stanley Kowalski. That Rojack is also literate is nothing more than an elegant finish upon the furniture of his "manhood" solidly based in the hard oaken grain of his mastery over any and every "broad" he can better, bludgeon, or bugger.

38 It would appear that the "pure flower of white womanhood" has at least at times been something of a disappointment to her lord as a fellow-racist. The historic connection of the Abolitionist and the Woman's Movement is some evidence of this, as well as the incidence of white female and black male marriages as compared with those of white male and black female. Figures on miscegenation are very difficult to obtain: Goode (*The Family*, p. 37) estimates the proportion of white women marrying black men to be between 3 to 10 times the proportion of white men marrying black women. Robert K. Merton "Intermarriage and the Social Structure" *Psychiatry*, Vol. 4, August 1941, p. 374, states that "most intercaste sex relations – not marriages – are between white men and Negro women." It is hardly necessary to emphasize that the more extensive sexual contacts between white males and black females have not only been extramarital, but (on the part of the white male) crassly exploitative. Under slavery it was simply a case of rape.

39 Sweden is an exception in considering housework a material service rendered and calculable in divorce suits, etc. Thirty-three to forty percent of the female population have market employment in Western countries: this leaves up to two thirds out of the market labor force. In Sweden and the Soviet Union that figure is lower.

40 US Department of Labor Statistics for 1966 (latest available figures). The proportion of women earning more than $10,000 a year in 1966 was 7/10 of 1%. See Mary Dublin Keyserling, "Realities of Women's Current Position in the Labor Force" in *Sex Discrimination in Employment Practices*, a report from the conference (pamphlet) University extension, U.C.L.A. and the Women's Bureau, September 19, 1968.

41 See *The 1965 Handbook on Women Workers*, United States Department of Labor, Women's Bureau: "In every major occupational group the median wage or salary income of women was less than that of men. This is true at all levels of educational attainment." A comparison of the income received by women and men with equal amounts of schooling revealed that women who had completed four years of college received incomes which were only 47% of those paid to men with the same educational training; high school graduates earned only 38%, and grade school graduates only 33%.

42 For the distribution of women in lower income and lower status positions see *Background Facts on Working Women* (pamphlet) US Department of Labor, Women's Bureau.

43 "For a married woman without children the irreducible minimum of work probably takes between fifteen to twenty hours a week, for a woman with small children the minimum is probably 70–80 hours a week." Margaret Benston, "The Political Economy of Women's Liberation," *Monthly Review*, Vol. XXI, September 1969.

44 See the publications of the Women's Bureau and particularly *Sex Discrimination in Employment Practices* (op. cit.) and Carolyn Bird, *Born Female* (New York: McKay, 1968).

45 Title VII of the 1964 Civil Rights Act. The inclusion of "sex" in the law upholding the civil right of freedom from discrimination in employment was half a joke and half an attempt on the part of Southern congressmen to force Northern industrial states to abandon passage of the bill.

46 We often forget how recent an event is higher education for women. In the US it is barely one hundred years old; in many Western countries barely fifty. Oxford did not grant degrees to women on the same terms as to men until 1920. In Japan and a number of other countries universities have been open to women only in the period after World War II. There are still areas where higher education for women scarcely exists. Women do not have the same access to education as do men. The Princeton Report stated that "although at the high school level more girls than boys receive grades of 'A,' roughly 50% more boys than girls go to college." *The Princeton Report to the Alumni on Co-Education* (pamphlet), Princeton, NJ, 1968, p. 10. Most other authorities give the national ratio of college students as two males to one female. In a great many countries it is far lower.

47 Since abortion is extralegal, figures are difficult to obtain. This figure is based on the estimates of abortionists and referral services. Suicides in pregnancy are not officially reported either.

48 Vivid exceptions come to mind in the wars of liberation conducted by Vietnam, China, etc. But through most of history, women have been unarmed and forbidden to exhibit any defense of their own.

49 They are still high. The number of rapes reported in the city of New York in 1967 was 2,432. Figure supplied by Police Department.

50 It is interesting that male victims of rape at the hands of other males often feel twice imposed upon, as they have not only been subjected to forcible and painful intercourse, but further abused in being reduced to the status of a female. Much of this is evident in Genet and in the contempt homosexual society reserves for its "passive" or "female" partners.

51 Masculine masochism is regarded as exceptional and often explained as latently homosexual, or a matter of the subject playing "the female role" – e.g., victim.

52 The literature of misogyny is so vast that no summary of sensible proportions could do it justice. The best reference on the subject is Katherine M. Rogers, *The Troublesome Helpmate, A History of Misogyny in Literature* (Seattle, University of Washington Press, 1966).

53 As well as the exquisite sonnets of love, Petrarch composed satires on women as the "De Remediis utriusque Fortunae" and *Epistolae Seniles*. Boccaccio too could balance the chivalry of romances (Filostrato, Ameto, and Fiammetta) with the vituperance of Corbaccio, a splenetic attack on women more than medieval in violence.

54 H. R. Hays, *The Dangerous Sex: The Myth of Feminine Evil* (New York: Putnam, 1964). Much of my summary in this section is indebted to Hays's useful assessment of cultural notions about the female.

55 The luxury conditions of the "better" restaurant affords a quaint exception. There not only the cuisine but even the table service is conducted by males, at an expense commensurate with such an occasion.

56 See Sigmund Freud, *Totem and Taboo*, and Ernest Crawley, *The Mystic Rose* (London, Methuen, 1902, 1927).

57 David Riesman, "Two Generations," in *The Woman in America*, ed. Robert Lifton (Boston, Beacon, 1967). See also James Coleman, *The Adolescent Society*.

58 Heinrich Schurtz, *Altersklassen und Männerbünde* (Berlin, 1902), and Lionel Tiger, *Men in Groups*.

59 Hays, *The Dangerous Sex*, p. 56.

60 Géza Róheim, "Psychoanalysis of Primitive Cultural Types," *International Journal of Psychoanalysis*, Vol. XIII, London, 1932.

61 All these traits apply in some degree to the bohemian circle which Miller's novels project, the Army which never leaves Mailer's consciousness, and the homosexual subculture on which Genet's observations are based. Since these three subjects of our study are closely associated with the separatist men's house culture, it is useful to give it special attention.

62 Genet demonstrates this in *The Screens*; Mailer reveals it everywhere.

63 Wherever one stands in the long anthropologists' quarrel over patriarchal versus matriarchal theories of social origins, one can trace a demotion of fertility goddesses and their replacement by patriarchal deities at a certain period throughout ancient culture.

64 Hesiod, *Works and Days*, translated by Richmond Lattimore (University of Michigan, 1959), p. 29.

65 Hesiod, *Theogony*, translated by Norman O. Brown (Indianapolis, Liberal Arts Press, 1953), p. 70.

66 Hesiod, *Works and Days*, phrases from lines 53–100. Some of the phrases are from Lattimore's translation, some from A. W. Mair's translation (Oxford, 1908).

67 It is impossible to assess how deeply embedded in our consciousness is the Eden legend and how utterly its patterns are planted in our habits of thought. One comes across its tone and design in the most unlikely places, such as Antonioni's film *Blow-Up*, to name but one of many striking examples. The action of the film takes place in an idyllic garden, loaded with primal overtones largely sexual, where, prompted by a temper with a phallic gun, the female again betrays the male to death. The photographer who witnesses the scene reacts as if he were being introduced both to the haggard knowledge of the primal scene and original sin at the same time.

68 Géza Róheim, "Eden," *Psychoanalytic Review*, Vol. XXVII, New York, 1940. See also Theodor Reik, *The Creation of Woman*, and the account given in Hays, *The Dangerous Sex*.

69 Languages outside the Indo-European group are instructive. Japanese, for example, has one word for man (***otōko***), another for woman (***ōnna***) and a third for human being (***ningen***). It would be as unthinkable to use the first to cover the third as it would be to use the second.

70 Philip Goldberg, "Are Women Prejudiced Against Women?" *Transaction*, April 1968.

71 Louis Wirth, "Problems of Minority Groups," in *The Science of Man in the World Crisis*, ed. Ralph Linton (New York, Appleton, 1945), p. 347. Wirth also stipulates that the group see itself as discriminated against. It is interesting that many women do not recognize themselves as discriminated against; no better proof could be found of the totality of their conditioning.

72 The productive handful in question include the following: Helen Mayer Hacker, "Women as a Minority Group," *Social Forces*, Vol. XXX, October 1951.

Gunnar Myrdal, *An American Dilemma*, Appendix 5 is a parallel of black minority status with women's minority status.

Everett C. Hughes, "Social Change and Status Protest: An Essay on the Marginal Man," *Phylon*, Vol. X, First Quarter, 1949.

Joseph K. Folsom, *The Family and Democratic Society*, 1943.

Godwin Watson, "Psychological Aspects of Sex Roles," *Social Psychology, Issues and Insights* (Philadelphia, Lippincott, 1966).

73 My remarks on the minority status of women are summarized from all the articles listed, and I am particularly indebted to an accomplished critique of them in an unpublished draft by Professor Marlene Dixon, formerly of the University of Chicago's Department of Sociology and the Committee on Human Development, presently of McGill University.

74 See The Commonwealth v. Daniels, 37 L.W. 2064, Pennsylvania Supreme Court, 7/1/68 (reversing 36 L.W. 2004).

75 See Helen Hacker, "Women as a Minority Group," and Carolyn Bird, *Born Female*.

76 "One study of fourth graders showed ten times as many girls wishing they could have been boys, as boys who would have chosen to be girls," Watson, "Psychological Aspects of Sex Roles," p. 477.

77 Amitai Etzioni, "Sex Control, Science, and Society," *Science*, September 1968, pp. 1107–12.

78 Myrdal, *An American Dilemma*, Hacker, "Women as a Minority Group," Dixon, n. 73 above.

79 Hughes, "Social Change."

5

Black Women: Shaping Feminist Theory

bell hooks

Feminism in the United States has never emerged from the women who are most victimized by sexist oppression; women who are daily beaten down, mentally, physically, and spiritually – women who are powerless to change their condition in life. They are a silent majority. A mark of their victimization is that they accept their lot in life without visible question, without organized protest, without collective anger or rage. Betty Friedan's *The Feminine Mystique* is still heralded as having paved the way for contemporary feminist movement – it was written as if these women did not exist. Friedan's famous phrase, "the problem that has no name," often quoted to describe the condition of women in this society, actually referred to the plight of a select group of college-educated, middle and upper class, married white women – housewives bored with leisure, with the home, with children, with buying products, who wanted more out of life. Friedan concludes her first chapter by stating: "We can no longer ignore that voice within women that says: 'I want something more than my husband and my children and my house.'" That "more" she defined as careers. She did not discuss who would be called in to take care of the children and maintain the home if more women like herself were freed from their house labor and given equal access with white men to the professions. She did not speak of the needs of women without men, without children, without homes. She ignored the existence of all non-white women and poor white women. She did not tell readers whether it was more fulfilling to be a maid, a babysitter, a factory worker, a clerk, or a prostitute, than to be a leisure class housewife.

She made her plight and the plight of white women like herself synonymous with a condition affecting all American women. In so doing, she deflected attention away from her classism, her racism, her sexist attitudes towards the masses of American women. In the context of her book, Friedan makes clear that the women she saw as victimized by sexism were college-educated, white women who were compelled by sexist conditioning to remain in the home. She contends:

> It is urgent to understand how the very condition of being a housewife can create a sense of emptiness, non-existence, nothingness in women. There are aspects of the housewife role that make it almost impossible for a woman of adult intelligence to retain a sense of human identity, the firm core of self

bell hooks, "Black Women: Shaping Feminist Theory," pp. 1–15 and 165 from *Feminist Theory: From Margin to Center*. Boston, MA: South End Press, 1984. Reprinted by permission of South End Press.

> or "I" without which a human being, man or woman, is not truly alive. For women of ability, in America today, I am convinced that there is something about the housewife state itself that is dangerous.

Specific problems and dilemmas of leisure class white housewives were real concerns that merited consideration and change but they were not the pressing political concerns of masses of women. Masses of women were concerned about economic survival, ethnic and racial discrimination, etc. When Friedan wrote *The Feminine Mystique*, more than one third of all women were in the work force. Although many women longed to be housewives, only women with leisure time and money could actually shape their identities on the model of the feminine mystique. They were women who, in Friedan's words, were "told by the most advanced thinkers of our time to go back and live their lives as if they were Noras, restricted to the doll's house by Victorian prejudices."[1]

From her early writing, it appears that Friedan never wondered whether or not the plight of college-educated, white housewives was an adequate reference point by which to gauge the impact of sexism or sexist oppression on the lives of women in American society. Nor did she move beyond her own life experience to acquire an expanded perspective on the lives of women in the United States. I say this not to discredit her work. It remains a useful discussion of the impact of sexist discrimination on a select group of women. Examined from a different perspective, it can also be seen as a case study of narcissism, insensitivity, sentimentality, and self-indulgence which reaches its peak when Friedan, in a chapter titled "Progressive Dehumanization," makes a comparison between the psychological effects of isolation on white housewives and the impact of confinement on the self-concept of prisoners in Nazi concentration camps.[2]

Friedan was a principal shaper of contemporary feminist thought. Significantly, the one-dimensional perspective on women's reality presented in her book became a marked feature of the contemporary feminist movement. Like Friedan before them, white women who dominate feminist discourse today rarely question whether or not their perspective on women's reality is true to the lived experiences of women as a collective group. Nor are they aware of the extent to which their perspectives reflect race and class biases, although there has been a greater awareness of biases in recent years. Racism abounds in the writings of white feminists, reinforcing white supremacy and negating the possibility that women will bond politically across ethnic and racial boundaries. Past feminist refusal to draw attention to and attack racial hierarchies suppressed the link between race and class. Yet class structure in American society has been shaped by the racial politic of white supremacy; it is only by analyzing racism and its function in capitalist society that a thorough understanding of class relationships can emerge. Class struggle is inextricably bound to the struggle to end racism. Urging women to explore the full implication of class in an early essay, "The Last Straw," Rita Mae Brown explained:

> Class is much more than Marx's definition of relationship to the means of production. Class involves your behavior, your basic assumptions about life. Your experience (determined by your class) validates those assumptions, how you are taught to behave, what you expect from yourself and from others, your concept of a future, how you understand problems and solve them, how you think, feel, act. It is these behavioral patterns that middle class women resist recognizing although they may be perfectly willing to accept class in Marxist terms, a neat trick that helps them avoid really dealing with class behavior and changing that behavior in themselves. It is these behavioral patterns which must be recognized, understood, and changed.

White women who dominate feminist discourse, who for the most part make and articulate feminist theory, have little or no understanding of white supremacy as a racial politic, of the psychological impact of class, of their political status within a racist, sexist, capitalist state.

It is this lack of awareness that, for example, leads Leah Fritz to write in *Dreamers and Dealers*, a discussion of the current women's movement published in 1979:

> Women's suffering under sexist tyranny is a common bond among all women, transcending the particulars of the different forms that tyranny takes. *Suffering cannot be measured and compared quantitatively*. Is the enforced idleness and vacuity of a "rich" woman,

which leads her to madness and/or suicide, greater or less than the suffering of a poor woman who barely survives on welfare but retains somehow her spirit? There is no way to measure such difference, but should these two women survey each other without the screen of patriarchal class, they may find a commonality in the fact that they are both oppressed, both miserable.

Fritz's statement is another example of wishful thinking, as well as the conscious mystification of social divisions between women, that has characterized much feminist expression. While it is evident that many women suffer from sexist tyranny, there is little indication that this forges "a common bond among all women." There is much evidence substantiating the reality that race and class identity creates differences in quality of life, social status, and lifestyle that take precedence over the common experience women share – differences which are rarely transcended. The motives of materially privileged, educated, white women with a variety of career and lifestyle options available to them must be questioned when they insist that "suffering cannot be measured." Fritz is by no means the first white feminist to make this statement. It is a statement that I have never heard a poor woman of any race make. Although there is much I would take issue with in Benjamin Barber's critique of the women's movement, *Liberating Feminism*, I agree with his assertion:

> Suffering is not necessarily a fixed and universal experience that can be measured by a single rod: it is related to situations, needs, and aspirations. But there must be some historical and political parameters for the use of the term so that political priorities can be established and different forms and degrees of suffering can be given the most attention.

A central tenet of modern feminist thought has been the assertion that "all women are oppressed." This assertion implies that women share a common lot, that factors like class, race, religion, sexual preference, etc. do not create a diversity of experience that determines the extent to which sexism will be an oppressive force in the lives of individual women. Sexism as a system of domination is institutionalized but it has never determined in an absolute way the fate of all women in this society. Being oppressed means the *absence of choices*. It is the primary point of contact between the oppressed and the oppressor. Many women in this society do have choices, (as inadequate as they are) therefore exploitation and discrimination are words that more accurately describe the lot of women collectively in the United States. Many women do not join organized resistance against sexism precisely because sexism has not meant an absolute lack of choices. They may know they are discriminated against on the basis of sex, but they do not equate this with oppression. Under capitalism, patriarchy is structured so that sexism restricts women's behavior in some realms even as freedom from limitations is allowed in other spheres. The absence of extreme restrictions leads many women to ignore the areas in which they are exploited or discriminated against; it may even lead them to imagine that no women are oppressed.

There are oppressed women in the United States, and it is both appropriate and necessary that we speak against such oppression. French feminist Christine Delphy makes the point in her essay, "For a Materialist Feminism," that the use of the term oppression is important because it places feminist struggle in a radical political framework:

> The rebirth of feminism coincided with the use of the term "oppression." The ruling ideology, i.e. common sense, daily speech, does not speak about oppression but about a "feminine condition." It refers back to a naturalist explanation: to a constraint of nature, exterior reality out of reach and not modifiable by human action. The term "oppression," on the contrary, refers back to a choice, an explanation, a situation that is political. "Oppression" and "social oppression" are therefore synonyms or rather social oppression is a redundance: the notion of a political origin, i.e. social, is an integral part of the concept of oppression.

However, feminist emphasis on "common oppression" in the United States was less a strategy for politicization than an appropriation by conservative and liberal women of a radical political vocabulary that masked the extent to which they shaped the movement so that it addressed and promoted their class interests.

Although the impulse towards unity and empathy that informed the notion of common oppression was directed at building solidarity, slogans like "organize around your own oppression" provided the excuse many privileged women needed to ignore the differences between their social status and the status of masses of women. It was a mark of race and class privilege, as well as the expression of freedom from the many constraints sexism places on working class women, that middle class white women were able to make their interests the primary focus of feminist movement and employ a rhetoric of commonality that made their condition synonymous with "oppression." Who was there to demand a change in vocabulary? What other group of women in the United States had the same access to universities, publishing houses, mass media, money? Had middle class black women begun a movement in which they had labeled themselves "oppressed," no one would have taken them seriously. Had they established public forums and given speeches about their "oppression," they would have been criticized and attacked from all sides. This was not the case with white bourgeois feminists for they could appeal to a large audience of women, like themselves, who were eager to change their lot in life. Their isolation from women of other class and race groups provided no immediate comparative base by which to test their assumptions of common oppression.

Initially, radical participants in women's movement demanded that women penetrate that isolation and create a space for contact. Anthologies like *Liberation Now, Women's Liberation: Blueprint for the Future, Class and Feminism, Radical Feminism*, and *Sisterhood Is Powerful*, all published in the early 1970s, contain articles that attempted to address a wide audience of women, an audience that was not exclusively white, middle class, college-educated, and adult (many have articles on teenagers). Sookie Stambler articulated this radical spirit in her introduction to *Women's Liberation: Blueprint for the Future*:

> Movement women have always been turned off by the media's necessity to create celebrities and superstars. This goes against our basic philosophy. We cannot relate to women in our ranks towering over us with prestige and fame. We are not struggling for the benefit of the one woman or for one group of women. We are dealing with issues that concern all women.

These sentiments, shared by many feminists early in the movement, were not sustained. As more and more women acquired prestige, fame, or money from feminist writings or from gains from feminist movement for equality in the workforce, individual opportunism undermined appeals for collective struggle. Women who were not opposed to patriarchy, capitalism, classism, or racism labeled themselves "feminist." Their expectations were varied. Privileged women wanted social equality with men of their class; some women wanted equal pay for equal work; others wanted an alternative lifestyle. Many of these legitimate concerns were easily co-opted by the ruling capitalist patriarchy. French feminist Antoinette Fouque states:

> The actions proposed by the feminist groups are spectacular, provoking. But provocation only brings to light a certain number of social contradictions. It does not reveal radical contradictions within society. The feminists claim that they do not seek equality with men, but their practice proves the contrary to be true. Feminists are a bourgeois avant-garde that maintains, in an inverted form, the dominant values. Inversion does not facilitate the passage to another kind of structure. Reformism suits everyone! Bourgeois order, capitalism, phallocentrism are ready to integrate as many feminists as will be necessary. Since these women are becoming men, in the end it will only mean a few more men. The difference between the sexes is not whether one does or doesn't have a penis, it is whether or not one is an integral part of a phallic masculine economy.

Feminists in the United States are aware of the contradictions. Carol Ehrlich makes the point in her essay, "The Unhappy Marriage of Marxism and Feminism: Can It Be Saved?," that "feminism seems more and more to have taken on a blind, safe, nonrevolutionary outlook" as "feminist radicalism loses ground to bourgeois feminism," stressing that "we cannot let this continue":

> Women need to know (and are increasingly prevented from finding out) that feminism is *not* about dressing for success, or becoming a corporate executive, or gaining elective office; it is *not* being able to share a two

> career marriage and take skiing vacations and spend huge amounts of time with your husband and two lovely children because you have a domestic worker who makes all this possible for you, but who hasn't the time or money to do it for herself; it is *not* opening a Women's Bank, or spending a weekend in an expensive workshop that guarantees to teach you how to become assertive (but not aggressive); it is most emphatically *not* about becoming a police detective or CIA agent or marine corps general.
>
> But if these distorted images of feminism have more reality than ours do, it is partly our own fault. We have not worked as hard as we should have at providing clear and meaningful alternative analyses which relate to people's lives, and at providing active, accessible groups in which to work.

It is no accident that feminist struggle has been so easily co-opted to serve the interests of conservative and liberal feminists since feminism in the United States has so far been a bourgeois ideology. Zillah Eisenstein discusses the liberal roots of North American feminism in *The Radical Future of Liberal Feminism*, explaining in the introduction:

> One of the major contributions to be found in this study is the role of the ideology of liberal individualism in the construction of feminist theory. Today's feminists either do not discuss a theory of individuality or they unself-consciously adopt the competitive, atomistic ideology of liberal individualism. There is much confusion on this issue in the feminist theory we discuss here. Until a conscious differentiation is made between a theory of individuality that recognizes the importance of the individual within the social collectivity and the ideology of individualism that assumes a competitive view of the individual, there will not be a full accounting of what a feminist theory of liberation must look like our Western society.

The ideology of "competitive, atomistic liberal individualism" has permeated feminist thought to such an extent that it undermines the potential radicalism of feminist struggle. The usurpation of feminism by bourgeois women to support their class interests has been to a very grave extent justified by feminist theory as it has so far been conceived. (For example, the ideology of "common oppression.") Any movement to resist the co-optation of feminist struggle must begin by introducing a different feminist perspective – a new theory – one that is not informed by the ideology of liberal individualism.

The exclusionary practices of women who dominate feminist discourse have made it practically impossible for new and varied theories to emerge. Feminism has its party line and women who feel a need for a different strategy, a different foundation, often find themselves ostracized and silenced. Criticisms of or alternatives to established feminist ideas are not encouraged, e.g. recent controversies about expanding feminist discussions of sexuality. Yet groups of women who feel excluded from feminist discourse and praxis can make a place for themselves only if they first create, via critiques, an awareness of the factors that alienate them. Many individual white women found in the women's movement a liberatory solution to personal dilemmas. Having directly benefited from the movement, they are less inclined to criticize it or to engage in rigorous examination of its structure than those who feel it has not had a revolutionary impact on their lives or the lives of masses of women in our society. Non-white women who feel affirmed within the current structure of feminist movement (even though they may form autonomous groups) seem to also feel that their definitions of the party line, whether on the issue of black feminism or on other issues, is the only legitimate discourse. Rather than encourage a diversity of voices, critical dialogue, and controversy, they, like some white women, seek to stifle dissent. As activists and writers whose work is widely known, they act as if they are best able to judge whether other women's voices should be heard. Susan Griffin warns against this overall tendency towards dogmatism in her essay, "The Way of All Ideology":

> when a theory is transformed into an ideology, it begins to destroy the self and self-knowledge. Originally born of feeling, it pretends to float above and around feeling. Above sensation. It organizes experience according to itself, without touching experience. By virtue of being itself, it is supposed to know. To invoke the name of this ideology is to confer truthfulness. No one can tell it anything new. Experience ceases

> to surprise it, inform it, transform it. It is annoyed by any detail which does not fit into its world view. Begun as a cry against the denial of truth, now it denies any truth which does not fit into its scheme. Begun as a way to restore one's sense of reality, now it attempts to discipline real people, to remake natural beings after its own image. All that it fails to explain it records as its enemy. Begun as a theory of liberation, it is threatened by new theories of liberation; it builds a prison for the mind.

We resist hegemonic dominance of feminist thought by insisting that it is a theory in the making, that we must necessarily criticize, question, re-examine, and explore new possibilities. My persistent critique has been informed by my status as a member of an oppressed group, experience of sexist exploitation and discrimination, and the sense that prevailing feminist analysis has not been the force shaping my feminist consciousness. This is true for many women. There are white women who had never considered resisting male dominance until the feminist movement created an awareness that they could and should. My awareness of feminist struggle was stimulated by social circumstance. Growing up in a Southern, black, father-dominated, working class household, I experienced (as did my mother, my sisters, and my brother) varying degrees of patriarchal tyranny and it made me angry – it made us all angry. Anger led me to question the politics of male dominance and enabled me to resist sexist socialization. Frequently, white feminists act as if black women did not know sexist oppression existed until they voiced feminist sentiment. They believe they are providing black women with "the" analysis and "the" program for liberation. They do not understand, cannot even imagine, that black women, as well as other groups of women who live daily in oppressive situations, often acquire an awareness of patriarchal politics from their lived experience, just as they develop strategies of resistance (even though they may not resist on a sustained or organized basis).

These black women observed white feminist focus on male tyranny and women's oppression as if it were a "new" revelation and felt such a focus had little impact on their lives. To them it was just another indication of the privileged living conditions of middle and upper class white women that they would need a theory to inform them that they were "oppressed." The implication being that people who are truly oppressed know it even though they may not be engaged in organized resistance or are unable to articulate in written form the nature of their oppression. These black women saw nothing liberatory in party line analyses of women's oppression. Neither the fact that black women have not organized collectively in huge numbers around the issues of "feminism" (many of us do not know or use the term) nor the fact that we have not had access to the machinery of power that would allow us to share our analyses or theories about gender with the American public negate its presence in our lives or place us in a position of dependency in relationship to those white and non-white feminists who address a larger audience.

The understanding I had by age thirteen of patriarchal politics created in me expectations of the feminist movement that were quite different from those of young, middle class, white women. When I entered my first women's studies class at Stanford University in the early 1970s, white women were revelling in the joy of being together – to them it was an important, momentous occasion. I had not known a life where women had not been together, where women had not helped, protected, and loved one another deeply. I had not known white women who were ignorant of the impact of race and class on their social status and consciousness (Southern white women often have a more realistic perspective on racism and classism than white women in other areas of the United States.) I did not feel sympathetic to white peers who maintained that I could not expect them to have knowledge of or understand the life experiences of black women. Despite my background (living in racially segregated communities) I knew about the lives of white women, and certainly no white women lived in our neighborhood, attended our schools, or worked in our homes.

When I participated in feminist groups, I found that white women adopted a condescending attitude towards me and other non-white participants. The condescension they directed at black women was one of the means they employed to remind us that the women's movement was "theirs" – that we were able to participate because they allowed it, even encouraged it; after all, we were needed to legitimate the process. They did not see us as equals. They did not treat us as equals. And though they expected us to provide first hand accounts of black experience, they felt it was their role to decide if these experiences were authentic. Frequently, college-educated black women (even those from poor and working class backgrounds) were dismissed as mere imitators. Our presence in movement activities did not count, as white women were convinced that "real" blackness meant speaking the patois of poor black people, being uneducated, streetwise, and a variety of other stereotypes. If we dared to criticize the movement or to assume responsibility for reshaping feminist ideas and introducing new ideas, our voices were tuned out, dismissed, silenced. We could be heard only if our statements echoed the sentiments of the dominant discourse.

Attempts by white feminists to silence black women are rarely written about. All too often they have taken place in conference rooms, classrooms, or the privacy of cozy living room settings, where one lone black woman faces the racist hostility of a group of white women. From the time the women's liberation movement began, individual black women went to groups. Many never returned after a first meeting. Anita Cornwall is correct in "Three for the Price of One: Notes from a Gay Black Feminist," when she states, "... sadly enough, fear of encountering racism seems to be one of the main reasons that so many black women refuse to join the women's movement."[3] Recent focus on the issue of racism has generated discourse but has had little impact on the behavior of white feminists towards black women. Often the white women who are busy publishing papers and books on "unlearning racism" remain patronizing and condescending when they relate to black women. This is not surprising given that frequently their discourse is aimed solely in the direction of a white audience and the focus solely on changing attitudes rather than addressing racism in a historical and political context. They make us the "objects" of their privileged discourse on race. As "objects," we remain unequals, inferiors. Even though they may be sincerely concerned about racism, their methodology suggests they are not yet free of the type of paternalism endemic to white supremacist ideology. Some of these women place themselves in the position of "authorities" who must mediate communication between racist white women (naturally they see themselves as having come to terms with their racism) and angry black women whom they believe are incapable of rational discourse. Of course, the system of racism, classism, and educational elitism remain intact if they are to maintain their authoritative positions.

In 1981, I enrolled in a graduate class on feminist theory where we were given a course reading list that had writings by white women and men, one black man, but no material by or about black, Native American Indian, Hispanic, or Asian women. When I criticized this oversight, white women directed an anger and hostility at me that was so intense I found it difficult to attend the class. When I suggested that the purpose of this collective anger was to create an atmosphere in which it would be psychologically unbearable for me to speak in class discussions or even attend class, I was told that they were not angry. *I* was the one who was angry. Weeks after class ended, I received an open letter from one white female student acknowledging her anger and expressing regret for her attacks. She wrote:

> I didn't know you. You were black. In class after a while I noticed myself, that I would always be the one to respond to whatever you said. And usually it was to contradict. Not that the argument was always about racism by any means. But I think the hidden logic was that if I could prove you wrong about one thing, then you might not be right about anything at all.

And in another paragraph:

> I said in class one day that there were some people less entrapped than others by Plato's picture of the world. I said I thought we, after fifteen years of education, courtesy of the ruling class, might be more entrapped than others who had not received a start in life so close to the heart of the monster. My classmate, once a close friend, sister, colleague, has not spoken to me since then. I think the possibility that we were not the best spokespeople for all women made her fear for her self-worth and for her Ph.D.

Often in situations where white feminists aggressively attacked individual black women, they saw themselves as the ones who were under attack, who were the victims. During a heated discussion with another white female student in a racially mixed women's group I had organized, I was told that she had heard how I had "wiped out" people in the feminist theory class, that she was afraid of being "wiped out" too. I reminded her that I was one person speaking to a large group of angry, aggressive people; I was hardly dominating the situation. It was I who left the class in tears, not any of the people I had supposedly "wiped out."

Racist stereotypes of the strong, superhuman black woman are operative myths in the minds of many white women, allowing them to ignore the extent to which black women are likely to be victimized in this society and the role white women may play in the maintenance and perpetuation of that victimization. In Lillian Hellman's autobiographical work *Pentimento*, she writes, "All my life, beginning at birth, I have taken orders from black women, wanting them and resenting them, being superstitious the few times I disobeyed." The black women Hellman describes worked in her household as family servants and their status was never that of an equal. Even as a child, she was always in the dominant position as they questioned, advised, or guided her; they were free to exercise these rights because she or another white authority figure allowed it. Hellman places power in the hands of these black women rather than acknowledge her own power over them; hence she mystifies the true nature of their relationship. By projecting onto black women a mythical power and strength, white women both promote a false image of themselves as powerless, passive victims and deflect attention away from their aggressiveness, their power, (however limited in a white supremacist, male-dominated state) their willingness to dominate and control others. These unacknowledged aspects of the social status of many white women prevent them from transcending racism and limit the scope of their understanding of women's overall social status in the United States.

Privileged feminists have largely been unable to speak to, with, and for diverse groups of women because they either do not understand fully the inter-relatedness of sex, race, and class oppression or refuse to take this inter-relatedness seriously. Feminist analyses of woman's lot tend to focus exclusively on gender and do not provide a solid foundation on which to construct feminist theory. They reflect the dominant tendency in Western patriarchal minds to mystify woman's reality by insisting that gender is the sole determinant of woman's fate. Certainly it has been easier for women who do not experience race or class oppression to focus exclusively on gender. Although socialist feminists focus on class and gender, they tend to dismiss race or they make a point of acknowledging that race is important and then proceed to offer an analysis in which race is not considered.

As a group, black women are in an unusual position in this society, for not only are we collectively at the bottom of the occupational ladder, but our overall social status is lower than that of any other group. Occupying such a position, we bear the brunt of sexist, racist, and classist oppression. At the same time, we are the group that has not been socialized to assume the role of exploiter/oppressor in that we are allowed no institutionalized "other" that we can exploit or oppress. (Children do not represent an institutionalized other even though they may be oppressed by parents.) White women and black men have it both ways. They can act as oppressor or be oppressed. Black men may be victimized by racism, but sexism allows them to act as exploiters and oppressors of women. White women may be victimized by sexism, but racism enables them to act as exploiters and oppressors of black people. Both groups have led liberation movements that favor their interests and support the continued oppression of other groups. Black male sexism has undermined struggles to eradicate racism just as white female racism undermines feminist struggle. As long as these two groups or any group defines liberation as gaining social equality with ruling class white men, they have a vested interest in the continued exploitation and oppression of others.

Black women with no institutionalized "other" that we may discriminate against, exploit, or oppress often have a lived experience that directly challenges the prevailing classist, sexist, racist social structure and its concomitant ideology. This lived experience may shape our consciousness in such a way that our world view differs from those who have a degree of privilege (however relative within the existing system). It is essential for continued feminist struggle that black women recognize the special vantage point our marginality gives us and make use of this perspective to criticize the dominant racist, classist, sexist hegemony as well as to envision and create a counter-hegemony. I am suggesting that we have a central role to play in the making of feminist theory and a contribution to offer that is unique and valuable. The formation of a liberatory feminist theory and praxis is a collective responsibility, one that must be shared. Though I criticize aspects of feminist movement as we have known it so far, a critique which is sometimes harsh and unrelenting, I do so not in an attempt to diminish feminist struggle but to enrich, to share in the work of making a liberatory ideology and a liberatory movement.

Notes

1 Betty Friedan, *The Feminine Mystique* (New York: W. W. Norten, 1997) , p. 15.

2 Friedan, "Progressive Dehumanization," ibid., p. 305.

3 Anita Cornwell, "Three for the Price of One: Notes from a Gay Black Feminist," in Jay Karla and Allen Young, eds, *Lavender Culture* (New York: New York University Press, 1994), p. 471.

Part II

What is Sexism?

Introduction to Part II

It is a central claim of feminism that women are systematically and unjustifiably disadvantaged by society. In many nations of the world, women are less well educated than men and are often economically dependent on them. Women everywhere occupy far fewer positions of power and authority – including positions as high ranking governmental officials. They are also underrepresented in most high paying and high status professions. As a result, women and their interests are often excluded from political and institutional policymaking. Indeed, in some parts of the world, women still lack full equality under the law. Moreover, women are often paid less than equally qualified men for similar types of work. In the context of the home, women still do a disproportionate amount of housework and childcare. Women must also fear a variety of types of violence – such as sexual harassment, rape, and battery – in virtue of their gender.

The examples listed above are meant to provide a brief, yet suggestive, summary of some reasonably uncontroversial examples of sexism in the world today. This is not to suggest, however, that it is easy to identify all cases of sexism – nor is it to suggest that it is easy to determine what sexism *is*. Sexism is a complex phenomenon, with a number of different possible meanings and causes. For example, sexism is sometimes characterized as unjust treatment on the basis of sex. Many feminists, however, prefer to characterize it in terms of the oppression of women. As for the causes of sexism, early liberal feminists focused on overt legal and institutional barriers to women's access to the public and professional realm. Some second wave feminists, on the other hand, turned their attention to the social structural causes of women's oppression. They argued that the causes of sexism are systematic – they infiltrate almost every aspect of social, political and economic life – and are often difficult to discern. Still others have focused on the biased attitudes (conscious and nonconscious) and subsequent actions of individual agents. These accounts need not be viewed as competing – although they sometimes are – but can be viewed as representing different aspects of sexism.

The readings in this part aim to characterize the nature of sexism, or sexist oppression. In "Sexism," Ann Cudd and Leslie Jones summarize three centuries of feminist theories of women's oppression and the evidence for the claim that sexism pervades contemporary society. They argue that the coining of the term "sexism" is a key event in this history, allowing us to unify a wide variety of experiences that might otherwise not be seen as having anything in common. They define sexism as a "systematic, pervasive, but often subtle, force that maintains the oppression of women, and that is at work through institutional structures, in interpersonal interactions, and the attitudes that are expressed in them, and in the cognitive, linguistic, and emotional processes of individual minds." Their view is thus that there are three levels at which sexism occurs and should be investigated: institutional, interpersonal, and unconscious. They characterize the two main types of feminist theories, equality feminism and difference feminism, by the ways that each type describes and prescribes remedies for each of these levels of sexism. Finally, Cudd and Jones respond to three main objections to the claim that sexism still exists or ought to be eradicated. The first objection, essentialism, maintains that the differences in the life outcomes of men and women is due to essential biological and psychological differences, and are therefore justifiable. But the authors reject this objection by arguing that the evidence is dubious and that the normative claim does not follow even if the descriptive essentialist claim holds. The second objection, skepticism, holds that women are not disadvantaged in contemporary society. Although this claim is easily countered by an appeal to the material facts, the authors cite influential adherents to the view. The third objection, defeatism, asserts that there is nothing to be done about sexism by individuals. Here the authors invoke particularly the interpersonal and unconscious levels of sexism to argue that individuals are morally obliged to avoid sexism in their own personal lives, even if they cannot make institutional changes.

As noted by Cudd and Jones, it is now commonplace in feminist theorizing to define sexism as a "historically and globally pervasive form of oppression against women." But what is oppression? The readings by Marilyn Frye and Iris Marion Young have become canonical feminist articles on the nature of oppression. In "Oppression," Frye characterizes oppression as a set of systematic forces that are often indiscernible – but are not accidental, occasional, or avoidable – which collectively immobilize, confine, and restrict the freedom of a group or category of people. She adds that oppression is both systematic and invisible: It is deeply woven into social, political, and economic structures in subtle and unforeseen ways. Frye uses an example of a birdcage as a metaphor for illustrating the systematic and invisible nature of oppression. If you inspect a bird cage one wire at a time, it is not possible to see how the bird's mobility can be limited. However, if you take a step back and look at all of the wires taken together, you see a system of barriers which collectively limit the bird's freedom and mobility. By analogy, women's oppression can be hard to recognize because individual social, political, or economic arrangements, when taken on their own, do not seem to limit a person's freedom. It is only when one studies the whole system that it becomes clear that such structures limit the lives of women.

Young begins her essay, "Five Faces of Oppression," by noting that at an abstract level, all oppressed people face a common set of limitations – i.e., in their freedom and ability to exercise their capacities and needs. Yet, she also argues that when one takes into account an individual's sociohistorical context, it is not possible to specify a common condition shared by all oppressed people – or all women for that matter. Young takes seriously the idea (discussed by hooks in Part 1 pp. 60–8) that women are a heterogeneous group – and, as a result, there are few, if any, attributes that all oppressed women share. Thus, instead of offering a strict definition of oppression – i.e., one that specifies necessary and sufficient conditions – Young discusses five "faces," or forms, of oppression; they include exploitation, marginality, powerlessness, cultural imperialism, and violence. She argues that none of these forms is necessary for oppression, but any one of them is sufficient. She also provides a number of examples to illustrate that women can, and often do, suffer each of these forms of oppression.

The accounts offered by Frye and Young make a valuable contribution to the feminist literature on oppression. Yet because they focus largely on the social, political, and economic aspects of oppression, some feminists would argue that they are incomplete. Missing from these accounts is an explicit formulation of the psychological aspects of oppression. In "On Psychological Oppression," Sandra Bartky provides just such an account. Bartky models her account after Frantz Fanon's account of racist oppression. In *Black Skin, White Masks*, Fanon describes a number of modes of racist oppression – stereotyping, cultural domination, and sexual objectification – as well as a characterization of what he calls "the psychic alienation of the black man" caused by colonialism and domestic racism. Bartky argues that the modes of sexist oppression resemble those of racist oppression: Not only do women experience stereotyping, cultural domination and sexual objectification; they also experience their own form of psychic alienation. She also highlights the harms of psychological oppression and illustrates the ways that women are co-opted into oppressing themselves through their internalization of inferiority.

6

Sexism

Ann E. Cudd and Leslie E. Jones

It is a pervasive, long-standing, and deeply disturbing fact that, by many ways of measuring well-being, women around the globe live lesser lives than men. In much of the world they are less well nourished, less healthy, and less well educated (UNIFEM 2000). Everywhere they are vulnerable to violence and abuse by men. It has been estimated that as a result of these facts, and because in many places girl babies are disproportionately aborted or killed, there are one hundred million missing women (Drèze and Sen 1989). Many more women in the world lack access to education and many more are illiterate. Jobs that are high paying are much less likely to be held by women. Tedious and menial work is much more likely to be done by women. Women in the workforce are paid less than their male counterparts, are more often harassed and intimidated in work, and are far more often responsible for childcare and housework "after work." Independently of their participation in the paying workforce, women suffer from domestic violence at much greater rates, bear primary responsibility for childrearing and housework, and are much more likely to be sick and poor in their old age. In much of the world women do not have access to safe abortion, or sometimes even to contraception, further putting women's health and well-being at risk. Women everywhere bear almost the full burden of unplanned pregnancies. Women in many nations of the world lack full formal equality under the law. Where they have it, they are less likely to be able to access the judicial system, and so still lack substantive equality. And almost nowhere in the world do women hold high government offices at anywhere near the rates of men. In short, when we compare the life prospects of women and men, we find that a woman is far more likely to be poor, unhealthy, abused, and politically disenfranchised, even while she works longer hours and is largely responsible for the primary care of future generations.

Ann E. Cudd and Leslie E. Jones, "Sexism," pp. 102–17 from R. G. Frey and C. H. Wellman (eds), *A Companion to Applied Ethics*. Oxford: Blackwell, 2003. Reprinted by permission of Blackwell Publishing Ltd.

Two general explanations could account for this remarkable disparity in life prospects: (1) women are by nature inferior to men, and so less worthy of concern or less able to benefit from equal concern, or (2) women are systematically disadvantaged by society. Under the first we include explanations based on psychology, biology, socio-biology, and so on that maintain that natural differences between men and women are sufficient to justify the comparatively sadder life prospects of women. As we will discuss below in "Objections," we suspect that many such claims depend on truant evidence (Fausto-Sterling 1985), and deny that any immediate normative implications follow from whatever differences might exist between men and women.

In what follows we proceed on the assumption that the more plausible course is to take some version of the second as true. To follow this line in investigating the ways in which women are systematically disadvantaged is to investigate sexism. We begin with a characterization of sexism. We then offer a brief history of its social recognition. We turn then to the levels at which sexism conditions human social life, and discuss some paradigm examples of sexism. We then set out the two principal types of feminist theories of sexism, and conclude with a brief discussion of three objections to struggle against sexism.

What is Sexism?

It is important to note at the outset that sexism is a highly complex notion. It is thus much easier to define conceptually, though this is no small task, than to concretely and unequivocally identify. Though there are certainly patent cases of sexism, on many definitions sexism is often only identifiable by its symptoms or consequences. We can quite readily explain that, if some distribution of opportunities systematically deprives women of what is offered to men, and there is no apparent overriding reason which justifies such a distribution, then we have a clear prima facie case of sexism. As a general claim this seems to us both undeniable and unassailable. The idea that sexism involves systematic inequality is, in short, a commonly recognized working definition. Yet those who deny that there is (much) sexism in the world, or in a particular case, often demand clear, ostensible evidence. Objective, operational criteria would be helpful here, and helpful for doing research or making policy as well. The task of finding such criteria is often quite difficult and comes from a wide array of theories covering the gamut of the social and psychological world. For sexism happens not only in explicitly institutionally structured settings, such as, for example, the denial of equal opportunity for jobs, but also in the daily and presumably much more spontaneous interactions between persons. As these latter interactions involve a wide variety of motives and causes, they may appear to be idiosyncratic and individualized rather than socially constructed. In such cases the charge of sexism might then appear less apt because less than obvious. Thus, the conceptual work of clarifying the nature of sexism is a far easier task than the practical work of showing that some particular concrete instance involving the mistreatment of women is the result of sexism or an instance of sexism. It is for this reason that much feminist work focuses on conceptual clarification and the organization of women's experience.

In its widest sense the term "sexism" can be used to refer to anything that creates, constitutes, promotes, sustains, or exploits an unjustifiable distinction between the sexes (Frye 1983: 18). In this wide sense the term "sexism" (and its nominative "sexist") can be used to refer to any purported though mistaken difference between the sexes. This neutral descriptive use of the term, however, is deeply unsatisfactory. First, because the history of the term (brief as it is) shows it to have been intentionally modeled on "racism." As "racism" does not merely describe attempts to differentiate between races, but instead refers to pernicious distinctions between races, the term "sexism" is better understood as referring to pernicious distinctions between the sexes. Second, a neutral use of the term implicitly denies its conceptual role in binding together and illuminating the various faces of women's social difference, and the ways in which these differences are harmful. Again, just as racism is most accurately used to refer to various forms of oppression against non-Caucasians (at least in Western societies), in the more accurate and more specific sense with which we will be concerned here, "sexism" refers to a historically and globally pervasive form of oppression against women. It is this more specific and explicitly normative sense of sexism that is the subject of feminist inquiry.

One catalyst for the identification of sexism was women's participation in struggles against racism. In fact, the first wave of the women's movement began with the participation of a number of thoughtful women in the abolition movement of the nineteenth century (Stanton and Anthony 1981), and the "second wave" can likewise trace its resurgence to the women of the civil rights movement in the twentieth century (Evans 1979). When contemplating a name for "the problem that has no name," as Betty Friedan (1983: Ch. 1) put it, there is little doubt that for many feminists the parallels with racism made the term "sexism" appealing. In some ways it might seem that this was an unfortunate start, for the differences between racism and sexism are sometimes obscured by the easy way in which they form lists of social wrongs. Perhaps the most important difference is that racism is based on dubious theories about the differences between the races, while sexual difference can hardly be denied. Racism seems often to be motivated by a hatred or fear of the other from which the conclusion comes that other "races" than one's own are inferior, a kind of racism that Kwame Anthony Appiah has called "intrinsic racism." Sexism, by contrast, is typically akin to what he calls "extrinsic racism," where the judgment that the other is inferior derives from the judgment that aspects or abilities of the other are inferior (Appiah 1990). Thus, many sexist men when so-charged can truly object that "I am not sexist; I love women," but this only means, at best, that they are not intrinsic sexists. However, there are many parallels between racism and sexism. For one thing, both are pervasive and have a high human cost. But, more importantly, the psychological mechanisms that make sexism and racism possible and desirable are similar: namely, our penchant for categorizing by social group, and making invidious distinctions between in-group and out-group members (Cudd 1998). Furthermore, the social mechanisms that maintain sexism and racism are similar. Both sexism and racism are maintained through systematic violence and economic disadvantage. Both are difficult to pinpoint, but can be statistically documented and are much more readily perceived by the victims than by the respective dominant social groups. Both sexism and racism can have devastating psychological effects on individuals. And both inspire enormously powerful backlash when they are publicly challenged. Considerable work remains to be done, however, on the relationship between the concepts of sexism and racism (Alcoff 1998).

If one holds, as we do, that sexism is pervasive, both historically and globally, then it will be no surprise that its ground will be both wide and deep. Institutions that are sexist will be both causes and effects of sexism. When regarded as a result of past sexism, such institutions will then carry on a tradition of, say, excluding women from available high-paying work. Managers and others who carry on this tradition may, of course, overtly maintain extrinsic sexism. They may sincerely, but falsely, believe women to be incapable of carrying on this work. This *intentional extrinsic sexism* should be distinguished from what might be called *individuated extrinsic sexism*, which maintains that while women (as a group) are capable of carrying on this work, no individual woman is. In either case it will be extremely difficult to persuasively establish such trenchant attitudes as sexist. In the latter case though women in general are held to be able to do this work, the technique of holding that each one now applying cannot do the job will effectively, if unintentionally, maintain the sexist tradition. Within that tradition such judgments are considered to be matters of keeping high standards, not sexism. As this practice requires an increasingly high degree of dubious judgment the longer it continues, over time it becomes correspondingly less reasonable to attribute to managers and others the sincere belief that women (as a group) are equally capable. In the case of intentional extrinsic sexism the fact that there are currently no or few women in the field contributes to the view that women cannot or do not want to do the work. The tradition of excluding women is, in this case, *intentional*, but is labeled by those who practice it "realism," not "sexism."

One important effect of the practice of excluding women in these ways is, of course, that women are made more dependent on others, usually men. By reducing the opportunities women have available to them, women are less able to clearly establish, both to themselves and to others, their general ability to accomplish high-paying (or high-status) tasks. Where these patterns are left unchallenged there is thus little to counter the claim that women are, by nature, more dependent. Moreover, these effects of sexist hiring practices are reinforced in a number of ways. They are reinforced by patterns of language which mark and delimit appropriate activities and attitudes on the basis of sex, and relegate the activities and attitudes of women to a lower status (i.e. sexist language). And they are reinforced by systems of education and enculturation which support, if not create and coerce, discrete proclivities for girls and boys, and relegate the proclivities of girls to a lower status. These social aspects of sexism are further mirrored in psychological dispositions, desires, and self-concepts. Accepting the activities, attitudes, and proclivities which are typically associated with men as "normal" or "standard" for human beings (i.e. the man standard) would render the activities, attitudes, and proclivities which are typically associated with women, when different, abnormal or substandard. For instance, women will appear "highly emotional" or "hysterical" when they display more emotion and concern than men, or "brooding" and "moody" when less. More pertinently, recognition of the man standard enables us to make as much sense as one can of the characterization of pregnancy as a form of illness or a temporary disability.

We stated earlier that sexism involves systematic inequality. Our discussion to this point has attempted to elucidate this notion. On our view sexism is a systematic, pervasive, but often subtle, force that maintains the oppression of women, and that is at work through institutional structures, in interpersonal interactions and the attitudes that are expressed in them, and in the cognitive, linguistic, and emotional processes of individual minds. In short, sexism structures our very experience of the world, and makes that world on the whole worse for women than for men.

Background: Language, Experience, and Recognition

Though sexism is a pervasive form of oppression, the term "sexism" is of surprisingly recent coinage, first appearing in print in 1968 (Shapiro 1985). Language and recognition are close allies when identifying social problems and investigating the possibility of social transformation. In naming this social phenomenon, and thus drawing attention to it, the second-wave feminists of the 1970s provided the conceptual space within which to recognize and reorganize long-standing moral, social, and political structures based on and affecting gender and biological sex. The resulting explorations into sexism have yielded considerable insights, and a number of difficulties.

Prior to the very recent coining of "sexism" there was simply no term to refer to the concept of women's oppression. Instead, authors identified various ways in which women seemed to be mistreated. Authors writing on this subject generally described fairly "local" forms of mistreatment. The primary focus of feminist arguments in the eighteenth and nineteenth centuries, for example, concerned the importance of education for women and an opposition to the absolute sovereignty of men within marriage (Astell 1694, 1700). These arguments, however, commonly held that any change in the position of women depended largely, if not solely, on a change in women. They also often agreed with the popular view that women had a naturally limited rational capacity (when compared with men), and that domestic life was women's naturally proper sphere.

At the end of the eighteenth century Mary Wollstonecraft focused on a comparatively greater variety of social factors contributing to women's subordinate position. Taking the radical stance that women are not inferior by nature, she held that women are naturally deserving of equal rights, and could, if properly educated, participate in "the theatre of politics." Like her predecessors, she held that women in general had an underdeveloped rational capacity. The vices that misogynist satires commonly attributed to women were, in her view, quite generally deserved: "it is your own conduct, O ye foolish women! which throws an odium on your sex!" (Wollstonecraft [1792] 1988: 302). Unlike them, however, she argued that it was not nature, but a lack of education that had contributed to women's focus on relatively trivial matters. Importantly, however, Wollstonecraft did not think that education would be sufficient to rectify women's subordinate position. She recognized that what she called the "stream of popular opinion" had an even stronger effect on women's social standing than did any characteristics actually possessed by individual women (Wollstonecraft [1792] 1988: 102). For bolstered by the stream of popular opinion and a socially produced reprehensible female character, she agreed that women's behavior often did "justify the authority that chains such a weak being to her duty" (Wollstonecraft [1792] 1988: 319). However, as women were just as capable as men of acquiring "human virtues," she argued that they were a social resource that was being squandered.

Like Wollstonecraft, J. S. Mill argued in the mid-nineteenth century that the various forms of mistreatment women suffered were contrary to general utility (Mill 1869). According to Mill, the opportunities offered to women and men should be based on a perfect equality of opportunity. That is, there should be nothing that is offered to men that is denied to women because they are women. Women, like men, will differ in aptitude and interest, but, like men, they should be allowed to win their social positions through fair and appropriate competition. On this position, the aim is to secure gender-neutral standards for all. As women have not been provided with the resources (for example, education, employment opportunities, political access, and social standing) to meet these standards, what is needed is a social transformation, which will give them the levels of access usually accorded men.

In 1949 Simone de Beauvoir reiterated the argument that women were not inferior to men by nature. However, de Beauvoir was interested in explaining not only the subordinate position of women in society, but also forms of female subjectivity that contribute to the durability of women's subordination. She thus gave greater weight to organizing "the lived experience" of women than did any of her predecessors. In her view both men's and women's natures have been socially constructed. However, the social construction of women has created a "second sex" in which women do not even regard themselves as a locus of dignity, as a self (de Beauvoir 1952). Instead, they regard themselves as "other," and, like men, reserve the notion of selfhood for men. The creation of a second sex is, moreover, the result of a primarily unconscious "desire for self-justification." That is, even the choices a woman believes she makes authentically, i.e. for herself, are the result of her constructed nature, the construction of which is for another, i.e. men. Alternatively, as the notion of "being a man" involves superiority, specifically superiority over women, men have a stake in maintaining women's inferiority. Women's subordination is thus explained and reinforced by men's and women's ways of experiencing the world. Though instructive in delineating aspects of female subjectivity, her work faces serious interpretive difficulties that mirror the main lines of feminist inquiry. These difficulties turn on the question of whether her position can be reconciled with some concept of gender-neutral standards. On the one hand, unless we can make sense of a self which is deeper than a constructed self, any notion of gender-neutral standards will be suspect. In other words, without an Archimedean point of view, gender neutrality will mean "equality with men" (i.e. the man standard) and women's differences will be detrimental to their well-being. On the other hand, if there is no deeper self, and the constructed differences between men and women must none the less be taken as "brute differences," then we are left with the difficult and somewhat uncomfortable goal of establishing "separate but equal" standards. To a large measure, feminist work on sexism has engaged in exploring, developing, and critically evaluating these complex lines of thought.

It would be difficult to deny that a sincere recognition of sexism will transform one's self-conception and one's conception of the world. Plato's allegory of the cave is a story of such experiential transformation, of coming to recognize something one would have not seen, and of coming to realize that what seems real is not real. For many women the recognition of sexism is just such a transformation. For like the cave-dwellers' first glimpse of the sun, the recognition of sexism is both revelatory and disorienting. Women sometimes describe their first recognition of sexism as a moment of realization, a "click" in which many previously disparate experiences, problems, reports, and issues become unified. What seemed previously to be simply one's own experiences, become a woman's experiences. What seemed previously to be personal problems, become women's problems. What were reports about others, or issues concerning others, become stories and issues about women like oneself. The recognition of sexism thus involves both a new way of conceptualizing experience and an identification with other women. It is also, unsurprisingly, a bewildering recognition (Bartky 1990). For once made it is difficult to determine which of one's reactions are, and which are not, the result of one's own idiosyncrasies. As the world of personal experience fades and the pervasiveness of sexism becomes more clear, few aspects of one's life remain in place. Fear, anger, and resentment at being insulted or threatened (however subtly) can no longer be regarded as simply personal reactions to personal affronts. They may, and often are, better apprehended as part of a system of oppression, in which individual perpetrators, perhaps even unknowingly, reaffirm the boundaries resulting from sexism.

The recognition of sexism for men is and has been both a slower and seemingly quite different process (Segal 1990). Few men report the recognition of sexism as a "click." It is more likely to take the form of a ploddingly arduous reconstruction of their own experience, which will require that they take responsibility for participation in sexist practices, and re-evaluate many of their beliefs and desires. Forms of male social interaction (e.g. jokes, chiding) come to be recognized as a mutual devaluing of women. Aspects and images of masculinity come to be recognized as compelling yet inconsistent with an aspiration for both inclusive social justice and uncoerced interpersonal cooperation. The recognition of sexism can thus also be transformative. As it is accompanied by an awareness that by forgoing forms of power and privilege the exercise of which determines one's relative social standing, the transformation carries considerable personal risk.

As it is accompanied by a realization of complicity the intentional nature of which is not always clear, it carries considerable moral risk. Different accounts of sexism will affect the degree of moral risk men face and the degree of personal risk which they ought to undertake.

Though the dynamics may be different, what is clear for both men and women is that the recognition of sexism, and its corresponding personal transformation, is a prerequisite for social transformation. Sexism, as noted above, works at a number of different levels whose interaction is, again, in need of further clarification.

Levels of Sexism

Sexism can be seen as a force responding to and molding human interactions. As a force, it can be seen, roughly, to operate at three levels: institutional sexism, which works on and through the level of social institutions; interpersonal sexism, which works on and through interactions among individuals who are not explicitly mediated by institutional structures; and unconscious sexism, which works at the personal level of the cognitive and affective processes of individuals. It is helpful to sort out these levels in order to explain why some charges of sexism are relatively uncontroversial, while others are difficult to see or evidence conclusively.

Institutional sexism

Institutional sexism refers to invidious sexual inequalities in the explicit rules and implicit norms governing and structuring social institutions. Religious institutions provide a useful example of how explicit rules and implicit norms structure institutions. In the Catholic Church, for instance, it is an explicit rule that all priests are men and all nuns are women. Only priests can run the church hierarchy, and priests outrank nuns in most decision-making situations. While it is clear how explicit rules can govern and structure institutions, this example can also help us to see that implicit norms also structure Catholic experience and create sexual inequality. While it is no longer widely accepted as an explicit rule that in heterosexual marriage the man is the head of the household and the woman is the helpmeet, it is implied by the relative rank of priests and nuns in the church and by its sacred writings. This implicit norm positions men above women in marriage (as in all other social institutions in which both sexes are present), clearly and invidious sexual inequality. In addition to the more explicitly rule-governed institutions of government, religion, family, health care, and education, there are crucially important informally or implicitly structured institutions prime among them being language, and the sites of cultural and artistic production. To say that sexism is a systematic social injustice based on one's sex (Radcliff Richards 1980), or a discriminatory sex-role differentiation (Bartky 1990), is to speak of institutional sexism. Sexism, then, must be understood as a part of the social order, similar to the economic order of capitalism or the political order of liberalism.

Interpersonal sexism

Whereas institutional sexism involves the explicit rules and their implicit norms that sustain oppressive social institutions, interpersonal sexism involves interactions between persons that are not governed by explicit rules. Interpersonal sexism comprises actions and other expressions between persons that create, constitute, promote, sustain, and/or exploit invidious sexual inequalities.

The person who is acting in a sexist way or making a sexist expression need not intend sexism; there are intentional and unintentional forms of interpersonal sexism. Here are some examples from our experiences:

- As a child, the girl is not allowed the free play of her brothers; she is prevented by her parents and teachers from engaging in rough-and-tumble play, not included in activities involving building, transportation, etc., not encouraged to try or expected to succeed at sports, mathematics, or leadership activities, and required, unlike her brothers, to do domestic chores.
- In school the teachers require her to speak less and restrain her behavior more than boys. Teachers reward her with better grades for her passivity, but boys exclude her from their games and begin to take the superior attitudes of their fathers.
- In sports she sees males and manhood extolled, females and womanhood ridiculed. Coaches and team-mates insult male athletes by calling

them "woman" or "girl," and praise them with the term "man."

- When a man and a woman negotiate a car loan or a home loan, or buy an expensive machine, the salesperson speaks only to the man. Supermarket ads are aimed, meanwhile, at women as housewives.
- In conversations between colleagues men are routinely deferred to while women's remarks are ignored. When a male colleague repeats what a female has said, he is complimented for his good idea.

Sexism is a key motif that unifies this otherwise seemingly disparate set of personal experiences. This list could, of course, be greatly expanded, and much feminist work has been devoted to increasing our stock of example experiences. This work is important because sexism is such an integral but unspoken part of the everyday world that both men and women have a difficult time recognizing it. For society's ground of legitimacy seems to require that injustice be recognized and socially opposed. Yet the injustice of sexism is built into the very fabric of everyone's everyday experiences from infancy on.

Unconscious sexism

"Unconscious sexism" refers to the psychological mechanisms and tacit beliefs, emotions, and attitudes that create, constitute, promote, sustain, and/or exploit invidious sexual inequalities. This category will be denied by many as vague, unprovable, or too easily invoked. But there are both conceptual and empirical arguments in favor of its existence. The conceptual argument is that the statistical evidence concerning the lesser lives that women live would be completely puzzling given the legal guarantees of equality for men and women in many countries were it not for the possibility of such unconscious sexism. Institutional and interpersonal sexism cannot alone account for all the data. That implies that there are unconscious attitudes and beliefs that allow persons in positions of power unconsciously to prefer men to women when social rewards are distributed, and yet not to see themselves or be seen as applying sexist standards.

The empirical argument is widely diffused, but accessible. It consists first of all in evidence for the existence of unconscious motivations, which is vast in the psychological literature. Second, there is evidence that when the same work is attributed to a woman it is judged of less value than when attributed to a man (Valian 1998). Third, there is evidence that women find it more painful to think of themselves as oppressed, and men find it more painful to think of themselves as the privileged gender. Thus, there is motivation for neither women nor men to think of women as oppressed and men as dominant (Branscombe 1998). Fourth, there is a great deal of evidence from social cognitive psychology to suggest that persons make invidious distinctions among salient social categories, that we tend to amplify them well beyond the real differences between individuals in those categories, and that sex is one of those categories (Tajfel 1981). Now since it surely cannot be argued that men get the worse end of this deal, this fact constitutes evidence for the claim that such cognitive processes tend to create unconscious sexist attitudes and beliefs. There is, no doubt, a great deal more evidence that could be cited, but this much should be sufficient to make the point that unconscious sexism is a real, documented, psychological phenomenon.

Having demonstrated its reality, however, some discussion and examples will be helpful to see how unconscious sexism is manifested and how one might go about discovering it. The key to recognizing unconscious motivations, especially unsavory ones that persons are reluctant to acknowledge in themselves, is to look for decisions or actions that could not be justified by a reasonable assessment of the available evidence. What counts as "reasonable" and "available" are crucial issues here, of course. By "reasonable" we mean consistent with one's other explicitly held beliefs and widely shared, non-sexist, knowledge in the community. We insist on explicit beliefs here because, of course, if one has tacit sexist beliefs the action could be reasonable but sexist, and yet not counted as unconscious. By "available evidence" we are referring to reports that would be made by a member of the community who does not have sexist beliefs or attitudes, or whose sexist beliefs played no role in the reports, or to widely shared, non-sexist, knowledge in the community. Of course, there may be no non-sexist members of any community. The practices of sexism affect one's self-conception. Internal critique may not be enough to free oneself from identification with those practices. But we must begin to identify sexist practices somewhere. Granting that it is possible that we will not recognize all unconscious (or, indeed, all conscious) sexism, we can still begin by finding the more obvious cases. Consider the following examples:

- A philosophy department is looking to hire a new faculty member. One-third of the applicants are women. One-third of the interview list is made up of women. In the interviews the women are judged as doing worse than the men. The comments afterwards are that they don't seem "as polished" or "professional" as the men. The fact is that the women do not meet the interviewers' expectations of what a philosopher or a faculty member is supposed to look like, a stereotype that includes being a man.
- A department is considering how to advise a female colleague and a male colleague concerning their chances for tenure. They have equal but modest publishing records, and roughly equal but modest teaching records. However, the female colleague has far more service. Both colleagues have been active participants in the departmental politics and have voiced strong opinions in departmental meetings. The male is judged to be an excellent colleague, while the female is judged to be uncollegial. They give the male colleague a very positive report for his tenure prospects, and the female is warned that she must publish more and improve her teaching to get tenure. In fact, the department has judged her to be worse because they feel uncomfortable with a strong, active woman, while the man is judged to have leadership qualities.
- A drug is being tested for its effectiveness in preventing heart disease. All the research subjects are men. When asked to account for this the research team leader responds that women's hormones would interfere with the study. While it is surely true that the drug could affect women differently from men as a result of female hormones, it is equally true that it could affect men differently from women as a result of male hormones. This symmetry is lost on the research team, who, like most of us, tend to think of women as the ones with the "interfering" or abnormal hormones.

Unconscious sexism often seems to be innocent, in the sense that the beliefs or feelings that make it up are never voiced, and often based on widely shared stereotypes. Whether or not it is innocent surely depends on the degree to which the individual has access to information that counters the unconscious sexist beliefs and attitudes, a condition that depends on larger social factors. Although we do believe that "sexism" names not only a mistake but a prima facie wrong, there are cases where one can commit this wrong and yet not be culpable.

These levels of sexism are, of course, interrelated. Understood as institutional discrimination, sexism concerns the interactions between men and women only as symptoms of a more pervasive problem. Social institutions guide, and on some accounts cause, our interpersonal attitudes. Our self-conceptions and our conception of others are at least partially a product of the social structures through which we interact with one another. How they are interrelated is a central question within feminism, feminist philosophy, and feminist social science. Different ways of understanding the interrelations between these levels result in different, and sometimes quite divergent, accounts. Two types of account are prominent in the feminist literature. In the next section we discuss these two types.

Two Feminist Views of Sexism

Though feminists agree that sexism structures our very experience of the world, feminist theories of sexism vary considerably. None the less, they can be very roughly divided into two categories. First, what can be labeled "equality feminism" maintains that social institutions are the primary medium of sexism. Men and women do not differ markedly in their potential capacities, interests, and abilities. Given similar training, men and women would develop fairly similar talents, at least as similar as those between men or between women. Thus if we are to transform society it will require that we resist and undermine those institutions that enforce sex differences and disproportionately deprive women of opportunities to develop highly valued social skills. Equality feminists need not accept what we have above called "the man standard." Rather, most contemporary equality feminists employ measures of social value such as utility, respect for human rights, or hypothetical agreement in order to develop gender-neutral standards by which to judge the opportunities, activities, and proclivities of men and women.

Alternatively, "difference feminists" maintain that unconscious desires are the primary medium of sexism. Accordingly, social institutions are the result, rather than the cause, of sexism. Recently a variety of feminists holding this view have attempted to both articulate the differences between men and women and re-evaluate equality feminism. Some, like Carol Gilligan (1982), Nel Noddings (1984), and Sara Ruddick (1989), have argued that women's "different voice" involves a greater emphasis on responsiveness, caring, and the maintenance of particular, concrete relationships. This voice is undervalued in society, they argue, because of the dominance of "responsibility" – a notion which involves a strict adherence to principle and which, they argue, typifies the male point of view. Others skeptical of gender neutrality are also skeptical of the idea that caring and relationship maintenance best characterize women's difference. They thus seek to identify a different difference. Catherine MacKinnon (1987: 39) writes: "women value care because men have valued us according to the care we give them, and we could probably use some." In her view, since women's subordinate position in society informs their experience of the world, and so requires concrete critical evaluation, it can also give them a unique, and privileged, position from which to criticize our social traditions. Somewhat similarly, Luce Irigaray argues that the critical revaluation of women should neither reassert what has traditionally been taken to be women's nature, nor strive for equality with men. She maintains that the law has a duty to "offer justice to *two genders that differ* in their needs, their desires, their properties" (Irigaray 1993: 4).

Both views aim to transform institutional sexism, interpersonal sexism, and unconscious sexism. They differ, however, over just what form such a transformation would take. For equality feminists the notion that there is a significant difference between men and women, a difference that makes a difference, seems more likely to sustain the global disparity existing between men and women since this disparity has been built on the basis of sex differentiation. For difference feminists, on the other hand, the notion that there is no significant difference between men and women, seems likely to undermine women's emancipation. Since women have been defined and have defined themselves in relation to men, as subordinate to dominant, women's independence depends on discovering, or perhaps imaginatively inventing, a different identity. Importantly, both equality feminists and difference feminists have the same worry. For both, the idea that an attempted transformation of society will result in a mere modification of sexism rather than its elimination is, given its evident though under-acknowledged depth and pervasiveness, a predominant, reasonable, and clearly practical concern.

Objections

Three kinds of objections have been raised to feminist struggles against sexism, which we shall call the objections from *essentialism*, *skepticism*, and *defeatism*. The objection from *essentialism* maintains that there are essential biological or psychological differences between men and women such that true equality or even equal evaluation of men and women will ultimately be impossible or will too greatly restrain our liberty. Such objections to feminist efforts to remedy the ravages of sexism have a long history, from Aristotle's view of woman as partial man through biological theories of inferiority propagated in the nineteenth and twentieth centuries to Freudian psychoanalytic theories of femininity. A recent and currently influential version of this objection appeals to evolutionary psychology to explain the differences between the status of men and women. According to evolutionary psychology, there are distinct male and female psychologies because of the different reproductive strategies that each sex pursues, and the resulting psychologies make males more competitive, independent, and aggressive, while females are more nurturing and concerned about interpersonal relations. In addition, at least one proponent of evolutionary psychology has claimed that male psychology makes it inevitable that men will "run to extremes – or, in other words, that men are disproportionately represented in the top and bottom of many measurements" (Guyot 2001: B15). Thus, the best lawyers, artists, politicians, businessmen, and so on must be men. So, Guyot argues, it would be inefficient and morally wrong to bring about parity in gender representation of these fields.

To this objection we have three responses. First, specifically regarding evolutionary psychology, it is a highly theorized but largely untested hypothesis at this point. Given its genealogy as another in a string of allegedly scientific proofs of women's inferiority, it is important to be skeptical until and unless it scores empirical successes. Second, and this response applies to any scientific theory about sexual difference, normative implications of difference are never directly implied by any descriptive differences. That is, it is fallacious to infer from the fact of sexual difference that women should therefore not have equal chances for social success. Finally, the ideals of liberal individualism and equality require each individual to be treated as a unique person, deserving of praise or social rewards based on his or her actual individual merit, and not based on the average merits of her class, caste, race, or gender. So even if it were true that women on average are less well suited to be lawyers, or whatever, it does not follow that there should be no safeguards in place to ensure that women are not discriminated against because of their sex. In fact, if women are on average less well suited to various occupations, it raises the likelihood that employers will unfairly judge individual women by their sex rather than their individual merits.

The objection from *skepticism* maintains that sexism is admittedly a serious problem in some other countries, but, though it has been a problem in our society in the past, sexism has largely been overcome. Women are not prevented from gaining an education, entering the workforce, or asserting their equal right to vote, to own property, or to divorce. In some cases women are treated preferentially and sometimes even outperform men. Therefore, there is no reason to pursue any remedies to sexism – it is already gone. This sort of objection has been leveled by Christina Hoff Sommers (2000). However, this objection overlooks a wealth of statistical information that proves that women's well-being is still compromised in contemporary American society. The gender wage gap hovers around 75 percent (Institute for Women's Policy Research 1997b) – up considerably from the 59 percent of the late 1970s, but still hardly something to be satisfied with. According to the Joint Center for Poverty Research, although the overall rate of poverty in the United States in 1997 was 13.3 percent, the rate for women was 24 percent. Women suffer from domestic violence at roughly four times the rate of men (US Department of Justice 2000). In 2001, 73 women served in the US Congress (13.6 percent): thirteen in the Senate, and 60 in the House, both all-time highs. Of course, no woman has ever been US President, and only two women are now and have ever been Justices of the Supreme Court. Women in state legislatures compose only 22.4 percent even of those bodies (Center for American Women in Politics 2001). Women own businesses at approximately half the rate of men, and of the top one hundred wealthiest people in *Forbes Magazine's* list for 2001, only ten were women. And this is only a partial list of the great inequalities suffered by women in contemporary US society. Finally, it is also important to point out to the skeptic that the fact that women are suffering from sexism in much of the world is itself harmful to all women. Women form a social group – a non-voluntary social group. They thereby share each other's fate to an extent. If women are harassed on the streets of Kabul, then American women who travel there will be harassed. If women are subjected to humiliating or violent treatment in East Asia, then American women who travel there will be as well. If women are not taken seriously in a country, then how can a woman diplomat from America hope to do her job there? The skeptic thus underestimates both the degree to which sexism still exists in Western society and the effects that sexism worldwide has on all women.

The *defeatist* argues that there is nothing that he or anyone personally can do to fight sexism. Defeatists often continue by arguing that since they are not themselves mistreating women, do not dislike women or hold them to be inferior, they should not therefore be required to do anything to combat sexism; nor do they think that anything constructive can be done to eliminate it. Defeatists overlook the existence of institutional and unconscious sexism. They fail to recognize that they can participate in sexism even without overt, conscious sexist attitudes. If they take seriously the problem of sexism, then they should examine their behaviors, choices, and preferences for what those express to the world. Perhaps they will find underneath a dislike of a certain co-worker, say, a prejudice against assertive women that they do not harbor against assertive men. This would be an example of unconscious sexism (made conscious). They should also examine how they respond to other people's overt interpersonal sexism. Do they laugh at wife jokes? Look the other way from sexual harassment in the office? Such behaviors support sexism, and thus injustice. Finally, the defeatist who acknowledges institutional sexism has the obligation not to support it: not to vote for it, not to buy from it, not to encourage it. The defeatist has no real defense, in other words, as long as he admits that there may be unconscious sexism, interpersonal sexism among others, or institutional sexism.

In conclusion, sexism is alive and well in contemporary Western society, and to an even greater degree in much of the rest of the world. Sexism is a serious form of oppression, and, as such, it is incumbent on decent people to oppose it, though the form that opposition should take remains a serious matter for theorists and activists alike.

References

Alcoff, L. M. (1998) Racism. In *A Companion to Feminist Philosophy*. Malden, MA: Blackwell.

Appiah, A. (1990) Racisms. In D. T. Goldberg (ed.), *Anatomy of Racism*. Minneapolis: University of Minnesota Press.

Astell, M. (1694) *A Serious Proposal to the Ladies for the Advancement of their True and Greatest Interest*. New York: New York University Press, 1997.

—— (1700) *Some Reflections on Marriage*. New York: Source Book Press, 1970.

Bartky, S. L. (1990) *Femininity and Domination*. New York: Routledge.

de Beauvoir, S. (1952) *The Second Sex*, trans. H. M. Parshley. New York: Random House (orig. pub. 1949).

Branscombe, N. (1998) Thinking about one's gender group's privileges or disadvantages: consequences for well-being in women and men. *British Journal of Social Psychology*, 37: 167–84.

Center for American Women in Politics (2001) www.rci.rutgers.edu/~cawp/facts/cawpfs.html.

Cudd, A. E. (1998) Psychological explanations of oppression. In C. Willett (ed.), *Theorizing Multiculturalism*. Malden, MA: Blackwell.

Drèze, J. and Sen, A. (1989) *Hunger and Public Action*. Oxford: Clarendon Press.

Evans, S. (1979) *Personal Politics: The Roots of Women's Liberation in the Civil Rights Movement and the New Left*. New York: Vintage Books.

Fausto-Sterling, A. (1985) *Myths of Gender: Biological Theories about Women and Men*. New York: Basic Books.

Friedan, B. (1983) *The Feminine Mystique*, 20th anniv. edn. New York: Dell.

Frye, M. (1983) *The Politics of Reality*. Trumansburg, New York: The Crossing Press.

Gilligan, C. (1982) *In a Different Voice: Psychological Theory and Women's Development*. Cambridge, MA: Harvard University Press.

Guyot, J. F. (2001) The defining moment for gender equity. *The Chronicle of Higher Education*. April 20.

—— (1997b) *The Wage Gap: Men's and Women's Earnings*. Briefing Paper. Washington, DC.

Irigaray, L. (1993) *Sexes and Genealogies*, trans. Gillian Gill. New York: Columbia University Press.

MacKinnon, C. (1987) *Feminism Unmodified: Discourses on Life and Law*. Cambridge, MA: Harvard University Press.

Mill, J. S. (1869) *The Subjection of Women*. New York: Source Books, 1970.

Noddings, N. (1984) *Caring: A Feminine Approach to Ethics and Moral Education*. Berkeley, CA: University of California Press.

Radcliff Richards, J. (1980) *The Sceptical Feminist*. London: Routledge and Kegan Paul.

Ruddick, S. (1989) *Maternal Thinking: Toward a Politics of Peace*. New York: Basic Books.

Segal, L. (1990) *Slow Motion: Changing Masculinities, Changing Men*. New Brunswick, NJ: Rutgers University Press.

Shapiro, F. R. (1985) Historical notes on the vocabulary of the Women's Movement. *American Speech*, 1: 3–16.

Sommers, C. H. (2000) *The War Against Boys: How Misguided Feminism is Harming our Young Men*. New York: Simon and Schuster.

Stanton, E. C. and Anthony, S. B. (1981) *Correspondence, Writings, Speeches*, ed. E. C. DuBois. New York: Schocken Books.

Tajfel, H. (1981) *Human Groups and Social Categories*. Cambridge: Cambridge University Press.

UNIFEM (2000) *Progress of the World's Women 2000*. New York: United Nations.

US Department of Justice, Office of Justice Programs (2000) *Extent, Nature, and Consequences of Intimate Partner Violence: Findings from the National Violence against Women Survey*. Washington, DC.

Valian, V. (1998) *Why So Slow? The Advancement of Women*. Cambridge, MA: MIT Press.

Wollstonecraft, M. (1792) *Vindication of the Rights of Woman*. New York: Penguin, 1988.

7

Oppression

Marilyn Frye

It is a fundamental claim of feminism that women are oppressed. The word "oppression" is a strong word. It repels and attracts. It is dangerous and dangerously fashionable and endangered. It is much misused, and sometimes not innocently.

The statement that women are oppressed is frequently met with the claim that men are oppressed too. We hear that oppressing is oppressive to those who oppress as well as to those they oppress. Some men cite as evidence of their oppression their much-advertised inability to cry. It is tough, we are told, to be masculine. When the stresses and frustrations of being a man are cited as evidence that oppressors are oppressed by their oppressing, the word "oppression" is being stretched to meaninglessness; it is treated as though its scope includes any and all human experience of limitation or suffering, no matter the cause, degree or consequence. Once such usage has been put over on us, then if ever we deny that any person or group is oppressed, we seem to imply that we think they never suffer and have no feelings. We are accused of insensitivity; even of bigotry. For women, such accusation is particularly intimidating, since sensitivity is one of the few virtues that has been assigned to us. If we are found insensitive, we may fear we have no redeeming traits at all and perhaps are not real women. Thus are we silenced before we begin: the name of our situation drained of meaning and our guilt mechanisms tripped.

But this is nonsense. Human beings can be miserable without being oppressed, and it is perfectly consistent to deny that a person or group is oppressed without denying that they have feelings or that they suffer.

We need to think clearly about oppression, and there is much that mitigates against this. I do not want to undertake to prove that women are oppressed (or that men are not), but I want to make clear what is being said when we say it. We need this word, this concept, and we need it to be sharp and sure.

I

The root of the word "oppression" is the element "press". *The press of the crowd; pressed into military service; to press a pair of pants; printing press; press the button.* Presses are used to mold things or flatten them or reduce them in bulk, sometimes to reduce

Marilyn Frye, "Oppression," pp. 1–16 from *The Politics of Reality*. Freedom, CA: The Crossing Press, 1983.

them by squeezing out the gasses or liquids in them. Something pressed is something caught between or among forces and barriers which are so related to each other that jointly they restrain, restrict or prevent the thing's motion or mobility. Mold. Immobilize. Reduce.

The mundane experience of the oppressed provides another clue. One of the most characteristic and ubiquitous features of the world as experienced by oppressed people is the double bind – situations in which options are reduced to a very few and all of them expose one to penalty, censure or deprivation. For example, it is often a requirement upon oppressed people that we smile and be cheerful. If we comply, we signal our docility and our acquiescence in our situation. We need not, then, be taken note of. We acquiesce in being made invisible, in our occupying no space. We participate in our own erasure. On the other hand, anything but the sunniest countenance exposes us to being perceived as mean, bitter, angry or dangerous. This means, at the least, that we may be found "difficult" or unpleasant to work with, which is enough to cost one one's livelihood; at worst, being seen as mean, bitter, angry or dangerous has been known to result in rape, arrest, beating and murder. One can only choose to risk one's preferred form and rate of annihilation.

Another example: It is common in the United States that women, especially younger women, are in a bind where neither sexual activity nor sexual inactivity is all right. If she is heterosexually active, a woman is open to censure and punishment for being loose, unprincipled or a whore. The "punishment" comes in the form of criticism, snide and embarrassing remarks, being treated as an easy lay by men, scorn from her more restrained female friends. She may have to lie and hide her behavior from her parents. She must juggle the risks of unwanted pregnancy and dangerous contraceptives. On the other hand, if she refrains from heterosexual activity, she is fairly constantly harassed by men who try to persuade her into it and pressure her to "relax" and "let her hair down"; she is threatened with labels like "frigid," "uptight," "manhater," "bitch" and "cocktease." The same parents who would be disapproving of her sexual activity may be worried by her inactivity because it suggests she is not or will not be popular, or is not sexually normal. She may be charged with lesbianism. If a woman is raped, then if she has been heterosexually active she is subject to the presumption that she liked it (since her activity is presumed to show that she likes sex), and if she has not been heterosexually active, she is subject to the presumption that she liked it (since she is supposedly "repressed and frustrated"). Both heterosexual activity and heterosexual nonactivity are likely to be taken as proof that you wanted to be raped, and hence, of course, weren't *really* raped at all. You can't win. You are caught in a bind, caught between systematically related pressures.

Women are caught like this, too, by networks of forces and barriers that expose one to penalty, loss or contempt whether one works outside the home or not, is on welfare or not, bears children or not, raises children or not, marries or not, stays married or not, is heterosexual, lesbian, both or neither. Economic necessity; confinement to racial and/or sexual job ghettos; sexual harassment; sex discrimination; pressures of competing expectations and judgments about *women, wives* and *mothers* (in the society at large, in racial and ethnic subcultures and in one's own mind); dependence (full or partial) on husbands, parents or the state; commitment to political ideas; loyalties to racial or ethnic or other "minority" groups; the demands of self-respect and responsibilities to others. Each of these factors exists in complex tension with every other, penalizing or prohibiting all of the apparently available options. And nipping at one's heels, always, is the endless pack of little things. If one dresses one way, one is subject to the assumption that one is advertising one's sexual availability; if one dresses another way, one appears to "not care about oneself" or to be "unfeminine." If one uses "strong language," one invites categorization as a whore or slut; if one does not, one invites categorization as a "lady" – one too delicately constituted to cope with robust speech or the realities to which it presumably refers.

The experience of oppressed people is that the living of one's life is confined and shaped by forces and barriers which are not accidental or occasional and hence avoidable, but are systematically related to each other in such a way as to catch one between and among them and restrict or penalize motion in any direction. It is the experience of being caged in: all avenues, in every direction, are blocked or booby trapped.

Cages. Consider a birdcage. If you look very closely at just one wire in the cage, you cannot see the other wires. If your conception of what is before you is determined by this myopic focus, you could look at that one wire, up and down the length of it, and be unable to see why a bird would not just fly around the wire any time it wanted to go somewhere. Furthermore, even if, one day at a time, you myopically inspected each wire, you still could not see why a bird would have trouble going past the wires to get anywhere. There is no physical property of any one wire, *nothing* that the closest scrutiny could discover, that will reveal how a bird could be inhibited or harmed by it except in the most accidental way. It is only when you step back, stop looking at the wires one by one, microscopically, and take a macroscopic view of the whole cage, that you can see why the bird does not go any-where; and then you will see it in a moment. It will require no great subtlety of mental powers. It is perfectly *obvious* that the bird is surrounded by a network of systematically related barriers, no one of which would be the least hindrance to its flight, but which, by their relations to each other, are as confining as the solid walls of a dungeon.

It is now possible to grasp one of the reasons why oppression can be hard to see and recognize: one can study the elements of an oppressive structure with great care and some good will without seeing the structure as a whole, and hence without seeing or being able to understand that one is looking at a cage and that there are people there who are caged, whose motion and mobility are restricted, whose lives are shaped and reduced.

The arresting of vision at a microscopic level yields such common confusion as that about the male door-opening ritual. This ritual, which is remarkably widespread across classes and races, puzzles many people, some of whom do and some of whom do not find it offensive. Look at the scene of the two people approaching a door. The male steps slightly ahead and opens the door. The male holds the door open while the female glides through. Then the male goes through. The door closes after them. "Now how", one innocently asks, "can those crazy womenslibbers say that is oppressive? The guy *removed* a barrier to the lady's smooth and unruffled progress." But each repetition of this ritual has a place in a pattern, in fact in several patterns. One has to shift the level of one's perception in order to see the whole picture.

The door-opening pretends to be a helpful service, but the helpfulness is false. This can be seen by nothing that it will be done whether or not it makes any practical sense. Infirm men and men burdened with packages will open doors for able-bodied women who are free of physical burdens. Men will impose themselves awkwardly and jostle everyone in order to get to the door first. The act is not determined by convenience or grace. Furthermore, these very numerous acts of unneeded or even noisome "help" occur in counterpoint to a pattern of men not being helpful in many practical ways in which women might welcome help. What *women* experience is a world in which gallant princes charming commonly make a fuss about being helpful and providing small services when help and services are of little or no use, but in which there are rarely ingenious and adroit princes at hand when substantial assistance is really wanted either in mundane affairs or in situations of threat, assault or terror. There is no help with the (his) laundry; no help typing a report at 4:00 a.m.; no help in mediating disputes among relatives or children. There is nothing but advice that women should stay indoors after dark, be chaperoned by a man, or when it comes down to it, "lie back and enjoy it."

The gallant gestures have no practical meaning. Their meaning is symbolic. The door-opening and similar services provided are services which really are needed by people who are for one reason or another incapacitated – unwell, burdened with parcels, etc. So the message is that women are incapable. The detachment of the acts from the concrete realities of what women need and do not need is a vehicle for the message that women's actual needs and interests are unimportant or irrelevant. Finally, these gestures imitate the behavior of servants toward masters and thus mock women, who are in most respects the servants and caretakers of men. The message of the false helpfulness of male gallantry is female dependence, the invisibility or insignificance of women, and contempt for women.

One cannot see the meanings of these rituals if one's focus is riveted upon the individual event in all its particularity, including the particularity of the individual man's present conscious intentions and motives and the individual woman's conscious perception of the event in the moment. It seems sometimes that people take a deliberately myopic view and fill their eyes with things seen microscopically in order not to see macroscopically. At any rate, whether it is deliberate or not, people can and do fail to see the oppression of women because they fail to see macroscopically and hence fail to see the various elements of the situation as systematically related in larger schemes.

As the cageness of the birdcage is a macroscopic phenomenon, the oppressiveness of the situations in which women live our various and different lives is a macroscopic phenomenon. Neither can be *seen* from a microscopic perspective. But when you look macroscopically you can see it – a network of forces and barriers which are systematically related and which conspire to the immobilization, reduction and molding of women and the lives we live.

II

The image of the cage helps convey one aspect of the systematic nature of oppression. Another is the selection of occupants of the cages, and analysis of this aspect also helps account for the invisibility of the oppression of women.

It is as a woman (or as a Chicana/o or as a Black or Asian or lesbian) that one is entrapped.

> "Why can't I go to the park; you let Jimmy go!"
> "Because it's not safe for girls."
>
> "I want to be a secretary, not a seamstress; I don't want to learn to make dresses."
> "There's no work for negroes in that line; learn a skill where you can earn your living."[1]

When you question why you are being blocked, why this barrier is in your path, the answer has not to do with individual talent or merit, handicap or failure; it has to do with your membership in some category understood as a "natural" or "physical" category. The "inhabitant" of the "cage" is not an individual but a group, all those of a certain category. If an individual is oppressed, it is in virtue of being a member of a group or category of people that is systematically reduced, molded, immobilized. Thus, to recognize a person as oppressed, one has to see that individual *as* belonging to a group of a certain sort.

There are many things which can encourage or inhibit perception of someone's membership in the sort of group or category in question here. In particular, it seems reasonable to suppose that if one of the devices of restriction and definition of the group is that of physical confinement or segregation, the confinement and separation would encourage recognition of the group as a group. This in turn would encourage the macroscopic focus which enables one to recognize oppression and encourages the individuals' identification and solidarity with other individuals of the group or category. But physical confinement and segregation of the group as a group is not common to all oppressive structures, and when an oppressed group is geographically and demographically dispersed the perception of it as a group is inhibited. There may be little or nothing in the situations of the individuals encouraging the macroscopic focus which would reveal the unity of the structure bearing down on all members of that group.[2]

A great many people, female and male and of every race and class, simply do not believe that *woman* is a category of oppressed people, and I think that this is in part because they have been fooled by the dispersal and assimilation of women throughout and into the systems of class and race which organize men. Our simply being dispersed makes it difficult for women to have knowledge of each other and hence difficult to recognize the shape of our common cage. The dispersal and assimilation of women throughout economic classes and races also divides us against each other practically and economically and thus attaches *interest* to the inability to see: for some, jealousy of their benefits, and for some, resentment of the others' advantages.

To get past this, it helps to notice that in fact women of all races and classes *are* together in a ghetto of sorts. There is a women's place, a sector, which is inhabited by women of all classes and races, and it is not defined by geographical boundaries but by function. The function is the service of men and men's interests as men define them, which includes the bearing and rearing of children. The details of the service and the working conditions vary by race and class, for men of different races and classes have different interests, perceive their interests differently, and express their needs and demands in different rhetorics, dialects and languages. But there are also some constants.

Whether in lower, middle or upper-class home or work situations, women's service work always includes personal service (the work of maids, butlers, cooks, personal secretaries),[3] sexual service (including provision for his genital sexual needs and bearing his children, but also including "being nice," "being attractive for him," etc.), and ego service (encouragement, support, praise, attention). Women's service work also is characterized everywhere by the fatal combination of responsibility and powerlessness: we are held responsible and we hold ourselves responsible for good outcomes for men and children in almost every respect though we have in almost no case power adequate to that project. The details of the subjective experience of this servitude are local. They vary with economic class and race and ethnic tradition as well as the personalities of the men in question. So also are the details of the forces which coerce our tolerance of this servitude particular to the different situations in which different women live and work.

All this is not to say that women do not have, assert and manage sometimes to satisfy our own interests, nor to deny that in some cases and in some respects women's independent interests do overlap with men's. But at every race/class level and even across race/class lines men do not serve women as women serve men. "Women's sphere" may be understood as the "service sector," taking the latter expression much more widely and deeply than is usual in discussions of the economy.

III

It seems to be the human condition that in one degree or another we all suffer frustration and limitation, all encounter unwelcome barriers, and all are damaged and hurt in various ways. Since we are a social species, almost all of our behavior and activities are structured by more than individual inclination and the conditions of the planet and its atmosphere. No human is free of social structures, nor (perhaps) would happiness consist in such freedom. Structure consists of boundaries, limits and barriers; in a structured whole, some motions and changes are possible, and others are not. If one is looking for an excuse to dilute the word "oppression", one can use the fact of social structure as an excuse and say that everyone is oppressed. But if one would rather get clear about what oppression is and is not, one needs to sort out the sufferings, harms and limitations and figure out which are elements of oppression and which are not.

From what I have already said here, it is clear that if one wants to determine whether a particular suffering, harm or limitation is part of someone's being oppressed, one has to look at it *in context* in order to tell whether it is an element in an oppressive structure: one has to see if it is part of an enclosing structure of forces and barriers which tends to the immobilization and reduction of a group or category of people. One has to look at how the barrier or force fits with others and to whose benefit or detriment it works. As soon as one looks at examples, it becomes obvious that not everything which frustrates or limits a person is oppressive, and not every harm or damage is due to or contributes to oppression.

If a rich white playbody who lives off income from his investments in South African diamond mines should break a leg in a skiing accident at Aspen and wait in pain in a blizzard for hours before he is rescued, we may assume that in that period he suffers. But the suffering comes to an end; his leg is repaired by the best surgeon money can buy and he is soon recuperating in a lavish suite, sipping Chivas Regal. Nothing in this picture suggests a structure of barriers and forces. He is a member of several oppressor groups and does not suddenly become oppressed because he is injured and in pain. Even if the accident was caused by someone's malicious negligence, and hence someone can be blamed for it and morally faulted, that person still has not been an agent of oppression.

Consider also the restriction of having to drive one's vehicle on a certain side of the road. There is no doubt that this restriction is almost unbearably frustrating at times, when one's lane is not moving and the other lane is clear. There are surely times, even, when abiding by this regulation would have harmful consequences. But the restriction is obviously wholesome for most of us most of the time. The restraint is imposed for our benefit, and does benefit us; its operation tends to encourage our *continued* motion, not to immobilize us. The limits imposed by traffic regulations are limits most of us would cheerfully impose on ourselves given that we knew others would follow them too. They are part of a structure which shapes our behavior, not to our reduction and immobilization, but rather to the protection of our continued ability to move and act as we will.

Another example: The boundaries of a racial ghetto in an American city serve to some extent to keep white people from going in, as well as to keep ghetto dwellers from going out. A particular white citizen may be frustrated or feel deprived because s/he cannot stroll around there and enjoy the "exotic" aura of a "foreign" culture, or shop for bargains in the ghetto swap shops. In fact, the existence of the ghetto, of racial segregation, does deprive the white person of knowledge and harm her/his character by nurturing unwarranted feelings of superiority. But this does not make the white person in this situation a member of an oppressed race or a person oppressed because of her/his race. One must look at the barrier. It limits the activities and the access of those on both sides of it (though to different degrees). But it is a product of the intention, planning and action of whites for the benefit of whites, to secure and maintain privileges that are available to whites generally, as members of the dominant and privileged group. Though the existence of the barrier has some bad consequences for whites, the barrier does not exist in systematic relationship with other barriers and forces forming a structure oppressive to whites; quite the contrary. It is part of a structure which oppresses the ghetto dwellers and thereby (and by white intention) protects and furthers white interests as dominant white culture understands them. This barrier is not oppressive to whites, even though it is a barrier to whites.

Barriers have different meanings to those on opposite sides of them, even though they are barriers to both. The physical walls of a prison no more dissolve to let an outsider in than to let an outsider in than to let an insider out, but for the insider they are confining and limiting while to the outsider they may mean protection from what s/he takes to be threats posed by insiders – freedom from harm or anxiety. A set of social and economic barriers and forces separating two groups may be felt, even painfully, by members of both groups and yet may mean confinement to one and liberty and enlargement of opportunity to the other.

The service sector of the wives/mommas/assistants/girls is almost exclusively a woman-only sector; its boundaries not only enclose women but to a very great extent keep men out. Some men sometimes encounter this barrier and experience it as a restriction on their movements, their activities, their control or their choices of "lifestyle." Thinking they might like the simple nurturant life (which they may imagine to be quite free of stress, alienation and hard work), and feeling deprived since it seems closed to them, they thereupon announce the discovery that they are oppressed, too, by "sex roles." But that barrier is erected and maintained by men, for the benefit of men. It consists of cultural and economic forces and pressures in a culture and economy controlled by men in which, at every economic level and in all racial and ethnic subcultures, economy, tradition – and even ideologies of liberation – work to keep at least local culture and economy in male control.[4]

The boundary that sets apart women's sphere is maintained and promoted by men generally for the benefit of men generally, and men generally do benefit from its existence, even the man who bumps into it and complains of the inconvenience. That barrier is protecting his classification and status as a male, as superior, as having a right to sexual access to a female or females. It protects a kind of citizenship which is superior to that of females of his class and race, his access to a wider range of better paying and higher status work, and his right to prefer unemployment to the degradation of doing lower status or "women's" work.

If a person's life or activity is affected by some force or barrier that person encounters, one may not conclude that the person is oppressed simply because the person encounters that barrier or force; nor simply because the encounter is unpleasant, frustrating or painful to that person at that time; nor simply because the existence of the barrier or force, or the processes which maintain or apply it, serve to deprive that person of something of value. One must look at the barrier or force and answer certain questions about it. Who constructs and maintains it? Whose interests are served by its existence? Is it part of a structure which tends to confine, reduce and immobilize some group? Is the individual a member of the confined group? Various forces, barriers and limitations a person may encounter or live with may be part of an oppressive structure or not, and if they are, that person may be on either the oppressed or the oppressor side of it. One cannot tell which by how loudly or how little the person complains.

IV

Many of the restrictions and limitations we live with are more or less internalized and self-monitored, and are part of our adaptations to the requirements and expectations imposed by the needs and tastes and tyrannies of others. I have in mind such things as women's cramped postures and attenuated strides and men's restraint of emotional self-expression (except for anger). Who gets what out of the practice of those disciplines, and who imposes what penalties for improper relaxations of them? What are the rewards of this self-discipline?

Can men cry? Yes, in the company of women. If a man cannot cry, it is in the company of men that he cannot cry. It is men, not women, who require this restraint; and men not only require it, they reward it. The man who maintains a steely or tough or laid-back demeanor (all are forms which suggest invulnerability) marks himself as a member of the male community and is esteemed by other men. Consequently, the maintenance of that demeanor contributes to the man's self-esteem. It is felt as good, and he can feel good about himself. The way this restriction fits into the structures of men's lives is as one of the socially required behaviors which, if carried off, contribute to their acceptance and respect by significant others and to their own self-esteem. It is to their benefit to practice this discipline.

Consider, by comparison, the discipline of women's cramped physical postures and attenuated stride. This discipline can be relaxed in the company of women; it generally is at its most strenuous in the company of men.[5] Like men's emotional restraint, women's physical restraint is required by men. But unlike the case of men's emotional restraint, women's physical restraint is not rewarded. What do we get for it? Respect and esteem and acceptance? No. They mock us and parody our mincing steps. We look silly, incompetent, weak and generally contemptible. Our exercise of this discipline tends to low esteem and low self-esteem. It does not benefit us. It fits in a network of behaviors through which we constantly announce to others our membership in a lower caste and our unwillingness and/or inability to defend our bodily or moral integrity. It is degrading and part of a pattern of degradation.

Acceptable behavior for both groups, men and women, involves a required restraint that seems in itself silly and perhaps damaging. But the social effect is drastically different. The woman's restraint is part of a structure oppressive to women; the man's restraint is part of a structure oppressive to women.

V

One is marked for application of oppressive pressures by one's membership in some group or category. Much of one's suffering and frustration befalls one partly or largely because one is a member of that category. In the case at hand, it is the category, *woman*. Being a woman is a major factor in my not having a better job than I do; being a woman selects me as a likely victim of sexual assault or harassment; it is my being a woman that reduces the power of my anger to a proof of my insanity. If a woman has little or no economic or political power, or achieves little of what she wants to achieve, a major causal factor in this is that she is a woman. For any woman of any race or economic class, being a woman is significantly attached to whatever disadvantages and deprivations she suffers, be they great or small.

None of this is the case with respect to a person's being a man. Simply being a man is not what stands between him and a better job; whatever assaults and harassments he is subject to, being male is not what selects him for victimization; being male is not a factor which would make his anger impotent – quite the opposite. If a man has little or no material or political power, or achieves little of what he wants to achieve, his being male is no part of the explanation. Being male is something he has going *for* him, even if race or class or age or disability is going against him.

Women are oppressed, *as women*. Members of certain racial and/or economic groups and classes, both the males and the females, are oppressed *as* members of those races and/or classes. But men are not oppressed *as men*.

. . . and isn't it strange that any of us should have been confused and mystified about such a simple thing?

Notes

1 This example is derived from *Daddy Was A Number Runner*, by Louise Meriwether (Prentice-Hall, Englewood Cliffs, New Jersey, 1970), p. 144.

2 Coerced assimilation is in fact one of the *policies* available to an oppressing group in its effort to reduce and/or annihilate another group. This tactic is used by the US government, for instance, on the American Indians.

3 At higher class levels women may not *do* all these kinds of work, but are generally still responsible for hiring and supervising those who do it. These services are still, in these cases, women's responsibility.

4 Of course this is complicated by race and class. Machismo and "Black manhood" politics seem to help keep Latin or Black men in control of more cash than Latin or Black women control; but these politics seem to me also to ultimately help keep the larger economy in *white* male control.

5 Cf., *Let's Take Back Our Space: "Female" and "Male" Body Language as a Result of Patriarchal Structures*, by Marianne Wex (Frauenliteratureverlag Hermine Fees, West Germany, 1979), especially p. 173. This remarkable book presents literally thousands of candid photographs of women and men, in public, seated, standing and lying down. It vividly demonstrates the very systematic differences in women's and men's postures and gestures.

8

Five Faces of Oppression

Iris Marion Young

Politics is partly a struggle over the language people use to describe social and political experience. Most people in the United States would not use the term "oppression" to name injustice in this society. For a minority of Americans, on the other hand – such as socialists, radical feminists, American Indian activists, black activists, gay and lesbian activists, and others identifying with new left social movements of the 1960s and 1970s – oppression is a central category of political discourse. Speaking the political language in which oppression is a central word involves adopting a whole mode of analyzing and evaluating social structures and practices which is quite incommensurate with the language of liberal individualism that dominates political discourse in the US.

Consequently, those of us who identify with at least one of the movements I have named have a major political project: we must persuade people that the discourse of oppression makes sense of much of our social experience. We are ill prepared for this task, however, if we have no clear account of the meaning of the concept of oppression. While we commonly find the term used in the diverse philosophical and theoretical literature spawned by radical social movements in the US, we find little direct discussion of the meaning of the concept of oppression as used by these movements.

Iris Marion Young, "Five Faces of Oppression," pp. 270–90 from *Philosophical Forum* 19(4), 1998. Reprinted by permission of Blackwell Publishing Ltd.

In this chapter I offer some explication of the concept as I understand its use by new social movements in the US since the 1960s. I offer you an explication of this concept, an unfolding of its meaning. I do not think the concept of oppression can be strictly defined, that is, corralled within one clear boundary. There is no attribute or set of attributes that all oppressed people have in common.

In the following account of oppression I reflect on the situation and experience of those groups said by new left social movements to be oppressed in US society: at least women, blacks, Chicanos, Puerto Ricans, and most other Spanish-speaking Americans, Native Americans, Jews, lesbians, gay men, Arabs, Asians, old people, working-class people, poor people, and physically or mentally disabled people.

Obviously, these groups are not oppressed to the same degree or in the same ways. In the most general sense, all oppressed people share some inhibition of their ability to develop and exercise their capacities and express their needs, thoughts, and feelings. Nevertheless, reflection on the concrete uses of the term "oppression" in radical political discourse convinces me that the term refers to several distinct structures or situations. I label these with five disparate categories: exploitation, marginality, powerlessness, cultural imperialism, and violence. Before I unfold these categories, though, I need to discuss some issues of social ontology relevant to placing the concept of oppression.

A New Left Revision of the Concept of Oppression

One of the reasons that many people would not use the term "oppression" to describe our society is that they do not understand the term in the same way as do radicals. In its traditional usage, which most people retain, "oppression" means the exercise of tyranny by a ruling group. Thus many Americans would agree with radicals in applying the term to the situation of black South Africans under apartheid. Traditionally, "oppression" also carries a strong connotation of conquest and colonial domination. The Hebrews were oppressed in Egypt, and many uses of the term in the West invoke this paradigm.

Dominant political discourse may use the term to describe societies other than our own, usually Communist or purportedly Communist societies. Within this anti-Communist rhetoric, both tyrannical and colonialist implications of the term appear. For the anti-Communist, communism denotes precisely the exercise of brutal tyranny over a whole people by a few rulers, and the will to conquer the world, bringing now independent peoples under that tyranny. In dominant political discourse, it is not legitimate to use the term to describe our society because "oppression" is the evil perpetrated by the Others.

New left social movements of the 1960s and 1970s, however, shifted the meaning of the concept. In its new usage, "oppression" designates the disadvantage and injustice some people suffer not because a tyrannical power intends to keep them down, but because of the everyday practices of a well-intentioned liberal society. In this new left usage, the tyranny of a ruling group over another, as in South Africa, must certainly be called oppressive. But "oppression" also refers to systemic and structural phenomena that are not necessarily the result of the intentions of a tyrant. Oppression in the structural sense is part of the basic fabric of a society, not a function of a few people's choice or policies. You won't eliminate this structural oppression by getting rid of the rulers or making some new laws, because oppressions are systematically reproduced in major economic, political, and cultural institutions. Thus one reason that "oppression" is not commonly used to describe injustice in our society is that the prevailing political discourse does not have a place in its social ontology for structuration and social groups.

Mirroring majority political discourse, philosophical discussions of justice and injustice rarely use the term "oppression," using instead the term "discrimination" to refer to some of the injustices radicals call "oppression." Even radical philosophers tend to avoid the term "oppression." Although his analysis is clearly influenced by Black Marxism and Black Power movements, Bernard Boxill, for example, consistently uses the term "discrimination" to designate the injustice that blacks have suffered and continue to suffer in US society.[1] This is a symptom of the old majority political discourse has over our thinking, perhaps especially over philosophers, who in turn help legitimate that discourse by using it and giving it technical precision. By "discrimination" I mean conscious actions and policies by which members of a group are excluded from institutions or confined to inferior positions. Discrimination is often an instrument of oppression, and discriminatory practices are certainly part of some oppressions, but the concept of oppression is neither coincident with nor reducible to discrimination.

Discrimination is a methodologically individualist concept.[2] In recent years most courts have found that there has been discrimination only if particular victims of discrimination can be individually identified, that a particular agent can be identified as responsible for discrimination, and it can be shown that the agent knew its actions or policies were discriminatory. To be sure, the concept of discrimination can make reference to groups insofar as a discriminatory policy excludes a whole class of persons from some position or activity. Even when concerning groups, however, discrimination is usually an individualist concept insofar as it presupposes an identifiable agent who discriminates, and that the sum of discrimination is the sum of discriminatory acts.

The difference between the concept of discrimination and the concept of oppression emerges most clearly with the insight that oppression often exists in the absence of overt discrimination. Though actions and policies that explicitly discriminated against members of particular groups were common in the United States not long ago, and have by no means disappeared, legislation and litigation in the past 20 years has greatly lessened overt policies of discrimination against most groups, with the outrageous exception of lesbians and gay men. Socialists, feminists, anti-racism activists, insist, however, that this serious reduction in overt and conscious policies of exclusion and segregation has done little to reduce the oppression that many groups have suffered and continue to suffer. This concept names the vast and deep injustices some groups suffer as a consequence of frequently unconscious assumptions and reactions of well-meaning people in ordinary interactions, media and cultural stereotypes, and structural features of bureaucratic hierarchy and market mechanisms, in short, the normal ongoing processes of everyday life. As Marilyn Frye puts it, oppression refers to "an enclosing structure of forces and barriers which tends to be the immobilization and reduction of a group or category of people."[3]

B The Concept of Social Group

Oppression refers to structural phenomena that immobilize or reduce a group. But what is a group? To be in a group is to share with others a way of life that defines a person's identity and by which other people identify him or her. Political philosophy typically has no place for a specific concept of social group. When philosophers and political theorists discuss groups, they tend to conceive them either on the model of aggregates or associations, both of which are methodologically individualist concepts. Along with Marilyn Friedman and Larry May, I think it is important to distinguish the concept of group from both aggregate and association.[4]

Liberal sentiments sometimes prompt us to assert that grouping by race, sex, religion, ethnicity, region, and so on, ought to carry no more significance than grouping by hair color, height, or the make of car we drive. Such an invocation calls for groups to be considered as mere aggregates, a classification of persons according to some attribute they share. The logic of aggregates presumes a substantial notion of the person to whom attributes are attached, and in that logical sense the person is prior to the collective. If we consider social groups as aggregates we imply that group membership does not define that person, but merely is a set of attributes, and that the collective is nothing other than the sum of the individuals with those attributes.

Political theorists tend to elide social groups more often with associations than aggregates.[5] By an association I mean a formally organized institution, such as a club, corporation, political party, church, college, union, etc. An individualist contract model of society applies to associations but not to groups. Individuals constitute associations, they come together as already formed persons and set them up, establishing rules, positions, and offices. Groups, on the other hand, constitute individuals. A subject's particular sense of history, sense of identity, affinity, and separateness, even the person's mode of reasoning, evaluating and expressing feeling are constituted at least partly by her or his group affinities. This does not mean that persons have no individual styles, or are unable to transcend or reject a group related identity, and it does not preclude persons having many aspects that are independent of these group identities. Since the form of group differentiation in modern societies implies that a single person usually belongs to several groups, it follows that individual subjects are not unified, but multiple, heterogeneous, and sometimes perhaps incoherent.

A person joins an association, and even if membership in it fundamentally affects one's life, one does not take that association membership to define one's very identity, in the way, for example, being Navajo might. Group affinity, on the other hand, has the character of what Heidegger calls "thrownness": one *finds oneself* as a member of a group, whose existence and relations one experiences as always already having been. For a person's identity is defined in relation to how others identify him or her, and they do so in terms of groups which always already have specific attributes, stereotypes, and norms associated with them, in reference to which a person's identity will be formed. From the thrownness of group affinity, it does not follow that one cannot leave groups and enter new ones. Many women become lesbian after identifying as heterosexual, and anyone who lives long enough becomes old. These cases illustrate thrownness precisely because such changes in group affinity are experienced as a transformation in one's identity.

Despite the modern myth of a decline of parochial attachments and ascribed identities, group differentiation is endemic to modern society. As markets and administration increase the web of social interdependency on a world scale, and as more people encounter one another as strangers in cities and states, they retain and renew ethnic, locale, age, sex, and occupations group identifications, and form new ones in the processes of encounter.[6] No social group, moreover, is itself homogeneous, but mirrors in its own differentiations many of the groups in the wider society. Patterns of group differentiation are fluid, often undergoing rapid change. Before the nineteenth century, for example, homosexuality did not serve as a basis of group ascription and identification.[7]

Some writers, such as Milton Fisk, understand class as a primary example of a social group.[8] Others might be inclined to distinguish the concept of group from class on the grounds that class is a structural concept that does not include subjectivity or identity, and a group as I have defined it includes reference to identity and interaction.[9] In a way I agree with both approaches. As used in technical Marxian economic theory, the concept of class is more abstract and structural than the concept of social group. It refers specifically to a relation to the major means of production, whether one owns them and/or has major decision-making power about the movement of capital, how it is invested, and so on. Class denotes a relation to capitalist profit: who gets it, who decides who gets it and how it will be gotten, who contributes to its getting without getting it, or does none of these. These structural positions in themselves are too narrow to define social groups.

In a more colloquial and empirical sense, however, the term "class" also refers to a basis for interaction and conflict, an identity by which people recognize one another, and to that degree class names social groups as well as structural positions. The ruling class in the US, and in most other societies, is a social group, whose members tend to bond with a shared culture and world view, to have common interests, and to move within specific institutions. There is, however, no single social group of the "working class" correlating with that ruling class.[10] Whatever the difficulties of locating it in technical Marxian analysis, "middle-class" professionals and managers must be understood as a social group distinct from "working-class" manufacturing, clerical and service workers and their families. Poor people, or what some theorists call the "underclass" may also constitute a social group.

Insofar as economic location and occupation significantly determine a person's self-understanding, perception of social relations and others, and insofar as such economic location in our society tends to be reproduced across generations, classes are certainly social groups in the sense I have discussed. Just how class will be defined will depend on the uses of the definition, for example, to understand the structural imperatives of accumulation, or to understand the motivation of particular persons to support certain policies.

Group differentiation does not necessarily imply oppression, however; groups can exist that are not oppressed. In the US, Catholics are a group in the sense I have discussed, but they are no longer an oppressed group. In Northern Ireland, on the other hand, Catholics are an oppressed group. Whether a group is oppressed depends on whether it is subject to one or more of the five conditions I shall discuss below. Despite the modern myth of a decline of parochial attachments and ascribed identities, I think that group differentiation is both an inevitable and desirable aspect of modern social processes. Social justice, then, requires not the melting away of differences, but institutions that promote reproduction of and respect for group difference without oppression.

I have suggested that oppression is the inhibition of a group through a vast network of everyday practices, attitudes, assumptions, behaviors, and institutional rules. Oppression is structural or systemic. The systemic character of oppression implies that an oppressed group need not have a correlate oppressing group. While structural oppression in our society involves relations among groups, these relations do not generally fit the paradigm of one group's consciously and intentionally keeping another down. Foucault suggests that to understand the meaning and operation of power in modern society we should look beyond the model of power as "sovereignty," a dyadic relation of ruler and subject, and instead analyze the exercise of power as the effect of liberal and humanized practices of education, bureaucratic administration, production and distribution of consumer goods, medical practice, and so on. The conscious action of many individuals daily contribute to maintaining and reproducing oppression, but those people are usually simply doing their jobs or living their lives, not understanding themselves as agents of oppression. Defining oppression as structural is an innovation of the new left usage of the term to describe our society. Many people understand oppression to refer only to a conscious tyranny of one individual or group over another, and for that reason will not use the term to describe injustices in our own society.

By denying that structural oppression is perpetrated by an identifiable agent of oppression I do not mean to suggest that within this system of oppression individual persons do not intentionally do things to harm others in oppressed groups. The raped woman, the beaten black youth, the locked-out worker, and the gay man harassed on the street are victims of intentional behavior by identifiable agents. Nor do I mean to suggest that specific groups are not beneficiaries of the oppression of other groups, and thus have an interest in their continued oppression. On the contrary, for every oppressed group there is a group that is *privileged* in relation to that group.

The concept of oppression has been used among radicals since the 1960s partly in reaction to some Marxist attempts to reduce the injustices of racism and sexism, for example, to the effects of class domination or bourgeois ideology. Racism, sexism, ageism, and homophobia, some social movements asserted, are distinct forms of oppression with their own dynamics apart from the dynamics of class, even though they might interact with class oppression. From often heated discussions among socialists, feminists, and anti-racism activists in the last ten years, a consensus is emerging that many different groups must be said to be oppressed in our society, and that no group's or form of oppression can claim causal or moral primacy.[11] The same discussion has also come to understand that group differences cross individual lives in a multiplicity of ways that can entail privilege and oppression for the same person in different respects. Only a plural explication of the concept of oppression can appropriately capture these insights (cf. Maynard and Brittan pp. 2–8).

Accordingly, in the following sections I offer an explication of five faces of oppression as a useful set of categories and distinctions which I believe is comprehensive, in the sense that it covers all the groups said by new left social movements to be oppressed and covers all the ways they are oppressed. I derive the five faces of oppression from reflection on the condition of these groups. Because different factors, or combinations of factors, constitute the oppression of different groups, making their oppression irreducible, I believe it is not possible to have one essential definition of oppression. With the following five categories, however, the oppression of any group can be described, as well as its similarities with and differences from the oppression of other groups.

1 Exploitation

The central function of Marx's theory of exploitation is to explain how class structure can exist in the absence of legally and normatively sanctioned class distinctions. In pre-capitalist societies domination is overt and carried on through direct political means. In both slave society and feudal society the right to appropriate the product of the labor of others partly defines class privilege, and these societies legitimate class distinctions with ideologies of natural superiority and inferiority.

Capitalist society, on the other hand, removes traditional juridically-enforced class distinctions and promotes a belief in the legal freedom of persons. Workers freely contract with employers, receive a wage, and no formal mechanisms of law or custom force them to work for that employer or any employer. Thus the mystery of capitalism arises: when everyone is formally free, how can there be class domination? Why does there continue to be class distinction between the wealthy, who own the means of production, and the mass of people, who work for them? The theory of exploitation answers this question.

Profit, the basis of capitalist power and wealth, is a mystery if we assume that in the market goods exchange at their values. Marx's use of the labor theory of value, however, dispels this mystery. Every commodity's value is a function of the labor time necessary for the production of labor power. Labor power is the one commodity which in the process of being consumed produces new value. Profit then comes from the difference between the actual labor and the value of that capacity to labor which the capitalist purchases and puts to work. The owner of capital appropriates this surplus value, which accounts for the possibility of realizing a profit.

In recent years there has been considerable controversy among Marxist scholars about the viability of the labor theory of value on which this account of exploitation relies.[12] John Roemer, for example, develops a theory of exploitation which claims to preserve the theoretical and practical purposes of Marx's theory, but without assuming a distinction between values and prices and without being restricted to a concept of abstract, homogeneous labor.[13] My purpose here is not to engage in technical economic disputes, but to indicate the place of a concept of exploitation in a conception of oppression.

Marx's theory of exploitation lacks an explicitly normative meaning, even though the judgment that workers are exploited clearly has normative as well as descriptive power in Marxian theory.[14] C. B. MacPherson reconstructs the Marxian idea of exploitation in a more explicitly normative form.[15] The injustice of capitalist society consists in the fact that some people exercise their capacities under the control, according to the purposes, and for the benefit of other people. Through the institutions of private ownership of the means of production, and through markets that allocate labor and the ability to buy goods, capitalism systematically transfers the powers of some persons to others, thereby augmenting their powers. In this process of the transfer of powers, moreover, according to MacPherson, the capitalist class acquires and maintains extractive power, which gives it the continued ability to extract benefits from workers. Not only are powers transferred from workers to capitalists, but also the powers of workers diminish by more than the amount of transfer, because workers suffer deprivation, a lack of control, and hence a lack of self-respect. Justice, then, requires eliminating the institutional forms that enable and enforce this process of transfer. Justice requires replacing them with institutional forms that enable all to develop and use their capacities in a way that do not inhibit, but rather enhance, others developing and using theirs.

The central insight expressed with the concept of exploitation, then, is that domination occurs through a steady process of the transfer of the results of the labor of some people to benefit others. The injustice of class division does not consist only in the fact that some people have great wealth while most people have little and some are severely deprived.[16] The theory of exploitation shows that this relation of power and inequality is produced and reproduced through a systematic process in which the energies of the have-nots are continuously expended to maintain and augment the power, status, and wealth of the haves.

Many writers have cogently argued that the Marxian concept of exploitation is too narrow to encompass all forms of domination and oppression.[17] In particular, by confining itself to examining class domination and oppression, the Marxian concept of exploitation does not contribute to an understanding of such group oppressions as sexism and racism. The question, then, is whether the concept of exploitation can be broadened to include other ways that the labor and energy expenditure of one group benefits another, thus reproducing a relation of domination between them.

Feminists have had little difficulty showing that women's oppression consists partly in a systematic and unreciprocated transfer of powers from women to men. Women's oppression consists not merely in an inequality of status, power, and wealth resulting from men's excluding women from privileged activities. The freedom, power, status, and self-realization of men is possible precisely because women work for them. Gender exploitation has two aspects, transfer of the fruits of material labor to men, and the transfer of nurturing and sexual energies to men.

Christine Delphy for example, theorizes marriage as a class relation in which women's labor benefits men without comparable remuneration.[18] She makes it clear that the exploitation consists not in the sort of work that women do in the home, for it might be various kinds of tasks, but the fact that they perform tasks for someone else on whom they are dependent. Thus, for example, in most systems of agricultural production in the world, men take to market goods women have produced, and more often than not men receive the status and often the entire income from this labor.

With the concept of sex-affective production, Ann Ferguson identifies another form of the transfer of women's energies to men.[19] Women provide men and children with emotional care, and provide men with sexual satisfaction, and as a class receive little of either from men.[20] The gender socialization of women makes us tend to be more attentive to interactive dynamics than men, and makes women good at providing empathy and support for people's feelings and at smoothing over interactive tensions. Both men and women look to women as nurturers of their personal lives, and women frequently complain that when they look to men for emotional support they do not receive it.[21] The norms of heterosexuality, moreover, are oriented around male pleasure, and consequently many women receive little satisfaction from their sexual interaction with men.[22]

Most feminist theories of gender exploitation have concentrated on the institutional structure of the patriarchal family. Recently, however, feminists have begun to theorize relations of gender exploitation enacted in the contemporary workplace and through the state. Carol Brown argues that as men have removed themselves from responsibility for children, many women have become dependent on the state for subsistence as they continue to bear nearly total responsibility for child rearing.[23] This creates a new system of the exploitation of women's domestic labor mediated by those state institutions, which she calls public patriarchy.

In twentieth-century capitalist economies, the workplaces that women have been entering in increasing numbers serve as another important site of gender exploitation. David Alexander argues that most typically feminine jobs have gender tasks involving sexual labor, nurturing, caring for a person's body, or smoothing over relations through personality.[24] In these ways, women's energies are expended in workplaces that enhance the status of, please, or comfort others, usually men; and these gender based labors of waitresses, clerical workers, nurses, and other caretakers often go unnoticed and under-compensated.

To summarize, women are exploited in the Marxian sense to the degree that they are wage workers. Some have argued that women's domestic labor is also a form of capitalist class exploitation insofar as it is labor covered by the wages a family receives. As a class, however, women undergo specific forms of gender exploitation – ways the energies and power of women are expended, often unnoticed and unacknowledged, usually to benefit men by releasing them for more important and creative work, enhancing their status or the environment around them, or providing men with sexual or emotional service.

Race is a structure of oppression at least as basic as class or gender. Are there, then, racially specific forms of exploitation? This is different from the question of whether racial groups are subjected to intense capitalist exploitation. Racial groups in the US, especially blacks and Latinos, are oppressed through capitalist superexploitation resulting from a segmented labor market that tends to reserve skilled, high-paying, unionized jobs for whites. There is wide disagreement about whether such superexploitation benefits whites as a group or only benefits the capitalist class, and I do not intend to resolve that dispute here.[25]

However one answers the question about capitalist superexploitation of racial groups, is it also possible to conceptualize a form of exploitation that is racially specific on analogy with the gender specific forms I have discussed? The category of *menial* labor might provide an opening for such conceptualization. In its derivation "menial" means the labor of servants. Wherever there is racism, including in the US today, there is the assumption, more or less enforced, that members of the oppressed racial groups are ought to be servants of those, or some of those, in the privileged group. In white racist societies this generally means that many white people have dark- or yellow-skinned domestic servants, and in the US today there remains significant race structuring of private household service.

In the US today much service labor has gone public: anybody can have servants if they go to a good hotel, a good restaurant, or hire a cleaning service. Servants often attend the daily – and nightly – activities of business executives, government officials, and other high status professionals. In our society there remains strong cultural pressure to fill servant jobs – like bell hop, porter, chamber maid, bus boy, and so on – with black and Latin workers. These jobs entail a transfer of energies whereby the servers enhance the status of the served, to place them in an aristocracy – the rule of the best.

Menial labor today refers to more than service, however, but to any servile, unskilled, low-paying work lacking in autonomy, and in which a person is subject to take orders from several people. Menial work tends to be auxiliary work, instrumental to another person's work, where that other person receives primary recognition for doing the job. Laborers on a construction site, for example, are at the beck and call of welders, electricians, carpenters, and other skilled workers, who receive recognition for the job done. In the history of the United States, explicit racial discrimination reserved menial work for blacks, Chicanos, American Indians, and Chinese, and menial work still tends to be linked to black and Latino workers.[26] I offer this category of menial labor as a form of racially specific exploitation, only as a proposal, however, which needs discussion.

2 *Marginalization*

Increasingly in the United States, racial oppression occurs more in the form of marginalization than exploitation. Marginals are people the system of labor markets cannot or will not employ. Not only in Third World capitalist countries, but also in most Western capitalist societies, there is a growing underclass of people permanently confined to lives of social marginality, the majority of whom are racially marked – blacks or Indians in Latin America, blacks, East Indians, Eastern Europeans, or North Africans in Europe.

Marginalization is by no means the fate only of racially marked groups, however. In the United States a shamefully large proportion of the population is marginal: old people, and increasingly people who are not very old but get laid off from their jobs and cannot find new work; young people, especially black or Latino, who cannot find first or second jobs; many single mothers and their children; other people involuntarily unemployed; many mentally or physically disabled people; and Americans Indians, especially those on reservations.

Marginalization is perhaps the most dangerous form of oppression. A whole category of people is expelled from useful participation in social life, potentially then subject to severe material deprivation and even extermination. The material deprivation marginalization often causes certainly is unjust, especially in a society where others have plenty. Contemporary advanced capitalist societies in principle have acknowledged the injustice of material deprivation caused by marginalization, and have taken some steps to address it by providing welfare payments and services. The continuance of this welfare state is by no means assured, and in most welfare state societies, especially the United States, benefits are not sufficient to eliminate large scale suffering and deprivation.

Material deprivation, which can be addressed by redistributive social policies, is not, however, the extent of the harm caused by marginalization. Two categories of injustice beyond distribution are associated with marginality in advanced capitalist societies. The provision of welfare itself produces new injustice when it deprives dependent persons of rights and freedoms that others have. If justice requires that every person have the opportunity to develop and exercise his or her capacities, finally, then marginalization is unjust primarily because it blocks such opportunity to exercise capacities in socially defined and recognized ways.

Liberalism traditionally asserts the right of all rational autonomous agents to equal citizenship. Early bourgeois liberalism made explicit that citizenship excluded all those whose reason was questionable or not fully developed, and all those not independent.[27] Thus poor people, women, the mad and the feeble minded, and children were explicitly excluded from citizenship, and many of these were housed in institutions modeled on the modern prison: poor houses, insane asylums, schools.

In our own society the exclusion of dependent persons from equal citizenship rights is only barely hidden beneath the surface. Because they are dependent on bureaucratic institutions for support or services, old people, poor people, and mentally or physically disabled people are subject to patronizing, punitive, demeaning, and arbitrary treatment by the policies and people associated with welfare bureaucracies. Being a dependent in this society implies being legitimately subject to often arbitrary and invasive authority of social service providers and other public and private bureaucrats, who enforce rules with which the marginal must comply, and otherwise exercise power over the conditions of her or his life. In meeting needs of the marginalized, with the aid of social scientific disciplines, the welfare agencies also construct the needs themselves. Medical and social service professionals know what is good for those they serve, and the marginals and dependents themselves do not have the right to claim to know what is good for them.[28] Dependency thus implies in this society, as it has in all liberal societies, a sufficient condition to suspend rights to privacy, respect, and individual choice.

Although dependency thus produces conditions of injustice in our society, dependency in itself should not and need not be oppressive. We cannot imagine a society in which some people would not need to be dependent on others at least some of the time: children, sick people, women recovering from childbirth, old people who have become frail, and depressed or otherwise emotionally needy persons have the moral right to be dependent on others for subsistence and support.

An important contribution of feminist moral theory has consisted in questioning the deeply held assumption that moral agency and full citizenship require that a person be autonomous and independent. Feminists have exposed such an assumption as inappropriately individualistic and derived from a specifically male experience of social relations, valuing competition, and solitary achievement.[29] Female experience of social relations, arising both from women's typical domestic care responsibilities and from the kinds of paid work that many women do, tends to recognize dependence as a basic human condition. Whereas on the autonomy model a just society would as much as possible give people the opportunity to be independent, the feminist model instead envisions justice as according respect and decision-making participation to those who are dependent as well as those who are independent.[30] Dependence should not be a reason to be deprived of choice and respect, and much of the oppression, many marginals experience would diminish if a less individualistic model of rights prevailed.

Marginalization does not cease to be oppressive when one has shelter and food. Many old people, for example, have sufficient means to live comfortably but remain oppressed in their marginal status. Even if marginals were provided a comfortable material life within institutions that respected their freedom and dignity, injustices of marginality would remain in the form of uselessness, boredom, and lack of self-respect. Most of this society's productive and recognized activities take place in contexts of organized social cooperation, and social structures and processes that close persons out of participation in such social cooperation are unjust.

The fact of marginalization raises basic structural issues of justice. In particular we must consider what is just about a connection between participation in productive activities of social cooperation, on the one hand, and acquisition of the means of consumption, on the other. As marginalization is increasing, with no sign of abatement, some social policy analysts have introduced the idea of a "social wage" as a guaranteed socially provided income not tied to the wage system. Restructuring activities of production and service provision to ensure that everyone able and willing has socially recognized work to do, moreover, also implies organization of socially productive activity at least partly outside of a wage system.[31]

3 *Powerlessness*

As I have indicated, the Marxian idea of class is important because it helps reveal the structure of exploitation: that some people have their power and wealth because they profit from the labor of others. For this reason I reject the claim some make that a traditional class exploitation model fails to capture the structure of contemporary society. It is still the case that the labor of most people in the society augments the power of a few; whatever their differences from non-professional workers, most professional workers share with them not being members of the capitalist class.

An adequate conception of oppression, however, cannot ignore the experience of social division colloquially referred to as the difference between the "middle class" and the "working class," a division structured by the social division of labor between professionals and non-professionals. Rather than expanding or revising the Marxian concept of class to take account of this experience, as some writers do, I suggest that we follow Weber and describe this as a difference in *status* rather than class.[32] Being a professional entails occupying a status position that non-professionals lack, creating a condition of oppression that non-professionals suffer. I shall call this kind of oppression "powerlessness."

The absence of genuine democracy in the US means that most people do not participate in making decisions that regularly affect the conditions of their lives and actions. In this sense most people lack significant power. Powerlessness, however, describes the lives of people who have little or no work autonomy, exercise little creativity or judgment in their work, have no technical expertise or authority, express themselves awkwardly, especially in public or bureaucratic settings, and do not command respect. Powerlessness names the oppressive situations Sennet and Cobb describe in their famous study of working class men.[33]

The clearest way for me to think of this powerless status is negatively: the powerless lack the status and sense of self that professionals tend to have. There are three aspects of status privilege that professionals have, the lack of which produces oppression for non-professionals.

First, acquiring and practicing a profession has an expansive, progressive character. Being professional usually requires a college education and learning a specialized knowledge that entails working with symbols and concepts. In acquiring one's profession, a person experiences progress in learning the expertise, and usually when one begins practicing one enters a career, that is, a working life of growth or progress in professional development. The life of the non-professional by comparison is powerless in the sense that it lacks this orientation toward the progressive development of one's capacities.

Second, while most professionals have supervisors and do not have power to affect many decisions or the action of very many people, most nevertheless have considerable day-to-day work autonomy. Professionals usually have some authority over others, moreover, either over workers they supervise, or over auxiliaries, or over clients. Non-professionals, on the other hand, lack autonomy, and both in their working lives and in their consumer-client lives, they often stand under the authority of professionals.

Though having its material basis in a division of labor between "mental" and "manual" work, the group division between "middle class" and "working class" designates not a division only in working life, but also in nearly all aspects of social life. Professionals and non-professionals belong to different cultures in the US. The two groups tend to live in segregated neighborhoods or even different towns, not least because of the actions and decisions of real estate people. They tend to have different tastes in food, decor, clothes, music, and vacations. Members of the two groups socialize for the most part with others in the same status group. While there is some intergroup mobility between generations, for the most part the children of professionals become professionals and the children of non-professionals do not.

Thus thirdly, the privileges of the professional extend beyond the workplace to elevate a whole way of life, which consists in being "respectable." To treat someone with respect is to be prepared to listen to what they have to say or to do what they request because they have some authority, expertise, or influence.

The norms of respectability in our society are associated specifically with professional culture. Professional dress, speech, tastes, demeanor, all connote respectability. Generally professionals expect and receive respect from others. In restaurants, banks, hotels, real estate offices, and many other such public places, professionals typically receive more respectful treatment than non-professionals. For this reason non-professionals seeking a loan or a job, or to buy a house or a car, will often try to look "professional" and "respectable" in these settings. The privilege of this professional respectability starkly appears in the dynamics of racism and sexism. In daily interchange women and men of color must prove their respectability. At first they are often not treated by strangers with respectful distance or deference. Once people discover that this woman or that Puerto Rican man is a college teacher or a business executive, however, people often behave more respectfully toward her or him. Working class white men, on the other hand, are often treated with respect until their working class status is revealed.

4 *Cultural imperialism*

Exploitation, marginality, and powerlessness all refer to relations of power and oppression that occur by virtue of the social division of labor: who works for whom, who does not work, and how the content of work in one position is defined in relation to others. These three categories refer to the structural and institutional relations that delimit people's material lives, including but not limited to the resources they have access to, the concrete opportunity they have or do not have to develop and exercise capacities in involving, socially recognized ways that enhance rather than diminish their lives. These kinds of oppression are a matter of concrete power in relation to others, who benefits from whom, and who is dispensable.

Recent theorists of movements of group liberation, especially feminists and black liberation theorists, have also given prominence to a rather different experience of oppression, which I shall call cultural imperialism.[34] This is the experience of existing with a society whose dominant meanings render the particular perspectives and point of view of one's own group invisible at the same time as they stereotype one's group and mark it out as the Other.

Cultural imperialism consists in the universalization of one group's experience and culture, and its establishment as the norm. Some groups have exclusive or primary access to what Nancy Fraser calls the means of interpretation and communication in a society.[35] As a result, the dominant cultural products of the society, that is, those most widely disseminated, express the experience, values, goals, and achievements of the groups that produce them. The cultural products also express their perspective on and interpretation of events and elements in the society, including the other groups in the society, insofar as they are noticed at all. Often without noticing they do so, the dominant groups project their own experience as representative of humanity as such.

An encounter with groups different from the dominant group, however, challenges its claim to universality. The dominant group saves its position by bringing the other group under the measure of its dominant norms. Consequently, the difference of women from men, Native Americans or Africans from Europeans, Jews from Christians, homosexuals from heterosexuals, or workers from professionals thus becomes reconstructed as deviance and inferiority. The dominant groups and their cultural expressions are the normal, the universal, and thereby unremarkable. Since the dominant group's cultural expressions are the only expressions that receive wide dissemination, the dominant groups construct the differences which some groups exhibit as lack and negation in relation to the norms, and those groups become marked out as Other.

Victims of cultural imperialism experience a paradoxical oppression, in that they are both marked out by stereotypes and rendered invisible. As remarkable, deviant beings, the culturally dominated are stamped with an essence. In contrast, the privileged are indefinable because they are individual; each is whatever he or she wants to be, they are in what they do, and by their doings they are judged. The stereotype marks and defines the culturally dominated, confines them to a nature which is usually attached in some way to their bodies, and thus which cannot easily be denied. These stereotypes so permeate the society that they are not noticed as contestable. Just as everyone knows that the earth goes around the sun, so everyone knows that gay people are promiscuous, that Indians are alcoholics, and that women are good with children.

Those living under cultural imperialism find themselves defined from the outside, positioned, and placed by a system of dominant meanings they experience as arising from elsewhere, from those with whom they do not identify and who do not identify with them. The dominant culture's stereotyped, marked, and inferiorized images of the group must be internalized by group members at least to the degree that they are forced to react to behaviors of others that express or are influenced by those images. This creates for the culturally oppressed the experience that W. E. B. DuBois called "double consciousness." "This sense of always looking at one's self through the eyes of others, of measuring one's soul by the tape of a world that looks on in amused contempt and pity."[36] This consciousness is double because the oppressed subject refuses to coincide with these devalued, objectified, stereotyped visions of herself or himself. The subject desires recognition as human, capable of activity, full of hope and possibility, but receives from the dominant culture only the judgment that he or she is different, marked, or inferior.

People in culturally oppressed groups often maintain a sense of positive subjectivity because they can affirm and recognize one another as sharing similar experiences and perspectives on social life. The group defined by the dominant culture as deviant, as a stereotyped Other, *is* culturally different from the dominant group, because the status of Otherness creates specific experiences not shared by the dominant group, and because culturally oppressed groups also are often socially segregated and occupy specific positions in the social division of labor. They express their specific group experiences and interpretations of the world to one another, developing and perpetuating their own culture. Double consciousness, then, occurs because one finds one's being defined by two cultures: a dominant and a subordinate culture.

Cultural imperialism involves the paradox of experiencing oneself as invisible at the same time that one is marked out and noticed as different. The perspective of other groups dominate the culture without their noticing it as a perspective, and their cultural expressions are widely disseminated. These dominant cultural expressions often simply pay no attention to the existence and experience of those other groups, only to mention or refer to them in stereotyped or marginalized ways. This, then, is the injustice of cultural imperialism: that the oppressed group's experience and interpretation of social life finds no expression that touches the dominant culture, while that same culture imposes on the oppressed group its experience and interpretation of social life.

5 *Violence*

Finally, many groups suffer the oppression of systematic and legitimate violence. The members of some groups live with the knowledge that they must fear random, unprovoked attacks on their persons or property, which have no motive but to damage, humiliate, or destroy the person. In US society women, blacks, Asians, Arabs, gay men, and lesbians live under such threat of violence, and in at least some regions Jews, Puerto Ricans, Chicanos, and other Spanish-speaking Americans must fear such violence as well. Violation may also take the form of name calling or petty harassment which intends to degrade or humiliate, and always signals an underlying threat of physical attack.

Such violence is systematic because it is directed at any member of the group simply because he or she is a member of that group. Any woman, for example, has reason to fear rape. The violence to which these oppressed groups are subject, moreover, is usually legitimate in the sense that most people regard it as unsurprising and it usually goes unpunished. Police beatings or killings of black youths, for example, are rarely publicized, rarely provoke moral outrage on the part of most white people, and rarely receive punishment.

An important aspect of the kind of random but systemic violence I am referring to here is its utter irrationality. Xenophobic violence is different from the violence of state or ruling class repression. Repressive violence has a rational, though evil, motive: rulers use it as a coercive tool to maintain their power. Many accounts of racist, sexist, or homophobic violence try to explain it as motivated by a desire to maintain group privilege or domination. I agree that fear of violence functions to help keep these oppressed groups subordinate. I think the causes of such violence must be traced to unconscious structures of identity formation which project onto some groups the fluid, bodily aspect of the subject that threatens the rigid unity of that identity.

C Conclusion

The five faces of oppression that I have explicated here function as criteria of oppression, not as a full theoretical account of oppression. With them we can tell whether a group is oppressed, according to objective social structures and behaviors. Being subject to any one of these five conditions is sufficient for calling a group oppressed. Most of the groups I listed earlier as oppressed in US society experience more than one of these forms and some experience all five.

Nearly all, if not all, groups said by contemporary social movements to be oppressed in our society suffer cultural imperialism. Which other oppressions are experienced by which groups, however, is quite variable. Working class people are exploited and powerless, for example, but if employed and white do not experience marginalization and violence. Gay men, on the other hand, are not *qua* gay exploited or powerless, but they experience severe cultural imperialism and violence. Similarly, Jews and Arabs as groups are victims of cultural imperialism and violence, though many members of these groups also suffer exploitation or powerlessness. Old people are oppressed by marginalization and cultural imperialism, and this is also true of physically or mentally disabled people. As a group women are subject to gender-based exploitation, powerlessness, cultural imperialism, and violence. Racism in the United States associates blacks and Latinos with marginalization, even though many members of these groups escape that condition; members of these groups often suffer all five forms of oppression.

With these criteria I have specifically avoided defining structures and kinds of oppression according to the groups oppressed: racism, classism, sexism, heterosexism, ageism. The forms of group oppression these terms name are not homologous, and the five criteria can help describe how and why not. The five criteria also help show that while no group oppression is reducible to or explained by any other group oppression, the oppression of one group is not a closed system with its own attributes, but overlaps with the oppression of other groups. With these criteria, moreover, we can claim that one group is more oppressed than another, insofar as it is subject to more of these five conditions, without thereby theoretically privileging a particular form of oppression or one oppressed group.

Are there any connections among these five forms of oppression? Why are particular groups subject to various combinations of them? The answers to these questions are beyond the scope of this chapter. My project here is analytical and descriptive, not explanatory. Answering these questions is important to the theoretical project of understanding oppression. I believe they cannot be answered by an a priori account, however, but require a specific explanatory account of the connections among forms of oppression for each social context and for each group.

Notes

1 Bernard Boxill, *Blacks and Social Justice* (Totowa, NJ: Rowman and Allenheld, 1984).
2 Marlene Fried, "The Invisibility of Oppression," *The Philosophical Forum*, Vol. XI, no. 1 (1979), pp. 18–29.
3 Marilyn Frye, "Oppression" in *The Politics of Reality* (Trumansburg, NY: The Crossing Press, 1983), pp. 1–16.
4 Marilyn Friedman and Larry May, "Harming Women as a Group," *Social Theory and Practice*, Vol. 11, no. 2 (1985), pp. 207–34.
5 Peter French, "Types of Collectivities and Blame," *The Personalist*, Vol. 56 (1975), pp. 160–9.
6 Cf. Jeffrey Ross, Introduction to *The Mobilization of Collective Identity*, ed. Ross and Cottrell (University Press of America, 1980); also, Joseph Rothschild, *Ethnopolitics* (New York: Columbia University Press, 1981).
7 Dennis Altman, *The Homosexualization of America* (Boston: Beacon Press, 1982).
8 Milton Fisk, *Ethics and Society* (New York: New York University Press, 1980), Part I.
9 E.g., Nicos Poulantzas, *Classes in Contemporary Capitalism* (London: Verso Books, 1975).
10 Cf. Manuel Castells, *The Economic Crisis and American Society* (Princeton University Press, 1980), pp. 138–61.
11 See Roger Gottlieb, *History and Subjectivity* (Philadelphia: Temple University Press, 1987).
12 See R. P. Wolff, *Understanding Marx* (Princeton University Press, 1984).
13 John Roemer, *A General Theory of Exploitation and Class* (Cambridge: Harvard University Press, 1982).
14 Alan Buchanan, *Marx and Justice* (Totowa, NJ: Rowman and Allenheld, 1980).
15 C. B. MacPherson, *Democratic Theory: Essays in Retrieval* (Oxford: Clarendon Press, 1973), especially Chapter III.
16 Cf. Alan Buchanan, pp. 44–9; Nancy Holmstrom, "Exploitation," *Canadian Journal of Philosophy*, Vol. VII, no. 2 (1977), pp. 353–69.
17 Anthony Giddens, *A Contemporary Critique of Historical Materialism* (Berkeley: University of California Press, 1981), p. 242; Arthur Vrittan and Mary Maynard, *Sexism, Racism and Oppression* (Oxford: Basil Blackwell, 1984), p. 93; Raymond Murphy, "Exploitation or Exclusion?" *Sociology*, Vol. 19, no. 2 (May 1985), pp. 225–43; Herbert Gintis and Samuel Bowles, *Capitalism and Democracy* (New York: Basic Books, 1986).
18 Christine Delphy, *Close to Home: A Materialist Analysis of Women's Oppression* (Amherst: University of Massachusetts Press, 1984).
19 See her "Women as a New Revolutionary Class" in *Between Labor and Capital*, ed. Pat Walker (Boston: South End Press, 1979), and "On Conceiving Motherhood and Sexuality: A Feminist Materialist Approach" in *Mothering: Essays in Feminist Theory*, ed. by Joyce Trebilcot (Totowa, NJ: Rowman and Allenheld, 1984).
20 Cf. Brittan and Maynard, pp. 142–8.
21 Barbara Easton, "Feminism and the Contemporary Family," *Socialist Review*, No. 39 (May/June 1978), pp. 11–36.
22 Rhonda Gottlieb, "The Political Economy of Sexuality," *Review of Radical Political Economy*, Vol. 16, no. 1 (1984), pp. 143–65.
23 Carol Brown, "Mothers, Fathers and Children: From Private to Public Patriarchy" in *Women and Revolution*, Sargent, ed. (Boston: South End Press, 1981), pp. 239–68; cf. Ellen Boris and Peter Bardaglio, "The Transformation of Patriarchy: The Historic Role of the State" in *Families, Politics and Public Policy*, Diamond, ed. (New York: Longman, 1983), pp. 79–93; Kathy Ferguson, *The Feminist Case Against Bureaucracy* (Philadelphia: Temple University Press, 1984).
24 David Alexander, "Gendered Job Traits and Women's Occupations" (PhD Dissertation, Economics, University of Massachusetts, 1987).
25 Michael Reich, *Racial Inequality* (Princeton University Press, 1981).
26 Al Symanski, "The Structure of Race," *Review of Radical Political Economy*, Vol. 17, no. 4 (1985), pp. 106–20.
27 Gintis and Bowles, 1986.
28 Nancy Fraser, "Women, Welfare, and the Politics of Need Interpretation," *Hypatia: A Journal of Feminist Philosophy*, Vol. 2, no. 1 (Winter 1987), pp. 103–22; Kathy Ferguson, 1984, Chapter 4.
29 Carol Gilligan, *In a Different Voice* (Cambridge: Harvard University Press, 1982); Marilyn Friedman, "Care and Context in Moral Reasoning" in Carol Harding, ed., *Moral Dilemmas: Philosophical and Psychological Issues in the Development of Moral Reasoning* (Chicago: Precedent, 1985).
30 Virginia Held, "A Non-Contractual Society" (paper given at the conference on Feminist Moral, Legal and Political Theory, at the University of Cincinnati, November, 1986).
31 Claus Offe, *Disorganized Capitalism: Contemporary Transformation of Work and Politics* (Cambridge: MIT Press, 1986), Chs 1–3.
32 Max Weber, "Classes, Status Groups and Parties" in *Weber: Selections in Translation*, ed. W. G. Runciman (Cambridge University Press, 1978), pp. 43–64; David Beetham, *Max Weber and the Theory of Modern Politics* (Oxford: Polity Press, 1985), pp. 79–82.

33 Richard Sennet and Jonathan Cobb, *The Hidden Injuries of Class* (New York: Vintage Books, 1972).
34 Maria C. Lugones and Elizabeth V. Spelman, "Have We Got a Theory for You! Feminist Theory, Cultural Imperialism and the Demand for 'The Woman's Voice'," *Women's Studies International Forum*, Vol. 6, no. 6 (1983), pp. 573–81.
35 Nancy Fraser, "Social Movements vs. Disciplinary Bureaucracies: The Discourses of Social Needs," CHS Occasional Paper #8 (Center for Humanistic Studies, University of Minnesota, 1987), pp. 1–37
36 W. E. B. Du Bois, *The Souls of Black Folks* (New York: Signet, 1903, 1969).

9

On Psychological Oppression

Sandra Bartky

In *Black Skin, White Masks*, Frantz Fanon offers an anguished and eloquent description of the psychological effects of colonialism on the colonized, a "clinical study" of what he calls the "psychic alienation of the black man." "Those who recognize themselves in it," he says, "will have made a step forward."[1] Fanon's black American readers saw at once that he had captured the corrosive effects not only of classic colonial oppression but of domestic racism too, and that his study fitted well the picture of black America as an internal colony. Without wanting in any way to diminish the oppressive and stifling realities of black experience that Fanon reveals, let me say that I, a white woman, recognize myself in this book too, not only in my "shameful livery of white incomprehension,"[2] but as myself the victim of a "psychic alienation" similar to the one Fanon has described. In this chapter I shall try to explore that moment of recognition, to reveal the ways in which the psychological effects of sexist oppression resemble those of racism and colonialism.

Sandra Bartky, "On Psychological Oppression," pp. 22–32 and 121–4 (notes) from *Femininity and Domination: Studies in the Phenomenology of Oppression*. New York: Routledge, 1990. Reproduced by permission of Routledge/Taylor & Francis Books, Inc.

To oppress, says Webster, is "to lie heavy on, to weigh down, to exercise harsh dominion over." When we describe a people as oppressed, what we have in mind most often is an oppression that is economic and political in character. But recent liberation movements, the black liberation movement and the women's movement in particular, have brought to light forms of oppression that are not immediately economic or political. It is possible to be oppressed in ways that need involve neither physical deprivation, legal inequality, nor economic exploitation;[3] one can be oppressed psychologically – the "psychic alienation" of which Fanon speaks. To be psychologically oppressed is to be weighed down in your mind; it is to have a harsh dominion exercised over your self-esteem. The psychologically oppressed become their own oppressors; they come to exercise harsh dominion over their own self-esteem. Differently put, psychological oppression can be regarded as the "internalization of intimations of inferiority."[4]

Like economic oppression, psychological oppression is institutionalized and systematic; it serves to make the work of domination easier by breaking the spirit of the dominated and by rendering them incapable of understanding the nature of those agencies responsible for their subjugation. This allows those who benefit from the established order of things to maintain their ascendancy with more appearance of legitimacy and with less recourse to overt acts of violence than they might otherwise require. Now, poverty and powerlessness can destroy a person's self-esteem, and the fact that one occupies an inferior position in society is all too often racked up to one's being an inferior sort of person. Clearly, then, economic and political oppression are themselves psychologically oppressive. But there are unique modes of psychological oppression that can be distinguished from the usual forms of economic and political domination. Fanon offers a series of what are essentially phenomenological descriptions of psychic alienation.[5] In spite of considerable overlapping, the experiences of oppression he describes fall into three categories: stereotyping, cultural domination, and sexual objectification. These, I shall contend, are some of the ways in which the terrible messages of inferiority can be delivered even to those who may enjoy certain material benefits; they are special modes of psychic alienation. In what follows, I shall examine some of the ways in which American women – white women and women of color – are stereotyped, culturally dominated, and sexually objectified. In the course of the discussion, I shall argue that our ordinary concept of oppression needs to be altered and expanded, for it is too restricted to encompass what an analysis of psychological oppression reveals about the nature of oppression in general. Finally, I shall be concerned throughout to show how both fragmentation and mystification are present in each mode of psychological oppression, although in varying degrees: fragmentation, the splitting of the whole person into parts of a person which, in stereotyping, may take the form of a war between a "true" and "false" self – or, in sexual objectification, the form of an often coerced and degrading identification of a person with her body; mystification, the systematic obscuring of both the reality and agencies of psychological oppression so that its intended effect, the depreciated self, is lived out as destiny, guilt, or neurosis.

The stereotypes that sustain sexism are similar in many ways to those that sustain racism. Like white women, black and brown persons of both sexes have been regarded as childlike, happiest when they are occupying their "place"; more intuitive than rational, more spontaneous than deliberate, closer to nature, and less capable of substantial cultural accomplishment. Black men and women of all races have been victims of sexual stereotyping: the black man and the black woman, like the "Latin spitfire," are lustful and hotblooded; they are thought to lack the capacities for instinctual control that distinguish people from animals. What is seen as an excess in persons of color appears as a deficiency in the white woman; comparatively frigid, she has been, nonetheless, defined by her sexuality as well, here her reproductive role or function. In regard to capability and competence, black women have, again, an excess of what in white women is a deficiency. White women have been seen as incapable and incompetent: no matter, for these are traits of the truly feminine woman. Black women, on the other hand, have been seen as overly capable, hence, as unfeminine bitches who threaten, through their very competence, to castrate their men.

Stereotyping is morally reprehensible as well as psychologically oppressive on two counts, at least. First, it can hardly be expected that those who hold a set of stereotyped beliefs about the sort of person I am will understand my needs or even respect my rights. Second, suppose that I, the object of some stereotype, believe in it myself – for why should I not believe what everyone else believes? I may then find it difficult to achieve what existentialists call an authentic choice of self, or what some psychologists have regarded as a state of self-actualization. Moral philosophers have quite correctly placed a high value, sometimes the highest value, on the development of autonomy and moral agency. Clearly, the economic and political domination of women – our concrete powerlessness – is what threatens our autonomy most. But stereotyping, in its own way, threatens our self-determination too. Even when economic and political obstacles on the path to autonomy are removed, a depreciated alter ego still blocks the way. It is hard enough for me to determine what sort of person I am or ought to try to become without being shadowed by an alternate self, a truncated and inferior self that I have, in some sense, been doomed to be all the time. For many, the prefabricated self triumphs over a more authentic self which, with work and encouragement, might sometime have emerged. For the talented few, retreat into the *imago* is raised to the status of art or comedy. Muhammad Ali has made himself what he could scarcely escape being made into – a personification of Primitive Man; while Zsa Zsa Gabor is not so much a woman as the parody of a woman.

Female stereotypes threaten the autonomy of women not only by virtue of their existence but also by virtue of their content.[6] In the conventional portrait, women deny their femininity when they undertake action that is too self-regarding or independent. As we have seen, black women are condemned (often by black men) for supposedly having done this already; white women stand under an injunction not to follow their example. Many women in many places lacked (and many still lack) the elementary right to choose our own mates; but for some women even in our own society today, this is virtually the only major decision we are thought capable of making without putting our womanly nature in danger; what follows ever after is or ought to be a properly feminine submission to the decisions of men. We cannot be autonomous, as men are thought to be autonomous, without in some sense ceasing to be women. When one considers how interwoven are traditional female stereotypes with traditional female roles – and these, in turn, with the ways in which we are socialized – all this is seen in an even more sinister light: White women, at least, are psychologically conditioned not to pursue the kind of autonomous development that is held by the culture to be a constitutive feature of masculinity.

The truncated self I am to be is not something manufactured out there by an anonymous Other which I encounter only in the pages of *Playboy* or the *Ladies' Home Journal*; it is inside of me, a part of myself. I may become infatuated with my feminine persona and waste my powers in the more or less hopeless pursuit of a *Vogue* figure, the look of an *Essence* model, or a home that "expresses my personality." Or I may find the parts of myself fragmented and the fragments at war with one another. Women are only now learning to identify and struggle against the forces that have laid these psychic burdens upon us. More often than not, we live out this struggle, which is really a struggle against oppression, in a mystified way: What we are enduring we believe to be entirely intrapsychic in character, the result of immaturity, maladjustment, or even neurosis.

Tyler, the great classical anthropologist, defined culture as all the items in the general life of a people. To claim that women are victims of cultural domination is to claim that all the items in the general life of our people – our language, our institutions, our art and literature, our popular culture – are sexist; that all, to a greater or lesser degree, manifest male supremacy. There is some exaggeration in this claim, but not much. Unlike the black colonial whom Fanon describes with such pathos, women *qua* women are not now in possession of an alternate culture, a "native" culture which, even if regarded by everyone, including ourselves, as decidedly inferior to the dominant culture, we could at least recognize as our own. However degraded or distorted an image of ourselves we see reflected in the patriarchal culture, the culture of our men is still our culture. Certainly in some respects, the condition of women is like the condition of a colonized people. But we are not a colonized people; we have never been more than half a people.[7]

This lack of cultural autonomy has several important consequences for an understanding of the condition of women. A culture has a global character; hence, the limits of my culture are the limits of my world. The subordination of women, then, because it is so pervasive a feature of my culture, will (if uncontested) appear to be natural – and because it is natural, unalterable. Unlike a colonized people, women have no memory of a "time before": a time before the masters came, a time before we were subjugated and ruled. Further, since one function of cultural identity is to allow me to distinguish those who are like me from those who are not, I may feel more kinship with those who share my culture, even though they oppress me, than with the women of another culture, whose whole experience of life may well be closer to my own than to any man's.

Our true situation in regard to male supremacist culture is one of domination and exclusion. But this manifests itself in an extremely deceptive way; mystification once more holds sway. Our relative absence from the "higher" culture is taken as proof that we are unable to participate in it ("Why are there no great women artists?"). Theories of the female nature must then be brought forward to try to account for this.[8] Thes plitting or fragmenting of women's consciousness which takes place in the cultural sphere is also apparent. While remaining myself, I must at the same time transform myself into that abstract and "universal" subject for whom cultural artifacts are made and whose values and experience they express. This subject is not universal at all, however, but *male*. Thus, I must approve the taming of the shrew, laugh at the mother-in-law or the dumb blonde, and somehow identify with all those heroes of fiction from Faust to the personae of Norman Mailer and Henry Miller, whose *Bildungsgeschichten* involve the sexual exploitation of women. Women of color have, of course, a special problem: The dominant cultural subject is not only male, but *white*, so their cultural alienation is doubled; they are expected to assimilate cultural motifs that are not only masculinist but racist.[9]

Women of all races and ethnicities, like Fanon's "black man," are subject not only to stereotyping and cultural depreciation but to sexual objectification as well. Even though much has been written about sexual objectification in the literature of the women's movement, the notion itself is complex, obscure, and much in need of philosophical clarification. I offer the following preliminary characterization of sexual objectification: A person is sexually objectified when her sexual parts or sexual functions are separated out from the rest of her personality and reduced to the status of mere instruments or else regarded as if they were capable of representing her. On this definition, then, the prostitute would be a victim of sexual objectification, as would the *Playboy* bunny, the female breeder, and the bathing beauty.

To say that the sexual part of a person is regarded as if it could represent her is to imply that it cannot, that the part and the whole are incommensurable. But surely there are times, in the sexual embrace perhaps, when a woman might want to be regarded as nothing but a sexually intoxicating body and when attention paid to some other aspect of her person – say, to her mathematical ability – would be absurdly out of place. If sexual relations involve some sexual objectification, then it becomes necessary to distinguish situations in which sexual objectification is oppressive from the sorts of situations in which it is not.[10] The identification of a person with her sexuality becomes oppressive, one might venture, when such an identification becomes habitually extended into every area of her experience. To be routinely perceived by others in a sexual light on occasions when such a perception is inappropriate is to have one's very being subjected to that compulsive sexualization that has been the traditional lot of both white women and black men and women of color generally. "For the majority of white men," says Fanon, "the Negro is the incarnation of a genital potency beyond all moralities and prohibitions."[11] Later in *Black Skin, White Masks*, he writes that "the Negro is the genital."[12]

One way to be sexually objectified, then, is to be the object of a kind of perception, unwelcome and inappropriate, that takes the part for the whole. An example may make this clearer. A young woman was recently interviewed for a teaching job in philosophy by the academic chairman of a large department. During most of the interview, so she reported, the man stared fixedly at her breasts. In this situation, the woman is a bosom, not a job candidate. Was this department chairman guilty only of a confusion between business and pleasure? Scarcely. He stares at her breasts for his sake, not hers. Her wants and needs not only play no role in the encounter but, because of the direction of his attention, she is discomfited, feels humiliated, and performs badly. Not surprisingly, she fails to get the job. Much of the time, sexual objectification occurs independently of what women want; it is something done to us against our will. It is clear from this example that the objectifying perception that splits a person into parts serves to elevate one interest above another. Now it stands revealed not only as a way of perceiving, but as a way of maintaining dominance as well. It is not clear to me that the sexual and nonsexual spheres of experience can or ought to be kept separate forever (Marcuse, for one, has envisioned the eroticization of all areas of human life); but as things stand now, sexualization is one way of fixing disadvantaged persons in their disadvantage, to their clear detriment and within a narrow and repressive eros.

Consider now a second example of the way in which that fragmenting perception, which is so large an ingredient in the sexual objectification of women, serves to maintain the dominance of men. It is a fine spring day, and with an utter lack of self-consciousness, I am bouncing down the street. Suddenly I hear men's voices. Catcalls and whistles fill the air. These noises are clearly sexual in intent and they are meant for me; they come from across the street. I freeze. As Sartre would say, I have been petrified by the gaze of the Other. My face flushes and my motions become stiff and self-conscious. The body which only a moment before I inhabited with such ease now floods my consciousness. I have been made into an object. While it is true that for these men I am nothing but, let us say, a "nice piece of ass," there is more involved in this encounter than their mere fragmented perception of me. They could, after all, have enjoyed me in silence. Blissfully unaware, breasts bouncing, eyes on the birds in the trees, I could have passed by without having been turned to stone. But I must be *made* to know that I am a "nice piece of ass": I must be made to see myself as they see me. There is an element of compulsion in this encounter, in this being-made-to-be-aware of one's own flesh; like being made to apologize, it is humiliating. It is unclear what role is played by sexual arousal or even sexual connoisseurship in encounters like these. What I describe seems less the spontaneous expression of a healthy eroticism than a ritual of subjugation.

Sexual objectification as I have characterized it involves two persons: the one who objectifies and the one who is objectified. But the observer and the one observed can be the same person. I can, of course, take pleasure in my own body as another might take pleasure in it and it would be naive not to notice that there are delights of a narcissistic kind that go along with the status "sex object." But the extent to which the identification of women with their bodies feeds an essentially infantile narcissism – an attitude of mind in keeping with our forced infantilization in other areas of life – is, at least for me, an open question. Subject to the evaluating eye of the male connoisseur, women learn to evaluate themselves first and best. Our identities can no more be kept separate from the appearance of our bodies than they can be kept separate from the shadow-selves of the female stereotype. "Much of a young woman's identity is already defined in her kind of attractiveness and in the selectivity of her search for the man (or men) by whom she wishes to be sought."[13] There is something obsessional in the preoccupation of many women with their bodies, although the magnitude of the obsession will vary somewhat with the presence or absence in a woman's life of other sources of self-esteem and with her capacity to gain a living independent of her looks. Surrounded on all sides by images of perfect female beauty – for, in modern advertising, the needs of capitalism and the traditional values of patriarchy are happily married – of course we fall short. The narcissism encouraged by our identification with the body is shattered by these images. Whose nose is not the wrong shape, whose hips are not too wide or too narrow? Anyone who believes that such concerns are too trivial to weigh very heavily with most women has failed to grasp the realities of the feminine condition.

The idea that women ought always to make themselves as pleasing to the eye as possible is very widespread indeed. It was dismaying to come across this passage in a paper written by an eminent Marxist humanist in defense of the contemporary women's movement:

> There is no reason why a woman's liberation activist should not try to look pretty and attractive. One of the universal human aspirations of all times was to raise reality to the level of art, to make the world more beautiful, to be more beautiful within given limits. Beauty is a value in itself; it will always be respected and will attract – to be sure various forms of beauty but not to the exclusion of physical beauty. A woman does not become a sex object in herself, or only because of her pretty appearance. She becomes a sexual object in relationship, when she allows a man to treat her in a certain depersonalizing, degrading way; and vice versa, a woman does not become a sexual subject by neglecting her appearance.[14]

It is not for the sake of mere men that we women – not just we women, but we women's liberation activists – ought to look "pretty and attractive," but for the sake of something much more exalted: for the sake of beauty. This preoccupation with the way we look and the fear that women might stop trying to make themselves pretty and attractive (so as to "raise reality to the level of art") would be a species of objectification anywhere; but it is absurdly out of place in a paper on women's emancipation. It is as if an essay on the black liberation movement were to end by admonishing blacks not to forget their natural rhythm, or as if Marx had warned the workers of the world not to neglect their appearance while throwing off their chains.

Markovic's concern with women's appearance merely reflects a larger cultural preoccupation. It is a fact that women in our society are regarded as having a virtual duty "to make the most of what we have." But the imperative not to neglect our appearance suggests that we can neglect it, that it is within our power to make ourselves look better – not just neater and cleaner, but prettier, and more attractive. What is presupposed by this is that we don't look good enough already, that attention to the ordinary standards of hygiene would be insufficient, that there is something wrong with us as we are. Here, the "intimations of inferiority" are clear: Not only must we continue to produce ourselves as beautiful bodies, but the bodies we have to work with are deficient to begin with. Even within an already inferiorized identity (i.e., the identity of one who is principally and most importantly a body), I turn out once more to be inferior, for the body I am to be, never sufficient unto itself, stands forever in need of plucking or painting, of slimming down or fattening up, of firming or flattening.

The foregoing examination of three modes of psychological oppression, so it appears, points up the need for an alteration in our ordinary concept of oppression. Oppression, I believe, is ordinarily conceived in too limited a fashion. This has placed undue restrictions both on our understanding of what oppression itself is and on the categories of persons we might want to classify as oppressed. Consider, for example, the following paradigmatic case of oppression:

> And the Egyptians made the children of Israel to serve with rigor; and they made their lives bitter with hard bondage, in mortar and in brick, and in all manner of service in the field; all their service wherein they made them serve, was with rigor.[15]

Here the Egyptians, one group of persons, exercise harsh dominion over the Israelites, another group of persons. It is not suggested that the Israelites, however great their sufferings, have lost their integrity and wholeness *qua* persons. But psychological oppression is dehumanizing and depersonalizing; it attacks the person in her personhood. I mean by this that the nature of psychological oppression is such that the oppressor and oppressed alike come to doubt that the oppressed have the capacity to do the sorts of things that only persons can do, to be what persons, in the fullest sense of the term, can be. The possession of autonomy, for example, is widely thought to distinguish persons from non-persons; but some female stereotypes, as we have seen, threaten the autonomy of women. Oppressed people might or might not be in a position to exercise their autonomy, but the psychologically oppressed may come to believe that they lack the capacity to be autonomous whatever their position.

Similarly, the creation of culture is a distinctly human function, perhaps the most human function. In its cultural life, a group is able to affirm its values and to grasp its identity in acts of self-reflection. Frequently, oppressed persons, cut off from the cultural apparatus, are denied the exercise of this function entirely. To the extent that we are able to catch sight of ourselves in the dominant culture at all, the images we see are distorted or demeaning. Finally, sexual objectification leads to the identification of those who undergo it with what is both human and not quite human – the body. Thus, psychological oppression is just what Fanon said it was – "psychic alienation" – the estrangement or separating of a person from some of the essential attributes of personhood.

Mystification surrounds these processes of human estrangement. The special modes of psychological oppression can be regarded as some of the many ways in which messages of inferiority are delivered to those who are to occupy an inferior position in society. But it is important to remember that messages of this sort are neither sent nor received in an unambiguous way. We are taught that white women and (among others) black men and women are deficient in those capacities that distinguish persons from nonpersons, but at the same time we are assured that we are persons after all. *Of course* women are persons; *of course* blacks are human beings. Who but the lunatic fringe would deny it? The Antillean Negro, Fanon is fond of repeating, is a *Frenchman*. The official ideology announces with conviction that "all men are created equal"; and in spite of the suspect way in which this otherwise noble assertion is phrased, we women learn that they mean to include us after all.

It is itself psychologically oppressive both to believe and at the same time not to believe that one is inferior – in other words, to believe a contradiction. Lacking an analysis of the larger system of social relations which produced it, one can only make sense of this contradiction in two ways. First, while accepting in some quite formal sense the proposition that "all men are created equal," I can believe, inconsistently, what my oppressors have always believed: that some types of persons are less equal than others. I may then live out my membership in my sex or race in *shame*; I am "only a woman" or "just a nigger." Or, somewhat more consistently, I may reject entirely the belief that my disadvantage is generic; but having still to account for it somehow, I may locate the cause squarely within myself, a bad destiny of an entirely private sort – a character flaw, an "inferiority complex," or a neurosis.

Many oppressed persons come to regard themselves as uniquely unable to satisfy normal criteria of psychological health or moral adequacy. To believe that my inferiority is a function of the kind of person I am may make me ashamed of being one of *this* kind. On the other hand, a lack I share with many others just because of an accident of birth would be unfortunate indeed, but at least I would not have to regard myself as having failed uniquely to measure up to standards that people like myself are expected to meet. It should be pointed out, however, that both of these "resolutions" – the ascription of one's inferiority to idiosyncratic or else to generic causes – produces a "poor self-image," a bloodless term of the behavioral sciences that refers to a very wide variety of possible ways to suffer.[16]

To take one's oppression to be an inherent flaw of birth, or of psychology, is to have what Marxists have characterized as "false consciousness." Systematically deceived as we are about the nature and origin of our unhappiness, our struggles are directed inward toward the self, or toward other similar selves in whom we may see our deficiencies mirrored, not outward upon those social forces responsible for our predicament. Like the psychologically disturbed, the psychologically oppressed often lack a viable identity. Frequently we are unable to make sense of our own impulses or feelings, not only because our drama of fragmentation gets played out on an inner psychic stage, but because we are forced to find our way about in a world which presents itself to us in a masked and deceptive fashion. Regarded as persons, yet depersonalized, we are treated by our society the way the parents of some schizophrenics are said by R. D. Laing to treat their children – professing love at the very moment they shrink from their children's touch.

In sum, then, to be psychologically oppressed is to be caught in the double bind of a society which both affirms my human status and at the same time bars me from the exercise of many of those typically human functions that bestow this status. To be denied an autonomous choice of self, forbidden cultural expression, and condemned to the immanence of mere bodily being is to be cut off from the sorts of activities that define what it is to be human. A person whose being has been subjected to these cleavages may be described as "alienated." Alienation in any form causes a rupture within the human person, an estrangement from self, a "splintering of human nature into a number of misbegotten parts."[17] Any adequate theory of the nature and varieties of human alienation, then, must encompass psychological oppression – or, to use Fanon's term once more, "psychic alienation."

Much has been written about alienation, but it is Marx's theory of alienation that speaks most compellingly to the concerns of feminist political theory. Alienation for Marx is primarily the alienation of labor. What distinguishes human beings from animals is "labor" – for Marx, the free, conscious, and creative transformation of nature in accordance with human needs. But under capitalism, workers are alienated in production, estranged from the products of their labor, from their own productive activity, and from their fellow workers.

Human productive activity, according to Marx, is "objectified" in its products. What this means is that we are able to grasp ourselves reflectively primarily in the things we have produced; human needs and powers become concrete "in their products as the amount and type of change which their exercise has brought about."[18] But in capitalist production, the capitalist has a right to appropriate what workers have produced. Thus, the product goes to augment capital, where it becomes part of an alien force exercising power over those who produced it. An "objectification" or extension of the worker's self, the product is split off from this self and turned against it. But workers are alienated not only from the products they produce but from their own laboring activity as well, for labor under capitalism is not, as labor should be, an occasion for human self-realization but mere drudgery which "mortifies the body and ruins the mind."[19] The worker's labor "is therefore not voluntary, but coerced; it is forced labor. It is therefore not the satisfaction of a need; it is merely a means to satisfy needs external to it."[20] When the free and creative productive activity that should define human functioning is reduced to a mere means to sustain life, to "forced labor," workers suffer fragmentation and loss of self. Since labor is the most characteristic human life activity, to be alienated from one's own labor is to be estranged from oneself.

In many ways, psychic alienation and the alienation of labor are profoundly alike. Both involve a splitting off of human functions from the human person, a forbidding of activities thought to be essential to a fully human existence. Both subject the individual to fragmentation and impoverishment. Alienation is not a condition into which someone might stumble by accident; it has come both to the victim of psychological oppression and to the alienated worker from without, as a usurpation by someone else of what is, by rights, *not his to usurp*.[21] Alienation occurs in each case when activities which not only belong to the domain of the self but define, in large measure, the proper functioning of this self, fall under the control of others. To be a victim of alienation is to have a part of one's being stolen by another. Both psychic alienation and the alienation of labor might be regarded as varieties of alienated productivity. From this perspective, cultural domination would be the estrangement or alienation of production in the cultural sphere; while the subjective effects of stereotyping as well as the self-objectification that regularly accompanies sexual objectification could be interpreted as an alienation in the production of one's own person.

All the modes of oppression – psychological, political, and economic – and the kinds of alienation they generate serve to maintain a vast system of privilege – privilege of race, of sex, and of class. Every mode of oppression within the system has its own part to play, but each serves to support and to maintain the others. Thus, for example, the assault on the self-esteem of white women and of black persons of both sexes prepares us for the historic role that a disproportionate number of us are destined to play within the process of production: that of a cheap or reserve labor supply. Class oppression, in turn, encourages those who are somewhat higher in the hierarchies of race or gender to cling to a false sense of superiority – a poor compensation indeed. Because of the interlocking character of the modes of oppression, I think it highly unlikely that any form of oppression will disappear entirely until the system of oppression as a whole is overthrown.

Notes

Several works that have appeared since the publication of this chapter may interest the reader. Linda Tschirhart Sanford and Mary Ellen Donovan have written a lucid, detailed, and powerful account of the many sources of women's low self-esteem: *Women and Self-Esteem* (New York: Doubleday, 1984). Also recommended is Ann Wilson Schaef, *Women's Reality* (New York: Harper and Row, 1981). In *Common Differences: Conflicts in Black and White Feminist Perspectives* (New York: Anchor/Doubleday, 1981), Gloria Joseph and Jill Lewis examine differences, including psychological differences, between black and white women. Linda LeMoncheck has written an analytically acute monograph on the subject of sexual objectification, *Dehumanizing Women: Treating Persons as Sex Objects* (Totowa, NJ: Rowman and Allanheld, 1985); she subjects my own view of sexual objectification to an extended discussion and critique. The exclusion of women in our society from cultural production, especially from art, literature, and music, has, of course, never been total. But since I wrote this chapter, there has been an enormous outpouring of work in these fields by creative women seeking very self-consciously to express a female and often a feminist perspective. Some of this work has reached a mass audience, for example, the art of Judy Chicago, the music of Holly Near and Tracey Chapman, and the novels of Toni Morrison, Marilyn French, Alice Walker, Marge Piercy, Erica Jong, and Gloria Naylor.

1 Frantz Fanon, *Black Skins, White Masks* (New York: Grove Press, 1967), p. 12.

2 Ibid.

3 For an excellent comparison of the concepts of exploitation and oppression, see Judith Farr Tormey, "Exploitation, Oppression and Self-Sacrifice," in *Women and Philosophy*, ed. Carol C. Gould and Marx W. Wartofsky (New York: G. P. Putnam's Sons, 1976), pp. 206–21.

4 Joyce Mitchell Cook, paper delivered at Philosophy and the Black Liberation Struggle Conference, University of Illinois, Chicago Circle, November 19–20, 1970.

5 Fanon's phenomenology of oppression, however, is almost entirely a phenomenology of the oppression of colonized *men*. He seems unaware of the ways in which the oppression of women by their men in the societies he examines is itself similar to the colonization of natives by Europeans. Sometimes, as in *A Dying Colonialism* (New York: Grove Press, 1968), he goes so far as to defend the clinging to oppressive practices, such as the sequestration of women in Moslem countries, as an authentic resistance by indigenous people to Western cultural intrusion. For a penetrating critique of Fanon's attitude toward women, see Barbara Burris, "Fourth World Manifesto," in *Radical Feminism*, ed. A. Koedt, E. Levine, and A. Rapone (New York: Quadrangle, 1973), pp. 322–57.

6 I have in mind Abraham Maslow's concept of autonomy, a notion which has the advantage of being neutral as regards the controversy between free will and determinism. For Maslow, the sources of behavior of autonomous or "psychologically free" individuals are more internal than reactive:

> Such people become far more self-sufficient and self-contained. The determinants which govern them are now primarily inner ones . . . They are the laws of their own inner nature, their potentialities and capacities, their talents, their latent resources, their creative impulses, their needs to know themselves and to become more and more integrated and unified, more and more aware of what they really are, of what they really want, of what their call or vocation or fate

is to be. *Toward a Psychology of Being*, 2nd edn. [New York: D. Van Nostrand Co., 1968], p. 35.

It would be absurd to suggest that most men are autonomous in this sense of the term. Nevertheless, insofar as there are individuals who resemble this portrait, I think it likelier that they will be men than women – at least white women. I think it likely that more white men than white women *believe* themselves to be autonomous; this belief, even if false, is widely held, and this in itself has implications that are important to consider. Whatever the facts may be in regard to men's lives, the point to remember is this: women have been thought to have neither the capacity nor the right to aspire to an ideal of autonomy, an ideal to which there accrues, whatever its relation to mental health, an enormous social prestige.

7 Many feminists would object vigorously to my claim that there has been no female culture (see, e.g., Burris, "Fourth World Manifesto"). I am not claiming that women have had no enclaves within the dominant culture, that we have never made valuable contributions to the larger culture, or even that we have never dominated any avenue of cultural expression – one would have to think only of the way in which women have dominated certain forms of folk art (e.g., quilting). What I am claiming is that none of this adds up to a "culture," in the sense in which we speak of Jewish culture, Arapesh culture, or Afro-American culture. Further, the fact that many women are today engaged in the self-conscious attempt to create a female culture testifies, I think, to the situation regarding culture being essentially as I describe it.

8 The best-known modern theory of this type is, of course, Freud's. He maintains that the relative absence of women from the higher culture is the consequence of a lesser ability to sublimate libidinal drives. See "Femininity" in *New Introductory Lectures in Psychoanalysis* (New York: W. W. Norton, 1933).

9 I take it that something like this forms the backdrop to the enjoyment of the average movie. It is daunting to consider the magnitude of the task of neutralization or transformation of hostile cultural messages that must fall constantly to the average female, non-white or even working class white male TV watcher or moviegoer. The pleasure we continue to take in cultural products that may disparage us remains, at least to me something of a mystery.

10 There might be some objection to regarding ordinary sexual relations as involving sexual objectification, since this use of the term seems not to jibe with its use in more ordinary contexts. For Hegel, Marx, and Sartre, "objectification" is an important moment in the dialectic of consciousness. My decision to treat ordinary sexual relations or even sexual desire alone as involving some objectification is based on a desire to remain within this tradition. Further, Sartre's phenomenology of sexual desire in *Being and Nothingness* (New York: Philosophical Library, 1966) draws heavily on a concept of objectification in an unusually compelling description of the experienced character of that state:

> The caress by realizing the Other's incarnation reveals to me my own incarnation; that is, I make myself flesh in order to impel the Other to realize for-herself and for-me her own flesh, and my caresses cause my flesh to be born for me in so far as it is for the Other flesh causing her to be born as flesh. I make her enjoy my flesh through her flesh in order to compel her to feel herself flesh. And so possession truly appears as a double reciprocal incarnation. (p. 508)

What I call "objectification," Sartre here calls "incarnation," a refinement not necessary for my purposes. What he calls "sadism" is incarnation without reciprocity. Most of my examples of sexual objectification would fall into the latter category.

11 Fanon, *Black Skin, White Masks*, p. 177. Eldridge Cleaver sounds a similar theme in *Soul on Ice* (New York: Dell, 1968). The archetypal white man in American society, for Cleaver, is the "Omnipotent Administrator," the archetypal black man the "Super-Masculine Menial."

12 Ibid., p. 180.

13 Erik Erikson, "Inner and Outer Space: Reflections on Womanhood," *Daedalus*, Vol. 93, 1961, pp. 582–606.

14 Mihailo Markovic, "Women's Liberation and Human Emancipation," in *Women and Philosophy*, pp. 165–6. In spite of this lapse and some questionable opinions concerning the nature of female sexuality, Markovic's paper is a most compelling defense of the claim that the emancipation of women cannot come about under capitalism.

15 Exod. 1:13–14.

16 The available clinical literature on the psychological effects of social inferiority supports this claim. See William H. Grier and Price M. Cobbs, *Black Rage* (New York: Grosset & Dunlap, 1969); Pauline Bart, "Depression in Middle-Aged Women," in *Women in Sexist Society*, ed. Vivian Gornick and Barbara Moran (New York: New American Library, 1971), pp. 163–86; also Phyllis Chesler, *Women and Madness* (New York: Doubleday, 1972).

17 Bertell Ollman, *Alienation: Marx's Conception of Man in Capitalist Society* (London and New York: Cambridge University Press, 1971), p. 135.

18 Ibid., p. 143.

19 Karl Marx, *The Economic and Philosophical Manuscripts of 1844*, ed. Dirk J. Struik (New York: International Publishers, 1964), p. 111.

20 Ibid.

21 The use of the masculine possessive pronoun is deliberate.

Part III

What is Gender?

Introduction to Part III

Since the beginning of the second wave, "gender" has been one of the most central concepts of feminism. The terms "sex" and "gender" were introduced into feminism in order to distinguish between the biological and the social aspects of sexual difference. According to a common formulation of this distinction, "sex" refers to the biological differences between males and females; "gender" refers to the socially caused differences. By embracing this distinction feminists hoped to displace the widely held assumption that most socially significant differences between men and women are primarily a function of biology with the idea that most of these differences are largely a product of culture. By the late 1980s, however, some feminists began to question the sex–gender distinction on the grounds that sex itself is a social construct and is not separate from gender.

Many questions about the meaning of gender and its relation to biological sex are still under debate today; they include: Do men and women have distinct natures – i.e., psychosocial differences that are grounded in biology? Or, are these differences largely a product of social conditioning? Should feminists resist the idea of human nature, or should they embrace this concept as liberatory? What does it mean to say that gender is a social construct, and how are gender differences constructed? Does the science of gender accurately depict women and their nature? If not, in what ways does it go wrong, and how should it be revised? Does it make sense to talk about the category "woman" as a single unified category, or do the differences in women's experiences (based on race, class, sexuality, etc.) undermine this assumption? Is the sex–gender distinction useful to feminism, or should it be abandoned? The chapters in this part take up many of these issues, including a critique of the science of gender, a discussion of the normative implications that follow from belief in human natures, a critical evaluation of gender (and of sex as well) as a foundation for feminism, and a pragmatic and normative account of gender as a social construct.

We begin with a critique of the science of sexual difference. Although feminists began to contest scientific representations of women as early as the eighteenth century, it wasn't until the latter part of the twentieth century that feminist philosophers fully established the depth of androcentric bias in the collection, organization, and interpretation of data on sex and gender differences. In "Pre-theoretical Assumptions in Evolutionary Explanations of Female Sexuality," Elisabeth Lloyd provides an example from contemporary evolutionary theory. She argues that evolutionary theories of sexuality often wrongly assume a direct link between reproduction and female sexuality. Lloyd attributes this assumption to two factors – adaptationism within biology and a long-standing social tradition of defining women in terms of their sexual and reproductive functions. She concludes that these factors have led to faulty science and an inaccurate depiction of female sexuality.

Philosophers have traditionally assumed that theories of human nature, including those that imply differences between men's and women's natures, have important political and ethical implications. One reason is that appeals to human nature have been, and sometimes still are, used to justify oppressive gender roles. As a result, some feminists challenge the very idea of human nature and, of course, the familiar corollary that men and women are different by nature. Other feminists, on the other hand, find the idea of human nature appealing. They argue that the existence of a nature that is common to men and women can provide a basis for feminist critiques of the subordination of women. In "Natures and Norms," however, Louise Antony takes quite a different view. She maintains that biological theories of human nature can tell us little about these types of normative issues. Her argument is that there is an ambiguity in the word "natural." The ethical arguments rely on one sense of natural – the scientific discussions of human nature rely on a different sense. As a result, the one has no bearing on the other.

It is (or has been) a central tenet of feminism that there is some existing identity, understood through the category "woman," that is represented by feminist goals and interests. Judith Butler, however, calls this assumption into question. In "Subjects of Sex/Gender/Desire," she begins her argument with the constructivist claim that the category "woman," far from being biologically based, is entirely a contingent product of patriarchal power structures. To this, she adds that the category "sex" is as constructed as gender. That is, sex does not precede gender as a separate category upon which gender is constructed. Rather, the two are intimately and ideologically intertwined. Moreover, Butler argues that gender intersects with other categories of oppression – race, class, ethnicity, sexuality, and so forth – and, therefore, concludes that the category "woman" cannot be understood as a single unified category. Collectively, these arguments lead Butler to skepticism about gender as a basis for feminism. Butler's conclusions, however, are not entirely negative. She thinks that feminist politics can succeed, but it must do so – not by asserting the commonalities shared by all women and not by insisting on a single unified feminism – but by recognizing and accepting a diversity of genders and a diversity of feminist aims.

Gender constructivism is roughly the view that, contrary to popular belief, gender differences are not biologically based. Rather, gender is a social construct that was invented for sociopolitical ends – such as reinforcing the existence of patriarchy. In "Gender and Race: (What) Are They? (What) Do We Want Them to Be?" Sally Haslanger develops the constructivist program by providing a normative account of gender, and of race as well. Thus, rather than trying to explain what our ordinary concepts refer to, her project is both pragmatic and revisionary. She asks what practical purposes, if any, do these concepts serve? What purposes should they serve? How might we revise them to better serve our purposes? Taking critical theory as her starting point, she aims to provide liberating accounts of race and gender – what they are and what they ought to be – such that they will be effective tools for fighting injustice.

10

Pre-theoretical Assumptions in Evolutionary Explanations of Female Sexuality

Elisabeth A. Lloyd

[...] In the second wave of the feminist movement in the United States, debates about women's identity have explicitly included sexuality; much feminist argument in the late 1960s and early 1970s involved an attempt to separate out an autonomous female sexuality from women's reproductive functions.

It is especially relevant, then, to examine biological arguments, particularly evolutionary arguments, to see what they say about *whether* and *how* women's sexuality is related to reproduction. We shall find that many evolutionary arguments seem to support the direct linking of female sexuality and reproduction. Yet I will argue that this support is not well-grounded. In fact, I think evolutionary explanations of female sexuality exemplify how social beliefs and social agendas can influence very *basic* biological explanations of fundamental physiological processes. In this chapter, I shall spend some time spelling out a few examples in which assumptions about the close link between reproduction and sexuality yield misleading results, then I shall conclude with a discussion of the consequences of this case study for issues in the philosophy of science.

The fundamental problem is that it is simply *assumed* that every aspect of female sexuality should be explained in terms of reproductive functions. But there is quite a bit of biological evidence that this is an empirically incorrect assumption to make. This raises the question of why autonomous female sexuality, distinct from reproductive functions, got left out of these explanations. I shall ultimately conclude that social context is playing a large and unacknowledged role in the practice of this science.

Perhaps the notion of the potential independence of female sexuality and reproduction may be unclear: I suggest thinking in terms of two distinct models, one in which all basic aspects of sexuality are *explained* in terms of reproduction, and the other in which sexuality is seen as an autonomous set of functions and activities, which are only *partially* explained in terms of reproductive functions. The difference may seem minor, but the two models have significantly disparate consequences when used in scientific explanation.

Let us begin with a classic and wide-spread model representing the hormonal determination of sexual behavior. In this model, female animals are only willing to have sexual intercourse when they are fertile – their sexual interest and activity are

Elisabeth A. Lloyd, "Pre-theoretical Assumptions in Evolutionary Explanations of Female Sexuality," pp. 139–53 from *Philosophical Studies* 69, 1993. Reproduced with kind permission from Kluwer Academic Publishers.

completely hormonally controlled. Typical and familiar examples of this type of set-up include rats, dogs, and cats. When these animals are in estrus, they are willing and eager to mate, otherwise not. Technically, estrus is defined hormonally – that is, estrus is a particular phase of the menstrual cycle, in which the animal is fertile, and certain hormone measures are very high. This model embodies a *very tight* link between sexuality and reproduction: female sexuality functions completely in the service of reproduction.

Some interesting problems arise, however, in the application of this hormonally deterministic picture to human and non-human primate behavior.

First of all, although estrus is biologically defined as a hormonal state, it is very common for estrus to be defined *operationally* as the period in which "the female is willing to participate in sex". In one species, the bonobos, this behavioral definition led to the comic conclusion that this species is in estrus 57–86% of the time.[1] Notice that identifying estrus in this manner amounts to an *enforcement* of the belief that sexual behavior is tightly linked to reproduction. It becomes impossible even to *ask* whether these primates have an active sexual interest outside of their peak hormonal periods.

It turns out that when independent studies are made, sexual activity is not confined to the fertile phase for a number of non-human primates, including rhesus monkeys, several species of baboons, and common chimpanzees.[2] Social factors such as partner preferences can be as influential as hormonal factors in regulating sexual behavior in several of these species.[3]

Female homosexual activity provides a good test for the assumed dependence of female sexuality on hormonal status. In addition, homosexual behaviors are clearly independent of reproduction *per se*, and might be interpreted as an indicator of an autonomous female sexuality. It turns out that female homosexual activities, which are widely observed in non-human primates, seem to be *independent* of the hormonal status of the participants. This independence has led some researchers to ignore such behaviors, or to declare that they are not, in fact, sexual. For example, pygmy chimpanzee females are commonly observed engaging in "genito-genital rubbing" (called "GG rubbing") in which two females hold each other and "swing their hips laterally while keeping the front tips of vulvae, where the clitorises protrude, in touch with each other."[4] Kano argues that this behavior is not sexual, because non-human primates can only be "sexual" during estrus; the fact that pygmy chimps engage in GG rubbing outside of estrus, claims Kano, itself "suggests that this behavior does not occur exclusively in a sexual context, but has some other social significance."[5] Generally, some caution about the interpretation of apparently sexual behaviors is appropriate; the misunderstanding of many dominance behaviors as sexual ones plagued primatology in its first decades. At stake in this case, however, is the very *possibility* of hormonally independent female sexuality. The issue was resolved in 1984, when Mori, using a detailed study of statistical relations among behaviors, concluded that GG rubbing was, in fact, sexual behavior, since the same cluster of behavior surrounded both mating and GG rubbing.[6]

A more blatant example of researcher bias typing reproduction and female sexuality tightly together appears in an experiment being done on female orgasm in stumptail macaques. The original studies on female macaque orgasm, completed in the 1970s, documented female orgasm in the context of female homosexual mounting – that is, one female mounts another female, and stimulates herself to orgasm.[7] One very interesting result of these studies was the finding that the mounting, orgasmic female was *never* in estrus when these orgasms occurred. This is a provocative result for several reasons. First, according to the hormonal determinism model, female macaques are not supposed to be interested in any sexual activity outside of estrus; Second, these same female macaques *never* evidenced any sign of orgasm when they were participating in heterosexual coitus. A later study of the same species documented the same basic patterns, with the exception that four out of ten females in the group seemed, occasionally, to have orgasm during heterosexual coitus.[8]

I was surprised, therefore, when I spoke with a researcher who was working on the evolution of female orgasm in stumptail macaques.[9] He described his experimental set-up to me with some enthusiasm: the females are radio-wired to record orgasmic muscle contractions and increased heartrate, etc. This sounds like the ideal experiment, because it can record the sex lives of the females mechanically, without needing a human observer. In fact, the project had been funded by the NIH, and had presumably gone through the outside referee and panel reviews necessary for funding. But then the researcher described to me the clever way he had set up his equipment to record the female orgasms – he wired up the heart rate of the *male* macaques as the signal to start recording the *female* orgasms. When I pointed out that the vast majority of female stumptail orgasms occurred during sex among the females alone, he replied that yes, he knew that, but he was only interested in the *important* orgasms.

Obviously, this is a very unfortunate case. But it is not an isolated incident. Observations, measurements, interpretations, and experimental design are all affected by the background assumptions of the scientists. There is a pervasive and undefended assumption that female sexuality in non-human primates is tightly linked to reproduction. I would like now to explore briefly the situation regarding human beings.

Human Cases

In most of the literature on the evolution of human sexuality, much attention is paid to the distinct attributes of human beings. The continual sexual "receptivity" of the human female is contrasted with the (supposed) strict hormonal restrictions on sexual activity in non-human animals. Human beings are supposed to be uniquely adapted to be sexually free from hormonal dictates, the possessors of a separate and self-constructed sexuality. When it comes to evolutionary explanations of women's sexuality, though, the tight connection between reproduction and sexuality remains firmly in place.

To continue with the hormonal theme, we can begin by looking at beliefs about the distribution of female sexual interest during the menstrual cycle. Many researchers, in evolutionary biology, behavior, and physiology, have *deduced* that it must be the case in human females that peak sexual interest and desire occur at the same time as peak fertility. This conclusion is a simple extension of the hormonal determinism model from mice and dogs. While this may have the ring of a reasonable assumption, it is not supported by the clinical literature. Kinsey, for example, found that 59% of his female sample experienced patterns of fluctuation in their sexual desire during their cycle – but only 11% experience a peak of sexual desire in mid-cycle, when they are most likely to be fertile.[10] More recently, Singer and Singer, in a survey of studies, found that only 6–8% of women experience an increase in sexual desire around the time of ovulation. Most studies found peaks of sexual desire right before and after menstruation, when the woman is almost invariably infertile.[11]

Hence, the majority of evidence supports a picture in which female sexual interest and activity is clearly *decoupled* from her reproductive state. Sexual interest and motivation is highest when the woman is least likely to conceive. Unfortunately, a number of researchers working in the area of the evolution of sexuality have not taken this on board, and continue to assert that peak sexual desire *must* be around the time of ovulation – otherwise it would not make any sense.

This "making sense" is precisely what I'm interested in. According to these researchers, female sexuality doesn't *make sense* unless it is in the service of reproduction. There is no scientific defense offered for this assumption. A similar assumption is also present in the evolutionary explanations offered for female orgasm.

I have examined thirteen stories for the evolution of human female orgasm, and all except one of these stories assume that orgasm is an evolutionary adaptation. That is, they assume that orgasm conferred a *direct selective* advantage on its possessors, and that is how it came to be prevalent among women. The most common general formula for explaining the evolution of human female orgasm is through the pair-bond. Here, the pair-bond means more-or-less monogamous heterosexual coupling, and it is argued that such coupling increases the potential reproductive success of both parties through mutual cooperation and assistance with rearing offspring. The idea is that the male and the female in the pair bond provide mutual support to one another, and assist each other in rearing offspring, and that offspring raised under these conditions will tend themselves to have higher survival and reproductive success than those raised under other circumstances.

Hence, pair-bonding is seen as an adaptation in the evolutionary sense – it exists *because* it confers better chances of surviving and reproducing to those who display the trait. Under the assumption that pair-bonds are adaptive, frequent intercourse is also seen as adaptive, since it helps "cement the pair bond". And this is where orgasm comes in. Orgasm evolved, according to these pair-bond theorists, because it gave the female a reward and motivation to engage in frequent intercourse, which is itself adaptive, because it helps cement the pair bond.

A number of different theorists have developed permutations of this basic story, but it remains the most widely accepted evolutionary story for female orgasm.[12]

Now, there is a glaring problem with this story – It assumes that intercourse is reliably connected to orgasm in females. All of the available clinical studies on women's sexual response indicate that this is a problematic assumption. Somewhere between 20 and 35% of women always or almost always experience orgasm with unassisted intercourse.[13] I should add that this figure is supported by what cross-cultural information exists.[14] This figure is very low, and it is especially striking given that somewhere around 90% of women do experience orgasm. Furthermore, about 30% of women *never* have orgasm with intercourse – this figure is taken from a population of women who do have regular intercourse, and of whom almost all are orgasmic.[15] What this means is that *not* to have orgasm from intercourse is the experience of the majority of women the majority of the time. Not to put too fine a point on it, if orgasm is an adaptation which is a reward for engaging in frequent intercourse, it does not seem to work very well.

Obviously, this observation does not rule out the possibility that there is some selective advantage to female orgasm, but the salient point is that *none of these pair bond theorists even address this problem*, which I call the orgasm-intercourse discrepancy. Rather they simply assume that when intercourse occurs, so does orgasm.[16]

In general, the association of intercourse with orgasm is relatively unproblematic among males. Hence, what is being assumed here is that female sexual response is like male sexual response to the same situation. There is little or no awareness, among the pair-bond theorists, of the orgasm-intercourse discrepancy, in spite of the fact that they cite or refer to the very studies which document this fact, including Kinsey's 1953 report on women's sexual response.

There is one obvious and understandable reason for this slip. They are, after all, trying to explain orgasm through evolutionary theory, which involves showing that the trait gave a reproductive advantage to its owner. It's easy to see how the equation of reproduction through intercourse and orgasm went by unnoticed. Nevertheless, this case does illustrate the main thesis, that female sexuality is unquestioningly equated with reproduction, and with the sort of sex that leads to reproduction.

There is another intriguing line of argument for the adaptive value of female orgasm, which was first published by Desmond Morris in 1967, though Shirley Strum tells me that Sherwood Washburn was teaching this in his classes at Berkeley earlier. Morris claimed that orgasm had a special function related to bipedalism (that is, walking on our hind legs), because it would increase chances of fertilization. Here again we have the direct link between female sexuality and reproduction.

> It does this in a rather special way that applies only to our own peculiar species. To understand this, we must look back at our primate relatives. When a female monkey has been inseminated by a male, she can wander away without any fear of losing the seminal fluid that now lies in the innermost part of her vaginal tract. She walks on all fours. The angle of her vaginal passage is still more or less horizontal. If a female of our own species were so unmoved by the experience of copulation that she too was likely to get up and wander off immediately afterwards, the situation would be different, for she walks bipedally and the angle of her vaginal passage during normal locomotion is almost vertical. Under the simple influence of gravity the seminal fluid would flow back down the vaginal tract and much of it would be lost. There is therefore... a great advantage in any reaction that tends to keep the female horizontal when the male ejaculates and stops copulation. The violent response of female orgasm, leaving the female sexually satiated and exhausted, has precisely this effect.[17]

Morris' view is in turn based on his understanding of physiological response – he says earlier... "after both partners have experienced orgasm [in intercourse] there normally follows a considerable period of exhaustion, relaxation, rest and frequently sleep."[18] Similarly, he claims, "once the climax has been reached, all the [physiological] changes noted are rapidly reversed and the resting, post-sexual individual quickly returns to the normal quiescent physiological state."[19]

Now let us refer to the clinical sex literature, which is cited by Morris and by others. According to this literature, the tendencies to states of sleepiness and exhaustion following orgasm, are, in fact, true for men but not for women. Regarding Morris's claim that the physiological changes are "rapidly reversed", this is also true for men but not for women – women return to the plateau phase of sexual excitement, and not to the original unexcited phase, as men do. This was one of the most noted conclusions of Masters and Johnson, whose picture of sexual response was enthusiastically adopted by Morris – but, it seems, only in part.[20]

In fact, Masters and Johnson publicized an interesting and important difference between men's and women's sexuality, and that is the capacity of many women to have more than one orgasm without a significant break. Forty-seven percent of the women in Hite's survey did not feel that a single orgasm was always satisfying to them, and many women wanted more, some as many as 15–25. If, at this point, you are concerned about Hite's bad reputation as a statistician and researcher, I'd like to point out that many of Hite's findings in that first study, published as the Hite report, were consistent with Kinsey's figures, and the Kinsey reports are considered, to this day, and in spite of any problems they might have, to be the best general studies ever done on the topic of women's sexuality.[21] Masters and Johnson contrast the ability of many women to have five or six orgasms within a matter of minutes with the adult male's usual inability to have more than one orgasm in a short period.[22] This female ability is linked to the fact that, following orgasm, women do not return to the pre-aroused state, as men do, but instead to the plateau phase of excitement.

Hence, Morris's story is in trouble. He claims that the physiological changes are rapidly reversed for women as well as for men. He also neglects the sizable percentage of women who are not satisfied by a single orgasm. Given the documented tendency in men to sleep and exhaustion following a single orgasm, it's not at all clear that a female desire to have orgasm wouldn't have exactly the opposite effect from that described by Morris – perhaps the woman would jump right up and cruise for a little more action at precisely the time when the sperm are most likely to leak out.

Actually, another serious problem with this story was recently pointed out by Shirley Strum, an expert on baboon behavior.[23] Supposedly, the selection pressure shaping female sexual response here is the potential loss of sperm that is threatened because human beings walk on two legs, and because the vaginal position is thus changed from horizontal to almost vertical. One would think, then, that our relatives walking on four legs would be protected against this occurrence, for anatomical reasons. But Strum says that immediately following intercourse, female baboons like to go off and *sit down* for ten or fifteen minutes. When they get up, she says, they inevitably leave a visible puddle of semen on the ground. Perhaps, then, the loss of semen is not the serious evolutionary challenge that Desmond Morris and others take it to be.

Summary

I claim that social agendas appear in these stories through the obliteration of any female sexual response that is independent from her function as a reproducer. Autonomous, distinct female sexual response just disappears.

In these explanations women are presumed to have orgasms nearly always with intercourse, as men do. Women are presumed to return to the resting state following orgasm, as men do. One could object that Morris is a relatively easy target, so I will offer the following tidbit in defense of my analysis. Gordon Gallup and Susan Suarez published, in 1983, a technical discussion on optimal reproductive strategies for bipedalism, and took up Morris' anti-gravity line of argument. They argue that orgasm would be adaptive because it would keep the woman lying down, and hence keep the semen from escaping. In the context of these paragraphs on female orgasm, they state, "it is widely acknowledged that intercourse frequently acts as a mild sedative. The average individual requires about five minutes of repose before returning to a normal state after orgasm."[24] The scientific reference they offer for this particular generalization is Kinsey 1948, which is, in fact, exclusively on *male* sexual response. In other words, this "average individual" which figures in their story about female orgasm, is, in fact, explicitly male.

An Alternative Explanation

Donald Symons, in his book *The Evolution of Human Sexuality* (1979), argues that female orgasm is not an adaptation. He develops a story parallel to the one about male nipples – female orgasm exists because orgasm is strongly selected in males, and because of their common embryological form, women are born with the potential for having orgasms, too.[25] Part of the story, then, is that orgasm is strongly selected in males; this is fairly plausible, since it is difficult for male mammals to reproduce without ejaculation, which requires a reflex response in certain muscles. These muscles are, in fact, the same (homologous) muscles that are involved in female orgasm. It is also significant that the intervals between contractions in orgasm is 4/5 of a second in both men and women. This is considered evidence that orgasm is a reflex with the same developmental origin in both sexes.

One of the consequences of Symons' theory is that it would be expected that similar stimulation of the clitoris and penis would be required to achieve the same reaction or reflex response. This similarity shows especially in the figures on masturbation. Only 1.5% of women masturbate by vaginal entry, which provides stimulation similar to the act of intercourse; the rest do so by direct or indirect stimulation of the clitoris itself.[26] Also, on the developmental theory, one would *not* expect similar reactions to intercourse, given the differences in stimulation of the homologous organs.

Finally, this theory is also supported by the evidence of orgasm in non-human primates. The observed orgasms occur almost exclusively when the female monkeys are themselves mounting other monkeys, and not during copulation. On the non-adaptive view of orgasm, this is almost to be expected. There, female orgasm is defined as a potential, which, if the female gets the right sort and amount of stimulation, is activated. Hence, it is not at all surprising that this does not occur often during copulation, which in these monkeys includes very little, if any, stimulation of the clitoris, but occurs rather with analogous stimulation of the homologous organs that they get in mounting.

Symons' proposal, which I found very powerful and plausible, has been sharply criticized by a number of feminists. For instance, a leading feminist sociobiologist, Sarah Blaffer Hrdy, claims that this non-adaptive explanation is dismissive of female sexuality.[27] Similarly, Mina Caulfield accuses Symons of denying the "significance of female pleasure."[28]

I view these criticisms as misguided, because they are based on the assumption that *only* adaptive explanations can provide for the significance of a trait. But why should we believe this? Musical and singing ability are not adaptations, but they are very important to human culture and human life. One must have adopted the idea, not merely that "what is natural is good", but further, that "only what is adaptive is good." The evolutionarily derivative role of female orgasm implies absolutely nothing about its importance unless you are a committed adaptationist. Finally, I wonder why these feminists are so eager to get orgasm defined as an adaptation – several of the serious evidential problems with evolutionary explanations about female orgasm arose, I have argued, from making an easy connection between sexuality and reproduction.

I would like to just mention a possible alternative interpretation. The conclusion that orgasm is not an adaptation *could* be interpreted as emancipatory. After all, the message here is that orgasm is a freebie. It can be used in any way that people want; there is no "natural" restriction on female sexual activities, nor is there any scientific ground for such a notion. Under the developmental view, the constraints are loosened on possible explanations about women's sexuality that are consistent with accepted clinical conclusions and with evolutionary theory. Hence, the realm formerly belonging exclusively to reproductive drive would now be open to much, much more.

Discussion

I would like to draw two conclusions.

First, I believe that prior assumptions have more influence in these areas of science than is commonly acknowledged in the usual philosophical and scientific pictures of scientific theorizing and testing. In the cases examined here, science is not very separate from the social and cultural context. Rather, social assumptions and prior commitments of the scientists play a major role in the practice of science itself, at many levels – experimental design, data collection, predictions, hypothesis formulation, and the evaluation of explanations.

To understand this area of scientific practice, we need a view of science that is more sophisticated, one that has more moving parts, than the pictures typically presented by philosophers of science. Under the usual approaches, science is seen as involving relations purely between theory and data, or between theory, data, and explainer. But this is not enough. We need a way to recognize and analyze the vital role of pre-theoretical beliefs and categories in *all* stages of scientific research.

One might object that the subject matter of this part of science makes social influence inevitable, and that one would not expect this same level of cultural bias in other scientific contexts. That's probably right. But we do not need to show social forces at work in every possible case of scientific inquiry in order to insist on having a theory of science with enough flexibility to work in many areas. The cases I have presented here are definitely "science", with plenty of funding, backing, authority, influence, and prestige. Philosophers who insist on a *pure* view of science, based on isolated and idealized examples of physics, are voting themselves out of the action. There are very interesting and important things going on in other areas as well, as the cases I have outlined above attest. Developing a view of science which can account for these other fields is vital.

My suggestion does *not* involve commitment to a relativist position. In a complete analysis of evolutionary explanations of human sexuality, I would adopt Helen Longino's general approach, in which she characterizes objectivity in science as resulting from the critical interaction of different groups and individuals with different social and cultural assumptions and different stakes. Under this view, the irreducibility of the social components of the scientific situation is accounted for – these social assumptions are, in fact, an essential part of the picture of scientific practice.

At any rate, I take it that the cases I have described above violate our common philosophical understandings of how we arrive at scientific beliefs, how knowledge is created, and how science works. If philosophers go the route of labeling as "science" *only* that which obeys the demands of current philosophy, we will end up discussing only some parts of physics and maybe some math. Meanwhile, what about the rest of science – biology, social sciences, anthropology, psychology, biochemistry? I suggest adopting and developing recent contextualist and feminist views of science, which take explicit account of pre-theoretical assumptions and preconceptions, and their social origins.

This case involving female sexuality is very interesting because there are *two* very strong forces working to put sex and reproduction together. Adaptationism, within biology, promotes the easy linking of all sexual activity with reproduction success, the measure of relative fitness. Secondly, the long social tradition of *defining* women in terms of their sexual and reproductive functions alone also tends to link sexuality and reproduction more tightly than the evidence indicates.

The long struggle by various women's movements to separate sex and reproduction seems to have had very little effect on the practice of the science we have examined in this chapter. This is especially ironic, because politically, ever since the late Nineteenth Century, scientific views about gender differences and the biology of women have been the single most powerful political tool against the women's movements. My second and more controversial conclusion is that current "purist" philosophy of science actually *contributes to* that political power by reinforcing myths of the insulation of scientific endeavors from social influences. A more sophisticated understanding of the production and evaluation of scientific knowledge would mean seeing science as (partly) a continuation of politics. Science would then lose at least *some* independent authority in the political arena. Judging by the scientific work that I have discussed in this chapter, I think that would be a good thing.

Notes

1 Kano, T. (1982) "The social group of Pygmy Chimpanzees of Wamba," *Primates* 23(2), 171–88.
2 Hafez, E. S. E. (1971) "Reproductive cycles," in *Comparative Reproduction of Non-human Primates*, ed. E. S. E. Hafez. Springfield, IL: Charles C. Thomas.
3 Wolfe, L. (1979) "Behavioral patterns of estrous females of the Arachiyama West troop of Japanese Macaques (*Macaca fuscata*)," *Primates* 20(4), 525-34.
4 Koruda, S. (1980) "Social behavior of the Pygmy Chimpanzees," *Primates* 21(2), 181–97. Quote from p. 189.
5 Kano, T. (1980) "Special behavior of wild Pygmy Chimpanzees (*Pan paniscus*) of Wambe: A preliminary report," *Journal of Human Evolution* 9, 243–60. Quote from p. 243.
6 Mori, A. (1984) "An ethological study of Pygmy Chimpanzees in Wambe Zaire: A comparison with Chimpanzees," *Primates* 25(3), 255–78.
7 Chevalier-Skolnikoff, S. (1974) "Male-female, female-female, and male-male sexual behavior in the Stumptail Monkey, with special attention to the female orgasm," *Archives of Sexual Behavior* 3(2), 95–116; (1976) "Homosexual behavior in a laboratory group of Stumptail monkeys (*Macaca arctoides*): Forms, contexts, and possible social functions," *Archives of Sexual Behavior* 5(6), 511–27.
8 Goldfoot, D., J. Westerborg-van Loon, W. Groeneveld, and A. Koos Slob (1980) "Behavioral and physiological evidence of sexual climax in the female

stump-tailed macaque (*Macaca arctoides*)," *Science* 208, 1477–9.

9 The identity of this researcher is not included for publication. The information stated here was obtained through personal communication.

10 Kinsey, A. C. *et al.* (1953) *Sexual Behavior in the Human Female*. Philadelphia: W. B. Saunders.

11 Singer, I. and J. Singer (1972) "Periodicity of sexual desire in relation to time of ovulation in women," *Journal of Biosocial Science* 4, 471–81.

12 Morris' work has been criticized by later researchers as being methodologically flawed (e.g., Wilson (1975) *Sociobiology*, Harvard UP; Crook (1972) "Sexual selection, dimorphism, and social organization in the primates," in *Sexual Selection and the Descent of Man*, ed. B. Campbell. Chicago: Aldine) but it is still widely cited, and its basic premises are accepted or slightly modified in other respected accounts such as: F. Beach (1973) "Human sexuality and evolution," in *Advances in Behavioral Biology*, eds. Wm. Montanga and Wm. Sadler. NY: Plenum Press, pp. 333–65; G. Pugh (1977) *Biological Origins of Human Values*, NY: Basic Books; Crook (1972); and B. Campbell (1967) *Human Evolution: An Introduction to Man's Adaptations*. Chicago: Aldine.

13 Hite, S. (1976) The Hite Report, NY: Macmillan; Kinsey, A. *et al. Sexual Behavior in the Human Female*.

14 See, for example Davenport, W. (1977) "Sex in cross-cultural perspective," in *Human Sexuality in Four Perspectives*, ed. F. Beach. Johns Hopkins U. Press, pp. 115–63.

15 Hite, S. The Hite Report.

16 Typically, in evolutionary explanations, if a trait is taken to have evolved as an adaptation, yet is rarely used in the adaptive context, some explanation of the details of the selection pressure or the extreme adaptive value of the trait is offered.

17 Morris, D. (1967) *The Naked Ape*. London: Jonathan Cape, p. 79.

18 Ibid., p. 55.

19 Ibid., p. 59.

20 Masters, W. H. and V. Johnson (1966) *Human Sexual Response*. Boston: Little, Brown.

21 Kinsey (1953, pp. 375–6); Hite (1976, p. 417); Masters and Johnson (1966, p. 65).

22 Masters, W. H. and V. Johnson (1961) "Orgasm, anatomy of the female," in *Encyclopedia of Sexual Behavior*, Vol. II, eds. A. Ellis and A. Abar-banal. New York: Hawthorn, p. 792.

23 Personal communication.

24 Gallup and Suarez (1983) "Optimal reproductive strategies for bipedalism," *Journal of Human Evolution* 12, 195.

25 This argument is spelled out in more detail by Stephen Jay Gould, in an essay that was based on my research and arguments ("Freudian Slip," *Natural History*, Feb. 1987, pp. 14–21).

26 Kinsey, 1953; Hite (1976), pp. 410–11.

27 Hrdy, S. B. (1981) *The Woman That Never Evolved*. Cambridge, MA: Harvard University Press, p. 165.

28 Caulfield, M. D. (1985) "Sexuality in human evolution: What is 'natural' in sex?" *Feminist Studies* 11(2), 343–63.

11

Natures and Norms

Louise M. Antony

Most feminists today are suspicious of any appeal to the notion of "human nature" in normative or political theory. This partly reflects the influence of postmodernism among feminist theorists: postmodernists reject foundationalism in general and are specifically critical of theories involving the universalistic category "humanity." But there is another, more prosaic explanation for this concern, and that is the fact that appeals to nature have been used historically, and continue to be used, to rationalize and justify the perpetuation of oppressive gender roles. Sometimes the theme is deterministic: there are things that we women cannot do because of our natures (govern, for example), as well as things that must be tolerated in men because of theirs (cheating on their wives, fighting in wars). At other times the appeal is to a sort of self-interest: given our natures, we will be unhappy, or unfulfilled, or simply "unfeminine" if we pursue certain goals or engage in certain activities. Often these two types of argument are combined, for a sort of lawyerly defense of gender roles: don't try to do X – in the first place, you can't do it, and in the second place, if you do it, you'll be sorry.

Consider, for example, a recent offering from syndicated columnist George Will, praising a new book by Danielle Crittenden, *What Our Mothers Didn't Tell Us: Why Happiness Eludes the Modern Woman*. Crittenden, according to Will, "says that feminism's androgyny project fails for an *intractable* reason: it is unnatural" (my emphasis). Laying on the determinism, he continues: "Today's feminism manifests liberalism's utopian streak, its aspiration to rid life of necessity. Feminism's grand dream is to escape the bonds of anatomy and refute the idea that biology is, in any sense, destiny."[1] But what exactly is the "necessity" that we feminists try vainly to eliminate? What is the "destiny" to which our anatomy "binds" us? Well, the "destiny" that Crittenden and Will seem to have in mind is for women to become stay-at-home mothers. To which the obvious objection is that this can't literally be destiny for all women, since many women – manifestly – have not taken this course. But here's where we change tack: indeed, many women have abjured the natural course, says Crittenden, says Will – that's why they're all so unhappy: "Crittenden sides with the anthropologist Lionel Tiger, who says, dryly, that if biology is not destiny, it certainly is 'good statistical probability.' Ignoring probability brings punishment. Feminism, having established that women are human, forgot that they are women, with distinctive desires, the ignoring of which causes unhappiness." Having established the general point, Will spins out the specific consequences for women: "Women who ignore the wisdom that 'we can have it all – but we

Louise M. Antony, "Natures and Norms," pp. 8–36 from *Ethics* 111(1), 2000. Reprinted by permission of the University of Chicago Press and the author.

cannot have it all at once' comprise a 'secret agony society.' Weary women trying to 'balance briefcase and baby' are failing to convince themselves that 'quality time' is a substitute for lots of time. They go to work to escape domestic worries, but instead are consumed by them."[2] So while our natures don't quite tell us what we have to do, they do tell us what we have to do to be happy.

It is hardly surprising, given the ubiquity and resilience of arguments of this sort, that many feminists see the whole idea of fixed "natures" as threatening – insisting, sometimes to the point of absurdity, on the malleability and contingency of all human characteristics.[3] But it does not serve feminist purposes well for us to embrace a dogmatic social constructivism. The question whether there is anything like human nature is, at least in large part, an empirical issue and is not one that can be settled either by a priori reasoning or by legislation. Failure to acknowledge this opens us to the charge of Lysenkoism and plays into pernicious stereotypes of feminists as dangerous loonies, zealots advocating "politically correct" views at the expense of science and common sense. We see the popular resonance of these stereotypes in Will's rhetoric: by invoking them, he is able to portray Crittenden (and, by association, himself), as a daring freethinker, a bold visionary able to cast off the blinders feminism has imposed on all the rest of us: "This indicates just how out of joint the times are: Human nature is startling news. Asserting that there is a human nature has become a radical political act, which today's feminists stigmatize as reactionary. This troubles Danielle Crittenden not at all."[4] Startling? Radical? The fact that biological determinism has never been without powerful champions troubles George Will not at all.

But the problem I've been speaking of is not simply rhetorical: the tactical rejection of the view that human beings have natures simply concedes too much to feminism's opponents. We need not agree – and should not give the appearance of agreeing – that the possibility of realizing feminist goals depends on there being nothing about us that is, in any sense, "true by nature," for in one perfectly good sense of the phrase, there's a great deal about us that falls into this category, and it would be a sad thing indeed if feminism required us to deny it. I believe that the fear that any concession to nativism can and will be used against us largely explains the unfortunate bias of many feminist and progressive theorists toward radically empiricist, social constructivist views of language and the mind, and their correlative hostility toward nativist accounts of the sort proposed by Noam Chomsky in linguistics and by many in cognitive psychology. The result, in my opinion, is a truly unfortunate disjunction between empirically well-grounded work in cognitive science and feminist discussions of language and the mind.[5] There's a particular irony in feminists claiming that nativist cognitive theory is expressive of a patriarchal point of view, and that is that many, if not most, of the leading theorists in developmental psychology who are pushing nativist accounts are women: Lila Gleitman, Susan Carey Elissa Newport, Barbara Landau, Elizabeth Spelke, Rochel Gelman, and Karen Wynn, to name but a few. Indeed, I'd venture to say that developmental psychology is the only branch of science dominated by women.

So, I would argue, there is no incompatibility between feminism and nativism, properly understood. But I used to go further. In an earlier essay, I argued not only that feminists had no reason to reject the notion of human nature but that they had strong positive reason to embrace it.[6] The notion of human nature could, I thought, provide a needed grounding for feminist critiques of the subordination of women. My reasoning was this: in order to explain what is wrong with patriarchy and to put forward our positive vision of equitable and sustaining human relationships, we need to affirm our humanity. We need, that is, to be able to assert two things: first, that we are essentially beings of a certain kind, and second, that there are modes of treatment that are appropriate, and others that are inappropriate, for beings of this kind. If we have no essential nature as human beings, how are we to understand the complaint that certain kinds of treatment are "dehumanizing"?

Something very like this line of reasoning is present in the recent work of Martha Nussbaum, who appeals to what she calls "Aristotelian Essentialism" as the grounding for her "capabilities approach" to human rights and social justice.[7] The capabilities approach proposes to assess the justice of a given society by assessing the degree to which its members are in possession of a variety of capacities for human functioning together with the opportunities for exercising and developing these capacities. Aristotelian essentialism is invoked in the generation of the list of these capabilities, by providing "an account of the most important functions of the human being, in terms of which human life is defined. The idea is that once we identify a group of especially important functions in human life, we are then in a position to ask what social and political institutions are doing about them. Are they giving people what they need in order to be capable of functioning in all these human ways? And are they making it possible for citizens to function *well?*" (HF p. 214). Nussbaum thus promotes the idea that we can somehow find within our common human nature the outlines of a good human life, a life that counts as a flourishing one for creatures of our kind.

I have recently come to the conclusion, however, that there is no plausible notion of human nature that can do quite this sort of normative work. This is not to say that Nussbaum is wrong to emphasize the enormous degree to which all human experience is conditioned by the same complement of biological and psychological characteristics. As will become clear, I think that the existence of such commonalities still has deep significance for ethics and politics. My current point is rather this: the fact – if it is one – that such human universals as exist are due to our *nature* as human beings is itself of no ethical importance.

To explain, I'll need to back up and look more closely at the argumentative strategies that I said have made many feminists wary of the very notion of a "nature."[8] All arguments of this type involve a premise that asserts that the possession (or lack) of some property is due to the "nature" of the individual involved:

> N: So-and-so possesses/lacks property *by nature*.

But the arguments differ in the way they move from this premise to their respective conclusions. "Deterministic" arguments (as I'll call them) are meant to show the outright impossibility of some course of action or state of being, while "paternalistic" arguments are meant to show something like its undesirability or inappropriateness. To obtain these conclusions, each argument must supplement N with an appropriate "linking" premise. Deterministic arguments must add a modal premise:

> D: What's true by nature *cannot* be changed.

And paternalistic arguments need a normative premise:

> P: What's true by nature is *good for you*.

But in order for the arguments to be valid, the notion of "nature" appealed to in N must be the same as the notion appealed to in D or P. This turns out to be the stumbling block. "Nature" is many-ways ambiguous. And while it is relatively easy to find senses of nature that make N true for various properties, and possible to find senses that make D or P true, it turns out to be mightily difficult to find a single notion of nature that makes N and D or N and P true together.

For example, one common meaning of "natural" is "independent of human agency." In this sense, it is uncontroversial that some people are nearsighted "by nature"; that is, without human intervention, these people would not be able to see very clearly or very far away. But if we plug this sense of nature into either premise D or premise P we get patent falsehoods, as the case of nearsightedness shows. Poor eyesight is hardly irremediable, and there is certainly no reason to regard it as desirable.

These examples do not show conclusively that there can be no good arguments from nature, but they do point to serious internal tensions plaguing arguments of these types. The trick in constructing a rhetorically effective argument from nature is to make premise N appear uncontroversial – to make what's "true by nature" seem a matter of simple observation or an uncontroversial finding from a neutral science – while at the same time preserving the modal or normative import that the term "nature" frequently carries. But these two goals are at cross purposes. The most plausible instances of N will use a notion of "nature" that is modally and normatively flat: notions like "independent of human agency" or "statistically normal," or even "part of our genetic endowment" (much more on this below). But the more purely descriptive the notion of nature – and hence the less controversial the resulting premise N – the less likely that the linking premises D or P will come out true without equivocation.

There is also a pragmatic peculiarity that afflicts arguments of both these types, pointed out over two centuries ago by John Stuart Mill. In both cases, the truth of the conclusion seems to obviate the argument itself. Take first the deterministic argument: as Mill notes, if something cannot be done, it is pointless to enjoin against its being attempted: "The anxiety of mankind to interfere in behalf of nature, for fear lest nature should not succeed in effecting its purpose, is an altogether unnecessary solicitude. What women by nature cannot do, it is quite superfluous to forbid them from doing."[9] Similarly, if one finds a particular social role or mode of life desirable, then one hardly needs to be argued into adopting it: "If women have a greater natural inclination for some things than for others, there is no need of laws of social inculcation to make the majority of them do the former in preference to the latter."[10] Mill finds these points so obvious that he indulges in some dark speculation as to the real motives of those who would enlist nature in these ways: "They might be supposed to think that the alleged natural vocation of women was of all things the most repugnant to their nature; insomuch that if they are free to do anything else – if any other means of living, or occupation of their time and faculties, is open, which has any chance of appearing desirable to them – there will not be enough of them who will be willing to accept the condition said to be natural to them."[11]

This all applies quite generally to arguments from nature. It applies, as should be obvious, to the Will-Crittenden brief summarized above, but it applies with equal force to progressive attempts to enlist the notion of human nature in the grounding of egalitarian philosophies. And herein lies the sad moral of my tale: there is no way of understanding "natures" that will disarm the pernicious appeals without simultaneously invalidating the liberatory ones. In particular, Nussbaum's appeal to human nature, her "Aristotelian Essentialism," can't work. Despite its far greater subtlety, her argument suffers the same liabilities as Will and Crittenden's: they stand or fall together.

1 Externalist and Internalist Appeals to Human Nature

I said above that arguments from nature tend to be plagued by internal tensions – that premise N needed a modally and normatively neutral sense of nature, while premises D and P needed a sense that retained modal or normative implications – and that this is no less true for arguments that appeal to "natures" to ground progressive political programs than it is for their evil twins. We can put the dilemma in different terms, terms that Nussbaum herself supplies.

In a discussion of Bernard Williams's writing on human nature, Nussbaum distinguishes "external" accounts of human nature from "internal" accounts. An external account, the sort of account that Williams attributes to Aristotle, treats facts about what is essentially human as "matters of natural scientific fact, not of ethical value." Such facts, it is imagined, can be ascertained "from the totally external standpoint of a neutral observer," an observer, that is, who has no knowledge of nor any commitment to human practices or values. It follows, on this conception, that the details of the account will "not be based (or not primarily or solely based) upon... ordinary beliefs and conceptions" and also that such details will be "uncontroversial in a way that ethical questions usually are not. Although the answers to such questions may be difficult to discover, the fact that they are matters for scientific inquiry means that they can, in principle, be settled in a more satisfyingly decisive way than questions of ethical value judgment" (HN p. 88). An external account of human nature will thus have the rhetorically attractive features of verifiability and objectivity. Beyond that, however, an external account might appear to offer real help to ethical theory. Because such an account provides a set of "fixed points" about what human beings are like – a set of facts neither relative to individual human interests nor subject to human choice or decision – it promises to (in Nussbaum's words) "effectively rule out certain ethical alternatives, and perhaps also give positive support for certain others" (HN p. 88). It could tell us what can and cannot be done to various kinds of beings by providing "hard, value-neutral constraints against 'atrocity'" (HN p. 88).

In contrast, Nussbaum tells us, an internal account of human nature makes no pretense of abjuring appeal to values. It constructs its account of what is essential to a human being by drawing explicitly on the norms and values embodied in human practices, using human beings' own judgments about what makes their lives "human" to sort human characteristics into the essential and the accidental. As Nussbaum explains in an earlier chapter,

> Such an account would say: take away properties X, Y, and Z (a suntan, let us say, or a knowledge of Chinese, or an income of $40,000 a year) and we will still have what we count as a human being on our hands. On the other hand, take away properties A, B, and C (the ability to think about the future, say, or the ability to respond to the claims of others, or the ability to choose and act) and we no longer have a human life at all. Separating these groups of properties requires an evaluative inquiry: for we must ask, which things are so important that we will not count a life as a human life without them? Such an evaluative inquiry into what is deepest and

> most indispensable in our lives need not presuppose an external metaphysical foundation, clearly: it can be a way of looking at ourselves, asking what we really think about ourselves and what holds our history together. (HF pp. 207–8)

Now it might be thought that an account of human nature based on what we human beings value most about ourselves is really just a different kind of external account – that instead of consulting science to see what the deep explanatory structure of the species *Homo sapiens* is, we might instead consult the pollsters to see what consensus we can achieve on the question, "What about yourself do you think is most important?" But I'm sure that this is not what Nussbaum has in mind. The upshot of such a sociological survey would yield purely descriptive information; it would carry no normative implications. Instead, I think that Nussbaum thinks it essential that the author of such a genuinely internal account of human nature not be a neutral observer of human society. The author must know human life "from the inside."

The point of Nussbaum's emphasis on the internal perspective is, in this context at least, to encourage us to interpret the claim that this or that aspect of human life is part of our nature as being as much an expression of the theorist's own self-conception as a description of how other human beings conceive themselves. This is how the internal account is meant to achieve its normativity, I think: for me to claim that, for example, practical reason is part of human nature is tantamount to my endorsing the evaluative judgment that the ability to consider reasons and to act in accordance with them is essential to a life worth living for beings like myself.

With this distinction between external and internal accounts of human nature, then, I can put my challenge this way: appeals to external accounts of human nature can be expected to garner interpersonal agreement that's independent of normative judgments but, for that very reason, will not be able to generate reasons for accepting ethical propositions about what human beings should or should not do. Appeals to internal accounts can generate ethical conclusions, but the crucial premise about human nature will only be acceptable to someone who antecedently endorses the value judgments embodied therein, rendering the appeal itself otiose.

Nussbaum, it turns out, agrees with the first part of my diagnosis but not the second. In discussing Williams's criticisms of external accounts, focusing on attempts to generate ethical conclusions from descriptive evolutionary accounts of human behavior, she finds Williams's worries decisive: the considerations Williams raises against sociobiology "cast doubt not only on some particular projects of giving ethics a scientific foundation, but on the whole idea that ethics could be meaningfully and convincingly grounded on an account given from the external perspective" (HN p. 90). Nonetheless, she thinks she can offer Williams – and, by implication, the rest of us who have championed externalist arguments – some reassurance: although we are right that externalist accounts will always be, just because of their externality, disconnected from ethics, we are wrong to think, therefore, that the project of grounding substantive ethical theory in an account of human nature is hopeless: "The external account, as Williams characterizes it, is neither necessary nor sufficient for providing ethics with a foundation" (HN p. 90). Nussbaum, in other words, wants to embrace the second horn of the dilemma I drew above: she thinks she can get an internalist account of human nature to do the work that an externalist account initially promised but cannot deliver.

To evaluate this suggestion of Nussbaum's, we'll need to look in much more detail both at the work that she thinks an internal account of human nature can and must do and at the specifics of the account she has to offer. I will argue that Nussbaum's account does not work; she appears to evade the dilemma only because she slides back and forth between external and internal accounts, depending on the work to be done or the dangers to be avoided. Before making my case in detail, though, let me digress briefly to say something about two kinds of "external" accounts of human nature that I think are plausibly available to us.

The first of these concerns what I'll call a "scientific nature." On this model, which derives from Locke's notion of a "real essence," a nature is an underlying (and possibly hidden) structure that plays a central role in the explanation of the thing's more superficial and manifest properties. Kripke and Putnam have argued persuasively that members of natural kinds have "natures" in this sense: the atomic number of elements and the molecular structure of chemical compounds, for example, serve to explain the distinctive profile of properties and dispositions of things of these kinds. I've argued elsewhere that genotype is a plausible candidate for being the "scientific essence" of a biological organism, since the organism's genes provide the categorical grounding for the hierarchy of dispositions that characterizes that particular organism.[12] This is not to endorse what's often called "biological determinism" – the doctrine that some phenotypic property or properties are fixed by an organism's genes. As every first-year biology student knows, an organism's set of observable features – its phenotype – is not determined by genotype alone but, rather, is the causal product of a particular genotype operating in a particular environment. What the genotype determines is only a very complex function from environmental circumstances to phenotypic properties – what's called in biology a "norm of reaction."[13]

There are two consequences of this view of the scientific natures of biological organisms that are worth noting in this context. First, on this view it will never be strictly correct to say that any phenotypic property is part of an organism's nature. This in itself is enough to refute most of the pernicious appeals to human nature, which typically involve a confusion between the disposition to display a certain property in certain circumstances, which may be fixed by the genotype, and the actual display of that property, which can never be attributed entirely to the genotype. This is not to say that we can make no sense out of claims that some phenotypic property is "genetic" or "innate." It frequently happens that the genetic mechanisms that underlie and direct the development of some physical organ or structure are relatively insensitive to variation in most environmental variables or at least to the variation present in (statistically) normal environments. This is what is meant – or what one ought to mean – in saying, for example, that it's part of a horse's nature to have four legs.

In the case of human phenotypic traits, we tend to be particularly interested in contrasting those traits whose development is systematically sensitive to variation in our cognitive or social environments with those traits whose development is not. Whether a person acquires the phenotypic property of playing a musical instrument or knowing the rules of chess depends crucially on whether the person has certain specific types of experience; whether a person comes to engage in what Aristotle would call "practical reasoning" is not so dependent. But this is not to say that human cognitive capacities are completely determined by our genes, independently of all experience. Thus, when Noam Chomsky says that the capacity to acquire language is part of our genetic endowment, as he frequently does, he is not saying that every human being will inevitably speak; he is perfectly aware that a certain amount of exposure to normal human speech within the first decade and a half of life is literally essential to normal linguistic development. (The "critical period" for language acquisition, after all, is part of his theory, and not of his non-nativist rivals.) Rather, Chomsky should be understood to be saying (*a*) that the development of language in humans is not dependent on the particular kinds and patterns of environmental contingencies that alternative accounts of language acquisition (e.g., behaviorism) have held to be causally necessary and (*b*) that the acquired competence is, at an interesting level of abstraction, the same across synchronic and diachronic variation in human belief systems and social organization, just as are the rough outlines of human physical development.

The second consequence of my view to which I'd like to call attention is that, for complex biological organisms, individual natures become logically and explanatorily prior to the natures of kinds. It's certainly true that there are many reliable regularities in the phenotypes of individuals grouped together as members of the same species. And there are also systematic differences between members of different species. Genetic similarity and variation, in these cases, explain the observed patterns. So it is not mere accident that (almost all) horses have four legs, whereas (almost all) human beings have two, nor that (almost all) human beings acquire a language by the time they are five years old, whereas no horses ever do. But this does not mean that there is anything like an ideal or even a typical genetic type that could serve to define equinity or humanity.[14] If there is any sense to be made of the notion of "the human genome," it must be done by generalizing over or abstracting from the genotypes of individuals antecedently identified as human.

But in that case, what does govern the identification of individuals as human? This question brings us to the second sort of external account of "natures" available to us, what I'll call "definitional natures." Natures in this sense are the necessary and sufficient conditions for being a thing of a certain kind. If Kripke and Putnam are right, then definitional natures coincide with scientific natures for some kinds of things. But there are many kinds of things that do not have scientific natures at all, and yet it is still the case that we can say what it is to be things of those types. The most persuasive examples I can offer are artifact kinds and socially constructed kinds. To be a knitting needle to have a certain characteristic shape, to have been constructed with a certain function in mind, to be able to perform a certain function, or some combination of these things; to be a US citizen is to satisfy conditions laid out explicitly in the US Constitution; to be a friend is to satisfy conditions implicitly defined through human social practices. If my arguments above are correct, then biological species do not themselves have scientific essences (though their members do) but have, instead, functional or historical essences, like artifacts. Indeed, they would be artifacts of a certain kind – groupings produced by human scientific interest in robust empirical regularities.

It's important to realize that, despite the fact that definitional natures are created, either explicitly or implicitly, by human practices and conventions, once these practices and conventions are in place, it is a perfectly objective matter what the definitional natures are. Furthermore, since human practices are not necessarily transparent, even to those who engage in them, it may take empirical investigation to find out what a definitional nature is. Finally, definitional natures need not have anything to do with values or norms – it's one thing to discover what the conditions of US citizenship are and quite another to decide if you think it's a good or a bad thing that they are as they are. For all these reasons, I think an account of the definitional nature of the kind "human being" should be classified as an external account, according to the criteria Nussbaum gives in her discussion of Williams.

It's also important to note that definitional natures can generate only *de dicto* necessities and not *de re* necessities. The conventions of English may determine that, as a matter of necessity, every mother is the parent of a child; that is, linguistic conventions ensure that if someone is a mother, then that person is the parent of a child. But it will not follow from this that any given person who is a mother had to have been the parent of a child; this will only be true if it's necessary for that person to have been a mother, and that's a matter that human conventions cannot determine. Another way of putting this: it may be part of the nature of being a mother to be the parent of a child; that doesn't entail that it's part of my nature to be the parent of a child, even if it happens to be true that I am a mother. Thus, the question of whether it is part of my individual nature to be a human being, a material object, a woman, a philosopher, or anything else is not a question that can be settled by appeal to the linguistic practices governing our use of the words "human being", "material object", and so on, even if those practices can settle the question of what it is to be a human being.

That raises the vexed question of what, if anything, does determine what constitutes the nature, in the definitional sense, of an individual. Philosophical tradition bids us settle the matter by thought experiment: what kinds of changes could I undergo and still be me? What properties could I have lacked and still have been me? By appeal to their own – generally referred to as "our" – intuitions, philosophers have defended a variety of conflicting claims about what is essential to a being like me: Descartes famously thinks it's only necessary that I be a thinking thing, while Kripke argues that I must have had the particular physical origin that I in fact had. Some feminist philosophers have argued that my gender is essential to me; others deny this.[15] Some philosophers think that my personhood is essential to me; I myself feel I can make sense of the possibility that (due, perhaps, to environmental contingencies that could have but fortunately did not obtain when I was an infant) I might have lacked the higher cognitive functions that I think are definitive of personhood.

Despite the lack of consistency in "results," however, the judgments elicited by these thought experiments are held to be, by those who engage in them, judgments of objective modal fact. And this is true whether these modal facts are taken to be "deep necessities" or, like definitional natures of kinds, the products of human convention. I mention this because as long as we defend claims about individual definitional essences by reference to these sorts of thought experiments, we are still in the realm of external accounts of the nature of individual human beings. There's another sort of thought experiment we can perform, however, that also tells us, in a sense, what we take to be essential to our existence, and that is to ask, instead of what changes I think I could not endure and still exist, what changes I think would make my life not worth living. A thought experiment of this sort – which, as we'll see, is the method Nussbaum endorses – cannot produce an external account of human nature, because it is an explicit appeal to my values.

Now let's turn to the matter of the inconsistency I find in Nussbaum's use of the notions of "internal" and "external" accounts. In her exegesis of

Williams, as we've seen, she makes the distinction between internal and external accounts essentially a matter of the distinction between the descriptive and the normative. Both my dilemma and Williams's concern internal and external accounts in this sense. But later in the essay on Williams, and in other work where she presents her positive "internalist" appeal to human nature, Nussbaum characterizes internal accounts in an importantly different way. Here's how the equivocation comes about.

In HF, Nussbaum surveys the objections that have been made to essentialist ethical theories (I'll present the full set of these objections below) and contends that many of these are really directed against a metaphysical view that is presumed to be a necessary part of any form of essentialism but which can in fact be separated from it. She explains that this metaphysical view, which she calls, following Putnam, "metaphysical realism," "claims that there is some determinate way that the world is apart from the interpretive workings of the cognitive faculties of living beings. A description of the world is true just in case it corresponds to that independently existing structure, false insofar as it does not so correspond" (HF p. 206). An essentialism that's backed by metaphysical realism will hold that "the way the human being essentially is will be a part of the independent furniture of the universe, something the gods can see and study independently of human life and human history" (HF p. 206). An essentialism of this sort, Nussbaum contends, is rightly criticized on the grounds that its metaphysical presuppositions are unacceptable, perhaps even incoherent: "If the only available (or perhaps even coherent) picture of reality is one in the derivation of which human interpretations play a part, if the only defensible conceptions of truth and knowledge hold truth and knowledge to be in certain ways dependent on human cognitive activity within history, then the hope for a pure unmediated account of our human essence as it is in itself, apart from history and interpretation, is no hope at all but a deep confusion" (HF p. 207). But one needn't be a metaphysical realist to be an essentialist, Nussbaum argues. One can be an internalist about human essences: "One might, that is, believe that the deepest examination of human history and human cognition *from within* still reveals a more or less determinate account of the human being, one that divides the essential from its accidental properties" (HF p. 207).

But there's independence from human cognitive activity and independence from human cognitive activity: the debate about metaphysical realism is, as Nussbaum is careful to note, a complex one, "involving technical issues in the philosophy of science and the philosophy of language" (HF p. 207). Specifically, the question is whether the fact that any thought or talk about extrahuman reality must employ human concepts and human terms means that we can sensibly conceive a reality that exists "prior to" or "independently of" the categorizations we impose on it. Partisans of metaphysical realism argue that stuff in the world is what it is, regardless of what we call it; opponents challenge the partisans to say what that way of being is. But the point here is that, whatever the upshot of this philosophical debate, it cannot turn out that there is no distinction to be made between matters that are up to human beings to determine (like what the rights of citizenship are or where we go to dinner) and matters that are quite out of our control (the age of the Earth, the amount of force exerted by a speeding car onto a concrete embankment). Such distinctions are, if you will, "internal," in the sense relevant to the metaphysical realism debate, to our descriptions of the world – they are part of the practice of human discourse, which recognizes the tininess of the region of space-time that human beings happen to occupy. (People do get confused about all this, of course. Here's a rule of thumb: if you find yourself saying that "it used to be true" that the Earth was flat, then you are not [as it were] getting the rules of our language game – either the rules involving "the Earth" and "flat," or the ones involving "true" and "used to be.")

So it shouldn't follow from a rejection of metaphysical realism that the distinction between that which is up to us and that which is not up to us completely collapses. The distinction may need to be characterized in some different way, some way that doesn't appeal to "unmediated" or "transcendent" reality, or perhaps should be relativized to a particular human language or to the human "conceptual scheme," but it must still be possible when all is said and done to assert truly that there were and would have been dinosaurs even if we had never evolved to name them "dinosaur", while there would not have been baseball players had we never evolved to invent the game of baseball. Neither should it follow from a rejection of metaphysical realism that the fact/value distinction collapses. If antirealism entails that there is no difference between saying "mothers do want to stay home with their kids" and "mothers ought to want to stay home with their kids," then so much the worse for antirealism. Once again, the issue should become a matter of how certain distinctions are to be explicated, not whether they can be drawn at all.

But in that case, if all the internalism of Nussbaum's account amounts to is a rejection of metaphysical realism, then her commitment to keeping her account internal won't preclude her from drawing elements of her account from conceptions of human nature that are externalist in the original, that is, nonnormative, sense to get her "fixed points" but then switching to a normative conception to generate the ethical conclusions. Then, too, her diagnosis of opposition to essentialist theories as misdirected opposition to metaphysical realism gives her a false sense of security about her vulnerability to the dilemma. As she herself makes clear, the apparent value of externalist accounts – in the original sense – derives from their independence from human values, not from their transcendental independence of all forms of human conceptualization. If Nussbaum's "internalism" is only the internalism of a committed antimetaphysical realist, then we have no assurance that the features of the account she offers that make it look attractive for foundationalist purposes are not the very features that will inevitably isolate it from the ethical principles and judgments of value it is supposed to ground.

I believe that this is exactly the case: the internalist account of human nature that Nussbaum finds in Aristotle, and which she offers to us as a replacement for the externalist account described by Williams, still falls prey to the dilemma. The more it invokes facts about human beings that are decidable independently of value judgments, the less the normative import; but the more normative material the account of human nature builds in, the less persuasive it becomes as a foundation for any particular ethical vision. That this latter point is true will be seen when we reflect on the similarities between the arguments Nussbaum offers and those of Crittenden and Will.

I turn, finally, to Nussbaum's account. Let's begin with the reasons why Nussbaum thinks an account of human nature is necessary at all and then consider whether her account is adequate by her own lights. She says, in general, that "I have said that we urgently need a version of essentialism in public life. If we reject it, we reject guidance that is crucial if we are to construct an adequate account of distributive justice to guide public policy in many areas" (HF p. 229). I can identify at least three areas where Nussbaum thinks we clearly need "guidance," and where she believes an account of human nature is what must provide it. Each of these areas provides the ground for one of the three main criticisms of essentialist theory that Nussbaum is concerned to address. So the adequacy of her internalist Aristotelian essentialism by her own lights is going to depend on whether the account of human nature it provides can do the work at hand while skirting the specific dangers endemic to each job.

2 A Substantive Theory of "Harm"

Perhaps the most important thing a theory of human nature can do, according to Nussbaum, is to tell us concretely and absolutely what kinds of treatment constitute damage to a human being. Here Nussbaum is concerned to oppose a particularly pernicious form of relativism, a form that parades as sensitivity and toleration but is really expressive of a kind of alienated indifference to what should be uncontroversially recognized as the mistreatment of fellow human beings. She refers, by way of illustration, to a presentation by a French anthropologist at an international conference, discussing the successful British campaign to eradicate smallpox in India. Because the campaign led to the demise of the cult of Sittala Devi, who had been thought to control the disease, the anthropologist thought that the campaign was a good example of Western insensitivity to difference. An audience member, an Indian, demurs: "Surely it is better to be healthy rather than ill, to live rather than die." Not necessarily at all, says the anthropologist; such preferences may simply be the result of a peculiarly Western way of conceiving the world (HF pp. 203–4). Nussbaum is appalled: is the anthropologist mad? It is as if one were to say, "Of course, I would find it insupportably awful to have painful, hemorrhaging sores covering my body, with premature death providing the only prospect of relief, but perhaps in other cultures, such things don't matter so much."[16]

What needs to be kept in focus, Nussbaum argues, is that we are all human beings. This entails that we are all subject to certain physical constraints and liabilities, whatever our historical and social location. If we forget this – if we persuade ourselves that difference is unbounded and unpredictable – then we lose our ability to recognize the suffering of others. I don't know if the following connection occurred to Nussbaum, but my mind was drawn immediately by her anthropologist case to the image of General

Westmoreland in the film *Hearts and Minds*, reassuring an American journalist that we didn't need to be too concerned about civilian casualties in Vietnam because "Asians just don't value life the same way we do."[17]

At the same time, though, Nussbaum acknowledges the legitimacy of the concern that the French anthropologist is raising, however inaptly in the particular case. The first of the three charges that "any good internalist account will need to answer" is thus the charge that essentialist theories neglect difference. As Nussbaum presents it, the complaint is this: "People... understand human life and humanness in widely different ways, and any attempt to produce a list of 'essential properties' is bound to enshrine certain understandings of the human and to demote others. Usually... this takes the form of enshrining the understanding of a dominant group at the expense of minority understandings" (HF p. 208). So what we must consider is whether Nussbaum's internalist essentialism can give her the tools she needs to block radical relativism about human harm and well-being, without committing her to an equally unjustified and pernicious chauvinism.

3 Justification of Normative Distinctions among People's Actual Preferences and Desires

Nussbaum wants to be able to do this because she is opposed – quite rightly, in my view – to bare utility-maximizing models of human flourishing and social justice, models that take no account of the ways in which oppressive conditions can shape desire and limit imagination. If we measure a society's success in providing for the well-being of its citizens purely by the levels of expressed satisfaction, we risk missing serious harms. Nussbaum illustrates the point with a case from India: "A poll of widowers and widows in India showed that the widowers were full of complaint about their health status; the widows, on the other hand, in most cases ranked their health status as 'good.' On the other hand, a medical examination showed that the widows were actually suffering far more than the males from diseases associated with nutritional deficiency. The point was that they had lived all their lives expecting that women will eat less, and the weakened health status produced in this way was second nature to them" (HF p. 230). A proper account of human nature, Nussbaum contends, will tell us that the widows' "satisfaction" was illusory, inauthentic, or otherwise inappropriate for human beings. By telling us what makes human life "human," such an account will tell us, inter alia, the amounts of nutrition a human being needs to engage in any of the projects characteristic of human life and, hence, what levels of nutrition one ought to expect. Anyone who is satisfied with less counts as an injured person.

I agree that any progressive political theory – feminism prominently included – is going to have to draw such distinctions and that it must say something in defense of the distinctions it draws. All such theories want an objective criterion of oppression; they want the injustice of a certain social arrangement to depend on something other than the subjective states of the individuals who are subject to the injustice, since it must be acknowledged that even severely oppressive conditions do not always produce subjective unhappiness. (And, of course, the converse is even more obviously true – it doesn't take oppression or injustice for one to be perfectly miserable.)[18] They all want to allow for the possibility, at least, of false consciousness – the condition wherein the oppressed internalize a theory that rationalizes and normalizes their own oppression – and to show that the creation of false consciousness is itself a form of injury. Feminists, in particular, do not want to have to deny that many women are, by any ordinary measure, perfectly happy within the gender roles prescribed for them by tradition or law. We do want to emphasize the extent and depth of the misery that sexism causes in the lives of many women. But we do not want to rest there. We want also to object to the ways in which patriarchal practices constrain women's goals and self-conceptions so that some options for being and living in the world are made, for women, practically unavailable and even unimaginable. This will require us to say something substantive about which kinds of options ought to be open to women and why.

But once again, there is lurking in the background a genuine concern: we ought not move too quickly to discount someone's stated preferences and values and should be suspicious of anyone who presumes to take over for some other individual the prerogative to define the individual's own life. Nussbaum calls this criticism the charge of "neglect of autonomy": "By determining in advance what elements of human life have most importance, the essentialist is failing to respect the right of people to choose a plan of life according to their own lights, determining what is most central and what is not" (HF p. 230). This charge must have resonance for any feminist, since it has been the position of most patriarchal authorities throughout history that women cannot be trusted to craft their own lives and values but must, for their own good, have these set for them by their superiors.

4 The Extent of our Normative Community

Here Nussbaum's idea is that an account of human nature which tells us which characteristics of human life are really essential to it can do extra duty by entailing that anyone who possesses these characteristics is human. Then, since the human nature we are considering is an avowedly normative notion, to conclude that someone is human is to conclude that that individual is part of our moral community and should be accorded appropriate respect.

Still and all, Nussbaum credits the worry that she calls the charge of "prejudicial application." The complaint is that to select any set of human properties or capacities and distinguish them as "essential" is to set the stage for denying precisely those properties or capacities to those people one wishes to keep subordinate. "If we operate with a determinate conception of the human being that is meant to have some normative moral and political weight, we must also, in applying it, ask which beings we take to fall under the concept. Here, the objector notes that all too easily the powerless can be excluded" (HF p. 209). This, again, is a charge that feminists must take especially seriously, for theorists of human nature historically have not constrained themselves to include women among the set of individuals whose "essential nature" is being described, and they quite sanguinely write of women's lacking the very properties they have just finished identifying as definitive of humanity.

So, finally, what is this internalist account of human nature, and how does Nussbaum get it? The details of the account are very easily given, a fact that belies the immense amount of research and reflection that clearly went into its construction. The account, as she offers it in HF, has two levels. The first is a list of factors common to all human lives, a list that includes, Nussbaum emphasizes, both capabilities and limitations. The list includes mortality, the fact of embodiment (together with the particular form of human embodiment, which itself generates a list of factors: the need for food and drink, the need for shelter, sexual desire, and the capacity for mobility), the capacity for pleasure and pain, various distinctive cognitive capabilities, prolonged neoteny, the capacity for and exercise of practical reason, the capacity and the desire for affiliation with other human beings, the fact of relatedness to other species and to nature, the capacity for humor and play, and the fact of separateness (HF pp. 216–20). These factors define, collectively, a "threshold of capability to function, beneath which a life will be so impoverished that it will not be human at all" (HF p. 220). The second level of the account itemizes the factors that define "a somewhat higher threshold, beneath which those characteristic functions are available in such a reduced way that although we may judge the form of life a human one, we will not think it a *good* human life" (HF p. 221). These factors basically spin out the consequences of recognizing the ubiquity of factors at the first level: insofar as mortality is an essential element of human life, so "being able to live to the end of a complete human life... not dying prematurely" is a level of function that is necessary for a good human life, a life that we would be satisfied to have (HF p. 222).

The methodology that produced this account is somewhat more difficult to explain, for while Nussbaum tells us that her internalist essentialism is Aristotelian, it is not the standard (or, at any rate, the most well-known) way of interpreting Aristotle's views on human nature. Nussbaum claims that the familiar passages in *Nicomachean Ethics* 1.7, where Aristotle presents his "human function" argument, are frequently misinterpreted so as to present Aristotle as attempting an externalist account of human nature, an account that will "move from natural fact to ethical value," but she argues that this is not Aristotle's aim at all. The difference between the two interpretations depends very largely on how we interpret Aristotle's method for finding the function of the human being. On both accounts, the argument begins the same way. Aristotle wants to know what constitutes happiness, or "flourishing" (*eudaimonia*), for a human being. He points out that, in general, if we can discover the distinctive functions of a kind of thing, we can answer the question what counts as "good" for a thing of that kind and so we can answer the question we want by discovering what, if anything, is the function of a human being. "For just as a flute-player, a sculptor, or any artist, and, in general, for all things that have a function or activity, the good and the 'well' is thought to reside in the function, so would it seem to be for man, if he has a function."[19] But now how do we go about discovering the function of a human being? On the received view, Aristotle recommends that we look for that activity or capacity that is distinctive of human beings, something which differentiates us from everything else. This differentiating capacity then turns out to be reason, and the function of human life is, accordingly, the exercise of reason. The good human life is, then, the life organized around reason, and a diminished or base human life is a life in which reason is damaged or ill-used.

Now this is clearly an externalist account of human nature in the original sense of "externalist," for the method it has Aristotle recommending for discovering the function of the human being is one that can be applied by any sufficiently careful observer – it simply involves learning what human beings can do that nothing else can do. We do not need to know anything about what any human being values in order to discover the essence of a human life. A reasonable extension of this method to human beings as we understand them today might even yield an account of either the scientific nature of an individual human being or the definitional nature of humankind. The externality of the account, in either case, would certify both the objectivity and the value neutrality of the properties on the list.

Nussbaum, however, contends that this is not the strategy Aristotle had in mind. In the first place, she argues, he never intended for us, in characterizing human function, to divorce the differentiating features of human life from all the other features that in fact make that life possible. "On this interpretation, 'the life of E-ing' means a life organized around E-ing, a life in which E-ing is the distinctive and guiding feature that gives the life its characteristic overall shape. On this reading, an E-*ike zoe* might well include G and H as well. What makes the life E-*ike* as opposed to G-*ike*, is that E is in some way its distinctive organizing principle; around E the other component activities are structured, or by E they are infused. G and H are done in an E-ish way, or according to E" (HF p. 113). The good for us, in that case, must involve more than just the exercise of reason, as if we might as well be disembodied spirits. It must involve all of our vital functions, presumed now to be all "infused" or "structured" by reason.

This much Nussbaum takes to show that Aristotle's conception of the human essence incorporates the whole of human existence, not just one isolated function. This will enable Nussbaum later to produce the rich list of human functions and common features that I reproduced above. But having shown this much, Nussbaum still wants to show that Aristotle's essentialism is internalist. To this end, she argues that the next step for Aristotle is to appeal to his audience's own sense of what's valuable about their own lives, rather than to the objective method of finding the differentia, to support the claim that a life without reason, a mindless or hedonistic life, would not be a truly human life. Aristotle, she says, makes this appeal by trying to show that the valuing of reason is implicit in all human activities, so that one who tried to deny the centrality of reason would stand convicted of a kind of pragmatic inconsistency: such a skeptic would betray his own commitment to the value of human reason simply by his engaging in almost any of the activities of routine human life, not to mention his willingness to enter into rational dispute. This means, then, that Aristotle does not depend on value-neutral, external facts to establish the nature of the good human life:

> The mindless life is not ruled out by external facts of nature; anthropomorphs [beings who resemble but are not really human beings] might lead it consistently, though most of Aristotle's opponents certainly do not lead it consistently with the rest of their values.... By participating at all in Aristotle's inquiry about *eudaimonia*, an inquiry that explicitly announces that its results will be drawn from the active practical reasoning of each participant, the interlocutor grants implicitly the importance of practical reasoning in a human life.... But still... the mindless life is not ruled out; what is established is the cost of the choice, and how deeply it is at odds with some of our firmest convictions concerning who we are. (HF p. 117)

At the same time, Aristotle appeals to our common judgment about how to regard others who reject what we deem so centrally valuable: "The argument establishes, furthermore, that an anthropomorph who does lead the mindless life will not be regarded by us as fully human" (HF p. 117).

Now I certainly am not going to presume to enter into rational disputation with Martha Nussbaum about Aristotle exegesis, so let's concede that she is right about what Aristotle is doing. What I want to point out is that the appeal to the audience's own values – the move that made the account internalist rather than externalist – completely obviates the reference to human nature. And this has two consequences for Nussbaum's view. First, it means that for those purposes that Nussbaum was looking to a theory of human nature to provide some kind of relatively "hard constraints," this internalist account is going to disappoint – we needed an external account for that. Second, it means that her argument for why we ought to value the human functions on her list and should expect our societies to facilitate their exercise is, on its face, just as question-begging as Crittenden and Will's. I'll defend these points in turn.

First, let's recall the purposes for which Nussbaum argued we needed some form of essentialism. The first was to set some kind of hard constraints on what counts as harm or damage to a human being. The pseudo-Aristotelian external account, as I said, looks reasonably promising on this count. After all, one and the same kind of treatment can count as damaging or as perfectly reasonable, depending on the kind of thing that's receiving it. Many things are destroyed by being banged on by a hammer, but banging on a nail doesn't count as damaging it – nails are meant to be banged on; that is the only way that they can perform their proper functions. So it seems sensible to see what it is that human beings are meant to do and then to count as damage anything which destroys or reduces a human being's capacity to do that.

This argument does not work, of course, because of its equivocation on the notions of "good" and "good for." A bomb is a good bomb if it explodes when and only when its owner wants it to – that much can be read off the bomb's distinctive function. But we reason fallaciously if we continue in either of two ways: if we say that that's a good bomb, good things are good, and, therefore, that's a good bomb; or if we say that keeping a bomb in a dry, good place preserves its capacity to fulfill its function, that is, explode, and, therefore, that keeping it in a cool, dark place is good for the bomb. The first equivocates between the syncategorematic use of "good" in the construction "good X," which means, roughly, "does what an X is supposed to do," and the categorical "good" which carries an overall evaluative price tag, often a moral one. I happen to think that whether a bomb is good or bad in the categorical sense depends entirely on the reason it's being deployed, and by this criterion, the vast majority of bombs are bad, and certainly no better, morally speaking, for performing their proper functions well. The second inference equivocates between, again, the syncategorematic "good" and the sense of good that means something like well-being: fiber is "good for" us to eat, meaning that fiber contributes to our well-being. To be the sort of thing that has a well-being to consider, an object must be some kind of conscious agent; there is, accordingly, nothing that is "good for" a bomb in this sense.

So we get the usual result. The externalist account can give us a plausible answer to questions about what, as a matter of fact, will be the consequences for a thing or a creature of this kind of doing X, Y, or Z, but it cannot tell us whether doing any of these things, even given those consequences, will be morally good, or good for the creature in question.

But what about the internalist account? The internalist account bids us answer the question, What counts as damage? by consulting our own and others' judgments about what we would find undesirable or intolerable, moreover, what kinds of things, if removed from our own lives, would render them significantly less worth living. And while the internalist account encourages us to express these judgments in terms of what is necessary to a human life, the fact that we are animals of this sort rather than another in fact puts no necessary constraints on the kinds of answers we can give.

Williams, I take it, wanted an account that could say something like this: an essential feature of the human animal is that certain things – fire, sharp edges, percussive blasts, or strong acid – produce pain, an inherently aversive experience, and, typically, damage, where damage can be cashed out in terms of the compromising of some evolutionarily determined function. Given that such liability to pain and damage is essential to human beings, the avoidance of pain is not just something we learn to do in particular cultures – it's built into us. It follows that everyone wants to avoid pain, and since everyone wants to avoid it, it is a prima facie bad thing to cause it to someone.

But here, too, the crucial work is being done by the premise that says that everyone wants to avoid pain – it is that fact, if it is one, that generates the moral imperative. And given that everyone wants to avoid pain, it doesn't matter much why everyone wants this. The fact that pain avoidance is instinctive, rather than acquired through acculturation, gives that disposition no special moral status. And on the other hand, the mere fact that some disinclination or dislike is socially induced does not give us moral leave to disregard it. Etiology is morally unimportant.

Does this mean that neither an internalist nor an externalist account can do the first job Nussbaum outlined? Well, yes. Neither kind of account can give us reason to regard some particular kind of treatment as morally wrong unless we antecedently grant a thoroughly normative premise about the value of the producing consequences of a given kind. And if we have that premise granted, we don't need anything else. Does that mean that accounts of nature have no role to play in combating the kind of relativism that would make us immobile in the face of patent human suffering? No. We can still use the normatively neutral facts provided by an externalist account; we can still use the strategy Nussbaum identifies as Aristotle's for securing agreement about issues of value. I'll explain what I mean by this presently. For now, let's move on to consider the second job Nussbaum wants her essentialism to do.

What can the internalist tell us about inauthentic desires or merely adaptive preferences? Can it give us grounds for saying that the widows' expressed satisfaction with the state of their health should not be taken completely at face value? The internalist will have no difficulty in securing my endorsement of the importance of a certain program of nutrition for leading the kind of life I consider to be a worthwhile one. But of course, that's not really the issue here. Remember that the challenge in constructing a substantive theory of human nature for the purpose of making normative distinctions among people's expressed desires was to avoid paternalistic or chauvinistic treatment of others and to respect other people's autonomy, their right to determine for themselves what makes their own lives worth living. Crittenden, after all, is making a kind of internalist appeal to me by her effusive proclamation that "the most animating aspect of motherhood" is that "we love our children more than anything else and want to be with them as much as we possibly can."[20] To which I say, what do you mean "we," Danielle? Crittenden is inviting me to endorse her conception of a life worth living for a mother, but in doing so, she gives me no reason to do so. Nor is she giving me or anyone else – except someone who agrees with her about the crucial issue already – any reason to think that there's anything wrong with the structure of preferences that I do have.

But what is the basis of our (mine and Nussbaum's anyway – I should let you, dear reader, speak for yourself) certainty that the widows who do not seem to mind being chronically undernourished are still being cheated – and cheated, in some sense, by their own lights? Here, once again, an externalist account in conjunction with a certain kind of internalist appeal can offer some help. The externalist account of human nature tells us mundane facts about how the human body is programmed to operate. This will enable us to determine various prerequisites for the functioning of various systems of the body. Now insofar as we can find anything that the widow does value that implicates one or more of these bodily systems, we have a point at which we might, with some justification, expect the widow's stated preferences to change. (This is, after all, a great deal of what is involved in education – not the changing of fundamental values so much as the clarification of the results and prerequisites for pursuing the values we do have.)

The externalist account, then, cannot generate for us the basis for making normative distinctions among values. But if such an account can be given at all – if it turns out that a good deal of the conditions of all human lives are set by facts about the kinds of creatures we are – then it can supply us with confidence that we can always find, with sufficient patience and humility, a point of entry for making an internalist appeal. Aristotle's bet – that the commonalities of human life mean that all such lives are apt to have implicated the same set of human functions – can bolster our confidence that some consensus on the question of what sort of human life has value can be achieved.

Things are looking up. But let's turn to the last job, which is perhaps both the most vital of the three and the trickiest, and that is the task of determining the extent of the moral community. Let's look first at how an externalist might have tried to approach this question. The idea would be that a scientific account of human nature would reveal a set of deep and explanatory properties shared by all human beings, in virtue of being members of the same species. Since these properties would include properties that grounded the possession of a number of morally important properties, like the ability to communicate and affiliate with other members of the species or the ability to reason, we could conclude that membership in the moral community coincides with membership in the species *Homo sapiens*. In a sense, we would be demonstrating a convergence between the explanatory nature of a biological kind and the definitional nature of a socially constructed kind.

But of course, once more, the externalist account is not going to be able to deliver just what it promises. In the first place, it's quite clear that we need the explicitly normative judgment about what properties are morally valuable in order to derive anything about the normative community from natural facts about human commonalities. Indeed, the convergence depends entirely on our defining the ethical kind, "person," in the right way. Just as the critics warned, there is serious danger of prejudicial application of this term: if we put the wrong properties on this list – that is, if we select properties that turn out not to be common to all human beings – then we will not get the desired result.

Nussbaum, however, thinks that her internalist account can do better. Once again, she proposes to invoke the strategy she attributes to Aristotle – if I try to exclude some fellow human being from my moral community, confront me with this person in a situation in which we must interact as people and then convict me in my own behavior of recognizing the humanness of the other. Nussbaum cites the research of Raul Hilberg on the behavior of Nazi functionaries toward Jews in support of the effectiveness of this strategy: "He argues that whenever circumstances arose that made it possible [*sic* – should surely be 'impossible'] to sustain this denial [that Jews were not human], what ensued was an emotional 'breakthrough.'...[These were] times, above all, when it became impossible to avoid the fact that one was interacting with a Jewish prisoner in a human manner: occasions of personal conversation or emotional connection that eluded the watchful protective mechanisms of denial" (HF p. 226). Because the salient humanness of these interactions stems from our common constitutions, concerns, and – at the relevant level of abstraction – circumstances, Nussbaum argues that the notion of "humanity" provides certain kinds of safeguards against prejudicial application that are not provided, or not provided as well by more purely normative notions like "person":

> Any moral conception may be withheld, out of ambition or hatred or shame. But the conception of the human being seems so much more difficult to withhold than other conceptions that have been put forward as the basis for ethical obligation. The notion of the "person," for example, has sometimes been preferred to the notion of the human being as a basis for ethics, on the grounds that it is clearly a normative conception.... I have argued that the conception of the human being is itself, in a certain way, a normative conception, in that it involves singling out certain functions as more basic than others.... On the other hand, we have far less flexibility in the application of the concept than we do with "person." (HF pp. 226–7)

Nussbaum goes on to explain that the content of the notion "person," because it is a purely normative construction, does not seem to be constrained by anything other than common custom or legal precedent, whereas application of the term "human being" is governed by functional criteria like the abilities to sense, to communicate, to form attachments to other human beings, and so on; such functions cannot plausibly be denied to people on the basis of whim or prejudice.

But Nussbaum is here being very slippery about what kind of concept of humanity provides advantages in this regard over a purely normative conception. As I pointed out above, the external account needs the normative notion "person" in order to obtain any normative consequences about the extent of the moral community. And this notion has just the kind of ungroundedness and lability that Nussbaum finds dangerous. But how is Nussbaum's internalist conception an improvement? It is normative, which means that its content is not fully determined by nonnormative facts about human beings. Nonetheless, Nussbaum thinks that the notion's being linked to a biological category gives some purchase.

But this is a mistake. Nussbaum presupposes a link between the category constructed by asking me what I value most deeply about my life and the biological category that will classify me together with many others whether I want to be so classified or not. But it is the link itself that needs explaining. Nussbaum has the internalist press her interlocutor with the question, "What makes your life a *human* life, a life worth living for a *human* being?" But the question could just as well be, "What makes your life important to you, what makes it a life worth living for someone like you?" As the term "humanity" functions in the context of an internalist theory, it is either an empty honorific, used to indicate especially important or valuable aspects of our lives as we see it, or it's not. If it's an empty honorific, then the question is harmless, but the answer will in no way connect me to others with whom I happen to be biologically related. If the term is meant instead in its nonnormative, biological sense, then I might rightly bridle at the question, for it presupposes that my answer will cite things that are common to all human beings, and I may happen to think that different kinds of lives are appropriate or desirable for different kinds of human beings.

Again, we can see the difficulty more clearly if we compare the analogous conception of flourishing that seems implicit in Crittenden and Will's argument. Quoting Crittenden, Will asserts that "men and women, by the very nature of their biology, have different and often opposing sexual agendas." This means, in their view, that women should not try to lead the same kinds of lives as men but should instead "'develop an appreciation for the mutual, if differing, contributions we make to marriage as man and woman,' and for the different compromises arising from sexual differences, especially compromises involving careers."[21] For Crittenden and Will, the existence of human commonalities is neither here nor there; in their view, the right question to ask is not, "What about your life makes it a truly human life?" but, rather, "What about your life makes it a truly feminine, or a truly masculine life?"

Actually, the Crittenden and Will argument makes vivid the consequences for normative theory of one aspect of the account of natures that I mentioned above, and that is the problem about the relative ontological priority of individuals and species. I said that, on the (externalist) account of natures that I offered, a species essence can be no more than a generalization over the genotypes of individual members of the species. But of course, the character of the generalization will be a function of the individuals chosen to generalize over. There will be nothing in nature that says that we must classify male humans together with female humans, black humans with white humans, or English-speaking humans with Swahili-speaking humans – nothing, that is, beyond the fact that some groupings will enable us to capture many more useful generalizations than will others. There is, furthermore, no natural level of abstraction at which to cease generalizing. We could stop well before the level of species; we could go on much further. (And of course, many animal-rights advocates argue that an ethical theory that stops at the level of theory is "speciesist.") Again, all nature can tell us is where we'll get the generalizations – the rest is up to us.

What this means, too, is that there is no "natural" sortal in terms of which I am in any way constrained to identify myself. Because nature does not tell us which groupings we ought to concern ourselves with, it won't divide properties for us into "essential" and "accidental." This, too, appears to be very largely up to us. Is my sex essential to me or accidental? If I feel that it's essential, does that mean that my moral community ought to be drawn differently than if I think that it isn't?

So Nussbaum's internalist conception of humanity is either just the externalist conception in disguise, in which case its presence simply begs the crucial normative question, or it's genuinely internal, in which case it provides no constraints at all on its application.

Where does this all leave us? Actually, we (would-be liberals) are not as badly off as it may appear. Neither the externalist accounts Nussbaum criticizes nor the internalist account she promotes can do quite the work we wanted from a theory of human nature. But as I suggested above, we can still deploy both sorts of accounts in useful ways. The externalist account can tell us two kinds of things that will be relevant to ethical thinking: the first is that we can indeed expect lots and lots of similarity among human beings. And insofar as we determine that the really valuable things (however we manage to do this) are properties connected to the sorts of capacities Nussbaum lists in the "Thick Vague Conception," we can have confidence that nearly all of our conspecifics (by purely biological criteria) will possess them. Second, it might also tell us that, given the way our embodiment works, we are extremely apt to have a variety of fundamental wants and needs in common. We are all going to find that pain hurts; although many of us, on many occasions, will choose to endure pain for the sake of something more valuable than the mere absence of discomfort, it will be overwhelmingly likely that other things equal, we'd rather not have the pain. Knowing that much, we can learn to look for that more valuable thing in situations in which some human being is clearly suffering and, in so inquiring, perhaps conceive a way for that person to preserve the value without having to endure the pain.

From the internalist account we get a guide for the process of ethical engagement. The strategy that Nussbaum finds in Aristotle (I have to confess at this point that I'm inclined to give Nussbaum more credit for this than she gives herself) is a strategy that bids us always find a basis, for any value that we recommend to another, in that other person's own current commitments and values. It also requires that we engage with others as members of a moral community. The question, "What do we value?" must be asked, not with the imperiousness of the person who knows, on the basis of his or her own answer, the answer that you too ought to accept but, rather, with a sense of identification and a presumption of common purpose.

The facts provided by the externalist account and the strategy provided by the internalist account work together. It is a great good thing that each one of us complicated, intelligent, striving, discouraged, hopeful, hurting, and celebrating creatures has so much in common with all the others. Moral community might not be impossible without powerful resemblances to facilitate our knowing and identifying with each other, but it would be vastly more difficult. The very happy fact is that our commonalities make it – if not easy, at least something well within our grasp – to figure out what we ought to do with respect to each other. All that's left is to do it.

Notes

1 George Will, "Marry Young and Have Youngsters Pronto," *Raleigh News and Observer* (February 5, 1999).

2 Both quotes from Will.

3 See Barbara Ehrenreich and Janet McIntosh, "The New Creationism: Biology under Attack," *Nation* (June 9, 1997), pp. 11–16.

4 Will.

5 See, for example, Andrea Nye's scurrilous, shockingly inaccurate, and altogether gratuitous attack on analytic philosophy of language and philosophy of mind, "Semantics in a New Key," in *Philosophy in a Feminist Voice*, ed. Janet Kourany (Princeton, NJ: Princeton University Press, 1998), pp. 263–95; see also Elizabeth Potter's empirically uninformed discussion of private language and language learning in her "Gender and Epistemic Negotiation," in *Feminist Epistemologies*, ed. Linda Alcoff and Elizabeth Potter (New York: Routledge, 1993), pp. 161–86. In her monograph, *What's Within: Nativism Reconsidered* (New York: Oxford University Press, 1999), philosopher Fiona Cowie tries to convict Chomskian nativism about language acquisition of guilt by association with crude biological determinist prejudices, asserting that such disturbing trends as "the growing obsession here and abroad with racial, national and sexual differences" and "the newly fashionable backlash against attempts to enforce ideals of equality and civil rights" all "find a fertile seeding ground in the New Nativism" (p. x). This is utter nonsense and an attempt on Cowie's part, I suspect, to enlist her reader's presumably liberal sympathies against a theory with which she has philosophical disagreements. I also see this dynamic at work in Naomi Scheman's essay, "Individualism and the Objects of Psychology," in *Discovering Reality*, ed. Sandra Harding and Merrill Hintikka (Dordrecht: Reidel, 1983), pp. 225–44. I reply to Scheman in "Is Psychological Individualism a Piece of Ideology?" *Hypatia* ("Special Issue on Analytical Feminism," ed. Ann Cudd and Virginia Klenk) 10 (1995): 157–74.

6 Louise Antony, "'Human Nature' and Its Role in Feminist Theory," in Kourany, ed., pp. 63–91.

7 I will focus on just two representative works: Martha Nussbaum, "Aristotle on Human Nature and the Foundations of Ethics," in *World, Mind, and Ethics: Essays on the Ethical Philosophy of Bernard Williams*, ed. J. E. J. Althan and Ross Harrison (Cambridge: Cambridge University Press, 1995), pp. 86–131 (hereafter cited as "HN"), and "Human Functioning and Social Justice: In Defense of Aristotelian Essentialism," *Political Theory* 20 (1992): 202–46 (hereafter cited as "HF").

8 For a more extensive discussion of these and other types of arguments from nature, see John Stuart Mill, *The Subjection of Women*, excerpted in *Philosophy and Women*, ed. Sharon Bishop and Marjorie Weinzweig (Belmont, Calif.: Wadsworth, 1979), pp. 52–9; Joyce Trebilcot, "Sex Roles: The Argument from Nature," in *Philosophy of Woman*, ed. Mary Mahowald (Indianapolis: Hackett, 1994), pp. 349–56; and Christine Pierce, "Natural Law Language and Women," in Mahowald, ed., pp. 357–68.

9 Mill, p. 55.

10 Ibid.

11 Ibid.

12 See, for example, Saul Kripke, "Identity and Necessity," in *Naming, Necessity, and Natural Kinds*, ed. Stephen P. Schwartz (Ithaca, New York: Cornell University Press, 1977); Hilary Putnam, "Is Semantics Possible?" in Schwartz, ed. Antony, "'Human Nature' and Its Role in Feminist Theory."

13 See Richard Lewontin, "The Analysis of Variance and the Analysis of Causes," in *The I.Q. Controversy*, ed. Ned Block and Gerald Dworkin (New York: Pantheon, 1976), pp. 179–93.

14 The fact that even the most ubiquitous species characteristic could fail to be expressed in some as-yet-unrealized environment, together with the fact that wide ranges of variation in certain traits are present within all complex species, show the folly and, perhaps, the confusion inherent in the idea of a genetic ideal form. For discussion, see Richard Lewontin, "The Dream of the Human Genome," in

his *Biology as Ideology: The Doctrine of DNA* (New York: HarperCollins, 1991), pp. 59–83; and Philip Kitcher, "Essence and Perfection," *Ethics* 110 (1999): 59–83. Thanks to John Deigh for calling the Kitcher article to my attention.

15 See Iris Young, "Humanism, Gynocentrism, and Feminist Politics," in her *Throwing like a Girl and Other Essays* (Bloomington: Indiana University Press, 1990).

16 To get a vivid idea of what the rigors of smallpox actually are, together with the amount of suffering the disease has visited on human populations, I refer the reader to Nicolau Barquet and Pere Domingo, "Smallpox: The Triumph over the Most Terrible of the Ministers of Death," *Annals of Internal Medicine* 127 (October 1997): 635–42. Also available on the internet at http://www.acponline.org/journals/annals/15oct97/smallpox.htm.

17 *Hearts and Minds*, mm, 112 min., BBS Productions, 1974.

18 See Marilyn Frye's discussion of this point in "Oppression," in her *The Politics of Reality* (Freedom, Calif.: Crossing, 1983).

19 Aristotle, *Nicomachean Ethics* 1.7, excerpted in Leslie Stevenson, ed., *The Study of Human Nature* (New York: Oxford University Press, 1981), p. 71.

20 See Will, quoting Danielle Crittenden, *What Our Mothers Didn't Tell Us: Why Happiness Eludes the Modern Woman* (New York: Simon & Schuster, 1999).

21 Will.

12

Subjects of Sex/Gender/Desire

Judith Butler

One is not born a woman, but rather becomes one.

Simone de Beauvoir

Strictly speaking, "women" cannot be said to exist.

Julia Kristeva

Woman does not have a sex.

Luce Irigaray

The deployment of sexuality... established this notion of sex.

Michel Foucault

The category of sex is the political category that founds society as heterosexual.

Monique Wittig

I "Women" as the Subject of Feminism

For the most part, feminist theory has assumed that there is some existing identity, understood through the category of women, who not only initiates feminist interests and goals within discourse, but constitutes the subject for whom political representation is pursued. But *politics* and *representation* are controversial terms. On the one hand, *representation* serves as the operative term within a political process that seeks to extend visibility and legitimacy to women as political subjects; on the other hand, representation is the normative function of a language which is said either to reveal or to distort what is assumed to be true about the category of women. For feminist theory, the development of a language that fully or adequately represents women has seemed necessary to foster the political visibility of women. This has seemed obviously important considering the pervasive cultural condition in which women's lives were either misrepresented or not represented at all.

Recently, this prevailing conception of the relation between feminist theory and politics has come under challenge from within feminist discourse. The very subject of women is no longer understood in stable or abiding terms. There is a great deal of material that not only questions the viability of "the subject" as the ultimate candidate for representation or, indeed, liberation, but there is very little agreement after all on what it is that constitutes, or ought to constitute, the category of women. The domains of political and linguistic "representation" set out in advance the criterion by which subjects themselves

Judith Butler, "Subject of Sex/Gender/Desire," pp. 3–14, 18–22, and 193–7 (notes) from *Gender Trouble*, 2nd edn. New York: Routledge, 1999. Reproduced by permission of Routledge/Taylor & Francis Books, Inc. and the author.

are formed, with the result that representation is extended only to what can be acknowledged as a subject. In other words, the qualifications for being a subject must first be met before representation can be extended.

Foucault points out that juridical systems of power *produce* the subjects they subsequently come to represent.[1] Juridical notions of power appear to regulate political life in purely negative terms – that is, through the limitation, prohibition, regulation, control, and even "protection" of individuals related to that political structure through the contingent and retractable operation of choice. But the subjects regulated by such structures are, by virtue of being subjected to them, formed, defined, and reproduced in accordance with the requirements of those structures. If this analysis is right, then the juridical formation of language and politics that represents women as "the subject" of feminism is itself a discursive formation and effect of a given version of representational politics. And the feminist subject turns out to be discursively constituted by the very political system that is supposed to facilitate its emancipation. This becomes politically problematic if that system can be shown to produce gendered subjects along a differential axis of domination or to produce subjects who are presumed to be masculine. In such cases, an uncritical appeal to such a system for the emancipation of "women" will be clearly self-defeating.

The question of "the subject" is crucial for politics, and for feminist politics in particular, because juridical subjects are invariably produced through certain exclusionary practices that do not "show" once the juridical structure of politics has been established. In other words, the political construction of the subject proceeds with certain legitimating and exclusionary aims, and these political operations are effectively concealed and naturalized by a political analysis that takes juridical structures as their foundation. Juridical power inevitably "produces" what it claims merely to represent; hence, politics must be concerned with this dual function of power: the juridical and the productive. In effect, the law produces and then conceals the notion of "a subject before the law"[2] in order to invoke that discursive formation as a naturalized foundational premise that subsequently legitimates that law's own regulatory hegemony. It is not enough to inquire into how women might become more fully represented in language and politics. Feminist critique ought also to understand how the category of "women," the subject of feminism, is produced and restrained by the very structures of power through which emancipation is sought.

Indeed, the question of women as the subject of feminism raises the possibility that there may not be a subject who stands "before" the law, awaiting representation in or by the law. Perhaps the subject, as well as the invocation of a temporal "before," is constituted by the law as the fictive foundation of its own claim to legitimacy. The prevailing assumption of the ontological integrity of the subject before the law might be understood as the contemporary trace of the state of nature hypothesis, that foundationalist fable constitutive of the juridical structures of classical liberalism. The performative invocation of a nonhistorical "before" becomes the foundational premise that guarantees a presocial ontology of persons who freely consent to be governed and, thereby, constitute the legitimacy of the social contract.

Apart from the foundationalist fictions that support the notion of the subject, however, there is the political problem that feminism encounters in the assumption that the term *women* denotes a common identity. Rather than a stable signifier that commands the assent of those whom it purports to describe and represent, *women*, even in the plural, has become a troublesome term, a site of contest, a cause for anxiety. As Denise Riley's title suggests, *Am I That Name?* is a question produced by the very possibility of the name's multiple significations.[3] If one "is" a woman, that is surely not all one is; the term fails to be exhaustive, not because a pregendered "person" transcends the specific paraphernalia of its gender, but because gender is not always constituted coherently or consistently in different historical contexts, and because gender intersects with racial, class, ethnic, sexual, and regional modalities of discursively constituted identities. As a result, it becomes impossible to separate out "gender" from the political and cultural intersections in which it is invariably produced and maintained.

The political assumption that there must be a universal basis for feminism, one which must be found in an identity assumed to exist cross-culturally, often accompanies the notion that the oppression of women has some singular form discernible in the universal or hegemonic structure of patriarchy or masculine domination. The notion of a universal patriarchy has been widely criticized in recent years for its failure to account for the workings of gender oppression in the concrete cultural contexts in which it exists. Where those various contexts have been consulted within such theories, it has been to find "examples" or "illustrations" of a universal principle that is assumed from the start. That form of feminist theorizing has come under criticism for its efforts to colonize and appropriate non-Western cultures to support highly Western notions of oppression, but because they tend as well to construct a "Third World" or even an "Orient" in which gender oppression is subtly explained as symptomatic of an essential, non-Western barbarism. The urgency of feminism to establish a universal status for patriarchy in order to strengthen the appearance of feminism's own claims to be representative has occasionally motivated the shortcut to a categorial or fictive universality of the structure of domination, held to produce women's common subjugated experience.

Although the claim of universal patriarchy no longer enjoys the kind of credibility it once did, the notion of a generally shared conception of "women," the corollary to that framework, has been much more difficult to displace. Certainly, there have been plenty of debates: Is there some commonality among "women" that preexists their oppression, or do "women" have a bond by virtue of their oppression alone? Is there a specificity to women's cultures that is independent of their subordination by hegemonic, masculinist cultures? Are the specificity and integrity of women's cultural or linguistic practices always specified against and, hence, within the terms of some more dominant cultural formation? If there is a region of the "specifically feminine," one that is both differentiated from the masculine as such and recognizable in its difference by an unmarked and, hence, presumed universality of "women"? The masculine/feminine binary constitutes not only the exclusive framework in which that specificity can be recognized, but in every other way the "specificity" of the feminine is once again fully decontextualized and separated off analytically and politically from the constitution of class, race, ethnicity, and other axes of power relations that both constitute "identity" and make the singular notion of identity a misnomer.[4]

My suggestion is that the presumed universality and unity of the subject of feminism is effectively undermined by the constraints of the representational discourse in which it functions. Indeed, the premature insistence on a stable subject of feminism, understood as a seamless category of women, inevitably generates multiple refusals to accept the category. These domains of exclusion reveal the coercive and regulatory consequences of that construction, even when the construction has been elaborated for emancipatory purposes. Indeed, the fragmentation within feminism and the paradoxical opposition to feminism from "women" whom feminism claims to represent suggest the necessary limits of identity politics. The suggestion that feminism can seek wider representation for a subject that it itself constructs has the ironic consequence that feminist goals risk failure by refusing to take account of the constitutive powers of their own representational claims. This problem is not ameliorated through an appeal to the category of women for merely "strategic" purposes, for strategies always have meanings that exceed the purposes for which they are intended. In this case, exclusion itself might qualify as such an unintended yet consequential meaning. By conforming to a requirement of representational politics that feminism articulate a stable subject, feminism thus opens itself to charges of gross misrepresentation.

Obviously, the political task is not to refuse representational politics – as if we could. The juridical structures of language and politics constitute the contemporary field of power; hence, there is no position outside this field, but only a critical genealogy of its own legitimating practices. As such, the critical point of departure is *the historical present*, as Marx put it. And the task is to formulate within this constituted frame a critique of the categories of identity that contemporary juridical structures engender, naturalize, and immobilize.

Perhaps there is an opportunity at this juncture of cultural politics, a period that some would call "postfeminist," to reflect from within a feminist perspective on the injunction to construct a subject of feminism. Within feminist political practice, a radical rethinking of the ontological constructions of identity appears to be necessary in order to formulate a representational politics that might revive feminism on other grounds. On the other hand, it may be time to entertain a radical critique that seeks to free feminist theory from the necessity of having to construct a single or abiding ground which is invariably contested by those identity positions or anti-identity positions that it invariably excludes. Do the exclusionary practices that ground feminist theory in a notion of "women" as subject paradoxically undercut feminist goals to extend its claims to "representation"?[5]

Perhaps the problem is even more serious. Is the construction of the category of women as a coherent and stable subject an unwitting regulation and reification of gender relations? And is not such a reification precisely contrary to feminist aims? To what extent does the category of women achieve stability and coherence only in the context of the heterosexual matrix? If a stable notion of gender no longer proves to be the foundational premise of feminist politics, perhaps a new sort of feminist politics is now desirable to contest the very reifications of gender and identity, one that will take the variable construction of identity as both a methodological and normative prerequisite, if not a political goal.

To trace the political operations that produce and conceal what qualifies as the juridical subject of feminism is precisely the task of *a feminist genealogy* of the category of women. In the course of this effort to question "women" as the subject of feminism, the unproblematic invocation of that category may prove to *preclude* the possibility of feminism as a representational politics. What sense does it make to extend representation to subjects who are constructed through the exclusion of those who fail to conform to unspoken normative requirements of the subject? What relations of domination and exclusion are inadvertently sustained when representation becomes the sole focus of politics? The identity of the feminist subject ought not to be the foundation of feminist politics, if the formation of the subject takes place within a field of power regularly buried through the assertion of that foundation. Perhaps, paradoxically, "representation" will be shown to make sense for feminism only when the subject of "women" is nowhere presumed.

II The Compulsory Order of Sex/Gender/Desire

Although the unproblematic unity of "women" is often invoked to construct a solidarity of identity, a split is introduced in the feminist subject by the distinction between sex and gender. Originally intended to dispute the biology-is-destiny formulation, the distinction between sex and gender serves the argument that whatever biological intractability sex appears to have, gender is culturally constructed: hence, gender is neither the causal result of sex nor as seemingly fixed as sex. The unity of the subject is thus already potentially contested by the distinction that permits of gender as a multiple interpretation of sex.[7]

If gender is the cultural meanings that the sexed body assumes, then a gender cannot be said to follow from a sex in any one way. Taken to its logical limit, the sex/gender distinction suggests a radical discontinuity between sexed bodies and culturally constructed genders. Assuming for the moment the stability of binary sex, it does not follow that the construction of "men" will accrue exclusively to the bodies of males or that "women" will interpret only female bodies. Further, even if the sexes appear to be unproblematically binary in their morphology and constitution (which will become a question), there is no reason to assume that genders ought also to remain as two.[8] The presumption of a binary gender system implicitly retains the belief in a mimetic relation of gender to sex whereby gender mirrors sex or is otherwise restricted by it. When the constructed status of gender is theorized as radically independent of sex, gender itself becomes a free-floating artifice, with the consequence that *man* and *masculine* might just as easily signify a female body as a male one, and *woman* and *feminine* a male body as easily as a female one.

This radical splitting of the gendered subject poses yet another set of problems. Can we refer to a "given" sex or a "given" gender without first inquiring into how sex and/or gender is given, through what means? And what is "sex" anyway? Is it natural, anatomical, chromosomal, or hormonal, and how is a feminist critic to assess the scientific discourses which purport to establish such "facts" for us?[9] Does sex have a history?[10] Does each sex have a different history, or histories? Is there a history of how the duality of sex was established, a genealogy that might expose the binary options as a variable construction? Are the ostensibly natural facts of sex discursively produced by various scientific discourses in the service of other political and social interests? If the immutable character of sex is contested, perhaps this construct called "sex" is as culturally constructed as gender; indeed, perhaps it was always already gender, with the consequence that the distinction between sex and gender turns out to be no distinction at all.[11]

It would make no sense, then, to define gender as the cultural interpretation of sex, if sex itself is a gendered category. Gender ought not to be conceived merely as the cultural inscription of meaning on a pregiven sex (a juridical conception); gender must also designate the very apparatus of production whereby the sexes themselves are established. As a result, gender is not to culture as sex is to nature; gender is also the discursive/cultural means by which "sexed nature" or "a natural sex" is produced and established as "prediscursive," prior to culture, a politically neutral surface *on which* culture acts. This construction of "sex" as the radically unconstructed will concern us again in the discussion of Lévi-Strauss and structuralism in Chapter 2. At this juncture it is already clear that one way the internal stability and binary frame for sex is effectively secured is by casting the duality of sex in a prediscursive domain. This production of sex as the prediscursive ought to be understood as the effect of the apparatus of cultural construction designated by *gender*. How, then, does gender need to be reformulated to encompass the power relations that produce the effect of a prediscursive sex and so conceal that very operation of discursive production?

III Gender: The Circular Ruins of Contemporary Debate

Is there "a" gender which persons are said to *have*, or is it an essential attribute that a person is said to *be*, as implied in the question "What gender are you?" When feminist theorists claim that gender is the cultural interpretation of sex or that gender is culturally constructed, what is the manner or mechanism of this construction? If gender is constructed, could it be constructed differently, or does its constructedness imply some form of social determinism, foreclosing the possibility of agency and transformation? Does "construction" suggest that certain laws generate gender differences along universal axes of sexual difference? How and where does the construction of gender take place? What sense can we make of a construction that cannot assume a human constructor prior to that construction? On some accounts, the notion that gender is constructed suggests a certain determinism of gender meanings inscribed on anatomically differentiated bodies, where those bodies are understood as passive recipients of an inexorable cultural law. When the relevant "culture" that "constructs" gender is understood in terms of such a law or set of laws, then it seems that gender is as determined and fixed as it was under the biology-is-destiny formulation. In such a case, not biology, but culture, becomes destiny.

On the other hand, Simone de Beauvoir suggests in *The Second Sex* that "one is not born a woman, but, rather, becomes one."[12] For Beauvoir, gender is "constructed," but implied in her formulation is an agent, a *cogito*, who somehow takes on or appropriates that gender and could, in principle, take on some other gender. Is gender as variable and volitional as Beauvoir's account seems to suggest? Can "construction" in such a case be reduced to a form of choice? Beauvoir is clear that one "becomes" a woman, but always under a cultural compulsion to become one. And clearly, the compulsion does not come from "sex." There is nothing in her account that guarantees that the "one" who becomes a woman is necessarily female. If "the body is a situation,"[13] as she claims, there is no recourse to a body that has not always already been interpreted by cultural meanings; hence, sex could not qualify as a prediscursive anatomical facticity. Indeed, sex, by definition, will be shown to have been gender all along.[14]

The controversy over the meaning of *construction* appears to founder on the conventional philosophical polarity between free will and determinism. As a consequence, one might reasonably suspect that some common linguistic restriction on thought both forms and limits the terms of the debate. Within those terms, "the body" appears as a passive medium on which cultural meanings are inscribed or as the instrument through which an appropriative and interpretive will determines a cultural meaning for itself. In either case, the body is figured as a mere *instrument* or *medium* for which a set of cultural meanings are only externally related. But "the body" is itself a construction, as are the myriad "bodies" that constitute the domain of gendered subjects. Bodies cannot be said to have a signifiable existence prior to the mark of their gender; the question then emerges: To what extent does the body *come into being* in and through the mark(s) of gender? How do we reconceive the body no longer as a passive medium or instrument awaiting the enlivening capacity of a distinctly immaterial will?[15]

Whether gender or sex is fixed or free is a function of a discourse which seeks to set certain limits to analysis or to safeguard certain tenets of humanism as presuppositional to any analysis of gender. The locus of intractability, whether in "sex" or "gender" or in the very meaning of "construction," provides a clue to what cultural possibilities can and cannot become mobilized through any further analysis. The limits of the discursive analysis of gender presuppose and preempt the possibilities of imaginable and realizable gender configurations within culture. This is not to say that any and all gendered possibilities are open, but that the boundaries of analysis suggest the limits of a discursively conditioned experience. These limits are always set within the terms of a hegemonic cultural discourse predicated on binary structures that appear as the language of universal rationality. Constraint is thus built into what that language constitutes as the imaginable domain of gender.

Although social scientists refer to gender as a "factor" or a "dimension" of an analysis, it is also applied to embodied persons as "a mark" of biological, linguistic, and/or cultural difference. In these latter cases, gender can be understood as a signification that an (already) sexually differentiated body assumes, but even then that signification exists only *in relation* to another, opposing signification. Some feminist theorists claim that gender is "a relation," indeed, a set of relations, and not an individual attribute. Others, following Beauvoir, would argue that only the feminine gender is marked, that the universal person and the masculine gender are conflated, thereby defining women in terms of their sex and extolling men as the bearers of a body-transcendent universal personhood. [...]

IV Theorizing the Binary, the Unitary, and Beyond

[...] Is it possible to identify a monolithic as well as a monologic masculinist economy that traverses the array of cultural and historical contexts in which sexual difference takes place? Is the failure to acknowledge the specific cultural operations of gender oppression itself a kind of epistemological imperialism, one which is not ameliorated by the simple elaboration of cultural differences as "examples" of the selfsame phallogocentrism? The effort to *include* "Other" cultures as variegated amplifications of a global phallogocentrism constitutes an appropriative act that risks a repetition of the self-aggrandizing gesture of phallogocentrism, colonizing under the sign of the same those differences that might otherwise call that totalizing concept into question.[16]

Feminist critique ought to explore the totalizing claims of a masculinist signifying economy, but also remain self-critical with respect to the totalizing gestures of feminism. The effort to identify the enemy as singular in form is a reverse-discourse that uncritically mimics the strategy of the oppressor instead of offering a different set of terms. That the tactic can operate in feminist and antifeminist contexts alike suggests that the colonizing gesture is not primarily or irreducibly masculinist. It can operate to effect other relations of racial, class, and heterosexist subordination, to name but a few. And clearly, listing the varieties of oppression, as I began to do, assumes their discrete, sequential coexistence along a horizontal axis that does not describe their convergences within the social field. A vertical model is similarly insufficient; oppressions cannot be summarily ranked, causally related, distributed among planes of "originality" and "derivativeness."[17] Indeed, the field of power structured in part by the imperializing gesture of dialectical appropriation exceeds and encompasses the axis of sexual difference, offering a mapping of intersecting differentials which cannot be summarily hierarchized either within the terms of phallogocentrism or any other candidate for the position of "primary condition of oppression." Rather than an exclusive tactic of masculinist signifying economies, dialectical appropriation and suppression of the Other is one tactic among many, deployed centrally but not exclusively in the service of expanding and rationalizing the masculinist domain.

The contemporary feminist debates over essentialism raise the question of the universality of female identity and masculinist oppression in other ways. Universalistic claims are based on a common or shared epistemological standpoint, understood as the articulated consciousness or shared structures of oppression or in the ostensibly transcultural structures of femininity, maternity, sexuality, and/or *écriture feminine*. The opening discussion in this chapter argued that this globalizing gesture has spawned a number of criticisms from women who claim that the category of "women" is normative and exclusionary and is invoked with the unmarked dimensions of class and racial privilege intact. In other words, the insistence upon the coherence and unity of the category of women has effectively refused the multiplicity of cultural, social, and political intersections in which the concrete array of "women" are constructed.

Some efforts have been made to formulate coalitional politics which do not assume in advance what the content of "women" will be. They propose instead a set of dialogic encounters by which variously positioned women articulate separate identities within the framework of an emergent coalition. Clearly, the value of coalitional politics is not to be underestimated, but the very form of coalition, of an emerging and unpredictable assemblage of positions, cannot be figured in advance. Despite the clearly democratizing impulse that motivates coalition building, the coalitional theorist can inadvertently reinsert herself as sovereign of the process by trying to assert an ideal form for coalitional structures *in advance*, one that will effectively guarantee unity as the outcome. Related efforts to determine what is and is not the true shape of a dialogue, what constitutes a subject-position, and, most importantly, when "unity" has been reached, can impede the self-shaping and self-limiting dynamics of coalition.

The insistence in advance on coalitional "unity" as a goal assumes that solidarity, whatever its price, is a prerequisite for political action. But what sort of politics demands that kind of advance purchase on unity? Perhaps a coalition needs to acknowledge its contradictions and take action with those contradictions intact. Perhaps also part of what dialogic understanding entails is the acceptance of divergence, breakage, splinter, and fragmentation as part of the often tortuous process of democratization. The very notion of "dialogue" is culturally specific and historically bound, and while one speaker may feel secure that a conversation is happening, another may be sure it is not. The power relations that condition and limit dialogic possibilities need first to be interrogated. Otherwise, the model of dialogue risks relapsing into a liberal model that assumes that speaking agents occupy equal positions of power and speak with the same presuppositions about what constitutes "agreement" and "unity" and, indeed, that those are the goals to be sought. It would be wrong to assume in advance that there is a category of "women" that simply needs to be filled in with various components of race, class, age, ethnicity, and sexuality in order to become complete. The assumption of its essential incompleteness permits that category to serve as a permanently available site of contested meanings. The definitional incompleteness of the category might then serve as a normative ideal relieved of coercive force.

Is "unity" necessary for effective political action? Is the premature insistence on the goal of unity precisely the cause of an ever more bitter fragmentation among the ranks? Certain forms of acknowledged fragmentation might facilitate coalitional action precisely because the "unity" of the category of women is neither presupposed nor desired. Does "unity" set up an exclusionary norm of solidarity at the level of identity that rules out the possibility of a set of actions which disrupt the very borders of identity concepts, or which seek to accomplish precisely that disruption as an explicit political aim? Without the pre-supposition or goal of "unity," which is, in either case, always instituted at a conceptual level, provisional unities might emerge in the context of concrete actions that have purposes other than the articulation of identity. Without the compulsory expectation that feminist actions must be instituted from some stable, unified, and agreed-upon identity, those actions might well get a quicker start and seem more congenial to a number of "women" for whom the meaning of the category is permanently moot.

This antifoundationalist approach to coalitional politics assumes neither that "identity" is a premise nor that the shape or meaning of a coalitional assemblage can be known prior to its achievement. Because the articulation of an identity within available cultural terms instates a definition that forecloses in advance the emergence of new identity concepts in and through politically engaged actions, the foundationalist tactic cannot take the transformation or expansion of existing identity concepts as a normative goal. Moreover, when agreed-upon identities or agreed-upon dialogic structures, through which already established identities are communicated, no longer constitute the theme or subject of politics, then identities can come into being and dissolve depending on the concrete practices that constitute them. Certain political practices institute identities on a contingent basis in order to accomplish whatever aims are in view. Coalitional politics requires neither an expanded category of "women" nor an internally multiplicitous self that offers its complexity at once.

Gender is a complexity whose totality is permanently deferred, never fully what it is at any given juncture in time. An open coalition, then, will affirm identities that are alternately instituted and relinquished according to the purposes at hand; it will be an open assemblage that permits of multiple convergences and divergences without obedience to a normative telos of definitional closure.

Notes

1 See Michel Foucault, "Right of Death and Power over Life," in *The History of Sexuality, Volume I, An Introduction*, trans. Robert Hurley (New York: Vintage, 1980), originally published as *Histoire de la sexualité 1:*

La volonté de savoir (Paris: Gallimard, 1978). In that final chapter, Foucault discusses the relation between the juridical and productive law. His notion of the productivity of the law is clearly derived from Nietzsche, although not identical with Nietzsche's will-to-power. The use of Foucault's notion of productive power is not meant as a simple-minded "application" of Foucault to gender issues. As I show in Chapter 3, section ii, of *Gender Trouble* "Foucault, Herculine, and the Politics of Sexual Discontinuity," the consideration of sexual difference within the terms of Foucault's own work reveals central contradictions in his theory. His view of the body also comes under criticism in the final chapter.

2 References throughout this work to a subject before the law are extrapolations of Derrida's reading of Kafka's parable "Before the Law," in *Kafka and the Contemporary Critical Performance: Centenary Readings*, ed. Alan Udoff (Bloomington: Indiana University Press, 1987).

3 See Denise Riley, *Am I That Name?: Feminism and the Category of "Women" in History* (New York: Macmillan, 1988).

4 See Sandra Harding, "The Instability of the Analytical Categories of Feminist Theory," in *Sex and Scientific Inquiry*, eds. Sandra Harding and Jean F. O'Barr (Chicago: University of Chicago Press, 1987), pp. 283–302.

5 I am reminded of the ambiguity inherent in Nancy Cott's title, *The Grounding of Modern Feminism* (New Haven: Yale University Press, 1987). She argues that the early twentieth-century US feminist movement sought to "ground" itself in a program that eventually "grounded" that movement. Her historical thesis implicitly raises the question of whether uncritically accepted foundations operate like the "return of the repressed"; based on exclusionary practices, the stable political identities that found political movements may invariably become threatened by the very instability that the foundationalist move creates.

6 I use the term *heterosexual matrix* throughout the text to designate that grid of cultural intelligibility through which bodies, genders, and desires are naturalized. I am drawing from Monique Wittig's notion of the "heterosexual contract" and, to a lesser extent, on Adrienne Rich's notion of "compulsory heterosexuality" to characterize a hegemonic discursive/epistemic model of gender intelligibility that assumes that for bodies to cohere and make sense there must be a stable sex expressed through a stable gender (masculine expresses male, feminine expresses female) that is oppositionally and hierarchically defined through the compulsory practice of heterosexuality.

7 For a discussion of the sex/gender distinction in structuralist anthropology and feminist appropriations and criticisms of that formulation, see chapter 2, section i, of *Gender Trouble* "Structuralism's Critical Exchange."

8 For an interesting study of the *berdache* and multiple-gender arrangements in Native American cultures, see Walter L. Williams, *The Spirit and the Flesh: Sexual Diversity in American Indian Culture* (Boston: Beacon Press, 1988). See also, Sherry B. Ortner and Harriet Whitehead, eds., *Sexual Meanings: The Cultural Construction of Sexuality* (New York: Cambridge University Press, 1981). For a politically sensitive and provocative analysis of the *berdache*, transsexuals, and the contingency of gender dichotomies, see Suzanne J. Kessler and Wendy McKenna, *Gender: An Ethnomethodological Approach* (Chicago: University of Chicago Press, 1978).

9 A great deal of feminist research has been conducted within the fields of biology and the history of science that assess the political interests inherent in the various discriminatory procedures that establish the scientific basis for sex. See Ruth Hubbard and Marian Lowe, eds., *Genes and Gender*, Vols 1 and 2 (New York: Gordian Press, 1978, 1979); the two issues on feminism and science of *Hypatia: A Journal of Feminist Philosophy*, Vol. 2, No. 3, Fall 1987, and Vol. 3, No. 1, Spring 1988, and especially The Biology and Gender Study Group, "The Importance of Feminist Critique for Contemporary Cell Biology" in this last issue (Spring 1988); Sandra Harding, *The Science Question in Feminism* (Ithaca: Cornell University Press, 1986); Evelyn Fox Keller, *Reflections on Gender and Science* (New Haven: Yale University Press, 1984); Donna Haraway, "In the Beginning was the Word: The Genesis of Biological Theory," *Signs: Journal of Women in Culture and Society*, Vol. 6, No. 3, 1981; Donna Haraway, *Primate Visions* (New York: Routledge, 1989); Sandra Harding and Jean F. O'Barr, *Sex and Scientific Inquiry* (Chicago: University of Chicago Press, 1987); Anne Fausto-Sterling, *Myths of Gender: Biological Theories About Women and Men* (New York: Norton, 1979).

10 Clearly Foucault's *History of Sexuality* offers one way to rethink the history of "sex" within a given modern Eurocentric context. For a more detailed consideration, see Thomas Laqueur and Catherine Gallagher, eds., *The Making of the Modern Body: Sexuality and Society in the 19th Century* (Berkeley: University of California Press, 1987), originally published as an issue of *Representations*, No. 14, Spring 1986.

11 See my "Variations on Sex and Gender: Beauvoir, Wittig, Foucault," in *Feminism as Critique*, eds. Seyla Benhabib and Drucilla Cornell (Basil Blackwell, dist. by University of Minnesota Press, 1987).

12 Simone de Beauvoir, *The Second Sex*, trans. E. M. Parshley (New York: Vintage, 1973), p. 301.

13 Ibid., p. 38.

14 See my "Sex and Gender in Beauvoir's *Second Sex*" *Yale French Studies, Simone de Beauvoir: Witness to a Century*, No. 72, Winter 1986.

15 Note the extent to which phenomenological theories such as Sartre's, Merleau-Ponty's, and Beauvoir's tend to use the term *embodiment*. Drawn as it is from theological contexts, the term tends to figure "the" body as a mode of incarnation and, hence, to preserve the external and dualistic relationship between a signifying immateriality and the materiality of the body itself.

16 Gayatri Spivak most pointedly elaborates this particular kind of binary explanation as a colonizing act of marginalization. In a critique of the "self-presence of the cognizing supra-historical self," which is characteristic of the epistemic imperialism of the philosophical cogito, she locates politics in the production of knowledge that creates and censors the margins that constitute, through exclusion, the contingent intelligibility of that subject's given knowledge-regime: "I call 'politics as such' the prohibition of marginality that is implicit in the production of any explanation. From that point of view, the choice of particular binary oppositions . . . is no mere intellectual strategy. It is, in each case, the condition of the possibility for centralization (with appropriate apologies) and, correspondingly, marginalization" (Gayatri Chakravorty Spivak, "Explanation and Culture: Marginalia," in *In Other Worlds: Essays in Cultural Politics* [New York: Routledge, 1987], p. 113).

17 See the argument against "ranking oppressions" in Cherríe Moraga, "La Güera," in *This Bridge Called My Back: Writings of Radical Women of Color*, eds. Gloria Anzaldúa and Cherríe Moraga (New York: Kitchen Table, Women of Color Press, 1982).

13

Gender and Race: (What) Are They? (What) Do We Want Them To Be?

Sally Haslanger

> If her functioning as a female is not enough to define woman, if we decline also to explain her through "the eternal feminine," and if nevertheless we admit, provisionally, that women do exist, then we must face the question: what is a woman?
>
> ***Simone de Beauvoir*, The Second Sex**

> I guess you could chuckle and say that I'm just a woman trapped in a woman's body.
>
> ***Ellen DeGeneres*,**
> **My Point . . . and I Do Have One**

> The truth is that there are no races: there is nothing in the world that can do all we ask race to do for us.
>
> ***Kwame Anthony Appiah*,**
> **In My Father's House**

It is always awkward when someone asks me informally what I'm working on and I answer that I'm trying to figure out what gender is. For outside a rather narrow segment of the academic world, the term "gender" has come to function as the polite way to talk about the sexes. And one thing people feel pretty confident about is their knowledge of the difference between males and females. Males are those human beings with a range of familiar primary and secondary sex characteristics, most important being the penis; females are those with a different set, most important being the vagina or, perhaps, the uterus. Enough said. Against this background, it isn't clear what could be the point of an inquiry, especially a philosophical inquiry, into "what gender is".

But within that rather narrow segment of the academic world concerned with gender issues, not only is there no simple equation of sex and gender, but the seemingly straightforward anatomical distinction between the sexes has been challenged as well. What began as an effort to note that men and women differ socially as well as anatomically has prompted an explosion of different uses of the term "gender". Within these debates, not only is it unclear what gender is and how we should go about understanding it, but whether it is anything at all.

The situation is similar, if not worse, with respect to race. The self-evidence of racial distinctions in everyday American life is at striking odds with the uncertainty about the category of race in law and the academy. Work in the biological sciences has informed us that our practices of racial categorization don't map neatly onto any useful biological

Sally Haslanger, "Gender and Race: (What) Are They? (What) Do We Want Them to Be?," pp. 31–55 from *Noûs* 34(1), 2000. Reprinted by permission of Blackwell Publishing Ltd.

classification; but that doesn't settle much, if anything. For what should we make of our tendency to classify individuals according to race, apparently on the basis of physical appearance? And what are we to make of the social and economic consequences of such classifications? Is race real or is it not?

This chapter is part of a larger project, the goal of which is to offer accounts of gender and race informed by a feminist epistemology. Here my aim is to sketch some of the central ideas of those accounts. Let me emphasize at the beginning that I do not want to argue that my proposals provide the *only* acceptable ways to define race or gender; in fact, the epistemological framework I employ is explicitly designed to allow for different definitions responding to different concerns. It is sometimes valuable to consider race or gender alone or to highlight the differences between them; however, here I will begin by exploring some significant parallels. Although there are dangers in drawing close analogies between gender and race, I hope my discussion will show that theorizing them together can provide us valuable resources for thinking about a wide range of issues. Working with a model that demonstrates some of the parallels between race and gender also helps us locate important differences between them.

I The Question(s)

It is useful to begin by reflecting on the questions: "What is gender?", "What is race?" and related questions such as: "What is it to be a man or a woman?"[1], "What is it to be White? Latino? or Asian?" There are several different ways to understand, and so respond to, questions of the form, "What is X?" or "What is it to be an X?" For example, the question "What is knowledge?" might be construed in several ways. One might be asking: What is *our* concept of knowledge? (looking to apriori methods for an answer). On a more naturalistic reading one might be asking: What (natural) kind (if any) does our epistemic vocabulary track? Or one might be undertaking a more revisionary project: What is the point of having a concept of knowledge? What concept (if any) would do that work best?[2] These different sorts of projects cannot be kept entirely distinct, but draw upon different methodological strategies. Returning to the questions, "What is race?" or "What is gender?" we can distinguish, then, three projects with importantly different priorities: *conceptual*, *descriptive*, and *analytical*.

A *conceptual* inquiry into race or gender would seek an articulation of our *concepts* of race or gender (Riley 1988). To answer the conceptual question, one way to proceed would be to use the method of reflective equilibrium. (Although within the context of analytic philosophy this might be seen as a call for a conceptual *analysis* of the term(s), I want to reserve the term "analytical" for a different sort of project, described below.)

In contrast to the conceptual project, a *descriptive* project is not concerned with exploring the nuances of our concepts (or anyone else's for that matter); it focuses instead on their extension. Here, the task is to develop potentially more accurate concepts through careful consideration of the phenomena, usually relying on empirical or quasi-empirical methods. Paradigm descriptive projects occur in studying natural phenomena. I offered the example of naturalistic approaches to knowledge above: the goal is to determine the (natural) kind, if any, we are referring to (or are attempting to refer to) with our epistemic talk. However, a descriptive approach need not be confined to a search for *natural* or *physical* kinds; inquiry into what it is to be, e.g., a human right, a citizen, a democracy, might begin by considering the full range of what has counted as such to determine whether there is an underlying (possibly social) kind that explains the temptation to group the cases together. Just as natural science can enrich our "folk" conceptualization of natural phenomena, social sciences (as well as the arts and humanities) can enrich our "folk" conceptualization of social phenomena. So, a descriptive inquiry into race and gender need not presuppose that race and gender are biological kinds; instead it might ask whether our uses of race and gender vocabularies are tracking social kinds, and if so which ones.

The third sort of project takes an *analytical* approach to the question, "What is gender?" or "What is race?" (Scott 1986). On this approach the task is not to explicate our ordinary concepts; nor is it to investigate the kind that we may or may not be tracking with our everyday conceptual apparatus; instead we begin by considering more fully the pragmatics of our talk employing the terms in question. What is the point of having these concepts? What cognitive or practical task do they (or should they) enable us to accomplish? Are they effective tools to accomplish our (legitimate) purposes; if not, what concepts would serve these purposes better?

In the limit case of an analytical approach the concept in question is introduced by stipulating the meaning of a new term, and its content is determined entirely by the role it plays in the theory. But if we allow that our everyday vocabularies serve both cognitive and practical purposes, purposes that might also be served by our theorizing, then a theory offering an improved understanding of our (legitimate) purposes and/or improved conceptual resources for the tasks at hand might reasonably represent itself as providing a (possibly revisionary) account of the everyday concepts.[3]

So, on an analytical approach, the questions "What is gender?" or "What is race?" require us to consider what work we want these concepts to do for us; why do we need them at all? The responsibility is ours to define them for our purposes. In doing so we will want to be responsive to some aspects of ordinary usage (and to aspects of both the connotation and extension of the terms). However, neither ordinary usage nor empirical investigation is overriding, for there is a stipulative element to the project: *this* is the phenomenon we need to be thinking about. Let the term in question refer to it. On this approach, the world by itself can't tell us what gender is, or what race is; it is up to us to decide what in the world, if anything, they are.

This essay pursues an analytical approach to defining race and gender. However, its analytical objectives are linked to the descriptive project of determining whether our gender and race vocabularies in fact track social kinds that are typically obscured by the manifest content of our everyday race and gender concepts.[4] Although the analyses I offer will point to existing social kinds (and this is no accident), I am not prepared to defend the claim that these social kinds are what our race and gender talk is "really" about. My priority in this inquiry is not to capture what we do mean, but how we might usefully revise what we mean for certain theoretical and political purposes.

My characterization of all three approaches remains vague, but there is one reason to be skeptical of the analytical approach that should be addressed at the outset. The different approaches I've sketched differ both in their methods and their subject matter. However, we come to inquiry with a conceptual repertoire in terms of which we frame our questions and search for answers: hence, the subject matter of any inquiry would seem to be set from the start. In asking what *race* is, or what *gender* is, our initial questions are expressed in *everyday* vocabularies of race and gender, so how can we meaningfully answer these questions without owing obedience to the everyday concepts? Or at least to our everyday usage? Revisionary projects are in danger of providing answers to questions that weren't being asked.

But ordinary concepts are notoriously vague; individual conceptions and linguistic usage varies widely. Moreover, inquiry often demonstrates that the ordinary concepts used initially to frame a project are not, as they stand, well-suited to the theoretical task at hand. (This is one reason why we may shift from a *conceptual* project to an *analytical* one.) But precisely because our ordinary concepts are vague (or it is vague which concept we are expressing by our everyday use of terms), there is room to stretch, shrink, or refigure what exactly we are talking about in new and sometimes unexpected directions.

However, in an explicitly revisionary project, it is not at all clear when we are warranted in appropriating existing terminology. Given the difficulty of determining what "our" concept is, it isn't entirely clear when a project crosses over from being explicative to revisionary, or when it is no longer even revisionary but simply changes the subject. If our goal is to offer an analysis of "our" concept of X, then the line between what's explication and what's not matters. But if our goal is to identify a concept that serves our broader purposes, then the question of terminology is primarily a pragmatic and sometimes a political one: should we employ the terms of ordinary discourse to refer to our theoretical categories, or instead make up new terms? The issue of terminological appropriation is especially important, and especially sensitive, when the terms in question designate categories of social identity such as "race" and "gender".

Are there principles that determine when it is legitimate to appropriate the terms of ordinary discourse for theoretical purposes? An answer, it seems to me, should include both a semantic and a political condition (though in some cases the politics of the appropriation will be uncontroversial). The semantic condition is not surprising: the proposed shift in meaning of the term would seem semantically warranted if central functions of the term remain the same, e.g., if it helps organize or explain a core set of phenomena that the ordinary terms are used to identify or describe.[5] Framing a political condition in general terms is much more difficult, however, for the politics of such appropriation will depend on the acceptability of the goals being served, the intended and unintended effects of the change, the politics of the speech context, and whether the underlying values are justified. We will return to some of these issues later in the chapter once my analyses have been presented.

II Critical (Feminist, Anti-Racist) Theory

In an analytical project we must begin by considering what we want the concept in question for. Someone might argue, however, that the answer is simple: our concepts must do the work of enabling us to articulate truths. But of course an unconstrained search for truth would yield chaos, not theory; truths are too easy to come by, there are too many of them. Given time and inclination, I could tell you many truths – some trivial, some interesting, many boring – about my physical surroundings. But a random collection of facts does not make a theory; they are a disorganized jumble. In the context of theorizing, some truths are more significant than others because they are relevant to answering the question that guides the inquiry (Anderson 1995).

Theorizing – even when it is sincerely undertaken as a search for truth – must be guided by more than the goal of achieving justified true belief. Good theories are systematic bodies of knowledge that select from the mass of truths those that address our broader cognitive and practical demands. In many contexts the questions and purposes that frame the project are understood and progress does not require one to investigate them. But in other contexts, e.g., especially when debate has seemed to break down and parties are talking at cross-purposes, an adequate evaluation of an existing theory or success in developing a new one is only possible when it is made clear what the broader goals are.

With this sketch of some of the theoretical options, I want to frame my own project as a *critical analytical* effort to answer the questions: "What is gender?", "What is race?", and the related questions "What is it to be a man?" "...a woman?", "...White?" "...Latino?", etc. "More specifically, the goal of the project is to consider what work the concepts of gender and race might do for us in a critical – specifically feminist and antiracist – social theory, and to suggest concepts that can accomplish at least important elements of that work (Geuss 1981). So to start: why might feminist antiracists want or need the concepts of gender and race? What work can they do for us?

At the most general level, the task is to develop accounts of gender and race that will be effective tools in the fight against injustice. The broad project is guided by four concerns:

(i) The need to identify and explain persistent inequalities between females and males, and between people of different "colors"[6]; this includes the concern to identify how social forces, often under the guise of biological forces, work to perpetuate such inequalities.

(ii) The need for a framework that will be ensitive to both the similarities and differences among males and females, and the similarities and differences among individuals in groups demarcated by "color"; this includes the concern to identify the effects of interlocking oppressions, e.g., the intersectionality of race, class, and gender (Crenshaw 1993).

(iii) The need for an account that will track how gender and race are implicated in a broad range of social phenomena extending beyond those that obviously concern sexual or racial difference, e.g., whether art, religion, philosophy, science, or law might be "gendered" and/or "racialized".

(iv) The need for accounts of gender and race that take seriously the agency of women and people of color of both genders, and within which we can develop an understanding of agency that will aid feminist and antiracist efforts to empower critical social agents.

In this chapter I will begin to address the first two concerns, though the fourth will become relevant later in the discussion. Let me emphasize, however, that my goal in this chapter is not to provide a thoroughgoing explanation of sexism and racism, if one wants by way of explanation a causal account of why and how females have come to be systematically subordinated throughout history, or why and how "color" has come to be a basis for social stratification. My goal here is in some ways more modest, and in other ways more contentious. Prior to explanation it is valuable to provide clear conceptual categories to identify the phenomenon needing explanation, e.g., categories that identify the kind of injustice at issue and the groups subject to it. In the case of racial and sexual subordination this is not as easy as it may seem. In the first place, the forms of racial and sexual subordination are tremendously heterogeneous and it would help to have accounts that enable us to distinguish *racial* subordination and *sexual* subordination from other sorts. But further, we must be cautious about treating familiar demarcations of "color" and "sex" as purely natural categories, as if the question at hand is simply why one's "color" or "sex" – where we take for granted our familiar understandings of these terms – has ever seemed to be socially significant. At least at this stage of the inquiry we must allow that the criteria for distinguishing "colors" or "sexes" differ across time and place, and that the boundaries are at least partly political; but in spite of this variation, we are still dealing with an overarching phenomenon of racial and sexual subordination.

III What is Gender?

Even a quick survey of the literature reveals that a range of things have counted as "gender" within feminist theorizing. The guiding idea is sometimes expressed with the slogan: "gender is the social meaning of sex". But like any slogan, this one allows for different interpretations. Some theorists use the term "gender" to refer to the subjective experience of sexed embodiment, or a broad psychological orientation to the world ("gender identity"[7]); others to a set of attributes or ideals that function as norms for males and females ("masculinity" and "femininity"); others to a system of sexual symbolism; and still others to the traditional social roles of men and women. My strategy is to offer a focal analysis that defines gender, in the primary sense, as a social class. A focal analysis undertakes to explain a variety of connected phenomena in terms of their relations to one that is theorized as the central or core phenomenon. As I see it, the core phenomenon to be addressed is the pattern of social relations that constitute the social classes of men as dominant and women as subordinate; norms, symbols, and identities are gendered in relation to the social relations that constitute gender.[8] As will become clearer below, I see my emphasis as falling within, though not following uncritically, the tradition of materialist feminism.[9]

Among feminist theorists there are two problems that have generated pessimism about providing any unified account of women; I'll call them the *commonality problem* and the *normativity problem*. Very briefly, the commonality problem questions whether there is anything social that females have in common that could count as their "gender". If we consider *all* females – females of different times, places, and cultures – there are reasons to doubt that there is anything beyond body type (if even that) that they all share (Spelman 1988). The normativity problem raises the concern that any definition of "what woman is" is valueladen, and will marginalize certain females, privilege others, and reinforce current gender norms (Butler 1990, Ch. 1).

It is important to note, even briefly, that these problems take on a different cast when they arise within a *critical analytical* project. The emphasis of an analytical project is not on discovering commonalities among females: although the empirical similarities and differences between females are relevant, the primary goal is an analysis of gender that will serve as a tool in the quest for sexual justice (see section II). Moreover, a critical project can accept the result that an effort to define "what women is" carries normative implications, for critical projects explicitly embrace normative results; the hope is that the account's implications would not reinforce but would help undermine the structures of sexual oppression. However, we will return to these issues below.

Given the priority I place on concerns with justice and sexual inequality, I take the primary motivation for distinguishing sex from gender to arise in the recognition that males and females do not only differ physically, but also systematically differ in their social positions. What is of concern, to put it simply, is that societies, on the whole, privilege individuals with male bodies. Although the particular forms and mechanism of oppression vary from culture to culture, societies have found many ways – some ingenious, some crude – to control and exploit the sexual and reproductive capacities of females.

The main strategy of materialist feminist accounts of gender has been to define gender in terms of women's subordinate position in systems of male dominance.[10] Although there are materialist feminist roots in Marxism, contemporary versions resist the thought that all social phenomena can be explained in or reduced to economic terms; and although materialist feminists emphasize the role of language and culture in women's oppression, there is a wariness of extreme forms of linguistic constructivism and a commitment to staying grounded in the material realities of women's lives. In effect, there is a concerted effort to show how gender oppression is jointly sustained by both cultural and material forces.

Critiques of universalizing feminisms have taught us to be attentive to the variety of forms gender takes and the concrete social positions females occupy. However it is compatible with these commitments to treat the category of gender as a genus that is realized in different ways in different contexts; doing so enables us to recognize significant patterns in the ways that gender is instituted and embodied. Working at the most general level, then, the materialist strategy offers us three basic principles to guide us in understanding gender:

(i) Gender categories are defined in terms of how one is socially positioned, where this is a function of, e.g., how one is viewed, how one is treated, and how one's life is structured socially, legally, and economically; gender is not defined in terms of an individual's intrinsic physical or psychological features.

(This allows that there may be other categories – such as sex – that are defined in terms of intrinsic physical features. Note, however, that once we focus our attention on gender as social position, we must allow that one can be a woman without ever (in the ordinary sense) "acting like a woman", "feeling like a woman", or even having a female body.)

(ii) Gender categories are defined hierarchically within a broader complex of oppressive relations; one group (viz., women) is socially positioned as subordinate to the other (viz., men), typically within the context of other forms of economic and social oppression.

(iii) Sexual difference functions as the physical marker to distinguish the two groups, and is used in the justification of viewing and reating the members of each group differently.

(Tentatively) we can capture these main points in the following analyses:

> S *is a woman* iff$_{df}$ S is systematically subordinated along some dimension (economic, political, legal, social, etc.), and S is "marked" as a target for this treatment by observed or imagined bodily features presumed to be evidence of a female's biological role in reproduction.[11]

> S *is a man* iff$_{df}$ S is systematically privileged along some dimension (economic, political, legal, social, etc.), and S is "marked" as a target for this treatment by observed or imagined bodily features presumed to be evidence of a male's biological role in reproduction.

It is a virtue, I believe, of these accounts, that depending on context, one's sex may have a very different meaning and it may position one in very different kinds of hierarchies. The variation will clearly occur from culture to culture (and sub-culture to sub-culture); so e.g., to be a Chinese woman of the 1790s, a Brazilian woman of the 1890s, or an American woman of the 1990s may involve very different social relations, and very different kinds of oppression. Yet on the analysis suggested, these groups count as women insofar as their subordinate positions are marked and justified by reference to (female) sex. (Also Hurtado 1994, esp. 142.) Similarly, this account allows that the substantive import of gender varies even from individual to individual within a culture depending on how the meaning of sex interacts with other socially salient characteristics (e.g., race, class, sexuality, etc.). For example, a privileged White woman and a Black woman of the underclass will both be women insofar as their social positions are affected by the social meanings of being female; and yet the social implications of being female vary for each because sexism is intertwined with race and class oppression.

There are points in the proposed analysis that require clarification, however. What does it mean to say that someone is "systematically subordinated" or "privileged", and further, that the subordination occurs "on the basis of" certain features? The background idea is that women are *oppressed*, and that they are oppressed *as women*. But we still need to ask: What does it mean to say that women are oppressed, and what does the qualification "as women" add?

Marilyn Frye's account of oppression with Iris Young's elaborations provides a valuable starting point (Frye 1983; Young 1990). Although these ideas are commonplace within certain intellectual circles, it is useful to summarize them very briefly here. There are of course unresolved difficulties in working out a satisfactory theory of oppression; I'm afraid I can't take on that further task here, so I can only invoke the rough outlines of the background view with the hope that an adequate account can at some point be supplied. Nonetheless, oppression in the intended sense is a structural phenomenon that positions certain groups as disadvantaged and others as advantaged or privileged in relation to them. Oppression consists of, "an enclosing structure of forces and barriers which tends to the immobilization and reduction of a group or category of people." (Frye 1983, 11). Importantly, such structures, at least as we know them, are not designed and policed by those in power, rather,

> oppression refers to the vast and deep injustices some groups suffer as a consequence of often unconscious assumptions and reactions of well-meaning people in ordinary interactions, media and cultural stereotypes, and structural features of bureaucratic hierarchies and market mechanisms – in short, the normal processes of everyday life. (Young 1990, 41)

Developing this concept of oppression, Young specifies five forms it can take: exploitation, marginalization, powerlessness, cultural imperialism, and (systematic) violence. The key point for us is that oppression comes in different forms, and even if one is privileged along some dimension (e.g., in income or respect), one might be oppressed in others.[12] In fact, one might be systematically subordinated along some social axis, and yet still be tremendously privileged in one's *overall* social position.

It is clear that women are oppressed in the sense that women are members of groups that suffer exploitation, marginalization, etc. But how should we understand the claim that women are oppressed *as women*. Frye explains this as follows:

> One is marked for application of oppressive pressures by one's membership in some group or category . . . In the case at hand, it is the category, *woman* . . . If a woman has little or no economic or political power, or achieves little of what she wants to achieve, a major causal factor in this is that she is a woman. For any woman of any race or economic class, being a woman is significantly attached to whatever disadvantages and deprivations she suffers, be they great or small . . . [In contrast,] being male is something [a man] has going *for* him, even if race or class or age or disability is going against him. (Frye 1983, 15–16)

But given the diffusion of power in a model of structural oppression how are we to make sense of one's being "marked" and the "application" of pressures? In the context of oppression, certain properties of individuals are socially meaningful. This is to say that the properties play a role in a broadly accepted (though usually not fully explicit) representation of the world that functions to justify and motivate particular forms of social intercourse. The significant properties in question – in the cases at hand, assumed or actual properties of the body – mark you "for application of oppressive pressures" insofar as the attribution of these properties is interpreted as adequate, in light of this background representation, to explain and/or justify your position in a structure of oppressive social relations. In the case of women, the idea is that societies are guided by representations that link being female with other facts that have implications for how one should be viewed and treated; insofar as we structure our social life to accommodate the cultural meanings of the female (and male) body, females occupy an oppressed social position.

Although I agree with Frye that in sexist societies social institutions are structured in ways that on the whole disadvantage females and advantage males, we must keep in mind that societies are not monolithic and that sexism is not the only source of oppression. For example, in the contemporary US, there are contexts in which being Black *and male* marks one as a target for certain forms of systematic violence (e.g., by the police). In those contexts, contrary to Frye's suggestion, *being male* is not something that a man "has going *for* him"; though there are other contexts (also in the contemporary US) in which Black males benefit from being male. In examples of this sort, the systematic violence against males *as males* is emasculating (and may be intended as such); but there are important differences between an emasculated man and a woman. On the sort of view we're considering, a woman is someone whose subordinated status is marked by reference to (assumed) *female* anatomy; someone marked for subordination by reference to (assumed) *male* anatomy does not qualify as a woman, but also, *in the particular context*, is not socially positioned as a man.

These considerations suggests that it may be useful to bring context explicitly into our account. Recent work on gender socialization also supports the idea that although most of us develop a relatively fixed gender identity by the age of three, the degree to which the marked body makes a difference varies from context to context. In her study of elementary school children, Barrie Thorne suggests:

> Gender boundaries are episodic and ambiguous, and *the notion of "borderwork"* [i.e., the work of contesting and policing gender boundaries] *should be coupled with a parallel term – such as "neutralization" – for processes through which girls and boys (and adults . . .) neutralize or undermine a sense of gender as division and opposition.* (Thorne 1993, 84)

Thorne's study is motivated by a recognition that gender is a well-entrenched system of oppression. However, her comments here are intended as an antidote to two problematic tendencies in speaking of girls and boys, men and women: first, the tendency to over-generalize gender differences based on paradigm or stereotyped interactions; second, the tendency to view individuals (specifically children) as passive participants in gender socialization and, more generally, gendered life.

In some respects, Frye's and Thorne's approaches appear to be in tension with one another. Frye is keen to highlight the structural facts of sexist oppression: like it or not, your body positions you within a social hierarchy. Thorne, on the other hand, examines how oppression is lived, enforced, and resisted at the micro-level. There are important advantages to both: without a recognition of oppressive structures and the overall patterns of advantage and disadvantage, individual slights or conflicts can seem harmless. But without a recognition of individual variation and agency, the structures take on a life of their own and come to seem inevitable and insurmountable. But can both perspectives be accommodated in an account of gender? The idea seems simple enough: there are dominant ideologies and dominant social structures that work together to bias the micro-level interactions, however varied and complex they may be, so that for the most part males are privileged and females are disadvantaged.

Although an adequate account of gender must be highly sensitive to contextual variation, if we focus entirely on the narrowly defined contexts in which one's gender is negotiated, we could easily lose sight of the fact that for most of us there is a relatively fixed interpretation of our bodies as sexed either male or female, an interpretation that marks us within the dominant ideology as eligible for only certain positions or opportunities in a system of sexist oppression. Given our priority in theorizing systems of inequality, it is important first to locate the social classes men and women in a broad structure of subordination and privilege:[13]

S *is a woman* iff

(i) S is regularly and for the most part observed or imagined to have certain bodily features presumed to be evidence of a female's biological role in reproduction;

(ii) that S has these features marks S within the dominant ideology of S's society as someone who ought to occupy certain kinds of social position that are in fact subordinate (and so motivates and justifies S's occupying such a position); and

(iii) the fact that S satisfies (i) and (ii) plays a role in S's systematic subordination, i.e., *along some dimension*, S's social position is oppressive, and S's satisfying (i) and (ii) plays a role in that dimension of subordination.

S *is a man* iff

(i) S is regularly and for the most part observed or imagined to have certain bodily features presumed to be evidence of a male's biological role in reproduction;

(ii) that S has these features marks S within the dominant ideology of S's society as someone who ought to occupy certain kinds of social position that are in fact privileged (and so motivates and justifies S's occupying such a position); and

(iii) the fact that S satisfies (i) and (ii) plays a role in S's systematic privilege, i.e., *along some dimension*, S's social position is privileged, and S's satisfying (i) and (ii) plays a role in that dimension of privilege.

These accounts are, however, compatible with the idea that (at least for some of us) one's gender may not be entirely stable, and that other systems of oppression may disrupt gender in particular contexts: a woman may not always function socially as a woman; a man may not always function socially as a man.[14] To return to a previous example, when systems of White supremacy and male dominance collide, a Black man's male privilege may be seen as so threatening that it must be violently wrested from him. In an effort to accommodate this variation, we can add:

S *functions as a woman* in context C iff$_{df}$

(i) S is observed or imagined in C to have certain bodily features presumed to be evidence of a female's biological role in reproduction;

(ii) that S has these features marks S within the background ideology of C as someone who ought to occupy certain kinds of social position that are in fact subordinate (and so motivates and justifies S's occupying such a position); and

(iii) the fact that S satisfies (i) and (ii) plays a role in S's systematic subordination in C, i.e., *along some dimension*, S's social position in C is oppressive, and S's satisfying (i) and (ii) plays a role in that dimension of subordination.

And mutatis mutandis for functioning as a man in context C.

It is important to note that the definitions don't require that the background ideology in question must use (assumed) reproductive function as itself the justification for treating men or women in the way deemed "appropriate"; (assumed) reproductive features may instead simply be "markers" of supposedly "deeper" (and morally relevant?) characteristics that the ideology supposes justifies the treatment in question (Appiah 1992, 13–15).

Although ultimately I will defend these analyses of *man* and *woman*, I'll argue below that there are reasons to modify the broader materialist strategy in defining *gender*. In short, I believe that gender can be fruitfully understood as a higher-order genus that includes not only the hierarchical social positions of man and woman, but potentially other non-hierarchical social positions defined in part by reference to reproductive function. I believe gender *as we know it* takes hierarchical forms as men and women; but the theoretical move of treating men and women as only two kinds of gender provides resources for thinking about other (actual) genders, and the political possibility of constructing non-hierarchical genders.

IV What is Race?

One advantage of this account of gender is the parallel it offers for race. To begin, let me review a couple of points that I take to be matters of established fact: First, there are no racial genes responsible for the complex morphologies and cultural patterns we associate with different races. Second, in different contexts racial distinctions are drawn on the basis of different characteristics, e.g., the Brazilian and US classification schemes for who counts as "Black" differ. For these reasons and others, it appears that race, like gender, could be fruitfully understood as a position within a broad social network.

Although suggestive, this idea is not easy to develop. It is one thing to acknowledge that race is *socially* real, even if a biological fiction; but it is another thing to capture in general terms "the social meaning of color". There seem to be too many different forms race takes. Note, however, that we encountered a similar problem with gender: is there any prospect for a unified analysis of "the social meaning of sex"? The materialist feminist approach offered a helpful strategy: don't look for an analysis that assumes that the meaning is always and everywhere the same; rather, consider how members of the group are *socially positioned*, and what *physical markers* serve as a supposed basis for such treatment.

How might we extend this strategy to race? Transposing the slogan, we might say that race is the social meaning of the geographically marked body, familiar markers being skin color, hair type, eye shape, physique. To develop this, I propose the following account.[15]

First definition:

> A group is *racialized* iff$_{df}$ its members are socially positioned as subordinate or privileged along some dimension (economic, political, legal, social, etc.), and the group is "marked" as a target for this treatment by observed or imagined bodily features presumed to be evidence of ancestral links to a certain geographical region.

Or in the more elaborate version:

> A group G is *racialized* relative to context C iff$_{df}$ members of G are (all and only) those:
>
> (i) who are observed or imagined to have certain bodily features presumed in C to be evidence of ancestral links to a certain geographical region (or regions);
>
> (ii) whose having (or being imagined to have) these features marks them within the context of the background ideology in C as appropriately occupying certain kinds of social position that are in fact either subordinate or privileged

(and so motivates and justifies their occupying such a position); and

(iii) whose satisfying (i) and (ii) plays (or would play) a role in their systematic subordination or privilege in C, i.e., who are *along some dimension* systematically subordinated or privileged when in C, and satisfying (i) and (ii) plays (or would play) a role in that dimension of privilege or subordination.[16]

In other words, races are those groups demarcated by the geographical associations accompanying perceived body type, when those associations take on evaluative significance concerning how members of the group should be viewed and treated. As in the case of gender, the ideology need not use physical morphology or geography as the entire basis for "appropriate" treatment; these features may instead simply be "markers" of other characteristics that the ideology uses to justify the treatment in question.

Given this definition, we can say that S is of the White (Black, Asian . . .) race [in C] iff Whites (Blacks, Asians . . .) are a racialized group [in C], and S is a member.[17] On this view, whether a group is racialized, and so how and whether an individual is raced, is not an absolute fact, but will depend on context. For example, Blacks, Whites, Asians, Native Americans, are currently racialized in the US insofar as these are all groups defined in terms of physical features associated with places of origin, and insofar as membership in the group functions socially as a basis for evaluation. However, some groups are not currently racialized in the US, but have been so in the past and possibly could be again (and in other contexts are), e.g., the Italians, the Germans, the Irish.

It is useful to note a possible contrast between race and ethnicity. I don't have a theory of ethnicity to offer; these are some preliminary comparisons. One's ethnicity concerns one's ancestral links to a certain geographical region (perhaps together with participation in the cultural practices of that region); often ethnicity is associated with characteristic physical features. For our purposes, however, it might be useful to employ the notion of "ethnicity" for those groups that are like races as I've defined them except that they do not experience systematic subordination or privilege in the context in question.[18] Ethnic groups can be (and are) racialized, however, and when they are, one's membership in the group positions one in a social hierarchy; but (on the view I'm sketching) the occurrence of this hierarchical positioning means that the group has gone beyond simply being an ethnic group and functions in that context as a race. In short, we can distinguish between grouping individuals on the basis of their (assumed) origins, and grouping them *hierarchically* on the basis of their (assumed) origins, and the contrast between race and ethnicity might be a useful way to capture this distinction.

V Normativity and Commonality

So what, if anything, is achieved by adopting the above analyses? Are they the tools we need? Let's first consider the problems of commonality and normativity, and begin with gender.

Remember, the problem of commonality questions whether there is anything social that all females can plausibly be said to have in common. If we ask whether females share any intrinsic (non-anatomical) features such as psychological make-up, character traits, beliefs, values, experiences or, alternatively, whether there is a particular social role that all females have occupied across culture and history, the answer seems to be "no".

On my analysis women are those who occupy a particular *kind* of social position, viz., one of sexually-marked subordinate. So women have in common that their (assumed) sex has socially disadvantaged them; but this is compatible with the kinds of cultural variation that feminist inquiry has revealed, for the substantive content of women's position and the ways of justifying it can very enormously. Admittedly, the account accommodates such variation by being very abstract; nonetheless, it provides a schematic account that highlights the interdependence between the material forces that subordinate women, *and* the ideological frameworks that sustain them.

One might complain, however, that there must be *some* women (or rather, females) who aren't oppressed, and in particular, aren't oppressed *as women*. Perhaps there are; e.g., some may "pass" as men, others may be recognizably female but not be subordinated in any way linked to that recognition. I'm not convinced that there are many cases (if any) of the latter, but I'll certainly grant that there *could be* females who did not satisfy the definition that I've offered. In fact, I believe it is part of the project of feminism to bring about a day when there are no more women (though, of course, we should not aim to do away with females!). I'm happy to admit that there could be females who aren't women in the sense I've defined, but these individuals (or possible individuals) are not counterexamples to the analysis. The analysis is intended to capture a meaningful political category for critical feminist efforts, and non-oppressed females do not fall within that category (though they may be interesting for other reasons).

But this leads us directly from the commonality problem to the normativity problem. The normativity problem raises the challenge that any effort to define *women* will problematically privilege some women and (theoretically) marginalize others, and will itself become normative. One worry is that bias inevitably occurs in deciding which experiences or social roles are definitive; a second worry is that if someone wants to be a "real" woman, she should conform to the definition of women provided, and this will reinforce rather than challenge male dominance.

On the account I've offered, it is true that certain females don't count as "real" women; and it is true that I've privileged certain facts of women's lives as definitive. But given the epistemological framework outlined above, it is both inevitable and important for us to choose what facts are significant on the basis of explicit and considered values. For the purposes of a critical feminist inquiry, oppression is a significant fact around which we should organize our theoretical categories; it may be that non-oppressed females are marginalized within my account, but that is because for the broader purposes at hand – relative to the feminist and antiracist values guiding our project – they are not the ones who matter. The important issue is not whether a particular account "marginalizes" some individuals, but whether its doing so is in conflict with the feminist values that motivate the inquiry. And as far as I can tell, *not* focusing our theoretical efforts on understanding the position of oppressed females would pose just such a conflict.

The question remains whether my definition of woman helps sustain gender hierarchy by implicitly offering a normative ideal of woman. Given that women on my definition are an oppressed group, I certainly hope not! Instead, the definition is more likely to offer a negative ideal that challenges male dominance.

I won't defend here my account of racialized groups against an extension of the normativity and commonality complaints, for I would simply repeat the strategy just employed. Although there are interesting nuances in adapting the arguments to apply to racialized groups, I don't see anything peculiar to race that would present an obstacle to developing the same sort of response.

VI Negotiating Terms

Let me now turn to summarize some of the advantages of the proposed definitions. At this point we could bracket the terminological issues and just consider whether the groups in question are ones that are important to consider given the goals of our inquiry. I hope it is clear from what I've already said how the analyses can help us identify and critique broad patterns of racial and sexual oppression (MacKinnon 1987), and how they accommodate the intersectionality of social categories. But a further and, I think, more interesting question is whether it is useful to think of these groups *in these terms*: Does it serve both the goal of understanding racial and sexual oppression, and of achieving sexual and racial equality to think of ourselves as *men* or *women*, or *raced* in the ways proposed?

By appropriating the everyday terminology of race and gender, the analyses I've offered invite us to acknowledge the force of oppressive systems in framing our personal and political identities. Each of us has some investment in our race and gender: I am a White woman. On my accounts, this claim locates me within social systems that in some respects privilege and in others subordinate me. Because gender and racial inequality are not simply a matter of public policy but implicate each of us at the heart of our self-understandings, the terminological shift calls us to reconsider who we think we are.

This point highlights why the issue of terminological appropriation is especially sensitive when the terms designate categories of social identity. Writing in response to a *NY Times* editorial supporting the terminological shift from "Black" to "African-American," Trey Ellis responded:

> When somebody tries to tell me what to call myself in all its uses just because they come to some decision at a cocktail party to which I wasn't even invited, my mama

> raised me to tell them to kiss my black ass. In many cases, *African-American* just won't do.[19]

The issue is not just what words we should use, and who gets to say what words to use, but who we take ourselves to be, and so, in some sense, who we are. Terms for social groups can function as descriptive terms: it may be accurate to say that someone is a woman when she satisfies certain conditions. However, terms for social groups serve other rhetorical purposes. Typically the act of classifying someone as a member of a social group invokes a set of "appropriate" (contextually specific) norms and expectations. It positions her in a social framework and makes available certain kinds of evaluation; in short, it carries prescriptive force. Accepting or identifying with the classification typically involves an endorsement of some norms and expectations, however, not always the socially sanctioned ones. The question whether I should be called a "woman" or a "womman", "White" or "Euro-American", is not just a matter of what words to use, but what norms and expectations are taken to be appropriate; to ask what I should be called is to ask what norms I should be judged by (Haslanger 1993, esp. 89–91).

Although "identifying" someone as a member of a social group invokes a set of "appropriate" norms, what these norms are is not fixed. What it means to be a woman, or to be White, or to be Latino, in this sense, is unstable and always open to contest. The instability across time is necessary to maintain the basic structure of gender and race relations through other social changes: as social roles change – prompted by the economy, immigration, political movements, natural disasters, war, etc. – the contents of normative race and gender identities adjust. The flexibility across contexts accommodates the complexity of social life: what norms are assumed to apply depends on the dominant social structure, the ideological context, and other dimensions of one's identity (such as class, age, ability, sexuality). But this instability and flexibility is exactly what opens the door for groups to redefine themselves in new ways. One strategy is for the group to adopt new names ("African-American", "woman"); another is to appropriate old names with a normative twist ("queer"); but in some cases the contest is over the meanings of the standard terms ("Ain't I a woman?"). Because individuals are so deeply invested in gender and, at least in the US, race categories, it remains of crucial importance to be and to be perceived as a "woman" or a "man" and as a member of one of the standard races. But even so, (although this is something of an exaggeration) it is possible to view our gender and race vocabulary as, in effect, providing terminological place-holders marking space for the collective negotiation of our social identities.

Given the normative force and political potential of identifying someone (or self-identifying) in racial or gendered terms, how do we evaluate a terminological appropriation of the kind I'm proposing? For example, isn't there something disingenuous about appropriating race and gender terminology *because* it is used to frame how we think of ourselves and each other, in order to use them for new concepts that are *not* part of our self-understandings?

This latter question is especially pressing because the appropriation under consideration intentionally invokes what many find to be positive self-understandings – being Latina, being a White man – and offers analyses of them which emphasize the broader context of injustice. Thus there is an invitation not only to revise one's understanding of these categories (given their instability, this happens often enough), but to revise one's relationship to their prescriptive force. By offering these analyses of our ordinary terms, I call upon us to reject what seemed to be positive social identities. I'm suggesting that we should work to undermine those forces that make being a man, a woman, or a member of a racialized group possible; we should refuse to be gendered man or woman, refuse to be raced. This goes beyond denying essentialist claims about one's embodiment and involves an active political commitment to live one's life differently (Stoltenberg 1989). In one sense this appropriation is "just semantics": I'm asking us to use an old term in a new way. But it is also politics: I'm asking us to understand ourselves and those around us as deeply molded by injustice and to draw the appropriate prescriptive inference. This, I hope, will contribute to empowering critical social agents. However, whether the terminological shift I'm suggesting is politically useful will depend on the contexts in which it is employed and the individuals employing it. The point is not to legislate what terms to use in all contexts, but to offer resources that should be used judiciously.

VII Lingering Concerns, Promising Alternatives

There is, nonetheless, a broader concern one might have about the strategy I've employed: Why build hierarchy into the definitions? Why not define gender and race as those social positions motivated and justified by cultural responses to the body, without requiring that the social positions are hierarchical? Wouldn't that provide what we need without implying (implausibly) that women are, by definition, subordinate, men, by definition, privileged, and races, by definition, hierarchically positioned?

If we were to remove hierarchy from the definitions, then there would be two other benefits: first, by providing a place in our model for cultural representations of the body *besides* those that contribute to maintaining subordination and privilege, we could better acknowledge that there are positive aspects to having a gender and a race. And second, the accounts would provide a framework for envisioning the sorts of constructive changes needed to create a more just world. The suggestion that we must eliminate race and gender may be a powerful rallying call to those who identify with radical causes, but it is not at all clear that societies can or should avoid giving meanings to the body, or organizing themselves to take sexual and reproductive differences into account. Don't we at least need a concept of gender that will be useful in the reconstructive effort, not only the destructive one?

Consider gender. I am sympathetic to radical rethinkings of sex and gender. In particular, I believe that we should refuse to use anatomy as a primary basis for classifying individuals and that any distinctions between kinds of sexual and reproductive bodies are importantly political and open to contest. Some authors have argued that we should acknowledge the continuum of anatomical differences and recognize at least five sexes (Fausto-Sterling 1993). And if sexual distinctions become more complex, we would also need to rethink sexuality, given that sexual desire would not fit neatly within existing homosexual/heterosexual paradigms.

However, one can encourage the proliferation of sexual and reproductive options without maintaining that we can or should eliminate *all* social implications of anatomical sex and reproduction. Given that as a species there are substantial differences in what human bodies contribute to reproduction, and what sorts of bodies bear the main physical burdens of reproduction, and given further that reproduction cannot really help but be a socially significant fact (it does, after all, produce children), it can seem difficult to imagine a functioning society, more specifically, a functioning *feminist* society, that doesn't acknowledge in some way the difference between those kinds of bodies that are likely able to bear children, and those that aren't. One could argue that we should work towards a society free of gender in a materialist sense – one in which sex-oppression does not exist – while still allowing that sexual and reproductive differences should be taken into account in a just society (Frye 1996; Gatens 1996).

I will not debate here the degree to which a just society must be attentive to sexual and reproductive differences. Whether we, as feminists, ought to recommend the construction of (new) non-hierarchical genders or work to abolish gender entirely is a normative issue I leave for another occasion. Nonetheless, at the very least it would help to have terminology to debate these issues. I propose that we use the definitions of *man* and *woman* offered above: it is clear that these dominant nodes of our current gender structures are hierarchical. But borrowing strategies employed before, we can define gender in generic terms under which the previous definitions of man and women fall,[20] thus allowing the possibility of non-hierarchical genders and breaking the binary opposition between man and woman.

> A group G is *a gender* relative to context C iff_{df} members of G are (all and only) those:
>
> (i) who are regularly observed or imagined to have certain bodily features presumed in C to be evidence of their reproductive capacities[21];
> (ii) whose having (or being imagined to have) these features marks them within the context of the ideology in C as motivating and justifying some aspect(s) of their social position; and
> (iii) whose satisfying (i) and (ii) plays (or would play) a role in C in their social position's having one or another of these designated aspects.

I offer this analysis as a way of capturing the standard slogan: gender is the social meaning of sex. Note, however, that in imagining "alternative" genders we should be careful not to take for granted that the relevant biological divisions will correspond to what *we* consider "sex".[22] (Alternative groupings could include: "pregnant persons," "lactating persons," "menstruating persons," "infertile persons," (perhaps "homosexuals," depending on the story given about physical causes)). Neither should we assume that membership in a gender will constitute one's personal or psychological identity to any significant degree. Recall that on the accounts of gender and race I am proposing, both are to be understood first and foremost as social groups defined within a structure of social relations; whatever links there might be to identities and norms are highly contingent and would depend on the details of the picture. For example, we might imagine that "after the revolution" gender is a component of one's overall social position because, for example, there are legal protections or medical entitlements granted to individuals classified as having a certain sort of "sexed" body; but this need not have broad implications for psychological identity or everyday social interactions, for the "sex" of bodies might not even be publicly marked.

Turning briefly to race, the parallel issue arises: Do we need a concept of non-hierarchical "races" in order to frame and debate different visions of a "racially" just society? It would seem that we have the terminological resources available without a further definition: let races be, as previously defined, those hierarchically organized groups that are defined (roughly) by physical features and (assumed) geographical origins, and call those that aren't hierarchically organized (in the context in question) "ethnicities". Admittedly, ethnicity as we know it does have implications for social status and power, so my proposal is to employ the term for a somewhat idealized conception.

As in the case of gender, the question arises whether it ought to be part of an anti-racist project to recommend the preservation of existing ethnic groups or the formation of "new" ethnicities. And more generally, we need to ask whether a feminist anti-racism should treat genders and ethno-racial groups in the same way over the long term. Should we seek, e.g., to eliminate all genders and ethno-racial groupings; to preserve and proliferate them; to eliminate gender but not ethnicity (or vice versa)? These questions deserve careful attention but I cannot address them here.

Because the structure of definitions has become quite complex, it may help at this point to provide a diagram:

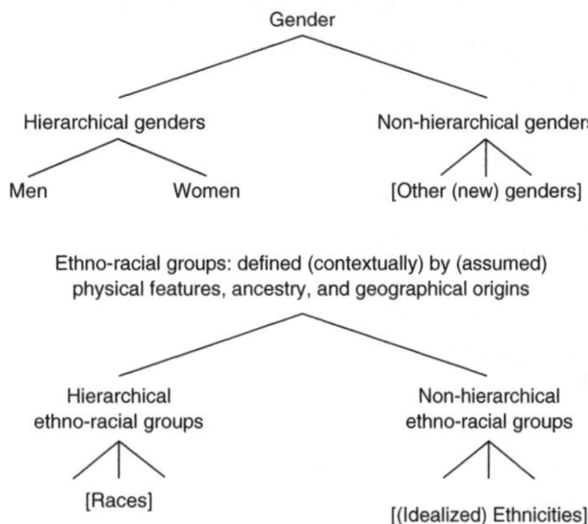

VIII Conclusion

On the accounts I've offered, there are striking parallels between race and gender. Both gender and race are real, and both are social categories. Neither gender nor race is chosen, but the forms they take can be resisted or mutated. Both race and gender (as we know it) are hierarchical, but the systems that sustain the hierarchy are contingent. And although the ideologies of race and gender and the hierarchical structures they sustain are substantively very different, they are intertwined.

There are many different types of human bodies; it is not the case that there is a unique "right" way of classifying them, though certain classifications will be more useful for some purposes than others. How we classify bodies can and does matter politically, for our laws, social institutions, and personal identities are profoundly linked to understandings of the body and its possibilities. This is compatible with the idea that what possibilities a human body has is not wholly a function of our understandings of it. Our bodies often outdo us, and undo us, in spite of the meanings we give them.

Within the framework I've sketched, there is room for theoretical categories such as *man, woman,* and *race* (and particular racial groups), that take hierarchy to be a constitutive element, and those such as *gender* and *ethnicity* that do not. As I have suggested before, I am willing to grant that there are other ways to define race or gender, man or woman, that are useful to answer different questions, motivated by different concerns and priorities. I'm sure we need several concepts to do all the work needed in understanding the complex systems of racial and gender subordination.

In short, (speaking of my analyses) I'm less committed to saying that *this* is what gender is and what race is, than to saying that *these* are important categories that a feminist antiracist theory needs. As I've explained above, I think there are rhetorical advantages to using the terms "gender", "man" and "woman," and "race" for the concepts I've defined, but if someone else is determined to have those terms, I'll use different ones. To return to the point made much earlier in characterizing analytic projects: it is our responsibility to define gender and race for our theoretical purposes. The world itself can't tell us what gender is. The same is true for race. It may be as Appiah claims that "there is nothing in the world that can do all we ask race to do for us" (Appiah 1992, 45), if our project inevitably inherits the concept's complex history; but we might instead ask "race" to do different things than have been asked before. Of course, in defining our terms, we must keep clearly in mind our political aims both in analyzing the past and present, and in envisioning alternative futures. But rather than worrying, "what is gender, really?" or "what is race, really?" I think we should begin by asking (both in the theoretical and political sense) what, if anything, we want them to be.

Notes

1 I use the terms "man" and "woman" to distinguish individuals on the basis of gender, the terms "male" and "female" to distinguish individuals on the basis of sex.

2 See Stich 1988. Stich uses the term "analytical epistemology" for what I would call a "conceptual" rather than an "analytical" project.

3 Cf. Appiah and Gutmann 1996, pp. 30–105. Appiah doesn't consider an analytical approach to race except rather elliptically on p. 42.

4 On the distinction between manifest and operative concepts, see my 1993, esp. p. 102.

5 It is important to keep in mind that what's at issue is not a criterion for *sameness* of meaning, but the boundary between what could count as a revisionary project and a new project altogether.

6 We need here a term for those physical features of individuals that mark them as members of a race. One might refer to them as "racial" features, but to avoid any suggestion of racial essences I will use the term "color" to refer to the (contextually variable) physical "markers" of race, just as I use the term "sex" to refer to the (contextually variable) physical "markers" of gender. I mean to include in "color" more than just skin tone: common markers also include eye, nose, and lip shape, hair texture, physique, etc. Although the term "people of color" is used to refer to non-Whites, I want to allow that the markers of "Whiteness" count as "color."

7 There are at least four different uses of the term "identity" that are relevant in considering the issue of gender or racial "identity"; here my comments about "gender identity" are admittedly superficial.

8 Very roughly, feminine norms are those that enable one to excel in the social position constituting the class *women*; feminine gender identity (at least in one sense of the term) is a psychological orientation to the world that includes the internalization of feminine norms; and feminine symbols are those that encode idealized feminine norms. What counts as a "feminine" norm, a "feminine" gender identity, or a "feminine" symbol is derivative (norms, symbols, and identities are not intrinsically feminine or masculine), and depends on how the social class of women is locally constituted.

9 For a sample of materialist feminist work, see Hennessy and Ingraham 1997.

10 Some theorists (Delphy, Hartmann) focus on the economic exploitation of women in domestic relations of production; others (Wittig) focus on sexual and reproductive exploitation under compulsory heterosexuality; others (MacKinnon) focus on sexual objectification.

11 These analyses allow that there isn't a common understanding of "sex" across time and place. On my account, gendered social positions are those marked by reference to features that are generally assumed *in the context in question* to either explain or provide evidence of reproductive role, whether or not these are features that *we* consider "sex".

12 On the importance of disaggregating power and oppression, see Ortner 1996.

13 This proposal depends on the claim that at least some societies have a "dominant ideology". Others have employed the notions of "background," "hegemony," "habitus," for the same purpose. Rather than debating what is the preferred notion, I'm happy to let the term "dominant ideology" serve as a placeholder for an account to be decided upon later. Given the strategy of my accounts, however, we must be sure to allow for multiple ideological strands in any society. See Geuss 1981, Hoy 1994.

14 We noted before that on a materialist account sex and gender don't always coincide. I'm making here a further claim: one may be gendered man or woman without functioning socially in that gender every moment of one's life.

15 On this I am deeply indebted to Stevens 1999, Ch. 4, and Omi and Winant 1994, esp. pp. 53–61.

16 There are aspects of this definition that need further elaboration or qualification. I will mention four here.

First, on my account, those who actually have the ancestral links to the specified region but who "pass", do not count as members of the racialized group in question. This is parallel to the case of a female functioning socially as a man or a male functioning socially as a woman. Because the goal is to define race and gender as social positions, I endorse this consequence of the definitions.

Second, as it stands the definition does not accommodate contexts such as Brazil in which membership in "racial" groups is partly a function of education and class. It excludes privileged ("Whitened") members from the subordinate races they might seem – considering only "color" – to belong to, and subordinated ("darkened") members from privileged races, because they don't satisfy the third condition. But it cannot handle the inclusion of the "Whitened" members in the privileged group or the "darkened" members in the subordinated group because they don't satisfy the first condition. However, we could take the definition to capture a *strong* version of racialization, and develop another version on which appropriate "color" is relevant but not necessary by modifying the second condition:

> ii*) having (or being imagined to have) these features – *possibly in combination with others* – marks them within the context of C's cultural ideology as appropriately occupying the kinds of social position that are in fact either subordinate or privileged (and so motivates and justifies their occupying such a position);

The first condition already allows that the group's members may have supposed origins in more than one region (originally necessary to accommodate the racialization of "mixed-race" groups); modifying the second condition allows that racialized groups may include people of different "colors", and depend on a variety of factors.

Third, need racialized groups be "marked" by actual or assumed body type? What about Jews, Native Americans, and Romanies? (Romanies are also interesting because it isn't entirely clear that there is a supposed place of origin, though I take "no place of origin" to be a factor in their racialization, and to serve as the limit case.) I would suggest that that there are *some* (perhaps imagined) physical features that are regarded as salient in contexts where Jews and Native Americans are racialized, though not every member of the group need have those features if there is other evidence of ancestral links. However, ultimately it might be more useful to allow racial membership to be determined by a cluster of features (such as physical appearance, ancestry, and class) weighted differently in different contexts.

Finally, I want the definition to capture the idea that members of racial groups may be scattered across social contexts and may not all actually be (immediately) affected by local structures of privilege and subordination. So, for example, Black Africans and African-Americans are together members of a group currently racialized in the US, even if a certain ideological interpretation of their "color" has not played a role in the subordination of all Black Africans. So I suggest that members of a group racialized in C are those who are *or would be* marked and correspondingly subordinated or privileged when in C. Those who think (plausibly) that all Blacks worldwide have been affected by the structures and ideology of White supremacy do not need this added clause; and those who want a potentially more fine-grained basis for racial membership can drop it.

17 As in the case of gender, I recommend that we view membership in a racial/ethnic group in terms of how one is viewed and treated regularly and for the most part in the context in question; though as before, one could distinguish *being* a member of a given race from *functioning as* one by considering the degree of one's entrenchment in the racialized social position (not on the basis of biology or ancestry).

18 We may want to allow there to be kinds of social stratification between ethnic groups that falls short of the kind of systematic subordination constitutive of race. My account remains vague on this point. Clarification might be gained by plugging in a more sophisticated account of social hierarchies. The body is also relevant: are ethnicities distinguishable from races by the degree to which they are perceived as capable of assimilation?

19 Trey Ellis, *Village Voice*, June 13, 1989; quoted in H. L. Gates 1992, "What's In a Name?", p. 139. Gates quotes the passage differently, leaving out "black" before "ass". Although he adds Ellis's conclusion, he robs the quote of its self-exemplifying power by the alteration.

20 Thanks to Geoff Sayre-McCord for suggesting this approach.

21 It is important here that the "observations" or "imaginings" in question not be idiosyncratic but part of a broader pattern of social perception; however, they need not occur, as in the case of *man*

and *woman*, "for the most part". They may even be both regular and rare.

22 I leave it an open question whether groups that have been identified as "third genders" count as genders on my account. Some accounts of gender that purport to include third genders pay inadequate attention to the body, so cannot distinguish, e.g., race from gender. See, for example, Roscoe 1996.

References

Anderson, Elizabeth (1995) "Knowledge, Human Interests, and Objectivity in Feminist Epistemology," *Philosophical Topics* 23:2: 27–58.

Appiah, K. Anthony and Amy Gutmann (1996) *Color Conscious*. Princeton, NJ: Princeton University Press.

Appiah, K. Anthony (1992) *In My Father's House*. New York: Oxford University Press.

Butler, Judith (1990) *Gender Trouble*. New York: Routledge.

Crenshaw, Kimberlé (1993) "Beyond Racism and Misogyny: Black Feminism and 2 Live Crew," *Words that Wound*, ed. M. Matsuda, C. Lawrence, R. Delgado, and K. Crenshaw. Boulder, CO: Westview, 111–32.

Fausto-Sterling, Anne (1993) "The Five Sexes: Why Male and Female Are Not Enough," *The Sciences* 33:2: 20–4.

Frye, Marilyn (1983) *The Politics of Reality*. Freedom, CA: Crossing Press.

Frye, Marilyn (1996) "The Necessity of Differences: Constructing a Positive Category of Women," *Signs* 21:4: 991–1010.

Gatens, Moira (1996) "A Critique of the Sex-Gender Distinction," *Imaginary Bodies*. New York: Routledge, 3–20.

Gates, Henry Louis Jr., (1992) *Loose Canons*. New York: Oxford University Press.

Geuss, Raymond (1981) *The Idea of a Critical Theory*. Cambridge: Cambridge University Press.

Haslanger, Sally (1993) "On Being Objective and Being Objectified," *A Mind of One's Own*, ed. L. Antony and C. Witt Boulder: Westview, 85–125.

Hennessy, Rosemary, and Chrys Ingraham, eds. (1997) *Materialist Feminism*. New York: Routledge.

Hoy, David (1994) "Deconstructing Ideology," *Philosophy and Literature* 18:1.

Hurtado, Aída (1994) "Relating to Privilege: Seduction and Rejection in the Subordination of White Women and Women of Color," *Theorizing Feminism*, ed. Anne Hermann and Abigail Stewart. Boulder, CO: Westview Press, 136–54.

MacKinnon, Catharine (1987) "Difference and Dominance: On Sex Discrimination," *Feminism Unmodified*. Cambridge, MA: Harvard University Press, 32–45.

Omi, M., and H. Winant (1994) *Racial Formation in the United States*. New York: Routledge.

Ortner, Sherry (1996) "Gender Hegemonies," *Making Gender*. Boston: Beacon Press, 139–72.

Riley, Denise (1988) *Am I That Name?* Minneapolis: University of Minnesota Press.

Roscoe, Will (1996) "How to Become a Berdache: Toward a Unified Analysis of Gender Diversity," *Third Sex, Third Gender*, ed. Gilbert Herdt. New York: Zone Books, 329–72.

Scott, Joan (1986) "Gender: A Useful Category of Historical Analysis," *American Historical Review* 91:5: 1053–75.

Spelman, Elizabeth (1988) *The Inessential Woman*. Boston: Beacon Press.

Stevens, Jacqueline (1999) *Reproducing the State*. Princeton: Princeton University Press.

Stich, Stephen (1988) "Reflective Equilibrium, Analytic Epistemology, and the Problem of Cognitive Diversity," *Synthese* 74: 391–413.

Stoltenberg, John (1989) *Refusing To Be a Man*. New York: Meridian Books.

Thorne, Barrie (1993) *Gender Play*. New Brunswick, NJ: Rutgers University Press.

Young, Iris (1990) *Justice and the Politics of Difference*. Princeton: Princeton University Press.

Part IV

Is Knowledge Gendered?

Introduction to Part IV

"Epistemology" derives from the Greek terms "episteme" and "logos," meaning "knowledge" and "explanation" respectively. Epistemology is thus a branch of philosophy that studies the nature, scope, and sources of knowledge. Some of the types of questions that epistemologists have traditionally concerned themselves with include: What is knowledge? Is it possible to have any knowledge? If so, what are its scope and limits? What conditions are required for knowledge? When and under what conditions is a belief justified? And so forth.

Philosophers of science have also expressed interest in the nature and limits of knowledge, but with a particular focus on scientific knowledge. Science often enjoys a privileged position in epistemology, due in large part to the assumption that the methods of science are truth-generating. Epistemologists and philosophers of science aim to explain the basis of this cognitive authority in part by examining the nature, justification, and confirmation of scientific theories.

The past several decades have brought a flurry of feminist criticisms of epistemology and philosophy of science. Epistemologists have traditionally treated gender as irrelevant to the study of knowledge. Yet, early research in feminist epistemology revealed androcentric bias in the characterization of many core epistemological concepts – such as knowledge, the knowing subject, rationality, emotion, and objectivity. Likewise, feminist philosophers of science have provided a host of examples of sexist bias in scientific theories, models, and experiments. In response to these discoveries, feminist philosophers began to defend the epistemic relevance of gender. Rather than seeing knowledge (and related concepts) as gender neutral, they argued that knowledge is often socially situated and, thus, reflects the gendered perspective of the knowing agent. However, because different feminists have different ideas about how gender situates knowers, the attitudes that they take towards epistemology and philosophy of science – as well as the revisions that they propose – are diverse. For example, some argue that bias in epistemology, science, and philosophy of science results in false, inaccurate, or distorted theories. Others, however, reject the ideal of value-free science. They maintain that it is not possible, nor is it desirable, to eliminate all biases from science. Feminist philosophers of science have also argued that the introduction of social and political values threatens the objectivity of science – but others deny that this is so. Still others question traditional representations of scientific objectivity and propose new ways of thinking about objectivity. Moreover, although most feminists agree that knowledge is socially situated, there is some disagreement over questions about epistemic privilege. Do some social groups, for example, have advantages as knowers? In response to this type of question, some feminists defend the epistemic privilege of women; others maintain that oppressed groups in general have advantages as knowers; and some deny that any group has an epistemic advantage over any other group. There is also disagreement over the form that feminist epistemology should take. Is a specifically feminist epistemology desirable, or can some version of traditional epistemology be modified for feminist ends?

In an essay that has become a classic in feminist epistemology, "The Man of Reason," Genevieve Lloyd draws the readers' attention to androcentric bias in seventeenth-century theories of rationality, knowledge, and emotion. In particular, she argues that seventeenth-century rationalism has characterized reason in ways that are culturally tied to being male. Moreover, in keeping with gender dichotomies and stereotypes, it has characterized emotion in ways that are culturally tied to being female. She adds that these assumptions have, in turn, resulted in masculinist conceptions of knowledge. Her critique, however, is not limited to seventeenth-century rationalism; it also extends to much of contemporary epistemology, which has been fundamentally influenced by seventeenth-century rationalism.

The next two chapters, by Elizabeth Anderson and Helen Longino, provide examples of a branch of feminist epistemology known as feminist empiricism. Empiricism is the view that knowledge claims are justified primarily (or solely) by experience. Feminist empiricism shares this basic assumption, but deviates from traditional empiricism by rejecting some of its other basic assumptions – such as the presumed value-neutrality of inquiry, the gender neutrality of the knowing subject, and the assumption that the ideal epistemic agent is a solitary individual who attains knowledge strictly through her own epistemic efforts.

In "Feminist Epistemology: An Interpretation and a Defense," Anderson addresses the question of how to revise epistemology for feminist ends. She argues that feminist epistemology is best understood as a social branch of naturalized epistemology that studies the ways in which conceptions of gender and associated norms influence, or ought to influence, the production of knowledge. Naturalized epistemologists see epistemology as closely connected to the empirical sciences and, thus, use empirical science to investigate epistemic activity. Social epistemology is a branch of naturalized epistemology that studies the ways that specifically social factors shape knowledge production. She defends this interpretation in part by arguing that it helps to elucidate many of the central problems of the field while, at the same time, avoiding dubious claims about feminine ways of knowing or women's epistemic privilege.

The next chapter, Helen Longino's "Can there be a Feminist Science?" addresses the question of whether it makes sense to talk about feminist science – or, is the very idea of feminist science an oxymoron? This question arises because philosophers of science have traditionally assumed that the best scientific inquiry is impersonal, objective, and value-free. The idea of a feminist science, on the other hand, suggests that social values and ideological commitment are important elements of scientific inquiry. Although contemporary philosophers of science have come to accept that social and political values sometimes influence the "context of discovery" (the process of hypothesis formation), many continue to defend the ideal of a value-free science by arguing that such values get screened out in the context of justification (the confirmation process). Longino, however, disagrees. Relying on the Quine-Duhem thesis – viz., the idea that scientific theories do not confront the evidence on their own, they make testable predictions only when conjoined with certain background assumptions – she argues that it is not possible to screen out all social or political values in the confirmation process. Part of the reason is that, aside from certain cognitive values (simplicity, entrenchment, testability, generality, etc.), there is little to prevent scientists from selecting assumptions according to their fit with their own value systems. Some philosophers might take this to be a unhappy conclusion for science. Longino, on the other hand, argues that value-neutrality should no longer be viewed as a desirable goal for science.

In contrast to the empiricist perspective adopted by Anderson and Longino, Sandra Harding advocates a position known as feminist standpoint epistemology. Early feminist standpoint epistemologists argued that knowledge is socially situated and that women's epistemic perspective is privileged. In "Rethinking Standpoint Epistemology: What is 'Strong Objectivity'?" Harding revises feminist standpoint theory and defends it against some objections. For example, some feminists reject the assumption that there is a single unified epistemic perspective shared by all women; they argue, instead, for a multiplicity of women's standpoints (black, Latina, lesbian, etc.). In response to this objection, Harding defends the epistemic authority of multiple marginalized groups, including those based on race, class, gender, sexuality, and so forth. She also responds to the worry that standpoint epistemology is inconsistent with the objectivity of knowledge. Not only does Harding deny that this is so, she argues that the methods of standpoint epistemology are better than traditional methods of research for achieving objectivity.

14

The Man of Reason

Genevieve Lloyd

By the Man of Reason I mean the ideal of rationality associated with the rationalist philosophies of the seventeenth century. And, secondly, something more nebulous – the residue of that ideal in our contemporary consciousness, our inheritance from seventeenth century rationalism. This is, I think, a substantial component in what reason has come to be. But it is not, of course, the only component. In focusing on it to the exclusion of many other developments in the notion of reason since the seventeenth century this chapter inevitably presents an incomplete picture of reason, but one which does highlight, I think, some aspects of reason which are of considerable relevance to philosophical aspects of feminism.

The main feature of the Man of Reason which I am concerned to bring into focus is his maleness. This in itself, I think, is a matter of philosophical interest. More is involved here than the supposedly "neutral" sense of "man" to include women. We are all familiar with the fact that linguistic usage commonly fails to recognize that humanity comprises two sexes. But there is something deeper to the maleness of the Man of Reason; something more deeply engrained in consciousness. He is after all a creation of reflective consciousness. When the Man of Reason is extolled, philosophers are not talking about idealizations of human beings. They are talking about ideals of manhood.

Genevieve Lloyd, "The Man of Reason," pp. 18–37 from *Metaphilosophy* 10(1), 1979. Reprinted by permission of Blackwell Publishing Ltd.

What I want to do in this chapter is to bring this undoubted maleness of the Man of Reason into clearer focus. There are, I think, reasons which belong in the history of philosophy for the association between reason and masculinity. Some parts of the history of philosophy can throw light here on a very confused and tension ridden area of human experience. Past philosophical reflection has after all helped form our present thought structures. And the creature I am calling the Man of Reason embodies some of the fundamental ideals of our culture. Let us try then to bring him into sharper focus.

The Association of "Male" with "Rational"

The associations between "male" and "rational" and between "female" and "non-rational" have, of course, a very long history. The idea that the rational is somehow specially associated with masculinity goes back to the Greek founding fathers of rationality as we know it. Aristotle thought that woman was "as it were an impotent male, for it is through a certain incapacity that the female is female".[1] This intrinsic female incapacity was a lack in the "principle of soul"[2] and hence associated with an incapacity in respect of rationality. The claim is not of course that women do not have rationality, but they have it in an inferior, fainter way. They have rationality; they are distinguished from the animals by being rational. Yet they are not equal to men. They are somehow *lesser* men, lesser in respect of the all important thing: rationality.

Later Augustine in *The Confessions* displays a similar reluctance to fully extend the privilege of male rationality to women:

> And finally we see man, made in your image and likeness, ruling over all the irrational animals for the very reason that he was made in your image and resembles you, that is because he has the power of reason and understanding. And just as in man's soul there are two forces; one which is dominant because it deliberates and one which obeys because it is subject to such guidance, in the same way in the physical sense, woman has been made for man. In her mind and her rational intelligence she has a nature the equal of man's, but in sex she is physically subject to him in the same way as our natural impulses need to be subjected to the reasoning power of the mind, in order that the actions to which they lead may be inspired by the principles of good conduct.[3]

And, two chapters later:

> Then you took man's mind, which is subject to none but you and needs to imitate no human authority, and renewed it in your own image and likeness. You made rational action subject to the rule of the intellect, as woman is subject to man.[4]

Being rational, woman ought to share a common nature with man and hence, unlike the animals, to be equal to him. But of course she is not equal to man. Augustine accommodates this tension by making a division within the rational faculty between a dominant and a passive mode of rationality, whose relationship mirrors that of woman to man.

These tensions surrounding woman's status as a rational being come to the surface during the Renaissance period, with prolonged debate centering on the vexed question "Does mankind include woman?" The rediscovery of ancient thought changed the character of education for the nobility and there was no lack of learned ladies. The acquisition of book learning by women was no doubt seen as a threat to male dominance and much of the debate of the period about woman's status as a rational being perhaps springs from this threat.

Charlotte de Brachart, in an attack on those who want to forbid knowledge to women, written in 1604, complains

> these gentlemen would like to see us plain imbeciles so that we could serve as shadows to set off better their fine wits.[5]

However that may be, the existence of women posed questions for the Renaissance world view. There was controversy over how they fitted into the scheme of things. The dignity, the perfection of man was a favorite theme of the age. For some, that meant the perfection of man alone. But there were many, men as well as women, at this period who insisted that "man" here covered the whole of the human race. Woman, her defenders of the period argue, cannot be called an imperfect animal, produced by chance through some error of nature. The divine image is perfect in her and in man equally. One man cannot be more wholly man than another, or the male more perfect in substance than the female, for both belong to the same species: man. As Marie de Gournay, a French woman writing on the equality of men and women early in the seventeenth century sums it up: "Nothing is more like a cat in a window than another cat."[6]

Such recognition of a common nature for men and women and the repudiation of Aristotle's views on the inferior natures of women did not however bring with them any automatic recognition of their equality. And widespread recognition of their common nature and equal capacities was small comfort to the ladies of the period. Nor did it prevent the endorsement of a different morality for women. There was an emphasis on different virtues, especially chastity, which was, for women, the central virtue around which all others revolved. Works on education for women at this time often focus on chastity as the principal justification for bothering with the education of women at all. A complex of social and economic factors, chiefly the fact that women were still the property of someone who therefore had special rights over them, ensured that they remained subject to a different array of moral restraints, obligations and correlative virtues. It was by no means critically assumed at this time that the dignity of man meant the dignity of males only. But the prolonged debate on the nature and rationality of women was of little consequence for sexual equality. Much of the debate in this Renaissance "war of the sexes" was conducted in theological terms, centering on the exegesis of Genesis. And what prevailed, in terms of the Genesis debate, was that *Man* was made in God's image. And that woman was made as his literal and metaphorical "offsider". Whether she also was made fully in the likeness of God paled into social insignificance compared with the fact that her *role* was to be man's companion and helpmate and hence subject to his rule.

But if reflection on the nature and extent of rationality did not help further the cause of sexual equality at this stage – as perhaps it should have done were rational considerations the only ones involved – it cannot be said that, in itself, it provided a hindrance either. In the seventeenth century, with the emergence of a special, more sharply defined, kind of reason, and the associated emergence of the Man of Reason as a character ideal, we find developing a rather different situation in the relationship between philosophical thought and social reality.

Reason in the Seventeenth Century

One of the most striking things that happens to reason in the seventeenth century is the attempt to encapsulate it in a systematic method for attaining certainty. The paradigm of this approach to reason is Descartes' *Regulae*, the *Rules for the Direction of the Mind*, written in 1628. Here there emerges a new conception of what is involved in knowledge. The acquisition of knowledge is a matter of the systematic pursuit of an orderly method. The essence of the method is to break down all the complex operations involved in reasoning into their most basic constituents and to render the mind adept in performing these simple operations – intuition and deduction. Intuition is the undoubting conception of an unclouded and attentive mind which comes from the light of reason alone. This is the basis for Descartes' later influential doctrine of clear and distinct ideas. Deduction is the process by which we extend knowledge beyond intuitions by connecting them in series. These are the only mental operations Descartes will admit into his method; but the proper understanding and use of them will, he thinks, yield all that lies within the province of knowledge. Anything else is in fact an impediment to knowledge:

> nothing can be added to the pure light of reason which does not in some way obscure it.[7]

The method is universally applicable, regardless of any difference in subject matter:

> we must not fancy that one kind of knowledge is more obscure than another, since all knowledge is of the same nature throughout, and consists solely in combining what is self evident.[8]

This universality of Cartesian method is emphasized in the *Discourse on Method* published in 1637:

> provided only that we abstain from receiving anything as true which is not so, and always retain the order which is necessary in order to deduce the one conclusion from the other, there can be nothing so remote that we cannot reach to it, nor so recondite that we cannot discover it.[9]

For Descartes, then, all knowledge consists in self evident intuition and necessary deduction. We are to break down the complex and obscure into what is simple and self evident, then combine the resultant units in an orderly manner. In order to know we must isolate the "simple natures", the objects of intuition, and "scrutinise them separately with steadfast mental gaze". We then combine them in chains of deductions. The whole of human knowledge consists in a distinct perception of the way in which these simple natures combine in order to build up other objects.[10]

There is a deeper, metaphysical, dimension to the Cartesian treatment of reason. In the course of elaborating a method for attaining certain knowledge Descartes thinks he is uncovering the unity of all the sciences, the unity of knowledge. For him this is identical with the order of thought itself, with the very structure of the knowing mind. And this order of thought is taken as transparently reflecting the order of things. In the *Regulae* there is no gap between intuitions and the simple natures which are their objective correlates. In the later *Meditations* (1641) the possibility of radical doubt opens a gap between ideas and the material world, between the structure of the mind and the structure of the reality it attempts to know. But this gap is then closed by the existence of a veracious God. Introspection of the nature of thought in an individual mind ultimately yields access to universal reason, God given and God guaranteed, and hence to the structure of reality itself, conceived by Cartesian rationalism to be identical with that of the mind.

This isomorphism between reason and reality, founded on a veracious God, gives reason a quasi divine character. Reason is God imbued, the divine spark in man. This is the seventeenth century version of the treatment of man's rational faculty as reflecting the godhead, as that in virtue of which man is made in God's image.

Another feature of Descartes' treatment of reason which is crucial here is its connection with his antithesis between mind and matter. The basic units of Cartesian method are discrete, sharp edged and self contained mental items. This becomes even more pronounced in his later works. The vehicles of knowledge are clear, precisely bordered mental states, sharply separated from one another:

> The distinct is that which is so precise and different from all other objects that it contains within itself nothing but what is clear.[11]

And this discrete, delineated character of the units of knowledge is grounded in Descartes' distinction between mind and matter. The absolute certainty which accompanies clear and distinct ideas derives from their purely mental character. Intuition, as Descartes puts it, is free of the "fluctuating testimony of the senses" and the "blundering constructions of imagination".[12] Cartesian method is essentially a matter of forming the "habit of distinguishing intellectual from corporeal matters". It is a matter of shedding the sensuous from thought.

The search for the "clear and distinct", the separating out of the emotional, the sensuous, the imaginitive, now makes possible polarizations of previously existing contrasts – intellect versus the emotions; reason versus imagination; mind versus matter. We have seen that the claim that women are somehow lacking in respect of rationality, that they are more impulsive, more emotional, than men is by no means a seventeenth century innovation. But these contrasts were previously contrasts *within* the rational. What ought to be dominated by reason had not previously been so sharply delineated from the intellectual. The conjunction of Cartesian down-grading of the sensuous with the use of the mind-matter distinction to establish the discrete character of Cartesian ideas introduces possibilities of polarization which were not there before.

Another relevant factor here is that shedding the non-intellectual from our mental states is something that demands training. In earlier centuries too, of course, it was thought appropriate to give the education of women a different character from that of men. And it was possible to present this as justified by their being different in respect of rationality. But with the seventeenth century there is a new dimension. Women can now be excluded from training *in* reason, that is, from the acquisition of method. And since this training is explicitly a matter of learning to leave one's emotions, imagination, etc. out of account, there now emerges a new dimension to the idea that women are more emotional or more impulsive, etc. than men. If they are excluded from training in rationality, women are perforce *left* emotional, impulsive, fancy ridden. They are not trained out of the "blundering constructions of the imagination" to enter the rarified air of reason. So thought styles, that are in the seventeenth century sense pre-rational, can survive in women. This *makes* is true, in a way it need not have been before, that women are less rational than men.

Also, it now becomes possible as it was not before, to have a reasoned basis for assigning the emotions, the imagination, the sensuous in general, to women as their special area of responsibility. The training of a Man of Reason does after all involve getting him to shed many of his normal characteristics. It can now be seen as woman's role to preserve for him the areas of warmth, and sensuousness which training in reason demands that he himself transcend. A great deal happens of course between the time of Descartes and that of Rousseau. But we can see this theme, elaborated almost to the point of parody, in Rousseau's views on the education of women in *Emile*, which so outraged Mary Wollstonecraft in the *Vindication of the Rights of Women*:

> To be pleasing in his sight, to win his respect and love, to train him in childhood, to tend him in manhood, to counsel and console, to make his life pleasant and happy, these are the duties of woman for all time, and this is what she should be taught while she is young.[13]

The contrast involved in the idea that man was made in God's image and woman was made to be a companion for man thus takes on a new dimension in the seventeenth century. We now have a separation of functions backed by a theory of mind. Given an already existing situation of sexual inequality, reason – the godlike, the spark of the divine in man – is assigned to the male. The emotions, the imagination, the sensuous are assigned to women. They are to provide comfort, relief, entertainment and solace for the austerity which being a Man of Reason demands. Something like this had of course been the case before. Different training was given to men and women to fit them for different life styles. But now the transcending of the sensuous can be seen as an end in itself. It is not in order to fit him for the heroic that the Man of Reason is to be trained out of his soft emotions and his sensuousness, but because that is precisely what it is to be rational. The division between reason and the non-rational can now be seen as reflecting and as being reenacted in the division between the sexes – in a way it was not before.

The stage is now set for the emergence of the Man of Reason as a male character ideal.

The Man of Reason as an Ethical Ideal

Cartesian method has its ethical correlate. Descartes' grandiose expectations of what can be gained by the elimination of sensuous intrusions on the intellect are paralleled by grandiose expectations of what can be acquired in the practical realm by gaining mastery of one's thoughts. In a letter to Princes Elizabeth, Descartes says:

> True philosophy teaches that even amid the saddest disasters and most bitter pains a man can always be content, provided that he knows how to use his reason.[14]

His own mastery of reason over the passions, he claims, has cured him of his hereditary dry cough and pale colour[15] and ensured that even his dreams are pleasant.[16]

But the full ethical dimensions of the seventeenth century cultivation of reason is found not in Descartes' works, but in Spinoza's *Ethics*. Here mastery of ones thoughts and the attaining of rational control over passion are no trivial pursuit of mental gymnastics for the maintenance of good health and pleasant dreams. Freeing oneself from the bondage of inadequate ideas to become a Man of Reason has as its goal nothing less than the attaining of eternity of the mind:

> the ignorant man is not only distracted in various ways by external causes without ever gaining the true acquiescence of his spirit, but moreover lives, as it were unwitting of himself, and of God, and of things, and as soon as he ceases to suffer ceases also to be.
>
> Whereas the wise man, in so far as he is regarded as such, is scarcely at all disturbed in spirit, but, being conscious of himself, and of God, and of things, by a certain eternal necessity, never ceases to be, but always possesses true acquiescence of his spirit.[17]

The details of Spinoza's account of the rewards to be gained from the cultivation of reason lie beyond the scope of this chapter. What I wish to focus on here are some features of his treatment of the relationship between reason and emotion.

It would not be true to say that Spinoza recommends that the Man of Reason ignore his passions. The task is not to ignore his emotions but, on the contrary, to understand them, thereby transforming them from passivities into active, rational emotions:

> An emotion, which is a passion, ceases to be a passion, as soon as we form a clear and distinct idea thereof.[18]
>
> An emotion therefore becomes more under our control, and the mind is less passive in respect of it, in proportion as it is more known to us.[19]

Emotions in their original state, that is as passions, are confused modes of perception of reality. When this confusion is replaced by clear and distinct perception the emotions cease to be passions. This process is bound up with the understanding of the causality of our passions and hence, for Spinoza, with the recognition of necessities. And this recognition of necessity is at the same time the means of attaining freedom. The transition from passion to active, intellectual emotion through the understanding of necessities is the transition to individual autonomy. Despite his metaphysical rejection of a plurality of individual substances, Spinoza's ethic is highly individualistic. But the achievement of individuality is at the cost of a detachment from the particular, the specific, the transient, in order to turn one's attention increasingly to the general, the universal, the unchanging, to what is common to all:

> an emotion which springs from reason is necessarily referred to the common properties of things, . . . which we always regard as present (for there can be nothing to exclude their present existence) and which we always conceive in the same manner. Wherefore an emotion of this kind always remains the same.[20]

So it is his increasing detachment from the transient and his increasing attachment to the unchanging that renders Spinoza's Man of Reason acquiescent and thereby free. The Man of Reason's attachments become increasingly directed away from the contingencies and vicissitudes of interactions with individuals and towards what is common to all. And he moves increasingly in a realm where the appearance of contingency gives way to the recognition of necessity:

> the strong man has ever first in his thoughts that all things follow from the necessity of the divine nature; so that whatsoever he deems to be hurtful and evil, and whatsoever, accordingly seems to him impious, horrible, unjust or base, assumes that appearance owing to his own disordered, fragmentary and confused view of the universe. Wherefore he strives before all things to conceive things as they really are, and to remove the hindrances to true knowledge, such as are hatred, anger, envy, derision, pride and similar emotions . . . Thus he endeavours, as far as in him lies, to do good and go on his way rejoicing.[21]

This sounds like a commendable exercise in tolerance of perception. And indeed it is that. The Man of Reason endeavours to transcend the distortions of his own self centred perception to perceive things as they really are. But if Spinoza's "strong man" recognizes the particular objects of his hate as seeming hateful only because of his own inadequate ideas, the same goes for the objects of his love. As Reason acquires dominance, changeable transient objects of affection are gradually cast aside:

> spiritual unhealthiness and misfortunes can generally be traced to excessive love for something which is subject to many variations, and which we never become masters of. For none is solicitous or anxious about anything, unless he loves it; neither do wrongs, suspicions, enmities, etc. arise, except in regard to things whereof no one can be really master.
>
> We may thus readily conceive the power which clear and distinct knowledge, and especially this third kind of knowledge . . . founded on the actual knowledge of God, possesses on the emotions: if it does not absolutely destroy them, in so far as they are passions; at any rate it causes them to occupy a very small part of the mind. . . . Further, it begets a love towards a thing immutable and eternal, whereof we may really enter into possession; neither can it be defiled by those faults which are inherent in ordinary love; but it may grow from strength to strength and may engross the greater part of the mind and deeply penetrate it.[22]
>
> Something else the Man of Reason sheds along the way is pity. Pity in a man who lives under the guidance of reason is in itself bad and useless.[23]
>
> He who rightly realizes that all things follow from the necessity of the divine nature, and come to pass in accordance with the eternal laws and rules of nature, will not find anything worthy of hatred, derision or contempt, nor will he bestow pity on anything. . . .[24]

In another section Spinoza described pity as "womanish".[25]

The ideal, again, is a masculine one. The ultimate horror for Spinoza's Man of Reason is to be "womanish", which is equated with being under the sway of passions, untransformed by reason. The full picture is of a man detached from changeable objects of passion to the point where temporal transience, including the fact of death is of no consequence:

> In so far as the mind conceives a thing under the dictates of reason, it is affected equally, whether the idea be of a thing future, past or present.[26]
>
> A free man thinks of death least of all things; and his wisdom is a meditation not of death but of life.[27]

Here we have the ultimate glorification of reason in its ethical dimension. But although the cultivation of reason is the means by which we attain to freedom; the motivating force for this effort is self-interest, the desire to persist in one's being. This emphasis on self-interest as the underlying ethical force is in some ways an anticipation of the more utilitarian spirit of the eighteenth century attitudes to the passions. The very essence of a man, according to Spinoza, resides in his endeavour to persist in his being. And, as a thinking being, his overriding self-interest is in preserving the coherence and continuity of his own thought against the flow of unconnected, fragmentary ideas that result from his limited, individual standpoint within the order of things. The more active his though processes the less he is at the mercy of the impingement of what is not himself, including, as we have seen, the demands of pity and the ravages of "meretricious" love. And the more autonomous, the more himself, he becomes. So integral is this connection between reason and the endeavour to persist in one's being that for Spinoza the rational mind simply cannot will not to be.[28]

All this gives to the *Ethics* a life affirming character and an emphasis on individuality that cannot be underestimated. But, as we have seen, this is in fact achieved at the cost of a detachment from changeable, individual objects of concern. It is true that the life style described by Spinoza contains positive compensations for the apparent impoverishment of individual life his ethical system involves. But what remains with us as the character ideal expressed in his Man of Reason is mainly the negative detachment from all that gives warmth and compassion to human existence – his ultimate detachment from the impingement of all that is not himself.

There is indeed much that is appealing and impressive in the picture Spinoza presents of the Man of Reason – the transcending of self-centered and hence dependent, jealous love; the pursuit of a detached perception of the truths of himself and his situation, transcending the distortions of his limited, unreflective perspective on things; the location of moral worth in a certain style of perception rather than in the will. Spinoza's attempt to combine a recognition of self interest as the basis of ethics – the rejection of false altruism and false sentiment – with the effort to transcend the distortions of a limited, individual perspective on the world remains of enduring significance. But the Man of Reason, we have seen, sheds not merely selfish, obsessive love, but also individuals as proper objects of love. This, along with his repudiation of "womanish" pity, may well seem too much to pay for liberation from the bondage of passion.

There is of course no suggestion that any man of reason will actually live like that. Pure specimens of the breed were no doubt non existent. "All things excellent are as difficult as they are rare", Spinoza says at the end of the *Ethics*. But it is the conception of the Man of Reason as an ideal that we are considering here. And we may well, I think, find the rarity of his particular kind of moral excellence no great cause for regret.

Reason and Intuition

Another area of relevance to the maleness of the Man of Reason concerns the relationship between reason and intuition. Spinoza identifies the pursuit of freedom with the cultivation of reason, in a broad sense. But, strictly, the higher levels of freedom which lead on to eternity of the mind are attained not through reason by which he means, roughly, ratiocination – the reason of Descartes' *Regulae* – but through what he calls "Scientia Intuitiva". This is a kind of knowledge superior to reason. It gives adequate knowledge of the essences of things and proceeds from an adequate idea of the absolute essence of the attributes of God. The exact nature of Spinoza's "intuition" need not concern us. What is important about it here is that Spinoza, in treating it as the highest form of knowledge, recognizes the limitations of the systematized reason of Cartesian method. This is of course a very different sense of the limitations of reason from that of later nineteenth century thought, which saw reason as limited in contrast to the access to reality provided by the will or the imagination. "Scientia intuitiva", whatever its exact nature, is clearly a mode of thought more closely related to Cartesian reason that to imagination. But Spinoza's treatment of intuition amounts nonetheless to a recognition of the limitations of the style of thinking systematized by Descartes. Intuitions for Descartes were the basic clear and distinct perceptions which were systematized by reason. For Spinoza intuition became a different form of thought, superior to reason.

Spinoza's recognition of the limitations of reason may seem surprising in a seventeenth century rationalist. But this is not as novel as it at first appears. In his letters to Princes Elizabeth, Descartes himself shows some awareness of the limitations of the style of thought he has developed. Although the purely intellectual can be separated out from the sensuous to yield clear and distinct ideas, the ideas thus obtained cannot, he admits, yield the whole truth. Clear and distinct perception demands the separation of mind from matter. But we have not grasped the whole truth unless we grasp also the union of mind and body. And to understand that, clearness and distinctness are of no use. Indeed, he goes on, it is only by refraining from metaphysical speculation that we can understand the union of mind and body.[29]

I am not sure how seriously Descartes should be taken here, though he is at pains to assure Elizabeth that he is not making fun of her. But there are in any case tensions within Descartes' treatment of the "intuitions" which are the very basis of his method, which give rise to some questions about the limitations of this style of reasoning.

Descartes saw himself as breaking with tradition, as shedding the stifling molds into which thought processes had been channelled by the excesses of the neo-scholastics. Method was to be above all a way of thinking originally, from one's own resources. This indeed was what his basic intuitions were supposed to be – the fresh, spontaneous, unclouded apprehensions of a mind operating in accordance with its understanding of its own nature. Yet in the fully developed Cartesian method, intuition becomes circumscribed by a process of ratiocination. Intuition becomes something the mind has to train itself to do; something it cannot be relied upon to do of its own untrained initiative. It becomes a legitimate question to ask, "Have I really managed to bring off in the approved manner a clear and distinct perception?" And with this arises the possibility of doubt about the reliability of reason itself. Authority, supposedly exorcised with the break from tradition, rears its head within method, intruding its demands into the inner recesses of consciousness itself. "This is how you must think if you wish to attain truth." Descartes begins from an emphasis on personal autonomous knowledge, the development of one's own judgments in a direct response to reality, untrammelled by appeals to authority. Yet Cartesian method itself shackles intuition within a method for knowing – a method in which the mind must be trained. This is partly of course just a matter of subjecting the erratic, unreliable vagaries of individual consciousness to the demands of rigour and discipline. But it is easy then to mistake the artificially created units Descartes has carved out of the flux of consciousness for the true nature of mind; as if mental life were really a succession of discrete, stabilized mental states.

This is partly why Descartes' "intuitions" break out of the bonds in which reason has put them. Descartes ties himself in knots attempting to validate the basic intuitions, to prove them reliable; moving, inevitably, in circles as he tries to establish the reliability of the mind's basic apprehensions by reasoning about them. The basic intuitions remain an unjustified base and Cartesian method is limited to ordering and systematizing them. A detailed critique of Descartes' attempt to justify the reliability of reason, on which a great deal has been written, is not my concern. What I want to emphasize is just that the rationalist's conception of reason does encapsulate thought artificially into discrete mental states, subject to rigorously disciplined order; and, especially from Descartes' treatment of reason, it then becomes easy to mistake this artificial creation for the real nature of consciousness.

Leibniz' treatment of knowledge shows a more explicit awareness of the pre-Rational underpinning of the sharply delineated constituents of seventeenth-century-style reasoning. His ideal of method coexists strikingly with a repeated insistence on the buzzing confusion of consciousness, incorporated into his system as the unconscious perceptions of the monads. Clean and distinct perception is a small isolated area of consciousness against a background of confusion:

> our confused sensations are the result of a variety of perceptions. This variety is infinite. It is almost like the confused murmuring which is heard by those who approach the shore of the sea. It comes from the continual beatings of innumerable waves.[30]

We have seen that the seventeenth century rationalists were aware of the limited, and limiting, character of systematized reason. Nonetheless what has come down to us as our unmistakeable inheritance from seventeenth century rationalism is the ideal of method, construed as expressing the true nature of the mind. Although much has happened since in the development of reason, this rationalist model still underlies our "rational" thought styles. Conversely, "intuition" has come to mean the negation of all this – a though style which is not sharpened and systematized in the manner of which Cartesian method is the paradigm. Intuition, inevitably, has come to be associated with specifically *female* thought styles.

If female minds are more intuitive, that is less rational, than male minds, it is mainly because rationality has been circumscribed to have no use for what, given the status quo, differentiates minds as female. If women's minds are less rational than mens', it is because the limits of reason have been set in a way that excludes qualities that are then assigned to women. It may well be true that thought styles that are not rational, in the seventeenth century sense, have survived more in women than in men as a result of their general exclusion from, at any rate, the more rarified levels of training in rationality. Here, in insisting on the existence and merits of "female intuition" women may in effect be trying to turn their own victimization into a false strength. "Female intuition" can, quite rightly, be a pejorative term.

An awareness of the claims of "intuition" can, nonetheless, be part of a constructive assessment of the claims and the ideals of reason. The Man of Reason is, after all, becoming in our times less able to bask in the glories of his self image, less confident in his self-styled dignity. There is, of course, a lot to be said in praise of the Man of Reason. But it *has* all been said. In the increasing self-questioning of the ideals of reason, the feminist challenge to male sovereignty – to women's exclusion from the power structure, which is in some ways identifiable with rationality – can be sterile and self defeating unless it is conjoined with a critical assessment of reason itself.

The Contemporary Man of Reason

The Man of Reason has, of course, had his crises before and been changed by them. In the eighteenth century he was stripped of his godlike character. The *philosophes* brought reason down to earth. No longer the spark of the divine in man, no longer dependent on nor guaranteed by God, reason was brought to bear critically on religion itself. But this did not really amount to a downgrading of reason. The result was rather, in some ways, to make a god of man himself. Optimism about reason survived the loss of its divine aura and much of the elitism associated with it in the seventeenth century. The *philosophes* were great popularizers of reason and this gave a new twist to women's relationship to reason in the eighteenth century. Woman was taken as the ultimate paradigm of "the common man".

The eighteenth century sees also a revaluation of the emotions. In the seventeenth century the passions were characteristically seen as a source of disorder and falsehood. Thought was the essence of the mind; the passions were seen as intruding distractions and disturbances resulting from the mind's union with the body. Although not necessarily disapproved of, they were seen as, at worst, threats to the purity and clarity of thought; and, at best, as confused modes of thought itself. They were to be either transcended and kept in subjugation by reason or else transformed by reason into higher modes of thought. The eighteenth century saw a defence of the passions as the well springs of action, with reason providing the means for achieving the dictates of passion. Something like this, we have seen, was already present in Spinoza's treatment of thought and emotion. But there it coexisted with an insistence on an inner weakness, a lack of reality in the passions; which made them amenable not just to domination by reason but to complete transformation by it. From the eighteenth century on, the passions, and the non-rational in general, are more assured of their own reality.

Even if controlled by reason, passion remains something different from thought, a motivating force in its own right. And by the nineteenth century, with the Romantic movement, it could be seen as challenging the supremacy of reason.

With the Romantic revaluation of the passions and exaltation of imagination and feeling we might expect a new evaluation of women along with the qualities associated with women. And so indeed there was, but one that proved disastrous for sexual equality – the pedestalizing of women, the revival of Romantic love. The Man of Reason stayed intact through the challenge of Romanticism, while going in search of his opposite to complete or complement his existence. The dichotomy between reason and feeling was preserved and in fact endorsed by the challenge of Romanticism.

What is distinctive about current disaffection with reason? It is not that the forces of unreason are stronger now. The Man of Reason was created in, and largely in response to, savage times. It is not that there is less faith in the basic reasonableness of human beings. What is new is the decline in optimism about the eventual victory of reason. Condorcet, an eighteenth century philosopher who died during the Terror, wrote the night before he left his hiding place in the expectation of his arrest, an affirmation of his faith in the eventual triumph of reason:

> How consoling for the philosopher who laments the errors, the crimes, the injustices which still pollute the earth and of which he is often the victim, is this view of the human race emancipated from its shackles, released from the empire of fate and from that of the enemies of its progress, advancing with a firm and sure step along the path of truth, virtue and happiness![31]

What is distinctive about current disaffection with reason is the sense that it will not all be solved by the progress of reason. It cannot any longer be said that the threats to humanity are threats posed by forces of unreason. Many of them have their source within reason itself. Man's reason is no longer an unequivocal object of his self-esteem.

The nineteenth century reactions against reason – the polarizations we associate with the exaltation of the non-rational – have, however, left a legacy in consciousness which makes it very difficult to engage in any critical assessment of the forms and structures of contemporary rationality. Critics of reason too easily fall into a sterile repudiation of the rational, a vacuous affirmation of the importance or superiority of feeling or imagination. A sense of the sterility of Romantic rejections of reason is no doubt a major reason for the lack of reasoned critiques of current forms of rationality. And any attempt to provide the notion of "intuition" with content can easily be seen in terms of such a repudiation of the rational.

This, for example, is a common reaction to Bergson's treatment of intuition and his associated critique of the limitations of rationality.[32] Bergson's "intuition" is not, as is often suggested, merely an aesthetic notion. For him it is the essential nature of metaphysics. His affirmation of intuition is not a repudiation of rationality but an attempt to get beneath the segmentation of thought involved in "clear and distinct" thinking. The project is not to reject clear and distinct Cartesian-style thought in favour of some non-rational mode of access to reality. Bergson sees clear and distinct conceptualized thought, which achieved its most self-conscious articulation in the seventeenth century, as a development in thought essential for utilitarian purposes – a development without which human beings could not have managed to cope with their environment; but, for all that, a limited thought style, especially for the purpose of speculative metaphysical understanding. Bergsonian intuition, then, is not meant to be anything mystical, but rather an attempt to get below the spatialized, discrete representations into which seventeenth-century rationalism has carved up reality; an attempt to grasp duration free of the spatializations which that form of reasoning has imposed on consciousness; an attempt to grasp the continuities rather than the separations.

More recently Robert Pirsig's book *Zen and the Art of Motor Cycle Maintenance* represents an attempt to get at the unity underlying "Classical" and "Romantic" thought styles. This is a very different kind of critique of reason from that attempted by the Romantics, who were concerned rather with affirming one side of the dichotomy. Pirsig's book points to the possibility of an expansion of reason, rather than an abandoning of it.

Another danger which besets any attempt to engage in a critique of the Man of Reason from a specifically feminist standpoint is that such critique becomes a catalogue of the atrocities he has perpetrated on women. It is easy to see the Man of Reason as just the post seventeenth century variant on the historical role of male oppressor. But men and women are jointly responsible for his continued status as an ideal of rationality, for he represents women's ideals too. What is needed is critique of his standing as an ideal, whether as an object of male self-esteem or of female envy. The impoverishment of woman through the imposition of sexual stereotypes is obvious. Exclusion from reason has meant exclusion from power. The corresponding impoverishment of men is rather less obvious, for what they miss out on has been downgraded. What is needed for the Man of Reason is realization of his limitations as a *human* ideal, in the hope that men and women alike might come to enjoy a more human life, free of the sexual stereotypes that have evolved in his shadow.

Notes

1 Aristotle: *Generation of Animals*, Book I, Ch. 20, 727a15.
2 Ibid., Book II, Ch. 3, 737a25.
3 Augustine: *The Confessions*, trans. R. S. Pine-Coffin (Penguin Classics), p. 344.
4 Ibid., p. 345.
5 Kelso, Ruth: *Doctrine for the Lady of the Renaissance* (University of Illinois Press), Urbana, 1956, p. 64. (This work is the source for much of the material in this section.)
6 Ibid., p. 17.
7 *Rules for the Direction of the Mind*, Rule IV in *Descartes: Philosophical Works*, trans. E. S. Haldane and G. R. T. Ross (Cambridge), 1968, Vol. 1, p. 10.
8 Ibid., Rule XIII, p. 47.
9 *Discourse on Method*, Part 11, op. cit., p. 92.
10 *Rules for the Direction of the Mind*, Rule XII, op. cit., p. 47.
11 Replies to the Second Set of Objections, op. cit., Vol. II, p. 32.
12 *Rules for the Direction of the Mind*, Rule III, op. cit., p. 7.
13 Rousseau, J. J.: *Emile*, Book V, trans. B. Foxley (Everyman), 1911, p. 328.
14 Descartes to Elizabeth, 6 October, 1645; in Kenny, A., ed. *Descartes' Philosophical Letters* (OUP), 1970, p. 180.
15 Descartes to Elizabeth, May or June 1645; ibid., p. 163.
16 Descartes to Elizabeth, 1 September 1645; ibid., p. 168.
17 Spinoza: *The Ethics*, trans. R. H. M. Elwes (Dover), 1955, Vol. II; Part V, Prop. XLII, p. 270.
18 Ibid., Part V, Prop. III, p. 248.
19 loc. cit.
20 Ibid., Part V, Prop. VII, p. 251.
21 Ibid., Part IV, Prop. LXXIII, p. 236.
22 Ibid., Part V, Prop. XX, p. 258.
23 Ibid., Part IV, Prop. L, p. 221.
24 loc. cit.
25 Ibid., Part IV, Prop. XXXVII, note 1, p. 213.
26 Ibid., Part IV, Prop. LXII, p. 229.
27 Ibid., Part IV, Prop. LXVII, p. 232.
28 Ibid.
29 Descartes to Elizabeth, 28 June 1643; op. cit., p. 141.
30 *Discourse on Metaphysics*, in *Leibniz: Basic Writings*, trans. G. R. Montgomery (Open Court), 1962, Ch. XXXIII, p. 57.
31 Quote in White, R. J.: *The Antiphilosophers* (Macmillan), 1970, p. 153.
32 See especially H. Bergson: *Creative Evolution* (Macmillan) 1913; *Introduction to Metaphysics* (Library of Liberal Arts) 1949. "Philosophical Intuition", in *The Creative Mind* (Citadel) 1946.

15

Feminist Epistemology: An Interpretation and a Defense

Elizabeth Anderson

[. . .] Feminist epistemology is about the ways gender influences what we take to be knowledge. Consider impersonal theoretical and scientific knowledge, the kind of knowledge privileged in the academy. Western societies have labeled this kind of knowledge "masculine" and prevented women from acquiring and producing it, often on the pretext that it would divert their vital energies from their "natural" reproductive labor (Schiebinger 1989; Hubbard 1990). Theoretical knowledge is also often tailored to the needs of mostly male managers, bureaucrats, and officials exercising power in their role-given capacities (Smith 1974; H. Rose 1987; Collins 1990). Feminist epistemologists claim that the ways gender categories have been used to understand the character and status of theoretical knowledge, whether men or women have produced and applied this knowledge, and whose interests it has served have often had a detrimental impact on its content. For instance, feminist epistemologists suggest that various kinds of practical know-how and personal knowledge (knowledge that bears the marks of the knower's biography and identity), such as the kinds of untheoretical knowledge that mothers have of children, are undervalued when they are labeled "feminine." Given the androcentric need to represent the "masculine" as independent of the "feminine," this labeling has led to a failure to use untheoretical knowledge effectively in theoretical reasoning (Smith 1974; H. Rose 1987).

Traditional epistemology finds these claims of feminist epistemology to be highly disturbing, if not plainly absurd. Some feminist epistemologists in turn have rejected empiricism (Harding 1986) or even traditional epistemology as a whole (Flax 1983) for its seeming inability to comprehend these claims. I argue, contrary to these views, that a naturalized empiricist epistemology offers excellent prospects for advancing a feminist epistemology of theoretical knowledge.

The project of feminist epistemology with respect to theoretical knowledge has two primary aims (Longino 1993a). First, it endeavors to explain the achievements of feminist criticism of science, which is devoted to revealing sexism and androcentrism in theoretical inquiry. An adequate feminist epistemology must explain what it is for a scientific theory or practice to be sexist and androcentric, how these features are expressed in theoretical inquiry and in the application of theoretical knowledge, and what bearing these

Elizabeth Anderson, "Feminist Epistemology: An Interpretation and a Defense," pp. 50–84 from *Hypatia* 10(3), 1995. Reprinted by permission of Indiana University Press, as the publisher.

features have on evaluating research. Second, the project of feminist epistemology aims to defend feminist scientific practices, which incorporate a commitment to the liberation of women and the social and political equality of all persons. An adequate feminist epistemology must explain how research projects with such moral and political commitments can produce knowledge that meets such epistemic standards as empirical adequacy and fruitfulness. I will argue that these aims can be satisfied by a branch of naturalized, social epistemology that retains commitments to a modest empiricism and to rational inquiry. Feminist naturalized epistemologists therefore demand no radical break from the fundamental internal commitments of empirical science. They may propose changes in our conceptions of what these commitments amount to, or changes in our methods of inquiry. But these can be derived from the core concept of reason, conjoined with perhaps surprising yet empirically supported hypotheses about social or psychological obstacles to achieving them, and the social and material arrangements required for enabling better research to be done. To see how such derivations are possible, modest conceptions of empiricism and reason must be explained before I outline a feminist epistemology that employs these notions.

A Modest Empiricism

I shall call "empiricism" the view that experience ultimately provides all the evidence we have about the world (Nelson 1990), or more modestly, that observation provides the least defeasible evidence we have about the world (Longino 1993a). No thought process operating independently of empirical evidence can rule out any conceivable hypothesis about the world. I believe that empiricism, so understood, is congenial to the puzzling and seemingly bizarre hypotheses of feminist epistemology because it implies two things. First, for all we know, *anything* can cause *anything*, and *anything* might provide an illuminating fruitful model for *any other phenomenon*. There are no sound a priori restrictions on the concepts or vocabulary we use in describing and explaining the world, so long as these concepts "turn wheels" in theories that have empirical implications. Second, empiricism implies that the discovery of the best theories demands the fullest and freest development of our imaginations. There is no reason to think our presently cramped and stunted imaginations set the actual limits of the world, but they do set the limits of what we now take to be possible. We can never know what further stretch of the imagination might uncover and explain what further expanse of the world. Since feminist epistemology and feminist criticism of science contain many empirical claims about the influence of gender on science that appear at first glance to be unimaginable, it is important to note that nothing in empiricism justifies dismissing such claims out of hand.

Empiricism is commonly taken to mean something else: a doctrine that imposes a priori substantive restrictions on the kinds of entities and concepts that can ultimately figure in science. Various self-described empiricists have tried to eliminate from science reference to unobservables, and use of intentional, modal, and evaluative concepts, or to reduce these to concepts thought to be more "naturalistic." These substantive commitments are simply bets as to how empirical science will actually turn out. Transformed into restrictions on the permissible content of theories, they are attempts to win the bets by rigging the game in advance, preventing the exploration of hypotheses that might show them wrong. This contradicts what I take to be the fundamental commitments of modest empiricism. Since feminist epistemology and feminist criticism of science contain many empirical claims couched in unreduced social, intentional, and evaluative vocabularies, it is important to note that modest empiricism is not committed to eliminating such claims from scientific theories.

I take modest empiricism, then, to be a purely methodological doctrine, which rejects a priori commitments to what the content of our theories and models must be. Empiricism is promiscuous in its permissible ontology and opportunistic in its methods and models. Any hypothesis or method is permitted that advances the goals of discovering and explaining novel phenomena consistent with the constraint that the theories produced seek empirical adequacy.

Rationality as Reflective Endorsability

Reason is the power to change our attitudes, intentions, and practices in response to reflection on the merits of having them or engaging in them. Theoretical reason is the power to acquire, reject, and revise our cognitive attitudes (beliefs and theoretical commitments) and our practices of inquiry through reflection on our reasons for holding them and engaging in them – that is, through reflection on arguments and evidence for our beliefs and about the consequences of our practices. Reflective endorsement is the only test for whether a consideration counts as a reason for having any attitude or engaging in any practice of inquiry: we ask, on reflecting on the ways the consideration could or does influence our attitudes and practices and the implications of its influencing us, whether we can endorse its influencing us in those ways. If we can reflectively endorse its influence, we count the consideration as a reason for our attitudes or practices (Anderson 1993, 91–8).

This conception of reason as reflective self-government rejects the ideal of individualistic self-sufficiency, which some feminists have argued is androcentric, or expressive of specifically male needs (Bordo 1987; Duran 1991). Rational inquiry is a social enterprise (Longino 1990; Nelson 1993). Anything that counts as evidence for a theory must be publicly accessible, and in experimental contexts, replicable by others. Individuals must use tools, methods, and conceptual frameworks developed by others in order to get their own inquiries under way. They must rely on the testimony of others to get evidence that is too costly or difficult for them to gather on their own, and even to interpret the evidence of their own senses (Coady 1992). Thus it is impossible for individuals to rely only on themselves, for the very reason and interpretations of their experience on which they rely and which seems most to be their own, is a social achievement, not an individual endowment (Scheman 1983; Nelson 1990).

The social character of rational inquiry suggests two things. First, the theories produced by our practices of inquiry may bear the marks of the social relations of the inquirers. To the extent that conceptions of gender inform these social relations, we might expect these conceptions to influence theoretical inquiry. Second, insofar as we reflectively reject certain ways that gender influences the practices and products of inquiry, we need not try to correct these problems by demanding that individual investigators somehow abstract from their gender or gender-related values and commitments. Each individual might be subject to perhaps ineradicable cognitive biases or partiality due to gender or other influences. But if the social relations of inquirers are well arranged, then each person's biases can check and correct the others'. In this way, theoretical rationality and objectivity can be expressed by the whole community of inquirers even when no individual's thought processes are perfectly impartial, objective, or sound (Longino 1990; Nelson 1990; Solomon 1994).

Feminist Epistemology as a Branch of Naturalized, Social Epistemology

Many theorists have proposed that we think of feminist epistemology as a social branch of naturalized epistemology (Harding 1986; Nelson 1990; Duran 1991; Tuana 1992; Antony 1993; Potter 1993). Naturalized epistemologists consider knowledge production as an activity in which inquirers are subject to the same causal forces that affect their objects of study (Quine 1969). They ask of science that it provide an account of its own activity. This point of view enables us to investigate empirically how knowledge changes as we change factors concerning the inquirers. Social epistemology is the branch of naturalized epistemology that investigates the influence of specifically social factors on knowledge production: who gets to participate in theoretical inquiry, who listens to whom, the relative prestige of different styles and fields of research, the political and economic conditions in which inquirers conduct their investigations, the social settings in which they interact with the subjects of study, their ideological commitments, the availability of models and narrative forms in the culture that can be used to structure scientific observation and explain phenomena, and so forth. Feminist epistemology can be regarded as the branch of social epistemology that investigates the influence of *socially constructed conceptions and norms of gender and gender-specific interests and experiences* on the production of knowledge. It asks how the historical exclusion of women from theoretical inquiry has affected the direction and content of research in fields such as anthropology, philosophy, and psychology; how the use of gender metaphors in biology has made some phenomena more salient than others; how history, economics, and medicine would change if we viewed phenomena from the standpoint of women's rather than men's lives; how the feminist movement has changed our data, our ways of describing the data, and our theories about differences between men and women.

These are all empirical questions. By framing the questions of feminist epistemology as empirical ones, feminist theorists can challenge mainstream theorists, who are largely empiricists, in a way that they cannot responsibly ignore or dismiss. This way of framing feminist epistemology also enables feminists to make arguments for reforming theoretical practice in terms internal to the self-critical commitments of science itself. Feminist criticisms and remedies can be seen as particular, if surprising, instances of general types of criticism and remedy already acknowledged and accommodated by scientific practice. For naturalized epistemology, considered as a tool for improving scientific practices, is already incorporated into the self-critical and self-reforming institutions of science.

How can naturalized epistemology, which studies how knowledge claims are actually produced, support normative views about how we ought to produce knowledge claims? This gap between "is" and "ought" is bridged by the reflective self-endorsement test. Naturalized epistemology considers inquirers in their social relations as systems of belief-formation processes, and theoretical inquiry as a social practice that uses these processes to generate new beliefs. These beliefs in turn are related to one another through various explanatory theories, models, or narratives that aim to produce understanding of the phenomena being studied. This two-level representation of theoretical inquiry suggests two ways naturalized epistemology can get critical leverage on our knowledge practices. First, we can examine our belief-formation processes. Some of these processes are such that, once we reflect on how they work or what they do, we lose confidence in the beliefs to which they give rise, since they do not reliably lead to true beliefs (consider optical illusions). Other processes satisfy the reflective endorsement test: reflecting on how they work or what they do leads us to endorse them and the beliefs to which they give rise (consider deductive inference). A knowledge practice is rational to the extent that it promotes such critical self-reflections and responds to them by checking or canceling out the unreliable belief-formation mechanisms and enabling the reliable ones.

The institution of placebo-controlled, double-blind, multi-center trials as the standard for testing drugs represents an exemplary critical achievement of naturalized epistemology. Each feature of this experimental standard was instituted in response to the discovery of an unreliable belief-formation mechanism that had to be checked. The well-known placebo effect, in which subjects report symptom improvement when they receive *any* intervention they believe may help them, is checked by requiring that the therapeutic effects of drugs be measured against a control group which is administered a placebo, and by requiring that subjects not know whether they belong to the control or the experimental group. Wishful thinking on the part of experimenters, which leads to exaggerated reports of the therapeutic effectiveness of drugs on trial, is checked by making the tests double-blind, so that even the experimenter does not know which group subjects belong to. Multi-center trials ensure that experimental outcomes are not merely an artifact of the micro-culture of researchers at a single site. These are all reforms scientific institutions have made in the past few decades, in response to scientific studies of its own practice.

The normative implications of much feminist epistemology and feminist criticism of science can be modeled on the case of double-blind testing. If a gendered norm is found to influence the production of knowledge claims in ways that cannot be reflectively endorsed, then we have epistemic reasons to reform our knowledge practices so that this norm is changed or its effects are blocked. Feminist empiricist epistemology thus produces arguments of the same logical type as those already accepted by our knowledge practices.

Feminist empiricist epistemology can generate normative implications for theory in a second way. The model of double-blind testing works only at the level of weeding out false beliefs. But getting an adequate understanding of phenomena is not simply a matter of removing sexist or androcentric bias from factual claims so as to allow scientists to see unvarnished truth. For theoretical inquiry does not aim simply to generate true beliefs. One can add to the stock of true beliefs without the aid of systematic theorizing. Although empirical adequacy poses a fundamental constraint on theorizing, the point of theory is to organize beliefs and generate understanding through models that explain phenomena that people find significant, important, or fundamental, and that abstract from phenomena thought to be unimportant. But whether a phenomenon is considered important or fundamental depends on practical needs and interests, which may be gendered or staked in other socially constructed positions such as class (Tiles 1987). Theories or models offer us only partial maps of the world. Thus different people may find different models satisfactory, depending on which aspects of the world the models highlight (Longino 1993b, 114–16).

This relativity of the value of a model to the socially conditioned interests and experiences of the people to whom it is offered does not imply that theoretical explanations must be false, or that all are equally good, or that there is no common basis for comparing their merits. Empirical adequacy provides the fundamental and common standard for comparing all theories. But a theory can be empirically adequate without being interesting or useful.

Thus, feminist naturalized epistemology uses reason both to constrain and to expand the range of acceptable theories, given what we know about how theories are formed. By raising the standards for evaluating methods of data collection and interpretation in the light of the reflective endorsement test, feminist epistemologists limit the field of credible theories. By legitimizing the explicit introduction of feminist interests to justify the choice of different models, feminist epistemologists use reason in its permissive mode to open up space for alternative theories oriented toward liberatory ends and to contest theories that close off possibilities for social change by representing the subjects of study as if they had no room to maneuver (Longino 1989, 210–13).

Such moves to multiply available explanatory models, like the moves to reform scientific practices on the lines of the double-blind experiment, are internal to the practices of science. These two types of critical activity correspond to the two goals of the feminist epistemology of theoretical knowledge: to legitimate science oriented toward feminist ends and to underwrite feminist criticism of sexist and androcentric science. The fact that these activities can be situated inside science does not mean that the changes feminist epistemology recommends for science must be modest. The sorts of criticisms that generate internal reform of scientific practices today focus on such matters as improving data-gathering instruments and technical features of experimental method. Feminist epistemology and feminist criticism of science focus on changing the background social conditions in which science is practiced. It is therefore an explicitly political enterprise, but one that is justified by epistemic values, such as reason and empirical adequacy, to which science already declares its allegiance.

The variety of claims made by feminist epistemologists and feminist critics of science is bewildering. Without attempting to account for or endorse all the conflicting claims made in the name of feminist epistemology, I shall follow the strategy of reading most of them as contributions to a research program in naturalized social epistemology. I propose that we can sort most of them into four categories, each specifying a particular type of gender influence on theoretical inquiry. Feminist epistemology has generally been better at identifying the ways gender is implicated in our knowledge practices than at explaining how these findings should affect our evaluations of the practices or the theories they produce (Longino 1993a). Naturalized epistemology provides a framework for developing such explanations. So I suggest some questions that probe the normative implications of each category of gender influence on theorizing.

First, studies that investigate *gender structures* focus on the ways gender norms structure the division of labor in society, including the divisions between intellectual and manual and service labor, and within the academy, among different disciplines and subfields, and among primary researchers, teachers, and assistants. These studies consider how the content of theories has been affected by historical discrimination against women entering the sciences, by the difficulties women scientists have getting their work recognized, and by the ways women have changed the orientation of fields of study once they have entered the elite ranks in significant numbers. These studies seek to answer the question, What difference does, or would, an equal representation and status of women researchers make to theoretical inquiry?

Second, some studies consider the uses of *gender symbolism*, which occurs when we represent nonhuman or inanimate phenomena as "masculine" or "feminine" and model them after gender ideals or stereotypes. Feminist epistemologists have found gender symbolism to be pervasive in theoretical inquiry. It is used to represent the relations of scientists to their subjects of study and the relations of different types of knowledge or of different disciplines and subfields to one another, to describe the character of scientific objectivity, and to model nonhuman and inanimate phenomena. These studies seek to answer the question, What difference does it make to our theories and our scientific practices that we conceive of theoretical inquiry itself and its subjects of study as gendered phenomena? How would our theories and practices of inquiry change if we altered our conceptions of the "masculine" and the "feminine," or ceased to employ gender symbolism in understanding our own theorizing or inanimate objects?

Third, some studies focus on *androcentrism* in biology, the social sciences, and cultural and literary studies. Androcentrism occurs when theories take males, men's lives, or "masculinity" to set the norm for humans or animals generally, with female differences either ignored or represented as deviant; when phenomena are viewed from the perspective of men's lives, without regard to how women see them differently; and when male activities or predicaments are represented as the primary causes or sites of important changes, without regard to the roles of females in initiating or facilitating changes or the ways the situation of females has been crucial to determining structural constraints and potentials for change. These studies ask, How would the content of theories be different if we viewed phenomena from the perspective of women's lives, or refused to accept either "masculinity" or "femininity" as setting the norm for humans or animals generally?

Fourth, some studies focus on *sexism* in theory, which can appear either in practices that apply the theory or in the content of the theory itself. Sexism is evident when theories are *applied* in ways that undermine women's interests or that reinforce their subordination to men. The *content* of a theory is sexist when it asserts that women are inferior to men, justly or inevitably subordinated to men, or properly confined to gender-stereotyped roles, or when it judges or describes women according to sexist ideals or double standards, or when it uses such claims as background assumptions to secure an evidential link between observations and theoretical claims. Feminist studies of sexism in theories explore the prospects for alternative scientific theories that meet criteria of empirical adequacy while seeking to serve women's interests and to promote universal equality.

The Gendered Division of Theoretical Labor

Feminist critics of science have carefully documented the history of women's exclusion from theoretical inquiry (Rossiter 1982; Schiebinger 1989). Although formal barriers to women's entry into various academic disciplines are now illegal in the United States, informal barriers at all levels remain. Girls are socialized by parents and peers to avoid studying or excelling in subjects considered "masculine," such as mathematics and the natural sciences. Teachers and school counselors actively discourage girls from pursuing these subjects (Curran 1980, 30–2). The classroom climate in mixed-gender schools favors boys. Teachers pay more attention and offer more encouragement to white boys than to girls, solicit their participation more, and expect them to achieve more, especially in mathematics courses (Becker 1981; AAUW 1992). Boys marginalize girls in class by interruption and sexual harassment (AAUW 1992). These behaviors in mixed-gender schools have a detrimental impact on girls' academic ambitions and performance. Girls in all-girl schools express a wider diversity of academic interests and perform better academically than girls in mixed-gender schools (Curran 1980, 34). The disadvantage to women's academic performance and interests from attending mixed-gender schools extends to college. The predominantly male faculty in mixed-gender colleges support women students' academic ambitions less than male and female faculty at women's colleges. Women's colleges produce 50 percent more high-achieving women relative to the number of their female graduates than coeducational institutions (Tidball 1980). Graduate schools present women with informal barriers or costs to advancement, including sexual harassment and exclusion from networks of male mentors and colleagues often vital to the advancement of aspiring academics (Reskin 1979; S. Rose 1989).

Women who overcome these obstacles and obtain advanced degrees are not treated as equals once they enter academic positions. Women whose qualifications are comparable to their male colleagues get lower pay, less research support, jobs in less prestigious institutions, lower-ranking positions, and positions that assign more and lower-level teaching (Astin and Beyer 1973; Fox 1981). The prestige of the graduate institution, publications, and having one's work cited aid men's career advancement much more than women's (Rosenfeld 1981). Women in scientific and engineering professions with publication rates equal to those of their male peers have higher unemployment rates, lower starting salaries, and lower academic rank than men. These differences cannot be explained by the greater impact on women of marriage and children

(Vetter 1981). The National Science Foundation (1984) found that after adjusting for factors such as women interrupting their careers to take care of children, half the salary differential between male and female scientists could be explained only by sex discrimination.

The gendered division of theoretical labor does not simply prevent women from doing research or getting published. It fits into a broader gendered structure of epistemic authority which assigns greater credibility, respect, and importance to men's than women's claims. Laboratory, field, and natural experiments alike show that the perceived gender of the author influences people's judgments of the quality of research, independent of its content. Psychologists M. A. Paludi and W. D. Bauer (1983) found that a group told that a paper's author was "John T. McKay" assigned it a much higher average ranking than a group told that the same paper's author was "Joan T. McKay." A group told that its author was "J. T. McKay" rated the paper between the other groups' evaluations, reflecting the suspicion that the author was a woman trying to conceal her gender identity. Academics are no less disposed than others to judge the quality of work higher simply because they believe a man has done it. L. S. Fidell (1970) sent vitae identical in all but name to heads of psychology departments that advertised open rank positions. The jobs the psychologists said they would offer to the purportedly male applicant were higher-ranking than those they were willing to offer to the purportedly female applicant. When the Modern Language Association reviewed papers submitted for their meetings with authors' names attached, men's submissions were accepted at significantly higher rates than women's. After the MLA instituted blind reviewing of papers, women's acceptance rates rose to equality with men's (Lefkowitz 1979).

The concerns raised by the influence of sexist norms on the division of theoretical labor and epistemic authority are not simply matters of justice. Feminist epistemology asks what impact these injustices toward women students and researchers have had on the content, shape, and progress of theoretical knowledge. In some cases, sex discrimination in the academy has demonstrably retarded the growth of knowledge. It took more than three decades for biologists to understand and recognize the revolutionary importance of Barbara McClintock's discovery of genetic transposition. Her attempts to communicate this discovery to the larger scientific community met with incomprehension and disdain. This failure can be partly explained by the fact that no biology department was willing to hire her for a permanent position despite her distinguished record of discoveries and publications. Lacking the opportunities such a position would have provided to recruit graduate students to her research program, McClintock had no one else doing research like hers who could replicate her results or help communicate them to a wider scientific community (Keller 1983).

Cases such as McClintock's demonstrate that the gendered structure of theoretical labor and cognitive authority sometimes slows the progress of knowledge. But does it change the content or shape of knowledge or the direction of knowledge growth? If the gender of the knower is irrelevant to the content of what is investigated, discovered, or invented, then the impact of removing sex discrimination would be to add to the pace of knowledge growth by adding more inquirers and by raising the average level of talent and dedication in the research community. Feminist epistemology would then recommend strictly "gender-blind" changes in the processes by which research jobs get assigned and epistemic authority distributed. The MLA's adoption of blind reviewing of papers to reduce cognitive bias due to sexism in the evaluation of research represents an exemplary application of this side of feminist epistemology. It is logically on a par with the institution of double-blind testing in drug research to reduce cognitive bias due to wishful thinking.

But if the gender of the inquirer makes a difference to the content of what is accepted as knowledge, then the exclusion and undervaluation of women's participation in theoretical inquiry does not merely set up randomly distributed roadblocks to the improvement of understanding. It imparts a systematic bias on what is taken to be knowledge. If the gender of the inquirer makes a difference to what is known, then feminist epistemology would not confine its recommendations to purely gender-blind reforms in our knowledge practices. It could recommend that these knowledge practices actively seek gender diversity and balance among inquirers and actively attend to the gender of the researchers in evaluating their products.

The gender of the researcher is known to make a difference to what is known in certain areas of social science. In survey research, subjects give different answers to questions depending on the perceived gender of the interviewer (Sherif 1987, 47–8). The perceived race of the interviewer also influences subjects' responses. It is a highly significant variable accounting for subjects' responses to questions about race relations (Schuman and Hatchett 1974). In anthropology, informants vary their responses depending on the gender of the anthropologist. In many societies, male anthropologists have less access to women's social worlds than female anthropologists do (Leacock 1982). The race of the researcher affects access to social worlds as well. Native Americans sometimes grant Asian anthropologists access to religious rituals from which they ban whites (Pai 1985).

Where the perceived gender and race of the researcher are variables influencing the phenomena being observed or influencing access to the phenomena, sound research design must pay attention to the gender and racial makeup of the researchers. In survey research, these effects can be analytically excised by ensuring a gender balanced and racially diverse research team and then statistically isolating the variations in responses due to factors other than subjects' responses to the characteristics of the interviewers. In anthropology, the method of reflexive sociology, instead of attempting to analyze away these effects, treats them as a subject of study in their own right. It advises researchers to interpret what informants tell them not as straightforward native observation reports on their own culture, but as reflections of a strategic interaction between informant and researcher and between the informant and other members of the community being studied (Bourdieu 1977). To obtain a complete representation of informants' report strategies with respect to gender, both male and female researchers must interact with both male and female informants and consider why informants varied their responses according to their own and the researcher's gender (see Bell, Caplan, and Karim [1993] for exemplary cases of feminist reflexive anthropology). Similar reasoning applies to factors such as race, class, nationality, and sexual orientation. So reflexive sociology, like survey research, requires a diversity of inquirers to obtain worthwhile results.

The phenomena just discussed concern the *causal* impact of the gender of the researcher on the *object* of knowledge. Many feminist epistemologists claim that the gender of the inquirer influences the *character* of knowledge itself by another route, which travels through the subjectivity of the researcher herself. The gender of the researcher influences what is known not just through her influence on the object of knowledge but by what are claimed to be gender-specific or gender-typical cognitive or affective dispositions, skills, knowledge, interests, or methods that she brings to the study of the object. The variety of claims of this type must be sorted through and investigated with great care. Some are local and modest. No one disputes that personal knowledge of what it is like to be pregnant, undergo childbirth, suffer menstrual cramps, and have other experiences of a female body is specific to women. Gynecology has certainly progressed since women have entered the field and have brought their personal knowledge to bear on misogynist medical practices. The claims get more controversial the more global they are in scope. Some people claim that women have gender-typical "ways of knowing," styles of thinking, methodologies, and ontologies that globally govern or characterize their cognitive activities across all subject matters. For instance, various feminist epistemologists have claimed that women think more intuitively and contextually, concern themselves more with particulars than abstractions, emotionally engage themselves more with individual subjects of study, and frame their thoughts in terms of a relational rather than an atomistic ontology (Smiths 1974; Gilligan 1982; Belenky, Clinchy, Goldberger and Tarule 1986; H. Rose 1987; Collins 1990).

There is little persuasive evidence for such global claims (Tavris 1992, Ch. 2). I believe the temptation to accept them is based partly on a confusion between gender symbolism – the fact that certain styles of thinking are *labeled* "feminine" – and the actual characteristics of women. It is also partly due to the lack of more complex and nuanced models of how women entering certain fields have changed the course of theorizing for reasons that seem connected to their gender or their feminist commitments. I will propose an alternative model toward the end of this essay, which does not suppose that women theorists bring some shared feminine difference to all subjects of knowledge. Controversies over supposed global differences in the ways men and women think have tended to overshadow other highly interesting work in feminist epistemology that does not depend on claims that men and women think in essentially different ways. The influence of gendered concepts and norms in our knowledge practices extends far beyond the ways male and female individuals are socialized and assigned to different roles in the division of labor. To see this, consider the role of *gender symbolism* in theoretical knowledge.

Gender Symbolism (I): The Hierarchy of Knowledge

It is a characteristic of human thought that our concepts do not stay put behind the neat logical fences philosophers like to erect for them. Like sly coyotes, they slip past these flimsy barriers to range far and wide, picking up consorts of all varieties, and, in astonishingly fecund acts of miscegenation shocking to conceptual purists, leave offspring who bear a disturbing resemblance to the wayward parent and inherit the impulse to roam the old territory. The philosophical guardians of these offspring, trying to shake off the taint of sexual scandal but feeling guilty about the effort, don't quite know whether to cover up a concept's pedigree or, by means of the discovery/justification distinction, deny that it matters. The latter strategy can work only if, like keepers of a zoo, the philosophers can keep their animals fenced in. Feminist epistemologists track these creatures sneaking past their fences while their keepers dream of tamed animals happy to remain confined.

The most cunning and promiscuous coyotes are our gender concepts. In a manner befitting their own links to sex, they will copulate with *anything*. Feminist epistemologists note that there is hardly any conceptual dichotomy that has not been modeled after and in turn used to model the masculine/feminine dichotomy: mind/body, culture/nature, reason/emotion, objective/subjective, tough-minded /soft-hearted, and so forth. These scandalous metaphorical unions generate conceptions of knowledge, science, and rational inquiry, as well as conceptions of the objects of these inquiries, that are shaped in part by sexist views about the proper relations between men and women. Feminist epistemologists investigate how these conceptions are informed and distorted by sexist imagery. They also consider how alternative conceptions are suppressed by the limits imposed by sexism on the imagination, or by the sexist or androcentric interests served by their present symbolic links to gender (Rooney 1991).

Gender symbolism appears on at least two levels of our knowledge practices: in the construction of a hierarchy of prestige and authority among kinds and fields of knowledge and in the content of theoretical inquiry itself. Consider first the ways different kinds and fields of knowledge are gendered. At the most general level, impersonal theoretical knowledge is coded "masculine." Personal knowledge – the kind of knowledge that is inseparable from the knower's identity, biography, and emotional experiences – is coded "feminine." Theoretical knowledge is thought to be masculine in part because it lays claims to objectivity, which is thought to be achieved through the rigorous exclusion from thought of feminine subjectivity – of emotions, particularity, interests, and values. These uses of gender symbolism have *epistemic* import because they structure a hierarchy of prestige and cognitive authority among kinds of knowledge, and hence of knowers, that is homologous with the gender hierarchy. As men in sexist society express contempt for women and enjoy higher prestige than women, so do theoretical knowers express contempt for those with "merely" personal knowledge of the same subject matters, and enjoy higher prestige than they. Echoing the sexist norms that women must obey men but men need not listen to women, the gender-coded hierarchy of knowledge embodies the norm that personal knowledge must submit to the judgments of impersonal theoretical knowledge, while theoretical knowledge has nothing to learn from personal knowledge and may ignore its claims.

These epistemic norms cannot withstand reflective scrutiny. Successful theorizing deeply depends on personal knowledge, particularly embodied skills, and often depends on emotional engagement with the subjects of study (Polanyi 1958; Keller 1983, 1985). Cora Diamond's (1991) insightful discussion of Vicki Hearne's personal knowledge as an animal trainer provides a particularly fine illustration of this point. Hearne's writings (1982) expose the failures of knowledge that occur when theorists ignore the experiences, skills, and language of animal trainers. In her animal training classes, Hearne observed that people's success in training their pets was inversely related to their training in the behavioral sciences. The anthropomorphic and value-laden language of animal trainers enables them to understand what animals are doing in ways not readily accessible to the impersonal, behavioristic language favored by most behavioral scientists. And their skills and personal knowledge of the animals they work with empower trainers to elicit from animals considerably more complex and interesting behaviors than scientists elicit. These powers are not irrelevant to theorizing about animals. Reflecting on Hearne's story about the philosopher Ray Frey, Diamond writes:

> [Frey] attempted to set up a test for his dog's capacity to rank rational desires. When, in order to see how the dog would rank desires, he threw a stick for his dog . . . and at the same time put food before the dog, the dog stood looking at him. Frey could not see that the dog wanted to know what Frey wanted him to do; Frey's conception of the dog as part of an experimental set-up (taken to include two possible desired activities but not taken to include queer behavior by the dog's master), with Frey as the observer, blocked his understanding. Frey's past experience with his dog did not feed an understanding of how the dog saw him; he could not grasp his own failure, as the dog's master, to make coherent sense, so could not see the dog as responding to that failure to make sense. (Diamond 1991, 1014, note 15)

Diamond diagnoses this epistemic failure as the product of Frey's attachment to a theory of knowledge that distrusts personal experience on the ground that it is distorted by the subject's emotional engagement with the object of knowledge. The theory supposes that we can't achieve objective knowledge of our object through such engagement because all it will offer is a reflection of the subject's own emotions. Subjectivity merely projects qualities onto the object and does not reveal qualities of the object. But the theory is mistaken. Love and respect for another being, animal or person, and trust in the personal experiences of engagement that are informed by such love and respect may be essential both for drawing out and for grasping that being's full potentialities. One of the reasons why behaviorists tend to elicit such boring behavior from animals and humans is that they don't give them the opportunities to exhibit a more impressive repertoire of behaviors that respect for them would require them to offer.

The gender-coded hierarchy of knowledge extends to specific subject matters and methods within theoretical knowledge. The natural sciences are "harder," more like the male body and hence more prestigious, than the social sciences or the "soft" humanities, supposed to be awash in feminine emotionality and subjectivity. Mathematics is coded masculine and is the language of physics, the most prestigious science. Through their closer association with physics, quantitative subfields of biology and the social sciences enjoy higher prestige than subfields of the same discipline or branch of science employing a qualitative, historical, or interpretive methodology. Experimentation asserts more control over subjects of study than observation does. So experimental subfields in biology and psychology are coded masculine and command more cognitive authority than observational subfields of the same disciplines. Values are designated feminine. So normative subfields in philosophy such as ethics and political philosophy enjoy less prestige than supposedly nonnormative fields such as philosophy of language and mind. Social interpretation is thought to be a feminine skill. So interpretive anthropology is designated less masculine, scientific, and rigorous than physical anthropology, which deals with "hard" facts like fossil bones. In each of these cases, the socially enforced norm for relations between fields of knowledge mirrors that of the relations between husband and wife in the ideal patriarchal family: the masculine science is autonomous from and exercises authority over the feminine science, which is supposedly dependent on the former's pronouncements to know what it should think next.

This gendered hierarchy of theoretical subfields produces serious cognitive distortions. Carolyn Sherif (1987) has investigated how the hierarchy of prestige generates cognitive biases in psychology. Forty years ago, experimental psychology dominated developmental and social psychology. The gendered character of this difference in cognitive authority is not difficult to read. Experimental psychologists, by imitating the methods of the "hard" sciences through manipulating quantified variables, claim some of the prestige of the natural sciences. Developmental and social psychologists engage in labor that looks more like the low-status labor conventionally assigned to women. Developmental psychologists work with children; social psychologists deal with human relationships, and forty years ago usually did so in settings not under the control of the researcher. Following the norm that "masculine" sciences need not pay attention to findings in "feminine" sciences, which it is assumed cannot possibly bear on their more "fundamental" research, experimental psychology has a history of constructing experiments that, like Ray Frey's, ignore the ways the social context of the experiment itself and the social relation between experimenter and subject influence outcomes. The result has been a history of findings that lack robustness because they are mere artifacts of the experimental situation. In experimental research on sex differences, this error has taken the form of ascribing observed differences in male and female behavior under experimental conditions to innate difference in male and female psychology rather than to the ways the experiment has socially structured the situation so as to elicit different responses from men and women.

The notorious claim in experimental psychology that women are more suggestible than men offers an instructive illustration of the perils of ignoring social psychology (Sherif 1987, 49–50). The original experiments that confirmed the hypothesis of greater suggestibility involved male researchers trying to persuade men and women to change their beliefs with respect to subject matters oriented to stereotypical male interests. Unaware of how their own gender-typical interests had imparted a bias in the selection of topics of persuasion, the predominantly male researchers confidently reported as a sex difference in suggestibility what was in fact a difference in suggestibility owing to the degree of interest the subjects had in the topics. Differences in the gender-typed cognitive authority of the researcher also affect subjects' responses. Men are more open to the suggestions of a female researcher when the topic is coded feminine, while women are more open to the suggestions of a male researcher when the topic is coded masculine.

Cognitive distortions due to the gender-coding of types and fields of knowledge are strictly separable from any claims about differences in the ways men and women think. Although it is true that the "feminine" sciences and subfields attract more women researchers than the "masculine" sciences do, the differences in cognitive authority between the various sciences and subfields were modeled on differences in social authority between men and women before women constituted a significant portion of the researchers in any field. Men still predominate even in fields of study that are designated feminine. And scientists' neglect of personal knowledge deprives many men who engage in stereotypically male activities of cognitive authority. For example, animal behaviorists ignore the personal knowledge male policemen have about their police dogs (Diamond 1991). For these reasons, Diamond and Sherif have questioned how gender figures into the cognitive distortions instituted by the hierarchy of knowledge and by scientistic conceptions of objectivity.[1] By shifting our focus from gender structure and supposed gender differences in ways of knowing to gender symbolism, we can see how ideas about gender can distort the relations between forms of knowledge independently of the gender of the knower. In the light of the cognitive distortions caused by the gender-coding of types and domains of knowledge, feminist naturalized epistemologists should recommend that we no longer model the relations between different kinds of knowledge on a sexist view of the authority relations between men and women.

Gender Symbolism (II): The Content of Theories

Gender symbolism figures in the *content* of theories as well as in their relations of cognitive authority whenever conceptions of human gender relations or gendered characteristics are used to model phenomena that are not gendered. Biology is particularly rich with gender symbolism – in models of gamete fertilization, nucleus-cell interaction, primatology, and evolutionary theory (Biology and Gender Study Group 1988; Haraway 1989; Keller 1985, 1992). Evelyn Fox Keller, a mathematical biologist and feminist philosopher of science, has explored gender symbolism in evolutionary theory most subtly (Keller 1992). Consider the fact that evolutionary theory tends to delineate the unit of natural selection, the entity accorded the status of an "individual," at the point where the theorist is willing to use complex and cooperative rather than competitive models of interaction. Among individuals, antagonistic competition predominates and mutualistic interactions are downplayed. The individual is considered "selfish" in relation to other individuals. Thus, theories that take the gene to be the unit of selection characterize the gene as a ruthless egoist ready to sacrifice the interests of its host organism for the sake of reproducing itself (Dawkins 1976). Where the organism is taken to be the unit of selection, it is represented as selfishly competitive with respect to other individual organisms. But within the individual, cooperation among constitutive parts prevails. Cooperation is modeled after the family, often a patriarchal family. The cells of an individual organism cooperate because of the bonds of kinship: they share the same genes. The constitutive parts of an individual cell cooperate because they are ruled by a wise and benevolent patriarch, the "master molecule" DNA, which autonomously tells all the other parts of the cell what to do, solely on the basis of information it contains within itself. Thus, evolutionary theory models the biological world after a sexist and androcentric conception of liberal society, in which the public sphere is governed by competition among presumably masculine selfish individuals and the private sphere of the family is governed by male heads of households enforcing cooperation among its members (Keller 1992, Ch. 8). This model is not rigidly or consistently applied in evolutionary theory, but it does mark theoretical tendencies that can be traced back to the fact that Darwin modeled his theory of natural selection after Malthus's dismal model of capitalist society.

Taken by itself, that evolutionary theory employs a sexist ideology of liberal society to model biological phenomena does not have any straight-forward normative implications. Defenders of the theory can appeal to the discovery/justification distinction here: just because a theory had its origins in politically objectionable ideas or social contexts does not mean that it is false or useless. Evolutionary theory is extraordinarily fruitful and empirically well confirmed. The model-theoretic view of theories, widely used by feminist empiricists and feminist postmodernists to analyze the roles of gender in the construction of theoretical knowledge, affirms the epistemic legitimacy of any coherent models, hence of any coherent sexist models, in science (Haraway 1986; Longino 1993b).

In the model-theoretic view, scientific theories propose elaborate metaphors or models of phenomena. Their virtues are empirical adequacy, simplicity, clarity, and fruitfulness. Theories are empirically adequate to the extent that the relations among entities in the model are homologous with the observed relations among entities in the world. Empirically adequate models offer a satisfactory explanation of phenomena to the extent that they model unfamiliar phenomena in ways that are simple, perspicuous and analytically tractable. They are fruitful to the extent that they organize inquirers' conceptions of their subjects in ways that suggest lines of investigation that uncover novel phenomena that can be accommodated by further refinements of the model. Empiricists place no a priori constraints on the things that may constitute useful models for phenomena. Anything might be an illuminating model for anything else. So, empiricists can offer no a priori epistemic objections to modeling nongendered phenomena after gendered ones, even if the models are overtly sexist or patriarchal. Such models may well illuminate and effectively organize important aspects of the objects being studied.

So the trouble with using sexist gender symbolism in theoretical models is not that the models are sexist. The trouble lies rather in the extraordinary political salience and rhetorical power of sexist gender ideology, which generates numerous cognitive distortions. Keller has carefully delineated several such distortions in evolutionary theory, especially with respect to its privileging of models of competitive over cooperative or mutualist interactions among organisms. First, to the extent that political ideology incorporates false conceptual identities and dichotomies, a scientific model borrowing its vocabulary and structure is likely to overlook the alternatives suppressed by that ideology or to elide distinctions between empirically distinct phenomena. The ideology of possessive individualism falsely identifies autonomy with selfishness and falsely contrasts self-interest with cooperation. When used to model phenomena in evolutionary biology, it leads to a false identification of peaceful, passive consumption activity with violent, competitive behavior, and to a neglect of mutualist interactions among organisms. Thus, the mathematical tools of population biology and mathematical ecology are rarely used to model cooperation among organisms although they could do so; in contrast with sociobiology, these mathematical subfields of biology have even neglected the impact of sexual intercourse and parenting behavior on the fitness of organisms (Keller 1992, 119–21). Although the technical definition of competition avoids false identities and dichotomies, biologists constantly turn to its colloquial meanings to explain their findings and frame research questions. In this way, "the use of a term with established colloquial meaning in a technical context permits the simultaneous transfer and denial of its colloquial connotations" (Keller 1992, 121). When the language used in a model has particularly strong ideological connotations, the cognitive biases it invites are particularly resistant to exposure and criticism.

The symbolic identification of the scientific with a masculine outlook generates further cognitive distortions. The ideology of masculinity, in representing emotion as feminine and as cognitively distorting, falsely assimilates emotion-laden thoughts – and even thoughts about emotions – to sentimentality. In identifying the scientific outlook with that of a man who has outgrown his tutelage, cut his dependence on his mother, and is prepared to meet the competitive demands of the public sphere with a clear eye, the ideology of masculinity tends to confuse seeing the natural world as indifferent in the sense of devoid of teleological laws with seeing the social world as hostile in the sense of full of agents who pursue their interests at others' expense (Keller 1992, 116–18). This confusion tempts biologists into thinking that the selfishness their models ascribe to genes and the ruthless strategic rationality their models ascribe to individual organisms (mere metaphors, however theoretically powerful) are more "real" than the actual care a dog expresses toward her pups. Such thoughts also reflect the rhetoric of unmasking base motivations behind policies that seem to be benevolent, a common if overused tactic in liberal politics and political theory. The power of this rhetoric depends on an appearance/reality distinction that has no place where the stakes are competing social *models* of biological phenomena, whose merits depend on their metaphorical rather than their referential powers. Thus, to the extent that the theoretical preference for competitive models in biology is underwritten by rhetoric borrowed from androcentric political ideologies, the preference reflects a confusion between models and reality as well as an unjustified intrusion of androcentric political loyalties into the scientific enterprise.

These are not concerns that can be relieved by deploying the discovery/justification distinction. To the extent that motivations tied to acquiring a masculine-coded prestige as a theorist induce mathematical ecologists to overlook the epistemic defects of models of natural selection that fail to consider the actual impact of sexual selection, parenting, and cooperative interactions, they distort the context of justification itself. Some of the criteria of justification, such as simplicity, are also distorted in the light of the androcentric distinction between public and private values. For example, simplicity in mathematical biology has been characterized so as to prefer explanations of apparently favorable patterns of group survival in terms of chance to explanations in terms of interspecific feedback loops, if straightforward individualistic mechanisms are not available to explain them (Keller 1992, 153). Finally, to the extent that gender ideologies inform the context of discovery by influencing the direction of inquiry and development of mathematical tools, they prevent the growth of alternative models and the tools that could make them tractable, and hence they bias our views of what is "simple" (Keller 1992, 160). The discovery/justification distinction, while useful when considering the epistemic relation of a theory to its confirming or disconfirming evidence, breaks down once we consider the relative merits of alternative theories. In the latter context, any influence that biases the development of the field of alternatives will bias the evaluation of theories. A theoretical approach may appear best justified not because it offers an adequate model of the world but because androcentric ideologies have caused more thought and resources to be invested in it than in alternatives.

So feminist naturalized epistemologists should offer a complex verdict on gender symbolism in the content of theories. They should leave open the possibility that gendered models of ungendered phenomena may be highly illuminating and successful, and hence legitimately used in theoretical inquiry. The impressive explanatory successes of evolutionary theory demonstrate this. At the same time, the ideological power of gender symbolism sometimes gets the better of otherwise careful theorists. It can generate conceptual confusion in ways that are hard to detect, and obscure theoretical possibilities that may be worth pursuing. The most reliable way to tell when the use of gender symbolism is generating such cognitive distortions is to critically investigate the gender ideology it depends on and the role this ideology plays in society. In other words, theorists who use gendered models would do well to consider how feminist theory can help them avoid cognitive distortion. Feminist naturalized epistemologists therefore should recommend that theorists attracted to gendered models of ungendered phenomena proceed with caution, in consultation with feminist theorists. It recommends an important change in the cognitive authority of disciplines, through its demonstration that biologists have something to learn from feminist theory after all.

Androcentrism

A knowledge practice is androcentric if it reflects an orientation geared to specifically or typically male interests or male lives. Androcentrism can appear in a knowledge practice in at least two ways: in the content of theories or research programs and in the interests that lead inquirers to frame their research in certain terms or around certain problems. Feminists in the natural and social sciences have advanced feminist epistemology most fully and persuasively by exposing androcentrism in the content of social-scientific and biological theories.

The content of theories can be androcentric in several ways. A theory may reflect the view that males, male lives, or "masculinity" set the norm for humans or animals generally. From this point of view, females, their lives, or "feminine" characteristics are represented as problematic, deviations from the norm, and hence in need of a type of explanation not required for their male counterparts. Androcentrism of this sort often appears in the ways theoretical questions are framed. For decades, psychological and biological research about sex differences has been framed by the question, "Why are women different from men?" and the presumed sex difference has cast women in a deviant position. Researchers have been preoccupied with such questions as why girls are more suggestible, less ambitious, less analytically minded, and have lower self-esteem than boys. Let us leave aside the fact that all these questions are based on unfounded beliefs about sex differences (Maccoby and Jacklin 1974). Why haven't researchers asked why boys are less responsive to others, more pushy, less synthetically minded, and more conceited than girls? The framing of the problem to be investigated reflects not just a commitment to asymmetrical explanation of men's and women's characteristics, but to an evaluation of women's differences as dimensions of inferiority (Tavris 1992, Ch. 1). It is thus sexist as well as androcentric.

Another way in which the content of theories can be androcentric is in describing or defining phenomena from the perspective of men or typically male lives, without paying attention to how they would be described differently if examined from the point of view of women's lives. Economists and political scientists have traditionally defined class and socioeconomic status from the point of view of men's lives: a man's class or socioeconomic status is defined in terms of his own occupation or earnings, whereas a women's status is defined in terms of her father's or husband's occupation or earnings. Such definitions obscure the differences in power, prestige, and opportunities between male managers and their homemaker wives, and between homemaker wives and female managers (Stiehm 1983). They also prevent an analysis of the distinctive economic roles and status of full-time homemakers and of adult independent unmarried women. The distinction between labor and leisure, central to standard economic analyses of the supply of wage labor, also reflects the perspective of male heads of households (Waring 1990). Classically, the distinction demarcates the public from the private spheres by contrasting their characteristic activities as having negative versus positive utility, or instrumental versus intrinsic value, or as controlled by others versus freely self-directed. From the standpoint of the lives of women with husbands or children, these demarcations make no sense. These women are not at leisure whenever they are not engaged in paid labor. Professional women often find much of their unpaid work to constitute a drudgery from which paid labor represents an escape with positive intrinsic value. Middle-class and working-class women who engage in paid labor and who cannot afford to hire others to perform their household tasks and child care are better represented as engaged in (sometimes involuntary) dual-career or double-shift labor than in trading off labor for leisure. Full-time mothers and homemakers often view what some consider to be their leisure activities as highly important work in its own right, even if it is unpaid.

The androcentrism implicit in the standard economic definition of productive labor has profound implications for national income accounting, the fundamental conceptual framework for defining and measuring what counts as economically relevant data for macroeconomic theory. It effectively excludes women's gender-typical unpaid domestic labor from gross national product (GNP) calculations, making women's work largely invisible in the economy. In the advanced industrialized nations, economists explain this omission by arguing that GNP figures properly measure only the economic value of production for market exchange. In developing nations, where only a modest proportion of productive activity shows up in market exchanges, economists have long recognized the uselessness of measures of national production that look only at the market; so they impute a market value to various unmarketed domestic production activities associated with subsistence agriculture, home construction, and the like. But which of these household activities do economists choose to count as productive? In practice, they have defined the "production boundary" in such societies by imposing an obsolete Western androcentric conception of the household. They assume that households consist of a productive primary producer, the husband, who supports a wife engaged in "housework," which is assumed to be economically unimportant or unproductive. "Housework" has no clear definition in societies where most production takes place within the household. So economists apply the concept of "housework" to whatever productive activities a society conventionally assigns to women. Thus, women's unmarketed labor in these societies counts as productive only if men usually perform it too, whereas men's unmarketed labor is usually counted in the national income statistics regardless of its relation to women's labor (Waring 1990, 74–87). The result is that in Africa, where women do 70 percent of the hoeing and weeding of subsistence crops, 80 percent of crop transportation and storage, and 90 percent of water and fuel collecting and food processing, these vital activities rarely appear in the national income accounts (Waring 1990, 84). Here, androcentrism is built into the very data for economic theorizing, in such a way that women's gender-typical activities become invisible.

Even when a theory does not go so far as to define the phenomena in a way that excludes female activities, it may still be androcentric in assuming that male activities or predicaments are the sole or primary sources of important changes or events. Until recently, primatologists focused almost exclusively on the behavior of male primates. They assumed that male sexual and dominance behaviors determined the basic structure of primate social order, and that the crucial social relationships among troop-dwelling primates that determined the reproductive fitness of individuals and maintained troop organization were between the dominant male and other males. The assumption followed from a sociobiological argument that claimed to show that females of any species will typically be the "limiting resource" for reproduction: most females will realize an equal and maximum reproductive potential, while males will vary enormously in their reproductive fitness. Natural selection, the driving force of evolutionary change, would therefore operate primarily on male characteristics and behavior (Hrdy 1986).

These assumptions were not seriously challenged until women, some inspired by the feminist movement, started entering the field of primatology in substantial numbers in the mid-1970s. Many studied female-female and female-infant interactions, female dominance and cooperative behavior, and female sexual activity. By turning their focus from male to female behaviors and relationships, they found that infant survival varied enormously, depending on the behavior and social status of the mothers, that troop survival itself sometimes depended on the eldest female (who would teach others the location of distant water holes that had survived droughts), and that female-directed social and sexual behaviors play key roles in maintaining and changing primate social organizations (Hrdy 1981; Haraway 1989). Today the importance of female primates is widely recognized and studied by both male and female primatologists.

What normative implications should be drawn about the epistemic status of androcentric theories? Some feminist epistemologists propose that theory can proceed better by viewing the world through the eyes of female agents. Gynocentric theory can be fun. What could be a more amusing retort to a study that purports to explain why women lack self-esteem than a study that explains why men are conceited? It can also be instructive. Richard Wrangham (1979) has proposed a gynocentric model of primate social organization that has achieved widespread recognition in primatology. The model assumes the centrality of female competition for food resources, and predicts how females will space themselves (singly or in kin-related groups) according to the distribution of the foods they eat. Males then space themselves so as to gain optimum access to females. The model is gynocentric both in defining the core of primate social groups around female kin-relations rather than around relations to a dominant male and in taking the situation of females to constitute the primary variable that accounts for variations in male and general primate social organization. According to the feminist primatologist Sarah Hrdy (1981, 126), Wrangham's model offers the best available explanation of primate social organization.

The three androcentric theoretical constructs mentioned correspond to three different ways in which a theory could be "gender-centric": in taking one sex or gender to set the norm for both, in defining central concepts with respect to the sex- or gender-typical characteristics, behaviors, or perspectives of males or females alone, and in taking the behaviors, situation, or characteristics of one sex or gender to be causally central in determining particular outcomes. These logical differences in gender-centric theorizing have different epistemic implications. As Wrangham's theory shows, gynocentric causal models can sometimes be superior to androcentric models. Whether they are superior in any particular domain of interest is an empirical question. It can only be answered by comparing rival gender-centric models to one another and to models that do not privilege either male- or female-typical activities or situations in their causal accounts, but rather focus on activities and situations common to both males and females. An important contribution of feminist scholarship in the social sciences and biology has been to show that the activities and situations of females have been far more causally important in various domains than androcentric theories have recognized.

The other two types of gender-centrism are much more problematic than this causal type. A theory that takes one gender to set the norm for both must bear an explanatory burden not borne by theories that refuse to represent difference as deviance. It must explain why an asymmetrical explanation is required for male- and female-specific characteristics. Given the dominant background assumption of modern science that the cosmos does not have its own telos, it is hard to justify any claim that one gender naturally sets the norm for both. Claims about norms must be located in human value judgments, which is to say that the only justification for normative gender-centrism would have to lie in a substantive sexist moral or political theory. As we shall see below, empiricism does not rule out the use of value judgments as background assumptions in scientific theories. Nevertheless, this analysis of normative gender-centrism suggests why feminists should not be satisfied with a table-turning, "why men are so conceited" type of gynocentric theorizing. Posing such questions may expose the androcentrism of standard ways of framing research problems in sex-differences research to healthy ridicule. But because feminists are interested in upholding the equality of all persons, not the domination of women over men, they have no interest in claiming that women set the norm for humans generally.

Theories that tailor concepts to the activities or positions specific to or typical of one gender only and then apply them to everyone are straightforwardly empirically inadequate. As the case of androcentric definitions of class showed, they obscure actual empirical differences between men and women and between differently situated women. As the case of the labor/leisure distinction showed, they overgeneralize from the typical situation of one gender to that of both. When conceptually androcentric theories guide public policy, the resulting policies are usually sexist, since theories cannot respond to phenomena they make invisible. Thus, when GNP statistics fail to count women's labor as productive, and public policies aim to increase GNP, they may do so in ways that fail to improve the well-being of women and their families and may even reduce it. In Malawi and Lesotho, where women grow most of the food for domestic consumption, foreign aid projects have provided agricultural training to the men who have no use for it, and offered only home economics education to women (Waring 1990, 232, 234). In the Sahel, a USAID drought-relief project forced women into economic dependency on men by replacing only men's cattle herds, on the androcentric assumption that women did not engage in economically significant labor (Waring 1990, 176–7).

Feminist naturalized epistemologists therefore pass different judgments on different kinds of gender-centrism in theoretical inquiry. Conceptual gender-centrism is plainly inadequate in any society with overlapping gender roles, because it leads to overgeneralization and obscures the differences between empirically distinct phenomena. It could work only in societies where men and women inhabit completely and rigidly segregated spheres, and only for concepts that apply exclusively to one or the other gender in such a society. Normative gender-centrism either depends on a problematic cosmic teleology or on sexist values. This does not automatically make it epistemically inadequate, but it does require the assumption of an explanatory burden (why men's and women's traits do not receive symmetrical explanatory treatment) that non-gender-centric theories need not assume. In addition, its dependence on sexist values give theorists who repudiate sexism sufficient reason to conduct inquiry that is not normatively gender-centric. Finally, causal gender-centrism may or may not be empirically justified. Some events do turn asymmetrically on what men or women do, or on how men or women are situated.

The chief trap in causal gender-centrism is the temptation to reify the domain of events that are said to turn asymmetrically on the actions or characteristics of one or the other gender. The selection of a domain of inquiry is always a function of the interests of the inquirer.[2] Failure to recognize this may lead androcentric theorists to construct their domain of study in ways that confine it to just those phenomena that turn asymmetrically on men's activities. They may therefore declare as an objective fact that, say, women have little causal impact on the "economy," when all that is going on is that they have not taken any interest in women's productive activities, and so have not categorized those activities as "economic." Feminist naturalized epistemologists caution against the view that domains of inquiry demarcate natural kinds. Following Quine, they question supposed conceptual barriers between natural and social science, analytic and synthetic knowledge, personal and impersonal knowledge, fact and value (Nelson 1990, Ch. 3). Their empiricist commitments enable them to uncover surprising connections among apparently distant points in the web of belief. If naturalized epistemologists use space-age technology to explore the universe of knowledge, feminist naturalized epistemologists could be said to specialize in the discovery of wormholes in that universe. Gender and science are not light-years apart after all; subspace distortions in our cognitive apparatus permit surprisingly rapid transport from one to the other, but feminist navigators are needed to ensure that we know the route we are travelling and have reason to take it.

Sexism in Scientific Theories

One frequently traveled route between gender and science employs normative assumptions about the proper relations between men and women, or about the respective characteristics and interests of men and women, in the content or application of scientific theories. When a theory asserts that women are inferior to men, properly subordinated to men, or properly confined to gender-stereotyped roles, or when it judges or describes women according to sexist or double standards, the content of the theory is sexist. When people employ such assumptions in applying theories, the application of the theory is sexist. Naturalized feminist epistemology considers how our evaluations of theories should change once their sexism is brought to light.

The application of theories can be sexist in direct or indirect ways. Theories may be used to provide direct ideological justification for patriarchal structures. Steven Goldberg (1973) uses his theory of sex differences in aggression to justify a gendered division of labor that deliberately confines women to low-prestige occupations. More usually, the application of theories is indirectly sexist in taking certain sexist values for granted rather than trying to justify them. For example, research on oral contraceptives for men and women uses a double standard for evaluating the acceptability of side effects. Oral contraceptives for men are disqualified if they reduce libido, but oral contraceptives for women are not rejected for reducing women's sexual desire.

In a standard positivist analysis, neither form of sexism in the application of theories has any bearing on the epistemic value of the theories in question. That a theory is used to support unpopular political programs does not show that the theory is false. At most, it reflects a failure of the proponents of the program to respect the logical gap between fact and value. But opponents of the program fail to respect this gap in attacking a theory for the uses to which it is put. According to this view, theories supply facts that all persons must accept, regardless of their political commitments. That a theory is indirectly applied in sexist ways provides even less ground for attacking its content. The question of truth must be strictly separated from the uses to which such truths are put.

Naturalized epistemology does not support such a sanguine analysis of theories that are applied in sexist ways. "Successful" technological applications of theories are currently taken to provide evidence of their epistemic merits. If knowledge is power, then power is a criterion of adequate understanding. The prevailing interpretation of this criterion does not consider whose power is enhanced by the theory and whose interests are served by it. Feminists urge that these considerations be taken explicitly into account when one evaluates whether technological applications of theories supply evidence of an adequate understanding of the phenomena they control (Tiles 1987). It maybe true that certain drugs would be effective in controlling the phenomena of women's hormonal cycles that are currently designated as pathologies constitutive of premenstrual syndrome. Such control may come at the expense of women's interests, not just because of undesirable side effects but also because the legitimation of drug treatment reinforces the medicalization of women's complaints, as if these complaints were symptoms to be medicated rather than as claims on others to change their behavior (Zita 1989). Doctors may be satisfied that such a "successful" drug treatment of PMS supplies evidence that the theory it applies provides them with an adequate understanding of women' menstrual cycles. But should women be satisfied with this understanding? Suppose the phenomena associated with PMS could also be eliminated, or revalued, by widespread acceptance of feminist conceptions of women's bodies or by egalitarian changes that would make social arrangements less frustrating to women. (This would be possible if women's symptoms of distress in PMS were partly caused by misogynist social expectations that represent women's menstrual cycles as pathological.) Such a successful "technological" application of feminist theory would provide women with an understanding of their own menstrual cycles that would empower them. Where the sexist medical technology would enable women to adapt their bodies to the demands of a sexist society, the feminist technology would empower women to change society so that their bodies were no longer considered "diseased." Thus, applications of theories may influence the content of theories whenever "success" in application is taken to justify the theory in question. Sexist or feminist values may inform criteria of success in application, which may in turn inform competing criteria of adequate understanding. The epistemic evaluation of theories therefore cannot be sharply separated from the interests their applications serve.

Feminist naturalized epistemology also rejects the positivist view that the epistemic merits of theories can be assessed independently of their direct ideological applications (Longino 1990; Antony 1993; Potter 1993). Although any acceptable ideology must make sure that it does not fly in the face of facts, theories do not merely state facts but organize them into systems that tell us what their significance is. Theories logically go beyond the facts; they are "underdetermined" by all the empirical evidence that is or ever could be adduced in their favor (Quine 1960, 22). The evidential link between an observed fact and a theoretical hypothesis can only be secured by background auxiliary hypotheses. This leaves open the logical possibility that ideological judgments may not be implications of an independently supported theory but figure in the justification of the theory itself, by supplying evidential links between empirical observations and hypotheses.

A particularly transparent example of this phenomenon may be found in theories about sex differences in intelligence. Girls scored significantly higher than boys on the first Stanford-Binet IQ tests developed by Lewis Terman. To correct for this "embarrassment," Terman eliminated portions of the test where girls scored higher than boys and inserted questions on which boys scored higher than girls. The substitution was considered necessary to ensure the validity of the test against school grades, the only available independent measures of children's intelligence, which did not differ by gender. But Terman did not adjust his test to eliminate sex differences on subtests of the IQ, such as those about quantitative reasoning. These differences seemed unproblematic because they conformed to prevailing ideological assumptions about appropriate gender roles (Mensh and Mensh 1991, 68–9). Today, that IQ scores are good predictors of a child's school grades is still taken to provide key evidence for the claim that differences in IQ scores measure differences in children's innate intelligence. But the evidential link tying school grades to this theoretical claim depends on the background value judgment that schools provide fair educational opportunities to all children with respect to all fields of study. Those schools that discourage girls from pursuing maths and science assume that girls have inferior quantitative reasoning ability; they do not recognize that lack of encouragement can cause relatively lower performance on maths tests.

From a positivist point of view, this reasoning is defective on two counts. First, it is circular to claim that IQ tests demonstrate innate sex differences in quantitative reasoning ability when the assumption of innate sex differences is built into the background hypotheses needed to validate the tests. Second, no reasoning is scientifically sound that incorporates value judgments into the background assumptions that link observations to theory. The salience of positivist views of science as well as their usefulness to feminists in criticizing research about sex differences has tempted some feminists to use the positivist requirement that science be value-free to discredit all scientific projects that incorporate sexist values in the explicit or implicit content of their theories. But this appropriation of positivism puts at odds the two aims of feminist epistemology – to criticize sexist science and to promote feminist science. If incorporating sexist values into scientific theories is illegitimate on positivist grounds, then so is incorporating feminist values into scientific theories (Longino 1993a, 259).

Feminist naturalized epistemologists offer a more nuanced response to the presence of value judgments in scientific inference. Even "good science" can incorporate such value judgments. The logical gap between theory and observation ensures that one cannot in principle rule out the possibility that value judgments are implicit in the background assumptions used to argue that a given observation constitutes evidence for a given hypothesis (Longino 1990). From the perspective of an individual scientist, it is not unreasonable to use any of one's firm beliefs, including beliefs about values, to reason from an observation to a theory. Nor does the prospect of circularity threaten the scientific validity of one's reasoning, as long as the circle of reasoning is big enough. In a coherent web of belief, every belief offers some support for every other belief, and no belief is perfectly self-supporting. Theories that incorporate value judgments can be scientifically sound as long as they are empirically adequate.

This reasoning underwrites the legitimacy of feminist scientific research, which incorporates feminist values into its theories. Such values may be detected in the commitment of feminist researchers to regard women as intelligent agents, capable of reflecting on and changing the conditions that presently constrain their actions. This commitment tends to support a theoretical preference for causal models of female behavior that highlight feedback loops between their intentional states and their social and physical environments, and that resist purely structuralist accounts of female "nature" that leave no room for females to resist their circumstances or maneuver among alternate possibilities (Haraway 1989, Ch. 13; Longino 1989, 210–13). In contrast, most behaviorist and some sociobiological theories favor models that highlight linear causal chains from fixed physiological or physical conditions to determinate behaviors, and that emphasize the structural constraints on action. The epistemic values of simplicity, prediction, and control might seem to support linear, structural causal models. But we have seen that control at least is a contested value; the kinds of control taken to warrant claims of adequate understanding depend on substantive value judgments about the importance of particular human interests. Is adequate understanding achieved when a theory empowers scientists to control women's lives, or when it empowers women to control their own lives? Rival interpretations of the other epistemic values also depend on contested nonepistemic values. The kind of simplicity one favors depends on one's aesthetic values. In any event, other epistemic values, such as fruitfulness, appear to favor complex, nonlinear causal models of human behavior. Such models support experiments that generate novel behaviors disruptive of presumed structural constraints on action.

Naturalized feminist epistemology thus permits scientific projects that incorporate feminist values into the content and application of theories. It does not provide methodological arguments against the pursuit of sexist theories. It does claim, however, that it is irrational for theorists to pursue sexist research programs if they do not endorse sexist values. Moral and political arguments about the rationality of particular values may therefore have a bearing on the rationality of pursuing particular research programs. In addition, the objectivity of science demands that the background assumptions of research programs be exposed to criticism. A scientific community composed of inquirers who share the same background assumptions is unlikely to be aware of the roles these assumptions play in licensing inferences from observations to hypotheses, and even less likely to examine these assumptions critically. Naturalized epistemology therefore recommends that the scientific community include a diversity of inquirers who accept different background assumptions. A community of inquirers who largely accept sexist values and incorporate them into their background assumptions could enhance the objectivity of the community's practice by expanding its membership to include researchers with feminist commitments (Longino 1993a, 267–9).

The Local Character of Naturalized Feminist Epistemology

In reading the project of feminist epistemology along naturalized, empiricist lines, I have tried to show how its interest and critical power do not depend on the global, transcendental claims that all knowledge is gendered or that rationality as a regulatory epistemic ideal is masculine. Naturalized feminist epistemologists may travel to distant locations in the universe of belief, but they always remain inside that universe and travel from gender to science by way of discrete, empirically discovered paths. They have an interest in constructing new paths to empirically adequate, fruitful, and useful forms of feminist science and in breaking up other paths that lead to cognitively and socially unsatisfactory destinations. All the paths by which naturalized epistemologists find gender to influence theoretical knowledge are local, contingent, and empirically conditioned. All the paths by which they propose to change these influences accept rationality as a key epistemic ideal and empirical adequacy as a fundamental goal of acceptable theories. This ideal and this goal are in principle equally open to pursuit by male and female inquirers, but may be best realized by mixed-gender research communities. Naturalized epistemologists find no persuasive evidence that indicates that all women inquirers bring some shared global feminine difference in ways of thinking to all subjects of study nor that such a feminine difference gives us privileged access to the way the world is.

In rejecting global, transcendental claims about differences in the ways men and women think, naturalized feminist epistemologists do not imply that the entry and advancement of significant numbers of women into scientific communities makes no systematic difference to the knowledge these communities produce. But, following their view of inquiry as a social, not an individual, enterprise, they credit the improvements in knowledge such entry produces to the greater diversity and equality of membership in the scientific community rather than to any purportedly privileged subject position of women as knowers (Tuana 1992; Longino 1993a). Men and women do have *some* gender-specific experiences and personal knowledge due to their different socialization and social status. We have seen that such experiences and forms of knowledge can be fruitfully brought to bear upon theoretical inquiry. So it should not be surprising that women researchers have exposed and criticized androcentrism in theories much more than men have. The diversity and equality of inquirers help ensure that social models do not merely reflect or fit the circumstances of a narrow demographic segment of the population when they are meant to apply to everyone. They correct a cognitive bias commonly found among inquirers belonging to all demographic groups, located in the habit of assuming that the way the world appears to oneself is the way it appears to everyone.

This survey of some findings of naturalized feminist epistemology has also identified improvements in knowledge that have or would come about through the entry of *feminist* theorists into various fields, and through revisions in the systems of cognitive authority among fields that would bring the findings of feminist theorists to bear upon apparently distant subjects.[3] We have seen that the use of gender symbolism to model nonhuman phenomena is fraught with cognitive traps. So it should not be surprising that feminist researchers, who make it their business to study the contradictions and incoherences in our conceptions of gender, can improve theories by exposing and clearing up the confusions they inherit from the gender ideologies they use as models. By pursuing feminist research in the humanities, social sciences, and biology, feminist researchers also pose challenges to prevailing theories. Here again, the kinds of changes we should expect in theoretical knowledge from the entry of feminist researchers into various fields do not typically consist in the production of specifically feminist ontologies, methodologies, standpoints, paradigms, or doctrines. Feminist contributions to theorizing are more usefully conceived as altering the field of theoretical possibilities (Haraway 1986, 81, 96). Research informed by feminist commitments makes new explanatory models available, reframes old questions, exposes facts that undermine the plausibility of previously dominant theories, improves data-gathering techniques, and shifts the relations of cognitive authority among fields and theories. In these and many other ways, it reconfigures our assessments of the prospects and virtues of various research programs. Without claiming that women, or feminists, have a globally different or privileged way of knowing, naturalized feminist epistemology explains how feminist theory can productively transform the field of theoretical knowledge.

Notes

1 Diamond (1991, 1009) writes that the exclusion of animal trainers' knowledge from the realm of authoritative knowledge "cannot in any very simple way be connected to gender." Pointing out that the terms "hard" and "soft" as applied to forms of knowledge are used by "men trying to put down other men," Sherif argues that for this reason it is "particularly misleading" to infer that these terms symbolize "masculine" and "feminine" (1987, 46–7). I would have thought that her observation supports

the gendered reading, since a standard way for men to put down other men is to insinuate that they are feminine.

2 The interests at stake need not be self-interests or even ideological interests of a broader sort. One might just be curious about how rainbows form, without seeking this knowledge for the sake of finding out: how to get the proverbial pot of gold at the end. Curiosity is one kind of interest we can express in a phenomenon.

3 The question of the impact of feminist theorists on knowledge is distinct from but related to the question of the impact of women theorists on knowledge. Not all women theorists are feminists, and some feminist theorists are men. At the same time, there could be no genuine feminist theory that was conducted by men alone. Feminist theory is theory committed to the liberation and equality of women. These goals can only be achieved through the exercise of women's own agency, especially in defining and coming to know themselves. Feminist theory is one of the vehicles of women's agency in pursuit of these goals, and therefore cannot realize its aims if it is not conducted by women. So it should not be surprising that most of the transformations of knowledge induced by feminist theory were brought about by women.

References

American Association of University Women. 1992. *The AAUW report: How schools shortchange girls.* Prepared by Wellesley College Center for Research on Women.

Anderson, Elizabeth. 1993. *Value in ethics and economics.* Cambridge: Harvard University Press.

Antony, Louise. 1993. Quine as feminist: The radical import of naturalized epistemology. In *A mind of one's own: Feminist essays on reason and objectivity*. See Antony and Witt 1993.

Antony, Louise, and Charlotte Witt. 1993. *A mind of one's own: Feminist essays on reason and objectivity.* Boulder, CO: Westview.

Astin, Helen S., and Alan E. Beyer. 1973. Sex discrimination in academe. In *Academic women on the move*, ed. Alice. S. Rossi and Ann Calderwood. New York: Russell Sage Foundation.

Becker, Joanne Rossi. 1981. Differential treatment of females and males in mathematics classes. *Journal for Research in Mathematics Education* 12(1): 40–53.

Belenky, Mary, Blythe Clinchy, Nancy Goldberger, and jill Tarule. 1986. *Women's ways of knowing*. New York: Basic Books.

Bell, Diane, Pat Caplan, and Wazir Karim, eds. 1993. *Gendered fields: Women, men, and ethnography*. New York: Routledge.

Biology and Gender Study Group. 1988. The importance of feminist critique for contemporary cell biology. *Hypatia* 3(1): 61–76.

Bordo, Susan. 1987. *The flight to objectivity: Essays on cartesianism and culture*. Albany: State University of New York Press.

Bourdieu, Pierre. 1977. *Outline of a theory of practice.* Cambridge: Cambridge University Press.

Coady, C. A. J. 1992. *Testimony*. Oxford: Clarendon Press.

Collins, Patricia Hill. 1990. *Black feminist thought: Knowledge, consciousness, and the politics of empowerment*. Boston: Unwin Hyman.

Curran, Libby. 1980. Science education: Did she drop out or was she pushed? In *Alice through the microscope*, ed. Brighton Women and Science Group. London: Virago.

Dawkins, Richard. 1976. *The selfish gene*. New York: Oxford University Press.

Diamond, Cora. 1991. Knowing tornadoes and other things. *New Literary History* 22: 1001–15.

Duran, Jane. 1991. *Toward a feminist epistemology*. Totowa, NJ: Rowman and Littlefield.

Fidell, L. S. 1970. Empirical verification of sex discrimination in hiring practices in psychology. *American Psychologist* 25(12); 1094–8.

Flax, Jane. 1983. Political philosophy and the patriarchal unconscious. In *Discovering reality*. See Harding and Hintikka 1983.

Gilligan, Carol. 1982. *In a different voice*. Cambridge: Harvard University Press.

Goldberg, Steven. 1973. *The inevitability of patriarchy*. New York: Morrow.

Haraway, Donna. 1986. Primatology is politics by other means. In *Feminist approaches to science*, ed. Ruth Bleier. New York: Pergamon.

———. 1989. *Primate visions*. New York: Routledge.

Harding, Sandra. 1986. *The science question in feminism*. Ithaca: Cornell University Press.

Hearne, Vicki. 1982. *Adam's task*. New York: Vintage.

Hrdy, Sarah. 1981. *The woman that never evolved*. Cambridge: Harvard University Press.

———. 1986. Empathy, polyandry, and the myth of the coy female. In *Feminist approaches to science*, ed. Ruth Bleier. New York: Pergamon.

Hubbard, Ruth. 1990. *The politics of women's biology*. New Brunswick, NJ: Rutgers University Press.

Keller, Evelyn Fox. 1983. *A feeling for the organism*. New York: Freeman.

———. 1985. The force of the pacemaker concept in theories of aggregation in cellular slime mold. In *Reflections on gender and science*. New Haven: Yale University Press.

———. 1992. *Secrets of life, secrets of death*. New York: Routledge.

Leacock, Eleanor. 1982. *Myths of male dominance*. New York: Monthly Review Press.

Lefkowitz, M. R. 1979. Education for women in a man's world. *Chronicle of Higher Education*, 6 August, p. 56.

Longino, Helen. 1989. Can there be a feminist science? In *Women, knowledge, and reality*, ed. Ann Carry and Marilyn Pearsall. Boston: Unwin Hyman.

———. 1990. *Science as social knowledge*. Princeton, NJ: Princeton University Press.

———. 1993a. Essential tensions – Phase two: Feminist, philosophical, and social studies of science. In *A mind of one's own*. See Antony and Witt 1993.

———. 1993b. Subjects, power, and knowledge: Description and prescription in feminist philosophies of science. In *Feminist epistemologies*. See Alcoff and Potter 1993.

Maccoby, Eleanor, and Carol Jacklin. 1974. *The psychology of sex differences*. Stanford: Stanford University Press.

Mensh, Elaine, and Harry Mensh. 1991. *The IQ mythology*. Carbondale: Southern Illinois University Press.

National Science Foundation. 1984. *Women and minorities in science and engineering*.

Nelson, Lynn. 1990. *Who knows? From Quine to a feminist empiricism*. Philadelphia: Temple University Press.

———. 1993. Epistemological communities. In *Feminist epistemologies*. See Alcoff and Potter 1993.

Pai, Hyung Il. 1985. (Anthropologist, University of California, Santa Barbara). Personal communication.

Paludi, Michele Antoinette, and William D. Bauer. 1983. Goldberg revisited: What's in an author's name. *Sex Roles* 9(3): 287–390.

Polanyi, Michael. 1958. *Personal knowledge*. Chicago: University of Chicago Press.

Potter, Elizabeth. 1993. Gender and epistemic negotiation. In *Feminist epistemologies*. See Alcoff and Potter 1993.

Quine, W. V. O. 1960. *Word and object*. Cambridge: MIT Press.

———. 1969. Epistemology naturalized. In *Ontological relativity and other essays*. New York: Columbia University Press.

Reskin, Barbara. 1979. Academic sponsorship and scientists' careers. *Sociology of Education* 52(3):129–46.

Rooney, Phyllis. 1991. Gendered reason: Sex metaphor and conceptions of reason. *Hypatia* 6(2): 77–103.

Rose, Hilary. 1987. Hand, brain, and heart: A feminist epistemology for the natural sciences. In *Sex and scientific inquiry*, ed. Sandra Harding and Jean O'Barr. Chicago: University of Chicago Press.

Rose, Suzanna. 1989. Women biologists and the "old boy" network. *Women's Studies International Forum* 12(3): 349–54.

Rosenfeld, Rachel. 1981. Academic career mobility for psychologists. In *Women in scientific and engineering professions*, ed. Violet Haas and Carolyn Perrucci. Ann Arbor: University of Michigan Press.

Rossiter, Margaret. 1982. *Women scientists in America: Struggles and strategies to 1940*. Baltimore: Johns Hopkins University Press.

Scheman, Naomi. 1983. Individualism and the objects of psychology. In *Discovering reality*. See Harding and Hintikka 1983.

Schiebinger, Londa. 1989. The *mind has no sex?* Cambridge: Harvard University Press.

Schuman, Howard, and Shirley Hatchett. 1974. *Black racial attitudes: Trends and complexities*. Ann Arbor: University of Michigan Press.

Sherif, Carolyn. 1987. Bias in psychology. In *Feminism and methodology*, ed. Sandra Harding. Bloomington: Indiana University Press.

Smith, Dorothy. 1974. Women's perspective as a radical critique of sociology. *Sociological inquiry* 44(1): 7–13.

Solomon, Miriam. 1994. Social epistemology. *Nous* 28: 325–43.

Stiehm, Judith. 1983. Our aristotelian hangover. In *Discovering reality*. See Harding and Hintikka 1983.

Tavris, Carol. 1992. *The mismeasure of woman*. New York: Simon and Schuster.

Tidball, M. Elizabeth. 1980. Women's colleges and women achievers revisited. *Signs* 5(3): 504–17.

Tiles, Mary. 1987. A science of Mars or of Venus? *Philosophy* 62(July): 293–306.

Tuana, Nancy. 1992. The radical future of feminist empiricism. *Hypatia* 7(1): 100–14.

Vetter, Betty. 1981. Changing patterns of recruitment and employment. In *Women in scientific and engineering professions*, ed. Violet Haas and Carolyn Perrucci. Ann Arbor: University of Michigan Press.

Waring, Marilyn. 1990. *If women counted*. San Francisco: HarperCollins.

Wrangham, Richard. 1979. On the evolution of ape social systems. *Biology and Social Life: Social Sciences Information* 18: 335–68.

Zita, Jacquelyn. 1989. The premenstrual syndrome: "Dis-easing" the female cycle. In *Feminism and science*, ed. Nancy Tuana. Bloomington: Indiana University Press.

16

Can there be a Feminist Science?

Helen E. Longino

I

The question of this title conceals multiple ambiguities. Not only do the sciences consist of many distinct fields, but the term "science" can be used to refer to a method of inquiry, a historically changing collection of practices, a body of knowledge, a set of claims, a profession, a set of social groups, etc. And as the sciences are many, so are the scholarly disciplines that seek to understand them: philosophy, history, sociology, anthropology, psychology. Any answer from the perspective of some one of these disciplines will, then, of necessity, be partial. In this essay, I shall be asking about the possibility of theoretical natural science that is feminist and I shall ask from the perspective of a philosopher. Before beginning to develop my answer, however, I want to review some of the questions that could be meant, in order to arrive at the formulation I wish to address.

The question could be interpreted as factual, one to be answered by pointing to what feminists in the sciences are doing and saying: "Yes, and this is what it is." Such a response can be perceived as questionbegging, however. Even such a friend of feminism as Stephen Gould dismisses the idea of a distinctively feminist or even female contribution to the sciences. In a generally positive review of Ruth Bleier's book, *Science and Gender*, Gould (1984) brushes aside her connection between women's attitudes and values and the interactionist science she calls for. Scientists (male, of course) are already proceeding with wholist and interactionist research programs. Why, he implied, should women or feminists have any particular, distinctive, contributions to make? There is not masculinist and feminist science, just good and bad science. The question of a feminist science cannot be settled by pointing, but involves a deeper, subtler investigation.

The deeper question can itself have several meanings. One set of meanings is sociological, the other conceptual. The sociological meaning proceeds as follows. We know what sorts of social conditions make misogynist science possible. The work of Margaret Rossiter (1982) on the history of women scientists in the United States and the work of Kathryn Addelson (1983) on the social structure of professional science detail the relations between a particular social structure for science and the kinds of science produced. What sorts of social conditions would make feminist science possible? This is an important question, one I am not

Helen E. Longino, "Can there be a Feminist Science?" pp. 51–64 from *Hypatia* 2(3), 1987. Reprinted by permission of Indiana University Press, as the publisher.

equipped directly to investigate, although what I can investigate is, I believe, relevant to it. This is the second, conceptual, interpretation of the question: what sort of sense does it make to about a feminist science? Why is the question itself not an oxymoron, linking, as it does, values and ideological commitment with the idea of impersonal, objective, value-free, inquiry? This is the problem I wish to address in this essay.

The hope for a feminist theoretical natural science has concealed an ambiguity between content and practice. In the content sense the idea of a feminist science involves a number of assumptions and calls a number of visions to mind. Some theorists have written as though a feminist science is one the theories of which encode a particular world view, characterized by complexity, interaction and wholism. Such a science is said to be feminist because it is the expression and valorization of a female sensibility or cognitive temperament. Alternatively, it is claimed that women have certain traits (dispositions to attend to particulars, interactive rather than individualist and controlling social attitudes and behaviors) that enable them to understand the true character of natural processes (which are complex and interactive).[1] While proponents of this interactionist view see it as an improvement over most contemporary science, it has also been branded as soft – misdescribed as non-mathematical. Women in the sciences who feel they are being asked to do not better science, but inferior science, have responded angrily to this characterization of feminist science, thinking that it is simply new clothing for the old idea that women can't do science. I think that the interactionist view can be defended against this response, although that requires rescuing it from some of its proponents as well. However, I also think that the characterization of feminist science as the expression of a distinctive female cognitive temperament has other drawbacks. It first conflates feminine with feminist. While it is important to reject the traditional derogation of the virtues assigned to women, it is also important to remember that women are *constructed* to occupy positions of social subordinates. We should not uncritically embrace the feminine.

This characterization of feminist science is also a version of recently propounded notions of a "women's standpoint" or a "feminist standpoint" and suffers from the same suspect universalization that these ideas suffer from. If there is one such standpoint, there are many: as Maria Lugones and Elizabeth Spelman spell out in their tellingly entitled article, "Have We Got a Theory for You: Feminist Theory, Cultural Imperialism, and the Demand for 'The Woman's Voice,'" women are too diverse in our experiences to generate a single cognitive framework (Lugones and Spelman 1983). In addition, the sciences are themselves too diverse for me to think that they might be equally transformed by such a framework. To reject this concept of a feminist science, however, is not to disengage science from feminism. I want to suggest that we focus on science as practice rather than content, as process rather than product; hence, not on feminist science, but on doing science as a feminist.

The doing of science involves many practices: how one structures a laboratory (hierarchically or collectively), how one relates to other scientists (competitively or cooperatively), how and whether one engages in political struggles over affirmative action. It extends also to intellectual practices, to the activities of scientific inquiry, such as observation and reasoning. Can there be a feminist scientific inquiry? This possibility is seen to be problematic against the background of certain standard presuppositions about science. The claim that there could be a feminist science in the sense of an intellectual practice is either nonsense because oxymoronic as suggested above or the claim is interpreted to mean that established science (science as done and dominated by men) is wrong about the world. Feminist science in this latter interpretation is presented as correcting the errors of masculine, standard science and as revealing the truth that is hidden by masculine "bad" science, as taking the sex out of science.

Both of these interpretations involve the rejection of one approach as incorrect and the embracing of the other as the way to a truer understanding of the natural world. Both trade one absolutism for another. Each is a side of the same coin, and that coin, I think, is the idea of a value-free science. This is the idea that scientific methodology guarantees the independence of scientific inquiry from values of value-related considerations. A science or a scientific research program informed by values is *ipso facto* "bad science." "Good science" is inquiry protected by methodology from values and ideology. This same idea underlies Gould's response to Bleier, so it bears closer scrutiny. In the pages that follow, I shall examine the idea of value-free science and then apply the results of that examination to the idea of feminist scientific inquiry.

II

I distinguish two kinds of values relevant to the sciences. Constitutive values, internal to the sciences, are the source of the rules determining what constitutes acceptable scientific practice or scientific method. The personal, social and cultural values, those group or individual preferences about what ought to be I call contextual values, to indicate that they belong to the social and cultural context in which science is done (Longino 1983c). The traditional interpretation of the value-freedom of modern natural science amounts to a claim that its constitutive and contextual features are clearly distinct from and independent of one another, that contextual values play no role in the inner workings of scientific inquiry, in reasoning and observation. I shall argue that this construal of the distinction cannot be maintained.

There are several ways to develop such an argument. One scholar is fond of inviting her audience to visit any science library and peruse the titles on the shelves. Observe how subservient to social and cultural interests are the inquiries represented by the book titles alone! Her listeners would soon abandon their ideas about the value-neutrality of the sciences, she suggests. This exercise may indeed show the influence of external, contextual considerations on what research gets done/supported (i.e., on problem selection). It does not show that such considerations affect reasoning or hypothesis acceptance. The latter would require detailed investigation of particular cases or a general conceptual argument. The conceptual arguments involve developing some version of what is known in philosophy of science as the underdetermination thesis, i.e., the thesis that a theory is always underdetermined by the evidence adduced in its support, with the consequence that different or incompatible theories are supported by or at least compatible with the same body of evidence. I shall sketch a version of the argument that appeals to features of scientific inference.

One of the rocks on which the logical positivist program foundered was the distinction between theoretical and observational language. Theoretical statements contain, as fundamental descriptive terms, terms that do not occur in the description of data. Thus, hypotheses in particle physics contain terms like "electron," "pion," "muon," "electron spin," etc. The evidence for a hypothesis such as "A pion decays sequentially into a muon, then a positron" is obviously not direct observations of pions, muons and positrons, but consists largely in photographs taken in large and complex experimental apparati: accelerators, cloud chambers, bubble chambers. The photographs show all sorts of squiggly lines and spirals. Evidence for the hypotheses of particle physics is presented as statements that describe these photographs. Eventually, of course, particle physicists point to a spot on a photograph and say things like "Here a neutrino hits a neutron." Such an assertion, however, is an interpretive achievement which involves collapsing theoretical and observational moments. A skeptic would have to be supplied a complicated argument linking the elements of the photograph to traces left by particles and these to particles themselves. What counts as theory and what as data in a pragmatic sense change over time, as some ideas and experimental procedures come to be securely embedded in a particular framework and others take their place on the horizons. As the history of physics shows, however, secure embeddedness is no guarantee against overthrow.

Logical positivists and their successors hoped to model scientific inference formally. Evidence for hypotheses, data, were to be represented as logical consequences of hypotheses. When we try to map this logical structure onto the sciences, however, we find that hypotheses are, for the most part, not just generalizations of data statements. The links between data and theory, therefore, cannot be adequately represented as formal or syntactic, but are established by means of assumptions that make or imply substantive claims about the field over which one theorizes. Theories are confirmed via the confirmation of their constituent hypotheses, so the confirmation of hypotheses and theories is relative to the assumptions relied upon in asserting the evidential connection. Conformation of such assumptions, which are often unarticulated, is itself subject to similar relativization. And it is these assumptions that can be the vehicle for the involvement of considerations motivated primarily by contextual values (Longino 1979, 1983a).

The point of this extremely telescoped argument is that one can't give an a priori specification of confirmation that effectively eliminates the role of value-laden assumptions in legitimate scientific inquiry without eliminating auxiliary hypotheses (assumptions) altogether. This is not to say that all scientific reasoning involves value-related assumptions. Sometimes auxiliary assumptions will be supported by mundane inductive reasoning. But sometimes they will not be. In any given case, they may be metaphysical in character; they may be untestable with present investigative techniques; they may be rooted in contextual, value-related considerations. If, however, there is no a priori way to eliminate such assumptions from evidential reasoning generally, and, hence, no way to rule out value-laden assumptions, then there is no formal basis for arguing that an inference mediated by contextual values is thereby bad science.

A comparable point is made by some historians investigating the origins of modern science. James Jacob (1977) and Margaret Jacob (1976) have, in a series of articles and books, argued that the adoption of conceptions of matter by seventeenth-century scientists like Robert Boyle was inextricably intertwined with political considerations. Conceptions of matter provided the foundation on which physical theories were developed and Boyle's science, regardless of his reasons for it, has been fruitful in ways that far exceed his imaginings. If the presence of contextual influences were grounds for disallowing a line of inquiry, then early modern science would not have gotten off the ground.

The conclusion of this line of argument is that constitutive values conceived as epistemological (i.e., truth-seeking) are not adequate to screen out the influence of contextual values in the very structuring of scientific knowledge. Now the ways in which contextual values do, if they do, influence this structuring and interact, if they do, with constitutive values has to be determined separately for different theories and fields of science. But this argument, if it's sound, tells us that this sort of inquiry is perfectly respectable and involves no shady assumptions or unargued intuitively based rejections of positivism. It also opens the possibility that one can make explicit value commitments and still do "good" science. The conceptual argument doesn't show that all science is value-laden (as opposed to metaphysics-laden) – that must be established on a case-by-case basis, using the tools not just of logic and philosophy but of history and sociology as well. It does show that not all science is value-free and, more importantly, that it is not necessarily in the nature of science to be value-free. If we reject that idea we're in a better position to talk about the possibilities of feminist science.

III

In earlier articles (Longino 1981, 1983b; Longino and Doell 1983), I've used similar considerations to argue that scientific objectivity has to be reconceived as a function of the communal structure of scientific inquiry rather than as a property of individual scientists. I've then used these notions about scientific methodology to show that science displaying masculine bias is not *ipso facto* improper or "bad" science; that the fabric of science can neither rule out the expression of bias nor legitimate it. So I've argued that both the expression of masculine bias in the sciences and feminist criticism of research exhibiting that bias are – shall we say – business as usual; that scientific inquiry should be expected to display the deep metaphysical and normative commitments of the culture in which it flourishes; and finally that criticism of the deep assumptions that guide scientific reasoning about data is a proper part of science.

The argument I've just offered about the idea of a value-free science is similar in spirit to those earlier arguments. I think it makes it possible to see these questions from a slightly different angle.

There is a tradition of viewing scientific inquiry as somehow inexorable. This involves supposing that the phenomena of the natural world are fixed in determinate relations with each other, that these relations can be known and formulated in a consistent and unified way. This is not the old "unified science" idea of the logical positivists, with its privileging of physics. In its "unexplicated" or "pre-analytic" state, it is simply the idea that there is one consistent, integrated or coherent, true theoretical treatment of all natural phenomena. (The indeterminacy principle of quantum physics is restricted to our understanding of the behavior of certain particles which themselves underlie the fixities of the natural world. Stochastic theories reveal fixities, but fixities among ensembles rather than fixed relations among individual objects or events.) The scientific inquirer's job is to discover those fixed relations. Just as the task of Plato's philosophers was to discover the fixed relations among forms and the task of Galileo's scientists was to discover the laws written in the language of the grand book of nature, geometry, so the scientist's task in this tradition remains the discovery of fixed relations however conceived. These ideas are part of the realist tradition in the philosophy of science.

It's no longer possible, in a century that has seen the splintering of the scientific disciplines, to give such a unified description of the objects of inquiry. But the belief that the job is to discover fixed relations of some sort, and that the application of observation, experiment and reason leads ineluctably to unifiable, if not unified, knowledge of an independent reality, is still with us. It is evidenced most clearly in two features of scientific rhetoric: the use of the passive voice as in "it is concluded that..." or "it has been discovered that..." and the attribution of agency to the data, as in "the data suggest...." Such language has been criticized for the abdication of responsibility it indicates. Even more, the scientific inquirer, and we with her, become passive observers, victims of the truth. The idea of a value-free science is integral to this view of scientific inquiry. And if we reject that idea we can also reject our roles as passive onlookers, helpless to affect the course of knowledge.

Let me develop this point somewhat more concretely and autobiographically. Biologist Ruth Doell and I have been examining studies in three areas of research on the influence of sex hormones on human behavior and cognitive performance: research on the influence of pre-natal, *in utero*, exposure to higher or lower than normal levels of androgens and estrogens on so-called "gender-role" behavior in children, influence of androgens (pre- and post-natal) on homosexuality in women, and influence of lower than normal (for men) levels of androgen at puberty on spatial abilities (Doell and Longino 1988).

The studies we looked at are vulnerable to criticism of their data and their observation methodologies. They also show clear evidence of androcentric bias – in the assumption that there are just two sexes and two genders (us and them), in the designation of appropriate and inappropriate behaviors for male and female children, in the caricature of lesbianism, in the assumption of male mathematical superiority. We did not find, however, that these assumptions mediated the inferences from data to theory that we found objectionable. These sexist assumptions did affect the way the data were described. What mediated the inferences from the alleged data (i.e., what functioned as auxiliary hypotheses or what provided auxiliary hypotheses) was what we called the linear model – the assumption that there is a direct one-way causal relationship between pre- or post-natal hormone levels and later behavior or cognitive performance. To put it crudely, fetal gonadal hormones organize the brain at critical periods of development. The organism is thereby disposed to respond in a range of ways to a range of environmental stimuli. The assumption of unidirectional programming is supposedly supported by the finding of such a relationship in other mammals; in particular, by experiments demonstrating the dependence of sexual behaviors – mounting and lordosis – on peri-natal hormone exposure and the finding of effects of sex hormones on the development of rodent brains. To bring it to bear on humans is to ignore, among other things, some important differences between human brains and those of other species. It also implies a willingness to regard humans in a particular way – to see us as produced by factors over which we have no control. Not only are we, as scientists, victims of the truth, but we are the prisoners of our physiology.[2] In the name of extending an explanatory model, human capacities for self-knowledge, self-reflection, self-determination are eliminated from any role in human action (at least in the behaviors studied).

Doell and I have therefore argued for the replacement of that linear model of the role of the brain in behavior by one of much greater complexity that includes physiological, environmental, historical and psychological elements. Such a model allows not only for the interaction of physiological and environmental factors but also for the interaction of these with a continuously self-modifying, self-representational (and self-organizing) central processing system. In contemporary neurobiology, the closest model is that being developed in the group selectionist approach to higher brain function of Gerald Edelman and other researchers (Edelman and Mountcastle 1978). We argue that a model of at least that degree of complexity is necessary to account for the human behaviors studies in the sex hormones and behavior research and that if gonadal hormones function at all at these levels, they will probably be found at most to facilitate or inhibit neural processing in general. The strategy we take in our argument is to show that the degree of intentionality involved in the behaviors in question is greater than is presupposed by the hormonal influence researchers and to argue that this degree of intentionality implicates the higher brain processes.

To this point Ruth Doell and I agree. I want to go further and describe what we've done from the perspective of the above philosophical discussion of scientific methodology.

Abandoning my polemical mood for a more reflective one, I want to say that, in the end, commitment to one or another model is strongly influenced by values or other contextual features. The models themselves determine the relevance and interpretation of data. The linear or complex models are not in turn independently or conclusively supported by data. I doubt for instance that value-free inquiry will reveal the efficacy or inefficacy of intentional states or of physiological factors like hormone exposure in human action. I think instead that a research program in neuroscience that assumes the linear model and sex-gender dualism will show the influence of hormone exposure on gender-role behavior. And I think that a research program in neuroscience and psychology proceeding on the assumption that humans do possess the capacities for self-consciousness, self-reflection, and self-determination, and which then asks how the structure of the human brain and nervous system enables the expression of these capacities, will reveal the efficacy of intentional states (understood as very complex sorts of brain states).

While this latter assumption does not itself contain normative terms, I think that the decision to adopt it is motivated by value-laden considerations – by the desire to understand ourselves and others as self-determining (at least some of the time), that is, as capable of acting on the basis of concepts or representations of ourselves and the world in which we act. (Such representations are not necessarily correct, they are surely mediated by our cultures; all we wish to claim is that they are efficacious.) I think further that this desire on Ruth Doell's and my part is, in several ways, an aspect of our feminism. Our preference for a neurobiological model that allows for agency, for the efficacy of intentionality is partly a validation of our (and everyone's) subjective experience of thought, deliberation, and choice. One of the tenets of feminist research is the valorization of subjective experience, and so our preference in this regard conforms to feminist research patterns. There is, however, a more direct way in which our feminism is expressed in this preference. Feminism is many things to many people, but it is at its core in part about the expansion of human potentiality. When feminists talk of breaking out and do break out of socially prescribed sex-roles, when feminists criticize the institutions of domination, we are thereby insisting on the capacity of humans – male and female – to act on perceptions of self and society and to act to bring about changes in self and society on the basis of those perceptions. (Not overnight and not by a mere act of will. The point is that we act.) And so our criticism of theories of the hormonal influence or determination of so-called gender-role behavior is not just a rejection of the sexist bias in the description of the phenomena – the behavior of the children studied, the sexual lives of lesbians, etc. – but of the limitations on human capacity imposed by the analytic model underlying such research.[3]

While the argument strategy we adopt against the linear model rests on a certain understanding of intention, the values motivating our adoption of that understanding remain hidden in that polemical context. Our political commitments, however, presuppose a certain understanding of human action, so that when faced with a conflict between these commitments and a particular model of brain-behavior relationships we allow the political commitments to guide the choice.

The relevance of my argument about value-free science should be becoming clear. Feminists – in and out of science – often condemn masculine bias in the sciences from the vantage point of commitment to a value-free science. Androcentric bias, once identified, can then be seen as a violation of the rules, as "bad" science. Feminist science, by contrast, can eliminate that bias and produce better, good, more true or gender free science. From that perspective the process I've just described is anathema. But if scientific methods generated by constitutive values cannot guarantee independent from contextual values, then that approach to sexist science won't work. We cannot restrict ourselves simply to the elimination of bias, but must expand our scope to include the detection of limiting and interpretive frameworks and the finding or construction of more appropriate frameworks. We need not, indeed should not, wait for such a framework to emerge from the data. In waiting, if my argument is correct, we run the danger of working unconsciously with assumptions still laden with values from the context we seek to change. Instead of remaining passive with respect to the data and what the data suggest, we can acknowledge our ability to affect the course of knowledge and fashion or favor research programs that are consistent with the values and commitments we express in the rest of our lives. From this perspective, the idea of a value-free science is not just empty, but pernicious.

Accepting the relevance to our practice as scientists of our political commitments does not imply simple and crude impositions of those ideas onto the corner of the natural world under study. If we recognize, however, that knowledge is shaped by the assumptions, values and interests of a culture and that, within limits, one can choose one's culture, then it's clear that as scientists/theorists we have a choice. We can continue to do establishment science, comfortably wrapped in the myths of scientific rhetoric or we can alter our intellectual allegiances. While remaining committed to an abstract goal of understanding, we can choose to whom, socially and politically, we are accountable in our pursuit of that goal. In particular we can choose between being accountable to the traditional establishment or to our political comrades.

Such accountability does not demand a radical break with the science one has learned and practiced. The development of a "new" science involves a more dialectical evolution and more continuity with established science than the familiar language of scientific revolutions implies.

In focusing on accountability and choice, this conception of feminist science differs from those that proceed from the assumption of a congruence between certain models of natural processes and women's inherent modes of understanding.[4] I am arguing instead for the deliberate and active choice of an interpretive model and for the legitimacy of basing that choice on political considerations in this case. Obviously model choice is also constrained by (what we know of) reality, that is, by the data. But reality (what we know of it) is, I have already argued, inadequate to uniquely determine model choice. The feminist theorists mentioned above have focused on the relation between the content of a theory and female values or experiences, in particular on the perceived congruence between interactionist, wholist visions of nature and a form of understanding and set of values widely attributed to women. In contrast, I am suggesting that a feminist scientific practice admits political considerations as relevant constraints on reasoning, which, through their influence on reasoning and interpretation, shape content. In this specific case, those considerations in combination with the phenomena support an explanatory model that is highly interactionist, highly complex. This argument is so far, however, neutral on the issue of whether an interactionist and complex account of natural processes will always be the preferred one. If it is preferred, however, this will be because of explicitly political considerations and not because interactionism is the expression of "women's nature."

The integration of a political commitment with scientific work will be expressed differently in different fields. In some, such as the complex of research programs having a bearing on the understanding of human behavior, certain moves, such as the one described above, seem quite obvious. In others it may not be clear how to express an alternate set of values in inquiry, or what values would be appropriate. The first step, however, is to abandon the idea that scrutiny of the data yields a seamless web of knowledge. The second is to think through a particular field and try to understand just what its unstated and fundamental assumptions are and how they influence the course of inquiry. Knowing something of the history of a field is necessary to this process, as is continued conversation with other feminists.

The feminist interventions I imagine will be local (i.e., specific to a particular area of research); they may not be exclusive (i.e., different feminist perspectives may be represented in theorizing); and they will be in some way continuous with existing scientific work. The accretion of such interventions, of science done by feminists as feminists, and by members of other disenfranchised groups, has the potential, nevertheless, ultimately to transform the character of scientific discourse.

Doing science differently requires more than just the will to do so and it would be disingenuous to pretend that our philosophies of science are the only barrier. Scientific inquiry takes place in a social, political, and economic context which imposes a variety of institutional obstacles to innovation, let alone to the intellectual working out of oppositional and political commitments. The nature of university career ladders means that one's work must be recognized as meeting certain standards of quality in order that one be able to continue it. If those standards are intimately bound up with values and assumptions one rejects, incomprehension rather than conversion is likely. Success requires that we present our work in a way that satisfies those standards and it is easier to do work that looks just like work known to satisfy them than to strike out in a new direction. Another push to conformity comes from the structure of support for science. Many of the scientific ideas argued to be consistent with a feminist politics have a distinctively non-production orientation.[5] In the example discussed above, thinking of the brain as hormonally programmed makes intervention and control more likely than does thinking of it as a self-organizing complexly interactive system. The doing of science, however, requires financial support and those who provide that support are increasingly industry and the military. As might be expected they support research projects likely to meet their needs, projects which promise even greater possibilities for intervention in and manipulation of natural processes. Our sciences are being harnessed to the making of money and the waging of war. The possibility of alternate understandings of the natural world is irrelevant to a culture driven by those interests. To do feminist science we must change the social and political context in which science is done.

So: can there be a feminist science? If this means: is it in principle possible to do science as a feminist?, the answer must be: yes. If this means: can we in practice do science as feminists?, the answer must be: not until we change present conditions.

Notes

1 This seems to be suggested in Bleier (1984), Rose (1983) and in Sandra Harding's (1980) early work.
2 For a striking expression of this point of view see Witelson (1985).
3 Ideological commitments other than feminist ones may lead to the same assumptions and the variety of feminisms means that feminist commitments can lead to different and incompatible assumptions.
4 Cf. note 1, above.
5 This is not to say that interactionist ideas may not be applied in productive contexts, but that, unlike linear causal models, they are several steps away from the manipulation of natural processes immediately suggested by the latter. See Keller (1985), especially Ch. 10.

References

Addelson, Kathryn Pine. 1983. The man of professional wisdom. In *Discovering Reay*, ed., Sandra Harding and Merrill Hintikka. Dordrecht: Reidel.

Bleier, Ruth. 1984. *Science and Gender*. Elmsford, NY: Pergamon.

Doell, Ruth and Longino, Helen. 1988. 'Sex hormones and human behavior: A critique of the linear model' *Journal of Homosexuality*, 15(3–4): 55–78.

Edelman, Gerald and Vernon Mountcastle. 1978. *The Mindful Brain*. Cambridge, MA: MIT Press.

Gould, Stephen J. 1984. Review of Ruth Bleier, *Science and Gender. New York Times Book Review*, VVI, 7(August 12): 1.

Harding, Sandra. 1980. The norms of inquiry and masculine experience. In *PSA 1980*, Vol. 2, ed. Peter Asquith and Ronald Giere. East Lansing, MI: Philosophy of Science Association.

Jacob, James R. 1977. *Robert Boyle and the English Revolution, A Study in Social and Intellectual Change*. New York: Franklin.

Jacob, Margaret C. 1976. *The Newtonians and the English Revolution, 1689–1720*. Ithaca, NY: Cornell University Press.

Keller, Evelyn Fox. 1985. *Reflections on Gender and Science*. New Haven, CT: Yale University Press.

Longino, Helen. 1979. Evidence and hypothesis. *Philosophy of Science* 46(1): 35–56.

———. 1981. Scientific objectivity and feminist theorizing. *Liberal Education* 67(3): 33–41.

———. 1983a. The idea of a value free science. Paper presented to the Pacific Division of the American Philosophical Association, March 25, Berkeley, CA.

———. 1983b. Scientific objectivity and logics of science. *Inquiry* 26(1): 85–106.

———. 1983c. Beyond "bad science." *Science, Technology and Human Values* 8(1): 7–17.

Longino, Helen and Ruth Doell. 1983. Body, bias and behavior. *Signs* 9(2): 206–27.

Lugones, Maria and Elizabeth Spelman. 1983. Have we got a theory for you! Feminist theory, cultural imperialism and the demand for "the woman's voice." *Hypatia 1*, published as a special issue of *Women's Studies International Forum* 6(6): 573–81.

Rose, Hilary. 1983. Hand, brain, and heart: A feminist epistemology for the natural sciences. *Signs* 9(1): 73–90.

Rossiter, Margaret. 1982. *Women scientists in America: Struggles and strategies to 1940*. Baltimore, MD: Johns Hopkins University Press.

Witelson, Sandra. 1985. An exchange on gender. *New York Review of Books* (October 24).

17

Rethinking Standpoint Epistemology: What is "Strong Objectivity"?

Sandra Harding

1 Both Ways

For almost two decades, feminists have engaged in a complex and charged conversation about objectivity. Its topics have included which kinds of knowledge projects have it, which don't, and why they don't; whether the many different feminisms need it, and if so why they do; and if it is possible to get it, how to do so.[1] This conversation has been informed by complex and charged prefeminist writings that tend to get stuck in debates between empiricists and intentionalists, objectivists and interpretationists, and realists and social constructionists (including poststructuralists).[2]

Most of these feminist discussions have *not* arisen from attempts to find new ways either to criticize or carry on the agendas of the disciplines. Frequently they do not take as their problematics the ones familiar within the disciplines. Instead, these conversations have emerged mainly from two different and related concerns. First, what are the causes of the immense proliferation of theoretically and empirically sound results of research in biology and the social sciences that have discovered what is not supposed to exist: rampant sexist and androcentric bias – "politics"! – in the dominant scientific (and popular) descriptions and explanations of nature and social life? To put the point another way, how should one explain the surprising fact that politically guided research projects have been able to produce less partial and distorted results of research than those supposedly guided by the goal of value-neutrality? Second, how can feminists create research that is *for* women in the sense that it provides less partial and distorted answers to questions that arise from women's lives and are not only about those lives but also about the rest of nature and social relations? The two concerns are related because recommendations for future scientific practices should be informed by the best accounts of past scientific successes. That is, how one answers the second question depends on what one thinks is the best answer to the first one.

Many feminists, like thinkers in the other new social liberation movements, now hold that it is not only desirable but also possible to have that apparent contradiction in terms – socially situated knowledge. In conventional accounts, socially situated beliefs only get to count as opinions. In order to achieve the status of knowledge, beliefs are supposed to break free of – to transcend – their original ties to

Sandra Harding, "Rethinking Standpoint Epistemology: What is Strong Objectivity"?, pp. 49–82 from Linda Alcoff and Elizabeth Potter (eds.), *Feminist Epistemologies*. New York: Routledge, 1993. Reproduced by permission of Routledge/Taylor & Francis Books, Inc. and the author.

local, historical interests, values, and agendas. However, as Donna Haraway has put the point, it turns out to be possible "to have *simultaneously* an account of radical historical contingency for all knowledge claims and knowing subjects, a critical practice for recognizing our own 'semiotic technologies' for making meanings, and a no-nonsense commitment to faithful accounts of a 'real' world...."[3]

The standpoint epistemologists – and especially the feminists who have most fully articulated this kind of theory of knowledge – have claimed to provide a fundamental map or "logic" for how to do this: "start thought from marginalized lives" and "take everyday life as problematic."[4] However, these maps are easy to misread if one doesn't understand the principles used to construct them. Critics of standpoint writings have tended to refuse the invitation to "have it both ways" by accepting the idea of real knowledge that is socially situated. Instead they have assimilated standpoint claims either to objectivism or some kind of conventional foundationalism or to ethnocentrism, relativism, or phenomenological approaches in philosophy and the social sciences.

Here I shall try to make clear how it really is a misreading to assimilate standpoint epistemologies to those older ones and that such misreadings distort or make invisible the distinctive resources that they offer. I shall do so by contrasting the grounds for knowledge and the kinds of subjects/agents of knowledge recommended by standpoint theories with those favored by the older epistemologies. Then I shall show why it is reasonable to think that the socially situated grounds and subjects of standpoint epistemologies require and generate stronger standards for objectivity than do those that turn away from providing systematic methods for locating knowledge in history. The problem with the conventional conception of objectivity is not that it is too rigorous or too "objectifying," as some have argued, but that it is *not rigorous or objectifying enough*; it is too weak to accomplish even the goals for which it has been designed, let alone the more difficult projects called for by feminisms and other new social movements.[5]

2 Feminist Standpoint versus Spontaneous Feminist Empiricist Epistemologies

Not all feminists who try to explain the past and learn lessons for the future of feminist research in biology and the social sciences are standpoint theorists. The distinctiveness of feminist standpoint approaches can be emphasized by contrasting them with what I shall call "spontaneous feminist empiricist epistemology."[6]

By now, two forms of feminist empiricism have been articulated: the original "spontaneous" feminist empiricism and a recent philosophical version. Originally, feminist empiricism arose as the "spontaneous consciousness" of feminist researchers in biology and the social sciences who were trying to explain what was and what wasn't different about their research process in comparison with the standard procedures in their field.[7] They thought that they were just doing more carefully and rigorously what any good scientist should do; the problem they saw was one of "bad science." Hence they did not give a special name to their philosophy of science; I gave it the name "feminist empiricism" in *The Science Question in Feminism* to contrast feminist standpoint theory with the insistence of empiricism's proponents that sexism and androcentrism could be eliminated from the results of research if scientists would just follow more rigorously and carefully the existing methods and norms of research – which, for practicing scientists, are fundamentally empiricist ones.

Recently, philosophers Helen Longino and Lynn Hankinson Nelson have developed sophisticated and valuable feminist empiricist philosophies of science (Longino calls hers "contextual empiricism") that differ in significant respects from what most prefeminist empiricists and probably most spontaneous feminist empiricists would think of as empiricism.[8] This is no accident, because Longino and Nelson both intend to revise empiricism, as feminists in other fields have fruitfully revised other theoretical approaches – indeed, as feminist standpoint theorists revise the theory from which they begin. Longino and Nelson incorporate into their epistemologies elements that also appear in the standpoint accounts (many would say that they have been most forcefully articulated in such accounts) – such as the inescapable but also sometimes positive influence of social values and interests in the content of science – that would be anathema to even the spontaneous feminist empiricists of the late 1970s and early 1980s as well as to their many successors today. These philosophical feminist empiricisms are constructed in opposition partly to feminist standpoint theories, partly to radical feminist arguments that exalt the feminine and essentialize "woman's experience" (which they have sometimes attributed to standpoint theorists), and partly to the prefeminist empiricists.

It would be an interesting and valuable project to contrast in greater detail these important philosophical feminist empiricisms with both spontaneous feminist empiricism and with feminist standpoint theory. But I have a different goal in this essay: to show how strongly feminist reflections on scientific knowledge challenge the dominant prefeminist epistemology and philosophy of science that are held by all of those people inside and outside science who are still wondering just what are the insights about science and knowledge that feminists have to offer. In my view, this challenge is made most strongly by feminist standpoint epistemology.

One can understand spontaneous feminist empiricism and feminist standpoint theory to be making competing arguments on two topics – scientific method and history – in order to explain in their different ways the causes of sexist and androcentric results of scientific research.[9] As already indicated, spontaneous feminist empiricists think that insufficient care and rigor in following existing methods and norms is the cause of sexist and androcentric results of research, and it is in these terms that they try to produce plausible accounts of the successes of empirically and theoretically more adequate results of research. Standpoint theorists think that this is only part of the problem. They point out that retroactively, and with the help of the insights of the women's movement, one can see these sexist or androcentric practices in the disciplines. However, the methods and norms in the disciplines are too weak to permit researchers *systematically* to identify and eliminate from the results of research those social values, interests, and agendas that are shared by the entire scientific community or virtually all of it. Objectivity has not been "operationalized" in such a way that scientific method can detect sexist and androcentric assumptions that are "the dominant beliefs of an age" – that is, that are collectively (versus only individually) held. As far as scientific method goes (and feminist empiricist defenses of it), it is entirely serendipitous when cultural beliefs that are assumed by most members of a scientific community are challenged by a piece of scientific research. Standpoint theory tries to address this problem by producing stronger standards for "good method," ones that can guide more competent efforts to maximize objectivity.[10]

With respect to history, spontaneous feminist empiricists argue that movements of social liberation such as the women's movement function much like the little boy who is the hero of the folk tale about the Emperor and his clothes. Such movements "make it possible for people to see the world in an enlarged perspective because they remove the covers and blinders that obscure knowledge and observation."[11] Feminist standpoint theorists agree with this assessment, but argue that researchers can do more than just wait around until social movements happen and then wait around some more until their effects happen to reach inside the processes of producing maximally objective, causal accounts of nature and social relations. Knowledge projects can find active ways incorporated into their principles of "good method" to use history as a resource by socially situating knowledge projects in the scientifically and epistemologically most favorable historical locations. History can become the systematic provider of scientific and epistemological resources rather than an obstacle to or the "accidental" benefactor of projects to generate knowledge.[12]

It is spontaneous feminist empiricism's great strength that it explains the production of sexist and nonsexist results of research with only a minimal challenge to the fundamental logic of research as this is understood in scientific fields and to the logic of explanation as this is understood in the dominant philosophies of science. Spontaneous feminist empiricists try to fit feminist projects into prevailing standards of "good science" and "good philosophy." This conservativism makes it possible for many people to grasp the importance of feminist research in biology and the social sciences without feeling disloyal to the methods and norms of their research traditions. Spontaneous feminist empiricism appears to call for even greater rigor in using these methods and following these norms. However, this conservatism is also this philosophy's weakness; this theory of knowledge refuses fully to address the limitations of the dominant conceptions of method and explanation and the ways the conceptions constrain and distort results of research and thought about this research even when these dominant conceptions are most rigorously respected. Nevertheless, its radical nature should not be underestimated. It argues persuasively that the sciences have been blind to their own sexist and androcentric research practices and results. And it thereby clears space for the next question: are the existing logics of research and explanation really so innocent in the commission of this "crime" as empiricism insists, or are they part of its cause?[13]

The intellectual history of feminist standpoint theory is conventionally traced to Hegel's reflections on what can be known about the master/slave relationship from the standpoint of the slave's life versus that of the master's life and to the way Marx, Engels, and Lukacs subsequently developed this insight into the "standpoint of the proletariat" from which have been produced marxist theories of how class society operates.[14] In the 1970s, several feminist thinkers independently began reflecting on how the marxist analysis could be transformed to explain how the structural relationship between women and men had consequences for the production of knowledge.[15] However, it should be noted that even though standpoint arguments are most fully articulated as such in feminist writings, they appear in the scientific projects of all of the new social movements.[16] A *social* history of standpoint theory would focus on what happens when marginalized peoples begin to gain public voice. In societies where scientific rationality and objectivity are claimed to be highly valued by dominant groups, marginalized peoples and those who listen attentively to them will point out that from the perspective of marginal lives, the dominant accounts are less than maximally objective. Knowledge claims are always socially situated, and the failure by dominant groups critically and systematically to interrogate their advantaged social situation and the effect of such advantages on their beliefs leaves their social situation a scientifically and epistemologically disadvantaged one for generating knowledge. Moreover, these accounts end up legitimating exploitative "practical politics" even when those who produce them have good intentions.

The starting point of standpoint theory – and its claim that is most often misread – is that in societies stratified by race, ethnicity, class, gender, sexuality, or some other such politics shaping the very structure of a society, the *activities* of those at the top both organize and set limits on what persons who perform such activities can understand about themselves and the world around them. "There are some perspectives on society from which, however well-intentioned one may be, the real relations of humans with each other and with the natural world are not visible."[17] In contrast, the activities of those at the bottom of such social hierarchies can provide starting points for thought – for *everyone's* research and scholarship – from which humans' relations with each other and the natural world can become visible. This is because the experience and lives of marginalized peoples, as they understand them, provide particularly significant *problems to be explained* or research agendas. These experiences and lives have been devalued or ignored as a source of objectivity-maximizing questions – the answers to which are not necessarily to be found in those experiences or lives but elsewhere in the beliefs and activities of people at the center who make policies and engage in social practices that shape marginal lives.[18] So one's social situation enables and sets limits on what one can know; some social situations – critically unexamined dominant ones – are more limiting than others in this respect, and what makes these situations more limiting is their inability to generate the most critical questions about received belief.[19]

It is this sense in which Dorothy Smith argues that women's experience is the "grounds" of feminist knowledge and that such knowledge should change the discipline of sociology.[20] Women's lives (our many different lives and different experiences!) can provide the starting point for asking new, critical questions about not only those women's lives but also about men's lives and, most importantly, the causal relations between them.[21] For example, she points out that if we start thinking from women's lives, we (anyone) can see that women are assigned the work that men do not want to do for themselves, especially the care of everyone's bodies – the bodies of men, babies, children, old people, the sick, and their own bodies. And they are assigned responsibility for the local places where those bodies exist as they clean and care for their own and others' houses and work places.[22] This kind of "women's work" frees men in the ruling groups to immerse themselves in the world of abstract concepts. The more successful women are at this concrete work, the more invisible it becomes to men as distinctively social labor. Caring for bodies and the places bodies exist disappears into "nature," as, for example, in sociobiological claims about the naturalness of "altruistic" behavior for females and its unnaturalness for males or in the systematic reticence of many prefeminist marxists actually to analyze who does what in everyday sexual, emotional, and domestic work, and to integrate such analyses into their accounts of "working class labor." Smith argues that we should not be surprised that men have trouble seeing women's activities as part of distinctively human culture and history once we notice how invisible the social character of this work is from the perspective of their activities. She points out that if we start from women's lives, we can generate questions about why it is that it is primarily women who are assigned such activities and what the consequences are for the economy, the state, the family, the educational system, and other social institutions of assigning body and emotional work to one group and "head" work to another.[23] These questions lead to less partial and distorted understandings of women's worlds, men's worlds, and the causal relations between them than do the questions originating only in that part of human activity that men in the dominant groups reserve for themselves – the abstract mental work of managing and administrating.

Standpoint epistemology sets the relationship between knowledge and politics at the center of its account in the sense that it tries to provide causal accounts – to explain – the effects that different kinds of politics have on the production of knowledge. Of course, empiricism also is concerned with the effects politics has on the production of knowledge, but prefeminist empiricism conceptualizes politics as entirely bad. Empiricism tries to purify science of all such bad politics by adherence to what it takes to be rigorous methods for the testing of hypotheses. From the perspective of standpoint epistemology, this is *far too weak a strategy* to maximize the objectivity of the results of research that empiricists desire. Thought that begins from the lives of the oppressed has no chance to get its critical questions voiced or heard within such an empiricist conception of the way to produce knowledge. Prefeminist empiricists can only perceive such questions as the intrusion of politics into science, which therefore deteriorates the objectivity of the results of research. Spontaneous feminist empiricism, for all its considerable virtues, nevertheless contains distorting traces of these assumptions, and they block the ability of this theory of science to develop maximally strong criteria for systematic ways to maximize objectivity.

Thus the standpoint claims that all knowledge attempts are socially situated and that some of these objective social locations are better than others as starting points for knowledge projects challenge some of the most fundamental assumptions of the scientific world view and the Western thought that takes science as its model of how to produce knowledge. It sets out a rigorous "logic of discovery" intended to maximize the objectivity of the results of research and thereby to produce knowledge that can be *for* marginalized people (and those who would know what the marginalized can know) rather than *for* the use only of dominant groups in their projects of administering and managing the lives of marginalized people.

3 What are the Grounds for Knowledge Claims?

Standpoint theories argue for "starting off thought" from the lives of marginalized peoples; beginning in those determinate, objective locations in any social order will generate illuminating critical questions that do not arise in thought that begins from dominant group lives. Starting off research from women's lives will generate less partial and distorted accounts not only of women's lives but also of men's lives and of the whole social order. Women's lives and experiences provide the "grounds" for this knowledge, though these clearly do not provide foundations for knowledge in the conventional philosophical sense. These grounds are the site, the activities, from which scientific questions arise. The epistemologically advantaged starting points for research do not guarantee that the researcher can maximize objectivity in her account; these grounds provide only a necessary – not a sufficient – starting point for maximizing objectivity. It is useful to contrast standpoint grounds for knowledge with four other kinds: the "God-trick," ethnocentrism, relativism, and the unique abilities of the oppressed to produce knowledge.

Standpoint theories versus the "God-trick"

First, for standpoint theories, the grounds for knowledge are fully saturated with history and social life rather than abstracted from it. Standpoint knowledge projects do not claim to originate in purportedly universal human problematics; they do not claim to perform the "God-trick."[24] However, the fact that feminist knowledge claims are socially situated does not in practice distinguish them from any other knowledge claims that have ever been made inside or outside the history of Western thought and the disciplines today; all bear the fingerprints of the communities that produce them. All thought by humans starts off from socially determinate lives. As Dorothy Smith puts the point, "women's perspective, as I have analyzed it here, discredits sociology's claim to constitute an objective knowledge independent of the sociologists's situation. Its conceptual procedures, methods, and relevances are seen to organize its subject matter from a determinate position in society."[25]

It is a delusion – and a historically identifiable one – to think that human thought could completely erase the fingerprints that reveal its production process. Conventional conceptions of scientific method enable scientists to be relatively good at eliminating those social interests and values from the results of research that differ *within* the scientific community, because whenever experiments are repeated by different observers, differences in the social values of individual observers (or groups of them from different research teams) that have shaped the results of their research will stand out from the sameness of the phenomena that other researchers (or teams of them) report.[26] But scientific method provides no rules, procedures, or techniques for even identifying, let alone eliminating, social concerns and interests that are shared by all (or virtually all) of the observers, nor does it encourage seeking out observers whose social beliefs vary in order to increase the effectiveness of scientific method. Thus culturewide assumptions *that have not been criticized within the scientific research process* are transported into the results of research, making visible the historicity of specific scientific claims to people at other times, other places, or in other groups in the very same social order. We could say that standpoint theories not only acknowledge the social situatedness that is the inescapable lot of all knowledge-seeking projects but also, more importantly, transform it into a systematically available scientific resource.

Standpoint theories versus ethnocentrism

Universalists have traditionally been able to imagine only ethnocentrism and relativism as possible alternatives to "the view from nowhere" that they assert grounds universal claims, so they think standpoint epistemologies must be supporting (or doomed to) one or the other of these positions. Is there any reasonable sense in which the ground for knowledge claimed by feminist standpoint theory is ethnocentric?

Ethnocentrism is the belief in the inherent superiority of one's own ethnic group or culture.[27] Do feminist standpoint theorists argue that the lives of *their own group or culture is superior* as a grounds for knowledge?[28] At first glance, one might think that this is the case if one notices that it is primarily women who have argued for starting thought from women's lives. However, there are several reasons why it would be a mistake to conclude from this fact that feminist standpoint theory is ethnocentric.

First, standpoint theorists themselves all explicitly argue that marginal lives that are not their own provide better grounds for certain kinds of knowledge. Thus the claim by women that women's lives provide a better starting point for thought about gender systems is not the same as the claim that *their own* lives are the best such starting points. They are not denying that their own lives can provide important resources for such projects, but they are arguing that other, different (and sometimes oppositional) women's lives also provide such resources. For example, women who are not prostitutes and have not been raped have argued that starting thought from women's experiences and activities in such events reveals that the state is male because it looks at women's lives here just as men (but not women) do. Dorothy Smith writes of the value of starting to think about a certain social situation she describes from the perspective of Native Canadian lives.[29] Bettina Aptheker has argued that starting thought from the everyday lives of women who are holocaust survivors, Chicana cannery workers, older lesbians, African-American women in slavery, Japanese-American concentration camp survivors, and others who have had lives different from hers increases our ability to understand a great deal about the distorted way the dominant groups conceptualize politics, resistance, community, and other key history and social science notions.[30] Patricia Hill Collins, an African-American sociologist, has argued that starting thought from the lives of poor and in some cases illiterate African-American women reveals important truths about the lives of intellectuals, both African-American and European-American, as well as about those women.[31] Many theorists who are not mothers (as well as many who are) have argued that starting thought in mother-work generates important questions about the social order. Of course some women no doubt do argue that their own lives provide the one and only best starting point for all knowledge projects, but this is not what standpoint theory holds. Thus, although it is not an accident that so many women have argued for feminist standpoint approaches, neither is it evidence that standpoint claims are committed to ethnocentrism.

Second, and relatedly, thinkers with "center" identities have also argued that marginalized lives are better places from which to start asking causal and critical questions about the social order. After all, Hegel was not a slave, though he argued that the master/slave relationship could better be understood from the perspective of slaves' activities. Marx, Engels, and Lukacs were not engaged in the kind of labor that they argued provided the starting point for developing their theories about class society. There are men who have argued for the scientific and epistemic advantages of starting thought from women's lives, European-Americans who understand that much can be learned about their lives as well as African-American lives if they start their thought from the latter, and so on.[32]

Third, women's lives are shaped by the rules of femininity or womanliness; in this sense they "express feminine culture." Perhaps the critic of standpoint theories thinks feminists are defending femininity and thus "their own culture." But all feminist analyses, including feminist standpoint writings, are in principle ambivalent about the value of femininity and womanliness. Feminists criticize femininity on the grounds that it is fundamentally defined by and therefore part of the conceptual project of exalting masculinity; it is the "other" against which men define themselves as admirably and uniquely human. Feminist thought does not try to substitute loyalty to femininity for the loyalty to masculinity it criticizes in conventional thought. Instead, it criticizes all gender loyalties as capable of producing only partial and distorted results of research. However, it must do this while also arguing that women's lives have been inappropriately devalued. Feminist thought is forced to "speak as" and on behalf of the very notion it criticizes and tries to dismantle – women. In the contradictory nature of this project lies both its greatest challenge and a source of its great creativity. It because the conditions of women's lives are worse than their brothers' in so many cases that women's lives provide better places from which to start asking questions about a social order that tolerates and in so many respects even values highly the bad conditions for women's lives (women's double-day of work, the epidemic of violence against women, women's cultural obligation to be "beautiful," and so on).[33] Thus research processes that problematize how gender practices shape behavior and belief – that interrogate and criticize both masculinity and femininity – stand a better chance of avoiding such biasing gender loyalties.

Fourth, there are many feminisms, and these can be understood to be starting off their analyses from the lives of different historical groups of women. Liberal feminism initially started off its analyses from the lives of women in the eighteenth- and nineteenth-century European and US educated classes; Marxist feminism, from the lives of wage-working women in the nineteenth- and early twentieth-century "industrializing" or "modernizing" societies; Third World feminism, from the lives of late twentieth-century women of Third World descent – and these different Third World lives produce different feminisms. Standpoint theory argues that each of these groups of women's lives is a good place to start in order to explain certain aspects of the social order. There is no single, ideal woman's life from which standpoint theories recommend that thought start. Instead, one must turn to all of the lives that are marginalized in different ways by the operative systems of social stratification. The different feminisms inform each other; we can learn from all of them and change our patterns of belief.

Last, one can note that from the perspective of marginalized lives, it is the dominant claims that we should in fact regard as ethnocentric. It is relatively easy to see that overtly racist, sexist, classist, and heterosexist claims have the effect of insisting that the dominant culture is superior. But it is also the case that claims to have produced universally valid beliefs – principles of ethics, of human nature, epistemologies, and philosophies of science – are ethnocentric. Only members of the powerful groups in societies stratified by race, ethnicity, class, gender, and sexuality could imagine that their standards for knowledge and the claims resulting from adherence to such standards should be found preferable by all rational creatures, past, present, and future. This is what the work of Smith, Hartsock, and the others discussed earlier shows. Moreover, standpoint theory itself is a historical emergent. There are good reasons why it has not emerged at other times in history; no doubt it will be replaced by more useful epistemologies in the future – the fate of all human products.[34]

Standpoint theory versus relativism, perspectivalism, and pluralism

If there is no single, transcendental standard for deciding between competing knowledge claims, then it is said that there can be only local historical ones, each valid in its own lights but having no claims against others. The literature on cognitive relativism is by now huge, and here is not the place to review it.[35] However, standpoint theory does not advocate – nor is it doomed to – relativism. It argues against the idea that all social situations provide equally useful resources for learning about the world and against the idea that they all set equally strong limits on knowledge. Contrary to what universalists think, standpoint theory is not committed to such a claim as a consequence of rejecting universalism. Standpoint theory provides arguments for the claim that some social situations are scientifically better than others as places from which to start off knowledge projects, and those arguments must be defeated if the charge of relativism is to gain plausibility.[36]

Judgmental (or epistemological) relativism is anathema to any scientific project, and feminist ones are no exception.[37] It is not equally true as its denial that women's uteruses wander around in their bodies when they take math courses, that only Man the Hunter made important contributions to distinctively human history, that women are biologically programmed to succeed at mothering and fail at equal participation in governing society, that women's preferred modes of moral reasoning are inferior to men's, that targets of rape and battering must bear the responsibility for what happens to them, that the sexual molestation and other physical abuses children report are only their fantasies, and so on – as various sexist and androcentric scientific theories have claimed. Feminist and prefeminist claims are usually not complementary but conflicting, just as the claim that the earth is flat conflicts with the claim that it is round. *Sociological* relativism permits us to acknowledge that different people hold different beliefs, but what is at issue in rethinking objectivity is the different matter of *judgmental* or epistemological relativism. Standpoint theories neither hold nor are doomed to it.

Both moral and cognitive forms of judgmental relativism have determinate histories; they appear as intellectual problems at certain times in history in only some cultures and only for certain groups of people. Relativism is not fundamentally a problem that emerges from feminist or any other thought that starts in marginalized lives; it is one that emerges from the thought of the dominant groups. Judgmental relativism is sometimes the most that dominant groups can stand to grant to their critics – "OK, your claims are valid for you, but mine are valid for me."[38] Recognizing the importance of thinking about who such a problem belongs to – identifying its social location – is one of the advantages of standpoint theory.

Standpoint theory versus the unique abilities of the oppressed to produce knowledge

This is another way of formulating the charge that standpoint theories, in contrast to conventional theories of knowledge, are ethnocentric. However, in this form the position has tempted many feminists, as it has members of other liberatory knowledge projects.[39] We can think of this claim as supporting "identity science" projects – the knowledge projects that support and are supported by "identity politics." In the words of the Combahee River Collective's critique of liberal and marxist thought (feminist as well as prefeminist) that failed to socially situate anti-oppression claims: "Focusing upon our own oppression is embodied in the concept of identity politics. We believe that the most profound and potentially the most radical politics come directly out of our own identity, as opposed to working to end somebody else's oppression."[40] (They were tired of hearing about how they should be concerned to improve others' lives and how others were going to improve theirs.)

To pursue the issue further, we will turn to examine just who is the "subject of knowledge" for standpoint theories. But we can prepare for that discussion by recollecting yet again that Hegel was not a slave, though he grasped the critical understanding of the relations between master and slave that became available only if he started off his thought from the slave's activities, and that Marx, Engels and Lukacs were not proletarians. Two questions are raised by these examples: What is the role for marginalized experience in the standpoint projects of members of dominant groups? And what are the special resources, but also limits, that the lives of people in dominant groups provide in generating the more objective knowledge claims standpoint theories call for? We shall begin to address these issues in the next section.

To conclude this one, marginalized lives provide the scientific problems and the research agendas – not the solutions – for standpoint theories. Starting off thought from these lives provides fresh and more critical questions about how the social order works than does starting off thought from the unexamined lives of members of dominant groups. Most natural and social scientists (and philosophers!) are themselves members of these dominant groups, whether by birth or through upward mobility into scientific and professional/managerial careers. Those who are paid to teach and contact research receive a disproportionate; share of the benefits of that very nature and social order that they are trying to explain. Thinking from marginal lives leads one to question the adequacy of the conceptual frameworks that the natural and social sciences have designed to explain (for themselves) themselves and the world around them. This is the sense in which marginal lives ground knowledge for standpoint approaches.

4 New Subjects of Knowledge

For empiricist epistemology, the subject or agent of knowledge – that which "knows" the "best beliefs" of the day – is supposed to have a number of distinctive characteristics. First, this subject of knowledge is culturally and historically disembodied or invisible because knowledge is by definition universal. "Science says . . . ," we are told. Whose science, we can ask? The drug and cigarette companies? The Surgeon General's? The National Institute of Health's? The science of the critics of the NIH's racism and sexism? Empiricism insists that scientific knowledge has no particular historical subject. Second, in this respect, the subject of scientific knowledge is different in kind from the objects whose properties scientific knowledge describes and explains, because the latter are determinate in space and time. Third, though the subject of knowledge for empiricists is transhistorical, knowledge is initially produced ("discovered") by individuals and groups of individuals (reflected in the practice of scientific awards and honors), not by culturally specific societies or subgroups in a society such as a certain class or gender or race. Fourth, the subject is homogeneous and unitary, because knowledge must be consistent and coherent. If the subject of knowledge were permitted to be multiple and heterogeneous, then the knowledge produced by such subjects would be multiple and contradictory and thus inconsistent and incoherent.

The subjects of knowledge for standpoint theories contrast in all four respects. First, they are embodied and visible, because the lives from which thought has started are always present and visible in the results of that thought. This is true even though the way scientific method is operationalized usually succeeds in removing all personal or individual fingerprints from the results of research. But personal fingerprints are not the problem standpoint theory is intended to address. The thought of an age is *of an age*, and the delusion that one's thought can escape historical locatedness is just one of the thoughts that is typical of dominant groups in these and other ages. The "scientific world view" is, in fact, a view of (dominant groups in) modern, Western societies, as the histories of science proudly point out. Standpoint theories simply disagree with the further ahistorical and incoherent claim that the content of "modern and Western" scientific thought is also, paradoxically, not shaped by its historical location.

Second, the fact that subjects of knowledge are embodied and socially located has the consequence that they are not fundamentally different from objects of knowledge. We should assume causal symmetry in the sense that the same kinds of social forces that shape objects of knowledge also shape (but do not determine) knowers and their scientific projects.

This may appear to be true only for the objects of social science knowledge, not for the objects that the natural sciences study. After all, trees, rocks, planetary orbits, and electrons do not constitute themselves as historical actors. What they are does not depend on what they think they are; they do not think or carry on any of the other activities that distinguish human communities from there constituents of the world around us. However, this distinction turns out to be irrelevant to the point here because, in fact, scientists never can study the trees, rocks, planetary orbits, or electrons that are "out there" and untouched by human concerns. Instead, they are destined to study something different (but hopefully systematically related to what is "out there"): *nature as an object of knowledge.* Trees, rocks, planetary orbits, and electrons always appear to natural scientists only as they are already socially constituted in some of the ways that humans and their social groups are already socially constituted for the social scientist. Such objects are already effectively "removed from pure nature" into social life – they are social objects – by, first of all, the contemporary general cultural meanings that these objects have for everyone, including the entire scientific community.[41] They also become socially constituted objects of knowledge through the shapes and meanings these objects gain for scientists because of earlier generations of scientific discussion about them. Scientists never observe nature apart from such traditions; even when they criticize some aspects of them they must assume others in order to carry on the criticism. They could not do science if they did not both borrow from and also criticize these traditions. Their assumptions about what they see are always shaped by "conversations" they carry on with scientists of the past. Finally, their own interactions with such objects also culturally constitute them; to treat a piece of nature with respect, violence, degradation, curiosity, or indifference is to participate in culturally constituting such an object of knowledge. In these respects, nature as an object of knowledge simulates social life, and the processes of science themselves are a significant contributor to this phenomenon. Thus the subject and object of knowledge for the natural sciences are also not significantly different in kind. Whatever kinds of social forces shape the subjects are also thereby shaping their objects of knowledge.

Third, consequently, communities and not primarily individuals produce knowledge. For one thing, what I believe that I thought through all by myself (in my mind), which I know, only gets transformed from my personal belief to knowledge when it is socially legitimated. Just as importantly, my society ends up assuming all the claims I make that neither I nor my society critically interrogate. It assumes the eurocentric, androcentric, heterosexist, and bourgeois beliefs that I do not critically examine as part of my scientific research and that, consequently, shape my thought and appear as part of my knowledge claims. These are some of the kinds of features that subsequent ages (and Others today) will say make my thought characteristic of my age, or society, community, race, class, gender, or sexuality. The best scientific thought of today is no different in this respect from the thought of Galileo or Darwin; in all can be found not only brilliant thoughts first expressed by individuals and then legitimated by communities but also assumptions we now regard as false that were distinctive to a particular historical era and not identified as part of the "evidence" that scientists actually used to select the results of research.[42]

Fourth, the subjects/agents of knowledge for feminist standpoint theory are multiple, heterogeneous, and contradictory or incoherent, not unitary, homogeneous, and coherent as they are for empiricist epistemology.[43] Feminist knowledge has started off from women's lives, but it has started off from many different women's lives; there is no typical or essential woman's life from which feminisms start their thought. Moreover, these different women's lives are in important respects opposed to each other. Feminist knowledge has arisen from European and African women, from economically privileged and poor women, from lesbians and heterosexuals, from Protestant, Jewish, and Islamic women. Racism and imperialism, local and international structures of capitalist economies, institutionalized homophobia and compulsory heterosexuality, and the political conflicts between ethnic and religious cultures produce multiple, heterogeneous, and contradictory feminist accounts. Nevertheless, thought that starts off from each of these different kinds of lives can generate less partial and distorted accounts of nature and social life.

However, the subject/agent of feminist knowledge is multiple, heterogeneous, and frequently contradictory in a second way that mirrors the situation for women as a class. It is the thinker whose consciousness is bifurcated, the outsider within, the marginal person now located at the center,[44] the person who is committed to two agendas that are by their nature at least partially in conflict – the liberal feminist, socialist feminist, Sandinista feminist, Islamic feminist, or feminist scientist – who has generated feminist sciences and new knowledge. It is starting off thought from a contradictory social position that generates feminist knowledge. So the logic of the directive to "start thought from women's lives" requires that one start one's thought from multiple lives that are in many ways in conflict with each other, each of which itself has multiple and contradictory commitments. This may appear an overwhelming requirement – or even an impossible one – because Western thought has required the fiction that we have and thus think from unitary and coherent lives. But the challenge of learning to think from the perspective of more than one life when those lives are in conflict with each other is familiar to anthropologists, historians, conflict negotiators, domestic workers, wives, mothers – indeed, to most of us in many everyday contexts.

Both empiricist philosophy and marxism could maintain the fiction that unitary and coherent subjects of knowledge were to be preferred only by defining one socially distinctive group of people as the ideal knowers and arguing that all others lacked the characteristics that made this group ideal. Thus, the liberal philosophy associated with empiricism insisted that it was the possession of reason that enabled humans to know the world the way it is and then defined as not fully rational women, Africans, the working class, the Irish, Jews, other peoples from Mediterranean cultures, and so on. It was said that no individuals in these groups were capable of the dispassionate, disinterested exercise of individual moral and cognitive reason that was the necessary condition for becoming the ideal subject of knowledge. Similarly, traditional marxism argued that only the industrial proletariat possessed the characteristics for the ideal subject of Marxist political economy. Peasants', slaves' and women's work, as well as bourgeois activities, made these people's lives inferior starting points for generating knowledge of the political economy.[45] In contrast, the logic of standpoint theory leads to the refusal to essentialize its subjects of knowledge.

This logic of multiple subjects leads to the recognition that the subject of liberatory feminist knowledge must also be, in an important if controversial sense, the subject of every other liberatory knowledge project. This is true in the collective sense of "subject of knowledge," because lesbian, poor, and racially marginalized women are all women, and therefore all feminists will have to grasp how gender, race, class, and sexuality are used to construct each other. It will have to do so if feminism is to be liberatory for marginalized women, but also if it is to avoid deluding dominant group women about their/our own situations. If this were not so, there would be no way to distinguish between feminism and the narrow self-interest of dominant group women – just as conventional androcentric thought permits no criterion for distinguishing between "best beliefs" and those that serve the self-interest of men as men. (Bourgeois thought permits no criterion for identifying specifically bourgeois self-interest; racist thought, for identifying racist self-interest; and so on.)

But the subject of every other liberatory movement must also learn how gender, race, class, and sexuality are used to construct each other in order to accomplish their goals. That is, analyses of class relations must look at their agendas from the perspective of women's lives, too. Women, too, hold class positions, and they are not identical to their brothers'. Moreover, as many critics have pointed out, agendas of the left need to deal with the fact that bosses regularly and all too successfully attempt to divide the working class against itself by manipulating gender hostilities. If women are forced to tolerate lower wages and double-days of work, employers can fire men and hire women to make more profit. Antiracist movements must look at their issues from the perspective of the lives of women of color, and so forth. Everything that feminist thought must know must also inform the thought of every other liberatory movement, and vice versa. It is not just the women in those other movements who must know the world from the perspective of women's lives. Everyone must do so if the movements are to succeed at their own goals. Most importantly, this requires that women be active directors of the agendas of these movements. But it also requires that men in those movements be able to generate original feminist knowledge from the perspective of women's lives as, for example, John Stuart Mill, Marx and Engels, Frederick Douglass, and later male feminists have done.[46]

However, if every other liberatory movement must generate feminist knowledge, it cannot be that women are the unique generators of feminist knowledge. Women can not claim this ability to be uniquely theirs, and men must not be permitted to claim that because they are not women, they are not obligated to produce fully feminist analyses. Men, too, must contribute distinctive forms of specifically feminist knowledge from their particular social situation. Men's thought, too, will begin first from women's lives in all the ways that feminist theory, with its rich and contradictory tendencies, has helped us all – women as well as men – to understand how to do. It will start there in order to gain the maximally objective theoretical frameworks within which men can begin to describe and explain their own and women's lives in less partial and distorted ways. This is necessary if men are to produce more than the male supremacist "folk belief" about themselves and the world they live in to which female feminists object. Women have had to learn how to substitute the generation of feminist thought for the "gender nativism" androcentric cultures encourage in them, too. Female feminists are made, not born. Men, too must learn to take historic responsibility for the social position from which they speak.

Patricia Hill Collins has stressed the importance to the development of Black feminist thought of genuine dialogue across differences, and of the importance of making coalitions with other groups if that dialogue is to happen.

> While Black feminist thought may originate with Black feminist intellectuals, it cannot flourish isolated from the experiences and ideas of other groups. The dilemma is that Black women intellectuals must place our own experiences and consciousness at the center of any serious efforts to develop Black feminist thought yet not have that thought become separatist and exclusionary. . . .
>
> By advocating, refining, and disseminating Black feminist thought, other groups – such as Black men, white women, white men, and other people of color – further its development. Black women can produce an attenuated version of Black feminist thought separated from other groups. Other groups cannot produce Black feminist thought without African-American women. Such groups can, however, develop self-defined knowledge reflecting their own standpoints. But the full actualization of Black feminist thought requires a collaborative enterprise with Black women at the center of a community based on coalitions among autonomous groups.[47]

It seems to me that Collins has provided a powerful analysis of the social relations necessary for the development of less partial and distorted belief by any knowledge community.

Far from licensing European-Americans to appropriate African-American thought or men to appropriate women's thought, this approach challenges members of dominant groups to make themselves "fit" to engage in collaborative, democratic, community enterprises with marginal peoples. Such a project requires learning to listen attentively to marginalized people; it requires educating oneself about their histories, achievements, preferred social relations, and hopes for the future; it requires putting one's body on the line for "their" causes until they feel like "our" causes; it requires critical examination of the dominant institutional beliefs and practices that systematically disadvantage them; it requires critical self-examination to discover how one unwittingly participates in generating disadvantage to them . . . and more. Fortunately, there are plenty of models available to us not only today but also through an examination of the history of members of dominant groups who learned to think from the lives of marginalized people and to act on what they learned. We can choose which historical lineage to claim as our own.

To conclude this section, we could say that since standpoint analyses explain how and why the subject of knowledge always appears in scientific accounts of nature and social life as part of the object of knowledge of those accounts, standpoint approaches have had to learn to use the social situatedness of subjects of knowledge systematically as a resource for maximizing objectivity. They have made the move from declaiming as a problem or acknowledging as an inevitable fact to theorizing as a *systematically accessible* resource for maximizing objectivity the inescapable social situatedness of knowledge claims.

5 Standards for Maximizing Objectivity

We are now in a position to draw out of this discussion of the innovative grounds and subject of knowledge for feminist standpoint theories the stronger standards for maximizing objectivity that such theories both require and generate. Strong objectivity requires that the subject of knowledge be placed on the same critical, causal plane as the objects of knowledge. Thus, strong objectivity requires what we can think of as "strong reflexivity." This is because culturewide (or nearly culturewide) beliefs function as evidence at every stage in scientific inquiry: in the selection of problems, the formation of hypotheses, the design of research (including the organization of research communities), the collection of data, the interpretation and sorting of data, decisions about when to stop research, the way results of research are reported, and so on. The subject of knowledge – the individual and the historically located social community whose unexamined beliefs its members are likely to hold "unknowingly," so to speak – must be considered as part of the object of knowledge from the perspective of scientific method. All of the kinds of objectivity-maximizing procedures focused on the nature and/or social relations that are the direct object of observation and reflection must also be focused on the observers and reflectors – scientists and the larger society whose assumptions they share. But a maximally critical study of scientists and their communities can be done only from the perspective of those whose lives have been marginalized by such communities. Thus, strong objectivity requires that scientists and their communities be integrated into democracy-advancing projects for scientific and epistemological reasons as well as moral and political ones.

From the perspective of such standpoint arguments, empiricism's standards appear weak; empiricism advances only the "objectivism" that has been so widely criticized from many quarters.[48] Objectivism impoverishes its attempts at maximizing objectivity when it turns away from the task of critically identifying all of those broad, historical social desires, interests, and values that have shaped the agendas, contents, and results of the sciences much as they shape the rest of human affairs.

Consider, first, how objectivism too narrowly operationalizes the notion of maximizing objectivity.[49] The conception of value-free, impartial, dispassionate research is supposed to direct the identification of all social values and their elimination from the results of research, yet it has been operationalized to identify and eliminate only those social values and interests that differ among the researchers and critics who are regarded by the scientific community as competent to make such judgments. If the community of "qualified" researchers and critics systematically excludes, for example, all African-Americans and women of all races and if the larger culture is stratified by race and gender and lacks powerful critiques of this stratification, it is not plausible to imagine that racist and sexist interests and values would be identified within a community of scientists composed entirely of people who benefit – intentionally or not – from institutionalized racism and sexism. This kind of blindness is advanced by the conventional belief that the truly scientific part of knowledge seeking – the part controlled by methods of research – occurs only in the context of justification. The context of discovery, in which problems are identified as appropriate for scientific investigation, hypotheses are formulated, key concepts are defined – this part of the scientific process is thought to be unexaminable within science by rational methods. Thus "real science" is restricted to those processes controllable by methodological rules. The methods of science – or rather, of the special sciences – are restricted to procedures for the testing of already formulated hypotheses. Untouched by these methods are those values and interests entrenched in the very statement of what problem is to be researched and in the concepts favored in the hypotheses that are to be tested. Recent histories of science are full of cases in which broad social assumptions stood little chance of identification or elimination through the very best research procedures of the day.[50] Thus objectivism operationalizes the notion of objectivity in much too narrow away to permit the achievement of the value-free research that is supposed to be its outcome.

But objectivism also conceptualizes the desired value-neutrality of objectivity too broadly. Objectivists claim that objectivity requires the elimination of *all* social values and interests from the research process and the results of research. It is clear, however, that not all social values and interests have the same bad effects upon the results of research. Democracy-advancing values have systematically generated less partial and distorted beliefs than others.[51]

Objectivism's rather weak standards for maximizing objectivity make objectivity a mystifying notion, and its mystificatory character is largely responsible for its usefulness and its widespread appeal to dominant groups. It offers hope that scientists and science institutions, themselves admittedly historically located, can produce claims that will be regarded as objectively valid without having to examine critically their own historical commitments from which – intentionally or not – they actively construct their scientific research. It permits scientists and science institutions to be unconcerned with the origins or consequences of their problematics and practices or with the social values and interests that these problematics and practices support. It offers the false hope of enacting what Francis Bacon erroneously promised for the method of modern science: "The course I propose for the discovery of sciences is such as leaves but little to the acuteness and strength of wits, but places all wits and understandings nearly on a level." His "way of discovering science goes far to level men's wits, and leaves but little to individual excellence, because it performs everything by surest rules and demonstrations."[52] In contrast, standpoint approaches requires the strong objectivity that can take the subject as well as the object of knowledge to be a necessary object of critical, causal – scientific! – social explanations. This program of strong reflexivity is a resource for objectivity, in contrast to the obstacle that de facto reflexivity has posed to weak objectivity.

Some feminists and thinkers from other liberatory knowledge projects have thought that the very notion of objectivity should be abandoned. They say that it is hopelessly tainted by its use in racist, imperialist, bourgeois, homophobic, and androcentric scientific projects. Moreover, it is tied to a theory of representation and concept of the self or subject that insists on a rigid barrier between subject and object of knowledge – between self and Other – which feminism and other new social movements label as distinctively androcentric or eurocentric. Finally, the conventional notion of objectivity institutionalizes a certain kind of lawlessness at the heart of science, we could say, by refusing to theorize any criteria internal to scientific goals for distinguishing between scientific method, on the one hand, and such morally repugnant acts as torture or ecological destruction, on the other. Scientists and scientific institutions disapprove of, engage in political activism against, and set up special committees to screen scientific projects for such bad consequences, but these remain ad hoc measures, extrinsic to the conventional "logic" of scientific research.

However, there is not just one legitimate way to conceptualize objectivity, any more than there is only one way to conceptualize freedom, democracy, or science. The notion of objectivity has valuable political and intellectual histories; as it is transformed into "strong objectivity" by the logic of standpoint epistemologies, it retains central features of the older conception. In particular, might should not make right in the realm of knowledge production any more than in matters of ethics. Understanding ourselves and the world around us requires understanding what others think of us and our beliefs and actions, not just what we think of ourselves and them.[53] Finally, the appeal to objectivity is an issue not only between feminist and prefeminist science and knowledge projects but also within each feminist and other emancipatory research agenda. There are many feminisms, some of which result in claims that distort the racial, class, sexuality, and gender relationships in society. Which ones generate less or more partial and distorted accounts of nature and social life? The notion of objectivity is useful in providing a way to think about the gap that should exist between how any individual or group wants the world to be and how in fact it is.[54]

6 An Objection Considered

"Why not just keep the old notion of objectivity as requiring value-neutrality and argue instead that the problem feminism raises is how to get it, not that the concept itself should be changed? Why not argue that it is the notion of scientific method that should be transformed, not objectivity?"

This alternative position is attractive for several reasons. For one thing, clearly feminist standpoint theorists no less than other feminists want to root out sexist and androcentric bias from the results of research. They want results of research that are not "loyal to gender" – feminine or masculine. In this sense, don't they want to maximize value-neutrality – that is, old-fashioned objectivity – in the results of research?

Moreover, in important respects an epistemology and a method for doing research in the broadest sense of the term have the same consequences or, at least, are deeply implicated in each other. What would be the point of a theory of knowledge that did not make prescriptions for how to go about getting knowledge or of a prescription for getting knowledge that did not arise from a theory about how knowledge can be and has been produced? So why not appropriate and transform what the sciences think of as scientific method, but leave the notion of objectivity intact? Why not argue that the standpoint theories have finally completed the quest for a "logic of discovery" begun and then abandoned by philosophers some decades ago? They are calling for an "operationalization" of scientific method that includes the context of discovery and the social practices of justification in the appropriate domain of its rules and recommended procedures.[55] Scientific method must be understood to begin back in the context of discovery, in which scientific "problems" are identified and bold hypotheses conjectured. Then "starting from marginalized lives" becomes part of the method of maximizing value-neutral objectivity. This possibility could gain support from the fact that some standpoint theorists consistently talk about their work interchangeably as an epistemology and a method for doing research.[56]

Attractive as this alternative is, I think it is not attractive enough to convince that only method and not also the concept of objectivity should be reconceptualized. For one thing, this strategy makes it look reasonable to think it possible to gain value-neutrality in the results of research. It implies that human ideas can somehow escape their location in human history. But this no longer appears plausible in the new social studies of science.

Second, and relatedly, this strategy leads away from the project of analyzing how our beliefs regarded as true as well as those regarded as false have social causes and thus, once again, to the assumption of a crucial difference between subjects and objects of knowledge. It would leave those results of research that are judged by the scientific community to be maximally objective to appear to have no social causes, to be the result only of nature's impressions on our finally well-polished, glassy-mirror minds. Objects of knowledge then become, once again, dissimilar for the subjects of knowledge. Subjects of real knowledge, unlike subjects of mere opinion, are disembodied and socially invisible, whereas their natural and social objects of knowledge are firmly located in social history. Thus the "strong method" approach detached from "strong objectivity" leaves the opposition between subjects and objects firmly in place – an opposition that both distorts reality and has a long history of use in exploiting marginalized peoples. The "strong objectivity" approach locates this very assumed difference between subject and object of knowledge in social history; it calls for a scientific account of this assumption, too.

Third, this strategy leaves reflexivity merely a perpetual problem rather than also the resource into which standpoint theorists have transformed it. Observers do change the world that they observe, but refusing to strengthen the notion of objectivity leaves reflexivity always threatening objectivity rather than also as a resource for maximizing it.

Finally, it is at least paradoxical and most certainly likely to be confusing that the "strong method only" approach must activate in the process of producing knowledge those very values, interests, and politics that it regards as anathema in the results of research. It is at least odd to direct would-be knowers to go out and reorganize social life – as one must do to commit such forbidden (and difficult) acts as starting thought from marginal lives – in order to achieve value-neutrality in the results of research. Standpoint approaches want to eliminate dominant group interests and values from the results of research as well as the interests and values of *successfully colonized* minorities – loyalty to femininity as well as to masculinity is to be eliminated through feminist research. But that does not make the results of such research value-neutral. It will still be the thought of this era, making various distinctive assumptions that later generations and others today will point out to us.

On balance, these disadvantages outweigh the advantages of the "strong method only" approach.

Can the new social movements "have it both ways"? Can they have knowledge that is fully socially situated? We can conclude by putting the question another way: if they cannot, what hope is there for anyone else to maximize the objectivity of *their* beliefs?

Notes

1 Important works here include Susan Bordo, *The Flight to Objectivity: Essays on Cartesianism & Culture* (Albany: SUNY Press, 1987); Anne Fausto-Sterling, *Myths of Gender* (New York: Basic Books, 1985); Elizabeth Fee, "Women's Nature and Scientific Objectivity," in *Woman's Nature: Rationalizations of Inequality*, ed. Marion Lowe and Ruth Hubbard (New York: Pergamon Press, 1981); Donna Haraway, op. cit. and *Primate Visions: Gender, Race and Nature in the World of Modern Science* (New York: Routledge, 1989); Ruth Hubbard, *The Politics of Women's Biology* (New Brunswick: Rutgers University Press, 1990); Evelyn Keller, *Reflections on Gender and Science* (New Haven: Yale University Press, 1984); Helen Longino, *Science as Social Knowledge* (Princeton, NJ: Princeton University Press, 1990); and Lynn Hankinson Nelson, *Who Knows: From Quine to a Feminist Empiricism* (Philadelphia: Temple University Press, 1990). These are just *some* of the important works on the topic; many other authors have made contributions to the discussion. I have addressed these issues in *The Science Question in Feminism* (Ithaca: Cornell University Press, 1986) and *Whose Science? Whose Knowledge? Thinking From Women's Lives* (Ithaca: Cornell University Press, 1991); see also the essays in Sandra Harding and Merrill Hintikka, eds., *Discovering Reality: Feminist Perspectives on Epistemology, Metaphysics, Methodology and the Philosophy of Science* (Dordrecht: Reidel 1983). An interesting parallel discussion occurs in the feminist jurisprudence literature in the course of critiques of conventional conceptions of what "the rational man" would do, "the objective observer" would see, and "the impartial judge" would reason; see, for example many of the essays in the special issue of the *Journal of Legal Education* on *Women in Legal Education – Pedagogy, Law, Theory, and Practice* 39, 1–2 (1988), ed. Carrie Menkel-Meadow, Martha Minow, and David Vernon; and Katharine T. Bartlett, "Feminist Legal Methods," *Harvard Law Review* 103, 4 (1990).

2 This literature is by now huge. For a sampling of its concerns, see Richard Bernstein, *Beyond Objectivism and Relativism* (Philadelphia: University of Pennsylvania Press, 1983); Martin Hollis and Steven Lukes, eds., *Rationality and Relativism* (Cambridge, Mass.: Harvard University Press, 1982); Michael Krausz and Jack Meiland, eds., *Relativism: Cognitive and*

Moral (Notre Dame, Ind.: University of Notre Dame Press, 1982); and Stanley Aronowitz, *Science and Power: Discourse and Ideology in Modern Society* (Minneapolis: University of Minnesota Press, 1988).

3 Haraway, "Situated Knowledges," loc. cit., 579. In the phrase "a critical practice for recognizing our own 'semiotic technologies' for making meanings," she also raises here the troubling issue of reflexivity, to which I shall return.

4 Dorothy Smith, *The Everyday World as Problematic: A Feminist Sociology* (Boston: Northeastern University Press, 1987) and *The Conceptual Practices of Power: A Feminist Sociology of Knowledge* (Boston: Northeastern University Press, 1990); Nancy Hartsock, "The Feminist Standpoint: Developing the Ground for a Specifically Feminist Historical Materialism," in Harding and Hintikka, eds., *Discovering Reality*; Hilary Rose, "Hand, Brain and Heart: A Feminist Epistemology of the Natural Sciences," *Signs* 9, 1 (1983); and my discussion of these writings in Ch. 6 of *The Science Question in Feminism*. Alison Jaggar also developed an influential account of standpoint epistemology in Chs 11 of *Feminist Politics and Human Nature* (Totowa, NJ: Rowman & Allenheld, 1983). For more recent developments of standpoint theory see Patricia Hill Collins, Chs 10 and 11 of *Black Feminist Thought: Knowledge, Consciousness and the Politics of Empowerment* (Boston: Unwin Hyman, 1990) and Chs 5, 6, 7, and 11 of my *Whose Science? Whose Knowledge*?

5 Chapter 6 of *Whose Science*?, "'Strong Objectivity' and Socially Situated Knowledge," addresses some of the issues I raise here. However, here I develop further the differences between the "grounds" and the subject of knowledge for standpoint theory and for other epistemologies. This is partly an archeology of standpoint theory – bringing to full light the obscured aspects of its logic – and partly a reformulation of some of its claims.

6 Scientists sometimes confuse the philosophy of science called "empiricism" with the idea that it is a good thing to collect information about the empirical world. All philosophies of science recommend the latter. Empiricism is that account of such practices associated paradigmatically with Locke, Berkeley and Hume and claiming that sensory experience is the only or fundamental source of knowledge. It contrasts with theological accounts that were characteristic of European science of the Middle Ages, with rationalism, and with Marxist philosophy of science. However, from the perspective of standpoint theory, it also shares key features with one or another of these three philosophies. For example, it borrows the monologic voice that seems proper if one assumes the necessity of a unitary and coherent subject of knowledge, as do all three.

7 Roy Bhaskar writes that although positivism mystifies the processes of science, nevertheless it has a certain degree of necessity in that it reflects the spontaneous consciousness of the lab bench – the tenets of positivism reflect how it feels like science is done when one is actually gathering observations of nature. Similarly, from the perspective of standpoint approaches, the "spontaneous" feminist empiricism I discuss here mystifies the processes of feminist research, although it has a certain necessity in that it just felt to these feminist empirical workers like what it was that they were doing as their work overturned the results of supposedly value-free prefeminist research. See Roy Bhaskar, "Philosophies as Ideologies of Science: A Contribution to the Critique of Positivism," in *Reclaiming Reality* (New York: Verso, 1989). Not all forms of empiricism are reasonably thought of as positivist, of course, but the most prevalent contemporary forms are. The philosophical feminist empiricism noted below is not positivist.

8 Longino, *Science as Social Knowledge*; Nelson, *Who Knows*.

9 There are many standpoint theorists and many spontaneous feminist empiricists. I present here ideal types of these two theories of knowledge. I have contrasted these two theories in a number of earlier writings, most recently on pp. 111–37 of *Whose Science: Whose Knowledge*? The following passage draws especially on pp. 111–20.

10 Dorothy Smith was right, I now think, to insist (in effect) that standpoint theory appropriates and transforms the notion of scientific method, not just of epistemology; see her comments on a paper of mine in *American Philosophical Association Newsletter on Feminism* 88, 3 (1989). It is interesting to note that by 1989, even the National Academy of Science – no rabble-rousing antiscience critic! – argues that the methods of science should be understood to include "the judgments scientists make about the interpretation or reliability of data . . ., the decisions scientists make about which problems to pursue or when to conclude an investigation," and even "the ways scientists work with each other and exchange information" [*On Being a Scientist* (Washington D.C.: National Academy Press, 1989), 5–6].

11 Marcia Millman and Rosabeth Moss Kanter, "Editor's Introduction" to *Another Voice: Feminist Perspectives on Social Life and Social Science* (New York: Anchor Books, 1975), vii. [Reprinted in S. Harding, ed., *Feminism and Methodology*, (Bloomington: Indiana University Press, 1987.)]

12 This description seems to imply that scientists are somehow outside of the history they are using – for example, capable of determining which are, in fact, the scientifically and epistemologically most favorable historical locations. This is not so, of course, and that is why the reflexivity project Haraway refers to is so important.

13 "Of course here and there will be found careless or poorly trained scientists, but no *real* scientist, no *good* scientist, would produce sexist or androcentric results of research." This line of argument has the consequence that there have been no real or good scientists except for feminists! See "What Is Feminist Science?," Ch. 12 of *Whose Science? Whose Knowledge?*, for discussions of this and other attempts to resist the idea that feminist science is exactly good science but that refusing to acknowledge the feminist component in good science obscures what makes it good.

14 Frederic Jameson has argued that the feminist standpoint theorists are the only contemporary thinkers fully to appreciate the Marxist epistemology. See "*History and Class Consciousness* as an 'Unfinished Project,'" *Rethinking Marxism* 1 (1988): 49–72. It should be noted that empiricist explanations of Marxist accounts are common: "Marx had this puzzle. . . . He made a bold conjecture and then attempted to falsify it. . . . The facts supported his account and resolved the puzzle." These make the accounts plausible to empiricists but fail to engage both with Marx's own different epistemology and with the additional "puzzle" of the historical causes of the emergence of his account, to which Marxist epistemology draws attention.

15 See note 5.

16 Cf., for example, Edward Said, *Orientalism* (New York: Pantheon Books, 1978); Samir Amin, *Eurocentrism* (New York: Monthly Review Press, 1989); Monique Wittig, "The Straight Mind," *Feminist Issues* 1, 1 (1980); Marilyn Frye, *The Politics of Reality* (Trumansburg, New York: The Crossing Press, 1983); and Charles Mills, "Alternative Epistemologies," *Social Theory and Practice* 14, 3 (1988).

17 Hartsock, "The Feminist Standpoint," 159. Hartsock's use of the term "real relations" may suggest to some readers that she and other standpoint theorists are hopelessly mired in an epistemology and metaphysics that have been discredited by social constructionists. This judgment fails to appreciate the way standpoint theories reject *both* pure realist and pure social constructionist epistemologies and metaphysics. Donna Haraway is particularly good on this issue.

18 We shall return later to the point that, for standpoint theorists, reports of marginalized experience or lives or phenomenologies of the "lived world" of marginalized peoples are not the *answers* to questions arising either inside or outside those lives, though they are necessary to asking the best questions.

19 For an exploration of a number of different ways in which marginal lives can generate more critical questions, see Ch. 5, "What is Feminist Epistemology?" in *Whose Science? Whose Knowledge?*

20 See, for example, *The Conceptual Practices of Power: A Feminist Sociology of Knowledge*, 54.

21 The image of knowledge seeking as a journey – "starting off thought from women's lives" – is a useful corrective to misunderstandings that more easily arise from the visual metaphor – "thinking from the perspective of women's lives." The journey metaphor appears often in writings by Hartsock, Smith, and others.

22 Some women are assigned more of this work than others, but even wealthy and aristocratic women with plenty of servants are left significantly responsible for such work in ways their brothers are not.

23 Of course body work and emotional work also require head work – contrary to the long history of sexist, racist, and class-biased views. See, for example, Sara Ruddick, *Maternal Thinking* (New York: Beacon Press, 1989). And the kind of head work required in administrative and managerial work – what Smith means by "ruling" – also involves distinctive body and emotional work, though it is not acknowledged as such. Think of how much of early childhood education of middle-class children is really about internalizing a certain kind of (gender-specific) regulation of bodies and emotions.

24 This is Donna Haraway's phrase in "Situated Knowledges".

25 Smith, "Women's Perspective as a Radical Critique of Sociology," in *Feminism and Methodology*, 91.

26 I idealize the history of science here as is indicated by recent studies of fraud, carelessness, and unconscious bias that is not detected. See, for example, Stephen Jay Gould, *The Mismeasure of Man* (New York: W. W. Norton, 1981); L. Kamin, *The Science and Politics of IQ* (Potomac, Md.: Erlbaum, 1974); and William Broad and Nicholas Wade, *Betrayers of the Truth* (New York: Simon & Schuster, 1982). The issue here can appear to be one about the sins of individuals, which it is. But far more importantly, it is an issue about both the unwillingness and impotence of scientific institutions to police their own practices. They *must* do so, for any other alternative is less effective. But science institutions will not want to or be competent to do so until they are more integrated into democratic social projects.

27 Richard Rorty is unusual in arguing that because social situatedness is indeed the lot of all human knowledge projects, we might as well embrace our ethnocentrism while pursuing the conversations of mankind. His defense of ethnocentrism is a defense of a kind of fatalism about the impossibility of people ever transcending their social situation; in a significant sense this comes down to and converges with the standard definition of ethnocentrism centered in my argument here. (I thank Linda Alcoff for helping me to clarify this point.) He does not imagine that one can effectively change one's "social situation" by, for example, participating in a feminist political movement, reading and producing feminist analyses, and

so on. From the perspective of his argument, it is mysterious how any woman (or man) ever becomes a feminist because our "social situation" is initially to be constrained by patriarchal institutions, ideologies, and the like. How *did* John Stuart Mill or Simone de Beauvoir ever come to think such thoughts as they did? See his *Objectivity, Relativism and Truth* (New York: Cambridge University Press, 1991).

28 Of course a gender is not an ethnicity. Yet historians and anthropologists write of women's cultures, so perhaps it does not stretch the meaning of ethnicity too far to think of women's cultures this way. Certainly some of the critics of standpoint theory have done so.

29 "Women's Perspective," cited in note 25.

30 Bettina Aptheker, *Tapestries of Life: Women's Work, Women's Consciousness, and the Meaning of Daily Life* (Amherst: University of Massachusetts Press, 1989).

31 *Black Feminist Thought*, cited in note 4.

32 The preceding citations contain many examples of such cases.

33 "So many," but not all. African-American and Latina writers have argued that in US society, at least, a poor African-American and Latino man cannot be regarded as better off than his sister in many important respects.

34 What are the material limits of standpoint theories? Retroactively, we can see that they require the context of scientific culture; that is, they center claims about greater objectivity, the possibility and desirability of progress, the value of causal accounts for social projects, and so on. They also appear to require that the barriers between dominant and dominated be not absolutely rigid; there must be some degree of social mobility. Some marginal people must be able to observe what those at the center do, some marginal voices must be able to catch the attention of those at the center, and some people at the center must be intimate enough with the lives of the marginalized to be able to think how social life works from the perspective of their lives. A totalitarian system would be unlikely to breed standpoint theories. So a historical move to antiscientific or to totalitarian systems would make standpoint theories less useful. No doubt there are other historical changes that would limit the resources standpoint theories can provide.

35 See the citations in note 2.

36 All of the feminist standpoint theorists and science writers insist on distinguishing their positions from relativist ones. I have discussed the issue of relativism in several places, most recently in Chs 6 and 7 of *Whose Science? Whose Knowledge?*

37 See S. P. Mohanty, "Us and Them: On the Philosophical Bases of Political Criticism," *Yale Journal of Criticism*, 2, 2 (1989); and Donna Haraway's "Situated Knowledges" for especially illuminating discussions of why relativism can look attractive to many thinkers at this moment in history, but why it should nevertheless be resisted.

38 Mary G. Belenky and her colleagues point out that the phrase "It's my opinion..." has different meanings for the young men and women they have studied. For men this phrase means "I've got a right to my opinion," but for women it means "It's just my opinion." Mary G. Belenky, B. M. Clinchy, N. R. Goldeberger, and J. M. Tarule, *Women's Ways of Knowing: the Development of Self, Voice, and Mind* (New York: Basic Books, 1986).

39 Critics of standpoint theories usually attribute this position to standpoint theorists. Within the array of feminist theoretical approaches, the claim that only women can produce knowledge is most often made by Radical Feminists.

40 The Combahee River Collective, "A Black Feminist Statement," in *This Bridge Called My Back: Writings by Radical Women of Color*, ed. Cherrie Moraga and Gloria Anzaldúa (Latham, New York: Kitchen Table: Women of Color Press, 1983), 212.

41 For example, mechanistic models of the universe had different meanings for Galileo's critics than they have had for modern astronomers or, later, for contemporary ecologists, as Carolyn Merchant and other historians of science point out. See Carolyn Merchant, *The Death of Nature: Women, Ecology and the Scientific Revolution* (New York: Harper & Row, 1980). To take another case, "wild animals" and, more generally, "nature" are defined differently by Japanese, Indian, and Anglo-American primatologists, as Donna Haraway points out in *Primate Visions* (cited in note 1). The cultural character of nature as an object of knowledge has been a consistent theme in Haraway's work.

42 Longino and Nelson's arguments are particularly telling against the individualism of empiricism. See Nelson's "Who Knows," Ch. 6 in *Who Knows*, and Longino's discussion of how the underdetermination of theories by their evidence insures that "background beliefs" will function as if they were evidence in many chapters of *Science as Social Knowledge* (cited in note 1) but especially in Chs 8, 9, and 10.

43 See Elizabeth Spelman, *Inessential Woman: Problems of Exclusion in Feminist Thought* (Boston: Beacon Press, 1988) for a particularly pointed critique of essentialist tendencies in feminist writings. Most of the rest of this section appears also in "Subjectivity, Experience and Knowledge: An Epistemology from/for Rainbow Coalition Politics," forthcoming in *Questions of Authority: The Politics of Discourse and Epistemology in Feminist Thought*, ed. Judith Roof and Robyn Weigman. I have also discussed these points in several other places.

44 These ways of describing this kind of subject of knowledge appear in the writings of, respectively, Smith ("Women's Perspective"), Collins (*Black Feminist Thought*) and Bell Hooks, *Feminist Theory From Margin to Center* (Boston: South End Press, 1983).

45 Consequently, a main strategy of the public agenda politics of the new social movements has been to insist that women, or peoples of African descent, or the poor, and so on do indeed possess the kinds of reason that qualify them as "rational men"; that women's, industrial, or peasant labor makes these groups also the "working men" from whose laboring lives can be generated less partial and distorted understandings of local and international economies.

46 I do not say these thinkers are perfect feminists – they are not, and no one is. But here and there one can see them generating original feminist knowledge as they think from the perspective of women's lives as women have taught them to do.

47 Collins, *Black Feminist Thought*, 35–6. Chs 1, 2, 10, and 11 of this book offer a particular rich and stimulating development of standpoint theory.

48 See the citations in note 2. The term "objectivism" has been used to identify the objectionable notion by Bernstein, Keller, and Bordo (see earlier citations), among others.

49 The following arguments are excerpted from pp. 143–8 in my *Whose Science? Whose Knowledge?*

50 See note 26.

51 Many Americans – even (especially?) highly educated ones – hold fundamentally totalitarian notions of what democracy is, associating it with mob rule or some at least mildly irrelevant principle of representation but never with genuine community dialogue. (A physicist asked me if by democracy I really meant that national physics projects should be managed by, say, fifty-two people, one selected randomly from each state! This made me think of the wisdom of William Buckley, Jr's desire to be governed by the first 100 people in the Boston phone book rather than the governors we have.) A good starting point for thinking about how to advance democracy is John Dewey's proposal: those who will bear the consequence of a decision should have a proportionate share in making it.

52 Quoted in Werner Van den Daele, "The Social Construction of Science," in *The Social Production of Scientific Knowledge*, ed. E. Mendelsohn, P. Weingart, and R. Whitley (Dordrecht: Reidel, 1977), 34.

53 David Mura puts the point this way in "Strangers in the Village," in *The Graywolf Annual Five: Multicultural Literacy* ed. Rick Simonson and Scott Walker (St Paul: Graywolf Press, 1988), 152.

54 These arguments for retaining the notion of objectivity draw on ones I have made several times before, most recently in *Whose Science? Whose Knowledge?* pp. 157–61.

55 The National Academy of Sciences recommends such an expansion, as indicated earlier.

56 For example. Smith and Hartsock, cited in note 4.

Part V

Is Value Gendered?

Introduction to Part V

The two most important contributions of feminism to ethics and political philosophy have been the development of an ethics of care and the debate over whether moral ideals or principles and/or human rights are universal. Each chapter in this part addresses one or both of these issues.

Contemporary feminist moral philosophy was deeply influenced by *In A Different Voice*, published in 1982 by the psychologist Carol Gilligan. In her research, Gilligan interviewed boys and girls, men and women, posing ethical problems for them and eliciting detailed responses. She interpreted their responses as evidence for the existence of a feminine gendered morality, which she called the "ethic of care," as distinct from the "ethic of justice," which she argued is gendered masculine, and which is the traditional subject of ethical theory. For a number of philosophers, most but not all of whom were women, this work was an epiphany. It opened up a whole set of female-centered experiences to the scrutiny of moral philosophy. As we see in the chapters in this part, the ethic of care seeks to, in Joan Tronto's apt phrase, "expand the moral domain" to consider practices, needs, virtues, attitudes and competencies that traditional moral theory had not focused on. This literature raises questions for the philosopher, such as: Is care ethics really new? Is it gendered female, that is, does care ethics arise from feminine experience and concerns? Is it compatible with the dominant conception of ethics as primarily focused on justice?

In the chapter, "The Need for More than Justice," Annette Baier summarizes and interprets Gilligan's empirical psychological work in the light of historical and contemporary moral theory. Her aim in this chapter is to show us how philosophers can use Gilligan's work to make a distinctly feminist contribution to ethical theory. Baier argues that while justice is clearly a primary subject of ethical theory, there are ethical concerns that women are more likely to be attuned to because of their different social location, that is, because they are required to give care and lead more interdependent lives than men, but that have been neglected by most (male) moral philosophers. Baier argues that these concerns are not just "optional extras" for a moral theory, but must be built into any satisfactory moral theory. She locates four specific challenges from Gilligan's work to what she sees as the dominant, Kantian liberal conception of morality. First, the ideal of individualism is neither plausible nor desirable; it is unattainable by humans, but in the pursuit of the ideal an elite few oppress many who are needed to orchestrate the illusion of independence. Second, it erects a pretense of equality, while ignoring the actual relations of inequality among persons. Third, it exaggerates the scope of freedom of choice for individuals, and bases responsibility largely on chosen relations, when many of our most important duties arise from unchosen relations to others. Fourth, it raises rationality above passion to the point of denigrating the role of emotion in moral behavior. Baier's chapter thus clarifies the feminist challenges to moral theory, and at the same time points to a possible future reconciliation of justice and care under a single comprehensive moral view.

The second chapter in this part, "An Ethic of Care" by Joan Tronto, argues that care must be seen as a central concern of any moral life. She analyzes care into four ethical elements: attentiveness, responsibility, competence, and responsiveness. Caring first requires attentiveness to need in the first instance, then second the recognition of one's responsibility for fulfilling certain needs of others, and third the ability to fulfill the needs one has accepted the responsibility for. As persons are both the carers and the cared for, the final ethical element of care involves responding to caregiving, and the recognition of the conditions of vulnerability and inequality that are inevitably a part of caring relationships. Although some of these notions are part of traditional moral theories, incorporating them into a theory that centers relations of care incorporates more of human experience, particularly women's experience, into the heart of moral theory. But Tronto does not wish to limit care to intimate relationships. Instead she argues that when we refocus our attention through the practice of care onto needs, vulnerabilities, and inequalities, our political theory will be transformed as well to focus more generally on "the process by which life is sustained."

In "Vulnerability and the Moral Nature of Dependency Relations," Eva Feder Kittay examines the obligations of dependents, caregivers (whom she calls "dependency workers"), and the larger society, and argues that coercion is a common problem in dependency relations. What, she asks, is the source of obligation to care for a dependent other? While the dominant tradition in ethics claims that obligations come from their voluntary acceptance, Kittay argues that this cannot explain our obligations in the many non-voluntary relations persons inhabit, both naturally and socially derived, most paradigmatically familial obligations. She appeals instead to Robert Goodin's vulnerability model of obligation, but argues that it fails to protect the obligated caregiver from coercion by dominant others or by social arrangements that systematically assign caregiving to certain classes of persons. She suggests that the problem can be solved by appealing to society's obligations to support caregivers and to prevent domination. "For the dependency worker to meet her responsibilities to another, it must be the responsibility of the larger social order to provide a structure whereby she, too, may be treated as a mother's child." The chapter leaves somewhat vague, however, how to recognize the coercive relations that are to be prevented, if the coercion is not to be defined in terms of a forced association, as it is on the voluntarist model.

While the first three chapters of the part are highly critical of the dominant Kantian and contractarian strands in contemporary moral theory, Jean Hampton defends a type of Kantian contractarianism in "Femininst Contractarianism." In her view feminism's most important contribution lies in revealing the distributive injustice in traditional intimate romantic and familial relationships, and she argues that contractarianism offers the best theory to illuminate that injustice. Hampton presents two forms of contractarian thought. Hobbesian contractarianism begins from the assumptions that individuals are self-interested and that no one ought to be able to coerce another to satisfy his interests. Morality is derived as norms for cooperative contract within these assumptions. She rejects this form of contractarianism for its failure to accord intrinsic value to individuals, but she argues that it contains one feminist insight, namely "the idea that morality should not be understood to require that we make ourselves prey of others." Kantian contractarianism differs in that it accords human individuals intrinsic value in deriving moral principles from the idea that each must be one that every person could rationally agree to. While some feminists would criticize this procedure as androcentric, Hampton argues that a feminist-informed understanding of the intrinsic moral worth of persons would provide a grounding for an ethics that avoids exploiting feminine tendencies to selflessness and unrecompensed caring.

The first four chapters in this part more directly address the issue of the ethics of care, but each of them is also concerned indirectly with the issue of universalism in that each addresses the question of whether there is a women's morality separate from that of men. While each of them sees unique contributions from women philosophers and from attention to the experiences of women to ethics, they have all implicitly embraced universalism in arguing for ethical theories that speak to both men and women. That is, none argues that their theory uniquely applies to women, or to women of a certain culture. Some feminist theories posit such relativist views, however, arguing that women are to be held to different moral standards than men, or that moral standards apply only locally. Such theorists accuse universalists of "essentialism," by which they mean a theory that holds that there are characteristics of persons that hold universally, regardless of culture. The final chapter in this part explicitly takes up the debate over universalism. In "Women and Cultural Universals" Martha Nussbaum argues for the universality of the value of what she calls, following Amartya Sen, "human capabilities." Human capabilities are general descriptions of the things that humans can choose to do and find value in doing, provided they have the required social freedom and support, the economic wherewithal, and the physical capacity. While no human being or culture values the functional use of all the capabilities equally, Nussbaum argues that we need to consider what humans are capable of and would ideally wish to do with their capabilities in order to judge whether the lives of some persons are being unjustly circumscribed. She proposes a comprehensive list of capabilities, and argues that societies can be judged for their morality by the degree to which they support these capabilities for all their members. While some may not choose to exploit certain capabilities, she argues that all must value the ability to choose which of their capacities they will use and how they will use them. She then defends the list, and the very idea of a list, against critics. The list allows her to argue against the idea that there should be two sets of moral and behavioral norms, one for men and one for women. First, she argues that empirical evidence shows that when women reject separate spheres they have been able to raise the quality of life for all. Second, she argues that the separate spheres and ideals deprive men and women of crucial capacities, such as emotional attachment and judgment, that all humans find valuable. In the end, then, Nussbaum rejects the idea the valuing of human capabilities, broadly construed, is gendered, while still leaving open the possibility that people will differ in the capacities that they value most highly.

18

The Need for More than Justice

Annette C. Baier

In recent decades in North American social and moral philosophy, alongside the development and discussion of widely influential theories of justice, taken as John Rawls takes it as the "first virtue of social institutions,"[1] there has been a countermovement gathering strength, one coming from some interesting sources. Some of the most outspoken of the diverse group who have in a variety of ways been challenging the assumed supremacy of justice among the moral and social virtues are members of those sections of society whom one might have expected to be especially aware of the supreme importance of justice: blacks and women. Those who have only recently won recognition of their equal rights, who have only recently seen the correction or partial correction of long-standing racist and sexist injustices to their race and sex, are among the philosophers now suggesting that justice is only one virtue among many, and one that may need the presence of the others in order to deliver its own undenied value. Among these philosophers of the philosophical counterculture, as it were – but an increasingly large counterculture – I include Alasdair MacIntyre,[2] Michael Stocker,[3] Lawrence Blum,[4] Michael Slote,[5] Laurence Thomas,[6] Claudia Card,[7] Alison Jaggar,[8] Susan Wolf,[9] and a whole group of men and women, myself included, who have been influenced by the writings of the Harvard educational psychologist Carol Gilligan, whose book *In a Different Voice* caused a considerable stir both in the popular press and, more slowly, in the philosophical journals.[10]

Annette C. Baier, "The Need for More than Justice," from *Canadian Journal of Philosophy,* supp. Vol. 13 (1987). Reprinted by the University of Calgary Press, Calgary, Alberta.

Let me say quite clearly at this early point that there is little disagreement that justice is *a* social value of very great importance, and injustice an evil. Nor would those who have worked on theories of justice want to deny that other things matter besides justice. Rawls, for example, incorporates the value of freedom into his account of justice, so that denial of basic freedoms counts as injustice. Rawls also leaves room for a wider theory of the right, of which the theory of justice is just a part. Still, he does claim that justice is the "first" virtue of social institutions, and it is only that claim about priority that I think has been challenged. It is easy to exaggerate the differences of view that exist, and I want to avoid that. The differences are as much in emphasis as in substance, or we can say that they are differences in tone of voice. But these differences do tend to make a difference in approaches to a wide range of topics not just in moral theory but in areas such as medical ethics, where the discussion used to be conducted in terms of patients' rights, of informed consent, and so on, but now tends to get conducted in an enlarged moral vocabulary, which draws on what Gilligan calls the ethics of *care* as well as that of justice.

"Care" is the new buzzword. It is not, as Shakespeare's Portia demanded, mercy that is to season justice, but a less authoritarian humanitarian supplement, a felt concern for the good of others and for community with them. The "cold jealous virtue of justice" (Hume) is found to be too cold, and it is "warmer," more communitarian virtues and social ideals that are being called in to supplement it. One might say that liberty and equality are being found inadequate without fraternity, except that "fraternity" will be quite the wrong word if, as Gilligan initially suggested, it is *women* who perceive this value most easily. ("Sorority" will do no better, since it is too exclusive, and English has no gender-neutral word for the mutual concern of siblings.) She has since modified this claim, allowing that there are two perspectives on moral and social issues that we all tend to alternate between, and which are not always easy to combine, one of them what she calls the justice perspective, the other the care perspective. It is increasingly obvious that there are many male philosophical spokespersons for the care perspective (Laurence Thomas, Lawrence Blum, Michael Stocker), so it cannot be the prerogative of women. Nevertheless Gilligan still wants to claim that women are most unlikely to take *only* the justice perspective, as some men are claimed to, at least until some mid-life crisis jolts them into "bifocal" moral vision (see *D.V.*, Ch. 6).

Gilligan in *In a Different Voice* did not offer any explanatory theory of why there should be any difference between the female and the male moral outlook, but she did tend to link the naturalness to women of the care perspective with their role as primary caretakers of young children, that is, with their parental and specifically maternal role. She avoided the question of whether it is their biological or their social parental role that is relevant, and some of those who dislike her book are worried precisely by this uncertainty. Some find it retrograde to hail as a special sort of moral wisdom an outlook that may be the product of the socially enforced restriction of women to domestic roles (and the reservation of such roles for them alone); that might seem to play into the hands of those who still favor such restriction. (Marxists, presumably, will not find it so surprising that moral truths might depend for their initial clear articulation on the social oppression, and memory of it, of those who voice the truths.) Gilligan did in the first chapter of *In a Different Voice* cite the theory of Nancy Chodorow (as presented in *The Reproduction of Mothering*[11]), which traces what appear as gender differences in personality to early social development, in particular to the effects of the child's primary caretaker being or not being of the same gender as the child. Later, both in "The Conquistador and the Dark Continent: Reflections on the Psychology of Love" and in "The Origins of Morality in Early Childhood Relationships," she develops this explanation.[12] She postulates two evils that any infant may become aware of, the evil of detachment or isolation from others whose love one needs, and the evil of relative powerlessness and weakness. Two dimensions of moral development are thereby set – one aimed at achieving satisfying community with others, the other aiming at autonomy or equality of power. The relative predominance of one development over the other will depend both upon the relative salience of the two evils in early childhood and on early and later reinforcement or discouragement in attempts made to guard against these two evils. This provides the germs of a theory about *why*, given current customs of child rearing, it should be mainly women who are not content with only the moral outlook that Gilligan calls the justice perspective, necessary though that was and is seen by them to have been to their hard-won liberation from sexist oppression. They, like the blacks, once used the language of rights and justice to change their own social position, but nevertheless now see limitations in that language, according to Gilligan's findings as a moral psychologist. She reports their discontent with the individualist, more or less Kantian moral framework which dominates Western moral theory and which influenced moral psychologists such as Lawrence Kohlberg,[13] to whose conception of moral maturity she seeks an alternative. Since the target of Gilligan's criticism is the dominant Kantian tradition, and since that has been the target also of moral philosophers as diverse in their own views as Bernard Williams,[14] Alasdair MacIntyre, Philippa Foot,[15] Susan Wolf, and Claudia Card, *In a Different Voice* is of interest as much for its attempt to articulate an alternative to the Kantian justice perspective as for its implicit raising of the question of male bias in Western moral theory, especially liberal-democratic theory. For whether the supposed blind spots of that outlook are due to male bias, or to nonparental bias, or to early traumas of powerlessness, or to early resignation to "detachment" from others, we need first to be persuaded that they *are* blind spots before we will have any interest in their cause and cure. Is justice blind to important social values, or at least only one-eyed? What is it that comes into view from the "care perspective" that is not seen from the "justice perspective"?

Gilligan's position here is most easily described by contrasting it with that of Kohlberg, against which she developed it. Kohlberg, influenced by Jean Piaget and the Kantian philosophical tradition as developed by John Rawls, developed a theory about typical moral development which saw it to progress from a preconventional level, where what is seen to matter is pleasing or not offending parental authority figures, through a conventional level in which the child tries to fit in with a group, such as a school community, and to conform to its standards and rules, to a postconventional critical level, in which such conventional rules are subjected to tests and where those tests are of a Utilitarian or, eventually, a Kantian sort – ones that require respect for each person's individual rational will, or autonomy, and conformity to any implicit social contract such wills are deemed to have made or to any hypothetical ones they would make if thinking clearly. What was found when Kohlberg's questionnaires (mostly by verbal response to verbally sketched moral dilemmas) were applied to female as well as male subjects, Gilligan reports, is that the girls and women not only scored generally lower than the boys and men but tended to *revert* to the lower stage of the conventional level even after briefly (usually in adolescence) attaining the postconventional level. Piaget's finding that girls were deficient in "the legal sense" was confirmed.

These results led Gilligan to wonder if there might not be a quite different pattern of development to be discerned, at least in female subjects. She therefore conducted interviews designed to elicit not just how far advanced the subjects were toward an appreciation of the nature and importance of Kantian autonomy but also to find out what the subjects themselves saw as progress or lack of it, what conceptions of moral maturity they came to possess by the time they were adults. She found that although the Kohlberg version of moral maturity as respect for fellow persons and for their rights as equals (rights including that of free association) did seem shared by many young men, the women tended to speak in a different voice about morality itself and about moral maturity. To quote Gilligan, "Since the reality of connection is experienced by women as given rather than as freely contracted, they arrive at an understanding of life that reflects the limits of autonomy and control. As a result, women's development delineates the path not only to a less violent life but also to a maturity realized through interdependence and taking care" (*D.V.*, p. 172). She writes that there is evidence that "women perceive and construe social reality differently from men and that these differences center around experiences of attachment and separation . . . because women's sense of integrity appears to be entwined with an ethic of care, so that to see themselves as women is to see themselves in a relationship of connection, the major transitions in women's lives would seem to involve changes in the understanding and activities of care" (*D.V.*, p. 171). She contrasts this progressive understanding of care, from merely pleasing others to helping and nurturing, with the sort of progression that is involved in Kohlberg's stages, a progression in the understanding, not of mutual care, but of mutual *respect*, where this has its Kantian overtones of distance, even of some fear for the respected, and where personal autonomy and *in*dependence, rather than more satisfactory interdependence, are the paramount values.

This contrast, one cannot but feel, is one which Gilligan might have used the Marxist language of alienation to make. For the main complaint about the Kantian version of a society with its first virtue justice, construed as respect for equal rights to formal goods such as having contracts kept, due process, equal opportunity including opportunity to participate in political activities leading to policy and lawmaking, to basic liberties of speech, free association and assembly, and religious worship, is that none of these goods does much to ensure that the people who have and mutually respect such rights will have any other relationships to one another than the minimal relationship needed to keep such a "civil society" going. They may well be lonely, driven to suicide, apathetic about their work and about participation in political processes, find their lives meaningless, and have no wish to leave offspring to face the same meaningless existence. Their rights, and respect for rights, are quite compatible with very great misery, and misery whose causes are not just individual misfortune and psychic sickness but social and moral impoverishment.

What Gilligan's older male subjects complain of is precisely this sort of alienation from some dimly glimpsed better possibility for human beings, some richer sort of network of relationships. As one of Gilligan's male subjects put it, "People have real emotional needs to be attached to something, and equality doesn't give you attachment. Equality fractures society and places on every person the burden of standing on his own two feet" (*D.V.*, p. 167). It is not just the difficulty of self-reliance which is complained of, but its socially "fracturing" effect. Whereas the younger men, in their college years, had seen morality as a matter of reciprocal noninterference, this older man begins to see it as reciprocal attachment. "Morality is... essential... for creating the kind of environment, interaction between people, that is prerequisite to the fulfillment of most individual goals. If you want other people not to interfere with your pursuit of whatever you are into, you have to play the game," says a young spokesman for traditional liberalism (*D.V.*, p. 98). But if what one is "into" is interconnection, interdependence rather than an individual autonomy that may involve "detachment," such a version of morality will come to seem inadequate. And Gilligan stresses that the interconnection that her mature women subjects, and some men, wanted to sustain was not merely freely chosen interconnection, nor interconnection between equals, but also the sort of interconnection that can obtain between a child and her unchosen mother and father, or between a child and her unchosen older and younger siblings, or indeed between most workers and their unchosen fellow workers, or between most citizens and their unchosen fellow citizens.

A model of a decent community different from the liberal one is involved in the version of moral maturity that Gilligan voices. It has in many ways more in common with the older religion-linked versions of morality and a good society than with the modern Western liberal ideal. That perhaps is why some find it so dangerous and retrograde. Yet it seems clear that it also has much in common with what we can call Hegelian versions of moral maturity and of social health and malaise, both with Marxist versions and with so-called right-Hegelian views.

Let me try to summarize the main differences, as I see them, between on the one hand Gilligan's version of moral maturity and the sort of social structures that would encourage, express, and protect it and on the other the orthodoxy she sees herself to be challenging. I shall from now on be giving my own interpretation of the significance of her challenges, not merely reporting them. The most obvious point is the challenge to the individualism of the Western tradition, to the fairly entrenched belief in the possibility and desirability of each person pursuing his own good in his own way, constrained only by a minimal formal common good, namely, a working legal apparatus that enforces contracts and protects individuals from undue interference by others. Gilligan reminds us that noninterference can, especially for the relatively powerless, such as the very young, amount to neglect, and even between equals can be isolating and alienating. On her less individualist version of individuality, it becomes defined by responses to dependency and to patterns of interconnection, both chosen and unchosen. It is not something a person *has*, and which she then chooses relationships to suit, but something that develops out of a series of dependencies and interdependencies, and responses to them. This conception of individuality is not flatly at odds with, say, Rawls's Kantian one, but there is at least a difference of tone of voice between speaking as Rawls does of each of us having our own rational life plan, which a just society's moral traffic rules will allow us to follow, and which may or may not include close association with other persons, and speaking as Gilligan does of a satisfactory life as involving the "progress of affiliative relationship" (*D.V.*, p. 170) where "the concept of identity expands to include the experience of interconnection" (*D.V.*, p. 173). Rawls can allow that progress to Gilligan-style moral maturity may be *a* rational life plan, but not a moral constraint on every life pattern. The trouble is that it will not do just to say "let this version of morality be an optional extra. Let us agree on the essential minimum, that is, on justice and rights, and let whoever wants to go further and cultivate this more demanding ideal of responsibility and care." For, first, the ideal of care cannot be satisfactorily cultivated without closer cooperation from others than respect for rights and justice will ensure, and, second, the encouragement of some to cultivate it while others do not could easily lead to exploitation of those who do. It obviously *has* suited some in most societies well enough that others take on the responsibilities of care (for the sick, the helpless, the young), leaving them free to pursue their own less altruistic goods. Volunteer forces of those who accept an ethic of care, operating within a society where the power is exercised and the institutions designed, redesigned, or maintained by those who accept a less communal ethic of minimally constrained self-advancement, will not be the solution. The liberal individualists may be able to "tolerate" the more communally minded, if they keep the liberals' rules, but it is not so clear that the more communally minded can be content with just those rules, nor be content to be tolerated and possibly exploited.

For the moral tradition which developed the concept of rights, autonomy, and justice is the same tradition that provided "justifications" of the oppression of those whom the primary rights-holders depended on to do the sort of work they themselves preferred not to do. The domestic work was left to women and slaves, and the liberal morality for rights-holders was surreptitiously supplemented by a different set of demands made on domestic workers. As long as women could be got to assume responsibility for the care of home and children and to train their children to continue the sexist system, the liberal morality could continue to be the official morality, by turning its eyes away from the contribution made by those it excluded. The long unnoticed moral proletariat were the domestic workers, mostly female. Rights have usually been for the privileged. Talking about laws, and the rights those laws recognize and protect, does not in itself ensure that the group of legislators and rights-holders will not be restricted to some elite. Bills of rights have usually been proclamations of the rights of some in-group, barons, landowners, males, whites, nonforeigners. The "justice perspective" and the legal sense that goes with it are shadowed by their patriarchal past. What did Kant, the great prophet of autonomy, say in his moral theory about women? He said they were incapable of legislation, not fit to vote, that they needed the guidance of more "rational" males.[16] Autonomy was not for them; it was only for first-class, really rational, persons. It is ironic that Gilligan's original findings in a way confirm Kant's views – it seems that autonomy really may not be for women. Many of them reject that ideal (*D.V.*, p. 48), and have been found not as good at making rules as are men. But where Kant concludes "so much the worse for women," we can conclude "so much the worse for the male fixation on the special skill of drafting legislation, for the bureaucratic mentality of rule worship, and for the male exaggeration of the importance of independence over mutual interdependence."

It is however also true that the moral theories that made the concept of a person's rights central were not just the instruments for excluding some persons but also the instruments used by those who demanded that more and more persons be included in the favored group. Abolitionists, reformers, women, used the language of rights to assert their claims to inclusion in the group of full members of a community. The tradition of liberal moral theory has in fact developed to include the women it had for so long excluded, to include the poor as well as rich, blacks as well as whites, and so on. Women such as Mary Wollstonecraft used the male moral theories to good purpose. So we should not be wholly ungrateful for those male moral theories, for all their objectionable earlier content. They were undoubtedly patriarchal, but they also contained the seeds of the challenge, or antidote, to this patriarchal poison.

But when we transcend the values of the Kantians, we should not forget the facts of history – that those values were the values of the oppressors of women. The Christian church, whose version of the moral law Aquinas codified in his very legalistic moral theory, still insists on the maleness of the God it worships, and jealously reserves for males all the most powerful positions in its hierarchy. Its patriarchal prejudice is open and avowed. In the secular moral theories of men, the sexist patriarchal prejudice is today often less open, not as blatant as it is in Aquinas, in the later natural law tradition, and in Kant and Hegel, but is often still there. No moral theorist today would say that women are unfit to vote, to make laws, or to rule a nation without powerful male advisors (as most queens had), but the old doctrines die hard. In one of the best male theories we have, Rawls's theory, a key role is played by the idea of the "head of a household." It is heads of households who are to deliberate behind a "veil of ignorance" of historical details, and of details of their own special situation, to arrive at the "just" constitution for a society. Now of course Rawls does not think or say that these "heads" are fathers rather than mothers. But if we have really given up the age-old myth of women needing, as Grotius put it, to be under the "eye" of a more "rational" male protector and master, then how do families come to have any one "head," except by the death or desertion of one parent? They will either be two-headed, or headless. Traces of the old patriarchal poison still remain in even the best contemporary moral theorizing. Few may actually say that women's place is in the home, but there is much muttering, when unemployment figures rise, about how the relatively recent flood of women into the work force complicates the problem, as if it would be a good thing if women just went back home whenever unemployment rose, to leave the available jobs for the men. We still do not have wide acceptance of the equal right of women to employment outside the home. Nor do we have wide acceptance of the equal duty of men to perform those domestic tasks which in no way depend on special female anatomy, such as cooking, cleaning, and the care of weaned children. All sorts of stories (maybe true stories) about children's need for one "primary" parent, who must be the mother if the mother breast-feeds the child, shore up the unequal division of domestic responsibility between mothers and fathers, wives and husbands. If we are really to transvalue the values of our patriarchal past, we need to rethink all of those assumptions, test those psychological theories. And how will men ever develop an understanding of the "ethics of care" if they continue to be shielded or kept from that experience of caring for a dependent child which complements the experience we all have had of being cared for as dependent children? These experiences form the natural background for the development of moral maturity as Gilligan's women saw it.

Exploitation aside, why would women, once liberated, not be content to have their version of morality merely tolerated? Why should they not see themselves as voluntarily, for their own reasons, taking on *more* than the liberal rules demand, while having no quarrel with the content of those rules themselves, nor with their remaining the only ones that are expected to be generally obeyed? To see why, we need to move on to three more differences between the Kantian liberals (usually contractarians) and their critics. These concern the relative weight put on relationships between equals, on freedom of choice, and on the authority of intellect over emotions. It is a typical feature of the dominant moral theories and traditions since Kant, or perhaps since Hobbes, that relationships between equals or those who are deemed equal in some important sense have been the relations that morality is primarily concerned to regulate. Relationships between those who are clearly unequal in power, such as parents and children, earlier and later generations in relation to one another, states and citizens, doctors and patients, the well and the ill, large states and small states, have had to be shunted to the bottom of the agenda and then dealt with by some sort of "promotion" of the weaker, so that an appearance of virtual equality is achieved. Citizens collectively become equal to states, children are treated as adults-to-be, the ill and dying are treated as continuers of their earlier more potent selves, so that their "rights" can be seen as the rights of equals. This pretense of an equality that is in fact absent may often lead to desirable protection of the weaker, or more dependent. But it somewhat masks the question of what our moral relationships *are* to those who are our superiors or our inferiors in power. A more realistic acceptance that we begin as helpless children, that at almost every point of our lives we deal with both the more and the less helpless, that equality of power and interdependency, between two persons or groups, is rare and hard to recognize when it does occur, might lead us to a more direct approach to questions concerning the design of institutions structuring these relationships between unequals (families, schools, hospitals, armies) and of the morality of our dealings with the more and the less powerful. One reason why those who agree with the Gilligan version of what morality is about will not want to agree that the liberals' rules are a good minimal set, the only ones we need pressure *everyone* to obey, is that these rules do little to protect the young or the dying or the starving or any of the relatively powerless against neglect, or to ensure an education that will form persons to be *capable* of conforming to an ethics of care and responsibility. Put baldly, and in a way Gilligan certainly has not put it, the liberal morality, if unsupplemented, may *unfit* people to be anything other than what its justifying theories suppose them to be, ones who have no interest in each other's interests. Yet some must take an interest in the next generation's interests. Women's traditional work, of caring for the less powerful, especially for the young, is obviously socially vital. One cannot regard any version of morality that does not ensure that caring for children gets well done as an adequate "minimal morality," anymore than we could so regard one that left any concern for more distant future generations an optional extra. A moral theory, it can plausibly be claimed, cannot regard concern for new and future persons as an optional charity left for those with a taste for it. If the morality the theory endorses is to sustain itself, it must provide for its own continuers, not just take out a loan on a carefully encouraged maternal instinct or on the enthusiasm of a self-selected group of environmentalists who make it their business or hobby to be concerned with what we are doing to mother earth.

The recognition of the importance for all parties of relations between those who are and cannot but be unequal, and of their effect on personality formation and so on other relationships, goes along with a recognition of the plain fact that not all morally important relationships can or should be freely chosen. So far I have discussed three reasons women have to be not content to pursue their own values within the framework of the liberal morality. The first was its dubious record. The second was its inattention to relations of inequality or its pretense of equality. The third reason is its exaggeration of the scope of choice, or its inattention to unchosen relations. Showing up the partial myth of equality among actual members of a community, and the undesirability of trying to pretend that we are treating all of them as equals, tends to go along with an exposure of the companion myth that moral obligations arise from freely *chosen* associations between such equals. Vulnerable future generations do not choose their dependence on earlier generations. The unequal infant does not choose its place in a family or nation, nor is it treated as free to do as it likes until some association is freely entered into. Nor do parents always choose their parental role or freely assume their parental responsibilities, anymore than we choose our power to affect the conditions in which later generations will live. Gilligan's attention to the version of morality and moral maturity found in women, many of whom had faced a choice of whether or not to have an abortion, and who had at some point become mothers, is attention to the perceived inadequacy of the language of rights to help in such choices or to guide them in their parental role. It would not be much of an exaggeration to call the Gilligan "different voice" the voice of the potential parents. The emphasis on care goes with a recognition of the often unchosen nature of responsibilities of those who give care, both of children who care for their aged or infirm parents and of parents who care for the children they in fact have. Contract soon ceases to seem the paradigm source of moral obligation once we attend to parental responsibility, and justice as a virtue of social institutions will come to seem at best only first equal with the virtue, whatever its name, that ensures that the members of each new generation are made appropriately welcome and prepared for their adult lives.

This all constitutes a belated reminder to Western moral theorists of a fact they have always known, that, as Adam Ferguson and David Hume before him emphasized, we are born into families, and the first society we belong to, one that fits or misfits us for later ones, is the small society of parents (or some sort of child-attendants) and children, exhibiting as it may relationships both of near equality and of inequality in power. This simple reminder, with the fairly considerable implications it can have for the plausibility of contractarian moral theory, is at the same time a reminder of the role of human emotions as much as human reason and will in moral development as it actually comes about. The fourth feature of the Gilligan challenge to liberal orthodoxy is a challenge to its typical *rationalism*, or intellectualism, to its assumption that we need not worry what passions persons have, as long as their rational wills can control them. This Kantian picture of a controlling reason dictating to possibly unruly passions also tends to seem less useful when we are led to consider what sort of person we need to fill the role of parent or, indeed, want in any close relationship. It might be important for father figures to have rational control over their violent urges to beat to death the children whose screams enrage them, but more than control of such nasty passions seems needed in the mother or primary parent, or parent-substitute, according to most psychological theories. Primary parents need to love their children, not just to control their irritation. So the emphasis in Kantian theories on rational control of emotions, rather than on cultivating desirable forms of emotion, is challenged by Gilligan, along with her challenge to the assumption of the centrality of autonomy, or relations between equals, and of freely chosen relations.

The same set of challenges to "orthodox" liberal moral theory has come not just from Gilligan and other women, who are reminding other moral theorists of the role of the family as a social institution and as an influence on the other relationships people want to sustain or are capable of sustaining, but also, as I noted at the start, from an otherwise fairly diverse group of men, ranging from those influenced by both Hegelian and Christian traditions (MacIntyre) to all varieties of other backgrounds. From this group I want to draw attention to the work of one philosopher in particular, Laurence Thomas, the author of a fairly remarkable article[17] in which he finds sexism to be a more intractable social evil than racism. In a series of articles and a book,[18] Thomas makes a strong case for the importance of supplementing a concern for justice and respect for rights with an emphasis on equally needed virtues, and on virtues seen as appropriate *emotional* as well as rational capacities. Like Gilligan (and unlike MacIntyre) Thomas gives a lot of attention to the childhood beginnings of moral and social capacities, to the role of parental love in making that possible, and to the emotional as well as the cognitive development we have reason to think both possible and desirable in human persons.

It is clear, I think, that the best moral theory has to be a cooperative product of women and men, has to harmonize justice and care. The morality it theorizes about is after all for all persons, for men and for women, and will need their combined insights. As Gilligan said (*D.V.*, p. 174), what we need now is a "marriage" of the old male and the newly articulated female insights. If she is right about the special moral aptitudes of women, then it will most likely be the women who propose the marriage, since they are the ones with the more natural empathy, with the better diplomatic skills, the ones more likely to shoulder responsibility and take moral initiative, and the ones who find it easiest to empathize and care about how the other party feels. Then, once there is this union of male and female moral wisdom, we maybe can teach each other the moral skills each gender currently lacks, so that the gender difference in moral outlook that Gilligan found will slowly become less marked.

Notes

1 John Rawls, *A Theory of Justice* (Cambridge, Mass.: Belknap Press of Harvard University Press, 1971).

2 Alasdair MacIntyre, *After Virtue* (Notre Dame, Ind.: Notre Dame University Press, 1980).

3 Michael Stocker, "The Schizophrenia of Modern Ethical Theories," *Journal of Philosophy*, 73 (1976): 453–66; and "Agent and Other: Against Ethical Universalism," *Australasian Journal of Philosophy*, 54 (December 1976): 206–20.

4 Lawrence Blum, *Friendship, Altruism, and Morality* (London: Routledge & Kegan Paul, 1980).

5 Michael Slote, *Goods and Virtues* (Oxford: Clarendon Press, 1983).

6 Laurence Thomas, "Love and Morality," in *Sociobiology and Epistemology*, ed. James Fetzer (Dordrecht and Boston: D. Reidel, 1985); "Justice, Happiness, and Self-Knowledge," *Canadian Journal of Philosophy*, 16 (March 1986): 63–82; "Beliefs and the Motivation to Be Just," *American Philosophical Quarterly*, 22 (1985): 347–52; and *Living Morally: A Psychology of Moral Character* (Philadelphia, Penna.: Temple University Press, 1989).

7 Claudia Card, "On Mercy," *Philosophical Review*, 81 (1972): 182–207; and *Choices and Values* (New York: Columbia University Press, 1994), and *Character and Moral Luck* (Philadelphia, Penna.: Temple University Press, expected 1995).

8 Alison Jaggar, *Feminist Politics and Human Nature* (London: Rowman & Allenheld, 1983).

9 Susan Wolf, "Moral Saints," *Journal of Philosophy*, 79 (August 1982): 419–39.

10 Carol Gilligan, *In a Different Voice: Psychological Theory and Women's Development* (Cambridge, Mass.: Harvard University Press, 1982). Hereafter cited as ***D.V.*** For a helpful survey article, see Owen Flanagan and Kathryn Jackson, "Justice, Care, and Gender: The Kohlberg-Gilligan Debate Revisited," *Ethics*, 97 (April 1987): 622–37.

11 Nancy Chodorow, *The Reproduction of Mothering* (Berkeley, Calif.: University of California Press, 1978).

12 Carol Gilligan, "The Conquistador and the Dark Continent: Reflections on the Psychology of Love," *Daedalus*, 113 (Summer 1984): 75–95; and "The Origins of Morality in Early Childhood Relationships," in *Mapping the Moral Domain*, ed. C. Gilligan, J. Ward, and J. Taylor (Cambridge, Mass.: Harvard University Press, 1988), pp. 111–37.

13 Lawrence Kohlberg, *Essays in Moral Development*, 2 vols (New York: Harper & Row, 1981, 1984).

14 Bernard Williams, *Ethics and the Limits of Philosophy* (New York: Cambridge University Press, 1985).

15 Philippa Foot, *Virtues and Vices* (Berkeley, Calif.: University of California Press, 1978).

16 Immanuel Kant, *The Metaphysics of Morals*, trans. Mary Gregor (New York: Cambridge University Press, 1991), sec. 46.

17 Laurence Thomas, "Sexism and Racism: Some Conceptual Differences," *Ethics*, 90 (1980): 239–50; reprinted in *Sexist Language: A Modern Philosophical Analysis*, ed. Mary Vetterling-Braggin (Totowa, NJ: Littlefield Adams, 1981).

18 See articles listed in note 6.

19

An Ethic of Care

Joan Tronto

People spend a large part of their lives giving and receiving care. If moral philosophy concerns the good in human life, then we might expect that care would play an important role in moral theory. Yet, except for some feminist thinkers, few moral philosophers have considered questions of care.[1] In this chapter I consider the moral implications of giving care a more central place in human life.

While the "ethic of care" has become part of the vocabulary of contemporary feminism, precisely what writers mean by the term "ethic of care" remains unclear. In many instances, writers who describe an ethic of care do little more than invoke the old forms of "women's morality." This association dooms an ethic of care to dismissal as a serious ethical idea. If care is tied to the "naturalness" of women's caring, then it is either instinctive, or deeply social or cultural behavior, and therefore not part of the realm of moral choice.

There are some points of agreement between my version of the ethic of care and other formulations of it. What distinguishes my approach to care is my insistence that we cannot understand an ethic of care until we place such an ethic in its full moral and political context. In this chapter I give an account of these contexts and of what will be required to change them and to accord care and its ethic a central place in our society. After we have recognized the complexities of care as a practice, and how completely care is implicated in structures of power in society, it will become clear that a meta-ethical position that starts from the standpoint of "the moral point of view" is incapable of making the kinds of judgments necessary for care.

The Practice of the Ethic of Care

An initial statement

To be a morally good person requires, among other things, that a person strives to meet the demands of caring that present themselves in his or her life. For a society to be judged as a morally admirable society, it must, among other things, adequately provide for care of its members and its territory.[2]

In claiming that to care adequately is a quality of the morally good person or society, I am not asserting that a person or society that *only* provided for care would then be automatically adjudged moral. This injunction to care is not meant to serve as a total account of morality. It is not meant to overthrow such moral precepts as do not lie, do not break promises, avoid harm to others. Keeping to all of

Joan Tronto, "An Ethic of Care," pp. 125–37, 141–52, and 208–13 (notes) from *Moral Boundaries*. New York: Routledge, 1993. Reproduced by permission of Routledge/Taylor & Francis Books, Inc. and the author.

those other moral precepts, though, still leaves an account of morality incomplete because it ignores the central role of caring in human life.

This initial statement of the ethic seems vague. In the first place, the language of striving suggests that the moral aspect of care does not necessarily turn upon the success or failure of caring. In the second place, the language "as it presents itself" seems to permit actors to escape from their failures to acknowledge needs for care. These qualities spring from the fact that the ethic of care is a practice, rather than a set of rules or principles. As a result, care's moral qualities will take a more ambiguous form than a list of carefully designed moral precepts.

The practice of an ethic of care is complex. It requires some specific moral qualities. It poses a different range of moral dilemmas than does current moral thinking. It involves both particular acts of caring and a general "habit of mind" to care that should inform all aspects of a practitioner's moral life. I elaborate on these aspects of care in the following sections.

Elements of an ethic of care

The four elements of care that Berenice Fisher and I identified provide a good starting point to describe some elements of an ethic of care. The four elements of care are: caring about, noticing the need to care in the first place; taking care of, assuming responsibility for care; care-giving, the actual work of care that needs to be done; and care-receiving, the response of that which is cared for to the care. From these four elements of care arise four ethical elements of care: attentiveness, responsibility, competence, and responsiveness.

Attentiveness. Since care requires the recognition of a need and that there is a need that be cared about, the first moral aspect of caring is attentiveness. If we are not attentive to the needs of others, then we cannot possibly address those needs. By this standard, the ethic of care would treat ignoring others – ignorance – as a form of moral evil. We have an unparalleled capacity to know about others in complex modern societies. Yet the temptations to ignore others, to shut others out, and to focus our concerns solely upon ourselves, seem almost irresistible. Attentiveness, simply recognizing the needs of those around us, is a difficult task, and indeed, a moral achievement.

That the absence of attentiveness is a moral failing has been remarked by a number of writers, especially those who have looked at the question of the atrocities committed during World War II. The notion of attention as a moral idea is perhaps most closely associated with the philosopher Simone Weil, who believed that the capacity for attention was crucial for any genuinely human interaction. Weil believed that the development of attention needed to become the focus of school studies, that it formed the basis for true relationships among people, and that it formed the opening to truth. That attention is, like care itself, other directed, is made clear in this passage:

> Attention consists in suspending thought, leaving it available, empty and ready to be entered by its object . . . thought must be empty, waiting, seeking nothing, but ready to receive in its naked truth the object that is about to penetrate it.[3]

Weil's account of attention obviously overstates the possibility of emptying the mind; thought is shaped after all, not in the least by language.[4] Nevertheless, the ideal that Weil described in this passage is useful in portraying the passivity – the absence of will – that is necessary for the first stage of care. One needs, in a sense, to suspend one's own goals, ambitions, plans of life, and concerns, in order to recognize and to be attentive to others.

The failure to be attentive is perhaps most chillingly described in Arendt's account of the "banality of evil" which she found personified in Adolf Eichmann.[5] Eichmann was unable to focus on anything except his own career and interests; he was simply inattentive and unable to grasp the consequences of what he did except in the most self-centered ways. Critics have accused Arendt of failing to note the monstrous qualities of the actions of Nazis. While this criticism is valid on one level, on another level Arendt has provided an important perspective on evil that we otherwise miss: evil can arise out of ignorance, either willful or established habits of ignorance. If people in the first world fail to notice everyday that the activities spurred by a global capitalist system result in the starvation of thousands, or in sexual slavery in Thailand,[6] are they inattentive? Is this a moral failing? I suggest that, starting from the standpoint of an ethic of care where noticing needs is the first task of humans, this ignorance is a moral failing.

Some dimensions of inattentiveness may be quickly sketched: it is probably more morally reprehensible to ignore willfully that which is close to one's own actions than to fail to be aware of a distant consequence of one's actions. When a boss orders all of the employees to arrive a half hour earlier tomorrow, knowing that some of the women who work for him have children who require care, we might suggest such inattentiveness is worse than if this same individual does not understand the moral dimensions of cutting medicaid benefits to working single parents, to an inattentiveness that is more remote. But when is ignorance simply ignorance, and when is it inattentiveness? If I do not know that rain forest destruction happens in order to provide the world with more beef, am I ignorant or inattentive? Suppose that ignorance is built into social structures? Some would argue that one of the consequences of racism, for example, is that Whites do not know, and do not think that they need to know, anything about the lives of Blacks, except for the self-serving myths that they have told themselves.[7]

The problem of attentiveness is not a new problem; moral philosophers have recognized it and alluded to its importance throughout Western history. In Book I of *The Republic*, Socrates and his cohorts briefly mention that unless one is willing to listen, the philosopher can have no effect.[8] Hume's example of the greater importance we would place on a broken mirror than someone else's burned down house also identifies someone who cannot suspend her or his own concerns and be attentive to the plight of others.[9] As many social theorists have noted, the increasing division of labor of modern societies both increases our material and impersonal interdependence upon others and reduces our personal dependence on particular others. Virtually all human needs can now be met through the market; if we only have enough money there is no need to depend upon others in any ongoing relationships. (We leave aside for the moment the question of whether such provisions are adequate.) The result of our changing ways of meeting our caring needs is a rise of insensitivity to others.

[...]

That caring has been so obscured in our current accounts of society helps to explain how the process of inattentiveness operates. But to increase attentiveness will require that caring become more prominent in social life. Further, in order for caring to become a more prominent part of social life, certain types of moral problems that are currently obscured by their peripheral location in contemporary theory will be made central. That "others" matter is the most difficult moral quality to establish in practice.

Yet the matter is still more complicated. In order to be able to recognize the needs of others, one must first be attentive to one's own needs for care. After all, in order to recognize that others have needs that are not being met, one needs to be in a position to recognize others; or in the spirit of Marx's argument in *The German Ideology*, it would mean that one's own needs have been sufficiently met so that one is able to glance around and notice others at all. Feminists have long recognized the problem of overidentifying with others, engaging in self-sacrifice, and then feeling angry and cheated by these forms of self-deprivation.[10] Psychologist Thomas Kitwood called this the need for free space psychologically,[11] and we can posit the need for "free space" provided by adequate care in order to devise an adequate ability to be attentive to others.

Responsibility. The second dimension of care, taking care of, makes responsibility into a central moral category. I do not claim that other theories of morality do not take questions of responsibility seriously, but responsibility is both central and problematic in an ethic of care; responsibility is among the handful of concepts that require constant evaluation. In this regard, the care approach is quite different from much contemporary political theory, which does not so emphasize responsibility.

The difficulty of situating the notion of "responsibility" in much of contemporary political theory is a good illustration of the way in which contextual moral theories differ from much contemporary moral theory. Often our responsibilities are conceived formally as the need to conform to obligations. Political theorists have devoted much attention to the question of how obligations arise, and usually our strongest obligations arise out of promises that we have made.[12]

Compared to obligation, responsibility has both a different connotation and a different context. It seems at first to be a more sociological or anthropological, rather than a political or philosophical, concept. Responsibility is a term that is embedded in a set of implicit cultural practices, rather than in a set of formal rules or series of promises. Nevertheless, it is certainly possible for questions of responsibility to become political, in that they can become matters of public debate. For example, we can debate what responsibilities do members of society, or the federal government in the United States, have in helping to rebuild violence-torn South Central Los Angeles? This is a different question from the question, what obligation do members of society owe to rebuilding Los Angeles? In the question of obligation, we might look for formal bonds, previously stated duties, formal agreements. We may conclude that we owe nothing. Concerning responsibility, we might look beyond formal or legal ties to try to understand: what role federal, state, and local politics played in creating the conditions for the disturbance; whether lack of jobs creates responsibilities for their consequences; and so forth. The question of responsibility to care is more ambiguous.

Ultimately, responsibility to care might rest on a number of factors; something we did or did not do has contributed to the needs for care, and so we must care. For example, if we are the parents of children, having become parents entails the responsibility of caring for these particular children. As a member of a family, we might feel our responsibility to elder relatives. At the other end of the spectrum, we might assume responsibility because we recognize a need for caring, and there is no other way that the need will be met except by our meeting it. In this way, some Europeans during World War II felt that simply by being human they owed a responsibility to try to rescue Jews and others from Nazis.[13]

But between these extremes of being responsible for everyone in every way, and thinking of responsibility as rooted in biology, there is a wide range of other possible assumptions of responsibility that are rooted in political motivations, cultural practices, and individual psychology. The notion of being overly responsible for others, especially for those in intimate relationships, has been widely discussed in recent years. "Responsibility" has different meanings depending upon one's perceived gender roles, and issues that arise out of class, family status, and culture, including cultural differences based on racial groupings.[14] In arguing for the inclusion of care as a political and philosophical notion, I am suggesting that we are better served by focusing on a flexible notion of responsibility than we are by continuing to use obligation as the basis for understanding what people should do for each other.

Competence. The third phase of caring gives rise to the importance of competence in care-giving as a moral notion. To include competence as a part of the moral quality of care, is obviously to align this approach with moral consequentialism. Intending to provide care, even accepting responsibility for it, but then failing to provide good care, means that in the end the need for care is not met. Sometimes care will be inadequate because the resources available to provide for care are inadequate. But short of such resource problems, how could it not be necessary that the caring work be competently performed in order to demonstrate that one cares?

An important reason for including competence as a moral dimension of care is to avoid the bad faith of those who would "take care of" a problem without being willing to do any form of care-giving. But clearly, making certain that the caring work is done competently must be a moral aspect of care if the adequacy of the care given is to be a measure of the success of care.

Many moral philosophers are made quite uncomfortable by this type of position. Consider an example: Imagine a teacher in an inadequately funded school system who is ordered to teach mathematics even though he does not know mathematics. Isn't there something wrong with morally condemning a teacher who does his best, since the fault is not of his own making, but of the inadequacy of resources?

This example explains why competence should be included in our sense of moral worthiness from a care perspective. If the teacher is absolved from responsibility because he is willing to try to do something beyond his competence (or perhaps he is willing to keep the students under control during the part of the day when they might otherwise learn math), then notice that good care becomes impossible. Those who have assigned the incompetent teacher can say that they have "taken care of" the problem, without actually following through to make certain that care, educating students about mathematics, is actually occurring. Especially in large bureaucracies, this type of "taking care of," with no concern about outcome or end result, seems pervasive.[15]

To look at the question of the competence of care-giving is a different way to look at another question central to ethics in recent years, the question of professional ethics. For the most part we do not associate the question of competence with the question of professional ethics. Nevertheless, the care perspective suggests a more integrative approach to questions of ethics in general and in professions as well. Professional ethics should be about more than teaching professionals that it is wrong to lie, to cheat, and to steal. The guiding thought that ethical questions occur in a context should centrally inform professional ethics. From a perspective of care, we would not permit individuals to escape from responsibility for their incompetence by claiming to adhere to a code of professional ethics.

Responsiveness. The fourth moral moment that arises out of caring is the responsiveness of the care-receiver to the care. Responsiveness signals an important moral problem within care: by its nature, care is concerned with conditions of vulnerability and inequality.

Caring is by its very nature a challenge to the notion that individuals are entirely autonomous and self-supporting. To be in a situation where one needs care is to be in a position of some vulnerability. What is interesting is that we do not always think about caring in this sense. An office worker does not feel vulnerable to the janitor who takes away the garbage and cleans the space in an office every day. But if those services stopped, the office worker's vulnerability would be exposed. In other forms of caring, the levels and types of vulnerabilities are perhaps more obvious. Children are extremely vulnerable, as are the old and infirm who rely on others to help them to meet their basic needs.

Robert Goodin's argument for "protecting the vulnerable"[16] reflects an awareness on the part of society of the need to protect the vulnerable. Because he starts from standard accounts of moral theory that assume the end of an autonomous moral actor, Goodin is unable to deal adequately with the dangers faced by the vulnerable at the hands of their care givers and other champions, who may come to assume that they can define the needs of the vulnerable.[17]

Vulnerability has serious moral consequences. Vulnerability belies the myth that we are always autonomous, and potentially equal, citizens. To assume equality among humans leaves out and ignores important dimensions of human existence. Throughout our lives, all of us go through varying degrees of dependence and independence, of autonomy and vulnerability. A political order that presumes only independence and autonomy as the nature of human life thereby misses a great deal of human experience, and must somehow hide this point elsewhere. For example, such an order must rigidly separate public and private life.

But one reason to presume that we are all independent and autonomous is to avoid the difficult questions that arise when we recognize that not all humans are equal. Inequality gives rise to unequal relationships of authority, and to domination and subordination. No society exists without such relationships, but neither can democratic order thrive when such inequalities exist.

The moral precept of responsiveness requires that we remain alert to the possibilities for abuse that arise with vulnerability. Indeed, as Patricia Benner suggests, the development of a capacity for responsiveness is an important moral quality in caring.[18] It also suggests the need to keep a balance between the needs of care-givers and care-receivers.

Responsiveness is not the same as reciprocity, but the parallel notion raises some interesting dimensions of responsiveness. Recall, for example, the centrality of the notion of reciprocity for Kohlberg's theory of moral development. Kohlberg believed that without reciprocity, moral growth could not occur. Responsiveness suggests a different way to understand the needs of others rather than to put our selves into their position. Instead, it suggests that we consider the other's position as that other expresses it. Thus, one is engaged from the standpoint of the other, but not simply by presuming that the other is exactly like the self. From such a perspective, we may well imagine that questions of otherness would be more adequately addressed than they are in current moral frameworks that presume that people are interchangeable.

Adequate responsiveness requires attentiveness, which again shows the way in which these moral elements of care are intertwined. We have often discovered that the explication of one of the dimensions of the ethical elements of care has involved other elements of care. As with our description of the caring process, we will now observe that the pieces of an ethic of care cannot be separated but must be considered as part of an integrated whole.

The integrity of care. Good care requires that the four phases of the care process must fit together into a whole. Similarly, to act properly in accordance with an ethic of care requires that the four moral elements of care, attentiveness, responsibility, competence, and responsiveness, be integrated into an appropriate whole. Such an integration of these parts of caring into a moral whole is not simple. Care involves conflict; to resolve this conflict will require more than an injunction to be attentive, responsible, competent, and responsive.

Care as a practice involves more than simply good intentions. It requires a deep and thoughtful knowledge of the situation, and of all of the actors' situations, needs and competencies. To use the care ethic requires a knowledge of the context of the care process. Those who engage in a care process must make judgments: judgments about needs, conflicting needs, strategies for achieving ends, the responsiveness of care-receivers, and so forth.

Care rests upon judgments that extend far beyond personal awareness. Despite the fact that many writers about care concern themselves with relationships of care that are now considered personal or private,[19] the kinds of judgments that I have described require an assessment of needs in a social and political, as well as a personal, context.

Moral Dilemmas in the Practice of Care

The moral question an ethic of care takes as central is not – What, if anything, do I (we) owe to others? but rather – How can I (we) best meet my (our) caring responsibilities? To meet one's caring responsibilities has both universal and particular components. On the one hand, it requires a determination of what caring responsibilities are, in general. On the other hand, it requires a focus upon the particular kinds of responsibilities and burdens that we might assume because of who, and where, we are situated. There are then both universal and particular moral issues that arise from this question. I have described some of the dilemmas about caring that arise along the way in this account of some elements of caring. In this section I delve more deeply into these problems. In general, caring will always create moral dilemmas because the needs for care are infinite. Beyond this dilemma, though, caring also poses moral problems that arise out of the particular location in which people find themselves in various processes of care. [...]

Particularity and moral dilemmas of care

The problems of evaluating proper levels of care, of anger and gratitude, and of providing smothering care as opposed to care that leads to autonomy, is intrinsic to the nature of care. In this section I detail some of these problems.

Some people make greater sacrifices of themselves than do other people; some will even sacrifice too much. Part of this moral problem is exacerbated by the fact that those who are most likely to be too self-sacrificing are likely to be the relatively powerless in society.[20]

Often, because people who care become enmeshed in the caring process, the great moral task for them is not to become involved with others (the problem of moral motivation, a fundamental problem in contemporary moral theory), but to be able to stand back from ongoing processes of care and ask, "What is going on here?" It requires honesty, and a non-idealized knowledge of selves and of others. Further it requires a constant ongoing assessment of how adequately care is being provided.

On the other hand, people who are needy, and who receive care, also need to recognize the structural difficulty of their situation. In contemporary American society, where a great emphasis is placed on autonomous individual life, we perceive neediness as being a burden on those who must help us meet our needs. We often resent needing the help of others, and translate that need into a resentment towards those who are in a position to help. Often such individuals will resent mightily "sacrifices" that are made on their behalf. This point is true of both individual and group forms of care.[21] We can resent individuals and social institutions that provide for our needs.

As eighteenth century thinkers recognized these moral problems of distance and inequality they abandoned theories of moral sentiments which started from daily moral life and moved towards moral theories that used universalistic rationality as the basis for moral judgments. In my advocacy of an ethic of care, I do not propose that we should return to the eighteenth century model of moral sentiments. Yet this ethic of care bears a family resemblance to those eighteenth century theories of moral sentiments, so perhaps it should not surprise us that the same issues that posed central moral dilemmas for those theories continue to be a source of trouble within an ethic of care.

Parochialism. In the way that I have described care, it necessarily involves an engagement with the concrete, the local, the particular. Indeed, I have suggested that simply to be concerned with care on an abstract and broad level, without paying attention to the actual practices of care-giving and care-receiving, is to misunderstand the nature of care. But a serious consequence of this commitment to the particular appears. How are we to guarantee that people, who are enmeshed in their daily rounds of care-giving and care-receiving, will be able to disengage themselves from their own local concerns and to address broader needs and concerns for care? If mothers care for their own children, why should they not take the needs of their own children more seriously than the needs of distant children? Why should

Americans worry about the distribution of food on a global level?[22]

The problem of partiality has been much discussed by contemporary moral theorists who operate within current moral theory paradigms. In general, however, their concern is to admit that some forms of partiality are compatible with a more general commitment to universalism. What this approach does less well, though, is to explain how the correct universal principles translate into individuals noticing how their moral imperatives might actually require them to change their daily lives.

Sublimated needs and the rage of care givers. The opposite problem may also arise; the process of care may leave too little distance between care-givers and care-receivers. One of the likely effects of any caring process is that the care-givers will have to struggle to separate their own needs from the needs of the ones who they care for. Especially if resources are insufficient, most care-givers will become enraged. Care-givers often must subordinate their own caring needs to those of the person, thing, or group to which they are providing care; the nurse may not have had a lunch break, but she still needs to take care of this patient. Further, care-givers need to respect the resistances that they are likely to encounter from care-receivers, who may resent their dependence upon another. As a result, care-givers are often enraged about their own unmet needs. If they are unable to recognize this rage, care givers are likely to vent their anger on those for whom they care.[23] Perhaps some rage is appropriate, but when it subverts the process of care itself, then it poses a serious moral problem. As I suggested in the last chapter, this rage not only subverts care, it is responsible for the contempt felt toward others who are care-receivers.

There is another side to the rage of care-givers, and that is what else they might do to try to change their circumstances besides vent their rage against the objects of their care. The most effective of the "powers of the weak" is to withhold. If, in a society that relied heavily upon domestic service, all of the servants ceased to work, the society would suffer immediately. But to go on strike is a relatively difficult task for care givers, because it requires that, in order to assert their power, they must not give care. In so doing, they undermine their own legitimacy and standing as care-givers. The more critical the presumed need for care, the more serious the contradiction between the care-giver's role and the care-giver's refusal to provide care. Consider, as an example, how nurses' strikes are viewed with a kind of horror. The care-givers face a serious problem, especially if they have limited social power in other forms, in trying to assert their own needs.

Because rational moral theories do not take notice of rage, it is easy to show that a care perspective, because it can take such a moral problem seriously, is more likely to be able to solve these types of problems.

Detached care and otherness. Another problem is that those who receive more detached care may come to be seen as "others." In a highly complex society, it is impossible that we will always be able to provide direct care to all of those to whom we might feel some responsibility. Hence, we often "take care of" many more things and people than to which we directly give care. By paying taxes, I help to take care of the environment, the homeless, people with AIDS. It would be impossible to live in a complex society where a fair amount of the care that we extended to others was not provided in this indirect manner. The consequence of such care, though, is that it is easy to become deluded about the nature of the care that is being provided, and about how and who we are helping. Thus, people with AIDS can, in the views of some, become the undeserving recipients of care, since they brought the virus upon themselves. Rather than eliminating otherness' being in a distant caring relationship can actually heighten a sense of the otherness of those for whom we must indirectly care.

The rational moral theory provides, through the mechanism of reciprocity, a seeming solution to this problem that turns out not to be a solution at all. It would seem that by putting oneself in the other's situation, this distance can be overcome. But the problem is that there is no way to guarantee that, in taking the place of the other as if in a game of "musical moral chairs," the moral actor will recognize all of the relevant dimensions of the other's situation. The result is more likely to be an imposition of an incomplete understanding on the situation than a morally sensitive response.[24]

Our best solution to understanding how these problems can be resolved, is to return to an Aristotelian insight. Aristotle argued that virtue lies in a mean that depends upon context.[25] What a care ethic requires from each individual or group in a caring process varies depending upon who are the involved people, groups, or objects. Aristotle's ideas further suggest this standard: since the task of care is to maintain, continue, and repair the world so that we can live in it as well as possible, we should do what will best achieve this end.

Care and equality

Care arises out of the fact that not all humans or others or objects in the world are equally able, at all times, to take care of themselves. Although much contemporary moral theory rests upon the convenient fiction of human equality, the fact of inequality in relations of care makes this assumption problematic. If we wish to maintain some commitment to democratic values, then we need to explain how equality can emerge out of inequality.

Otherness. I suggested in the last chapter that our desire not to be unequal and dependent results in a treatment of those who need care as inherently different and unequal.[26] The result is that those who receive care are often transformed into the "other," and identified by whatever marks them as needing care: their economic plight, their seeming physical disability, and so forth. The question of how others might be treated without such alienation is a serious problem, and it remains a serious problem from the standpoint of a theory of care.

Paternalism. As we have previously observed, care is not an activity that occurs between equal and autonomous actors or objects, but between those who have needs and those who can provide for those needs. We can well imagine that those who are care-givers, as well as those who have decided to take care of a particular need, will come to accept their own account of what is necessary to meet the caring need as definitive. In this way, care-receivers are ignored, as the tension between competence and met needs works out in favor of experts, of those with resources to meet caring needs, and so forth. By its very nature, care is rarely an activity engaged in by equals; the fact that A needs care and that B provides it, means that A is in B's power. A and B are not in this situation equals. Nor is A at this moment, needing B's assistance, autonomous. There is always implicit in care the danger that those who receive care will lose their autonomy and their sense of independence. Similarly, the question of whether the temporary absence of equality and autonomy translate into a permanent state of dependency on the one hand and a condition of privilege on the other, or of denying some the ability to make decisions for themselves, is a moral question that is always implicit in the provision of care.

Privileged irresponsibility. We have already noted that, at present, the caring needs of some are met more completely than the caring needs of others, and that this pattern follows the distribution of power in society. What is to keep the relatively powerful from continuing to define their needs as the most important, and to dismiss the concerns of those who are less well off? Indeed, this is precisely the way that privilege functions, because there is no necessary reason why the privileged will recognize that more of their needs are being met than the needs of others. Further, care's parochialism, its concern with the local, means that there will be no reason why the privileged need to look beyond how their own caring needs are met in order to believe that they are caring.[27] Here, parochialism reveals itself to be more than simply an inconvenience or prejudice, but a way to excuse the inattention of the privileged.

In the context of the American ideology of individualism, universal morality is no automatic solution to these problems of indifference, inattention, and caring more about one's own situation. Moral theories are not generally designed to notice inequalities of power.[28] Where the notion, "I made it on my own, you should make it on your own," appears to have the formal quality of a morally correct and universalizable judgment, it can also serve to disguise the inequality of resources, powers, and privileges that have made it possible for some to "make it" while others have not.

These problems are difficult ones to solve. One way to think about them is to acknowledge that, throughout their lives, all people need care; so the inequality that emerges when some are care-givers and others are care-receivers should not be so morally significant. Furthermore, despite the intractability of the problems of otherness, privilege, and paternalism, I suggest that a moral theory that can recognize and identify these issues is preferable to a moral theory that, because it presumes that all people are equal, is unable even to recognize them.

Expanding our Moral Terrain

If care is not an unproblematic moral theory, that does not distinguish it from all other moral theories. All moral theories are better able to address some moral questions than others. Different questions will seem more pressing at some times and in some circumstances than at other times. The ability to recognize widespread starvation in a distant part of the globe, for example, only occurs in fairly recent times, and raises the moral question of what to do to alleviate it.[29] An argument that we owe nothing to future generations[30] would make no sense in a culture that believed ancestors are present among us, and that former and future generations require our continuing respect.

One of the framing aspects of the existing debate about an ethic of care is the starting point that an ethic of care, because it is a moral practice, relies upon a different metaethical theory, and is therefore incompatible with universalistic moral reasoning.[31] Thus, care, seemingly based on some type of Aristotelian metaethic, and justice, based on a deontological or utilitarian metaethic, seem to be diametrically opposed, and any attempts to make the two compatible are viewed as philosophically unsophisticated.

As long as the discussion between care and justice occupies this terrain it is not fruitful. Such a discussion prevents us from paying attention to the substantive concerns raised by an ethic of care while we spend time analyzing the appropriateness of epistemological positions. Often philosophers start and stop at the metaethical level in considering disputes such as the value of care and justice.[32] Not only is this seeming dispute between justice and care not best resolved at this level, it cannot be resolved at this level at all.

On the one hand, the argument that justice reasoning rests upon a universalistic metaethical position seems to decide the question for those who believe that "the moral point of view" demands the application of universalizable rules.[33] From this standpoint, care will always be a type of moral fill-in.

The strongest argument for universalistic moral theory, from the standpoints of its advocates, is that it cannot be undermined by political or cultural fortune. It stands above, or apart from, the vicissitudes of political life and of daily (perhaps corrupt) moral practice.[34] Thus, universalistic morality, unlike more pragmatic theories of morality, maintains a strict boundary between politics and morality. It maintains that our moral principles can be established and defended regardless of context. That their application requires a sensitivity to context does not change their pristine truth. To such moral thinkers, if those in the world do not act morally, so much the worse for them, but it should not be the task of philosophy to change this situation.

On the other hand, the notion that a universalistic approach to morality could address all conceivable moral questions has been under attack for a long time by moral philosophers. Several moral philosophers have noted that the commitment to universal morality seems to be waning.[35] As Betty Sichel summarizes this discussion, it is now clear that the hegemony of Neo-Kantian ethics has been challenged by moral theories that rely upon compassion, care, the emotions, and to some extent, communication.[36] Since mid-century, Stuart Hampshire has insisted that Kant had asked the wrong moral questions,[37] and the number of philosophers who would now say that they subscribe to a non-Kantian meta-ethic seems large indeed; they include Thomists,[38] eudaemonists,[39] pragmatists,[40] those who would call themselves advocates of character or virtue ethics,[41] and other assorted Aristotelians.[42] This discussion has shaped a lively philosophical debate about partiality and impartiality, resulting in a more nuanced discussion of relativism.[43] Finally, the post-structuralist, post-modern challenge to any form of metaethical argument does not claim to substitute an alternative metaethic, but to deny the very possibility of such an approach to ethics.

The reason this discussion continues to prove so unsatisfying and unresolved is because the participants within the discussion presume, for the most part,[44] that the question of metaethical adequacy is a question that can be resolved within the framework of philosophical discussion itself.[45] After all, the kind of metaethical theory that we find convincing reveals a great deal about who we are, what moral problems we think are significant, and how we view the world. I have illustrated this point earlier by noting that the disfavor with which late eighteenth century thinkers viewed Scottish conventional morality grew out of changed circumstances in which that account of moral life was no longer so relevant. As Habermas put it, "Moral universalism is a historical result."[46]

It is ironic that the challenge to Western moral theory seems to arise at a time when the question of "otherness" has become a central moral problem. The challenge that "the rights of man" posed to its adherents, to accept all others as equal, was a central piece of Western moral belief.[47] The problem has not been in the theory, but in the fact that the theory allowed exceptions around many forms of difference. As these exceptions seem no longer legitimate, the theory that allowed these exceptions has also seemed less legitimate.

This change in our perception of the validity of moral theories derived from rational foundations has been accompanied by a change in historical circumstance and in the kinds of moral questions that we are therefore likely to find salient. Political changes also point to the need for us to redraw moral boundaries. [. . .]

The separation of public and private life that might have served as an ideological description of life in the nineteenth century can no longer be sustained.[48] The separation of household and economic life no longer describes reality, and much of the household activity that was previously "private," such as caring for small children, tending the ill, preparing meals and clothing, etc., have now been absorbed into social and market spheres. With these changed circumstances, the political and moral underpinnings that accompanied the gendered division of labor have also been eroded. The rise of universal education and some opportunity for class mobility, combined with recognitions that religious, racial, and gendered preferences are wrong, have made a mixed and heterogeneous society into a moral norm.[49]

This emerging moral order does not require that we abandon previous moral commitments, for example, to universalizablity, or to a moral point of view that rejects special pleading to serve one's interests. What it also requires, though, is that we recognize that humans are not only autonomous and equal, but that they are also beings who require care. [. . .]

Notes

1 Martin Heidegger is among the exceptions. Lawrence A. Blum has explored questions related to care in *Friendship, Altruism and Morality* (London: Routledge & Kegan Paul, 1980).
Although I shall discuss my notions of care vis a vis other writers who have addressed care, I will not try to describe the place of the care ethic in relation to other questions in feminist ethics. A large and good literature has emerged on this topic; I shall mention a few of these works here: Clandia Card, ed., *Feminist Ethics* (Lawrence, KS: University of Kansas Press, 1990); Cole and Coultrap-McQuin, eds, *Explorations in Feminist Ethics* (Bloomington: Indiana University Press, 1992); Porter, *Women and Moral Identity*; Larrabee, ed., *An Ethic of Care*. See also Pollitt, "Are Women Morally Superior to Men?" *The Nation* (Dec. 28, 1992).

2 Readers on the lookout for an inconsistency in my argument may note that this statement has the ring of a universalistic moral principle, so that my argument that the ethic of care is a different type of moral theory must therefore be wrong. Even if this statement were acceptable as a moral principle, though, that point does not make my position inconsistent. It means that the dichotomy between universalistic moral theory and moral theories that are more sensitive to context is not an absolute one. It has been a hallmark of feminist thinking throughout the second wave of feminism to distrust rigid dichotomies of thought; here is another one that we have inherited that does not serve our intellectual purposes well. I return to this issue at the end of this chapter.

3 Quoted by Pat Little, *Simone Weil: Waiting on Truth* (New York: St. Martin's Press, 1988), p. 130.

4 Feminist theorists, among others, have articulated the view that language can shape us to be inattentive to some kinds of social problems. See especially Elizabeth V. Spelman, *Inessential Woman*.

5 Hannah Arendt, *Eichmann in Jerusalem: A Report on the Banality of Evil*, rev. ed. (New York: Viking, 1964).

6 Murray Kempton, "A New Colonialism," *New York Review of Books* 39, 19 (November 19, 1992), p. 39.

7 For example, if one believes that Blacks are simple-minded, then it seems perfectly fair to relegate them to domestic service. This belief was a strong part of American racial ideology.

8 Plato, *The Republic*, tr. F. M. Cornford (New York: Oxford University Press, 1941), p. 3.

9 David Hume, *A Treatise of Human Nature*, 2 ed. (Oxford: Oxford University Press, 1978), p. 429.

10 A thoughtful account of this process appears in Susan Wendell, "A (Qualified) Defense of Liberal Feminism," *Hypatia* 2, 2 (Summer 1987), pp. 65–93.

11 Thomas Kitwood, *Concern for Others: A New Psychology of Conscience and Morality* (New York: Routledge, 1990).

12 For an excellent feminist account of the nature of obligation, see Nancy Hirschmann, *Rethinking Obligation* (Ithaca: Cornell University Press, 1992).

13 See Kristen R. Monroe, Michael C. Barton, and Ute Klingermann, "Altruism and the Theory of Rational Action: Rescuers of Jews in Nazi Europe," *Ethics* 101 (October 1990), pp. 103–22.

14 For example, Carol Stack's discussion of the Clyde dilemma is perhaps closer to a concern with responsibility than with obligation. Stack, "Different Voices, Different Visions," in Faye Ginsberg and Anna Tsing, eds, *Uncertain Terms* (Boston: Beacon Press, 1990), pp. 19–27.

15 See Larry Spence, "Moral Judgment and Bureaucracy," in R. W. Wilson and G. J. Schochet, eds, *Moral Development and Politics* (New York: Praeger, 1980), pp. 137–71.

16 Robert Goodin, *Protecting the Vulnerable: A Reanalysis of Our Social Responsibilities* (Chicago: University of Chicago Press, 1985).

17 Goodin addresses this issue as: is it better to protect the vulnerable, or to render them invulnerable? He argues that invulnerability is impossible, because humans are interdependent. Goodin's construction of the question precludes any other possible answer, though I believe my account of care stands in contrast to his views. There remains something disturbing in the way that Goodin seems to identify himself, and moral philosophers, with the protectors, and to think of the vulnerable as "other." See *Protecting the Vulnerable*, ibid., Ch. 6.

18 See Patricia Benner and Judith Wrubel, *The Primacy of Caring* (Menlo Park, Ca: Addison–Wesley, 1989). I am indebted to Patricia Benner for our discussions of these matters, though my treatment of this question in this text is necessarily too brief and inadequate.

19 Noddings discusses our care relations with animals and plants in *Caring: A Feminine Approach*, Ch. 7; see especially, pp. 159–61. I have criticized the parochialism of Noddings' work in Tronto, "Feminism and Caring." Even Sara Ruddick's admirable work, because of its focus on the particular care practice of mothering, is often misunderstood and reduced to a privatized context. See *Maternal Thinking* (Boston: Beacon Press, 1989).

20 This self-sacrifice has often been a reading of women's caring, especially their caring for men. Hence, consider Sarah Hoagland's critique of Noddings that we need to consider and to recognize oppression when we examine the morality of care. Sarah Lucia Hoagland, "Some Thoughts About 'Caring'" in *Feminist Ethics*, op.cit., pp. 246–63.

This argument is carried still further to see the corrupting effect of self-sacrifice by Susan Wendell:

> Self-sacrifice as over-identifying with others also interferes with women's abilities to work together, to co-operate in opposing oppressive social institutions and creating alternatives to them. Too often we carry self-sacrifice into the women's movement when we have stopped sacrificing ourselves for men but have not learned to take our own needs and desires seriously. Such self-sacrifice is not a gift freely given; it carries with it the same load of resentment and unrealistic expectations of reward that were there when it was given to men. "A (Qualified) Defense of Liberal Feminism." p. 83.

21 The Freudian version of this argument is presented by Eli Sagan:

> Human nurturing, however, presents us with one profound problematic: it is ambivalent from the start. The human child receives not only love, affection, and concern from the adults who care for it, but also anger, animosity, and hostility. It is the ambivalent nature of human nurturing that makes morality an absolute necessity of both our biological and our psychological existence. Moral action is essential for psychic health because *all* critical human relationships are ambivalent: Within them love and aggression struggle for hegemony, and it is one of the fundamental functions of morality to resolve such conflicts on the side of Eros. *Freud, Women, and Morality: The Psychology of Good and Evil* (New York: Basic Books, 1988), p. 28.

22 For a more sustained treatment of this problem, see Joan Tronto, "Woman and Caring," in Susan Bordo and Alison Jaggar, eds., *Gender/Body/Knowledge* (New Brunswick: Rutgers University Press, 1989), pp. 172–87, and Sarah Hoagland, "Some Thoughts About Caring," op.cit.

23 Levels of abuse of children are best understood as a sign of the inadequacy of the types of care that we provide for children: why have we organized society in such a way that children are left with care givers who can abuse them?

24 See John Kekes, "Moral Sensitivity," in *The Examined Life* (Lewisburg, Pa: Buckness University Press, 1988).

25 Aristotle, *Ethics*, pp. 101–3.

26 See, among others, Michael Oliver, *The Politics of Disablement: A Sociological Approach* (New York: St. Martin's Press, 1990).

27 This is the central starting problem for Goodin's *Protecting the Vulnerable*. Although I have disagreed with Goodin's characterization of the vulnerable as insufficiently responsive, he is surely right to recognize the seriousness of this problem.

28 Cf. Rooney, "A Different Different Voice."

29 See, for example, Thomas L. Haskell, "Convention and Hegemonic Interest;" Onora O'Neill, *Faces of Hunger: An Essay on Poverty, Justice and Development* (London: Allen & Unwin, 1986).

30 See the discussion of this question in Rawls, *A Theory of Justice*; also see R. I. Sikora and Brian Barry, eds, *Obligations to Future Generations* (Philadelphia: Temple University Press, 1978).

31 See, for example, Herbert E. Dreyfus and Stuart E. Dreyfus who find "radically anti-cognitivist implications" in the work of Carol Gilligan; see "What Is Morality?," in David Rasmussen, ed. *Universalism Vs. Communitarianism* (Cambridge: MIT Press, 1990), pp. 237–64.

In my earlier writings I drew perhaps too much on the metaethical difference between a theory of care and more common accounts of morality; see, for example, "Beyond Gender Difference to a Theory of Care," *Signs* 12(1987), pp. 644–63. Rather than see this opposition as a battle between incompatible metaethical positions, I suggest that a political and moral practice of care can coexist with an account of moral principles.

32 An equally dismaying approach is to invoke two levels of morality, one that informs daily life, and one which is more reflective, and to assume that one better accounts for moral life than the other. Jonathan Adler, "Moral Development and the Personal Point of View," in *Women and Moral Theory*, ed., Eva F. Kittay and Diana T. Meyers (Totowa, NJ: Rowman and Littlefield, 1987), pp. 205–34. The problems with this approach are most severe when the levels are gendered, or in some other way, the higher level remains a preserve for the possessors of privilege and leisure. Even if this were morally acceptable, it does not seem to be acceptable in the context of democratic life.

33 Cf., for example, Habermas, *Moral Consciousness and Communication Action* (Cambridge: MIT Press, 1990).

34 Habermas thus views philosophy's prime task as the defense of rationality. *Moral Consciousness*.

35 See, Christopher W. Gowans, ed., *Moral Dilemmas* (New York: Oxford University Press, 1987).

36 See Betty A. Sichel, *Moral Education: Character, Community and Ideals* (Philadelphia: Temple University Press, 1988). Some theorists of a communicative ethic still hold to the prospect of universalistic morality of some sort; especially Habermas. Others are more willing to accept the possibilities of the role of care and emotion. See, for example, Benhabib, *Situating the Self*; and Young, *Justice and the Politics of Difference*.

37 Stuart Hampshire, "Fallacies in Moral Philosophy," *Mind* 58 (1949), pp. 466–82.

38 See Alasdair MacIntyre, *After Virtue* 2ed. (Notre Dame: University of Notre Dame Press, 1984), and *Whose Justice? Which Rationality?* (Notre Dame: University of Notre Dame Press, 1988) .

39 Such as David Norton, *Democracy and Moral Development*; John Kekes, *Moral Tradition and Individuality* (Princeton: Princeton University Press, 1989); and perhaps, Marilyn French, *Beyond Power: On Women, Men, and Morals* (New York: Summit Books, 1985).

40 Most notably, though not solely, Richard Rorty, *Philosophy and the Mirror of Nature* (Princeton: Princeton University Press, 1979); and "Feminism and Pragmatism," *Michigan Quarterly Review* 30, 2 (Spring 1991), pp. 231–58.

41 For example, Rosalind Hursthouse, "Virtue Theory and Abortion," *Philosophy and Public Affairs* 20, 3 (Summer 1991), pp. 223–46; and Sichel, *Moral Education*.

42 Among them, Nussbaum; see especially "Human Functioning and Social Justice: In Defense of Aristotelian Essentialism," *Political Theory*, 20 (May 1992), pp. 202–46."

43 I cannot do justice to this rich discussion here, but see, among others, Thomas Nagel, "Moral Luck," *Mortal Questions* (Cambridge: Cambridge University Press, 1979); Adina Schwartz "Against Universality," *Journal of Philosophy* 78, 3 (March 1981), pp. 127–43; Owen Flannagan and Jonathan E. Adler, "Impartiality and Particularity," *Social Research* 50, 3 (Autumn 1983), pp. 576–96; Jonathan Adler, "Particularity, Gilligan, and the Two Levels View, A Reply," *Ethics* 100 (October 1989), pp. 149–56; Jonathan Dancy, "Ethical Particularism and Morally Relevant Properties," *Mind* 92 (1983), pp. 530–47; and Marilyn Friedman, "The Social Self and the Partiality Debates," in *Feminist Ethics*, op.cit. pp. 161–79.

This debate is no longer about solely Kant's views; but see, for example, Tom Sorell's appreciation of Kant's view of the personal in "Self, Society and Kantian Impersonality," *The Monist* 74, 1 (January 1991), pp. 30–42 and Thomas Nagel, *The View From Nowhere* (Oxford: Oxford University Press, 1986); and the anti-Kantian position of Schott, *Cognition and Eros* (Boston: Beacon Press, 1988).

44 Three notable exceptions are Calhoun, "Justice, Care and Gender Bias," *Journal of Philosophy* 85 (1988), pp. 451–63. Rooney, "A Different Different Voice," *The Philosophical Forum* 2 (Summer 1991), pp. 344–9 and Margaret Urban Walker, "Moral Understandings: Alternative 'Epistemology' For a Feminist Ethics," *Hypatia* 4 (Summer 1989), pp. 15–28.

45 It is, of course, important to acknowledge what can be accomplished within the philosophical discourse. Here, the nuanced discussion of whether partiality stands as a convincing defeat of a Kantian universalistic metatheory is a good example of the fact that philosophers can distinguish between good and bad arguments. It is possible, recent philosophical discussion shows, to have a universalistic moral theory without excluding some conditions for partiality.

My point is quite different. I am interested in pointing to the kinds of assumptions that come to be accepted by philosophers in the daily practice of their craft. I believe that an important part of philosophical practice is revealed if we look more closely at the examples and philosophical devices that philosophers think that it is interesting to use: why is the question, "If a building is on fire, should you save the brain surgeon or your Mother?" an important questions for philosophers to answer? Notice the remarkable array of cultural questions that have gone into asking this question. These are the kinds of concerns that I have in mind when I argue that philosophical study needs to be more contextual. As I have suggested throughout this book, power and privilege are important parts of any idea's context.

46 *Moral Consciousness*, op.cit. p. 208.

47 And the notion of treating all as equals remains a benchmark of liberal, democratic thought. As jaded as some professional philosophers may be in its presence, undergraduate students are always deeply impressed by John Rawls's argument for equality in *A Theory of Justice*.

48 Of course, the image of the bourgeois separation of life into public and private spheres in which men engaged in commerce and women in raising families was never an accurate description of life in the United States; at most it described the White, bourgeois middle class. See among others, Alice Kessler Harris, *Out To Work: A History of Wage-Earning Women in the United States* (New York: Oxford, 1982); on African American life, see Brewer, "Black Women in Poverty."

49 Once again there is a difference between the ideological commitments and the realities of class mobility, the end of religious and racial hatreds, and so forth. See Herbert Gintis and Samuel Bowles, *Schooling in Capitalist America: Educational Reform and the Contradictions of Economic Life* (New York: Basic Books, 1976) on educational inequalities; and Andrew Hacker, *Two Nations: Black and White, Separate, Hostile, Unequal* (New York: Scribner's, 1992). Klanwatch has reported a rise in the number of racial hate groups (*Oakland Tribune* February 19, 1992, A8), but polling data on race and anti-Semitism from the American Jewish Committee suggests that tolerance levels are increasing. (*San Francisco Chronicle* January 10, 1992, A12). The open expression of anti-Semitic and racist comments are generally perceived as wrong, even though they occur. The change between the present and 40 years ago is remarkable.

20

Vulnerability and the Moral Nature of Dependency Relations

Eva Feder Kittay

[...]

The Transparent Self of the Dependency Worker

The demands of dependency work favor a self accommodating to the wants of another; that is, a self that defers or brackets its own needs in order to provide for another's. Within the past decade or so, feminists have attempted to characterize a *feminine* sense of self – a self fashioned by a set of relationships and constraints imposed on (or chosen by) women within patriarchal societies. This construction of the self has been variously conceived as a *self-in-relationship*,[1] a *soluble self*,[2] and a *giving self*.[3] Each expression is useful in highlighting a different aspect of this self. I will want to add the idea of a *transparent self* – a self through whom the needs of another are discerned, a self that, when it looks to gauge its own needs, sees first the needs of another.

Such a self may seem too servile to be the autonomous[4] agent of moral actions. Many feminists have argued that to miss the significance of the relational self is to miss a whole dimension of moral life. Furthermore, recent feminist writings extol distinctive features of a self that is relational and giving. Its permeable ego boundaries, many have argued, facilitate not only caretaking responsibilities, but also deep friendships, intimate relations, a less exploitative relation to the natural world, an epistemological stance distinctive to women *and* a form of moral decision making that has inherent value.

Other feminists have disputed this valorization of the "feminine self." They argue against what they take to be the political liability of developing a relational or giving self. My concern here is not to enter the debate about the superiority or inferiority – moral or otherwise – of this "feminine" self. My concern is to consider the moral requirements of the self of the dependency worker in a dependency relation. We will see that this self contrasts with the self represented as participating as an equal in the social relations of liberal political theory. Whether or not it is desirable to be a relational, giving self, my argument rests on the moral requirements of dependency work that make such

Eva Feder Kittay, "Vulnerability and the Moral Nature of Dependency Relations," pp. 51–73 and 198–202 (notes) from *Love's Labor: Essays on Women, Equality, and Dependency*. New York: Routledge, 1999. Reproduced by permission of Routledge/Taylor & Francis Books, Inc. and the author.

a self indispensable. As dependency work, in turn, is an indispensable feature of any human society, every society must count on certain persons adopting such a moral self. In focussing on the requirements of the self of the dependency worker, my concern is not only with the responsiveness of a giving self, and not only with the lack of separation experienced by the soluble self. I want to think about the extent to which this self does not allow its own needs to obscure its perception of another's needs nor to have its own needs offer a resistance to its response to another.

This is what I propose with the idea of a transparent self: The perception of and response to another's needs are neither blocked out nor refracted through our own needs. Of course, no self is ever truly transparent in this sense, but such transparency is a benchmark for the self-conception of the dependency worker qua dependency worker. It is a regulatory ideal for the dependency worker qua dependency worker. It is an altruistic ideal. But while altruism is often seen as morally supererogatory, this ideal is *required* of the labor I have called dependency work.

Where the vulnerability of the charge is absolute, such as that of an infant, an interference with the transparency of self can have dire consequences. An infant's caregiver who is more attuned to her own needs than to those of her charge can fail to notice – or can disregard – important, even life-threatening needs. It is neither capricious nor misogynist nor disrespectful of individual rights when we insist that individuals who mother[5] infants or young children defer their own desires, and even needs, to meet those of their dependent child. The child who awakes in the night, hungry, sick, or terrified, has the claim of the attention of her caregiver, even if that caregiver is herself exhausted and unwilling to be awakened. I will shortly discuss the basis of that claim. For now I want simply to point to the intuitions that prioritize the needs of the dependent over the needs of the dependency worker. The degree to which this prioritization is absolute diminishes as the dependency of the charge diminishes. As a child gets older, as a sick person recovers, as a disabled person mends or acquires self-reliant tools and skills, the dependency worker gains a measure of relief from the overbearing nature of the other's needs. The self of the dependency worker retains a transparency to the needs of the charge to the degree that the charge must depend on her.

The transparency of this self is placed in stark contrast to the self of the liberal tradition of rights and utilities. The self of the liberal tradition is a rationally self-interested agency, rather than an agency in the service of the interests of another. This is not to say that altruism is merely irrational and goes entirely unrecognized in this tradition. But the claim has been that altruistic actions, actions benefiting another at the expense of oneself that do not fall within our contractual obligations, are supererogatory. In any case, acting in the interests of another presents a *problem*: "The problem . . . is not how the interests of others can motivate us to some specific policy of altruistic conduct, but how they can motivate us at all," writes Thomas Nagel (1970, p. 79). As a matter of course, dependency work requires actions often deemed supererogatory when the actor is the autonomous self of liberal theory. Unlike the self of the participant in the Rawlsian original position, the transparent self of the dependency worker is neither moderately self-interested nor disinterested. It is often passionately interested – but the interest is vested in the well-being of another.

Moral Obligations of Dependency Workers and an Ethics of Care

Just as the selves in dependency relationships are not the selves of contracting parties, neither can ties between a dependency worker and her charge be represented as contractual relations. Ties of affection and concern bind dependency worker and her charge. The ties are not between generalizable others, but between non-fungible concrete others.[6] The relations and moral obligations between the parties are not the general obligations we bear to another person, whoever they may be, but special relations. In the case of special relations, we have obligations that are particular to the individual in that relationship. Unlike obligations incurred in special relations spoken of in traditional voluntaristic moral theories, they may not be voluntarily assumed. They are rarely the consequences of an explicit agreement – some performative utterance such as "I promise to . . ." Frequently they involve obligations with no discrete endpoint. These special relations and their attendant obligations do not fit easily within a moral theory that understands justice as the primary virtue. When a parent saves her own child first, is she being unjust or is she meeting her parental responsibility?[7] When a parent, indifferent to a child's wishes, refuses her an innocent pleasure, is it a matter of rights or is it a failure of response? Yet, justice is not a virtue to be ignored in asymmetric relations.[8]

The character of the moral self, the asymmetry of the relationship, the partiality of its participants, and its nonvoluntary nature make the moral demands of the dependency relationship more amenable to an ethic of care than to a rights-based or an utilitarian-based morality. An ethic of care regards the moral subject as inherently relational. It understands moral reasoning to be contextual and responsive rather than a calculus performed on rights or utilities. And an ethic of care centers not on impartial judgments, but on judgments partial to participants within a caring relation. While a long history attaches to the moral claims in an ethic where the first virtue is justice, the *source* of moral claims in an ethic of care has not been made sufficiently explicit.[9] What are the moral claims of a relational subject? On what normative grounds can we accept contextual reasoning and responsiveness as bases for moral judgments? And how can the partiality exhibited in a caring relation, which might not even have been voluntarily assumed, have a moral character – especially when obligations that are not self-assumed and partiality have so often been the mark of heteronomy, i.e., of actions which fail to express our moral essence?

In what follows, the reader may object that I address myself only to those obligations that attach themselves to dependency workers with respect to their charge. I do not speak of obligations of the charge to the dependency worker. That is not because I think none exist. In the limiting case of a wholly dependent being, however, it makes no sense to speak about the obligation of the charge to the dependency worker. I begin with the most helpless charge so that we can glean certain moral features of the dependency relationship. Ultimately I am interested in addressing the obligations that are owed the dependency worker. Some of the obligations owed the dependency worker arise out of the moral obligations that devolve on the dependency worker to care for the charge. By beginning with the most helpless charge, we see how grave these obligations may be, how much they exact from the dependency worker, and how the charge, at least in the limiting case, cannot reciprocate the care or concern the dependency worker devotes to her. This is not to say that even the most dependent person does not reciprocate in some way – through love and affection perhaps. Nonetheless, the obligation to redress the "cost" that duties of dependency work exact from the dependency worker must fall on those outside the relationship itself. Of course, the responsibilities and costs of dependency work for the caregiver are graduated, and hang in part on the degree of the dependency. Where the charge is able to respond morally to the dependency worker, she too has an obligation. But the nature and extent of that obligation can be bracketed for the purposes of this discussion.

The "Vulnerability Model"

Justificatory ground for a relation of care can be located in Robert Goodin's work *Protecting the Vulnerable*. Although Goodin's concern is not specifically with an ethic of care, he sees the moral claim for special relations as situated in the vulnerability of another to our actions. In other words, while his own aim is not a foundation for an ethic of care, the point at which he situates the moral claims of special relations shares the moral ground of an ethic of care.

Goodin contrasts a Vulnerability Model of special relations to the Voluntaristic Model, whose paradigm is the promise. In the case of the promise, I assume a special obligation to another when I give my word to do that which I promised. Although the obligation is to a particular other, the form of the obligation is perfectly general: I would have that obligation to whomsoever I made that promise. The obligation is also self-assumed. Because I made such a promise out of my own free choice, and because I would expect anyone freely incurring such an obligation to honor their promises, I assume the obligation to fulfill my promise.

On the Vulnerability Model, the moral basis of special relations between individuals arises from the vulnerability of one party to the actions of another. The needs of another call forth a moral obligation on our part when we are in a special position vis-à-vis that other to meet those needs. We can call such obligations *vulnerability-responsive obligations*. Goodin argues that all special relations, business relations, relations between a professional and a client or patient, family relations, friendships, benefactor-beneficiary relations, even promises and contractual relations, are better described on the Vulnerability Model.[10]

Goodin's model can be described in strikingly relational terms. The moral claim is a claim upon *me* only if I am so situated as to be able to answer the need. It is a moral claim upon me, only if the other is vulnerable to *my* actions. What is striking about this model is that the moral claim arises not by virtue of the properties of an individual – construed as rights, needs, or interests – but out of a *relationship* between one in need and one who is situated to meet the need.[11] Given the earlier discussion of dependency relations, we see immediately how the vulnerability model speaks directly to the moral claim the dependent has upon the dependency worker. The dependency worker is positioned so as to be *the* individual best situated, or exclusively situated to meet the needs of the dependent.

Who can oblige whom by their vulnerability?

The vulnerability model is not without difficulties. On the one hand, it is open to the charge of making our obligations too general and so obliging us to more than is reasonable. If, for example, a distant admirer declares his love for you and claims to be unable to live unless you extend yourself in some way, it is not at all clear that you have an obligation to that person. But the vulnerability model, on first blush, appears to put the power of obliging you into the hands of whosoever wishes to exercise that power. Upon further thought, the model can be charged with unreasonably limiting our responsibility. If our responsibility arises from being in a unique position to meet the need of another, then it seems we have no obligation to meet any needs which could as well be met by anyone else. Goodin's principles of individual and group responsibility (see Goodin 1985, pp. 118, 136, 139) make our obligation to another depend upon the degree to which the vulnerable party can be affected by our actions. The principles are meant to delimit the sphere and scope of vulnerability-responsive obligations. Assigning a degree of responsibility resolves some of the difficulty but not all. The distant admirer can threaten suicide by your neglect and therefore the degree to which the vulnerable party can be affected is very great indeed. But it is less intuitively clear that this distant lover should have the power to thus oblige you in the first place. It also seems clear that to take the vulnerability model as the sole way in which we become obligated makes it odd that I should have any obligation to persons who simply do not need me to benefit them. And yet, I may well feel an obligation to a kin member, even when there is virtually nothing that I might do that another kin could not do equally well. Nor does it explain why I may feel a stronger obligation to kin than a non-kin who may be at least as vulnerable to my actions.

Two responses are possible to this last objection – and neither is satisfactory. On the one hand, one may reply that such a sense of obligation is simply a parochialism that the vulnerability model is intended to address. One of the attractions of this model is the result that obligations to kin are not to be preferred to those of other individuals who may be more vulnerable to your actions. However, it is not at all clear that we can just discard such conventions. A great deal relies on the historical and cultural circumstances and practices that determine our relationships to others in our community. On the other hand, one could argue that kinship defines a relationship in which kin are already vulnerable to the actions of each other. Much depends on the degrees of vulnerability, which must be weighed in each circumstance. But then the vulnerability model would just be begging the question of moral responsibility, for we can give whatever weight we choose to affinitive relations, and invoking vulnerability adds little to our considerations.

To resolve these various quandaries, we need first to acknowledge that who is responsible for whom is often a matter of absolute judgment and less a matter of degree; second, to accept that responsibility in special relations arises in multiple ways;[12] and third, to recognize that obligations, however formed, arise in a set of cultural practices. Many of the most binding relations and responsibilities arise out of a confluence of different practices and different obliging conditions. A relationship is set within a number of cultural determinations establishing who meets whose needs – modulated, necessarily, by exigencies not foreseen in the culturally established conventions. If I encounter a bleeding stranger and there is no one else around, then the fact of my being there creates a unique relation that calls forth an obligation on my part to do something to help the stranger. If, however, my child is hungry, then while there are many others around who can feed the child, the presumption is that I am responsible to see that she gets fed. As long as I am able to fulfill that obligation, it falls upon me to do so. Alternatively I can assign the responsibility to another to fulfil an obligation on my behalf – but the ultimate responsibility remains mine. It is an obligation that arises out of the relationship between parent and child.[13]

Most pertinent for our purposes, however, is that in the case of dependency work, a relationship is already given – either by familial ties, friendship, or the obligations of employment. These bases of the dependency relationship legitimate the situation whereby the charge is vulnerable to the actions of the dependency worker. The charge, unlike the distant admirer, is in a position that legitimates her obliging the dependency worker. The charge is vulnerable. Familial ties, friendships, and certain paid employment serve as socially acknowledged justifications for the charge being vulnerable to the actions of this particular individual – her dependency worker.

The legitimacy of needs in vulnerability-responsive obligations

The vulnerability model has not only to solve the problem of who gets to oblige whom by their vulnerability, it also has to question what sort of needs legitimately impose obligations. Neither what is construed as need nor what is understood as an appropriate response can go unexamined. While the need of the hungry infant for food unquestionably calls for a response to provide food, the appropriate response to an alcoholic's need for drink is less clear.[14]

A person accustomed to riches and servants all her life may experience these as needs of such urgency that their absence is intolerable. Toni Morrison, in her novel *Song of Solomon*, explores the effect of such a need in a story told by Circe, the only remaining servant of Miss Butler, the daughter of a formerly wealthy but highly exploitative family. Miss Butler, whose wealth was eventually dissipated, commits suicide rather than face total destitution. A midwife as well as a servant, Circe helped birth Miss Butler and Miss Butler's mother before her. She remains on the estate after her mistress's death, tending to the dogs and presiding over the total decay of the former mansion. "The last few years we ate out of the garden," recounts Circe. "Finally she [Miss Butler] couldn't take it anymore. The thought of having no help, no money – well, she couldn't take that. She had to let everything go." In response to an interlocutor who mistakes Circe's abiding relationship to her mistress for a reciprocal and enduring loyalty, Circe exclaims, "I said she killed herself rather than do the work I'd been doing all my life! . . . Do you hear me? She saw the work I did all her days and *died*, you hear me, *died* rather than live like me." Circe stays on, not out of a misplaced loyalty, but out of a commitment to see all her masters' beloved property – "They loved it. Stole for it, lied for it, killed for it" –undergo a material decadence commensurate with the moral decadence that formerly sustained it.

While there may well be fundamental, primary needs, needs without which no individual could survive, needs that would have a prima facie moral claim to response, all other needs are identifiable only within certain practices. The extent to which such needs have a moral weight depends upon a moral evaluation of the practice, as well as the urgency of the need as understood within that practice. A critical understanding of needs requires not only a sensitivity to the neediness of another and an understanding of how another may be vulnerable to one's own actions, but also a knowledge of when fulfilling those needs would morally diminish oneself or the other. Within a relation of dependency, false needs can be generated either by the charge or by societal expectations on the dependency worker. The critically assessed practices in which dependency work takes place offer a means by which to formulate a critical discourse about needs. Circe's understanding that her mistress's needs are predicated on the devaluation of her own person – that Miss Butler would rather die than lead the life that she, Circe, has lived – offers her a critical perspective of the practices in which she engaged as a dependency worker. These practices themselves originated in a set of false needs, diminishing the dependency worker and rendering the one for whom she labored hopelessly, but unnecessarily, vulnerable. Circe, a woman who had done dependency work both in the primary and extended senses, understood well the difference between a need to which a response was moral and a need that can be met only by diminishing oneself.

Limiting how one becomes obliged in the vulnerability model

Circe, a slave in the Butler household for the better part of her life, was in the unique position to meet her mistress's need only because of a practice that unjustly allocated responsibilities to her. Even after she was freed, she continued to be the one to whose actions her mistress, having become so dependent upon her during slavery, was vulnerable. Is the question of *how* someone comes to be in a position where another is vulnerable to their actions relevant to the moral warrant of the vulnerability-responsive obligation? Goodin claims it is never relevant. He writes:

> [T]he existing allocation of responsibilities, whatever its initial basis, should now be treated as a "social fact." Whether or not the existing allocation of responsibilities itself has any moral warrant, it has made some people vulnerable to others; and that fact, if no other, provides a moral warrant for discharging those responsibilities. The pragmatic "ought"... attaches to the vulnerabilities... And...stays attached until and unless responsibilities – and the expectations and vulnerabilities surrounding them – are redefined (Goodin 1985, p. 125).

However, the justice of Goodin's position is questionable, and the "pragmatic ought" he invoked may be at odds with a "moral ought" that proscribes *self-demeaning behavior* or one that puts us at unjustifiable risk. Goodin does insist that we are always vulnerable to our own actions, and therefore have obligations to ourselves as well. Is this response adequate to Circe's problem? First, the appeal to an obligation to ourselves cannot help much here since responding to the vulnerability of a dependent other will often put us at risk. Still we expect to bracket our own interests if they conflict with those of a vulnerable dependent for whom we are caring. Second, we can say that responding to the needs of another unjustly thrust upon us is, in itself, demeaning. It requires that we place a lower value on ourselves than on those who would unjustly demand a response from us making us vulnerable to their needs or those of another. This, however, would hold in all cases where the pragmatic ought is in conflict with a moral obligation that arises out of a just allocation of responsibilities. If then, our obligations to ourselves trump the obligations to others in cases of unjust allocations of responsibility, there is no pragmatic ought and I have no quarrel with Goodin.

Appeal to obligations to ourselves then either defeat the pragmatic ought or conflict with the other demands of the vulnerability model. If Goodin insists on the pragmatic ought, so that an unjust allocation of responsibilities nonetheless obliges us, then he must agree that it can do so even in the face of coercive conditions. This is both counterintuitive and an undesirable feature in a moral theory. It seems more reasonable to insist that the injustice trumps any moral obligation induced by the vulnerability of the one-in-need to the actions of the coerced person.[15] Perhaps this is why even many opponents of abortion tend to agree that a pregnancy caused by a rape is legitimately aborted. A slave coerced into caring for an ailing master would be thought justifiable if she took the occasion of his incapacity as an opportunity to escape.

Nonetheless, if we are to judge from some accounts of slavery, not all slaves, in fact, viewed the moral situation in such stark terms. Margaret Walker's novel of the lives of slaves during the Civil War, *Jubilee*, invokes the reckonings of Jim, a house slave in the Dutton home who accompanied the plantation heir to the front lines. He contemplates what he is to do with his mortally wounded young master:

> "Marster Johnny dying and he can't get home by hisself. I'll carry him home to his Maw where he can die in peace, but I sho ain't staying there." If Jim had been a field hand, such a delicate conflict would not have disturbed him. He would have felt no ties to the Dutton household, but he had nursed the old man and he had watched the children grow. Contemptuous as he was of Big Missy he was nevertheless tied to a strange code of honor, duty, and noblesse oblige which he could not have explained. So he was taking Johnny home (Walker 1967, p. 184).

Judith Jarvis Thomson's notorious argument for the permissibility of abortion is worth considering here. Thomson (1971) contends that granting the personhood of a fetus does not preclude a woman's right to an abortion. In her famous analogy, she likens an unintended pregnancy to a scenario in which a hospital patient awakens from an operation only to find himself attached by tubes to a famous violinist whose life is temporarily sustained by the hookup. Thomson's point is that it cannot be unjust for the recruited party to refuse the obligation to aid the violinist no matter how vulnerable the violinist is to such a refusal, since the association was not undertaken voluntarily. To insist that the hospital patient stay hooked up to the violinist would be coercive and unjust. Similarly, goes the argument, the pregnant woman who is not voluntarily assuming the association with the fetus is under no obligation to lend her body to the fetus's development.

Although I do not dispute the right of a woman to have an abortion, nor do I wish to have my remarks so interpreted, the argument from voluntarism is troubling here. Surely there are many obligations that appear to have the force of the moral, yet do not follow from voluntarily assumed associations: obligations to parents, to neighbors, to strangers in need whom we happen upon. Thomson, it is worth noting, argues that it is only the moral virtue of justice which is contravened when the demand is made that we assume the life support of the violinist. A less exacting moral virtue such as moral decency – less exacting in what it insists upon before an obligation is posited – would urge that there is an obligation to sustain the violinist, at least as long as the cost to oneself is not too great.

The intuitions that are called upon to sustain Thomson's distinction here between the demands of justice and the demands of moral decency, however, are problematic. Many would argue that the demands of justice bear heavily on filial responsibilities, for instance.[16] Thomson's example of a person who is *kidnapped* in order to be the source of another's life-sustaining treatment is so effective, I propose, because kidnapping is a particularly compelling form of coercion (even if it is not "blood and gore" violence). If kidnapped, few would think that they have any sort of obligation to meet the needs of the one on whose behalf the kidnapping was done. Clearly coercive situations, situations in which one is *forced* to come to the aid of another, seem not only to be unjust, but the injustice also can be sufficient cause to cancel any moral obligation to respond as one might otherwise in the face of need. In Thomson's example an individual becomes the unique person to satisfy the need by virtue of the coercion. Once hooked up to another person's body, the other individual is so much more Vulnerable to your refusal than he might have been before. If one were in fact the only person who could satisfy the need – if, for example, some rare blood type in combination with a particular set of antibodies were required and only one person was identified with these – the one in need would, I believe, have a great deal of moral suasion over the one capable of helping. But here, too, *someone* must determine if the moral claim of one life is greater than that of another.

Voluntarism has a great deal of appeal because we tend to think that the person called upon to help must make the decision that she wishes to forego her interest for another's sake. But a previous relationship between these two persons can alter those intuitions. If the person called upon to make the sacrifice of time, energy, money or even life itself is a mother or father, voluntarism has less appeal. We expect the parent to be willing to make the sacrifice. Contrary to Goodin, then, our intuitions about whose needs we have obligations to respond to partly depends on how or why we find ourselves in the position to meet those needs. Contrary to the voluntarist, however, voluntarily undertaken obligations are not the only source of obligations in relationships.

Thomson might agree that voluntarily undertaken obligations are not the only source of obligations in relationships. Nevertheless, she would want to argue, they are the source of all obligations we incur that pertain to justice. Think, however, of an encounter between a well-fed person with plenty of food and a starving person. Would we not want to say that a refusal to give the hungry person food is a matter of injustice and not just indecency? Here the vulnerability model seems to issue obligations that are matters of justice. The appropriate moral distinctions are not between what is just and what is decent, but between conditions which, when they place a person in a "privileged" position to respond to need, are either morally benign or morally unacceptable. Where these positions are voluntarily chosen, it is both a matter of justice and decency that we honor such obligations. Where these positions are coerced, then such obligations have no moral standing. Most common and interesting situations, however, are those which are neither coerced (either at all or in an obvious sense), nor voluntarily chosen.[17]

There is a sufficiently large class of such responsibilities and obligations. These noncoerced *yet not voluntarily chosen* associations fill our lives. They range from the most intimate familial relations to those of fellow citizen and fellow traveler. Duties incurred by these associations arise out of a whole network of expectations, bonds, and responsibilities, most of whose validity we do not question, even if we question some specific obligations they impose. This is to say that just because coerced responsibilities do not carry a moral warrant does not mean we can only admit obligations voluntarily assumed – even if we limit moral considerations to justice. By virtue of our acceptance of these nonvoluntary, but noncoerced relationships (whether formed by longstanding convention or mere happenstance), we question our capacity for acting justly and well. We question the kind of person we are[18] when we fail to meet a primary need, when we are uniquely situated to meet that need.

The "coercion problem"

The voluntaristic model offers a consistent reason for refusing a duty imposed through coercion, even if it cannot account for the intuition that it is unjust to refuse aid in an unchosen, but noncoercive situation. On the voluntaristic model, no one can legitimately exercise any claims against us unless we can aver to *some* consensual arrangement, hence neither the violinist in Thomson's analogy – nor an unwanted fetus has any claims against us.[19] We suggested that there were frequent instances of relations to others, non-voluntary but not coerced, in which many would think it unjust not to offer the needed assistance. The vulnerability model accounts for these intuitions. The switch to a vulnerability model, however, raises a different concern.

I have resisted Goodin's insistence that the moral warrant of an antecedent allocation of responsibilities is irrelevant to the moral warrant for carrying out vulnerability-responsive obligations. In arguing against Goodin's pragmatic ought, we needed to evoke a conception of justice – a justice that pertains to how "the existing allocation of responsibilities itself" came to be. We have argued that in special relationships, obligations (even obligations demanded by justice) can arise – whether or not the relationships are voluntary – just as long as they are not coerced. But we argued against any moral warrant of obligations within a relationship that is coerced by appealing to the injustice of such coercion. If justice, as it pertains to the institutions and practices through which special relationships arise, always requires some consensual, voluntaristic basis, then the vulnerability model faces a genuine difficulty. Either it must accept Goodin's pragmatic ought – and so cannot accept that coerced obligations carry no moral weight – or it cannot get off the ground.

Arguably, the theory that most comprehensively provides justification for such institutions and practices is social contract theory. Social contract theory, however, is a voluntaristic theory, in which social institutions derive their legitimacy from the voluntary agreement of an association of equally situated and empowered parties.

The voluntarism of social contract theory assumes individuals who act out of an elevated self-interest, who are rational and mutually disinterested, and who are equally situated to engage in moral interactions with each other.[20] The suitability of such a concept is what is at stake in this book. Such a view, I have claimed, fails to take into account the circumstance that some individuals will always be dependent, does not explain the moral commitment of those who care for dependents, and employs an unhelpful conception of equality. We hoped to find a more suitable basis for an ethic of care (an ethic that applies to dependency relations) in the Vulnerability Model proposed by Goodin. To again resort to a Voluntaristic Model to ground our obligations to vulnerable dependents undoes our efforts.

This difficulty leads us to what I call the *coercion problem* of the vulnerability model. The coercion problem is this: Either we reject Goodin's pragmatic ought, but find that we must rely on voluntarism after all, or we accept Goodin's pragmatic ought and accept that dependency relationships formed by coercing the dependency worker to take on these obligations have a moral warrant. Neither option is attractive to a feminist position with respect to dependency. Granting that a vulnerability model without Goodin's pragmatic ought must accept voluntarism also means granting that even the vulnerability model (the moral model best suited to dependency relations) must begin with the premise that the dependency critique disputes: that society is appropriately or ideally thought to be an association of those equally situated and empowered. Accepting the pragmatic ought, however, deflects from the urgency to see how often those responsibilities have unfairly been allocated to women. Women, and others who have done dependency work because of coercive conditions or without adequate compensation, have too long simply accepted these unfair allocations as social facts, thereby colluding with an oppressive and exploitative situation. Challenging the justice of the social facts is precisely what feminists must do, but accepting the pragmatic ought leaves no place from which to challenge unfair allocations, without, once again, resorting to the voluntarism that undercuts the validity of the vulnerability model. Is there a way out of the coercion problem? Is there room for a notion of justice within a vulnerability model?

With the coercion problem, our focus is not on how the person who is in the position to address the vulnerabilities of another behaves with respect to her responsibilities, but on what obligations others have to that person. The problem, as we have repeatedly indicated, is especially acute for those dealing with what we have called primary needs, since those with such needs make very compelling demands – ones that are met in relationships of dependency and that are potentially very costly to the dependency worker. Both the ground of the dependency workers' obligation to care and the obligations to the dependency worker need to be clarified. The coercion problem needs to be seen in the context of what is owed to those who meet the needs of others, most especially dependent others. To solve the problem of coercion, then, we need to shift the inquiry, deferring a resolution until we understand more generally what are the moral obligations to the dependency worker.

Moral Obligations to the Dependency Worker

We have said that dependency relations, especially in the primary sense we are privileging here, begin with the needs of a charge who is vulnerable, whose needs are legitimate, and who may stand in a prior relation to the person assuming the role of dependency worker. Because the dependency worker is charged with the welfare of her charge, the latter becomes vulnerable to the actions of the dependency worker. The vulnerability model gives us a basis for understanding the moral pull of being in a relation with another who is vulnerable to one's actions. It must be said that an individual has an unqualified obligation to assume the responsibilities of dependency work when the following conditions are met: (1) the needs are basic; (2) the vulnerability is extensive; and (3) the prior relation, which puts a particular individual into position of having to assume such a vulnerability-responsive obligation, has a moral warrant. Furthermore, this obligation has to be assumed even when there is a substantial cost to the dependency worker's own interests and projects. This is what every mother and every father who gets up at four o'clock in the morning to tend to a sick child knows so well.

What about the obligations owed to the dependency worker? Who is to care for the caregiver? How are her needs to be recognized? To the extent that the dependency worker is vulnerable to the actions of the charge, the charge is obliged to behave in ways that address those vulnerabilities. Not only is the charge vulnerable to the actions of the dependency worker, but the dependency worker may also be vulnerable to the actions of the charge. The elder-care worker who tends to a frail elderly man may be vulnerable to sexual abuse, economic exploitation, and poor treatment. The vulnerability is aggravated where the dependency worker is poor, a woman, a person of color, an immigrant, and so forth. Again, here the vulnerability model is just right. The charge may not have chosen her dependency worker or may not even want one, but she has an obligation to understand the extent to which the dependency worker may be vulnerable to her actions and act so as to avoid harm.

The response of the charge can also provide deep fulfillment to the dependency worker. The loving gaze and laughter of a child with profound cognitive disabilities can offer a special joy to her attendant, even if the child is unable to utter a "thank you." How vulnerable the dependency worker is to the actions of the charge is, in part, a function of what actions the charge is capable of. The newborn infant who is not yet capable of much, or a person with profound mental and physical impairments who is able to control very few of her actions clearly cannot be held responsible for vulnerabilities imposed by her. But now the circle of the dependency obligations must expand to include the vulnerability of the dependency worker, which is itself a consequence of her deferred interests as well as needs pertaining to her affective bond to her charge and her concern for her charge's well-being.

First and foremost, the obligation owed to a person who must defer her own interests and projects is that her responsibilities to another not be unjustly thrust upon her. To disregard such an obligation is to treat her as someone of lesser moral worth than either the person she cares for or those who placed her in the obliging position. It seems as if in decrying the injustice of being *compelled* to care, we have made an appeal to equality, a basic moral parity. Here we begin our thoughts of equality from the relationship of dependency.

Connection-based equality

If we start not with individuals in their separateness, but in their connectedness, we can read their demands for equality through these connections. If we can see each individual nested within relationships of care, we can envision relationships that embrace the needs of each. This leads us to an alternative understanding of equality.

The equality that begins with the interests of an independent self and is extended to others by virtue of an elevated self-interest is an individual-based equality. This is the equality registered in the equal right of each to form his or her own conception of the good and to compete for the resources needed to attain that good. It is the equality which is based upon the recognition of each person's individuality and independence – each one's own conception of one's own good – and the individually held rights and powers.[21]

The alternative conception that I propose – the equality claimed in the assertion that we are all some mother's child – is instead a connection-based equality. This alternative equality assumes a fundamental need for relationship, and it gives rise to a distinctive set of claims. The claims generated by a connection-based equality derives not from the rights we hold as independent individuals, but from what is due us by virtue of our connection to those with whom we have had and are likely to have relations of care and dependency. They are claims made not necessarily on our own behalf alone, and they are made not necessarily by those to whom they are due. Such claims are *entitlements* first to a relationship in which one can be cared for if and when appropriate, and second to a socially supported situation in which one can give care without the caregiving becoming a liability to one's own well-being. The last is an entitlement that goes beyond, and has different properties than, the entitlement to the care itself.

Family leave policies are a fine example of entitlements characteristic of this concept of equality.[22] The worker who claims an entitlement to a family leave not only claims it on her own behalf – for the release time from work – but primarily claims it for the sake of the dependent who receives the benefit, the care and attention made possible by the release time. Furthermore, this is often a claim that the dependent cannot make on her own behalf. In the case of the dependent who cannot voice the legitimate demand to have her needs attended to, a dependency worker must make the claim on the dependent's part – and the claim includes the time and resources of the dependency worker to attend to the needs of her charge. Furthermore, a claim based on a connection-based equality is a claim to have the need attended to by one genuinely, perhaps uniquely, concerned with the well-being of the dependent. That sort of claim is really what justifies and lies behind the moral soundness of a family leave policy.

"What goes round, comes round" – reciprocity-in-connection

Connection-based equality is not characterized by reciprocity in the standard sense. In standard relationships of parity, reciprocity requires that efforts I exert on your behalf will be met by some equivalent exertion on your part, immediately, at some specified time in the future, or when the need arises. I expect my act to be reciprocated by the same individual to whom I directed my action. The reciprocity has the nature of an exchange – it is an *exchange reciprocity*. Connection-based equality eschews this exchange reciprocity for another sort, one based on different kinds of expectations.

In studies indicating that women, whether employed or not, provide more hours of care and more care of every sort than do men, the sociologist Naomi Gerstel found that the expectations of others that they will give care was among the reasons the subjects gave for the time spent caring. But their willingness to respond to these expectations was based on an understanding of reciprocity characteristic of a connection-based equality. A fifty-year-old lawyer voiced a typical response:

> Well, my mother may be a pain sometimes but she is very frail now and needs me. She *expects* me to help her. And you know, she took care of her mother. So I have to help her. Nobody else will (Gerstel 1991, p. 18).[23]

Her mother's expectation is one that she accepts: Since her mother gave care to her mother, her mother is now owed care. And as the care her mother's mother received was meted out by the daughter, so that daughter now deserves care from her own daughter. Significantly, the reciprocation is based *not* on the care her mother gave her daughter and which she now expects her daughter to return.[24] That would turn the mother's care for her daughter into a sort of advance payment for later care – a maneuver typical of exchange reciprocity. The daughter instead invokes a set of nested obligations. The fulfillment of those obligations is now her responsibility and her's uniquely. If she does not do the caring, "no one else will."

Within the African-American community, Gerstel found that "especially women, but also men spend far more time helping people they know, especially kin, and volunteering than do whites" (1991, p. 20). She explains this finding in terms of a greater commitment of African-Americans to community life than that of similarly situated whites. Gerstel cites the words of one African-American woman who was justifying the large number of hours she spends on caregiving: "Well, what goes round comes round" (Gerstel 1991, p. 20). This chain of obligations linking members of a community creates a sense of reciprocity between those who give and those who receive that raises the expectation that when one is in the position to give care, one will, and when that person is in need another who is suitably situated to give care will respond. It is a reciprocity of those who see their equality in their connection with, and obligation toward, others.

Such reciprocity depends upon a linked and nested set of social relations, sometimes reciprocal in the standard sense, but not always. In Chapter Four, this connection-based reciprocity is brought to bear on the concept of social cooperation. Standard notions of social cooperation tend to invoke what I have here called exchange-based reciprocity. In dependency relations, however, the dependent is seldom in a position to reciprocate in kind. Reciprocation from the charge may never be possible. The dependency worker is entitled not to a reciprocity from the charge herself, but to a relationship that sustains her as she sustains her charge. Connection-based equality yields a nested set of reciprocal relations and obligations. It is the social cooperation that depends on these nested relationships and obligations that I call *doulia* – a term that improvises on the name of a postpartum caregiver (a *doula*) who assists the new mother as the mother cares for the infant. Just as the *doula* gives care to the one who cares for the dependent infant, the direction of the obligation in connection-based reciprocity goes from those in position to discharge the obligations to those to whom they are relevantly connected.

The dependency worker as some mother's child

The maxim that "we are all some mother's child" supplies not only a notion of equality through connection, but also something substantial about the treatment each one is warranted to receive by virtue of the connection. To assert that "I, too, am a mother's child" is to assert that I am due treatment compatible with or analogous to the treatment a mother renders to a child. To be recognized as a mother's child is to be treated in a fashion that is compatible with or analogous to maternal practice: It is to be deemed worthy of such treatment. This worthiness is inalienable.

Our own behavior can render us less worthy, so that the full treatment as a mother's child may be justifiably overridden by other societal needs, but it can never be fully relinquished. The case of inalienable rights is analogous. There are some rights, such as the freedom to move about unhindered or the right to vote, which we maintain only if we are citizens in good standing – criminal behavior strips us of these rights, at least temporarily. But there are certain rights no one may be deprived of – we not only feed, clothe, house, give medical treatment to convicted criminals, but we also allow even the most vicious to have visitation rights. This indicates the societal recognition that nothing can take from an individual his or her worthiness for a certain amount of care and connection.

That nothing can fully alienate the responsibility of others to recognize us as some mother's child resides in that feature of human existence that demands connection as a fundamental condition for human survival. No one can survive and become a member of the human community without the interest of some mothering person(s) who has provided a degree of a preservative love, a concern in fostering the individual's growth, and a training for social acceptability.[25] When we respect an individual as some mother's child, we honor the efforts of that mothering person and symbolically of all mothering persons. When we do not, not only are rights belonging to the abused individual violated, but the efforts of the mothering persons are dishonored. The sanctity of the relation that makes possible all human connection is violated. The importance of human connection *per se* is thereby disavowed.

A connection-based equality depends on grasping an analogy: The relation between a needy child and the mother who tends to those needs is analogous to the mother's own neediness and those who are in a position to meet those needs. The maternal relation becomes a paradigm, an analogue, for social relations in which vulnerability is central. It is important to emphasize that I am talking about an *analogical* move. I am not suggesting that everyone be treated as a mother treats a child. That would constitute a maternalism as objectionable as paternalism. The role of analogical thinking seems crucial to the concept of equality-in-connection. The procedure by which we go from one situation to another is not a procedure of generalization or universalization, nor is it a deduction from a general rule. It is instead a process of analogical extension.

We have looked at the moral nature both of the self and of the relationship in the case of dependency work, but we still need to provide a critical understanding of the moral nature of the response called for by the relationship itself. The response must not only be possible but must be considered in light of the prior relationship between the individuals, the prior commitment of care, and the tensions between the needs of the charge and the condition of vulnerability in which the dependency worker is placed when meeting those needs. Connection-based equality, which is grounded in our understanding of ourselves as inherently related to others, can serve as a guide to thinking and even to policy.

If we think of each person as some mother's child, then we consider what is owed to a mother's child by virtue of its being vulnerable to the extent that the child is dependent upon the mother for its well-being. We need then to think analogically: Who stands in the position of the mother, who stands in the position of the child and what would be the analogue of the maternal practice?[26] The maternal paradigm is extended analogically to whatever situation we may be in where we *need* to be cared for – where our survival, our flourishing and our well-being as social creatures depend on the extension of another's care, concern, and connection to us. When I respond to the vulnerabilities of another, when I as a dependency worker tend to my charge, this concept of equality requires that it be remembered that I, too, am some mother's child. However my needs may be deferred, they cannot be permitted to languish. For the dependency worker to meet her responsibilities to another, it must be the responsibility of the larger social order to provide a structure whereby she, too, may be treated as a mother's child. Otherwise, she is both treated unequally and hindered in meeting her obligations to her charge.

Connection-based equality, partly justified by the vulnerability model, at the same time marks a limit to the morally acceptable sacrifice on the part of the caregiver or dependency worker – even without questioning the legitimacy of the needs of the vulnerable. A connection-based equality calls upon those within the nested set of social relations to support the dependency worker sufficiently, so that she is not made unduly vulnerable as she answers to the vulnerability of another. Just as the one-in-need is to be assisted and cared for, social relations must be arranged to meet her needs – especially, but not exclusively, those needs and vulnerabilities that result from the other-directed nature of her toils.

We can deduce other consequences from a connection-based equality that takes maternal practice as a paradigm for moral relations between two individuals who are not equally situated from the perspective of an individual-based equality. Some consequences will be further considered in the later chapters when we discuss policy proposals emanating from a connection-based equality and a public concept of *doulia*.

Maternal practice – providing for children – requires that we provide caring institutions while recognizing that the work itself often demands the commitment of a self transparent to the needs of the charge. The recognition of equality inherent in the understanding that we all are some mother's child – or connection-based equality – has implications for responses appropriate to the requirements of dependency work. Dependency work makes moral claims not only on the dependency worker, but also on the larger society. It falls upon the larger social order to permit the flourishing and preservation of dependency relations by providing for the dependency worker without creating the secondary dependency so debilitating to women today.

The vulnerability model is the one that best accords with the moral claims of the dependent on the dependency worker and of the dependency worker on those whose actions she becomes vulnerable to by virtue of this work. Goodin has argued that the vulnerability model is fundamental for all moral claims of special relationships. We have interpreted this model as fundamentally relational, or one in which the moral claim arises out of the relationships themselves. If these views are correct, then dependency relations are *the* paradigmatic moral relations.[27]

Revisiting the coercion problem

We are now in a position to justify limiting the moral responsibility for another when that responsibility is not the result of voluntarism but of a coerced special relation. A mother, acting in a manner compatible with the norms of maternal practice, does not force her child to sacrifice the child's own well-being for another's benefit. Such coercion is not commensurate with a maternal practice that remains true to the well-being of the child. At the extreme of coercion is the experience of the slave. It is no coincidence that the lament of the slave goes: "Sometimes I feel like a motherless child."

If we take the maternal relation as a paradigm of a connection-based equality, we see that when someone takes on the care of another we cannot ignore the fact that the dependency worker is also some mother's child. Working from the analogy of a maternal practice, we see that vulnerability-responsive obligations, which fall upon one by virtue of a coerced situation, cannot, under this conception, become morally binding. Coercion should no more be directed at the caregiver, than at the cared for, given that the caregiver is also a mother's child. This is not to say that a caregiver or dependency worker whose labor is coerced is incapable of providing care to another consistent with maternal practice. Empirical evidence tells us that the coerced dependency worker is capable of providing care consistent with maternal practice. But it is the moral status of her situation that is at issue. The individual coerced into doing dependency work is not being treated in a manner that is consistent with a conception of her as some mother's child. The presumptive obligations of a person so coerced are cancelled because that coercion is not consistent with a paradigm derived from an analogy with maternal practice. An ethic that makes maternal practice a paradigm with this normative force can no more countenance coercion than can a justice-based voluntaristic ethic. And yet the sanction does not presuppose that obligations take their moral force from their status as self-assumed obligations.

We are now in a position to resolve the coercion problem, a problem that appeared to undo the vulnerability model, which is otherwise well suited to the moral conditions of the dependency relationship. Within a moral framework that is voluntaristic there is no problem with coerced responsibilities, for as Thomson's arguments demonstrate, within a voluntaristic framework, it is against such coercion that moral obligation gets defined. But if moral obligation arises when the well-being of one party is vulnerable to the actions of another, then a relation resulting from a coerced situation seems no less able to generate morally binding obligations. Hence Goodin's pragmatic ought.

Goodin's pragmatic ought, however, provides a moral warrant to relationships of dependency – in both the primary sense and the extended sense – that are intuitively unjust. To think that the slave Jim was under a moral obligation to return his master to his home rather than take the opportunity to gain his freedom seems counterintuitive.[28] Here we appeal to justice. This is precisely Thomson's strategy in the arguments defending the right of one to unhook oneself from the violinist, or to abort an undesired pregnancy. Thomson's argument relies heavily on the fact that, when we are hooked up to the violinist against our consent or find ourselves host to an uninvited fetus, we have had no say in the arrangement. In such situations, she contends, justice does not demand that the one vulnerable to our actions has any claim on us, although moral decency may. My response has been that it is not the nonvoluntary nature of this arrangement that vitiates the moral claim of the one dependent on our actions, but its coercion. The argument that justice requires the association to be voluntary is rooted on a mistaken view of social arrangements and an individual-based equality. This view holds that to get at moral obligation we need to start with individuals equally situated and determine how they come together and interact in morally justifiable ways. Whatever determines how this is possible becomes the defining character of moral relationships. Here voluntarism plays a crucial role. Instead the picture that results when we focus on dependency compels us to start with persons firstly connected through relationships of dependency, and then take the moral commitments needed for such relationships as prior to all subsequent moral relationships. But these relationships are often nonvoluntary, and therefore whether or not a relationship is voluntary fails to play the vital role in establishing moral obligations.

Furthermore, if dependency relations form the first model for moral relationships, then the vulnerability model with its emphasis on the response to need is the appropriate one for moral relations – but need is not solely a property of the dependent. The dependency worker is also a person with needs. The mother who feeds her child also needs to eat. The echo of the dinnertime remark returns: My mother is also a mother's child. Just as well-done dependency work requires that the dependency worker not act coercively toward the charge – coercion, like domination is exercised for benefit of someone other than the one upon whom it is imposed – so, too, an equality that begins with caring relationships can give no moral warrant to actions or relationships that are coerced. The proscription against coercion and domination inheres in the moral vision that begins with relationships no less than one that begins with individuals. We can have a vulnerability model without giving a moral warrant to a coercive allocation of responsibilities; we can have a vulnerability model without Goodin's pragmatic ought. But we need the vulnerability model to be situated in a moral, social, and political theory that repudiates the notion that the founding obligations of a social order are derived from the voluntary association of equally situated and empowered individuals.

Notes

1 Nancy Chodorow, C. Keller, Carol Gilligan, Diana Meyers, M.F. Belenky, Luce Irigaray, Rita Manning, Susan Hekman are among the many writers who speak of the relational self in some way.

2 Catherine Keller, *From a Broken Web* (Boston: Beacon Press, 1986).

3 Robin West, "The Difference in Women's Hedonic Lives," *Wisconsin Womens Law Journal* 3 (1987), pp. 81–145.

4 See Marilyn Friedman, "Autonomy and Social Relationship: Rethinking the Feminist Critique," in D. T. Meyers, ed., *Feminists Rethink the Self* (Boulder, CO: Westview Press, 1997) for a review and discussion of feminist critiques of the idea of autonomy and of attempts to develop relationally conceived ideas of autonomy. Such efforts treat "social relations and human community as central to the realization of autonomy" p. 40.

5 I use the term in the extended sense that Sarah Ruddick, *Maternal Thinking* (New York: Beacon Press, 1989), gives to it. For Ruddick, the term "mother" includes any individual, regardless of gender, who does the primary caretaking. Nonetheless, I adopt a convention of using the feminine pronoun for the dependency worker, reflecting at once the predominance of women who do this work *and* the possibility of generalizing the feminine as well as the masculine pronoun to speak of someone whose gender is not specified.

6 See Seyla Benhabib, "The Generalized and the Concrete Other," in Kittay and Meyers, eds, *Women and Moral Theory* (Totowa, NJ: Rowman and Littlefield, 1987).

7 Similar points have received a great deal of philosophical attention, especially since Bernard Williams made his now famous remark with respect to the utilitarian calculator who considers if he should save his drowning wife before he saves others, that he asks one question too many. See Bernard Williams, *Utilitarianism, For and Against,* J. Smart and Bernard Williams, eds (Cambridge: Cambridge University Press, 1973).

8 This is a point I argue below. It is also a point nicely argued in Sarah Ruddick, "Injustice in Families: Assault and Domination" in Virginia Held, ed., *Justice and Care* (Boulder, CO: Westview Press, 1995), pp. 203–23

9 One writer who has attended to this is Nel Noddings. She speaks of responses of care coming out of memories of our best caring, *Caring: A Feminist Approach to Ethics* (Berkeley: University of California Press, 1984). I believe that this identification is (and is meant as) a psychological and not a normative source – that is, not a source of the obligation, but of the desire to care for another. Accordingly, she identifies the distinctly moral character of caring actions as those responses that are generated not simply by that desire but by our sense that we have the obligation to care. My approach is somewhat different: I want to identify the source in a normative sense, but say that a response motivated by another need is already a moral response.

10 We ought to note that the parties in the relationships discussed are individuals. However, there is no reason not to talk about the parties as groups – social groups or ethnic groups or groups formed on a given occasion, bystanders at an accident, let us say. Goodin discusses the responsibilities codified in professional codes, group responsibilities more generally, and the responsibility of an individual as a member of a group. To think in terms of group responsibility may be a useful way in considering how different systems of oppression interact, given that there are important dependency relations achieved among distinct social groups. Furthermore, when we understand what it is for an individual to be especially well-situated to meet the needs of another, it may be a situatedness that is mediated by her membership in a particular social group. Thus, for example, when the earthquake in Armenia occurred, Armenia-Americans were the ones who were most

vigorous in their response. By virtue of their membership in that ethnic group, they saw it as their special responsibility to meet that need. Stereotyping, unfortunately, will create expectations that members of a particular group will assume certain responsibilities. Women sometimes find themselves with responsibilities foisted upon them that are the result of other's expectations of them as women. Once these expectations are in place, a person can find herself so situated that another is now vulnerable to her actions merely in virtue of stereotyped expectations of the group to which she belongs.

11 The move to a relational construal of notions previously considered on an individualistic model is found in several authors. Earlier we cited relational accounts of autonomy. Martha Minow, *Making All the Difference* (Cambridge: Harvard University Press, 1990) attempts a reconstruction of rights along a relational model. A right, she emphasizes, is not something we possess regardless of the actions of another. Rights are what we hold against the actions of another. While compatible with my own position, Minow still supposes a ethical model in which the obligations and responsibilities incurred are *reciprocal* in a standard sense. In focusing on dependency relations, I am considering moral relations that often *cannot* be reciprocal.

12 See Stephen Scheffler, "Relationship and Responsibilities," *Philosophy and Public Affairs* 26 (Summer 1997), pp. 189–209, for a defense of a non-reductive account of obligations in special relations.

13 Goodin's own Principle of Group Responsibility (see Robert Goodin, *Protecting the Vulnerable* (Chicago: University of Chicago Press, 1985, p. 136)), does acknowledge if not cultural practices as such, group-based obligations. I think we require something stronger, namely, an answer to the question "who in a group is vulnerable to whom as a matter of (cultural) practice?" However, it may be possible to refine the principle in ways that satisfy the stronger requirements to which I point.

14 In a very tender scene in the movie *Fried Green Tomatoes*, the responsiveness of the heroine is portrayed in her willingness to treat the town alcoholic to a shot of whiskey. Her action is depicted as an act of kindness that transcends moralizing when, during dinner, the poor fellow excuses himself from the table to avoid the humiliation and miserable exposure of the shakes. In the absence of other available means of response, giving an alcoholic a drink may be the most compassionate action. For the alcoholic struggling with the pain of abstinence, but determined to stay dry, giving her a drink is a very poor response to an apparent need.

15 I speak primarily of coercion here, but I use the term to cover all sorts of unjust circumstances that might result in our being in, and staying in, positions where we are the one upon whom seemingly vulnerable-responsive obligations fall.

16 See Christina Sommers, "Filial Morality" in E. F. Kittay and D. T. Meyers, 1987, op. cit., and Norman Daniels, *Am I my Parents Keeper?* (New York: Oxford University Press, 1988), for examples.

17 See Margaret Gilbert, *Living Together* (Lanham, MD: Rowman and Littlefield, 1996) for an interesting discussion of the formation of obligation as a consequence of relations. Gilbert, however, is not confining her discussion to moral obligation.

18 In *Subjection and Subjectivity* (New York: Routledge, 1994), Diana Meyers suggests that in such cases we question the "kind of person" we would be if we failed to respond appropriately. The question gets framed precisely this way in Doctorow's novel (most recently made into a musical play) *Ragtime*. The female protagonist, wife of a successful fireworks manufacturer and adventurer, residing in an allwhite suburban town, finds a newly buried yet still alive black infant as she digs in her garden. She tries to understand what she ought to do. As a dutiful wife, she knows that her husband – away on an adventure to the North Pole – would want her to give the child away immediately to a charity that would handle such a case. As a caring woman, who knows all too well the indifferent treatment such a throwaway child would receive, she cannot determine to do her wifely duty to obey what she knows would be her husband's wishes. In the musical, she sings in one chorus, "What kind of wife would I be?" if she kept the child, and responds in the next with: "What kind of woman would I be?" if she gave up the child. She resolves to keep the child and raise it in her own home. She responds to the pressing need of one who, by mere happenstance, is totally vulnerable to her actions rather than to an unquestioned duty to obey her husband.

19 While intuitions may be less uniform with respect to the fetus, I take it to be a desideratum of a model of moral obligation that an argument defending a woman's right to an abortion can be made plausibly. My quarrel with Thomson is not with her conclusion, but with the argument. The situation of pregnancy is not, I believe, adequately analogized to other situations that lend themselves to voluntaristic models. Historically, pregnancy has not been a consciously-consented-to-action that is characteristic of voluntarism. More often, a woman just finds herself pregnant and must respond to the situation in some way. But an adequate defense of abortion is not within the scope of the present project. Nonetheless it is an interesting challenge to the vulnerability model to attempt to mount a defense of abortion that respects the largely involuntary nature of the relation between pregnant woman and fetus.

20 See Eva Feder, Love's Labor (New York: Routledge, 1999) Part Two for a defense of this claim with respect to the liberal tradition of contract theory as revived by John Rawls. For a feminist critique of obligations based on the social contract, See Nancy Hirshman and Christine DiStefano, *Revisioning the Political* (Boulder, CO: Westview Press, 1996).

21 In Kittay (1999), ibid., Chapter Three, I make the case for the limitations of this conception in the face of dependency.

22 See Kittay (1999), ibid., Chapter Five, p. 133ff., for a discussion of the Family and Medical Leave Act of 1993.

23 It is interesting to hear the vulnerability model echoed in this response. The assumption of obligation is neither freely chosen nor coerced. It is, however, expected. The expectation arises out of the fact that the speaker's mother cared for her own mother. The speaker's mother is vulnerable to the speaker's actions first because of the expectation, and second because there is no one else who can help. The demand is morally warranted moreover because of an expectation backed by a similar response on the part of the one who now needs care – the care was justly deserved and justly demanded of the speaker. Also see note below.

24 At the same time the response is situated in a context where dependency work is gendered by social convention. What is the moral justification for the gendered assignment of care? Does the speaker have any male siblings who could share her obligations? That the mother has a justifiable claim to care from her children seems plausible enough, but the further question can be asked, why is there no one else who can do the care?

25 See Ruddick (1989) op. cit..

26 This method is not discussed in ethical reasoning frequently enough, but it is doubtless of great importance for ethical judgments. It is a separate project to work out the precise nature of such analogical moral thinking.

27 Virginia Held suggests that the maternal relation be substituted for the contractual relation as the fundamental model of moral relations. My suggestion follows upon that of Held except that I generalize these to dependency relations and do not confine them to maternal relations. See Virginia Held, "Non-Contractual Society: A Feminist View," *Canadian Journal of Philosophy* 13 (1987), pp. 111–35.

28 On the other hand, *in spite* of the condition of slavery, a certain fellow feeling may have developed between his master and him. This fellow feeling may become a more legitimate basis for an obligation arising out of his master's vulnerability to his actions. Such fellow feeling could only come about if the master had similarly provided evidence of fellow feeling toward the slave. A truly brutal master could not even warrant such a basis for response. Relationships of dependency often invoke some affective bonds which make clear-cut moral injunctions difficult – especially since (I want to insist) these affective bonds (of which fellow feeling is perhaps the mildest and most general) are themselves the ground of moral obligation.

21

Feminist Contractarianism

Jean Hampton

Like any good theory, {a woman's moral theory} will need not to ignore the partial truth of previous theories. So it must accommodate both the insights men have more easily than women, and those women have more easily than men. It should swallow up its predecessor theories. Women moral theorists, if any, will have this very great advantage over the men whose theories theirs supplant, that they can stand on the shoulders of men moral theorists, as no man has yet been able to stand on the shoulders of any woman moral theorist. There can be advantages, as well as handicaps, in being latecomers.

***Annette C. Baier*[1]**

Is it possible to be simultaneously a feminist and a partisan of the contractarian approach to moral and political theory? The prospects for a successful marriage of these two positions look dubious if one has read recent feminist criticisms of contemporary contractarian theories. Moreover, this brand of moral theory has been suffused with the technical machinery of game theory, logic, and economics of the sort often thought to attract male philosophers and repel female ones, making such theorizing, in the words of one feminist philosopher, a "big boys' game" and a "male locker room" that few female philosophers have "dared enter."[2]

But this seemingly inhospitable philosophical terrain has been my intellectual home for some years now. And I have been persistently attracted to contractarian modes of theorizing not merely because such theorizing offers "good clean intellectual fun"[3] but also because it holds out the promise of delivering a moral theory that will answer to my political – and in particular my feminist – commitments. This is not to say that particular contractarian moral theories don't deserve much of the feminist criticism they have received. In this chapter, I will explore and acknowledge the legitimacy of these feminist challenges. Nonetheless I want to argue that one version of this method of moral theorizing offers us what may be the keystone of any truly adequate moral theory.

In a nutshell I will be contending that contractarianism illuminates distributive justice, and this form of justice is required not only in relationships between strangers but also in relationships between intimates, including husbands and wives, parents and children, friend and friend. In making this

Jean Hampton, "Feminist Contractarianism," pp. 337–68 from Louise M. Antony and Charlotte E. Witt (eds.), *A Mind of One's Own: Feminist Essays on Reason and Objectivity*, 2nd edn. Boulder, CO: Westview Press, 2002.

argument I am opposing conventional philosophical wisdom going back as far as Aristotle, who writes, "If people are friends, they have no need of justice."[4] Among contemporary theorists, David Hume's claim that justice is only necessary in circumstances in which people have limited feelings of benevolence or friendship toward one another has been accepted by virtually every political philosopher since then, including Karl Marx and John Rawls. But I will contend that distributive justice, understood in its deepest sense, is inherent in any relationship that we regard as morally healthy and respectable – particularly in a friendship. Indeed, Aristotle himself hinted at this idea immediately after the passage just quoted – he says not only that those who are just also require friendship but also that "the justice that is most just seems to belong to friendship."[5] The reflection in this chapter might be taken as a way of exploring this enigmatic passage.

Hearing Voices

Recent work by Carol Gilligan has reinforced the general tendency of philosophers to see the concerns of justice and friendship as distinct from one another. Using interviews with older children and adults that address real or hypothetical moral problems, Gilligan attempts to display two different "moral voices" – voices she calls the "ethic of justice" and the "ethic of care" – and finds some evidence (albeit controversial) associating the first with men and the second with women.[6]

Two of her interviews with older children have always struck me as highly interesting. Eleven-year-old Jake, whose answers to the interviewers earned him high marks on Lawrence Kohlberg's moral maturity scale, gave the following answer when asked, "When responsibility to oneself and responsibility to others conflict, how should one choose?" He replied with great self-assurance, "You go about one-fourth to the others and three-fourths to yourself."[7] Contrast the following answer to the same question given by eleven-year-old Amy, whose answers to the interviewers earned poorer marks on Kohlberg's scale:

> Well, it really depends on the situation. If you have a responsibility with somebody else [*sic*], then you should keep it to a certain extent, but to the extent that it is really going to hurt you or stop you from doing something that you really, really want, then I think maybe you should put yourself first. But if it is your responsibility to somebody really close to you, you've just got to decide in that situation which is more important, yourself or that person, and like I said, it really depends on what kind of person you are and how you feel about the other person or persons involved.[8]

This rather tortured reply indicates considerable sensitivity and beneficent concern for others. Unsurprisingly, Amy's discussion of other moral problems reveals an interest in maintaining the well-being of others and in keeping relationships intact, which, according to Gilligan, shows that Amy values care. In contrast, Jake's remarks take for granted the importance of following rules that preclude interference in other people's pursuit of their interests, which, according to Gilligan, shows that Jake values justice. When asked to explain his answer to the question about responsibility to himself and others, Jake replies, "Because the most important thing in your decision should be yourself, don't let yourself be guided totally by other people, but you have to take them into consideration. So, if what you want to do is blow yourself up with an atom bomb, you should maybe blow yourself up with a hand grenade because you are thinking about your neighbors who would die also."[9]

As Jake's remarkable example shows, he regards "being moral" as pursuing one's own interests without damaging the interests of others, and he takes it as a matter of moral strength not to allow the interests of others to dictate to him what he ought or ought not to do. ("Don't let yourself be guided totally by other people," he warns.) In contrast, "being moral" for Amy means being responsive to the needs of others who are close to you or to whom you have made a commitment. Each child therefore makes a different assumption about the extent to which any of us is self-sufficient. Jake assumes that we are and ought to be interested in and capable of caring for ourselves, so that interaction with others is likely to be perceived either as interference or as an attempt to compromise one's independence. In contrast, Amy takes it for granted that we are not self-sufficient and that service to others will be welcomed as a sign of care and commendable concern.

Many feminist theorists maintain that the kind of moral voice that Amy exemplifies is clearly preferable to that of Jake. Annette Baier, for example, writes,

> Gilligan's girls and women saw morality as a matter of preserving valued ties to others, of preserving the conditions for that care and mutual care without which human life becomes bleak, lonely, and after a while, as the mature men in her study found, not self affirming, however successful in achieving the egoistic goals which had been set. The boys and men saw morality as a matter of finding workable traffic rules for self asserters, so that they do not needlessly frustrate one another, and so that they could, should they so choose, cooperate in more positive ways to mutual advantage.[10]

Certainly Baier is right that a "traffic rule" perspective on morality is neither a sophisticated nor a mature moral perspective. It appears to derive from the mistaken assumption that each of us is self-sufficient, able and desirous of "going it alone." Amy is surely right that this is false. In contrast, a perspective on morality that emphasizes caring for and fostering the well-being of others appears to be not only a richer, sounder theory of what genuine moral behavior is all about but also a better guide to behavior that enables one to live a life full of friendship and love. Such a perspective is one that women (and especially mothers) are frequently thought to exhibit more than men. Baier concludes, "It would not be much of an exaggeration to call the Gilligan 'different voice' the voice of the potential parent."[11]

Baier's way of responding to Jake's answer makes him into an archetype for a (commonly male) brand of moral immaturity. But one can respond to Amy's answer in a way that makes her an archetype for a quite different (and commonly female) brand of moral immaturity. Consider that Jake's answer is 13 words; Amy's is 109 words, and it is neither clear nor self-assured. *Maybe* she can put herself first, she says, if not doing so would mean losing out on something that she "really, really" wants. But only maybe. Jake is convinced not only that his interests count, but that they count far more than other people's (three-quarters to one-quarter). Amy appears to be having trouble figuring out whether or not her interests count at all. Consider her answer to the responsibility question:

> Some people put themselves and things for themselves before they put other people, and some people really care about other people. Like, I don't think your job is as important as somebody that you really love, like your husband or your parents or a very close friend. Somebody that you really care for – or if it's just your responsibility to your job or somebody that you barely know, then maybe you go first.[12]

Again, note her "maybe." Even in a situation in which she takes her responsibility to others to be minimal, she is having trouble asserting the priority of her own interests. Here is a child who appears very much guided by the interests of other people and takes that guidance to be what "being moral" means. One worries that she will find it difficult to plan a life that takes into consideration what she alone wants, because she is highly susceptible to being at the beck and call of others.

These interpretations are harsh and are probably not fair to the real children. But the fact that they are not only possible but natural shows the immature directions in which each child's thinking tends. Jack is susceptible to a brand of moral immaturity that manifests itself in an insensitivity to the needs of others and a failure to see himself as a fellow caretaker in a relationship. His remarks define a morality only in the most minimal sense: There is too much distance between him and others to enable him to be aware of and responsive to the needs or interests of others. In contrast, Amy is susceptible to a moral perspective that makes her too sensitive to other people, and her concern to meet their needs borders on outright servility. Whereas the authority and importance of others' needs are clear for her, the authority and importance of her own needs appear not to be. Indeed, unlike Jake she can offer no principle upon which to adjudicate the conflict between her claims and the claims of others, presumably because she has difficulty seeing herself as entitled to make any claim at all. And because she is so readily able to appreciate and be responsive to the needs of others, she is potentially a highly exploitable person. Thus if we interpret Amy's remarks as typifying a brand of moral immaturity quite different from that of Jake, they define an "ethic of care" that is really just a mimicry of genuine morality insofar as "caring" actions are generated out of the assumption that the agent is worth less than (and hence the servant of) the people she serves. Such caring cannot be moral because it is born of self-abnegation rather than self-worth.[13]

Although she respects Amy's concern for care, Gilligan herself admits the immaturity of Amy's response (while also stressing the immaturity of Jake's perspective). Moreover, that this brand of caring is an imitation of a genuinely moral response to others has also been noticed by other feminist writers,[14] and it is a surprisingly common theme in literature by women. For example, Charlotte Brontë's heroine in *Shirley* begins the journey to genuine maturity when she comes to question her own propensity to offer to care for others:

> "What was I created for, I wonder? Where is my place in the world?" She mused again. "Ah! I see," she pursued presently, "that is the question which most old maids are puzzled to solve: other people solve it for them by saying, 'Your place is to do good to others, to be helpful whenever help is wanted.' That is right in some measure, and a very convenient doctrine for the people who hold it; but I perceive that certain sets of human beings are very apt to maintain that other sets should give up their lives to them and their service, and then they requite them by praise: they call them devoted and virtuous. Is this enough? Is it to live? Is there not a terrible hollowness, mockery, want, craving, in that existence which is given away to others, for want of something of your own to bestow it on? I suspect there is. Does virtue lie in abnegation of self? I do not believe it. Undue humility makes tyranny: weak concession creates selfishness.... Each human being has his share of rights. I suspect it would conduce to me happiness and welfare of all, if each knew his allotment and held to it as tenaciously as a martyr to his creed."[15]

And there is Virginia Woolf's well-known description of "the angel in the house" who threatens to take over and destroy a woman's soul:

> She was intensely sympathetic. She was immensely charming. She was utterly unselfish. She excelled in the difficult art of family life. She sacrificed herself daily. If there was chicken, she took the leg: if there was a draught she sat in it – in short she was so constituted that she never had a mind or a wish of her own, but preferred to sympathize always with the minds and wishes of others. Above all – I need not say it – she was pure.... I turned upon her and caught her by the throat. I did my best to kill her. My excuse, if I were to be had up in a court of law would be that I acted in self-defence. Had I not killed her she would have killed me.[16]

Both novelists believe that a genuine moral agent has to have a good sense of her own moral claims if she is going to be a person at all and thus a real partner in a morally sound relationship.[17] She must also have some sense of what it is to make a legitimate claim if she is to understand and respond to the legitimate claims of others and resist attempts to involve herself in relationships that will make her the mere servant of others' desires. Both philosophical and commonsense understandings of morality have been so fixated on the other-regardingness of moral life that they have encouraged us to mistake archetypal Amy's response for a moral response.[18]

What happens when archetypal Jake and archetypal Amy grow up? If they were to marry, wouldn't Amy take it upon herself to meet the needs of Jake and do the work to maintain their relationship (giving up her career if necessary, insofar as she thinks that a job isn't as important as "someone you really love")? And wouldn't Jake naturally take it for granted that his interests should predominate (three-fourths to one fourth) and be ignorant of many of the needs of others around him that might prompt a caring response? I find it striking that these children's answers betray perspectives that seem to fit them perfectly for the kind of gendered roles that prevail in our society. In their archetypal forms, I hear the voice of a child who is preparing to be a member of a dominating group and the voice of another who is preparing to be a member of the group that is dominated. Neither of these voices should be allowed to inform our moral theorizing if such theorizing is going to be successful at formulating ways of interacting that are not only morally acceptable but also attack the oppressive relationships that now hold in our society.

Two Forms of Contractarian Theory

So how do we set about defining an acceptable formulation of morality? The idea that the essence not only of human rationality but also of human morality is embodied in the notion of contract is the heart of what is called the "contractarian" approach to moral thinking. Advocates of this approach ask us to imagine a group of people sitting around a bargaining table; each person is interested only in himself. This group is to decide answers to moral or political questions by determining what they can all agree to or what they would all be unreasonable to reject.

However, both proponents and opponents of this style of argument have failed to appreciate just how many argumentative uses of the contract idea have appeared over the centuries. Arguments that self-consciously invoke a social contract can differ in what they aim to justify or explain (for example, the state, conceptions of justice, morality), what they take the problem of justification to be, and whether or not they presuppose a moral theory or purport to be a moral theory. Thus, even though theorists who call themselves "contractarians" have all supposedly begun from the same reflective starting point – namely, what people could "agree to" – these differences and disagreements among people who are supposedly in the same philosophical camp show that contractarians are united not by a common philosophical theory but by a common *image*. Philosophers hate to admit it, but sometimes they work from pictures rather than ideas. And in an attempt to get a handle on the nature of the state, the reasons for its justification, and the legitimate moral claims each of us can make on our behalf against others, the contract imagery has struck many as enormously promising. But how that image has been translated into argument has varied considerably, and philosophers have disagreed about what political or moral issue that image can profitably illuminate.

A number of feminist theorists reject out of hand the idea that this could be an acceptable approach to defining morality precisely because of what they take to be the unattractiveness of the contract image.[19] Virginia Held, for example, insists:

> To see contractual relations between self-interested or mutually disinterested individuals as constituting a paradigm of human relations is to take a certain historically specific conception of 'economic man' as representative of humanity. And it is, many feminists are beginning to agree, to overlook or to discount in very fundamental ways the experience of women.[20]

And at first glance this way of thinking about morality does seem rather Jake-like. People are postulated to be self-regarding rather than other-regarding and their project is to define rules that enable them to live in harmony – which sounds a great deal like constructing (to quote Baier again) "traffic rules for self assertors."[21] Moreover, their distance from one another seems to prevent them from feeling emotional bonds of attachment or concern that would prompt care without the promise of pay.

I will be arguing that this type of attack on contractarian theory is importantly misguided. But before I can begin that argument, I want to clarify in this section exactly what kind of contractarian argument I will be defending in the rest of the chapter. There are two kinds of moral argument that one contract image has spawned in modern times – the first has its roots in Thomas Hobbes and is exemplified in the work of David Gauthier, James Buchanan, Gilbert Harman, and John Mackie; the second has its roots in Immanuel Kant and is exemplified in the work of John Rawls and T. M. Scanlon. I will review these two forms of contractarian theory and the criticisms to which each is subject before I go on, in the next section, to locate my own contractarian approach in this conceptual space.

Hobbesian contractarianism

Although Hobbes himself never repudiated a divine origin for moral laws, he and the moral philosophers who followed him have attempted to develop an entirely *human* justification of morality.[22] Hobbesians start by insisting that what is valuable is what a person desires or prefers, not what he ought to desire (for no such prescriptively powerful object exists); and rational action is action that achieves or maximizes the satisfaction of desires or preferences. They then go on to insist that moral action is rational for a person to perform if and only if such action advances the satisfaction of his desires or preferences. And usually, they argue, for most of us the moral action will be rational. Because moral actions lead to peaceful and harmonious living conducive to the satisfaction of almost everyone's desires or preferences, moral actions are rational for almost everyone and thus "mutually agreeable." But in order to ensure that no cooperative person becomes the prey of immoral aggressors, Hobbesians believe that moral actions must be the conventional norms in a community, so that each person can expect that if she behaves cooperatively, others will do so too, and vice versa. These conventions constitute the institution of morality in a society.

So the Hobbesian moral theory is committed to the idea that morality is a human-made institution that is justified only to the extent that it effectively furthers human interests. Hobbesians explain the existence of morality in society by appealing to the convention-creating activities of human beings; they also argue that the justification of morality in any human society depends upon how well its moral conventions serve individuals' desires or preferences. So Hobbesians do not assume that existing conventions are, in and of themselves, justified. By considering "what we *could* agree to" if we had the chance to reappraise and redo the cooperative conventions in our society, we are able to determine the extent to which our present conventions are mutually agreeable and thus rational for us to accept and act on. Consequently, Hobbesians invoke both actual agreements (or rather, conventions) and hypothetical agreements (which involve considering what conventions would be mutually agreeable) at different points in their theory. The former are what they believe our moral life consists in; the latter are what they believe our moral life *should* consist in – that is, what our actual moral life should model.[23]

This means the notion of contract does not do justificational work *by itself* in the Hobbesian moral theory – this term is only used metaphorically. What we "could agree to" has moral force for the Hobbesians not because make-believe promises in hypothetical worlds have any binding force but because this sort of agreement is a device that (merely) reveals the way in which the agreed-upon outcome is rational for all of us. In particular, thinking about "what we could all agree to" allows us to construct a deduction of practical reason to determine what politics are mutually advantageous. Thus the justificational force of this kind of contract theory is carried within but is derived from sources other than the contractor agreement in the theory.

As I've noted, many theorists are attracted to this theory because of its sensible metaphysics: It doesn't base morality on strange, nonnatural properties or objects; nor does it credit human beings with what Mackie calls "magical" powers capable of discerning the moral truth "out there."[24] Instead it sees morality as a human invention that we commend to the extent that it is mutually advantageous for those who would use it. But such a metaphysical foundation is attractive only if what is built upon it counts as a genuine morality. And there are good reasons for complaining that Hobbesian contractarianism yields considerably less than the real thing. When *Leviathan* was originally published in 1651, some readers sympathetic to Aristotelian ideas were shocked by the idea that the nature of our ties to others was interest based and contended that Hobbes's theory went too far in trying to represent us as radically separate from others. Their worries are also the worries of many twentieth-century critics, including feminists, who insist that any adequate moral theory must take into account our emotion-based connections with others and the fact that we are socially defined beings.[25]

But I would argue that what disqualifies it at a more fundamental level as an acceptable moral theory is its failure to incorporate the idea that individuals have what I will call "intrinsic value." It has not been sufficiently appreciated, I believe, that by answering the "Why be moral?" question by invoking self-interest in the way that Hobbesians do, one makes not only cooperative action but also the human beings with whom one will cooperate merely of *instrumental value*. That is, if you ask me why I should treat you morally, and I respond by saying that it is in my interest to do so, I am telling you that my regard for you is something that is merely instrumentally valuable to me; I do not give you that regard because there is something about you yourself that merits it, regardless of the usefulness of that regard to me. Now Hobbes is unembarrassed by the fact that on his view, "the *Value*, or WORTH of a man, is as of all other things, his Price; that is to say, so much as would be given for the use of his Power: and therefore is not absolute; but a thing dependent on the need and judgment of another."[26]

But this way of viewing people is not something that we, or even some Hobbesians, can take with equanimity. In the final two chapters of his book, Gauthier openly worries about the fact that the reason why we value moral imperatives on this Hobbesian view is that they are instrumentally valuable to us in our pursuit of what we value. But why are they instrumentally valuable? Because, in virtue of our physical and intellectual weaknesses that make it impossible for us to be self-sufficient, we need the cooperation of others to prosper. If there were some way that we could remedy our weaknesses and become self-sufficient – for example, by becoming a superman or a superwoman, or by using a Ring of Gyges to make ourselves invisible and so steal from the stores of others with impunity – then it seems we would no longer value or respect moral constraints because they would no longer be useful to us – unless we happened to like the idea. But in this case, sentiment rather than reason would motivate kind treatment. And without such sentiment, it would be rational for us to take other people as "prey."

Even in a world in which we are not self-sufficient, the Hobbesian moral theory gives us no reason outside of contingent emotional sentiment to respect those with whom we have no need of cooperating or those whom we are strong enough to dominate, such as the elderly, the physically handicapped, mentally disabled children whom we do not want to rear, or people from other societies with whom we have no interest in trading. And I would argue that this shows that Hobbesian moral contractarianism fails in a serious way to capture the nature of morality. Regardless of whether or not one can engage in beneficial cooperative interactions with another, our moral intuitions push us to assent to the idea that one owes that person respectful treatment simply in virtue of the fact that she is a *person*. It seems to be a feature of our moral life that we regard a human being, whether or not she is instrumentally valuable, as always intrinsically valuable. Indeed, to the extent that the results of a Hobbesian theory are acceptable, this is because one's concern to cooperate with someone whom one cannot dominate leads one to behave in ways that mimic the respect one ought to show her simply in virtue of her worth as a human being.

Kantian contractarianism

To abandon the idea that the only value human beings have is instrumental is to abandon the Hobbesian approach to morality and to move in the direction of what I will call "Kantian contractarianism." In his later writings Immanuel Kant proposed that the "ideal" of the "Original Contract" could be used to determine just political policies:

> Yet this contract, which we call *contractus originarius or pactum sociale*, as the coalition of every particular and private will within a people into a common public will for purposes of purely legal legislation, need by no means be presupposed as a fact.... It is rather a *mere idea* of reason, albeit one with indubitable practical reality, obligating every lawmaker to frame his laws so that they *might* have come from the united will of an entire people, and to regard any subject who would be a citizen as if he had joined in voting for such a will. For this is the touchstone of the legitimacy of public law. If a law is so framed that all the people *could not possibly* give their consent – as, for example, a law granting the hereditary *privilege of master status* to a certain class of subjects – the law is unjust.[27]

As I interpret this passage, when Kant asks us to think about what people could agree to, he is not trying to justify actions or policies by invoking, in any literal sense, the consent of the people. Only the consent of *real* people can be legitimating, and Kant talks about hypothetical agreements made by hypothetical people. But he does believe these make-believe agreements have moral force for us, not because we are under any illusion that the make-believe consent of make-believe people is obliging for us, but because the process by which these people reach agreement is morally revealing.

Kant's contracting process has been further developed by subsequent philosophers, such as John Rawls and T. M. Scanlon, convinced of its moral promise. Rawls, in particular, concentrates on defining the hypothetical people who are supposed to make this agreement to ensure that their reasoning will not be tarnished by immorality, injustice, or prejudice and thus that the outcome of their joint deliberations will be morally sound (although not all contractarians have agreed with his way of defining the parties to get this result). The Kantians' social contract is therefore a device used in their theorizing to reveal what is just or what is moral. So like the Hobbesians, their contract talk is really just a way of reasoning that allows us to work out conceptual answers to moral problems. But whereas the Hobbesians' use of contract language expresses the fact that, on their view, morality is a human invention that (if it is well invented) ought to be mutually advantageous, the Kantians' use of the contract language is meant to show that moral principles and conceptions are provable theorems derived from a morally revealing and authoritative contractarian reasoning process or "moral proof procedure."[28]

There is a prominent feminist criticism of Rawls's version of this form of contractarianism. These feminists charge (along with certain Hegelian critics) that Rawls's stripping people of their socially defined identities and sending them off to an "Archimedean point" to choose among or between moral conceptions asks us to do the impossible – namely, to abstract from our socially defined identities in order to reveal some sort of transcultural truth.[29] Because we are socially defined, these critics contend that any intuitions remaining after people are supposedly stripped to their bare essentials will still be permeated with the assumptions of a sexist society, producing (not surprisingly) "patriarchal outcomes."[30]

There is good reason to think that this feminist complaint is importantly misguided, particularly in view of the feminists' own political commitments (and at least one feminist has already argued this point).[31] Although feminists often insist that our natures are to a high degree socially defined – which means that, on their view, theorizing about what we are "really like" will tend to be informed by intuitions that reflect the society that forms us – it is part of the feminist challenge to our society that some ways in which our society forms us are *wrong* – producing human beings whose development is stunted or distorted and whose connection with other human beings is problematic (because they are either too inclined to want to master others or too likely to wind up being mastered). So although many feminists call themselves "pluralists" who advocate the recognition of many points of view and the legitimacy of many kinds of theorizing about the world, in fact there are some points of view that they reject outright, including sexist and racist views and inegalitarian conceptions of human treatment. Whether or not they explicitly recognize it, this rejection is motivated by an implicit appeal to objective ideals of human interaction and optimal socialization of men and women. The pluralists' vision of a better world, in which the oppression of women does not exist, is a vision of human beings developing in the right – that is, objectively right – way, such that they can flourish and interact well with one another rather than in ways that precipitate oppression or abuse. Accordingly, it is ironic that a Rawlsian Archimedean point is exactly what feminists require to carry out their form of social criticism.

Some feminists will insist that although they do attack some of the practices and points of view in their society, nonetheless the values they use in their criticisms are still authored by their society. Hence, they argue, their society is sufficiently pluralistic to produce mutually inconsistent value-schemes. But even if that is so, what bearing does this sociological fact have on what ought to happen in the sociopolitical arena? In particular, what justifies the feminists in thinking that their values should come to predominate? Merely appealing to consistency or social stability isn't sufficient to justify that predominance, because these reasons could just as easily justify the predominance of racist/sexist values. Feminists not only want their values to predominate, they want them to do so because they are the right values. Hence to argue for their values, they must have an Archimedean point from which to survey and critically assess the value-schemes in their societies. The Rawlsian Archimedean point "forces one to question and consider traditions, customs, and institutions from all points of view"[32] and thus attempts to go beyond mere shared understandings, common beliefs, or social practices that may be oppressive or exploitative. Hence, it seems to offer feminists the perspective they need to be able to identify and attack unjust social practices.[33]

Feminists, however, have an important counter-response to this defense of the Rawlsian method. They can grant that an Archimedean point would be highly desirable for them given their political agenda, but go on to complain that no Kantian contractarian, including Rawls, has convincingly demonstrated that his contractarian theory provides one, because no contractarian has specified his theory sufficiently such that we can be sure it relies only upon "morally pure" starting points and not the sort of "biased" (for example, sexist or racist) ideas or intuitions that an unjust society can encourage in its citizens. There are two ways in which feminists could charge that these morally suspect intuitions might be intruding into Rawls's theory. First, these intuitions may be covertly motivating the particular constraints, assumptions, or features that are supposed to apply in the contract situation. Feminists are implicitly criticizing Rawls's theory on this basis when they charge that his assumption that parties in the original position are self-interested is motivated by intuitions about what counts as a plausibly "weak" psychology, intuitions that actually derive from a discredited Hobbesian view of human nature. According to these critics, this Jake-like component of Rawls's thinking drives out of his theory both our emotion-based attachments to others' well-being and our other-regarding, duty-based commitments to them, demonstrating the extent to which even this high-minded Kantian appears heavily in the grip of outmoded and distorting individualistic intuitions. Second, suspect intuitions may be illicitly operating within the original-position reasoning procedure and thereby playing a direct role in the justification of Rawls's political conclusions. Critics who charge that Rawls's reliance on the maximin rule cannot be justified will note that if the rule is removed from the argument, only vague intuitive appeals could explain how the parties would reach the political conclusions Rawls recommends, appeals that might not withstand sustained moral scrutiny if they were better understood.[34]

Although Scanlon does not presume that his contract approach defines an Archimedean point, his approach is even more susceptible to the charge that it is covertly relying on ill-defined or ill-defended intuitions. Scanlon argues that (what he calls) the "contractualist" account of the nature of moral wrongdoing goes as follows: "An act is wrong if its performance under the circumstances would be disallowed by any system of rules for the general regulation of behavior which no one could reasonably reject as a basis for informed, unforced general agreement."[35] This definition is intended as "a characterization of the kind of property which moral wrongness is."[36] In this statement of contractualism, the reader is inevitably drawn to the word "reasonably", yet Scanlon never explicitly cashes out the term. He claims, for example, that a policy A that would pass an average utilitarian test but that would cause some to fare badly is, prima facie, a policy that the "losers" would be reasonable to reject.[37] He goes on to say, however, that ultimately the reasonableness of the losers' objection to A is not established simply by the fact that they are worse off under A than they would be under some alternative policy E in which no one's situation is as bad. Instead, says Scanlon, the complaint against A by the A losers must be weighed against the complaints made by those who would do worse under E than under A. "The question to be asked is, is it unreasonable for some one to refuse to put up with the Losers' situation under A in order that someone else should be able to enjoy the benefits which he would have to give up under E?"[38]

But on what grounds, or using what criteria, can we provide the right answer to this question? Scanlon gives us no directions for adjudicating the complaints of the two groups in this situation, and one begins to worry that his appeal to "reasonableness" as a way of determining the solution is an appeal to inchoate intuitions. Occasionally, he seems to link the term to the purported desire that people in the hypothetical contract are supposed to have to reach an agreement with one another: "The only relevant pressure for agreement comes from the desire to find and agree on principles which no one who had this desire could reasonably reject."[39] But what is this desire? It seems to be more than just the desire to reach an agreement, for Scanlon says later that the desire is one to "find principles which none could reasonably reject."[40] So, because the desire is defined in terms of reasonableness, it cannot be taken to explicate it. And if reasonableness is defined using moral notions such as fairness (as in, "It is only reasonable for me to reject proposals that are unfair"), Scanlon's moral project is circular, because on his view moral properties are supposed to be defined by the contract test, thereby precluding a central component of that test that presupposes one or more moral properties.[41]

So we don't know what is really doing the work in Scanlon's test, and this generates at least three problems for his theory. First, we can't be sure that everyone who uses Scanlon's test will rely on the same conception of reasonableness to arrive at the same answer. Second, unless his conception of reasonableness is fully (and acceptably) explicated, feminists have good reason to worry about what might seem reasonable to people raised in a sexist patriarchal society. And third, unless this conception is fully explicated, those of us loyal to contractarianism as a distinctive form of moral argument have reason to worry that there is so much reliance on intuition in the operation of Scanlon's test that his approach ultimately reduces to some other ethical theory. For example, if these intuitions are understood as foundational, his theory would seem to amount to nothing more than a version of ethical intuitionism. Or if they are understood to be generated by some other moral theory, such as utilitarianism, the contract method would appear to be merely a way of marshaling ideas generated by that other theory. Thus a utilitarian might argue that "reasonable rejection" should be understood as rejection on the grounds that what is being proposed is not utility-maximizing for the group. But Scanlon wants to be able to draw upon and generate antiutilitarian ideas in his contractarian argument through argument rather than through an appeal to intuition alone.[42] Because neither he nor, for that matter, any Kantian contractarian has given us any sense of what these ideas are, or why they are appropriate to rely upon, or how they work together to form a nonintuitionistic moral reasoning procedure, we begin to wonder whether or not this or indeed any Kantian's appeal to "what we could agree to" is just a way to fabricate a defense for moral or political conceptions that these Kantian theorists happen to like but for which they cannot provide a valid argument resting on plausible and well-explicated premises.

A Feminist Form of Kantian Contractarian Theory

In view of these criticisms against both Hobbesian and Kantian contractarianism, it might seem that the whole approach is a theoretical dead end not only for feminists but also for any philosopher interested in developing a successful theory of our moral life. But I want to try to rehabilitate this approach in the eyes of its critics by outlining what might be called a "Hobbesian" brand of Kantian contractarianism that is responsible both to the meta-ethical and to the feminist criticisms I have outlined and that holds the promise of being at least part (but only part) of a complete theory outlining a mature morality.

"Private" relationships and the contractarian test

As I tried over the years to determine the source of my own support for the contractarian approach, I found myself increasingly convinced that the contract test was highly appropriate for the evaluation of exactly the kinds of relationships feminists assumed they could not illuminate: personal, intimate ones. It is a testament to the powerful control that the public-private distinction has over even its most ardent feminist critics that they resist the appropriateness of what they take to be a "public" metaphor to evaluate the morality of a "private" relationship. I want to propose that by invoking the idea of a contract we can make a moral evaluation of any relationship, whether it is in the family, the marketplace, the political society, or the workplace[43] – namely, an evaluation of the extent to which that relationship is just ("just" in a sense I shall define below).

A necessary condition of a relationship's being just is that no party in that relationship or system is exploited by another. But exploitation is possible even in the most intimate relationship if one party relies upon the affection or duty felt by another party to use that other party to her detriment. In Gauthier's words, our sociality

> becomes a source of exploitation if it induces persons to acquiesce in institutions and practices that but for their fellow-feeling would be costly to them. Feminist thought has surely made this, perhaps the core form of exploitation, clear to us. Thus the contractarian insists that a society could not command the willing allegiance of a rational person if, without appealing to her feelings for others, it afforded her no expectation of benefit.[44]

As I understand Gauthier's remarks, he is not suggesting that one should never give gifts out of love or duty without insisting on being paid for them; rather, he is suggesting that one's propensity to give gifts out of love or duty *should not become the lever that another party who is capable of reciprocating relies upon to get one to maintain a relationship to one's cost.*

Perhaps this is most deeply true within the family. A woman whose devotion to her family causes her to serve them despite the fact that they do little in return is in an exploitative relationship. Of course, infants cannot assume any of her burdens; fairness cannot exist between individuals whose powers and capacities are so unequal. (Note that this relationship is not unfair either; the infant does not use the mother's love in order to exploit her.) But older children can. Indeed, as children become able to benefit those who have cared for them, it becomes increasingly unacceptable to see them failing to return these benefits. Unless they are encouraged to reciprocate the care they have received as they become able to do so, they are being allowed to exploit other human beings by taking advantage of their love for them.

So our ties (for example, of friendship or marriage) to those who are able to reciprocate what we give to them (as opposed to victims of serious diseases, impoverished people, or infants) are morally acceptable, healthy, and worthy of praise only insofar as they do not involve, on either side, the infliction of costs or the confiscation of benefits over a significant period that implicitly reveals disregard rather than respect for that person.

In order to test for the presence of such disregard, I want to argue that we should apply a version of a contractarian test to the relationship by asking: "Given the fact that we are in this relationship, could both of us reasonably accept the distribution of costs and benefits (that is, the costs and benefits that are not themselves side effects of any affective or duty-based tie between us) if it were the subject of an informed, unforced agreement in which we think of ourselves as motivated solely by self-interest?" Note, first, that the self-interested motivation is assumed for purposes of testing the moral health of the relationship; one is essentially trying to put aside the potentially blinding influence of affection or duty to see whether costs and benefits are distributed such that one is losing out to the other party. Second, note that the costs and benefits that the test inquires about are not ones that come from the affection or duty holding the parties together in the relationship – for among other things, these cannot be distributed and are outside the province of justice. One cannot distribute the pain that a parent feels when her teenage child gets into trouble, the happiness felt by someone because of the accomplishments of her friend, the suffering of a woman because of the ill-ess of a parent. But one can distribute the burdens of caring for an infant or running a household, the costs of correspondence, the work involved in a project jointly undertaken by two friends. These nonaffective costs and benefits that the relationship itself creates or makes possible must be distributed fairly if the relationship is to be just.

But how does this test actually work? In par ticular, how do we give content to the word "reasonable" such that it is not just a covert appeal to our (perhaps morally suspect) intuitions?

A simple appeal to equality won't do. Exploitation doesn't loom every time a person gets a present from a friend and then forgets her friend's birthday, or when she pays less in long-distance phone calls than her friend does. Nor would the test be reliable if it relied only upon feelings of "being used"; such feelings are all too likely to be wrong, or exaggerated, or inappropriately weak for us to put full moral faith in them. So I shall now argue that the test must be informed by a set of normative concepts that, taken together, enable us to define exploitation and recognize it when it occurs.

The concept behind the test

I claim that at the base of the Kantian contract theory is not a collection of inchoate and perhaps morally suspect intuitions that might vary among human beings; rather, it is a particular set of defensible concepts composing what I will call, after Rawls, a "conception of the person." As I understand it, in a successful contractarian theory the contract is a (mere) device that, if used in the right circumstances, will call to mind and organize these concepts in a way that will enable us to apply them to diagnose successfully the presence of injustice in a relationship. The contractarian conception of the person includes a list of characteristics of personhood. But it is more than just a list. It also includes two normative conceptions that are central to understanding how we are to respond to a person: namely, a conception of human worth and a conception of a person's legitimate interests.

A conception of human worth tells one what sort of treatment is appropriate or required or prohibited for certain types of individuals on the basis of an assessment of how valuable these individuals are. Some philosophers follow Hobbes in thinking that any assessments of our value as individuals can only be instrumental, whereas other philosophers such as Kant believe that, regardless of our price, our worth is non-instrumental, objective, and equal. Kant also has opponents who, while agreeing that our value is noninstrumental and objective, reject the idea that all humans are of equal value – for example, those who think human beings of a certain gender or race or caste are higher in value (and so deserving of better treatment) than those of a different gender, race, or caste.

I want to argue that animating the contract test is a certain very Kantian conception of human worth. To say that a policy must be "agreed to" by all is to say that in formulating a just policy, we must recognize that none of us can take only herself to "matter" such that she can dictate the solution alone, and also that none of us is allowed to ignore or disregard her own importance in the formulation of the right policy. Therefore, the self-interested perspective each person takes when she uses the test to assess a relationship shouldn't be seen as arrogant selfishness but as a way of symbolizing (as Jake would wish) the proper self-regard each of us should have in view of our worth, in view of the fact that, as Kant would put it, we are "ends in ourselves." However, by requiring that a policy be one that we could all agree to, the contractarian doesn't merely ask each of us to insist on our own worth; he also asks us (as Amy would wish) to recognize and come to terms with the fact that others are just as valuable as we ourselves. So without being an explicit theory of how we are valuable relative to one another, the contract device nonetheless "pictures" that relative value.

It was because the contractarian image implicitly calls forth a certain conception of relative human worth that Rawls was drawn to it as a way of combating the sacrificial tendencies of utilitarianism. The Amy-like insistence of the utilitarian that we should put the group first and accommodate ourselves to the well-being of others even if it would mean substantial and serious sacrifices either on our part or on the part of others has been the central reason why so many have rejected it as an adequate moral theory. If, on the other hand, we evaluate policies, actions, or treatments in any relationship by asking whether each individual, from a self-interested point of view, could reasonably reject them, we are letting each person "count" in a certain way. And I am proposing that we can give content to a Scanlon-like contract test as long as we develop the conception of how human beings ought to count – that is, the conception of human worth that implicitly informs the contract image.[45]

Because the contract image is ultimately animated by this conception of worth, a contractarian doesn't even need to appeal to "what we could agree to" if she has another device that is animated by the same conception. In this regard, it is important to note that although Rawls is called a contractarian, he makes minimal use of the contract device in *A Theory of Justice* and relies on another method of accomplishing the morally revealing representation of relative worth.[46] Although he says that each party to the original position must agree with all the rest on which available alternative is the best conception of justice, in fact that agreement is otiose because each party in his original position follows the same reasoning procedure and reaches the same conclusion – namely, that the Rawlsian conception of justice is preferable to all others. This reasoning procedure requires those who use it to appraise policies, rules, or principles without knowing which person she will become in the society that will be subject to these policies, rules, or principles. But note that, as with the contract device, this "I could be anybody" device requires that I reason in such a way that each person matters, so that I will be reluctant to permit any one of them (who might turn out to be *me*) to be sacrificed for the benefit of the group. So although Rawls relies on a noncontractarian device in *A Theory of Justice*, he is nonetheless a "real" contractarian because the device he uses taps into the same conception of worth as the contract device.[47] And this shows that it isn't the contract device that is the substance of a contractarian theory but the conception of worth that informs that device.

But, the reader may ask, if the conception of the person you're developing is the *real* moral theory and the contract talk only a heuristic device useful for picturing or suggesting this conception, are you really a contractarian?

In a way I don't care about the answer to this question: I am ultimately uninterested in labels, and if my insistence that the substantive roots of my theory are not found in the idea of a contract convinces readers that the label "contractarian" is inappropriate for that theory, then so be it. But, as I've discussed, every contract theory, whether Hobbesian or Kantian, has used the idea of a contract as a heuristic tool that points us toward the correct form of moral reasoning and has not relied on the idea of contract in any literal way to do any justificatory work. Moreover, there is not enough in the notion of a contract to constitute an adequate moral reasoning procedure in and of itself, as the discussion of Scanlon's theory shows. Hence, in my theory (and, I would argue, in Kant's), the idea of a contract serves as a device that points to, or suggests, the concepts (in particular, the concept of human worth) at the substantive heart of morality. And I would argue that it is because of its suggestiveness that philosophers like me have been persistently attracted to talk of contract and have used the term to label their theories.

Clarifying the concept

On my view, the way to develop a successful Kantian contractarian argument so that it is not worryingly "intuitive" is to understand and make precise the conception of the person, and particularly the conception of human worth, implicitly underlying the contract image. I regard this as a tough, lengthy and long-term project. Nonetheless, I can at least make a few preliminary remarks here to show how I believe we can read off from the contract image aspects of the conception of human worth that animates it.

The most important idea invoked by the image is the Kantian idea that people have *intrinsic, non-instrumental value* (which is why I take it that Kant himself invoked the image in his political writings). But some readers may wonder why the contract image doesn't imply, instead, the idea that the people involved in the contract, or the services they would provide, are mere commodities. This is the assumption of many Marxists and some feminists: Carol Pateman, for example, has argued that the "logic" of contractual thinking would effect a morally offensive "universal market in bodies and services" in which people would contract for the services they desired (many of which they now get "for free" in a marriage – for example, sex, surrogate parenting, selling human eggs, renting wombs, and so on).[48]

But my understanding of the contract image suggests nothing of the sort. This is because, first, the contract image I invoke is deliberately meant to be an *ideal* agreement between equals. I do not regard the contract test as a morally neutral device (as Rawls, for example, suggests); rather, I see it as an image fed by normative ideas that one is ultimately relying on when using the test to make moral evaluations. And it is not true that in an ideal contract each party responds to the other solely as instrumentally valuable. Think literally about what one means when one says a person is instrumentally valuable: One is saying that the person is valuable in the way that a pen or a typewriter or a hammer is valuable. That person has the value *and the status* of a tool. But in an ideal contract among relative strangers, neither party responds to the other only in that way. I don't get you to paint my house simply by whistling and pointing to the paint, as if you were some kind of automated paint machine. I believe that to get you to paint my house I must get your *consent* to do so, and I also believe (if I think our contractual relationship is ideal and hence just) that I can only get your consent if you are sure that I am not asking you to bear the costs of doing so without any reciprocating benefit from me to you. But note that this attitude implicitly rejects the view that the other person has only instrumental standing. In an ideal contract between equals, each person must respect the wishes of the other in order to achieve the agreement; hence, requiring mutual consent under these circumstances means requiring respect.

So understood, the contract test could be successfully used to disallow the commodization of certain aspects of our person. It could be used, for example, to preclude the commodization of a womb: Before a group of people could even consider the question, "What terms could we reasonably accept for our surrogacy contract?" they would have to ask the question, "Is the very idea of a surrogacy contract something that each of us could reasonably accept?" And it is plausible to suppose that people equally situated and motivated to secure their legitimate interests could not all agree to such a contract (in particular, the prospective surrogate mother could not). Remember that both Kant and Rawls have argued that the contract idea, when invoked, precludes certain institutional structures and social practices (for example, aristocratic social orders or slavery) that are degrading; similarly, I argue for an understanding of the contract test that forbids a variety of social arrangements that are demeaning – that is, inconsistent with the worth of all the parties involved.

As these remarks show, the conception of worth informing the contract device, understood ideally, is an *egalitarian* conception: Contractarians aim to idealize parties in a relationship so that each of them not only is an equal participant in the agreement process but also possesses equal bargaining power. And this is a way of expressing the idea that no person's intrinsic worth is greater than any other's. Finally, it is a *nonaggregative* conception. Although utilitarians grant people value, and can even be called "egalitarians" about value insofar as they allow each person to count equally in the utilitarian calculation, this way of "counting" still isn't good enough for the contractarian, who would note that each person appears in the utilitarian calculation as a number representing how much he contributes to the total good. This means that it is not really the individual so much as the summable units of good that he contributes (and, in the final analysis, represents in the calculation) that the utilitarian takes seriously. Each individual is therefore valued by that theory (only) to the extent that he will respond to any resources by contributing units of good to the total. In contrast, the contractarian gives each person the ability to veto an arrangement that he believes will unreasonably disadvantage him relative to the others, and this reflects the contractarian's view that each of us has a value that resists aggregation and that makes demands on us regardless of how advantageous a group might find it to ignore those demands.

The other component of the conception of the person informing the contract device is the conception of a person's legitimate interests. If one has something of great value, that value requires that one, for example, preserve it, treat it carefully so as not to hurt it, and, if it is sentient, minimize its experience of pain. That is, its value requires that one care for it in view of its importance. These responses presuppose a theory of what a valued object requires such that its value can be both preserved and respected. Human beings' unique and considerable value requires that they be properly cared for. But what does such care involve? I believe that the answer to such a question would involve detailing who we are and what interests of ours are urgent given our nature. These interests would include not only having enough to eat but also have the psychological conditions that allow us to function well and the liberty that, as autonomous beings, we need. To put it in Aristotelian terms, the answer involves constructing a normative theory formulating what is good for human beings (both as a species and as distinctive individuals).[49] This normative theory is, however, connected to the contractarian's theory of human worth. If we regard a certain set of sentient creatures as relatively unimportant, what we take to be their legitimate interests will differ sharply from what we take to be the legitimate interests of those to whom we attribute great worth. Of course, a conception of human good will also be informed by a host of physiological and psychological facts about human beings, but how we respond to those facts is fundamentally dependent upon how we understand human beings to be valuable.

To the extent that we can pin down what our legitimate interests are, we can also pin down some of the ideas to which we are implicitly appealing in the contract test. When we ask, "Could all of us reasonably accept this if it were proposed as the subject of unforced, informed agreement?" we must assume that each of us is consulting interests that we are legitimately entitled to have respected. Rawls's theory is famous for trying to define these interests in a political context, and many critics have noted that despite his demurrers to the contrary, his is a normatively loaded conception. But of course it must be, because not all of our interests are good ones and thus count as grounds for "reasonable rejections." Contractarians have thus far been unable to get philosophical control over the concept of legitimate interests to which they must appeal if their test is going to have real bite; I am proposing that to do so, they must not rely upon vaguely defined intuitions called forth by the contract device but must instead develop and defend in its own right the concept of legitimate interests generating these intuitions.

Contractarianism and feminist politics

The development of this theory depends upon the development and defense of the conception of the person informing the contract test. I believe feminist theorizing can be a highly useful resource for this development and defense. Feminist writings have a lot to say about questions surrounding worth, status, and honor. They also have a lot to say about the pain and damage human beings experience when they are considered second class and subject to discrimination and prejudice, or when they are denied not only economic opportunities but decent housing and food. Implicit in these writings, on my view, is a conception of how people can go wrong not only in how they treat others but also in how they regard these others such that this treatment is permitted (and even, at times, encouraged). So both contractarians and many feminists are concerned to clarify the right kind of regard that any human being, in any human relationship, must be paid by others. Once that regard, and the treatment associated with it, are better understood, we will be able to clarify what each party to the contract wants when she is motivated to secure "what is best for her." Feminist theorizing can therefore do much to help the development and analytical precision of Kantian contractarian theory.

But contractarian theory can also help the feminist cause, and it can do so because it unabashedly insists on the worth of each of us. The reliance on self-interest in my formulation of the contract test is not an unfortunate remnant of Hobbes's moral theory; rather, it is a deliberate attempt to preserve what may be the only right-headed aspect of

Hobbes's thought – namely, *the idea that morality should not be understood to require that we make ourselves the prey of others.* The self-interested concern that each party to a Kantian social contract brings to the agreement process symbolizes her morally legitimate concern to prevent her exploitation and have the value of her interests and her person respected. My insistence that each party to a relationship take a self-concerned perspective in his or her evaluation of its moral health is really the insistence that each of us is right to value ourselves, our interests, and our projects and right to insist that we not become the prey of other parties in the pursuit of their projects. The contractarian method grants us what Charlotte Brontë in the passage quoted earlier seems to want: a way to be tenacious advocates of ourselves. What has attracted so many to this form of argument and what makes it worthy of further pursuit is precisely the fact that by granting to each individual the ability to be his or her own advocate, this method enables us to conceive of both public and private relationships without exploitative servitude.

Nonetheless, a philosopher's call for all of us to insist that our interests be accorded proper weight in a relationship will sound foolish indeed to a mother caring for three kids alone after her husband has left her and who ends up taking in an aging mother too ill to take care of herself. Women in this society are in trouble largely because society has defined roles for them to play in a variety of relationships that involve them bearing a disproportionately larger share of the costs and receiving a disproportionately smaller share of the benefits than others.

The strength and downright bravery many women display as they endure their burdens is considerable and impressive, but such strength is, in the eyes of one feminist, also a roadblock to ending the abuse: "Certain values described as feminine virtues may get some women through but they do not seem to offer most women the resources for fighting the enemy – for genuine resistance. They do not, that is, push one to 'cripple' or 'damage' or stop the enemy…or at least to try."[50] However impressive the heroic service women have traditionally provided – to the extent that it is soul destroying for them and for the women who will follow them – they must develop forms of thinking and acting that prevent their propensity to care from being the source of their abuse and exploitation. Thus it is precisely because its self-interested perspective is so alien to their other-regarding modes of thinking that feminist critics of contractarianism should welcome it as they pursue changes not merely in intimate relationships but in society at large. It is a form of thinking about moral relationships that not only encourages individuals to insist on the acknowledgment of their own interests and concerns but also (as a Rawlsian would wish) encourages them to attack societal and political sources of the exploitative roles in which women fine themselves.

The Uses and Limits of Contractarian Moral Theory

I have been arguing that if we understand the structure and role of the contractarian device in our moral thinking, the contract idea isn't in any sense foundational, or even necessary, for effective moral reasoning. It is merely a test that is heuristically valuable for the moral agent in virtue of the fact that it is informed by ideas that are the real source of moral reasoning. In particular, *the contract device is effective at illuminating the nature of distributive justice, which I understand to be the, "distribution of benefits and burdens in a relationship consistent with the contractarian conception of the person."* Thus exploitation, or distributive injustice, is a distribution inconsistent with that conception. So understood, the concern to realize distributive justice is a species of moral concern generally, which I define as *treating people consistent with the contractarian conception of the person.* In this section I shall explore how and when the contract test works and when it is not appropriate to use it.

There are three different ways exploitation can exist and thus three ways that the contract test can be used to search for it. First, as I've emphasized, exploitation can exist within a relationship when it evolves such that the distribution of nonaffective costs and benefits is unfair. In this situation, there is nothing inherent in the relationship itself that creates the exploitation; instead, the behavior of the parties involved precipitates it. Consider a relationship held together by bonds of affection. Although the contract test is misapplied if someone were to try to use it to evaluate directly those affective bonds (such as love or sympathetic concern), it might nonetheless be instrumental to preserving these affective bonds by enabling the parties to locate and correct ways in which they have been behaving unfairly toward one another. In a good friendship, for example, each friend naturally accords the other noninstrumental value. In response to this value, each is prepared to give gifts to the other. A "pay for service" mentality exists between business partners; but between genuine friends, there is only a concern to serve the other insofar as she is (each believes) the sore of valuable being for whom such service or such gift-giving is appropriate. Note, however, that when both friends take this kind of interest in the other, the gift-giving will be roughly reciprocal, and each will be loathe even to appear to use the other as a means.

In contrast, when a friendship starts to get corrupted, one of the parties begins to enjoy the gifts being given more than he does the giver of those gifts, thereby evaluating the one who is giving the gifts as a gift-giver, as a servant of his desires, as the one who ministers to his needs or desires. And if her affection for him is sufficiently strong to motivate her to continue to give the gifts without being paid, why should he reciprocate? He gets what he wants "for free" (or perhaps with minimal cost on his part). This is an example of the kind of exploitation that, as Gauthier notes, can exist in the context of an affective relationship. One party uses the other party's affection to get her to serve him, according her mere instrumental worth. This is not only unjust; it is also a sign that the love in the relationship has been corrupted.

So although philosophers have generally believed that distributive justice has little to do with friendship or love, in fact a concern to locate and eradicate this kind of exploitation can be understood to derive not only from an interest in securing justice between the parties but also from an interest in preserving a genuinely caring relationship. Or to put it another way, insofar as I am arguing that "being just" in a distributive sense means "distributing benefits and burdens in a relationship such that each person's worth is properly respected," then love and distributive justice so understood are not opposing responses because the former is only possible if the latter prevails.

Second, the contract test can function as a test, not of the operation of a relationship, but of the relationship itself, to determine whether exploitation is inherent in the design of some of the roles played by those involved in it. The master-slave relationship is an example of a relationship that would fail the test, "Could all of us reasonably accept the idea of entering into or remaining in any of the roles in this relationship if doing so were the subject of an informed, unforced agreement in which we think of ourselves as motivated solely by self-interest?" Yet another example is given by Charlotte Brontë's account of society's role for spinster women: "Your place is to do good to others, to be helpful whenever help is wanted." As she notes, this is "a very convenient doctrine for the people who hold it," but one that results in "a terrible hollowness, mockery, want, craving, in that existence which is given away to others, for want of something of your own to bestow it on." It is a good example of a social role that could not be agreed upon by those called upon to assume it were they freed of social pressures and imagined obligations and encouraged instead to consult (and regard as legitimate) their own wishes and aspirations.

Third, even if no injustice would occur within a relationship, it might occur as a result of one's decision to enter into it. A relationship can be nonexploitative in its nature and in its operation but still precipitate exploitation if one's decision to participate in it will result in someone (for example, oneself or third parties) getting less than her due. So the contract test can be used to explore whether everyone involved could agree to one's participation in that relationship. Suppose, for example, that you were considering whether to become a parent, teacher, doctor, or minister. The contract test would evaluate whether, if you took on one of these roles and, as a result, developed obligations and affective connections toward others, you could remain fair to yourself and/or to others toward whom you already had obligations or affection. ("If I have this child, can I still do what I need to do for myself?" "If I adopt this profession, will I be able to give to my family what I owe them?") There may be nothing unjust in, say, a parent-child relationship in and of itself, but there may be injustice in the adult's decision to become a parent in the first place.

There are also times, however, when the contract test is not appropriate to use. In particular, it is not appropriate for morally evaluating relationships between people radically unequal in capacity.[51] There is something absurd about inquiring into the morality of the relationship between, say, a mother and her newborn infant by asking, "What services could each agree to? What would they be unreasonable to reject?" For, so long as this radical inequality prevails, such a relationship is outside the province of distributive justice – in part because an infant or anyone severely infirm is incapable of reciprocating the benefit, making it ridiculous for any moral theory to require it, and in part because such people are not manipulating the situation to extract "free care" from others.[52] The contract test is not useful in helping to determine the obligations parties have to one another in these relationships because there are no issues of distributive justice involved in them. However, the conception of the person animating that device is directly relevant to defining those duties.

As I have discussed, it is part of what it means to respect someone's worth that one attend to her legitimate interests. So a traveler who, like the Samaritan, sees someone bleeding to death on the roadside and refuses to help him is failing to honor that person's worth, and a society that fails to define or develop institutional or social responses to those who are in serious need is failing to respond to the worth of its own citizens effectively. In such "Good Samaritan" cases, we commend the caregivers precisely because they unselfishly provide care for the needy person, without thinking of any benefits for themselves. It is not only permissible but also appropriate to give one's services as a gift to those who are in trouble. But note that what we are concerned about when we test relationships for their justice – namely, that each party's worth is properly acknowledged – is never compromised in these sorts of relationships. We are able to commend the service provided by the Good Samaritan because the person being benefited receives the aid without ever taking advantage of the benefactor's affection for or feeling of duty toward him in order to receive the service. He has a great need to which the Samaritan responds insofar as she is respectful of his value as a human being.

Suppose the incapacitated person regains (or develops) his capacities. Once that happens, the use of the contract test becomes appropriate to determine the response he ought to make toward his benefactor. Normally we say that such a person should feel "gratitude" toward his benefactor and take steps to benefit her in some way in order to thank her for his care. I would argue that gratitude is at least partly generated by a concern to be just: Gratitude contains within it the appreciation of the worth of the person who would provide such care, engendering in the genuinely moral person the desire to give benefits in return as a way of showing that he desires to honor, rather than take advantage of, his benefactor's services. An ungrateful recipient of a Good Samaritan's care is therefore unjust, not because he did anything to manipulate the situation such that he received care for which he did not have to pay, but because he is now acquiescing in the uneven distribution of benefits and burdens that could not have been agreed to by self-interested parties had such agreement been possible before the care. This acquiescence may not be as bad as actions that have manipulated the exploitation, but it is still an unjust reaction to the benefactor – a way of responding to his benefactor solely as instrumentally valuable to his needs and interests.[53]

But let me stress once again that the return needn't be equal to the gift received in order for justice to be realized. Even after one gains capacities roughly equal to those of one's benefactor, an equal return might be impossible. The impoverished widow who gave her mite to the Lord in gratitude surely indicates by her actions that she honors the one who benefited her and does not view him merely as a means. Even a bare "thank you" from one who can give little else may be sufficient to show this person's desire to honor rather than take advantage of the one who helped him.[54] The bottom line for those who use the contract test is not whether the distribution of costs and benefits between them has been equal, but whether the distribution is such that either of them is exploiting the other. Given the complexities of human circumstances, there is no formula applicable in all situations to decide the answer to this question. It is for this reason that Scanlon's imprecise word *reasonable* may be a good one to use to characterize what we are looking for in an acceptable distribution of costs and benefits – assuming, of course, that it is nonetheless given content by the conception of the person defined earlier – because *reasonable* implies both that there is no set of rules we can invoke that decisively determines how to distribute costs and benefits and that there are still right and wrong answers as to how to do it.

Communitarian Concerns

Suppose the conception of the person required by the contract test can be developed successfully. Nonetheless, is this the sort of theory upon which our moral and political theorizing should rest?

There are two interesting reasons why certain communitarian political theorists might argue it should not.

Consider, first, Michael Sandel's criticism of Rawls's contract theory as one that presupposes an implausible metaphysical conception of the person. In his recent work, Rawls has tried to back away from grounding his argument in any metaphysical claims at all. So a communitarian might argue that my theory takes on the sort of metaphysical baggage other contractarians don't (and shouldn't) want. I would insist, however, that the metaphysical claims made in my theory are the strength of that theory and not an embarrassment to it. There is nothing in the contractarian conception of the person as I understand it that would deny our deep sociality as a species; indeed, like Rawls, who stressed our sociality as a reason for beginning moral philosophy at the level of the basic structure of society, I agree that it is this structure that plays a primary role in forming us. But I would also insist that, regardless of the society we develop in, we are autonomous beings possessing a worth that is noninstrumental and equal, with certain needs that ought to be met. So on this view, a society that teaches its members to believe that some of them are inherently more valuable than others by virtue of their birth, or gender, or race is importantly *wrong*. I will not dispute that this metaphysical claim requires a defense, and in a forthcoming work I aim to propose one; but I will insist that there is nothing "unattractive" about this metaphysics. Indeed, a communitarian who is ready to embrace whatever views about relative value his culture communicates to him will have to swallow views (for example, about women or people of color) that many of us believe are unacceptable. The driving force behind the contractarian theory is what might be called a "socially responsible metaphysics" that insists on the equal intrinsic worth of all people. I would argue that we owe this idea our allegiance, even as we strive to construct philosophical arguments that develop and defend it.

Which brings us to the communitarian's second concern: Isn't a contract test likely to generate a liberal political theory hostile to the interests of a community? In answering this concern I admit – and welcome – the idea that it would do so, although I do not have time to spell out in detail the structure of the political liberalism it would generate. Nonetheless, it is not a morally neutral form of political liberalism but rather (and quite deliberately) a morally loaded liberalism informed by a conception of the person prescribing the creation and sustenance of institutions that respect the worth and legitimate interests of persons. Thus a society that has an unregulated market economy, or wholesale allegiance to the doctrine of freedom of contract, or patriarchal institutions, or racist practices will not function so that each gets what she is due as a persons; accordingly, it would be criticized as unjust by this theory. Of course, individuals, not groups, are the fundamental concern of this theory; in this sense, the theory might be thought anticommunitarian. But insofar as our legitimate needs include the need to function as part of a collective, the interests of a collective will be recognized insofar as they are instrumental to the aims of (intrinsically worthy) individuals. (So, on this view, collectives are protected only to the extent that they have instrumental value for the individuals who compose them.) And the operation at these collectives – the roles they define for people and the institutions they adopt – are the appropriate subjects of a contract test concerned with locating the presence of exploitative injustice, subjects ranging from the monogamous nuclear family to market society, from democratic polities to social practices defining gender. It is a fundamental (and liberal) tenet of this view that a community's practices must answer to the worth of individuals and not the other way around.

Beyond Morality

Let me conclude on a note sympathetic to some of the feminist criticisms I reviewed earlier. Suppose we had a complete moral theory founded on the contractarian's conception of the person and, as part of this theory, a conception of distributive justice effectively revealed by the contract test. Would we have arrived at a fully mature or (perhaps better) genuinely wise perspective regarding how we should live our lives with one another?

I think not, because we would still not understand certain important reasons why individuals forge relationships or the full nature of the affective or duty-based connections holding our relationships together. Contra the beliefs of Hobbesians, in our various relationships with others we are not simply concerned with gaining the advantages of cooperation from people we take to be instrumentally valuable to the pursuit of our own interests. Moreover, even if our relationships are subject to the demands of justice, most of them are not undertaken in order to realize justice. A person doesn't become a parent so that she can be just toward her children. None of us fosters a friendship with another out of a concern to be fair. Joining a church or a charity organization, volunteering in one's community, organizing charities for people in other countries, committing oneself in the manner of Mother Theresa to the needs of the desperately poor, are ways of creating a role for oneself that are prompted by interests that may have a good deal to do with honoring the worth of these individuals but perhaps have much more to do with the love one feels toward others.

I believe that if we begin to theorize in a more complete way about the values inherent in human relationships, we will find that the concepts of justice as well as morality are too limp to help us understand many of the responses we commend when we praise human beings. Consider, for example, the response of a Texas farm woman to a tornado that destroyed her family's home. As the destruction was occurring she sat in a shelter with her family and worked on a quilt, explaining, "I made my quilt to keep my family warm. I made it beautiful so my heart would not break."[55] To describe this woman as "moral" seems evaluatively inept. In fact, there is no traditional ethical theory (except perhaps Aristotle's) that could shed much light on what this woman was aiming at by her actions with respect to her family or herself. Yet here is someone whose response to herself and those around her is impressive and important; the story surely brings to mind memories of what our families and friends have done for themselves and for us, not merely because they were "moral" and concerned to respect us as persons, but because they loved us, and themselves, and those aspects of the world around us that are worth loving. The intrinsic value morality tells us to respect in our dealings with other persons is probably not the only kind of value each of us has, and to love someone may be to appreciate them in a quite special way – to accord them a particular nonmoral value (think of how parents cherish their children, or how people take delight in their friends' company).

Nonetheless, real love can exist only if there is also moral respect. The contract device therefore gives us a way to evaluate one moral component of any human relationship. It helps us to understand what to protect in our relationships with others, but it doesn't tell us all the ways we should respond to human beings in order to build a fine friendship, a loving marriage, a bond with our children. It tells us the harmful emotional responses we must control in order to accord people their worth; it does not tell us the emotions we ought to cultivate if we wish to develop enriching ties to others. And outside of explaining their instrumental value, it can never tell us what our lives, and our relationships with others, are *for*.

So contractarian theorizing is the beginning of wisdom about how we should relate to our fellow human beings – but it is only the beginning.[56]

Notes

1 Annette C. Baier, "What Do Women Want in a Moral Theory?" *Nous* 19, 1 (March 1985): 56.

2 Ibid., p. 54. And see Ian Hacking, "Winner Take Less: A Review of *The Evolution of Cooperation* by Robert Axelrod," in *New York Review of Books*, June 28, 1984.

3 Baier, "What Do Women Want in a Moral Theory?" p. 55.

4 Aristotle, *Nicomachean Ethics*, tr. by T. E. Irwin (Indianapolis: Hackett, 1985), 1155a22 (p. 208).

5 See 1155a27 (Irwin translation, p. 208). It may be, however, that Aristotle is primarily arguing that if one is just, one is also friendly (as part of his concept of civic friendship), whereas I want to emphasize that if one is friendly, one is also just.

6 Carol Gilligan's classic work is *In a Different Voice: Psychological Theory and Women's Development* (Cambridge, Mass.: Harvard University Press, 1982). She has revised and expanded her ideas since then. See a variety of articles about Gilligan's recent work in *Mapping the Moral Domain*, ed. Carol Gilligan, Victoria Ward, and Jill McLean, with Betty Bandige (Cambridge, Mass.: Center for the Study of Gender, Education, and Human Development, 1988). See also Carol Gilligan, "Moral Orientation and Moral Development," in *Women and Moral Theory*, ed. by Eva Feder Kittay and Diana T. Meyers (Totowa, NJ: Rowman and Littlefield, 1987), pp. 19–33.

7 Gilligan, *In a Different Voice*, pp. 35–6.

8 Ibid.

9 Ibid., p. 36.

10 Baier, "What Do Women Want in a Moral Theory," p. 62.

11 Annette Baier, "The Need for More Than Justice," this volume, p. 248.

12 Gilligan, *In a Different Voice*, p. 36.

13 See Marcia Homiak, "Feminism and Aristotle's Rational ideal," *in A Mind of One's Own*, 2nd ed.,

Antony and Witt, eds. (Boulder: Westview Press, 2002), pp. 3–20.

14 See, for example, L. Blum, M. Homiak, J. Housman, and N. Scheman, "Altruism and Women's Oppression," in *Women and Philosophy*, ed. Carol Gould and Marx Wartofsky (New York: G. P. Putnam's Sons, 1976), pp. 222–47.

15 Charlotte Brontë, *Shirley*, quotation taken from edition of Andrew and Judith Hook (Harmondsworth: Penguin, 1987) p. 190.

16 From "Professions for Women" in *The Virginia Woolf Reader*, ed. Mitchell A. Leaska (San Diego: Harcourt Brace, 1984), pp. 278–9.

17 See Blum *et al.*, "Altruism and Women's Oppression," for a discussion of the way altruism must be accompanied by autonomy if it is going to be a morally healthy response.

18 I take this to be an idea suggested by Susan Wolf in her "Moral Saints," *Journal of Philosophy*, 79, 8 (August 1982): 419–39. Ironically, this fixation has been more the product of theories developed by males (e.g., Immanuel Kant and Jeremy Bentham) than by females. Perhaps such a fixation is the natural result of male dissatisfaction with a Jake-like moral perspective and an attempt to redirect the largely self-regarding focus of that perspective. But theorists such as Kant, who stress the other-regarding nature of morality, invariably start from an assumption of self-worth and personal autonomy. In a paper that celebrates interdependence and connection, Baier notes that Kant thought women were incapable of full autonomy and then remarks, "It is ironic that Gilligan's original findings in a way confirm Kant's views – it seems that autonomy really may not be for women. Many of them reject that ideal" ("Need for More Than Justice," p. 50). But such a rejection may actually be evidence of these women's development into servile and dependent beings rather than free, self-respecting, and claim-making persons. For discussions on this general topic, see the contributions by DuBois, Dunlap, Carol Gilligan, Catharine MacKinnon and Menkel-Meadow in "Feminist Discourse, Moral Values, and the Law," *Buffalo Law Review* 34 (1985): 11 ff.

19 Virginia Held, "Noncontractual Society: A Feminist View," in Hanen and Nielsen, eds., *Science, Morality, and Feminist Theory*, p. 111.

20 Ibid., p. 113. For similar criticisms, see Carole Pateman, *The Sexual Contract* (Palo Alto, Calif: Polity/Stanford University Press, 1988).

21 Baier, "What Do Women Want in a Moral Theory?," p. 62.

22 Hobbes believed that moral imperatives were also justified by virtue of being commanded by God. However, his contractarian justification seeks to define the nature and authority of moral imperatives solely by reference to the desires and reasoning abilities of human beings, so that regardless of their religious commitments, all people will see that they have reason to act morally.

23 Hobbes believes he performed the latter project in Chs 14 and 15 of *Leviathan*, ed. C. B. MacPherson (Harmondsworth: Penguin, 1968).

24 However, I have argued elsewhere that Hobbesian contractarians implicitly assume the kind of problematic metaphysical ideas they criticize in the theories of others. See my "Normativity and Naturalism," unpublished manuscript.

25 Gauthier himself has been moved by these kinds of worries, inspired, he says, by Hegel. See his "Social Contract as Ideology," *Philosophy and Public Affairs* (1977): 130–64.

26 Hobbes, *Leviathan*, Ch. 10, paragraph 16 (p. 42 in MacPherson edition).

27 Immanuel Kant, On the Common Saying: "This May Be True in Theory, But It Doesn't Apply in Practice," in *Kant's Political Writings*, ed. Hans Reiss (Cambridge: Cambridge University Press, 1970), p. 63. Emphasis in original.

28 Rawls, for example, explicitly compares his original position procedure to Kant's Categorical Imperative procedure (see Rawls, *A Theory of Justice* [Cambridge, Mass.: Harvard University Press, 1971], section 40). And Scanlon suggests that the contractarian form of argument is a kind of proof procedure for ethics that is analogous to proof procedures in mathematics; its basis is in human reason, and we use it to construct moral laws in a way that gives them objectivity. See Scanlon's "Contractualism and Utilitarianism," in *Utilitarianism and Beyond*, ed. A. Sen and B. Williams (Cambridge: Cambridge University Press, 1982).

29 Sarah Ruddick, for example, writes, "Especially masculine men (and sometimes women), fearful of physicality and needs of care, develop a transcendence based on a 'tradition of freeing the thinking brain from the depths of the most pressing situations and sending it off to some (fictive) summit for a panoramic overview.' From this perch they promulgate views that are inimical to the values of caring labor. They imagine a truth abstracted from bodies and a self detached from feelings. When faced with concrete seriousness, they measure and quantify. Only partially protected by veils of ignorance that never quite hide frightening differences and dependencies, they forge agreements of reason and regiment dissent by rules and fair fights." From Ruddick, *Maternal Thinking: Toward a Politics of Peace* (Boston: Beacon, 1989); quotation in passage taken from Klaus Thewelweit, *Male Fantasies* (Minneapolis: University of Minnesota Press, 1987), p. 364. Ruddick's criticism is similar to those made by Rawls's Hegel-inspired communitarian critics (e.g., Michael Sandel).

30 See Kathryn Morgan, "Women and Moral Madness," in Hanen and Nielsen, eds., *Science, Morality and Feminist Theory*, pp. 201–26.

31 Susan Moller Okin, *Justice, Gender, and the Family*, (New York: Basic Books, 1989).

32 Ibid., p. 101.

33 Indeed, as I have reflected on Archimedean thinking in the literature, it has struck me that it is interestingly akin to a certain kind of thinking of mothers as they raise their children. In the words of one novelist, mothers are "Conscious Makers of People" who strive to develop an environment for their children that will allow them to grow up well (i.e., confident rather than fearful, fulfilled rather than miserable, capable rather than dependent) and try to ensure that the institutions with which their children come into contact will operate in a way that fosters that end. The Rawlsian contractarian also wants us to play a role in shaping the people of our society by asking us to formulate principles that will animate the social institutions that make any of us who we are. Members of a Rawlslike Archimedean position have as their primary concern the development of an environment in which future members of the society can grow up well, and insofar as they are aware of the powerful effect society and its institutions have on shaping the kind of people any of us become, they are just as interested as any mother in constructing or changing social institutions to foster the development of mature and morally healthy human beings. Far from being antithetical to the perspective of mothering, Rawls's Archimedean point is a way to encourage mothering-like concerns in a political context.

34 For a review of the problems with Rawls's maximin rule, see John Harsanyi, "Can the Maximin Principle Serve as a Basis for Morality? A Critique of John Rawls's *A Theory of Justice*," *American Political Science Review* 69 (1975): 594–606. And for a discussion of these problems from a philosophical standpoint, see D. Clayton Hubin, "Minimizing Maximin," *Philosophical Studies* 37 (1980): 363–72.

35 Scanlon, "Contractualism and Utilitarianism," p. 110.

36 Ibid.

37 Ibid., pp. 123–4.

38 Ibid., p. 123.

39 Ibid., p. 111.

40 Ibid., p. 127.

41 In "Contractualism and Utilitarianism," Scanlon seems to vacillate between regarding the test as defining moral properties and regarding it as a test that presupposes and uses those properties. He begins the essay by pushing the first position, arguing that we should follow Mackie in being suspicious of moral properties that are supposed to be instances of "intrinsic 'to-be-doneness' and 'not-to-be-doneness'" (p. 118), and he proposes instead that moral properties be defined via a reasoning procedure (and in particular, a contractualist procedure) that would define rather than presuppose such properties (making the view the moral equivalent of mathematical intuitionism). But later Scanlon cannot help but appeal to properties that are right- and wrong-making independent of the contractualist agreement test, properties that he relies upon in order to define that reasoning procedure. "There are also right- and wrong-making properties which are themselves independent of the contractualist notion of agreement. I take the property of being an act of killing for the pleasure of doing so to be a wrong-making property of this kind" (p. 118). But immediately after stating this, Scanlon writes, "Such properties are wrong-making because it would be unreasonable to reject any set of principles which permitted the acts they characterise" (ibid.). But now it sounds as if their wrong-making character is *derived from* the contractualist test, such that it cannot be independent of the test after all.

42 Scanlon is prepared to allow that contractarian reasoning might endorse the utilitarian principle, but he would have to insist that it would do so in a "contractarian way"– i.e., a way that was not itself a form of utilitarian reasoning. Hence, he needs to give us the structure of this uniquely contractarian way of reasoning.

43 See also Marilyn Friedman, "Beyond Caring: The Demoralization of Gender," in Hanen and Nielsen, eds., *Science, Morality, and Feminist Theory*, p. 100. I am in substantial agreement with Friedman's arguments that the "justice perspective" properly understood is just as concerned with and relevant to the health of a variety of human relationships – including intimate ones – as is the "care perspective."

44 David Gauthier, *Morals by Agreement* (Oxford: Oxford University Press, 1986), p. 11.

45 Moreover, to make a meta-ethical point, although I am understanding this notion of dignity or worth to be the source of moral rightness and wrongness, it may not itself be a moral notion. So if "reasonableness" is cashed out using this notion, we may be able to interpret the contractarian test as Scanlon wished – i.e., as that which defines moral rightness and moral wrongness while being informed by something nonmoral.

46 See Jean Hampton, "Contracts and Choices: Does Rawls Have a Social Contract Theory?" *Journal of Philosophy* 77, 6 (June 1980).

47 Thus I disagree with Scanlon ("Contractualism and Utilitarianism," pp. 124–8), who argues that Rawls is not a real contractarian because of his reliance on the "I could be anyone" device. Both devices aim to bring others' needs to bear on your deliberations such that your choice takes them into account in the right way. Whether the others are there "in person" around an agreement table in your thought experiment,

or whether they are there in virtue of the fact that you are forced to choose as if you were any one of them, does not seem to matter at all in the final result.

48 Carol Pateman, *The Sexual Contract* (Stanford, Calif.: Stanford University Press, 1988), p. 184; see also p. 187. Patemen lays out the peculiarities of the marriage contract on pp. 163–7. Feminist advocates of contractualization include Marjorie Schultz, "Contractual Ordering of Marriage: A New Model for State Policy," *California Law Review* 70 (1982): 207–334.

49 Such an Aristotelian theory needn't say that all of us have the same legitimate interests. This theory could ascribe to us a certain set of interests but insist that the different psychological and physiological natures of each of us generate different needs.

50 Joan Ringelheim, "Women and the Holocaust: A Reconsideration of Research," *Signs* 10, 4 (1985): 741–61; quoted by Barbara Houston, "Rescuing Womanly Virtues: Some Dangers of Moral Reclamation," in Hanen and Nielsen, eds., *Science, Morality, and Feminist Theory*, p. 248.

51 Annette Baier writes: "It is a typical feature of the dominant moral theories and traditions, since Kant, or perhaps since Hobbes, that relationships between equals or those who are deemed equal in some important sense, have been the relations that morality is concerned primarily to regulate. . . . This pretence of an equality that is in fact absent may often lead to desirable protection of the weaker, or more dependent. But it somewhat masks the question of what our moral relationships are to those who are our superiors or our inferiors in power. A more realistic acceptance of the fact that we begin as helpless children, that at almost every point of our lives we deal with both the more and the less helpless, that equality of power and interdependency, between two persons or groups, is rare and hard to recognize when it does occur, might lead us to a more direct approach to questions concerning the design of institutions structuring these relationships between unequals (families, schools, hospitals, armies) and of the morality of our dealings with the more and the less powerful" ("Need for More Than Justice," pp. 52–3).

52 See also Will Kymlicka, "Two Theories of Justice," *Inquiry* 33, 109–10: "In an important sense, the 'ethic of care' advanced by recent feminists does reverse these questions, replacing the contractual relationship between adults with the mother-child relationship as their paradigm of a morally responsible relationship. But the conclusion they reach is that our responsibilities to dependents can only be met if we replace the appeal to impartiality with attention to particularity, and replace justice with care."

53 Of course, a person is grateful for what the benefactor did, not for his worth. Gratitude is a reaction to the beneficial deed; but the benefited one feels it to the extent that he appreciates that his benefactor's services came about not because the benefactor was a servant or tool of his desires, but because the benefactor freely chose to bestow these services upon him. So an acknowledgment of that choice – and thus of the noninstrumental standing of the benefactor – is implicit in the emotion of gratitude.

54 There is a reason why those benefited by Good Samaritans may want to benefit their benefactors in return – they desire to preserve their own worth. Those who are in extreme need, although equal in worth to those who help them, are nonetheless not equal in circumstance or capacity, and in this sense they do not have the equal standing necessary for justice to demand that they make a return. But many find this inequality a painful and humiliating experience. They wish to be in a position to return the favor in order to establish themselves as equal in capacity and circumstance to those who benefited them. Thus they want to respond as justice would require in order to show that they have the standing that the demands of justice presuppose. I am told by a family counselor that this attitude of wishing to return the benefits to parents who have freely given their care is frequent among teenagers desiring to manifest equal status with their parents (sometimes even leading them to insist that all future benefits and burdens in the family be the subject of contracts).

55 Sara Ruddick, "Maternal Thinking," in *Women and Values*, ed. M. Pearsall (Belmont, Calif.: Wadsworth, 1986), p. 344 and note 8.

56 Portions of this chapter were read at Texas Technical University, Yale Law School, and the 1991 Pacific Division Meeting of the American Philosophical Association, and I wish to thank those audiences. I also wish to thank the members of the Los Angeles Law and Philosophy Group; the members of my graduate seminar at the University of California, Davis, in the fall of 1990; and Marcia Homiak, for their help during the writing of this chapter.

22

Women and Cultural Universals

Martha C. Nussbaum

> We shall only solve our problems if we see them as human problems arising out of a special situation; and we shall not solve them if we see them as African problems, generated by our being somehow unlike others.
>
> ***Kwame Anthony Appiah,***
> *Africa in the Philosophy of Cultures*

> Being a woman is not yet a way of being a human being.
>
> ***Catharine MacKinnon***

I A Matter of Survival

"I may die, but still I cannot go out. If there's something in the house, we eat. Otherwise, we go to sleep." So Metha Bai, a young widow in Rajasthan, India, with two young children, described her plight as a member of a caste whose women are traditionally prohibited from working outside the home – even when, as here, survival itself is at issue. If she stays at home, she and her children may shortly die. If she attempts to go out, her in-laws will beat her and abuse her children. For now, Metha Bai's father travels from 100 miles away to plow her small plot of land. But he is aging, and Metha Bai fears that she and her children will shortly die with him.[1]

In this case, as in many others throughout the world, cultural traditions pose obstacles to women's health and flourishing. Depressingly, many traditions portray women as less important than men, less deserving of basic life support or of fundamental rights that are strongly correlated with quality of life, such as the right to work and the right to political participation. Sometimes, as in the case of Metha Bai, the women themselves resist these traditions. Sometimes, on the other hand, the traditions have become so deeply internalized that they seem to record what is "right" and "natural," and women themselves endorse their own second-class status.

Such cases are hardly confined to non-Western or developing countries. As recently as 1873, the US Supreme Court upheld a law that forbade women to practice law in the state of Illinois, on the grounds that "[t]he constitution of the family organization, which is founded in the divine ordinance, as well as in the nature of things, indicates the domestic sphere as that which properly belongs to the domain and functions of

Martha C. Nussbaum, "Women and Cultural Universals," pp. 29–54 and 377–84 (notes) from *Sex and Social Justice*, Oxford: Oxford University Press, 1999.

womanhood."[2] And in 1993, a woman who was threatened and grossly harassed by her male coworkers, after becoming the first woman to work in the heavy metal shop in the General Motors plant in Indiana, was described by a federal district judge as having provoked the men's conduct by her "unladylike" behavior – behavior that consisted in using a four-letter word a few times in a five-year period.[3] Clearly our own society still appeals to tradition in its own way to justify women's unequal treatment.

What should people concerned with justice say about this? And should they say anything at all? On the one hand, it seems impossible to deny that traditions, both Western and non-Western, perpetrate injustice against women in many fundamental ways, touching on some of the most central elements of a human being's quality of life – health, education, political liberty and participation, employment, self-respect, and life itself. On the other hand, hasty judgments that a tradition in some distant part of the world is morally retrograde are familiar legacies of colonialism and imperialism and are correctly regarded with suspicion by sensitive thinkers in the contemporary world. To say that a practice endorsed by tradition is bad is to risk erring by imposing one's own way on others, who surely have their own ideas of what is right and good. To say that a practice is all right whenever local tradition endorses it as right and good is to risk erring by withholding critical judgment where real evil and oppression are surely present. To avoid the whole issue because the matter of proper judgment is so fiendishly difficult is tempting but perhaps the worst option of all. It suggests the sort of moral collapse depicted by Dante when he describes the crowd of souls who mill around in the vestibule of hell, dragging their banner now one way, now another, never willing to set it down and take a definite stand on any moral or political question. Such people, he implies, are the most despicable of all. They cannot even get into hell because they have not been willing to stand for anything in life, one way or another. To express the spirit of this chapter very succinctly, it is better to risk being consigned by critics to the "hell" reserved for alleged Westernizers and imperialists – however unjustified such criticism would in fact be – than to stand around in the vestibule waiting for a time when everyone will like what we are going to say. And what we are going to say is: that there are universal obligations to protect human functioning and its dignity, and that the dignity of women is equal to that of men. If that involves assault on many local traditions, both Western and non-Western, so much the better, because any tradition that denies these things is unjust. Or, as a young Bangladeshi wife said when local religious leaders threatened to break the legs of women who went to the literacy classes conducted by a local NGO (nongovernmental organization), "We do not listen to the *mullahs* any more. They did not give us even a quarter kilo of rice."[4]

The situation of women in the contemporary world calls urgently for moral standtaking. Women, a majority of the world's population, receive only a small proportion of its opportunities and benefits. According to the *Human Development Report*, in no country in the world is women's quality of life equal to that of men, according to a complex measure that includes life expectancy, educational attainment, and GDP (gross domestic product) per capita.[5] Some countries have much larger gender disparities than others. (Among prosperous industrial countries, for example, Spain and Japan perform relatively poorly in this area; Sweden, Denmark, and New Zealand perform relatively well.[6]) If we now examine the Gender Empowerment Measure, which uses variables chosen explicitly to measure the relative empowerment of men and women in political and economic activity,[7] we find even more striking signs of gender disparity. Once again, the Scandinavian nations do well; Japan and Spain do relatively poorly.[8]

If we turn our attention to the developing countries we find uneven achievements but, in the aggregate, a distressing situation. On average, employment participation rates of women are only 50% those of men (in South Asia 29%; in the Arab states only 16%).[9] Even when women are employed, their situation is undercut by pervasive wage discrimination and by long hours of unpaid household labor. (If women's unpaid housework were counted as productive output in national income accounts, global output would increase by 20–30%.) Outside the home, women are generally employed in a restricted range of jobs offering low pay and low respect. The percentage of earned income that goes to women is rarely higher than 35%. In many nations it is far lower: in Iran, 16%; Belize, 17%; Algeria, 16%; Iraq, 17%; Pakistan, 19%. (China at 38% is higher than Japan at 33%; highest in the world are Sweden at 45%, Denmark at

42%, and the extremely impoverished Rwanda at 41%, Burundi at 42%, and Mozambique at 42%.) The situation of women in the workplace is frequently undermined by sex discrimination and sexual harassment.

Women are much less likely than men to be literate. In South Asia, female literacy rates average around 50% those of males. In some countries the rate is still lower: in Nepal, 35%; Sierra Leone, 37%; Sudan, 27%; Afghanistan, 32%.[10] Two-thirds of the world's illiterate people are women. In higher education, women lag even further behind men in both developing and industrial nations.[11]

Although some countries allowed women the vote early in this century, some still have not done so. And there are many informal obstacles to women's effective participation in political life. Almost everywhere, they are underrepresented in government: In 1980, they made up only around 10% of the world's parliamentary representatives and less than 4% of its cabinet officials.[12]

As Metha Bai's story indicates, employment outside the home has a close relationship to health and nutrition. So too, frequently, does political voice. And if we now turn to the very basic issue of health and survival, we find compelling evidence of discrimination against females in many nations of the world. It appears that when equal nutrition and health care are present women live, on average, slightly longer than men – even allowing for a modest level of maternal mortality. Thus, in Europe the female/male ratio in 1986 was 105/100, in North America 104.7/100.[13] But it may be objected that for several reasons it is inappropriate to compare these developed countries with countries in the developing world. Let us, therefore, with Jean Drèze and Amartya Sen, take as our baseline the ratio in sub-Saharan Africa, where there is great poverty but little evidence of gender discrimination in basic nutrition and health.[14] The female/male ration in 1986 was 102.2/100. If we examine the sex ratio in various other countries and ask the question, "How many more women than are now in country C would be there if its sex ratio were the same as that of sub-Saharan Africa?," we get a number that Sen has graphically called the number of "missing women." The number of missing women in Southeast Asia is 2.4 million; in Latin America, 4.4; in North Africa, 2.4; in Iran, 1.4; in China, 44.0; in Bangladesh, 3.7; in India, 36.7; in Pakistan, 5.2; in West Asia, 4.3. If we now consider the ratio of the number of missing women to the number of actual women in a country, we get, for Pakistan, 12.9%; for India, 9.5%; for Bangladesh, 8.7%; for China, 8.6%; for Iran, 8.5%; for West Asia, 7.8%; for North Africa, 3.9%; for Latin America, 2.2%; for Southeast Asia, 1.2%. In India, not only is the mortality differential especially sharp among children (girls dying in far greater numbers than boys), the higher mortality rate of women compared to men applies to all age groups until the late thirties.[15]

Poverty alone does not cause women to die in greater numbers than men. This is abundantly clear from comparative regional studies in India, where some of the poorest regions, for example, Kerala, have the most equal sex ratios, and some far richer regions perform very poorly.[16] When there is scarcity, custom and political arrangement frequently decree who gets to eat the little there is and who gets taken to the doctor. And custom and political arrangement are always crucial in deciding who gets to perform wage labor outside the home, an important determinant of general status in the family and the community. As Sen has argued, a woman's perceived contribution to the well-being of the family unit is often determined by her ability to work outside, and this determines, in turn, her bargaining position within the family unit.[17] Custom and politics decree who gets access to the education that would open job opportunities and make political rights meaningful. Custom and politics decree who can go where in what clothing in what company. Custom and politics decree who gets to make what sorts of protests against ill treatment both inside and outside the family and whose voice of protest is likely to be heard.

Customs and political arrangements, in short, are important causes of women's misery and death. It seems incumbent on people interested in justice, and aware of the information about women's status that studies such as the *Human Development Reports* present, to ask about the relationship between culture and justice and between both of these and legal-political arrangements. It then seems incumbent on them to try to work out an account of the critical assessment of traditions and political arrangements that is neither do-gooder colonialism or an uncritical validation of the status quo.

One might suppose that any approach to the question of quality of life assessment in development economics would offer an account of the relationship between tradition and women's equality that would help us answer these questions. But in fact such an account is sorely lacking in the major theoretical approaches that, until recently, dominated the development scene. (Here I do not even include what has been the most common practical approach, which has been simply to ask about GNP (gross national product) per capita. This crude approach does not even look at the distribution of wealth and income; far less does it ask about other constituents of life quality, for example, life expectancy, infant mortality, education, health, and the presence or absence of political liberties, that are not always well correlated with GNP per capita.[18] The failure to ask these questions is a particularly grave problem when it is women's quality of life we want to consider. For women have especially often been unable to enjoy or control the fruits of a nation's general prosperity.)

The leading economic approach to the family is the model proposed by Nobel Prize-winning economist Gary Becker. Becker assumes that the family's goal is the maximization of utility, construed as the satisfaction of preference or desire, and that the head of the household is a beneficent altruist who will adequately take thought for the interests of all family members.[19] In real life, however, the economy of the family is characterized by pervasive "cooperative conflicts," that is, situations in which the interests of members of a cooperative body split apart, and some individuals fare well at the expense of others.[20] Becker deserves great credit for putting these issues on the agenda of the profession in the first place. But his picture of male motivation does not fit the evidence, and in a way substantial enough to affect the model's predictive value – especially if one looks not only at women's stated satisfactions and preferences, which may be deformed by intimidation, lack of information, and habit,[21] but at their actual functioning.[22] Furthermore, the model prevents those who use it from even getting the information about individual family members on which a more adequate account might be based.[23]

Suppose we were to retain a utilitarian approach and yet to look at the satisfactions of all family members – assuming, as is standardly done in economics, that preferences and tastes are exogenous and independent of laws, traditions, and institutions rather than endogenously shaped by them. Such an approach – frequently used by governments polling citizens about well-being – has the advantage of assessing all individuals one by one. But the evidence of preference endogeneity is great, and especially great when we are dealing with people whose status has been persistently defined as second class in laws and institutions of various sorts. There are many reasons to think that women's perception even of their health status is shaped by traditional views, such as the view that female life is worth less than male life, that women are weaker than men, that women do not have equal rights, and so forth. In general, people frequently adjust their expectations to the low level of well-being they think they can actually attain.[24] This approach, then, cannot offer a useful account of the role of tradition in well-being, because it is bound by its very commitments to an uncritical validation of the status quo.

More promising than either Becker's model or the standard utilitarian approach is one suggested by John Rawls's liberalism, with its account of the just distribution of a small list of basic goods and resources.[25] This approach does enable us to criticize persistent inequalities, and it strongly criticizes the view that preferences are simply given rather than shaped by society's basic structure. But in one way the Rawlsian approach stops short. Rawls's list of "primary goods," although it includes some capacity-like items, such as liberty and opportunity, also includes thing-like items, particularly income and wealth, and it measures who is least well off simply in terms of the amount of these thing-like resources an individual can command. But people have varying needs for resources: a pregnant woman, for example, needs more calories than a nonpregnant woman, a child need more protein than an adult. They also have different abilities to convert resources into functioning. A person in a wheelchair will need more resources to become mobile than a person with unimpaired limbs; a woman in a society that has defined employment outside the home as off limits to women needs more resources to become a productive worker than one who does not face such struggles. In short, the Rawlsian approach does not probe deeply enough to show us how resources do or do not go to work in making people able to function. Again, at least some of our questions about the relationship between tradition and quality of life cannot be productively addressed.

Workers on such issues have therefore increasingly converged on an approach that is now widely known as "the capabilities approach." This approach to quality-of-life measurement and the goals of public policy[26] holds that we should focus on the question: What are the people of the group or country in question actually able to do and to be? Unlike a focus on opulence (say, GNP per capita), this approach asks about the distribution of resources and opportunities. In principle, it asks how each and every individual is doing with respect to all the functions deemed important. Unlike Becker's approach, the capability approach considers people one by one, not as parts of an organic unit; it is very interested in seeing how a supposed organic unit such as the family has constructed unequal capabilities for various types of functioning. Unlike a standard utilitarian approach, the capability approach maintains that preferences are not always reliable indicators of life quality, as they may be deformed in various ways by oppression and deprivation. Unlike the type of liberal approach that focuses only on the distribution of resources, the capability approach maintains that resources have no value in themselves, apart from their role in promoting human functioning. It therefore directs the planner to inquire into the varying needs individuals have for resources and their varying abilities to convert resources into functioning. In this way, it strongly invites a scrutiny of tradition as one of the primary sources of such unequal abilities.[27]

But the capabilities approach raises the question of cultural universalism, or, as it is often pejoratively called, "essentialism." Once we begin asking how people are actually functioning, we cannot avoid focusing on some components of lives and not others, some abilities to act and not others, seeing some capabilities and functions as more central, more at the core of human life, than others. We cannot avoid having an account, even if a partial and highly general account, of what functions of the human being are most worth the care and attention of public planning the world over. Such an account is bound to be controversial.

II Anti-Universalist Conversations

The primary opponents of such an account of capability and functioning will be "antiessentialists" of various types, thinkers who urge us to begin not with sameness but with difference – both between women and men and across groups of women – and to seek norms defined relatively to a local context and locally held beliefs. This opposition takes many forms, and I shall be responding to several distinct objections. But I can begin to motivate the enterprise by telling several true stories of conversations that have taken place at the World Institute for Development Economics Research (WIDER), in which the anti-universalist position seemed to have alarming implications for women's lives.[28]

At a conference on "Value and Technology," an American economist who has long been a leftwing critic of neoclassical economics delivers a paper urging the preservation of traditional ways of life in a rural area of Orissa, India, now under threat of contamination from Western development projects. As evidence of the excellence of this rural way of life, he points to the fact that whereas we Westerners experience a sharp split between the values that prevail in the workplace and the values that prevail in the home, here, by contrast, exists what the economist calls "the embedded way of life," the same values obtaining in both places. His example: Just as in the home a menstruating woman is thought to pollute the kitchen and therefore may not enter it, so too in the workplace a menstruating woman is taken to pollute the loom and may not enter the room where looms are kept. Some feminists object that this example is repellant rather than admirable; for surely such practices both degrade the women in question and inhibit their freedom. The first economist's collaborator, an elegant French anthropologist (who would, I suspect, object violently to a purity check at the seminar room door), replies: Don't we realize that there is, in these matters, no privileged place to stand? This, after all, has been shown by both Derrida and Foucault. Doesn't he know that he is neglecting the otherness of Indian ideas by bringing his Western essentialist values into the picture?[29]

The same French anthropologist now delivers her paper. She expresses regret that the introduction of smallpox vaccination to India by the British eradicated the cult of Sittala Devi, the goddess to whom one used to pray to avert smallpox. Here, she says, is another example of Western neglect of difference. Someone (it might have been me) objects that it is surely better to be healthy rather than ill, to live rather than to die. The answer comes back; Western essentialist medicine conceives of things in terms of binary oppositions: life is opposed to death, health to disease.[30] But if we cast away this binary way of thinking, we will begin to comprehend the otherness of Indian traditions.

At this point Eric Hobsbawm, who has been listening to the proceedings in increasingly uneasy silence, rises to deliver a blistering indictment of the traditionalism and relativism that prevail in this group. He lists historical examples of ways in which appeals to tradition have been politically engineered to support oppression and violence.[31] His final example is that of National Socialism in Germany. In the confusion that ensues, most of the relativist social scientists – above all those from far away, who do not know who Hobsbawm is – demand that Hobsbawm be asked to leave the room. The radical American economist, disconcerted by this apparent tension between his relativism and his affiliation with the left, convinces them, with difficulty, to let Hobsbawm remain.

We shift now to another conference two years later, a philosophical conference on the quality of life.[32] Members of the quality-of-life project are speaking of choice as a basic good, and of the importance of expanding women's sphere of choices. We are challenged by the radical economist of my first story, who insists that contemporary anthropology has shown that non-Western people are not especially attached to freedom of choice. His example: A book on Japan has shown that Japanese males, when they get home from work, do not wish to choose what to eat for dinner, what to wear, and so on. They wish all these choices to be taken out of their hands by their wives. A heated exchange follows about what this example really shows. I leave it to your imaginations to reconstruct it. In the end, the confidence of the radical economist is unshaken: We are victims of bad universalist thinking, who fail to respect "difference."[33]

The phenomenon is an odd one. For we see here highly intelligent people, people deeply committed to the good of women and men in developing countries, people who think of themselves as progressive and feminist and antiracist, people who correctly argue that the concept of development is an evaluative concept requiring normative argument[34] – effectively eschewing normative argument and taking up positions that converge, as Hobsbawm correctly saw, with the positions of reaction, oppression, and sexism. Under the banner of their fashionable opposition to universalism march ancient religious taboos, the luxury of the pampered husband, educational deprivation, unequal health care, and premature death.

Nor do these anti-universalists appear to have a very sophisticated conception of their own core notions, such as "culture," "custom," and "tradition." It verges on the absurd to treat India as a single culture, and a single visit to a single Orissan village as sufficient to reveal its traditions. India, like all extant societies, is a complex mixture of elements[35]: Hindu, Muslim, Parsi, Christian, Jewish, atheist; urban, suburban, rural; rich, poor, and middle class; high caste, low caste, and aspiring middle caste; female and male; rationalist and mystical. It is renowned for mystical religion but also for achievements in mathematics and for the invention of chess. It contains intense, often violent sectarianism, but it also contains Rabindranath Tagore's cosmopolitan humanism and Mahatma Gandhi's reinterpretation of Hinduism as a religion of universal nonviolence. Its traditions contain views of female whorishness and childishness that derive from the Laws of Manu[36]; but it also contains the sexual agency of Draupadi in the *Mahabharata*, who solved the problem of choice among Pandava husbands by taking all five, and the enlightened sensualism and female agency of the *Kama Sutra*, a sacred text that foreign readers wrongly interpret as pornographic. It contains women like Metha Bai, who are confined to the home; it also contains women like Amita Sen (mother of Amartya Sen), who fifty years ago was among the first middle-class Bengali women to dance in public, in Rabindranath Tagore's musical extravaganzas in Santiniketan. It contains artists who disdain the foreign, preferring, with the Marglins, the "embedded" way of life, and it also contains Satyajit Ray, that great Bengali artist and lover of local traditions, who could also write, "I never ceased to regret that while I had stood in the scorching summer sun in the wilds of Santiniketan sketching *simul* and *palash* in full bloom, *Citizen Kane* had come and gone, playing for just three days in the newest and biggest cinema in Calcutta."[37]

What, then, is "the culture" of a woman like Metha Bai? Is it bound to be that determined by the most prevalent customs in Rajasthan, the region of her marital home? Or, might she be permitted to consider with what traditions or groups she wishes to align herself, perhaps forming a community of solidarity with other widows and women, in pursuit of a better quality of life? What is "the culture" of Chinese working women who have recently been victims of the government's "women go home" policy, which appeals to Confucian traditions about woman's "nature"?[38] Must it be the one advocated by Confucius, or may they be permitted to form new alliances – with one another, and with other defenders of women's human rights? What is "the culture" of General Motors employee Mary Carr? Must it be the one that says women should be demure and polite, even in the face of gross insults, and that an "unladylike" woman deserves the harassment she gets? Or might she be allowed to consider what norms are appropriate to the situation of a woman working in a heavy metal shop, and to act accordingly? Real cultures contain plurality and conflict, tradition, and subversion. They borrow good things from wherever they find them, none too worried about purity. We would never tolerate a claim that women in our own society must embrace traditions that arose thousands of years ago – indeed, we are proud that we have no such traditions. Isn't it condescending, then, to treat Indian and Chinese women as bound by the past in ways that we are not?

Indeed, as Hobsbawm suggested, the vision of "culture" propounded by the Marglins, by stressing uniformity and homogeneity, may lie closer to artificial constructions by reactionary political forces than to any organic historical entity. Even to the extent to which it is historical, one might ask, exactly how does that contribute to make it worth preserving? Cultures are not museum pieces, to be preserved intact at all costs. There would appear, indeed, to be something condescending in preserving for contemplation a way of life that causes real pain to real people.

Let me now, nonetheless, describe the most cogent objections that might be raised by a relativist against a normative universalist project.

III The Attack on Universalism

Many attacks on universalism suppose that any universalist project must rely on truths eternally fixed in the nature of things, outside human action and human history. Because some people believe in such truths and some do not, the objector holds that a normative view so grounded is bound to be biased in favor of some religious/metaphysical conceptions and against others.[39]

But universalism does not require such metaphysical support.[40] For universal ideas of the human do arise within history and from human experience, and they can ground themselves in experience. Indeed, those who take all human norms to be the result of human interpretation can hardly deny that universal conceptions of the human are prominent and pervasive among such interpretations, hardly to be relegated to the dustbin of metaphysical history along with recondite theoretical entities such as phlogiston. As Aristotle so simply puts it, "One may observe in one's travels to distant countries the feelings of recognition and affiliation that link every human being to every other human being."[41] Kwame Anthony Appiah makes the same point, telling the story of his bicultural childhood. A child who visits one set of grandparents in Ghana and another in rural England, who has a Lebanese uncle and who later, as an adult, has nieces and nephews from more than seven different nations, finds, he argues, not unbridgeable alien "otherness," but a great deal of human commonality, and comes to see the world as a "network of points of affinity."[42] But such a metaphysically agnostic, experiential and historical universalism is still vulnerable to some, if not all, of the objections standardly brought against universalism.

Neglect of historical and cultural differences

The opponent charges that any attempt to pick out some elements of human life as more fundamental than others, even without appeal to a transhistorical reality, is bound to be insufficiently respectful of actual historical and cultural differences. People, it is claimed, understand human life and humanness in widely different ways, and any attempt to produce a list of the most fundamental properties and functions of human beings is bound to enshrine certain understandings of the human and to demote others. Usually, the objector continues, this takes the form of enshrining the understanding of a dominant group at the expense of minority understandings. This type of objection, frequently made by feminists, can claim support from many historical examples in which the human has indeed been defined by focusing on actual characteristics of males.

It is far from clear what this objection shows. In particular it is far from clear that it supports the idea that we ought to base our ethical norms, instead, on the current preferences and the self-conceptions of people who are living what the objector herself claims to be lives of deprivation and oppression. But it does show at least that the project of choosing one picture of the human over another is fraught with difficulty, political as well as philosophical.

Neglect of autonomy

A different objection is presented by liberal opponents of universalism. The objection is that by determining in advance what elements of human life have most importance, the universalist project fails to respect the right of people to choose a plan of life according to their own lights, determining what is central and what is not.[43] This way of proceeding is "imperialistic." Such evaluative choices must be left to each citizen. For this reason, politics must refuse itself a determinate theory of the human being and the human good.

Prejudicial application

If we operate with a determinate conception of the human being that is meant to have some normative moral and political force, we must also, in applying it, ask which beings we take to fall under the concept. And here the objector notes that, all too easily – even if the conception itself is equitably and comprehensively designed – the powerless can be excluded. Aristotle himself, it is pointed out, held that women and slaves were not full-fledged human beings, and because his politics were based on his view of human functioning, the failure of these beings (in his view) to exhibit the desired mode of functioning contributed to their political exclusion and oppression.

It is, once again, hard to know what this objection is supposed to show. In particular, it is hard to know how, if at all, it is supposed to show that we would be better off without such determinate universal concepts. For it could be plausibly argued that it would have been even easier to exclude women and slaves on a whim if one did not have such a concept to combat.[44] On the other hand, it does show that we need to think not only about getting the concept right but also about getting the right beings admitted under the concept.

Each of these objections has some merit. Many universal conceptions of the human being have been insular in an arrogant way and neglectful of differences among cultures and ways of life. Some have been neglectful of choice and autonomy. And many have been prejudicially applied. But none of this shows that all such conceptions must fail in one or more of these ways. At this point, however, we heed to examine a real proposal, both to display its merits and to argue that it can in fact answer these charges.

IV A Conception of the Human Being: The Central Human Capabilities

The list of basic capabilities is generated by asking a question that from the start is evaluative: What activities[45] characteristically performed by human beings are so central that they seem definitive of a life that is truly human? In other words, what are the functions without which (meaning, without the availability of which) we would regard a life as not, or not fully, human?[46] We can get at this question better if we approach it via two somewhat more concrete questions that we often really ask ourselves. First is a question about personal continuity. We ask ourselves which changes or transitions are compatible with the continued existence of that being as a member of the human kind and which are not. Some functions can fail to be present without threatening our sense that we still have a human being on our hands; the absence of others seems to signal the end of a human life. This question is asked regularly, when we attempt to make medical definitions of death in a situation in which some of the functions of life persist, or to decide, for others or (thinking ahead) for ourselves, whether a certain level of illness or impairment means the end of the life of the being in question.[47]

The other question is a question about kind inclusion. We recognize other humans as human across many differences of time and place, of custom and appearance. We often tell ourselves stories, on the other hand, about anthropomorphic creatures who do not get classified as human, on account of some feature of their form of life and functioning. On what do we base these inclusions and exclusions? In short, what do we believe must be there, if we are going to acknowledge that a given life is human?[48] The answer to these questions points us to a subset of common or characteristic human functions, informing us that these are likely to have a special importance for everything else we choose and do.

Note that the procedure through which this account of the human is derived is neither ahistorical nor a priori. It is the attempt to summarize empirical findings of a broad and ongoing cross-cultural inquiry. As such, it is both open-ended and humble; it can always be contested and remade. Nor does it claim to read facts of "human nature" from biological observation; it takes biology into account as a relatively constant element in human experience.[49] It is because the account is evaluative from the start that it is called a conception of the good.

It should also be stressed that, like John Rawls's account of primary goods in *A Theory of Justice*,[50] this list of good functions, which is in some ways more comprehensive than his own list, is proposed as the object of a specifically political consensus.[51] The political is not understood exactly as Rawls understands it because the nation state is not assumed to be the basic unit, and the account is meant to have broad applicability to cross-cultural deliberations. This means, given the current state of world politics, that many of the obligations to promote the adequate distribution of these goods must rest with individuals rather than with any political institution, and in that way its role becomes difficult to distinguish from the role of other norms and goals of the individual. Nonetheless, the point of the list is the same as that of Rawlsian primary goods: to put forward something that people from many different traditions, with many different fuller conceptions of the good, can agree on, as the necessary basis for pursuing their good life. That is why the list is deliberately rather general.[52] Each of its components can be more concretely specified in accordance with one's origins, religious beliefs, or tastes. In that sense, the consensus that it hopes to evoke has many of the features of the "overlapping consensus" described by Rawls.[53]

Having isolated some functions that seem central in defining the very presence of a human life, we do not rest content with mere bare humanness. We want to specify a life in which fully human functioning, or a kind of basic human flourishing, will be available. For we do not want politics to take mere survival as its goal; we want to describe a life in which the dignity of the human being is not violated by hunger or fear or the absence of opportunity. (The idea is very much Marx's idea, when he used an Aristotelian notion of functioning to describe the difference between a merely animal use of one's faculties and a "truly human use."[54]) The following list of central human functional capabilities is an attempt to specify this basic notion of the good: All citizens should have these capabilities, whatever else they have and pursue.[55] I introduce this as a list of capabilities rather than of actual functionings, because I shall argue that capability, not actual functioning, should be the goal of public policy.

Central human functional capabilities

1. *Life*. Being able to live to the end of a human life of normal length[56]; not dying prematurely or before one's life is so reduced as to be not worth living
2. *Bodily health and integrity*. Being able to have good health, including reproductive health; being adequately nourished[57]; being able to have adequate shelter[58]
3. *Bodily integrity*. Being able to move freely from place to place; being able to be secure against violent assault, including sexual assault, marital rape, and domestic violence; having opportunities for sexual satisfaction and for choice in matters of reproduction
4. *Senses, imagination, thought*. Being able to use the senses; being able to imagine, to think, and to reason – and to do these things in a "truly human" way, a way informed and cultivated by an adequate education, including, but by no means limited to, literacy and basic mathematical and scientific training; being able to use imagination and thought in connection with experiencing and producing expressive works and events of one's own choice (religious, literary, musical, etc.); being able to use one's mind in ways protected by guarantees of freedom of expression with respect to both political and artistic speech and freedom of religious exercise; being able to have pleasurable experiences and to avoid nonbeneficial pain
5. *Emotions*. Being able to have attachments to things and persons outside ourselves; being able to love those who love and care for us; being able to grieve at their absence; in general, being able to love, to grieve, to experience

longing, gratitude, and justified anger; not having one's emotional developing blighted by fear or anxiety. (Supporting this capability means supporting forms of human association that can be shown to be crucial in their development.[59])

6. *Practical reason.* Being able to form a conception of the good and to engage in critical reflection about the planning of one's own life. (This entails protection for the liberty of conscience.)
7. *Affiliation.* (a) Being able to live for and in relation to others, to recognize and show concern for other human beings, to engage in various forms of social interaction; being able to imagine the situation of another and to have compassion for that situation; having the capability for both justice and friendship. (Protecting this capability means, once again, protecting institutions that constitute such forms of affiliation, and also protecting the freedoms of assembly and political speech.) (b) Having the social bases of self-respect and nonhumiliation; being able to be treated as a dignified being whose worth is equal to that of others. (This entails provisions of nondiscrimination.)
8. *Other species.* Being able to live with concern for and in relation to animals, plants, and the world of nature[60]
9. *Play.* Being able to laugh, to play, to enjoy recreational activities
10. *Control over one's environment.* (a) *Political*: being able to participate effectively in political choices that govern one's life; having the rights of political participation, free speech, and freedom of association (b) *Material*: being able to hold property (both land and movable goods); having the right to seek employment on an equal basis with others; having the freedom from unwarranted search and seizure.[61] In work, being able to work as a human being, exercising practical reason and entering into meaningful relationships of mutual recognition with other workers.

The "capabilities approach," as I conceive it,[62] claims that a life that lacks any one of these capabilities, no matter what else it has, will fall short of being a good human life. Thus it would be reasonable to take these things as a focus for concern, in assessing the quality of life in a country and asking about the role of public policy in meeting human needs. The list is certainly general – and this is deliberate, to leave room for plural specification and also for further negotiation. But like (and as a reasonable basis for) a set of constitutional guarantees, it offers real guidance to policymakers, and far more accurate guidance than that offered by the focus on utility, or even on resources.[63]

The list is, emphatically, a list of separate components. We cannot satisfy the need for one of them by giving a larger amount of another one. All are of central importance and all are distinct in quality. This limits the trade-offs that it will be reasonable to make and thus limits the applicability of quantitative cost-benefit analysis. At the same time, the items on the list are related to one another in many complex ways. Employment rights, for example, support health, and also freedom from domestic violence, by giving women a better bargaining position in the family. The liberties of speech and association turn up at several distinct points on the list, showing their fundamental role with respect to several distinct areas of human functioning.

V Capability as Goal

The basic claim I wish to make – concurring with Amartya Sen – is that the central goal of public planning should be the *capabilities* of citizens to perform various important functions. The question that should be asked when assessing quality of life in a country – and of course this is a central part of assessing the quality of its political arrangements – is, How well have the people of the country been enabled to perform the central human functions? And, have they been put in a position of mere human subsistence with respect to the functions, or have they been enabled to live well? Politics, we argue (here concurring with Rawls), should focus on getting as many people as possible into a state of capability to function, with respect to the interlocking set of capabilities enumerated by that list.[64] Naturally, the determination of whether certain individuals and groups are across the threshold is only as precise a matter as the determination of the threshold. I have left things deliberately somewhat open-ended at this point, in keeping with the procedures of the *Human Development Report*, believing that the best way to work toward a more precise determination, at present, is to focus on comparative information and to allow citizens to judge for themselves whether their policymakers have done as well as they should have. Again we will have to answer various questions about the costs we are willing to pay to get all citizens above the threshold, as opposed to leaving a small number below and allowing the rest a considerably above-threshold life quality. It seems likely, at any rate, that moving all citizens above a basic threshold of capability should be taken as a central social goal. When citizens are across the threshold, societies are to a great extent free to choose the other goals they wish to pursue. Some inequalities, however, will themselves count as capability failures. For example, inequalities based on hierarchies of gender or race will themselves be inadmissible on the grounds that they undermine self-respect and emotional development.

The basic intuition from which the capability approach starts, in the political arena, is that human capabilities exert a moral claim that they should be developed. Human beings are creatures such that, provided with the right educational and material support, they can become fully capable of the major human functions. That is, they are creatures with certain lower-level capabilities (which I call "basic capabilities"[65]) to perform the functions in question. When these capabilities are deprived of the nourishment that would transform them into the high-level capabilities that figure on my list, they are fruitless, cut off, in some way but a shadow of themselves. They are like actors who never get to go on the stage, or a person who sleeps all through life, or a musical score that is never performed. Their very being makes forward reference to functioning. Thus, if functioning never arrives on the scene they are hardly even what they are. This may sound like a metaphysical idea, and in a sense it is (in that it is an idea discussed in Aristotle's *Metaphysics*). But that does not mean it is not a basic and pervasive empirical idea, an idea that underwrites many of our daily practices and judgments in many times and places. Just as we hold that a child who dies before getting to maturity has died especially tragically – for her activities of growth and preparation for adult activity now have lost their point – so too with capability and functioning more generally: We believe that certain basic and central human endowments have a claim to be assisted in developing, and exert that claim on others, and especially, as Aristotle saw, on government. Without some such notion of the basic worth of human capacities, we have a hard time arguing for women's equality and for basic human rights. Think, for example, of the remark of Catharine MacKinnon that I quoted as my epigraph. If women were really just trees or turtles or filing cabinets, the fact that their current status in many parts of the world is not a fully human one would not be, as it is, a problem of justice. In thinking of political planning we begin, then, from a notion of the basic capabilities and their worth, thinking of them as claims to a chance for functioning, which give rise to correlated political duties.

I have spoken both of functioning and of capability. How are they related? Getting clear about this is crucial in defining the relation of the capabilities approach to liberalism. For if we were to take functioning itself as the goal of public policy, the liberal would rightly judge that we were precluding many choices that citizens may make in accordance with their own conceptions of the good. A deeply religious person may prefer not to be well nourished but to engage in strenuous fasting. Whether for religious or for other reasons, a person may prefer a celibate life to one containing sexual expression. A person may prefer to work with an intense dedication that precludes recreation and play. Am I saying that these are not fully human or flourishing lives? Does the approach instruct governments to nudge or push people into functioning of the requisite sort, no matter what they prefer?

Here we must answer: No, capability, not functioning, is the political goal. This is so because of the very great importance the approach attaches to practical reason, as a good that both suffuses all the other functions, making them human rather than animal,[66] and figures, itself, as a central function on the list. It is perfectly true that functionings, not simply capabilities, are what render a life fully human: If there were no functioning of any kind in a life, we could hardly applaud it, no matter what opportunities it contained. Nonetheless, for political purposes it is appropriate for us to shoot for capabilities, and those alone. Citizens must be left free to determine their course after that. The person with plenty of food may always choose to fast, but there is a great difference between fasting and starving, and it is this difference we wish to capture. Again, the person who has normal opportunities for sexual satisfaction can always choose a life of celibacy, and we say nothing against this.

What we do speak against, for example, is the practice of female genital mutilation, which deprives individuals of the opportunity to choose sexual functioning (and indeed, the opportunity to choose celibacy as well).[67] A person who has opportunities for play can always choose a workaholic life; again, there is a great difference between that chosen life and a life constrained by insufficient maximum-hour protections and/or the "double day" that makes women in many parts of the world unable to play.

The issue will be clearer if we recall that there are three different types of capabilities that figure in the analysis.[68] First, there are *basic capabilities*: the innate equipment of individuals that is the necessary basis for developing the more advanced capability. Most infants have from birth the basic capability for practical reason and imagination, though they cannot exercise such functions without a lot more development and education. Second, there are *internal capabilities*: states of the person herself that are, as far as the person herself is concerned, sufficient conditions for the exercise of the requisite functions. A woman who has not suffered genital mutilation has the internal capability for sexual pleasure; most adult human beings everywhere have the internal capability to use speech and thought in accordance with their own conscience. Finally, there are *combined capabilities*, which we define as internal capabilities *combined with* suitable external conditions for the exercise of the function. A woman who is not mutilated but is secluded and forbidden to leave the house has internal but not combined capabilities for sexual expression (and work and political participation). Citizens of repressive nondemocratic regimes have the internal but not the combined capability to exercise thought and speech in accordance with their conscience. The aim of public policy is the production of *combined capabilities*. This means promoting the states of the person by providing the necessary education and care; it also means preparing the environment so that it is favorable for the exercise of practical reason and the other major functions.[69]

This clarifies the position. The approach does not say that public policy should rest content with *internal capabilities* but remain indifferent to the struggles of individuals who have to try to exercise these in a hostile environment. In that sense, it is highly attentive to the goal of functioning, and instructs governments to keep it always in view. On the other hand, we are not pushing individuals into the function: Once the stage is fully set, the choice is up to them.

The approach is therefore very close to Rawls's approach using the notion of primary goods. We can see the list of capabilities as like a long list of opportunities for life functioning, such that it is always rational to want them whatever else one wants. If one ends up having a plan of life that does not make use of all of them, one has hardly been harmed by having the chance to choose a life that does. (Indeed, in the cases of fasting and celibacy it is the very availability of the alternative course that gives the choice its moral value.) The primary difference between this capabilities list and Rawls's list of primary goods is its length and definiteness, and in particular its determination to place on the list the social basis of several goods that Rawls has called "natural goods," such as "health and vigor, intelligence and imagination."[70] Since Rawls has been willing to put the social basis of self-respect on his list, it is not at all clear why he has not made the same move with imagination and health.[71] Rawls's evident concern is that no society can guarantee health to its individuals – in that sense, saying that our goal is full combined capability may appear unreasonably idealistic. Some of the capabilities (e.g., some of the political liberties) can be fully guaranteed by society, but many others involve an element of chance and cannot be so guaranteed. We respond to this by saying that the list is an enumeration of political *goals* that should be useful as a benchmark for aspiration and comparison. Even though individuals with adequate health support often fall ill, it still makes sense to compare societies by asking about actual health capabilities, because we assume that the comparison will reflect the different inputs of human planning and can be adjusted to take account of more and less favorable natural situations.

Earlier versions of the list appeared to diverge from the approach of Rawlsian liberalism by not giving as central a place as Rawls does to the traditional political rights and liberties – although the need to incorporate them was stressed from the start.[72] This version of the list corrects that defect of emphasis. These political liberties have a central importance in making well-being human. A society that aims at well-being while overriding these has delivered to its members a merely animal level of satisfaction.[73] As Amartya Sen has recently written, "Political rights are important not only for the fulfillment of needs, they are crucial also for the formulation of needs. And this idea relates, in the end, to the respect that we owe each other as fellow human beings."[74] This idea has recently been echoed by Rawls: Primary goods specify what citizens' needs are from the point of view of political justice.[75]

The capability view justifies its elaborate list by pointing out that choice is not pure spontaneity, flourishing independently of material and social conditions. If one cares about people's powers to choose a conception of the good, then one must care about the rest of the form of life that supports those powers, including its material conditions. Thus the approach claims that its more comprehensive concern with flourishing is perfectly consistent with the impetus behind the Rawlsian project, which has always insisted that we are not to rest content with merely formal equal liberty and opportunity but must pursue their fully equal worth by ensuring that unfavorable economic and social circumstances do not prevent people from availing themselves of liberties and opportunities that are formally open to them.

The guiding thought behind this Aristotelian enterprise is, at its heart, a profoundly liberal idea,[76] and one that lies at the heart of Rawls's project as well: the idea of the citizen as a free and dignified human being, a maker of choices. Politics has an urgent role to play here, getting citizens the tools they need, both to choose at all and to have a realistic option of exercising the most valuable functions. The choice of whether and how to use the tools, however, is left up to them, in the conviction that this is an essential aspect of respect for their freedom. They are seen not as passive recipients of social planning but as dignified beings who shape their own lives.[77]

Let us now return to the Marglins and to Metha Bai. What would this universalist approach have to say about these concrete cases? Notice how close the Marglin approach is, in its renunciation of critical normative argument, to the prevailing economic approaches of which it presents itself as a radical critique. A preference-based approach that gives priority to the preferences of dominant males in a traditional culture is likely to be especially subversive of the quality of life of women, who have been on the whole badly treated by prevailing traditional norms. And one can see this clearly in the Marglins' own examples. For menstruation taboos, even if endorsed by habit and custom, impose severe restrictions on women's power to form a plan of life and to execute the plan they have chosen.[78] They are members of the same family of traditional attitudes that make it difficult for women like Metha Bai to sustain the basic functions of life. Vulnerability to smallpox, even if someone other than an anthropologist should actually defend it as a good thing, is even more evidently a threat to human functioning. And the Japanese husband who allegedly renounces freedom of choice actually shows considerable attachment to it, in the ways that matter, by asking the woman to look after the boring details of life. What should concern us is whether the woman has a similar degree of freedom to plan her life and to execute her plan.

As for Metha Bai, the absence of freedom to choose employment outside the home is linked to other capability failures, in the areas of health, nutrition, mobility, education, and political voice. Unlike the type of liberal view that focuses on resources alone, my view enables us to focus directly on the obstacles to self-realization imposed by traditional norms and values and thus to justify special political action to remedy the unequal situation. No male of Metha Bai's caste would have to overcome threats of physical violence in order to go out of the house to work for life-sustaining food.

The capabilities approach insists that a woman's affiliation with a certain group or culture should not be taken as normative for her unless, on due consideration, with all the capabilities at her disposal, she makes that norm her own. We should take care to extend to each individual full capabilities to pursue the items on the list – and then see whether they want to avail themselves of those opportunities. Usually they do, even when tradition says they should not. Martha Chen's work with widows like Metha Bai reveals that they are already deeply critical of the cultural norms that determine their life quality. One week at a widows' conference in Bangalore was sufficient to cause these formerly secluded widows to put on forbidden colors and to apply for loans; one elderly woman, "widowed" at the age of seven, danced for the first time in her life, whirling wildly in the center of the floor.[79] In other cases, especially when a woman must negotiate a relationship with a surviving husband, it takes longer for her real affiliations and preferences to emerge. Chen's related study of a rural literacy project in Bangladesh[80] shows that it took a good deal of time for women previously illiterate to figure out, in consultation with development workers, that literacy might offer something to their own concrete lives. Nonetheless, what we do not see in any of these cases is the fantasy that the Marglins describe, a cultural monolith univocally repudiating the outsider and clinging to an "embedded way of life." Why should women cling to a tradition, indeed, when it is usually not their voice that speaks or their interests that are served?

VI Answering the Objections: Human Functioning and Pluralism

We still need to show that this approach has answers to the legitimate questions that confronted it. Concerning *neglect of historical and cultural difference*, we can begin by insisting that this normative conception of human capability is designed to make room for a reasonable pluralism in specification. The capabilities approach urges us to see common needs, problems, and capacities, but it also reminds us that each person and group faces these problems in a highly concrete context. The list claims to have identified in a very general way some components that are fundamental to any human life. But it makes room for differences of context in several ways. First, it is open ended and nonexhaustive. It does not say that these are the only important things, or that there is anything unimportant (far less, bad) about things not on the list. It just says that this is a group of especially important functions on which we can agree to focus for political purposes.

Further, the list allows in its very design for the possibility of multiple specifications of each of the components. Good public reasoning about the list will retain a rich sensitivity to the concrete context, to the characters of the agents and their social situation. Sometimes what is a good way of promoting education in one part of the world will be completely ineffectual in another. Forms of affiliation that flourish in one community may prove impossible to sustain in another. Arriving at the best specification will most reasonably be done by a public dialogue with those who are most deeply immersed in those conditions. We should use the list to criticize injustice, but we should not say anything at all without rich and full information.

We see this, for example, in Martha Chen's account of the Bangladeshi literacy project.[81] An initial approach that simply offered the women adult literacy materials met with no response. It was only after a period of "participatory dialogue," during which the local women told their stories and the development workers gave them rich narrative information about the lives of women elsewhere, that a picture of literacy for these women in these circumstances began to emerge and to make sense. Given the opportunity, they made for themselves a concrete local specification of this vague end. And it was clearly no external imposition: The women's narratives express a joy in self-command and agency that seems to come from something very deep in themselves. Rohima, of the West Shanbandha women's group, comments:

> Even my mother said yesterday: "You did not use to visit others' homes, did not speak to others. How have you learnt to speak so many things?" I said: "Ma, how I have learnt I cannot say. Whenever I am alone I sit with the books." Mother asked: "What do you see in the books?" I said: "Ma, what valuable things there are in the books you will not understand because you cannot read and write." If somebody behaves badly with me, I go home and sit with the books. When I sit with the books my mind becomes better.[82]

The books had to have some relation to the women's concrete situation, but it was equally important that the development workers did not back off when they saw that the women's local traditions contained no history of female literacy.

We can say the same of the related value of autonomy. It would have been very wrong to assume, with the Marglins, that these women did not want separateness and choice, that they really wanted to submerge their own aims in those of husband and family. This, again, emerges retrospectively, in their moving accounts of their newfound feeling of selfhood and mental awareness. "My mind was rusty," says one young wife, "and now it shines." On the other hand, it also would have done no good to go into that village and deliver a lecture on Kant – or on human capabilities! The universal value of practical reason and choice would have meant little in the abstract. To make sense, it had to become concretely situated in the stories they told about themselves and their lives.

If we turn to the difficult story of Metha Bai, something similar emerges. Metha Bai's is the story of age-old traditions regarding widowhood in India.[83] Any approach to her situation would have to be based on an understanding of these traditions and their special connection with issues of caste in an upwardly mobile Hindu family. Talk of "the right to work" would have been no use without a concrete local understanding. On the other hand, if the workers in the widows project had simply backed off, saying that the local values did not include a value of right to work for widows, they would have missed the depth at which Metha Bai herself longed for choice and autonomy, both as means to survival for herself and her children and as means to selfhood. These are typical examples of the fruitful ways in which an abstract value can be instantiated in a concrete situation, through rich local knowledge.

One further observation is in order. This objector is frequently worried about the way in which universalist projects may erode the values that hold communities together. We have already seen that traditional community values are not always so good for women. We can now add that universalist values build new types of community. All the women studied by Chen stressed the solidarity promoted by the literacy project, the comfort and pleasure they had in consulting with a group of women (some local, some from the development project) rather than each being isolated in the home. Mallika, a young widow in Dapunia, vigorously expresses this idea:

> The group helped us and taught us many things. I have learned how to live unitedly. Before if any rich person abused or criticized, we could not reply. But now if anybody says anything bad, we, the 17 members of the group, go together and ask that person why he or she passed this comment. This is another kind of help we have gotten. Before we did not know how to get together and help each other.... Each one was busy with their own worries and sorrows, always thinking about food for their children and themselves. Now we, the 17 members of the group, have become very close to one another.[84]

This story is no isolated phenomenon. In women's groups I have visited in both India and China, the first benefit that is typically mentioned is that of affiliation and friendship with other women in pursuit of common goals. This shows us something highly pertinent to the Marglins' nostalgic tale of embeddedness. We do not have to choose between "the embedded life" of community and a deracinated type of individualism. Universal values build their own communities, communities of resourcefulness, friendship, and agency, embedded in the local scene but linked in complex ways to groups of women in other parts of the world. For these women the new community was a lot better than the one they had inhabited before.

The liberal charges the capability approach with *neglect of autonomy*, arguing that any such determinate conception removes from the citizens the chance to make their own choices about the good life. We have already said a good deal about this issue, but let us summarize, stressing three points. First, the list is a list of capabilities, not a list of actual functions, precisely because the conception is designed to leave room for choice. Government is not directed to push citizens into acting in certain valued ways; instead, it is directed to make sure that all human beings have the necessary resources and conditions for acting in those ways. By making opportunities available, government enhances, and does not remove, choice.[85] It will not always be easy to say at what point someone is really capable of making a choice, especially when there are traditional obstacles to functioning. Sometimes our best strategy may well be to look at actual functioning and infer negative capability (tentatively) from its absence.[86] But the conceptual distinction remains critical. Even in the rare case in which the approach will favor compulsory measures – particularly in primary and secondary education – it does so because of the huge role education plays in opening other choices in life.

Second, this respect for choice is built deeply into the list itself, in the role it gives to practical reasoning, to the political liberties, and also to employment, seen as a source of opportunity and empowerment. One of the most central capabilities promoted by the conception will be the capability of choosing itself.[87]

The examples we have considered show the truth of these claims. In the literacy project, a concern for autonomy was fundamental in the method of participatory dialogue itself, which constructed a situation free from intimidation and hierarchy in which the women's own concerns could gradually emerge and develop on the basis of the information they received. Their ex post facto satisfaction with their new situation, in which life choices were greatly enhanced, indicates, I believe, that the focus on a general capability goal was not a violation of their autonomy. (Rohima comments: "It is good now. . . . As my knowledge and understanding are good now, I will be able to do many things gradually."[88]) Indeed, we can see in the project as a whole the construction of full autonomy out of a more inchoate sense of the self. Metha Bai already had a robust sense of her own interests and how they diverged from the expectations of those around her. But the widows project, which extended her thoughts by providing information and advice, was crucial to the further development of her own conception of life.

Finally, the capability view insists that choice is not pure spontaneity, flourishing independently of material and social conditions. If one cares about autonomy, then one must care about the rest of the form of life that supports it and the material conditions that enable one to live that form of life. Thus, the approach claims that its own comprehensive concern with flourishing is a better way of promoting choice than is the liberal's narrower concern with spontaneity alone, which sometimes tolerates situations in which individuals are cut off from the fully human use of their faculties.

We now face the objection about *prejudicial application*. Catharine MacKinnon once claimed that "being a woman is not yet a way of being a human being."[89] As this remark suggests, most traditional ways of categorizing and valuing women have not accorded them full membership in the human species, as that species is generally defined. If this is so, one might well ask, of what use is it to identify a set of central human capabilities? For the basic (lower-level) capacity to develop these can always be denied to women, even by those who grant their centrality – for example, by denying women "rational nature," or by asserting that they are connected to dangerous or unclean animality. Does this problem show that the human function idea is either hopelessly in league with patriarchy or, at best, impotent as a tool for justice?

I believe that it does not. For if we examine the history of these denials we see, I believe, the great power of the conception of the human as a source of moral claims. Acknowledging the other person as a member of the very same kind would have generated a sense of affiliation and a set of moral and educational duties. That is why, to those bent on shoring up their own power, the stratagem of splitting the other off from one's own species seems so urgent and so seductive. But to deny humanness to beings with whom one lives in conversation and interaction is a fragile sort of self-deceptive stratagem, vulnerable to sustained and consistent reflection, and also to experiences that cut through self-deceptive rationalization. Any moral conception can be withheld, out of ambition or hatred or shame. But the conception of the human being, spelled out, as here, in a roughly determinate way, seems much harder to withhold than others that have been made the basis for ethics, such as "rational being" or "person."

VII Women and Men: Two Norms or One?

But should there be a single norm of human functioning for men and women? One might grant that human capabilities cross cultures while still maintaining that in each culture a division of labor should be arranged along gender lines.

One such position, which I shall call Position A, assigns to both males and females the same general normative list of functions but suggests that males and females should exercise these functions in different spheres of life: men in the public sphere, for example, and women in the home. The second, which I shall call Position B, insists that the list of functions, even at a high level of generality, should be different: for men, citizenship and rational autonomy; for women, family love and care.

Position A is compatible with a serious interest in equality and in gender justice. For what it says, after all, is that males and females have the same basic needs for capability development and should get what they need. It is determined to ensure that both get to the higher (developed) level of capability with respect to all the central functions. It simply holds that this can (and perhaps should) be done in separate spheres. Is this any more problematic than to say that human functioning in India can, and even should, take a different concrete form from functioning in England? Or that some people can realize musical capacities by singing; others by playing the violin?

The trouble comes when we notice that Position A usually ends up endorsing a division of duties that is associated with traditional forms of hierarchy.

Even Mill, who made so many fine arguments against women's subordination, did not sufficiently ask how the very perpetuation of separate spheres of responsibility might reinforce subordination. It is hard to find plausible reasons for perpetuating functional distinctions that coincide with traditional hierarchy. Even in the fourth century B.C.E., Plato was able to see that women's role in childbearing does not require, or even suggest, that women be confined to the home.[90] Advances in the control of reproduction are making this less and less plausible. The disability imposed by childbearing on a member of the labor force is to a large extent socially constructed, above all by the absence of support for child care, from the public sphere, from employers, and from male partners.

Sometimes clinging to traditional divisions is a prudent way of promoting social change. Neither Chen nor her colleagues proposed to jettison all gender divisions within the Bangladeshi villages. Instead, they found "female jobs" for the women that were somewhat more dignified and important than the old jobs, jobs that looked continuous with traditional female work but were outside the home and brought in wages. The "revolution" in women's quality of life never would have taken place but for the caution of the women, who at each stage gave the men of the village reason to believe that the transformations were not overwhelmingly threatening and were good for the well-being of the entire group. But such pragmatic decisions in the face of recalcitrant realities do not tell us how things ought to be. And it is likely that women's subordination will not be adequately addressed as long as women are confined to a sphere traditionally devalued, linked with a low "perceived well-being contribution."[91] *The Human Development Report's* Gender Empowerment Measure rightly focuses, therefore, on the ability of women to win entry into the traditional male spheres of politics and administration.

I turn, then, to Position B, which has been influentially defended by many philosophers, including Rousseau and some of his followers in today's world.[92] Insofar as B relies on the claim that there are two different sets of basic innate capacities, we should insist, with John Stuart Mill, that this claim has not been borne out by any responsible scientific evidence. Experiments that allegedly show strong gender divisions in basic (untrained) abilities have been shown to contain major scientific flaws; these flaws removed, the case for such differences is altogether inconclusive.[93] Experiments that cross-label babies as to sex have established that children are differentially handled, played with, and talked to straight from birth, in accordance with the handler's beliefs about the child's biological sex. It is therefore impossible at present to separate "nature" from "culture."[94] There may be innate differences between the sexes, but so far we are not in a position to know them – any more than we were when Mill first made that argument in 1869.[95]

Second, we should note that even what is claimed in this body of scientific material without substantiation usually does not amount to a difference in what I have been calling the central basic capabilities. What is alleged is usually a differential statistical distribution of some specific capacity for a high level of excellence, not for crossing a basic threshold, and excellence in some very narrowly defined function (say, geometrical ability), rather than in one of our large-scale capabilities such as the capability to perform practical reasoning. Thus, even if the claim were true it would not be a claim about capabilities in our capacious sense; nor, because it is a statistical claim, would it have any implications for the ways in which individuals should be treated. The political consequences of such alleged sex differences in our scheme of things, even had they been established, would be nil.

But we can also criticize Position B in a different way, arguing that the differentiated conceptions of male and female functioning characteristically put forward by B are internally inadequate and fail to give us viable norms of human flourishing.[96]

What do we usually find, in the versions of B that our philosophical tradition bequeaths to us? (Rousseau's view is an instructive example.) We have, on the one hand, males who are "autonomous," capable of practical reasoning, independent and self-sufficient, allegedly good at political deliberation. These males are brought up not to develop strong emotions of love and feelings of deep need that are associated with the awareness of one's own lack of self-sufficiency. For this reason they are not well equipped to care for the needs of their family members or, perhaps, even to notice those needs. On the other hand, we have females such as Rousseau's Sophie,[97] brought up to lack autonomy and self-respect, ill equipped to rely on her own practical reasoning, dependent on males, focused on pleasing others, and good at caring for others. Is either of these viable as a complete life for a human being?

It would seem not. The internal tensions in Rousseau's account are a good place to begin.[98] Rousseau places tremendous emphasis on compassion as a basic social motivation. He understands compassion to require fellow feeling and a keen responsiveness to the sufferings of others. And yet, in preparing Emile for autonomous citizenship, he ultimately gives emotional development short shrift, allocating caring and responsiveness to the female sphere alone. It appears likely that Emile will be not only an incomplete person but also a defective citizen, even by the standards of citizenship recognized by Rousseau himself.

With Sophie, things again go badly. Taught to care for others but not taught that her life is her own to plan, she lives under the sway of external influences and lacks self-government. As Rousseau himself shows in his fascinating narrative of the end of her life,[99] Sophie comes to a bad end through her lack of judgment. Moreover, in the process she proves to be a bad partner and deficient in love. For love, as we come to see, requires judgment and constancy. Thus each of them fails to live a complete human life, and each fails, too, to exemplify fully and well the very functions for which they were being trained, because those functions require support from other functions for which they were not trained. The text leads its thoughtful reader to the conclusion that the capabilities that have traditionally marked the separate male and female spheres are not separable from one another without a grave functional loss. Society cannot strive for completeness by simply adding one sphere to the other. It must strive to develop in each and every person the full range of the human capabilities.

This more inclusive notion of human functioning admits tragic conflict. For it insists on the separate value and the irreplaceable importance of a rich plurality of functions. And the world does not always guarantee that individuals will not be faced with painful choices among these functions, in which, in order to pursue one of them well they must neglect others (and thus, in many cases, subvert the one as well). But this shows once again, I believe, the tremendous importance of keeping some such list of the central functions before us as we assess the quality of life in the countries of the world and strive to raise it. For many such tragedies – like many cases of simple capability failure – result from unjust and unreflective social arrangements. One can try to construct a society in which the tragic choices that faced Emile and Sophie would not be necessary, in which both males and females could learn both to love and to reason.

In April 1994, Metha Bai went to Bangalore for the widows' conference. She met widows from all over India, and they spent a week discussing their common problems. During that week, Metha Bai began to smile a lot. She bought beads in the forbidden color of blue, and she seemed pleased with the way she looked. With advice from a local NGO involved in the conference, she applied for and obtained a loan that enabled her to pay off the mortgage on the small property she still owns. Although her economic situation is not secure and she still does not hold a job outside the home, she has managed to stave off hunger. Like many women all over the world, she is fighting for her life, with resilience and fortitude.

Women belong to cultures. But they do not choose to be born into any particular culture, and they do not really choose to endorse its norms as good for themselves, unless they do so in possession of further options and opportunities – including the opportunity to form communities of affiliation and empowerment with other women. The contingencies of where one is born, whose power one is afraid of, and what habits shape one's daily thought are chance events that should not be permitted to play the role they now play in pervasively shaping women's life chances. Beneath all these chance events are human powers, powers of choice and intelligent self-formation. Women in much of the world lack support for the most central human functions, and this denial of support is frequently caused by their being women. But women, unlike rocks and plants and even horses, have the potential to become capable of these human functions, given sufficient nutrition, education, and other support. That is why their unequal failure in capability is a problem of justice. It is up to all human beings to solve this problem. I claim that a conception of human functioning gives us valuable assistance as we undertake this task.

Notes

I have discussed the capabilities approach in several other papers, to which I shall refer: "Nature, Function, and

Capability: Aristotle on Political Distribution," *Oxford Studies in Ancient Philosophy* Supplementary Volume 1 (1988), 145–84, hereafter NFC; "Aristotelian Social Democracy," in *Liberalism and the Good*, ed. R. B. Douglass *et al.* (New York: Routledge, 1990), 203–52, hereafter ASD; "Non-Relative Virtues: An Aristotelian Approach," in *The Quality of Life*, ed. M. Nussbaum and A. Sen (Oxford: Clarendon Press, 1993), hereafter NRV; "Aristotle on Human Nature and the Foundations of Ethics," in *World, Mind and Ethics: Essays on the Ethical Philosophy of Bernard Williams*, ed. J. E. J. Altham and Ross Harrison (Cambridge: Cambridge University Press, 1995), 86–131, hereafter HN; "Human Functioning and Social Justice: In Defense of Aristotelian Essentialism," *Political Theory* 20 (1992), 202–46, hereafter HF; "Human Capabilities, Female Human Beings," in *Women, Culture, and Development*, ed. M. Nussbaum and J. Glover (Oxford: Clarendon Press, 1995), 61–104, hereafter HC; "The Good as Discipline, the Good as Freedom," in *The Ethics of Consumption and Global Stewardship*, ed. D. Crocker and T. Linden (Lanham, MD: Rowman and Littlefield, 1998), 312–41, hereafter GDGF; "Capabilities and Human Rights," *Fordham Law Review* 66 (1997), 273–300, hereafter CHR.

1 For this case and others like it, see Martha Chen, "A Matter of Survival: Women's Right to Employment in India and Bangladesh," in *Women, Culture, and Development* (hereafter WCD), ed. M. Nussbaum and J. Glover (Oxford: Clarendon Press, 1995), 37–57. See also M. Chen, *Perpetual Mourning: Widowhood in Rural india*, (Philadelphia, PA: University of Pennsylvania Press, 2002).

2 *Bradwell v. Illinois*, 83 US (16 Wall.) 130 (1873).

3 *Carr v. Allison Gas Turbine Division, General Motors Corp.*, 32 F.3d 1007 (1994). Mary Carr won her case on appeal.

4 Martha Chen, A *Quiet Revolution: Women in Transition in Rural Bangladesh* (Cambridge, MA: Schenkman, 1983), 176.

5 *Human Development Report* (New York: United Nations Development Program, 1996) (hereafter *Report*); see also the 1995 *Report*, which focuses on gender. The countries in which women do best in life quality, according to the Gender Development Index (GDI), a measure using the same variables as the HDI (Human Development Index) but adjusted according to disparities between the sexes (see *Report*, 107, for the technical formulation) are, in order, Sweden, Canada, Norway, the United States, Finland, Iceland, Denmark, France, Australia, New Zealand, the Netherlands, Japan, Austria, the United Kingdom, and Belgium.

6 If we subtract the GDI rank from the HDI rank, we get –10 for Spain, –9 for Japan, 8 for Sweden, 10 for Denmark, and 4 for New Zealand.

7 These variables include percentage shares of administrative and managerial positions, percentage shares of professional and technical jobs, and percentage shares of parliamentary seats.

8 The ranking at the top: Norway, Sweden, Denmark, Finland, New Zealand, Canada, Germany, the Netherlands, the United States, Austria, Barbados, and Switzerland. Spain ranks 25; Japan, 37; France, 40; and Greece, 60.

9 These data are from the 1993 report; later reports disaggregate employment data into jobs of various specific kinds and no longer count unpaid agricultural labor as employment.

10 Again, these are 1993 data; the 1996 report gives the absolute percentages, which are, for these examples, Sierra Leone, 16.7%; Afghanistan, 13.5%; Sudan, 32%; Nepal, 13%. Nations in which the female literacy rate is strikingly out of step with the general level of economic development include Saudi Arabia, 47.6%; Algeria, 45.8%; Egypt, 37.0%; Iraq, 42.3%; Pakistan, 23.0%; and India, 36.0%. Striking progress in female literacy, on the other hand, if one can rely on the figures, has been made in Cuba, 94.6%; Sri Lanka, 86.2%; Philippines, 93.9%; most of the former constituent states of the Soviet Union, in the 90s; Vietnam, 89.5%; and China, 70.9%. On the disparity of achievement between China and India, see Jean Drèze and Amartya Sen, *India: Economic Development and Social Opportunity* (Oxford: Clarendon Press, 1996).

11 Numbers of female students in tertiary education per 100,000 people: Hong Kong, 1,022; Barbados, 1,885; Republic of Korea, 2,866; Philippines, 3,140; Egypt, 499; China, 132; Iran, 764; Laos, 60; Pakistan, 149; Ethiopia, 24; and Rwanda, 19.

12 Countries where women hold a high percentage of parliamentary seats: Norway, 39.4%; Sweden, 40.4%; and Denmark, 33.0%. Bangladesh at 10.6% is ahead of the United States at 10.4%, and India at 8.0% is ahead of Japan at 6.7%.

13 The statistics in this paragraph are taken from Jean Drèze and Amartya Sen, *Hunger and Public Action* (Oxford: Clarendon Press, 1989).

14 This is very likely due to the central role women play in productive economic activity. For a classic study of this issue, see Esther Boserup, *Women's Role in Economic Development* (New York: St Martin's Press, 1970), 2nd edn (Aldershot: Gower Publishing, 1986). For a set of valuable responses to Boserup's work, see *Persistent Inequalities*, ed. Irene Tinker (New York: Oxford University Press, 1990).

15 See Drèze and Sen, *Hunger*, 52.

16 See Drèze and Sen, *India*.

17 See Sen, "Gender and Cooperative Conflicts," in Tinker, 123–49.

18 See Drèze and Sen, *India*, for graphic evidence of the relative independence of educational and health attainment from economic growth, in comparative regional studies.

19 Gary Becker, *A Treatise on the Family* (Cambridge, MA: Harvard University Press, 1981; 2nd edn 1991).

20 See Sen, "Gender and Cooperative Conflicts"; Partha Dasgupta, *An Inquiry Into Well-Being and Destitution* (Oxford: Clarendon Press, 1993), Ch.11; on food allocation, see Lincoln C. Chen, E. Huq, and S. D'Souza, "Sex Bias in the Family Allocation of Food and Health Care in Rural Bangladesh," *Population and Development Review* 7 (1981), 55–70. Bargaining models of the family are now proliferating; for two valuable recent examples, see Shelly Lundberg and Robert A. Pollak, "Bargaining and Distribution in Marriage," *Journal of Economic Perspectives* 10 (1996), 139–58, and S. Lundberg, R. Pollak, and T. J. Wales, "Do Husbands and Wives Pool Their Resources? Evidence from the U.K. Child Benefit," *Journal of Human Resources* (1997), 463–80.

21 See, now, Gary Becker, "The Economic Way of Looking at Behavior," the Nobel Address 1992, in *The Essence of Becker*, ed. Ramón Febrero and Pedro S. Schwartz (Stanford, CA: Hoover Institution Press, 1995), 647, on the role of childhood experiences in shaping preferences.

22 Sen, "Gender and Cooperative Conflicts," argues that Becker's account is much stronger as an account of actual preferences in the household than as an account of the real interests (life and death, good and bad health, good and bad nutrition) that underlie the preferences. (He provides evidence that people's perception of their health and nutritional status may be severely distorted by informational deficiencies.)

23 Becker now admits deficiencies in the model: "Many economists, including me, have excessively relied on altruism to tie together the interests of family members." Motives of "obligation, anger, and other attitudes usually neglected by theories of rational behavior" should be added to the models. Becker, "The Economic Way of Looking at Behavior," 648. Elsewhere, Becker mentions guilt, affection, and fear – his example being a woman's habitual fear of physical abuse from men. Ibid., 647. It is unclear whether he still supports an organic one-actor model, with a more complicated motivational structure, or a "bargaining model," of the sort increasingly used by family economists. See Becker, *A Treatise on the Family*.

24 See Sen, "Gender and Cooperative Conflicts"; Jon Elster, *Sour Grapes* (Cambridge: Cambridge University Press, 1993).

25 See John Rawls, *A Theory of Justice* (hereafter TJ) (Cambridge, MA: Harvard University Press, 1970); *Political Liberalism* (hereafter PL) (New York: Columbia University Press, 1993, paper ed. 1996).

26 The "capabilities approach" was pioneered within economics by Amartya Sen and has been developed by both Sen and me in complementary but not identical ways. For an overview, see David Crocker, "Functioning and Capability: the Foundations of Sen's and Nussbaum's Development Ethic," in WCD, 152–98.

27 See Amartya Sen, "Equality of What?," in *Choice, Welfare, and Measurement* (Oxford: Basil Blackwell, 1982), 353–72; and Nussbaum, ASD.

28 Much of the material described in these examples is now published in *Dominating Knowledge: Development, Culture, and Resistance*, ed. Frédérique Apffel Marglin and Stephen A. Marglin (Oxford: Clarendon Press, 1990). The issue of "embeddedness" and menstruation taboos is discussed in S. A. Marglin, "Losing Touch: The Cultural Conditions of Worker Accommodation and Resistance," 217–82, and related issues are discussed in S. A. Marglin, "Toward the Decolonization of the Mind," 1–28. On Sittala Devi, see F. A. Marglin, "Smallpox in Two Systems of Knowledge," 102–44; and for related arguments see Ashis Nandy and Shiv Visvanathan, "Modern Medicine and Its Non-Modern Critics," 144–84. I have in some cases combined two conversations, into one; otherwise things happened as I describe them.

29 For Sen's own account of the plurality and internal diversity of Indian values, one that strongly emphasizes the presence of a rationalist and critical strand in Indian traditions, see M. Nussbaum and A. Sen, "Internal Criticism and Indian Relativist Traditions," in *Relativism: Interpretation and Confrontation*, ed. M. Krausz (Notre Dame: Notre Dame University Press, 1989), 299–325 (an essay originally presented at the same WIDER conference and refused publication by the Marglins in its proceedings); and A. Sen, "India and the West," *The New Republic*, June 7, 1993. See also Bimal K. Matilal, *Perception* (Oxford; Clarendon Press, 1995) (a fundamental study of Indian traditions regarding knowledge and logic); and B. K. Matilal, "Ethical Relativism and the Confrontation of Cultures," in Krausz, ed., *Relativism*, 339–62.

30 S. A. Marglin, "Toward the Decolonization," 22–3, suggests that binary thinking is peculiarly Western. But such oppositions are pervasive in Indian, Chinese, and African traditions (see HC). To deny them to a culture is condescending: for how can one utter a definite idea without bounding off one thing against another?

31 See Eric Hobsbawm and Terence Ranger, eds., *The Invention of Tradition* (Cambridge: Cambridge University Press, 1983). In his *New Republic* piece, Sen makes a similar argument about contemporary India: The Western construction of India as mystical and "other" serves the purposes of the fundamentalist Bharatiya Janata Party (BJP), who are busy refashioning history to serve the ends of their own political power. An eloquent critique of the whole notion of the "other" and of the associated "nativism," where

Africa is concerned, can be found in Kwame Anthony Appiah, *In My Father's House: Africa in the Philosophy of Cultures* (New York: Oxford University Press, 1991).

32 The proceedings of this conference are now published as M. Nussbaum and A. Sen, eds., *The Quality of Life* (Oxford: Clarendon Press, 1993).

33 Marglin has since published this point in "Toward the Decolonization." His reference is to Takeo Doi, *The Anatomy of Dependence* (Tokyo: Kodansha, 1971).

34 See S. A. Marglin, "Toward the Decolonization."

35 See Nussbaum and Sen, "Internal Criticism," and A. Sen, "Human Rights and Asian Values," *The New Republic*, July 10/17, 1997, 33–40.

36 See Roop Rekha Verma, "Femininity, Equality, and Personhood," in WCD.

37 Satyajit Ray, "Introduction," *Our Films, Their Films* (Bombay: Orient Longman, 1976, reprinted New York: Hyperion, 1994), 5.

38 Personal communication, scholars in women's studies at the Chinese Academy of Social Sciences, June 1995.

39 Note that this objection itself seems to rely on some universal values such as fairness and freedom from bias.

40 See HF for a longer version of this discussion.

41 Aristotle, *Nicomachean Ethics* VIII.I. I discuss this passage in HN and NRV.

42 "If my sisters and I were 'children of two worlds,' no one bothered to tell us this; we lived in one world, in two 'extended' families divided by several thousand miles and an allegedly insuperable cultural distance that never, so far as I can recall, puzzled or perplexed us much." Appiah, vii–viii. Appiah's argument does not neglect distinctive features of concrete histories; indeed, one of its purposes is to demonstrate how varied, when concretely seen, histories really are. But his argument, like mine, seeks a subtle balance between perception of the particular and recognition of the common.

43 This point is made by the Marglins, as well as by liberal thinkers, but can they consistently make it while holding that freedom of choice is just a parochial Western value? It would appear not; on the other hand, F. A. Marglin (here differing, I believe, from S. A. Marglin) also held in oral remarks delivered at the 1986 conference that logical consistency is simply a parochial Western value.

44 See Noam Chomsky, in *Cartesian Linguistics* (New York: Harper and Row, 1966). Chomsky argues that Cartesian rationalism, with its insistence on innate essences, was politically more progressive, more hostile to slavery and imperialism, than empiricism, with its insistence that people were just what experience had made of them.

45 The use of this term does not imply that the functions all involve doing something especially "active." See here A. Sen, "Capability and Well-Being," in *The Quality of Life*, ed. M. Nussbaum and A. Sen (Oxford: Clarendon Press, 1993), 30–53. In Aristotelian terms, and in mine, being healthy, reflecting, and being pleased are all "activities."

46 For further discussion of this point, and for examples, see HN.

47 Could one cease to be one's individual self without ceasing to be human? Perhaps, in cases of profound personality or memory change, but I shall leave such cases to one side here. This is ruled out, I think, in Aristotle's conception but is possible in some other metaphysical conceptions.

48 See HN for a more extended account of this procedure and how it justifies.

49 Nor does it deny that experience of the body is shaped by culture. See NRV.

50 Rawls, TJ, 90–95, 396–7.

51 This was implicit in ASD but has become more prominent in recent essays. See A. Sen, "Freedoms and Needs," *New Republic*, January 10/17, 1994, 31–8; Nussbaum GDGF.

52 In ASD I call it "the thick vague theory of the good."

53 Rawls, PL. Note that the consensus is defined in terms of a normative notion of reasonableness. Thus, the failure of some real individuals to agree will not be fatal to the view.

54 On this relationship, see HN.

55 The current version of this list reflects changes suggested to me by discussions during my visits to women's development projects in India. These include a new emphasis on bodily integrity, on employment, on property rights, and on dignity and nonhumiliation.

56 Although "normal length" is clearly relative to current human possibilities and may need, for practical purposes, to be to some extent relativized to local conditions, it seems important to think of it – at least at a given time in history – in universal and comparative terms, as the *Human Development Report* does, to give rise to complaint in a country that has done well with some indicators of life quality but badly on life expectancy. And although some degree of relativity may be put down to the differential genetic possibilities of different groups (the "missing women" statistics, for example, allow that on the average women live somewhat longer than men), it is also important not to conclude prematurely that inequalities between groups – for example, the growing inequalities in life expectancy between blacks and whites in the United States – are simply genetic variation, not connected with social injustice.

57 The precise specification of these health rights is not easy, but the work currently being done on them in drafting new constitutions in South Africa and Eastern Europe gives reasons for hope that the combination of a general specification of such a right with a tradition

of judicial interpretation will yield something practicable. It should be noticed that I speak of health, not just health care; and health itself interacts in complex ways with housing, with education, with dignity. Both health and nutrition are controversial as to whether the relevant level should be specified universally, or relatively to the local community and its traditions. For example, is low height associated with nutritional practices to be thought of as "stunting" or as felicitous adaptation to circumstances of scarcity? For an excellent summary of this debate, see S. R. Osmani, ed., *Nutrition and Poverty* (Oxford: Clarendon Press, WIDER series, 1990), especially the following papers: on the relativist side, T. N. Srinivasan, "Undernutrition: Concepts, Measurements, and Policy Implications," 97–120; on the universalist side, C. Gopalan, "Undernutrition: Measurement and Implications," 17–48; for a compelling adjudication of the debate, coming out on the universalist side, see Osmani, "On Some Controversies in the Measurement of Undernutrition," 121–61.

58 There is a growing literature on the importance of shelter for health; for example, that the provision of adequate housing is the single largest determinant of health status for HIV-infected persons. Housing rights are increasingly coming to be constitutionalized, at least in a negative form – giving squatters grounds for appeal, for example, against a landlord who would bulldoze their shanties. On this as a constitutional right, see proposed Articles 11, 12, and 17 of the South African Constitution, in a draft put forward by the African National Congress (ANC) committee adviser Albie Sachs, where this is given as an example of a justiciable housing right.

59 Some form of intimate family love is central to child development, but this need not be the traditional Western nuclear family. In the development of citizens it is crucial that the family be an institution characterized by justice as well as love. See Susan Moller Okin, *Justice, Gender, and the Family* (New York: Basic Books, 1989).

60 In terms of cross-cultural discussion, this item has proven the most controversial and elusive on the list. It also properly raises the question whether the list ought to be anthropocentric at all, or whether we should seek to promote appropriate capabilities for all living things. I leave further argument on these questions for another occasion.

61 ASD argues that property rights are distinct from, for example, speech rights, in the sense that property is a tool of human functioning and not an end in itself. See also Nussbaum, CHR.

62 Sen has not endorsed any such specific list of the capabilities.

63 See Sen, "Gender Inequality and Theories of Justice," in WCD, 259–73; Becker, "The Economic Way of Looking at Behavior."

64 With Sen, I hold that the capability set should be treated as an interlocking whole. For my comments on his arguments, see NFC.

65 See ibid., with reference to Aristotle.

66 See HN. This is the core of Marx's reading of Aristotle.

67 See Ch. 4.

68 See NFC, referring to Aristotle's similar distinctions.

69 This distinction is related to Rawls's distinction between social and natural primary goods. Whereas he holds that only the social primary goods should be on the list, and not the natural (such as health, imagination), we say that *the social basis of* the natural primary goods should most emphatically he on the list.

70 TJ, 62.

71 Rawls comments that "although their possession is influenced by the basic structure, they are not so directly under its control." TJ, 62. This is of course true if we are thinking of health, but if we think of the social basis of health, it is not true. It seems to me that the case for putting these items on the political list is just as strong as the case for the social basis of self-respect. In "The Priority of Right and Ideas of the Good," *Philosophy and Public Affairs* 17 (1988), 251–76, Rawls suggests putting health on the list.

72 See ASD and GDGF.

73 See HN. For the relation of capabilities to human rights, see CHR.

74 Sen, "Freedoms and Needs," 38.

75 PL 187–8.

76 Though in one form Aristotle had it too. See also GDGF; and CHR.

77 Compare Sen, "Freedoms and Needs," 38: "The importance of political rights for the understanding of economic needs turns ultimately on seeing human beings as people with rights to exercise, not as parts of a 'stock' or a 'population' that passively exists and must be looked after. What matters, finally, is how we see each other."

78 Chapter 3, "Introduction from *The Second Sex*," argues that religious norms should not be imposed without choice on individuals who may not have opted for that religious tradition. In that sense, any religiously based employment restriction is questionable.

79 Chen, *The Lives of Widows in Rural India*. Girls in some regions of India are betrothed at a very young age and at that point become members of their husband's family, although the marriage will not be consummated until puberty. Such a girl is treated as widowed even if the male dies before consummation.

80 Chen, *A Quiet Revolution*.

81 Ibid.

82 Ibid., 202. Married at age seven, abandoned by her husband many years later, Rohima lives with her brother. Four of her children have died; one son and one daughter survive. Her son gives her some financial support.

83 See the account of these in Chen, *The Lives of Widows*.

84 Chen, *A Quiet Revolution*, 216.

85 Sen has stressed this throughout his writing on the topic. For an overview, see "Capability and Well-Being." And for some complications, see GDGF.

86 This is the strategy used by Robert Erikson's Swedish team when studying inequalities in political participation. See Robert Erikson, "Descriptions of Inequality," in Nussbaum and Sen, eds., *The Quality of Life*.

87 Rawls proceeds in a similar way, insisting that satisfactions that are not the outgrowth of one's very own choices have no moral worth. He conceives of the "two moral powers" (analogous to our practical reasoning) and of sociability (corresponding to our affiliation) as built into the definition of the parties in the original position, and thus as necessary constraints on any outcome they will select. See ASD.

88 Chen, *A Quiet Revolution*, 199.

89 The remark was cited by Richard Rorty in "Feminism and Pragmatism," *Michigan Quarterly Review* 30 (1989), 263; it has since been confirmed and repeated by MacKinnon herself.

90 Plato, *Republic*, Book V. Although Plato's proposal is theoretical and Utopian, it is closely based on observation of the functioning of women in Sparta. See S. Halliwell, *Plato: Republic V* (Warminster: Aris & Phillips, 1994).

91 See Sen, "Gender and Cooperative Conflicts."

92 On Rousseau, see Susan Moller Okin, *Women in Western Political Thought* (Princeton: Princeton University Press, 1979), and Jane Roland Martin, *Reclaiming a Conversation* (New Haven: Yale University Press, 1985). On some related recent arguments, for example, those of Allan Bloom, see Okin, *Justice*, Ch. 1.

93 See the convincing summary in Anne Fausto-Sterling, *Myths of Gender*, 2nd edn (New York: Basic Books, 1992).

94 Ibid.

95 John Stuart Mill, *The Subjection of Women* (1869), ed. Susan Moller Okin (Indianapolis, IN: Hackett, 1988).

96 Here I am in agreement with the general line of argument in Okin, *Women*; and Martin, *Reclaiming*, and with the related arguments in Nancy Chodorow, *The Reproduction of Mothering* (Berkeley: University of California Press, 1978).

97 Jean-Jacques Rousseau, *Emile: or On Education*, trans. Allan Bloom (New York: Basic Books, 1979), Book V.

98 See Okin, *Women*; and Martin, *Reclaiming*.

99 See the discussion in Okin, *Women*.

Part VI

What is a Self?

Introduction to Part VI

Questions of the self, including the issues of personal identity (what makes a person a single unified being through time? what makes a human being a person?) and of autonomy (what is freedom or self-determination?) have a long history in philosophy. Although these questions may at first seem to belong in different philosophical domains, there is also a long history of connecting the metaphysical with the ethical issues. Locke, for instance, developed his theory of personal identity in part to explain the possibility of moral responsibility. Feminism, as a movement for human freedom, has an important stake in these issues. First because women have been seen as lesser humans, in part because they have been seen as inconstant or lacking in the central qualities of autonomy – the ability to live according to a self-imposed law. As women have been denied the ability to develop capacities or coerced into servility, they have often failed to attain the characteristics of autonomy. Second, as women have been more dependent on men than the reverse, they have been made victims of cultures that extol autonomy for men, permitting men to neglect their dependents in the name of freedom of self-determination. Feminist theory has challenged the ideal of autonomy thus presented, as well as the conditions that have prevented women from attaining it. As we saw in the previous part, one of the fundamental feminist criticisms of the dominant strain of Kantian liberal moral theory is the conception of persons as independent, unconnected selves. A burgeoning feminist literature has developed to address the question of what autonomy is for a socially connected, interdependent self, that is, a self that more closely resembles actual women and men.

Although this literature is too vast to do it justice in a short space, this part includes two chapters that sample the rich feminist discussions of autonomy through essays that either challenge traditional conceptions of autonomy or uphold the traditional conception at least in part as a feminist ideal. The other two chapters of the part explore ways in which the self is socially constructed through our experience with others, either supportive of or hostile to our personal projects.

The first chapter in this part, Jean Grimshaw's "Autonomy and Identity in Feminist Thinking," challenges traditional notions of the self that informed early second wave feminist theory. Such feminists argued in part that women's desires and personality have been deformed by patriarchy, implying that in order to achieve liberation, women need to peel away the false layers of personality to find their true selves. The assumption that there is an underlying, coherent, autonomous and asocial self forms the basis of what Grimshaw calls the humanist paradigm of the self. She argues that the humanist paradigm is unable to account for key experiences of women, such as the pleasure that women find in sexual fantasies that they would never want to live out, our focus on appearance or style, or the capacity for self-deception. She claims that there is no asocial, autonomous core that is one's "true self," rather, the self is constantly under construction in our attempts to make sense of our lives, a process which is heavily influenced by our gender. Still, the humanist paradigm is appealing because it posits a self that would be under control and free of contradictions between our ideals and our desires. She concludes that a feminist theory of autonomy should conceptualize the self as a constant search for coherence and control balanced against a realistic portrayal of our psychic lives.

Marilyn Friedman's "Autonomy, Social Disruption, and Women" explores an influential feminist critique of autonomy to devise four guidelines for the construction of a feminist theory of autonomy. According to that critique, autonomy disrupts personal relationships in ways that tend to harm women. Friedman illustrates the critique with the story of Paul Gauguin, who, in pursuit of artistic freedom, abandoned his wife and five children to paint in the South Pacific. However, she argues that autonomy is valuable for all persons, and that feminists must find a way to balance the values of community and relationships with personal autonomy. One guideline for improvement is to develop narratives of autonomy that feature women. The second is to redefine autonomy without stereotypically masculine traits. The third is to bring out the relational character of autonomy. Relational theories of autonomy have become dominant among feminist inspired theories. Such theories take seriously the importance of our social relationships in defining who we are, and claim that we are autonomous to the degree that these relationships provide structure for fulfilling, positive, and non-coercive relations with others. The final guideline is to portray the disruption of social relationships as a potentially valuable, though also possibly destructive, aspect of autonomy for women. Friedman argues that women should come to see autonomy as valuable in their pursuit of freedom from oppression, although that is to be balanced by the value of community and the responsibility to make relationships and communities worthwhile.

The next chapter explores how social group membership involves internalizing norms for behavior, which, when temporarily forgotten, induce an experience of shock and shame. In "Forgetting Yourself" Anita Allen explores the idea of how one can sometimes "forget" oneself, in the sense of losing sight of one's ascribed place in society or in a gender and/or racial hierarchy. Forgetting oneself is a metaphor that captures the sense of identity as given and yet as possible to transcend. The ways in which we can thus "forget" ourselves reveal many things about our social structures, and about how those structures shape our personalities. By investigating these forgettings and social structures we can, as Allen suggests, examine the structures of oppression and the degrees of autonomy that persons have who belong to social groups who can forget themselves in certain ways that others of the society cannot.

Susan Brison, in "Outliving Oneself," discusses the cognitive and emotional consequences of trauma on the self. Brison considers and critiques Locke's theory of personal identity in light of what has recently been learned about post-traumatic stress disorder and her personal experience of extreme violence. Victims of extreme violence not only suffer serious memory lapses, but also often feel themselves to be different persons after violence. Telling their story to others who believe them is essential to their personal re-integration. Where an entire social group is singled out for violence, such as the Jewish Holocaust, victimization goes beyond the direct object of the violence to include all who belong to the group. Brison argues that these facts of trauma and recovery reveal the relational nature of the self, that is, the importance of a social web of others who accept and reinforce one to one's very sense of self. Autonomy is only possible when one has this sense of an integrated self that can plan a future and act with some confidence that one's world will not be arbitrarily crushed in the next instant.

23

Autonomy and Identity in Feminist Thinking

Jean Grimshaw

Issues about women's autonomy have been central to feminist thinking and action. Women have so often been in situations of powerlessness and dependence that any system of belief or programme of action that could count as 'feminist' must in some way see this as a central concern. But what is meant by 'autonomy' and under what conditions is it possible? This has been an important and contentious question in philosophy. But questions about autonomy, and related questions about self and identity have also been important to feminism, and within feminist thinking it is possible to find radically different ways of thinking about these things. In this chapter, I want to look at one kind of way in which some feminists have tried to conceptualise what it is for a woman to be 'autonomous', and at the implications this has for ways of thinking about the human self. I shall argue that this conception is not only philosophically problematic, but also has an implicit politics which is potentially damaging. And I shall try to suggest some ways of beginning to think about 'autonomy' which seem to me to be more fruitful and adequate, and to draw on different traditions of thinking about the self which have become influential in some recent feminist thinking.

Jean Grimshaw, "Autonomy and Identity in Feminist Thinking," pp. 90–108 from Morwenna Griffiths and Margaret Whitford (eds.), *Feminist Perspectives in Philosophy*. Indianapolis, IN: Indiana University Press, 1988. Reproduced with permission of Palgrave Macmillan.

Feminist thinking does not, of course, exist in a vacuum, and in thinking about women's autonomy, feminists have drawn on different (and conflicting) approaches to questions about the human self, some of which have a long history. I want to begin by going back to an argument that Aristotle put forward in the *Ethics*, since I think that the point at which his argument breaks down can illuminate the nature of the problem some feminist thinking has faced.

Aristotle's argument concerns the question of what it is that makes an action 'voluntary', done of a person's own free will, and in order to answer this question, he distinguished between actions whose origin was 'inside' a person, and those whose origin was 'outside', which resulted from external influences or pressure or compulsion. He discussed at some length the problems that arise over trying to define ideas such as 'compulsion', and in estimating the degree of severity of pressure that could make an action not voluntary. But in this sort of model of autonomy, what defines an action as autonomous is seen as its point of *origin*; it must have an 'immaculate conception', as it were, from *within* the self.

Now ultimately I think that it is this definition of 'autonomy' in terms of origin, and the associated distinction between an 'inner' self which can in some way spontaneously generate its 'own' actions, and 'external' influences which are not 'part' of the self, that will need challenging. But I think it is possible to defend the Aristotelian version of autonomy up to a point, provided notions of 'inside' and 'outside' the self are defined in a certain way. If a person is prevented from doing what they would otherwise intend or desire to do, or if they are coerced into doing what they would *not* otherwise want or desire to do, they are not acting autonomously. Under this interpretation, actions which originate from 'inside' the self are those which are seen as in accordance with conscious desires or intentions, and those which originate from 'outside' the self are those which one would not do if one were not coerced. The pressure here is to consider the sorts of circumstances which do, in fact, coerce people in these sorts of ways. And, of course, a central concern of feminism has been to identify and fight against the kinds of coercion to which women have been subjected, including things like physical violence and economic dependence.

But it is at this point that an Aristotelian-type argument fails to be able to deal with the most difficult questions about autonomy. The Aristotelian view, as I have interpreted it, 'works' only to the extent that it is assumed that there is no problem about what I shall call 'the autonomy of desires'. Autonomy is defined as acting in accordance with desire (or intention). But what of the desires themselves? Are there *desires* (or intentions) which are not 'autonomous', which do not originate from 'within' the self, which are not authentic, not really 'one's own'?

Feminist writers have wanted, of course, to indict the various forms of brutality and coercion from which women have suffered. But this brutality and coercion has been seen not merely as a question of physical or 'external' coercion or constraint; the force of subjection has also been seen as a psychic one, invading women's very selves. The language of 'conditioning', 'brainwashing', 'indoctrination', and so forth, has been used to describe this force. The female self, under male domination, is riddled through and through with false or conditioned desires. But set against this conditioned, non-autonomous female self are various images of a female self that would be authentic, that would transcend or shatter this conditioning. I want now to look at some of these images of the female self in feminist discourse: my particular examples are from the work of Mary Daly, Marilyn Frye and Kate Millett.

Daly, Frye and Millett all stress the way in which women have been subject to the *power* of men. Much of Daly's book, *Gyn/Ecology* (1979), is an account of the barbarities inflicted on women such as suttee, clitorectomy, foot-binding and other forms of mutilation. Millett, in *Sexual Politics* (1977), sees patriarchal power as something so historically all-embracing that it has totally dominated women's lives. Frye, in *The Politics of Reality* (1983), uses the situation of a young girl sold into sexual slavery and then systematically brutalised and brainwashed into a life of service to her captors as an analogy for the situation of all women. And all three writers stress the way in which they see the female self as 'invaded' by patriarchal conditioning. Millett writes:

> When, in any group of persons, the ego is subjected to such invidious versions of itself through social beliefs, ideology and tradition, the effect is bound to be pernicious. This should make it no very special cause for surprise that women develop group characteristics common to those who suffer minority status and a marginal existence. (Millett, 1977, p. 55)

Women, she argues, are deprived of all but the most trivial sources of dignity or self-respect. In her discussion of Lawrence's depiction of Connie in *Lady Chatterley's Lover*, what she sees Connie as relinquishing is 'self, ego, will, individuality' (p. 243); all those things which, Millett argues, women had but recently achieved, (and for which Lawrence had a profound distaste).

Mary Daly's picture of the way in which women's selves are invaded by patriarchal conditioning is even more striking. She describes women, for example, as 'moronised', 'robotised', 'lobotomised', as 'the puppets of Papa'. At times she seems to see women as so 'brainwashed' that they are scarcely human; thus she describes them as 'fembots', even as 'mutants'. In Millett, Daly and Frye, women are seen primarily as *victims*: the monolithic brutality and psychological pressures of male power have reduced women almost to the state of being 'non-persons'. And indeed, as Daly sees women as having become 'mutants' or 'fembots', so Millett sees them as not having been allowed to participate in fully 'human' activities (which she characterises as those that are most remote from the biological contingencies of life), and Frye sees them as simply 'broken' and then 'remade' in the way that suits their masters.

But behind this victimised female self, whose actions and desires are assumed to be not truly 'her own', since they derive from processes of force, conditioning or psychological manipulation, there is seen to be an authentic female self, whose recovery or discovery it is one of the aims of feminism to achieve. The spatial metaphor implicit in the word 'behind' is not accidental, since this model of self is premised on the possibility of making a distinction between an 'inner' and an 'outer' self. Ibsen's Peer Gynt compared his quest for identity to the process of peeling layers off an onion; but after shedding all the 'false selves', he found that there was nothing inside, no 'core'. The sort of spatial metaphor implicit in Peer Gynt's account of himself is also apt in the accounts of self given by Daly, Millett and Frye, except that there *is* assumed to be a 'core'. This is clearest in the work of Daly. In *Gyn/Ecology*, discovering or recovering one's own self is seen as akin to a process of salvation or religious rebirth, and Daly writes of what she calls the unveiling or unwinding of the 'shrouds' of patriarchy to reveal the authentic female Spirit-Self underneath. And this Self is seen as a unitary and harmonious one. Splits and barriers within the psyche, she argues, as well as those between Selves, are the result of patriarchal conditioning. In the unitary and harmonious female Spirit-Self there will be no such splits.

Millett's picture of the authentic female self is rather different from that of Daly. It does not draw, as Daly's does, on religious metaphors of salvation and rebirth. It derives, rather, from a picture of the self as fundamentally a unitary, conscious and rational thing, a picture which, in Western philosophy, can be traced back to Descartes. It emerges most clearly in her discussion of Freud. She describes Freud's theory of the Unconscious as a major contribution to human understanding, but her account of the self owes, in fact, scarcely anything to Freud. She is scathingly critical of Freud's theory of penis envy: Freud, she argued, 'did not accept his patient's symptoms as evidence of a justified dissatisfaction with the limiting circumstances imposed on them by society, but as symptomatic of an independent and universal feminine tendency' (Millett, 1977, p. 179). He made a major (and foolish) confusion between biology and culture. Girls, Millett argues, are fully cognisant, of male supremacy long before they see their brother's penis; and what they envy is not the penis, but the things to which having a penis gives the boy access – power, status and rewards. Freud ignored the more likely 'social' hypothesis for feminine dissatisfaction, preferring to ascribe it to a biologically based female nature. What we should be studying, Millett argues, are the effects of male-supremacist culture on the female ego. And what will undo these effects, she writes in the Postscript, is altered consciousness, and a process of 'human growth and true re-education' (p. 363).

The 'social' factors of which Millett writes are here seen as pressures which are 'external' to the self, and which have the effect of thwarting the conscious and unitary rationality of female individuality, or the female ego. And the task is that of *removing* their influence. If, in *Lady Chatterley's Lover*, the scales were to fall from Connie's eyes and she were to see the worship of Mellor's phallus for what it is, a means of subordinating and oppressing women, she could free herself and develop her authentic will, ego and individuality.

The paradigm of coercion, writes Frye, is *not* the direct application of physical force. Rather, it is a situation in which choice and action *do* take place, and in which the victim acts under her own perception and judgement. Hence, what the exploiter needs is that

> the will and intelligence of the victim be disengaged from the projects of resistance and escape but that they not be simply broken or destroyed. Ideally, the disintegration and misintegration of the victim should accomplish the detachment of the victim's will and intelligence from the victim's own interests and their attachment to the interests of the exploiter. This will effect a displacement or dissolution of self-respect and will undermine the victim's intolerance of coercion. With that, the situation transcends the initial paradigmatic form or structure of coercion; for if people don't mind doing what you want them to do, you can't really be *making* them do it. (Frye, 1983, p. 60)

And, she writes:

> The health and integrity of an organism is a matter of its being organised largely towards its own interests and welfare. *She* is healthy

> and 'working right' when her substance is organised primarily on principles which align it to *her* interests and welfare. Co-operation is essential of course, but it will not do that I arrange everything so that *you* get enough exercise: for me to be healthy, *I* must get enough exercise. My being adequately exercised is logically independent of your being so. (Ibid., p. 70)

Frye is writing here as if it were possible to distinguish the interests of one self sharply from those of another, and as if, were the effects of male domination to be undone, it would not be too much of a problem for the self to know what its interests were.[1]

In various ways then, underlying much of the work of these three writers is a set of assumptions about the self. First, that it is, at least potentially, a unitary, rational thing, aware of its interests. Second, that 'splits' within the psyche should be seen as resulting from the interference of patriarchal or male-dominated socialisation or conditioning. Third, that the task of undoing this conditioning is one that can be achieved solely by a rational process of learning to understand and fight against the social and institutional effects of male domination. And implicit in these assumptions about the self, I think, is a conception of autonomy. Frye writes that 'left to themselves' women would not want to serve men. Daly writes of unveiling or unwinding the 'shrouds' of patriarchy. Millett writes of the individuality and ego that women can discover in themselves once they recognise the effects of their patriarchal socialisation. And in all three, what is autonomous (or authentic) is what is seen as originating in some way from *within* the self; what is in some way *untainted* by the conditioning or manipulation to which a woman has previously been subjected.

Before I come to discuss the philosophical problems that are raised by this sort of account of self and autonomy, I want to look at what I have called its implicit politics; and what I mean by this primarily is its possible consequences for the way in which women might think about their relationships to each other, and the way in which they might think about themselves. The first consequence seems to me to be this. Any view which sees self-affirmation in terms of an 'authentic' inner self arising from the smashing of a socially conditioned 'false self', or which sees autonomy as a question of the origin of actions from 'inside' rather than 'outside', is almost bound to adopt, however implicitly, a derogatory attitude towards those who are not yet 'authentic'. The precise nature and tone of this attitude may vary. But Mary Daly, for example, in *Gyn/Ecology*, sometimes writes as if most women were really little more than the programmed, robotic puppets to which women were reduced in Ira Levin's novel *The Stepford Wives*; the language of 'fembots' and 'mutants' and 'puppets', whilst intended, I am sure, to enunciate a critique of women's oppressors, veers perilously near to sounding like contempt for those who are subject to that oppression. And this is related, for example, to Daly's scorn for 'tokenism' – for those women who participate in what are seen as patriarchal institutions. Kate Millett's language is less obviously extreme. But the picture she paints of women is nevertheless often a derogatory one. She describes them, for example, as 'infantilised'; she accepts without question research which purported to show that most women despised each other (Millett, 1977, p. 55); she sees women as having little 'self-respect', and as devoting almost all their time and attention to pleasing and flattering men.

This implicitly derogatory attitude to women is linked both to an overmonolithic account of male power, and to a failure to give much attention to the ways in which women have, in fact, often spent much of their lives, and to the activities which have been particularly theirs (such as the rearing of children, for example). Sometimes women are depicted almost as a caricature of a male stereotype of themselves – they *are* servile, weak, powerless, etc. (Millett even suggests (p. 56) that the fact that women commit less 'crime' than men is due to their patriarchal conditioning in passivity.) Millett basically dismisses the activities which have tended to dominate women's lives as 'infantilising', because they restrict women to the level, she argues, of the merely biological, and do not allow them to enter upon the 'fully human' activities which have been the province of men. And it is interesting, as Toril Moi (1985) points out, that in her discussion of literature, Millett concentrates almost wholly on male authors, with the exception of Charlotte Brontë, of whose work she tends to be very dismissive. Furthermore, as Moi suggests, she seems to avoid much in the way of recognition or acknowledgement of feminist work prior to her own, or of the existence of female traditions and strengths which might have tended to challenge or subvert the supposedly monolithic nature of the male power which it is the main aim of her book to describe.

Mary Daly's indictment of male power and brutality similarly allows little space for a consideration of the patterns of women's lives, or the strengths and capacities that these might have enabled them to develop. Her female Spirit-Self simply seems to rise mysteriously like a phoenix from the ashes of patriarchal conditioning. And Frye is sceptical about the possibility of women looking to their foremothers as a source of inspiration; of seeing some women, at least, as having led lives that were not wholly male-mediated. Feminist vision or imagination has no real resource to turn to.

Now these kinds of accounts (or perhaps one might say *failures* to give an adequate account?) of women's lives are implicitly divisive and threatening. They are divisive because they have a tendency to divide women into two camps; those who have and those who have not shaken the dust of patriarchal conditioning from their feet. And they are threatening, because it is offensive and undermining to be told that the life one has led has merely been one of servility, that it has not been of truly 'human' value, that one has been a 'fembot' or a 'puppet'. I think that one important strand in the rejection of feminism by many women has been a feeling that feminists are saying that their lives have been of no value, and that their activities and concerns have been trivial.

But this image of autonomy and of the self can be threatening, too, to women who *do* have a strong allegiance to feminism; and the threat intersects with assumptions that have been made in some feminist discourse about who is or is not 'really' a feminist. The threat arises because this account of autonomy is in fact often a strongly *normative* one; it presents an image of what a 'feminist self' should be like. To be autonomous or authentic one should be strong, independent, rational, coherent or consistent, able to distinguish clearly those aspects of one's previous self which derive from male-dominated conditioning and reject them. If one is ambivalent, conflicted, uncertain, confused, unwilling to make wholesale rejections, one stands to be accused, whether by oneself or by others, of bad faith, of lack of courage, of 'selling out', of tokenism.

I am here giving an account of just one (influential) strand in feminist discourse. There are other strands which have rejected this account of self and autonomy.[2] As I have said before, a picture of the self as conscious, unitary and rational can be traced back, in Western philosophy, to Descartes. I do not have space here to discuss the various ways in which versions of this conception of self have been influential, in philosophy and psychology, for instance. But the major tradition which has queried this view of self has been that which derives from psychoanalysis. Feminism has had a complex relation to psychoanalysis. Freud's theories have been the target of a great deal of feminist criticism. In *Sexual Politics*, for example, Kate Millett sees Freud simply as the proponent of a biologistic theory of male supremacy, and as one of the arch-villains in the male plot of patriarchy. Other feminist writers, however, have tried to reevaluate the significance of psychoanalytic theory for feminism. And they have argued that, whilst feminism should indeed always have a critical relationship to psychoanalytic theory, the latter has within it the potential for allowing a better understanding of the complexities of human desires and of the psychological construction of 'masculinity' and 'femininity'.

Now any adequate account of self needs to be able, I think, to encompass and try to make intelligible the ways in which women and men experience themselves. And the central reasons for rejecting the 'humanist' paradigm of the self – as I have outlined it above – are, firstly, that there may be aspects of the development of self which are not easily accessible to consciousness, and secondly, that there are conscious experiences which are not easy to make intelligible within the humanist paradigm.[3] I want now to look at some aspects of self-experience that I think should be central to any theory of self, and hence to any discussion of women's autonomy.

Fantasy

The dream (on which we may try hard to impose a narrative structure, to make sense of it) is unlike much fantasy in that it often doesn't, of itself, contain any such structure, and the 'story', if it tells one, may be deeply unintelligible to us. Much conscious fantasy is different; we may 'tell a story' to ourselves (or listen to a story and fantasise it as about ourselves); and sometimes we may attempt an imagined resolution, through fantasy, of some aspect of our social situation. One might, thus, fantasise the death of someone seen as a threat, or imagine oneself as possessing enormous fame or wealth. But fantasies, not always in the form of a coherent narrative, may irrupt or intervene; one can be plagued, dominated or obsessed by them. Freud wrote of the way in which fantasies or desires, often seen as evil or dangerous, could come to dominate a person's life. Fantasy may be a threat; it may be inexplicable, bizarre and intrusive. Discovering the fantasies of others, too, may be threatening; the discovery, for example, as Rosalind Coward (1984) suggests, that the 'mild' man one lives with is a secret addict of sadomasochistic pornography. Female sexual fantasies can be disturbing as well. Why do many women find *The Story of O* erotic, and why is there a 'split' between sexual fantasy and that which one might find pleasurable or erotic in real life?

Fantasy may be experienced both as pleasurable and as dangerous. But sometimes it can just be pleasurable. Coward discusses, for instance, the importance of the fact that one of the biggest growth areas in publishing in recent years has been women's romantic fiction. Unlike the 'modern' women's novel in which, usually after a series of disastrous sexual misadventures, the female heroine ends up (more or less) 'her own person', romantic fiction is stylised, formulaic and unrealistic. It offers women, Coward argues, the fantasised pleasure (and apotheosis of sexual desire) of finding security in the strong arms of the hard-bitten patriarchal hero, along with the pleasure of having 'tamed' him and domesticated his wild ways by the power one enjoys over him in being a woman.

We have to understand the pleasure there is for women in such fantasies. We have to understand what seems often to attract women more than men to soap operas, or to a passionate interest in the doings of the Royal Family. We need to understand how and why male fantasies may commonly differ from female ones, and why the sorts of fantasies I have mentioned, which may in some ways seem antithetical to feminism, may still have a strong appeal to women who have a feminist allegiance.

The 'Split' Between Reason and Desire

I will suggest, as a first example of this, a book by Suzanne Lowry, on Princess Diana, called *The Princess in the Mirror* (1985). The appearance of the book is at first glance like that of any other glossy book about the Royals. But it sets out, its author says, to deconstruct the image and appeal of the Princess. At the end of the book, Lowry states that the image of the Princess is conformist and reactionary, that it acts as a powerful form of social control, and that Diana is an unwitting agent of that. Yet the presentation of the book, and Lowry's text, often speak of a fascination with the Princess that is more than simply the fascination one can derive from the exercise of deconstructing an image. And this fascination is often in tension with the attempt to articulate a critique.

Or think about the Fonda phenomenon. The text of Fonda's book, *Women Coming of Age* (1984), exhorts women not to 'think thin', and its theme is mainly that of health. Yet the illustrations are nearly all of women who are pencil-thin enough not to be out of place on the catwalk in a Paris fashion show. The discourse of 'health' is almost inextricably intertwined, in the case of women, with discourse about youth and beauty and sexual attractiveness. The reasons women have for concern about fitness and health are often multiply overdetermined. Notions, for example, of *Ageless Ageing* (Kenton, 1986) *slide* between discussions of how to preserve a youthful skin and a young-looking body and how to stave off the ravages of *appearing* older, with discussions of mental vitality and energy, and so forth. A young-looking body is a *sign* of an alert mind.

There is a type of feminist criticism, both in literature and other media (and in fields such as education), which has been called 'Images of Women' criticism.[4] This has supposed that feminist effort should be devoted, first, to showing how the 'images' in question oppress or denigrate women, and second, to offering positive images of women to replace these. One problem with this kind of criticism is that the 'images' in question have often been misinterpreted, since they have been discussed without reference to the context or narrative structure in which they may appear. But there are two other problems with this type of criticism which I want to focus on here. First, what this approach often fails to recognise is the importance of understanding the *appeal* of the 'images' that are criticised; the relations they may have to women's pleasures, desires, fantasies, fears and conceptions of themselves. Second, it fails to recognise what is signally obvious in the experience of many women, myself of course included, namely that it is perfectly possible to agree 'in one's head' that certain images of women might be reactionary or damaging or oppressive, while remaining committed to them in emotion and desire. I suspect that this 'split' happens at times in all women, and perhaps particularly in those who have some commitment to feminism. And what it suggests is that structures of desire, emotion and fantasy have deep roots of some sort in the self which are not necessarily amenable in any simple way to processes of conscious rational argument. An adequate theory of subjectivity has to recognise and try to understand these roots.

Contradictions

I have already identified more than one type of contradiction; those that can exist between one's fantasies and what one would actually do or enjoy in real life, and those that can exist between one's understanding of the oppressive nature of some discourse or practice and one's continuing investment of desire and finding of pleasure in it.

In his *Introductory Lectures on Psychoanalysis* (1973), Freud discussed the way in which symptoms are experienced in certain forms of obsessional neurosis. He wrote:

> Obsessional neurosis is shown in the patient's being occupied with thoughts in which he is in fact not interested, in his being aware of impulses which appear very strange to him and his being led to actions the performance of which give him no enjoyment, but which it is quite impossible for him to omit. The thoughts (obsessions) may be senseless in themselves, or merely a matter of indifference to the subject; often they are completely silly, and invariably they are the starting-point of a strenuous mental activity, which exhausts the patient and to which he only surrenders himself most unwillingly. (p. 297)

Obsessional neurosis is characterised, Freud argued, by the fact that the symptoms are not only debilitating, but are experienced by the person as *alien*; they do not seem 'part' of him or her, and they seem discrepant with an everyday or normal sense of the self. In the case of many of Freud's patients the disruption and debilitation caused by the symptoms was so extreme that they were scarcely able to carry on their lives adequately at all. But Freud insisted that there was no sharp dividing line between 'normal' and 'neurotic' people, and would have argued that similar, though less extreme, obsessions and apparently inexplicable compulsions can be found in all of us. In these cases, the self is, as it were, split against itself, subject to desires and impulses that seem 'out of character'.

But one cannot assume that an everyday 'coherent' sense of self is readily available. One reason for this is that women (and men, of course) are often faced with the problem of negotiating contradictory or conflicting conceptions of themselves. Women may, for example, be required to be *both* sexually exciting and available, *and* modest and chaste. And gender relationships may be subject to the problems that can arise from conflicting discourses about femininity or masculinity. Men may, for example, *both* see themselves as 'stronger' than women and tend to see women as more weak and passive, but *also* see women as having a power over them that can seem to engulf the man in forms of emotional dependence by which he may feel threatened.[5] Discourse about femininity and masculinity is by no means a homogeneous or stable thing.

In the twentieth century, the advent of a 'consumer culture' and of mass communications has given questions about self and identity a peculiar intensity and difficulty in some respects. They have led, for example, to a focus on appearance and 'style', and the way in which these may 'express' one's individuality, that is historically novel. The clothes one wears, the 'room of one's own' in the Sunday Supplements: one may, apparently, now 'try on' identities as if they really were clothes. And women have often tended to be the main target of fashion and 'lifestyle' talk. For all the rejection of what was sometimes called 'woman garbage' by American feminists, the issue of appearance is something that no woman can wholly avoid. Feminists too, of course, have used style of dress and demeanour to express a sense of self and of political commitment. (Elizabeth Wilson recorded once realising that she was more than usually anxious about the question of what to wear when she was going to talk to a feminist group.)

Self-knowledge and Self-deception

The concept of self-deception is one that has constantly puzzled philosophers. How can one both know and yet not know something about oneself. I do not have space here to discuss the question of self-deception in detail. But an important thing to recognise at the outset is that knowing about oneself can never be a matter of 'mere information'. One cannot be distanced from or emotionally neutral about issues of self-knowledge. (Freud stressed this in his account of the transference in the analytic situation.) Herbert Fingarette (1959) uses the concept of 'avowal' to give an account of the concept of self-deception. We do not see everything that we think or do or fantasise or desire as equally 'central' to ourselves. It is quite common, in everyday discourse, to say things like 'I wasn't really myself 'or' 'It wasn't like *me* to do that'. Sometimes this process of rejection, of not avowing, is quite conscious. At other times it may be barely admitted to consciousness, if whatever it was is seen as threatening to the self. And sometimes it is, I think, not conscious at all. Psychoanalysis have talked, for example, about the process of 'projection', in which aspects of oneself of which one is fearful may be projected on to other people.[6] (A number of writers have seen 'projection' as involved in the problem of masculinity, and have suggested that men may sometimes project their own fears of such things as emotional intimacy on to women, who are then seen as 'bad' because they cause these problems.)

Self-knowledge can never be a matter of easy or immediate introspection. This is partly because aspects of oneself may be disavowed, sometimes unconsciously, and partly because the 'meaning' of the deliverances of introspection is always dependent on an interpretation. One may be *aware* of feelings, sexual ones for example, that one is not able to conceptualise *as* sexual at the time. Freud believed that at the root of all neuroses lay repressed sexual desires, but even if one does not follow him in this, it would be hard to resist the conclusion that this was true of some of his patients. Sometimes his patients lacked the kind of knowledge that would have enabled them to interpret the experience as 'sexual' at all. Sometimes they possessed knowledge about sex, but could not admit that *this* was sexual, or that *they* had those sorts of desires.

I have outlined above some of the experiences and the problems about subjectivity that any adequate theory of self must be able to encompass, in a way that the 'humanist' paradigm is, I think, unable to do. There are approaches to understanding and theorising self which depart radically from the humanist paradigm. I shall not attempt to enumerate them all here, nor do I think that feminism should accept any of them uncritically. What they share, despite their differences, is an insistence that there is no 'original' wholeness or unity in the self, nor a 'real self' which can be thought of as in some way *underlying* the self of everyday life. The self is *always* a more or less precarious and conflictual construction out of, and compromise between, conflicting and not always conscious desires and experiences, which are born out of the ambivalences and contradictions in human experience and relationships with others.

Accounts of the construction of the self vary, in the degree of stress, for example, that they lay on the period of infancy and early childhood, and on the importance given to sexuality. But it seems to me that the theories of Freud must be seen as centrally important. It is sometimes argued that Freud's theories must be accepted or rejected all of a piece, and that one cannot simply accept or reject 'bits' of them as one fancies. It is true, I think, that there is a certain sort of eclecticism, practised for example by some neo-Freudian writers such as Erich Fromm or by the American 'ego psychologists', which may undermine anything useful that Freudian theory really has to offer. But whatever we may take or reject from Freud, what I think we should not lose is the way in which he raises questions and problematises things which are sometimes taken for granted. Freud questions any easy (or utopian) idea or ideal of the unity of the self, he questions the idea that self-knowledge could ever be a matter of simple introspection, and he sees issues about desire and fantasy as central to subjectivity. He stresses the way in which the acquisition of a *gendered* subjectivity is necessarily conflictual and involves struggle. And above all, perhaps, he forces a radical questioning of the concepts of the 'individual' and the 'social'. Nothing could be further from the truth than Kate Millett's accusation that Freud believed that women's destiny was a simple outcome of their biology. In Freudian theory, there is a constant concern with the way in which entry into culture and human relationships, and the conflicts and struggle this causes, should be seen as *constitutive* of the human self.

Freud's particular view of human culture was problematic. He stressed that psychoanalysis was never concerned solely with desires seen as arising unmediated from the body, but always with psychic representations of these. But he also believed in a sort of Lamarckian view of the inheritance of a 'primal schema' of desires and fantasies which determined the form taken by the Oedipal situation. The French psychoanalyst, Jacques Lacan, argued that Freud himself (as well as virtually all the psychoanalysis who revised Freud's theories) never managed to escape fully from the assumption of an already existing gendered subjectivity which entered into the Oedipal situation. And Lacan argued that the human subject must be seen as constituted through language, through entry into the Symbolic Order. According to Lacan, the aim of psychoanalysis should be rigorously to deconstruct and expose the contradictions and radical tissues in which human subjectivity is born.[7]

Feminism, as I have said, needs to preserve a critical distance from all theories of self. But it needs also to engage with those theories which deconstruct the distinction between the 'individual' and the 'social', which recognise the power of desire and fantasy and the problems of supposing any 'original' unity in the self, while at the same time preserving its concern with lived experience and the practical and material struggles of women to achieve more autonomy and control over their lives.

The appeal of what I have called the 'humanist paradigm' lies, I think, in the way it can seem to conceptualise the need women have experienced for this greater degree of autonomy and control, for overcoming the fragmentation and contradictions in their lives, and for a capacity for self-definition. No theory of self should lose sight of these things. I have argued, however, that there are also aspects of women's experience which the humanist paradigm is unable to conceptualise adequately; hence the appeal of theories which attempt to 'deconstruct' the self in more radical ways. But the danger in some 'deconstructionist' theories, however, is that they seem to leave no space for the material struggles or ordinary aspirations of women. Thus it seems that Lacanian psychoanalysis, both in theory and practice, aims *merely* to show what a fragmented, decentred thing the human subject is, and Lacan has dismissed all talk of 'unity' or 'identity' as an illusion. It can be argued (though I do not have space to do it here), that there is an incoherence in a view of the subject which regards all notions of unity as an illusion. But there is also a practical and political problem, since it is difficult to see how such a theory could speak in any way to the practical or material concerns of women.

The problem, then, is not to be seen as one of whether we should continue to use concepts like 'identity' or 'autonomy' at all, or simply reject them out of hand. It is a problem, rather, of how to offer an interpretation of them which neither assumes the original unitary self of the humanist paradigm, nor ignores the needs of women. And Freud can again provide a useful starting point. It is true that Freudian theory questions any notion of the original unity of the self. But it is not true that Freudian theory has no space for ideas of unity or autonomy. The purpose of psychoanalytic therapy, according to Freud, was to remove the power of the symptom by making it intelligible, by showing the *sense* that it had. Psychoanalysis aimed to trace its roots in unconscious desires (though this was not a process merely of intellectual understanding). The unintelligible, alien quality of the symptom will be removed. But for this to happen, a person's conception of themselves must also be transformed. They must, for example, be able to think of themselves as 'the sort of person who *does* have incestuous sexual desires', is prepared to avow them as 'part' of the self, and ceases to be so threatened by them. Part of this process of change is a greater tolerance of certain aspects of oneself, and a lesser propensity for these to cause guilt or anxiety. But, paradoxically perhaps, this greater tolerance may result in *less* fragmentation, more coherence, and less subjection to the forms of anxiety or guilt or compulsive behaviour that may once have been so deeply disturbing or threatening.

It seems to me that there is a sort of dialectic we need to preserve when thinking about autonomy. There is no authentic or unified 'original' self which can simply be recovered or discovered as the source of 'autonomous' actions. But we are often faced with the experienced need to make 'sense' of our lives and our feelings and goals, to relate confused fragments of ourselves into something that seems more coherent and of which we feel more in control. We are often also faced, however, with the need to tolerate contradictions, not to strive for an illusory or impossible ideal, and to avoid self-punishing forms of anxiety, defence and guilt (and feminist guilt can be as punishing as any other kind). The dialectic of autonomy is one in which a constant (but never static or final) search for control and coherence needs balancing against a realism and tolerance born out of efforts to understand ourselves (and others) better.

Notes

1 Further discussion of some of the philosophical traditions which have influenced this type of view, and of the problems with such a conception of 'interests', can be found in Jaggar (1983) and Grimshaw (1986).
2 Two in particular are important. First, there is the strand in feminist thinking which rejects what it sees as a typically male 'individualism'. (For discussion of this see Flax, 1983; and Grimshaw, 1986, Ch. 6.) Second, there is the strand which sees psychoanalytic accounts of the self as having a great deal to offer to feminist analysis. A great deal has been written about this, but for two influential accounts, see Mitchell (1975) and Mitchell and Rose (1982).
3 The words 'humanism' and 'humanist' have a complex history which I do not have space to go into in this chapter. For a clear and interesting discussion of this, see Soper (1986).
4 There is an interesting discussion of 'Images of Women' literary criticism in Moi (1985).
5 Wendy Hollway discusses such contradictions in her article 'Gender Differences and the Production of Subjectivity', in Henriques *et al.* (1984).
6 Nancy Chodorow (1978), for example, discusses and uses the notion of 'projection'.
7 For accessible discussions of the work of Lacan and of his influence on French feminist thought, see Duchen (1986), Sayers (1986), and Soper (1986). See also Whitford (1986) for an interesting discussion of the work of the French feminist writer Luce Irigaray.

References

Chodorow, Nancy (1978), *The Reproduction of Mothering: Psychoanalysis and the Sociology of Gender* (Berkeley: University of California Press).

Coward, Rosalind (1984), *Female Desire: Women's Sexuality Today* (London: Paladin).

Daly, Mary (1979), *Gyn/Ecology: The Metaethics of Radical Feminism* (London: The Women's Press).

Duchen, Claire (1986), *Feminism in France: From May '68 to Mitterrand* (London: Routledge & Kegan Paul).

Fingarette, Herbert (1959), *Self-deception* (London: Routledge & Kegan Paul).

Flax, Jane (1983), 'Political Philosophy and the Patriarchal Unconscious: A Psychoanalytic Perspective on Epistemology and Metaphysics', in S. Harding and M. Hintikka (eds), pp. 245–81.

Fonda, Jane (1984), *Women Coming of Age* (Harmondsworth: Penguin).

Freud, Sigmund (1973), *Introductory Lectures on Psychoanalysis* (Harmondsworth: Penguin).

Frye, Marilyn (1983), *The Politics of Reality: Essays in Feminist Theory* (Trumansburg, New York: Crossing Press).

Grimshaw, Jean (1986), *Feminist Philosophers: Women's Perspectives on Philosophical Traditions* (Brighton: Wheatsheaf).

Harding, Sandra and Hintikka, Merrill B. (eds) (1983), *Discovering Reality: Feminist Perspectives on Epistemology, Metaphysics, Methodology, and Philosophy of Science* (Dordrecht: Reidel).

Henriques, Julian, Hollway, Wendy, Urwin, Cathy, Venn, Couze and Walkerdine, Valerie (1984), *Changing the Subject: Psychology, Social Regulation and Subjectivity* (London: Methuen).

Jaggar, Alison M. (1983), *Feminist Politics and Human Nature* (Brighton: Harvester).

Kenton, Leslie (1986), *Ageless Ageing* (London: Century Arrow).

Lowry, Suzanne (1985), *The Princess in the Mirror* (London: Chatto & Windus).

Millett, Kate (1977), *Sexual Politics* (London: Virago).

Mitchell, Juliet (1975), *Psychoanalysis and Feminism* (Harmondsworth: Penguin).

Mitchell, Juliet and Rose, Jacqueline (eds) (1982), *Feminine Sexuality: Jacques Lacan and the École Freudienne* (London: Macmillan).

Moi, Toril (1985), *Sexual/Textual Politics: Feminist Literary Theory* (London: Methuen).

Sayers, Janet (1986), *Sexual Contradictions: Psychology, Psychoanalysis, and Feminism* (London: Tavistock).

Soper, Kate (1986), *Humanism and Anti-Humanism* (London: Hutchinson).

Whitford, Margaret (1986), 'Speaking as a Woman: Luce Irigaray and the Female Imaginary', *Radical Philosophy*, Vol. 43, pp. 3–8.

24

Autonomy, Social Disruption, and Women[1]

Marilyn Friedman

Of Autonomy and Men

Are women in Western societies alienated by the ideal of autonomy? Many feminist philosophers have recently suggested that women find autonomy to be a notion inhospitable to women, one that represents a masculine-style preoccupation with self-sufficiency and self-realization at the expense of human connection.

Paul Gauguin's life epitomizes what many feminists take to be the masculine ideal of autonomy. Gauguin abandoned his family and middle-class life as a banker in Denmark to travel to Mediterranean France, Tahiti, and Martinique in search of artistic subjects and inspiration. He deserted his wife and five children, one might say, to paint pictures in sunny locales. Biographies of Gauguin's life reveal that he agonized for some time over the decision to leave his family. He once wrote: "One man's faculties can't cope with two things at once, and I for one can do *one thing only*: paint. Everything else leaves me stupefied."[2] Gauguin's self-reflective agonies, I believe, would qualify as autonomous, according to many contemporary definitions.

Marilyn Friedman, "Autonomy, Social Disruption, and Women," pp. 35–51 from Catriona Mackenzie and Natalie Stoljar (eds.), *Relational Autonomy: Feminist Perspectives on Autonomy, Agency, and the Self*. New York: Oxford University Press, 2000.

How has Western culture assessed Gauguin's life and work? Gauguin was *canonized* by Western art history. Of course, he had the moral good luck to have painted important pictures, something that Bernard Williams might call a "good for the world."[3] Whereas his fame is certainly based on his paintings and not on his familial desertion, nevertheless, the fact of his having left behind a wife and five children for sunnier prospects has done nothing to tarnish his stature. If anything, it has added a romantic allure to his biography.

Narratives of this sort suggest that autonomy in practice is antithetical to women's interests because it prompts men to desert the social relationships on which many women depend for the survival and well-being of themselves and their children. In the past, because of women's restricted opportunities, the loss of support suffered by abandoned women has often been worse than the heterosexual relationships on which they depended.

Men are supposed to "stand up like a man" for what they believe or value, including the simple assertion of their self-interests. Women are instead supposed to "*stand by* your man." The maxim "stand up like a *woman*!" has no serious meaning. It conjures up imagery that is, at best, merely humorous. There is no doubt which model of behavior as exhibited by which gender receives the highest honors in Western public culture.

Still today, women in general define themselves more readily than men in terms of personal relationships. In addition, women's moral concerns tend to focus more intensely than those of men on sustaining and enhancing personal ties.[4] Also, popular culture still presumes that women are more concerned than men to create and preserve just the sorts of relationships, such as marriage, that autonomy-seeking men sometimes want to abandon.[5] Feminist analysis has uncovered ways in which close personal involvement and identification with others have been culturally devalued, in tandem with the devaluation of women, by comparison with the public world of impersonal relationships that men have traditionally monopolized.[6] Focusing on the importance of the social is one feminist strategy for combating these traditions of thought and for elevating social esteem for women. Many feminist philosophers have thus emerged as champions of social relationships and of relational approaches to diverse philosophical concepts.[7]

The cultural understanding of autonomy needs to change if the concept is to be relevant for women. I discuss three such changes: new paradigms of autonomy that involve female protagonists, redefinitions of autonomy that avoid stereotypically masculine traits, and redefinitions of autonomy that somehow involve social relationships or are at least not antithetical to them. Indeed such an account has been under development for some time in philosophical literature, and my suggestions on these points are not new. Of course, nothing guarantees a priori that we will find an account of autonomy that synthesizes these elements consistently with the core notion of self-determination that sets limits to our understanding of autonomy. I am optimistic, however, that a female-friendly account of autonomy can be, and has in part already been, developed.

At any rate, I mention these points merely to set the stage for my fourth, and primary, thesis: at the same time that we embrace relational accounts of autonomy, we should also be cautious about them. Autonomy increases the risk of disruption in interpersonal relationships. Although this is an empirical and not a conceptual claim about autonomy, nevertheless, the risk is significant. It makes a difference in whether the ideal of autonomy is genuinely hospitable to women.

After providing a capsule characterization of autonomy that is typical of accounts in the contemporary philosophical literature, I address each of the preceding points in turn.

Personal Autonomy: A Capsule Account

Autonomy involves choosing and living according to standards or values that are, in some plausible sense, one's "own." A plausible sense of "ownness" involves at least two dimensions. First, someone must reflect in an autonomy-conferring manner on the particular choices she makes and the standards or values by which she will be guided. Autonomy-conferring reflection, in my view, is not confined to rational reflection. Such terms as "critical," "reflection," "consideration," "evaluation," "scrutiny," and "choice," as I use them, encompass emotional as well as strictly rational or narrowly cognitive dimensions of personal processes.[8]

Second, the reflection itself must be relatively free of those varieties of interference that impede the achievement of autonomy. What varieties these are I do not specify except to say that socialization does not as such impede autonomy, whereas coercion as such does do so.[9] These circular terms ("autonomy-conferring reflection" and "autonomy-impeding interference") are not meant to articulate the notions in question but merely to serve as placeholders for a fully fleshed account of the nature of autonomy, which is not my present concern.

For the most part, my discussion focuses on personal autonomy, something best defined by reference to moral autonomy. Moral autonomy has to do with what one regards either as morally required or as morally permissible. It involves choosing and living according to rules that one considers to be morally binding. Personal autonomy involves acting and living according to one's own choices, values, and identity within the constraints of what one regards as morally permissible.[10]

Of Autonomy and Women

First, I consider the historic association of autonomy with men. Autonomy, its constituent traits, and the actions and lives that seem to manifest it are publicly esteemed much more often in men than in women. As noted earlier, the preponderance of men in narratives of autonomy could easily cast a masculine shadow over the concept.

Does a concept become irrevocably shaped by the paradigms that initially configure its usage? I believe that it does not and that autonomy can accordingly be freed of its historically near exclusive association with male biographies and male-identified traits. Doing so will require systematic rethinking. In part, we need new paradigms of autonomy that feature female protagonists.[11]

A particularly *feminist* appropriation of the concept of autonomy requires narratives of women who strive in paradigmatically or distinctively female situations against patriarchal constraints to express and refashion their deepest commitments and senses of self. Such narratives are already widely available. Susan Brison, for example, writes of regaining autonomous control over her life after she was tragically raped and almost murdered.[12] Patricia Hill Collins explains the power and importance of self-definition to African-American women, who are fighting the dominating cultural images of themselves as mammies, matriarchs, and welfare mothers.[13] Minnie Bruce Pratt tells of how she struggled to live as a lesbian while at the same time renouncing the racism and antisemitism that she had derived from her family and community of origin.[14]

In addition, there are women's autonomy narratives that are not particularly about overcoming patriarchal constraints. Sara Ruddick's account of maternal thinking, for example, draws heavily on stories of women who reflected deeply on how to care well for their children, an otherwise conventional female task.[15] In short, there is already available a large variety of narratives that exemplify women's autonomous struggles, both feminist and non-feminist.

It is, in addition, helpful to remember that autonomy is not always valued in men. Whole groups of minority men have had their autonomous aspirations crushed by white Western societies. Moreover, white men do not always tolerate autonomy from one another. In traditional, patriarchal hierarchies, such as military or corporate structures, even many *white* men are routinely punished for being autonomous, for challenging accepted norms and authoritative dictates, for not being a "team player."[16]

Some male philosophers, in addition, criticize the ideal of autonomy in at least some of its versions. Male communitarians challenge what they take to be the overly individualistic and ungrounded autonomy of the liberal tradition.[17] Sounding a different note, Loren Lomasky regards autonomy as a source of "massive dislocation" and "widespread human misery." He criticizes autonomy as a rallying cry of the "Red Guards" and of proponents of the welfare state who reject the "traditional ways" of family life.[18]

Thus, the historical link between autonomy and men is not uniform. It is being further challenged today by the growing diversity of women's lives. Autonomy is now available to, and sometimes celebrated in, women, and it is not always celebrated in men. The gender paradigms of autonomy are shifting. On the basis of paradigms alone, autonomy is no longer straightforwardly male-oriented or alien to women.

Autonomy and Gender Stereotypes

My second point is that we should seek redefinitions of autonomy that avoid stereotypically masculine traits. Autonomy has often been conceptualized in terms of traits that suggest an antifemale bias. Traditional ideals of autonomy, for example, have been grounded in reason. Genevieve Lloyd and others have argued that traditional conceptions of reason have excluded anything deemed "feminine," such as emotion.[19] The exclusion of emotion from the concept of reason, however, is less prominent a view today than it once was. Some recent accounts of rationality by both feminists and mainstream philosophers blur the boundary between reason and emotion and thus promise to undermine this traditional dichotomy.[20] In case those accounts prove to be well grounded, this particular philosophical basis for thinking that autonomy is an antifemale ideal would have been eliminated.[21]

Besides connecting autonomy to reason, popular Western culture has also associated autonomy with other masculine-defined traits, for example, independence and outspokenness.[22] Traits popularly regarded as feminine, by contrast, have no distinctive connection to autonomy – social interactiveness, for example.[23] Thus popular gender stereotypes have associated autonomy with men but not with women; these stereotypes might invidiously infect philosophical thinking about autonomy.

To be sure, because of gender differences in socialization, autonomy might actually occur less often in women than in men. As Diana Meyers has documented, male socialization still promotes autonomy competency more effectively than does female socialization.[24] Overall, men have had far greater opportunities than women to act and live autonomously.[25] Such modes of action and living have in the past been closed to most women because they required unavailable (to women) resources such as political power, financial independence, or the freedom to travel unmolested in public space – to jog safely, for example, through New York City's Central Park.

The more frequent appearance of autonomy in men than in women, combined with the association of stereotypically masculine but not feminine traits with autonomy, might unwittingly bias philosophical investigations of autonomy. Together with their nonphilosophical peers, philosophers might fail to recognize manifestations of autonomy by women. Philosophers who try to conceptualize autonomy might do so with autonomous males in mind as paradigm cases. They might go on to mistake what are merely masculine traits for the traits that make up autonomy competency as such. Thus contemporary philosophical accounts of autonomy should be scrutinized particularly with a view to eliminating any covert masculine paradigms that might lie behind them.

In addition to creating a male bias that might influence philosophical reflections on autonomy, male stereotypes are also easy to exaggerate in ways that could further distort the conception of autonomy. The male-stereotyped traits of independence and self-sufficiency have often been interpreted, both in general culture and in philosophical traditions, in asocial, atomistic terms that seem to sanction detachment from close personal relationships with others.[26] Many feminists have argued that this illusory goal of atomistic self-sufficiency has indeed structured male development and male perspectives in those cultures that require men to repudiate the feminine to consolidate their own masculine gender identity.[27] Some feminists worry that the very concept of autonomy has been irremediably contaminated by this atomistic approach, which neglects the social relationships that are vital for developing the character traits required for mature autonomy competency.[28] Much of that socialization consists of women's traditional child-care labor.

Philosophical accounts might err in this regard more by omission than by commission. Some contemporary accounts, for example, fail to mention how the human capacity for autonomy develops in the course of socialization.[29] By neglecting to mention the role of socialization in the development of mature autonomy competency, traditional accounts of autonomy ignore one crucial way in which autonomous persons are ultimately dependent persons after all, and in particular, dependent on women's nurturing. This philosophical omission does nothing to undermine the conceited cultural illusion of the "self-made man" as a paradigm of autonomy.

To be sure, no respectable philosopher today would *explicitly* deny that a social upbringing and ongoing personal interaction are necessary to become autonomous. These conditions impart the self-concept and resources for critical reflection that autonomy requires. Also, no respectable philosopher would deny that women's labors still make up the lion's share of child care, especially in the crucial years of early formative socialization. Careful philosophical thought on these issues should correct the pop-cultural view of some men as impossibly "self-made," a view that denies women their proper share of credit for nurturing or supporting the autonomy competency found in those men. The point is that philosophers must actively take pains to weed out inappropriate male paradigms that might contaminate their own or a wider cultural understanding of key philosophical notions.

In virtue of disregarding the fundamentally social nature of autonomy and autonomous persons, the myth of the self-made man rests on a mistake. The fact that mistaken conceptions of autonomy are male-biased, however, does not show that autonomy *properly understood* is male-biased or antifemale.

Social Reconceptualizations of Autonomy

My third point is that we need an account of autonomy that brings out its relational character. Fortunately, a relational approach to autonomy has been emerging for some time. Two developments are relevant to this issue: a procedural conception of autonomy and a relational or intersubjective conception of autonomy.[30]

According to a procedural account, personal autonomy is realized by the right sort of reflective self-understanding or internal coherence along with an absence of undue coercion or manipulation by others. Autonomy, in this sort of view, is not a matter of living substantively in any particular way.[31] My own capsule account of autonomy in the previous section is a procedural account. Although this sort of account can be debated,[32] it is nevertheless common in philosophy today. In a procedural conception, avoiding or abandoning close personal relationships is in no sense required by autonomy. Nor is it for any reason inherently a better way for any individual to strive for autonomy.

Although the language of autonomy in popular culture might still suggest asocial atomistic images of the self-made man, academic philosophers now seldom share this view. The atomistic "self-made" conception of autonomy is a substantive conception of a particular sort of life or mode of behaving that someone must choose in order to realize autonomy. Such an ideal falls outside the bounds of procedural accounts of autonomy. It is not a proper part of them.

In addition to focusing mainly on procedural matters, many contemporary philosophers of autonomy have also tended to gravitate toward relational or intersubjective accounts of autonomy. This is true of both feminist and mainstream philosophers. At present, both construe autonomy in social, relational, interpersonal, or intersubjective terms.[33]

According to the relational approach, persons are fundamentally social being who develop the competency for autonomy through social interaction with other persons. These developments take place in a context of values, meanings, and modes of self-reflection that cannot exist except as constituted by social practices. Also, according to some theorists, autonomy is itself the capacity for a distinctive form of social and, in particular, dialogical engagement.[34]

Autonomy is no longer thought to require someone to be a social atom, that is, radically socially unencumbered, defined merely by the capacity to choose, or to be able to exercise reason prior to any of her contingent ends or social engagements.[35] It is now well recognized that our reflective capacities and our very identities are always partly constituted by communal traditions and norms that we cannot put entirely into question without at the same time voiding our very capacities to reflect.

We are each reared in a social context of some sort, typically although not always that of a family, itself located in wider social networks such as community and nation. Nearly all of us remain, throughout our lives, involved in social relationships and communities, at least some of which partly define our identities and ground our highest values. These relationships and communities are fostered and sustained by varied sorts of ties that we share with others, such as languages, activities, practices, projects, traditions, histories, goals, views, values, and mutual attractions – not to mention common enemies and shared injustices and disasters.

Someone who becomes more autonomous concerning some tradition, authority, view, or value in her life does not stop depending on other persons or relationships, nor does she evade her own necessarily social history of personal development. Her initial detached questioning does not arise in a social vacuum but is likely to be prompted by commitments reflecting still other relationships that for the present time remain unquestioned and perhaps heteronomous. A shift in social relationships or commitments is not equivalent to, nor need it betoken, wholesale social detachment.

Autonomy does not require self-creation or the creation of law ex nihilo, a limitation that we need not join Richard Rorty in lamenting.[36] Becoming more procedurally autonomous concerning particular standards, norms, or dictates involves reflecting on them in a language that one did not create – according to further norms and standards that one has almost surely taken over from others – in light of what is most central to that product of social development that is oneself.[37] Also, autonomy is always a matter of degree, of more or less. Reflective consideration still counts as a gain in autonomy even if done in the light of other standards and relationships not simultaneously subjected to the same scrutiny.

How Autonomy Disrupts Personal Relationships

Feminists have sought a relational account of autonomy to render it relevant to women. Philosophers in general have sought such an account to make good on a widely shared intuition that autonomy is not antithetical to other social values and virtues that concern us all, such as love, friendship, care, loyalty, and devotion.[38] Many philosophers seem to expect that most of what we want or value in interpersonal relationships will prove to be consistent with the ideal of autonomy, once we develop an appropriately social conception of it.

That conviction, however, may be unfounded. It underestimates, I believe, the disruption that autonomy can promote in close personal relationships and in communities. Although autonomy is not inherently antithetical to social relationships, nevertheless, in practice autonomy often contingently disrupts particular social bonds. How it sometimes interferes with social relationships and what this implies about its value for women make up the fourth and primary theme of this chapter.

Human relationships and communities, as noted, are held together by a variety of ties that persons share, including languages, practices, traditions, histories, goals, views, and values. Any of these elements in someone's life can become the focus of her critical scrutiny. Whenever someone questions or evaluates any tie or commitment that binds her to others, the possibility arises that she may find that bond unwarranted and begin to reject it. Rejecting values that tie someone to others may lead her to try to change the relationships in question or simply to detach herself from them. Someone might also reflect on the very nature of her relationships to particular others and come to believe that those ties are neglecting or smothering important dimensions of herself. To liberate those aspects of herself, she might have to distance herself from the problematic relationships.

Most personal and communal relationships are multifaceted and based on more than one sort of tie. Kinship, for example, keeps many people in contact with relatives whose values would otherwise repel them. Childhood friends who travel disparate paths in life may retain shared memories that keep them ever fondly in touch with each other. A shared ethnic identity may link economically diverse people in the pursuit of collective political ends or cultural self-affirmation. Thus, friends, relatives, or other associates who diverge over important values may still remain related to each other in virtue of other shared ties.

The resilience of social relationships is, of course, not always a blessing. Relationships in which one partner exploits or abuses the other can also, and regrettably, last for years.[39] Sometimes, however, a person becomes so disenchanted with her relationships or their underlying values that they become, to her, unbearable. At that level of discontent, and assuming viable alternatives, she may begin to withdraw from the relationships. In so doing, she displays just the sort of relational disconnection that can stem from a person's autonomous reflections on (and growing dissatisfaction with) her prior commitments.

Alternatively, someone's increasing autonomy might result in the breakup of a relationship not because she rejects it but rather because other parties to the relationship reject her. They might despise the changes in her behavior that they are witnessing. Some parents, for example, disown children who rebel too strongly against deeply held parental values. Peer groups often ostracize their members for disregarding important norms that prevail in their own subcultures.

Strictly speaking, to say that autonomy unqualified (sometimes) disrupts social relationships is misleading. The mere capacity for autonomy is not intrinsically socially disruptive. What disrupts a social relationship in a particular case is the actual exercise of the capacity. More strictly still, the differences that arise between people as a result of one party's autonomous rejection of values or commitments that the other party still holds may lead one party to draw away from or reject the other. Thus, to borrow a rhetorical turn of phrase from the US lobbying group the National Rifle Association (!), it is not *autonomy* (as a dispositional capacity) that disrupts social relationships; it is *people* who disrupt social relationships.

The exercise of autonomy, it should be emphasized, is not sufficient as such to disrupt particular relationships. The connection between autonomy and social disruption is merely contingent. Someone's autonomous reflections increase the chances of disruption in her social relationships but do not make it a necessary consequence. In certain sorts of circumstances, autonomy may not even make social disruption more likely than it already is. Someone's reflective consideration might lead her to appreciate in a new light the worth of her relationships or the people to whom she is socially attached and to enrich her commitment to them. In such cases, autonomy would strengthen rather than weaken relational ties. Even if someone began to disagree with significant others about important matters, their relationship might still not suffer. People use many interpersonal strategies to keep differing commitments from disrupting social harmony – "never discuss religion or politics," for example.[40]

Thus, someone's autonomy is not a *sufficient* condition for the disruption of her social relationships. Nor is it a *necessary* condition. A person might end a relationship because of new commitments that she has reached heteronomously. Peer pressure, for example, can promote knee-jerk rebelliousness that disrupts personal relationships as much as the greatest soul searching and critical self-reflection. Someone's attitudes can also change as the result of traumatic experiences over which she had no control. These changes may occasion deep rifts in her relationships with close others.[41] Someone's increasing autonomy is thus neither a sufficient nor a necessary cause of disruption in social relationships.

Nevertheless, the contingently possible connection between autonomy and social disruption is of noteworthy importance. When a culture places great value on autonomy, members of that culture are thereby encouraged to question their prior allegiances and the standards that impinge on them. Autonomy as a cultural ideal creates a supportive climate for personal scrutiny of traditions, standards, and authoritative commands.[42] Public discourse in such a culture will tend to promote open dialogue and debate over values and traditions. Autonomy-idealizing societies may protect such discourse, and the normative critiques it can foster, with a legal right to a substantial degree of freedom of expression.

Thus, other things being equal, in a culture that prizes autonomy, all traditions, authorities, norms, views, and values become more vulnerable to rejection by at least some members of the society than they would be in a society that devalued autonomy. No commitment in such a culture remains entirely immune to critical scrutiny, whether the commitment concerns religion, sex, family, government, economy, art, education, race, ethnicity, gender, or anything else.

Once such scrutiny takes place, the likelihood increases that people who are socially linked to each other will begin to diverge over views or values they previously shared, including the value of their social ties. Once people begin to diverge over important matters, they are more likely than they were before to disagree and quarrel with each other or to lose mutual interest and drift apart. In this way (other things being equal), an autonomy-idealizing culture increases the risk of (though it certainly does not guarantee) ruptures in social relationships.

To be sure, cultures that idealize autonomy do not always extend this ideal to all social groups. Sometimes certain sorts of people, white men, for example, receive the lion's share of the social protections and rewards for being autonomous. Also, even an autonomy-idealizing culture may shield certain norms or values from critical scrutiny. In such a society, values that protect dominant social groups, those privileged to enjoy the value of autonomy, might not get as much critical attention as they deserve. Whereas limitations on rampant autonomy might be necessary to prevent wholesale social breakdown, they can also create bastions of unquestioned autonomous privilege. In such a culture, autonomy might well be a restricted, domesticated, socially nonthreatening luxury.

Nevertheless, as long as autonomy is culturally valued even for only some groups and for only certain issues, its very cultural availability opens up the possibility for wide social transformation. Even if idealized for only a privileged few, it can always fall into the "wrong" hands. New groups might coincidentally acquire autonomy competency in virtue of social changes, such as the spread of literacy and formal education. They might then go on to contest norms and values previously left unscrutinized. This possibility has been historically crucial for women and other subordinated groups. The ideal of autonomy is thus always a potential catalyst for social disruption in interpersonal relationships.

Notice also that the rupture that autonomy can promote in any one particular social relationship does not necessarily amount to an overall decline in the societal quantity of relationality, to put the point inelegantly. Typically, when someone questions some prior commitment, such as a religious commitment, which cemented certain relationships in her life, she is probably doing so in company with other skeptics whose reflections prompt and reinforce her own rising doubts. When she turns away from her prior religious community, she is likely to be turning toward a different community, perhaps a religiously neutral secular community or a new religious group. Those with whom someone shares her new commitments may have given her a vocabulary or perspective for reflecting on her central concerns. Without any empirical backing for this claim, I nevertheless estimate that in most cases in which autonomous reflection does lead people to reject the commitments that bound them to particular others, they are at the same time taking up new commitments that link them through newly shared conviction to *different* particular others. This is one important reason for thinking of autonomy as social in character.

Although people in an autonomy-valuing society might have as many interpersonal relationships as those in a society that devalued autonomy, it is reasonable to speculate that the nature of people's relationships would differ in the two cases. Where people are permitted with relative ease to leave relationships that have become dissatisfying to them, we should expect attachments to be less stable, to shift and change with greater frequency, than in societies in which personal autonomy (or relational mobility) is discouraged. The types and qualities of relationships in an autonomy-promoting culture would also probably differ from those of an autonomy-discouraging culture. Relationships into which people are born and in which they are first socialized – those of family, church, neighborhood, friendship, and local communities – would probably be disrupted first, if any, by widespread individually autonomous reflections on basic values and commitments. In a culture that values autonomy, it is likely that more people than otherwise would gravitate toward voluntary relationships formed in adult life around shared values and attitudes.[43]

Women and the Social Disruptions of Autonomy

What difference should it make to our theory of autonomy that autonomy, however social its nature or origin, might promote the disruption of social relationships? More precisely in the present context, what difference does this possibility make to *women*? If autonomy is sometimes socially disruptive, does that make it inimical to the relational orientation that many feminists celebrate in women and display in their own moral concerns?

Some people exhibit what I call autonomophobia, or fear of autonomy. What they usually fear is not their own autonomy; it is the autonomy of *others* that scares them. Their concern is that autonomous people will disrupt or desert valuable, *shared* relationships. Which relationships are thought to be valuable will be specified differently from distinct critical perspectives. Feminists, and many women in general, often worry about the relationships on which many women depend for material and emotional sustenance.

Whether or not any particular woman benefits or suffers in virtue of the exercise of autonomy depends on how she is positioned in relation to it. When a woman is connected to someone else whose autonomous pursuits disrupt their relationship, the immediate effect on her is likely to be simply a loss – of whatever benefits she derived from their relationship. Autonomophobia is thus a legitimate concern. It arises from the ways in which our lives are intertwined with those of other persons. When others who are close to use reflect on their own deepest commitments, they might well find grounds for challenging or abandoning the relationships and communities that we share with them. We might find ourselves helpless as a result. Social relationships and communities are collective projects. They function best when sustained jointly by people with important values or norms in common. In a culture that idealizes autonomy, each individual faces the insecurity of investing herself in relationships and communities that the other participants might, on critical reflection, come to reject.

Historically, the disruption of personal relationships has had a different impact on men than on women. Because women were usually limited to dependence on men for financial support, whereas men had no comparable limitation, women doubtless suffered more than they benefited from the cultural idealization of autonomy. Men have been historically better situated than women to forsake personal relationships that came to seem dissatisfying to them. Unlike most women, many men have had the material and cultural resources with which to support themselves, as well as greater opportunities to seek more satisfying relationships elsewhere. Men were able to abandon their responsibilities to women and children to pursue forms of personal fulfillment unavailable to women.

Men who, like Gauguin, produced good enough subsequent works have been celebrated for autonomous pursuits that involved neglecting or abandoning relationships that supported women and children. Dependent women and children have suffered greatly from these male desertions. Women's own autonomous living, by contrast, brought them much more censure and hardship than praise.[44] Since women tend to be more financially dependent on men than men are on women even today, autonomophobia is understandably still more often a female than a male concern. Thus, men's autonomy would have done women little direct good and could have imposed serious harm.

On the other hand, many social relationships constrain and oppress women, indeed the very women who work to sustain them. Apart from whether or not women *want* to devote their lives to maintaining close personal ties, gender norms have required it of them. Women have been expected to make the preservation of certain interpersonal relationships such as those of family their highest concern regardless of the costs to themselves. Women who have had important commitments other than those of taking care of family members were nevertheless supposed to subordinate such commitments to the task of caring for loved ones. Many men, by contrast, have been free to choose or affirm their highest commitments from among a wide panorama of alternatives. Indeed, men are sometimes lauded for just the sort of single-minded pursuit of an ideal that imposes sacrifices on all the people close to them.

Traditionally, the majority of women derived their primary adult identities from their marriages and families. For at least some groups of women, however, social and economic opportunities have broadened in the late twentieth century. Because of expanding financial opportunities in the West, many women no longer need to accommodate themselves *uncritically* to traditional marriages or other relational ties to sustain themselves. As many feminists have well recognized, there is no reason to defend social relationships without qualification. There is nothing intrinsic to each and every social relationship that merits female or feminist allegiance.[45] The traditional relational work of women has included sublime joy and fulfillment but also abuse, exploitation, and subordination. There are some, perhaps many, relationships that women, too, should want to end.

Thus, the disruption of social relationships that can follow someone's growing autonomy is not itself inherently alien to women, nor is it a dimension of the ideal of autonomy that women today should automatically reject. What should matter to any particular woman in any given case is the worth of the relationship in question and how its disruption would bear on herself and on innocent others. The old question, "can this marriage be saved?" should be revised to, "can this marriage be saved from *oppressiveness*?" Some relationships should be preserved and others should be abolished. Even relationships that should be preserved can always be improved. Sometimes what disrupts social relationships is good for particular women. Since the socially disruptive potential of autonomy can at least sometimes be good for women, it does not constitute a reason for women to repudiate the ideal of autonomy.

Indeed, reflecting on one's relationships or the norms or values that underlie them might be the *only* way someone can determine for herself the moral quality of those relationships. A woman who does not reflect on her relationships, communities, norms, or values is incapable of recognizing for herself where they go wrong or of aiming on her own to improve them. Her well-being depends on those who control her life and on their wisdom and benevolence – regrettably, not the most reliable of human traits. Autonomy is thus crucial for women in patriarchal conditions, in part *because* of its potential to disrupt social bonds. That autonomy is sometimes antithetical to social relationships is oftimes a good for women. With all due respect to Audrey Lorde, the "master's tools" *can* "dismantle the master's house."[46]

Thus, although women still have occasion to fear *men's* autonomy, it seems that many women have good reason to welcome our *own*. When a woman is the one who is exercising autonomy, even if its exercise disrupts relationships in her life the value of her gain in autonomous living might well make the costs to her worth her while. She may plausibly fear what increasingly autonomous others might do to the relationships between herself and them, but it would not make sense for her to reject autonomy for herself. A woman might choose not to *exercise* autonomy under certain conditions. She might, for example, devote herself loyally to an ideal that she can only serve by working with a group of persons who sometimes take specific actions she does not understand or endorse. She can hardly want to give up, however, the very option of so devoting herself. To reflect on the standards or values according to which one will behave or live one's life, as one does when resolving to dedicate oneself to a particular ideal, is already to exercise a degree of autonomy. It would be self-defeating, at the same time, to reject autonomy altogether as a value for oneself.

Once women admit that autonomy might be a value for us, it would be difficult to deny its value for persons in general. The capacity for autonomy seems instrumentally valuable as a means for resisting oppression and intrinsically valuable as part of the fullest humanly possible development of moral personality. In these respects it seems valuable for anyone. The problem arises with the need for reciprocity. We cannot esteem autonomy in women while deprecating it in men. Yet men's autonomy and the social disruption it can promote does sometimes threaten women's well-being. I have argued that when women have access to means for their own material support, this risk is lessened.[47]

Women can then gain at least as much from a generalized cultural idealization of autonomy as they risk by it.

There are, as well, certain mitigating possibilities that reduce, even though they do not eliminate, the likelihood that autonomy might cause social disruption. Autonomy does not necessarily lead someone to reject her prior commitments. Someone else's increasing autonomy might instead enhance her appreciation of her close relationships. Even if she comes to regard a relationship as seriously flawed, she might work to improve it rather than abandoning it.

These possibilities suggest that alongside autonomy as a cultural ideal, we should also idealize the values and responsibilities that make relationships and communities worthwhile.[48] We can emphasize, for example, the ways in which close relationships are vital sources of care for the most vulnerable members of our society.[49] We should articulate these values in public dialogues in which all can participate, including those who might become autonomously skeptical about those social ties.

This balanced pursuit of the values of community along with the ideal of autonomy is a partial response to the concern that the empirical social disruptiveness of autonomy lessens the value of autonomy for women. There is no way, however, to alleviate this concern fully. The possibility of social disruptiveness is one risk that must be faced by persons and cultures who would idealize personal autonomy.[50] I have argued that social disruptiveness is, at least, a mixed curse, one that harbors the potential for good, as well as bad, consequences.

In addition, the mantra of "family values" that is invoked uncritically in so much public debate in the United States should remind us as feminists of the hazards of allowing any relationships, including those we most cherish, to be entirely insulated from the critical reflection of all their participants. Even care for the most vulnerable can usually be improved. It is a form of respect toward those with whom we most want affiliation to want *them* to find forms of commitment to us that reflect *their* most cherished values.

Notes

1 I am grateful to Natalie Stoljar and Catriona Mackenzie for helpful editorial suggestions on an earlier draft of this chapter.

2 Yann le Pichon, *Gauguin: Life, Art, Inspiration* (New York: Abrams, 1987), p. 26.

3 Bernard Williams's discussion of moral luck deploys the hypothetical biography of an artist whose life resembles that of the historic Gauguin; see Williams, "Moral Luck," in *Moral Luck* (Cambridge: Cambridge University Press, 1981), p. 37. See my discussion of Williams on the Gauguin-like example in my *What Are Friends For?: Feminist Perspectives on Personal Relationships and Moral Theory* (Ithaca, New York: Cornell University Press, 1993), pp. 163–70.

4 See the germinal work on this topic by Carol Gilligan, *In a Different Voice* (Cambridge, Mass.: Harvard University Press, 1982), and Nel Noddings, *Caring: A Feminine Approach to Ethics and Moral Education* (Berkeley: University of California Press, 1984).

5 See Susan Faludi's discussion of the popularization of research results alleging that women's chances of marrying fall precipitously after age forty, in *Backlash: The Undeclared War against American Women* (New York: Crown Publishers, 1991), Ch. 1. Faludi argues persuasively that the conclusions were misrepresented in the mass media. My point is a different one: these research results would not have received popular attention if it hadn't been for the presumption that people, including women, would want to know about them.

6 See Gilligan, *In a Different Voice*, Ch. 1.

7 See, for example, Helen Longino, *Science as Social Knowledge* (Princeton, NJ: Princeton University Press, 1990).

8 For an account of emotion as a source of autonomy, see Bennett W. Helm, "Freedom of the Heart," *Pacific Philosophical Quarterly* 77 (1996): 71–87. Harry Frankfurt discusses caring and love as sources of autonomy but uses those terms to refer to states of will rather than of emotion; see, for example, *The Importance of What We Care About* (Cambridge: Cambridge University Press, 1988), and "Autonomy, Necessity, and Love," in *Vernunftbegriffe in der Moderne: Stuttgarter Hegel-Kongress 1993*, ed. Hans Friedrich Fulda and Rolf-Peter Horstmann (Stuttgart: Klett-Cotta, 1994), pp. 433–47.

9 Of course, socialization might itself be coercive. See John Christman's approach to this problem in "Autonomy and Personal History," *Canadian Journal of Philosophy* 20 (1991): 1–24.

10 Diana T. Meyers, *Self, Society, and Personal Choice* (New York: Columbia University Press, 1989), pp. 13–17.

11 Morwenna Griffiths explores the importance of narratives in the cultural understanding of autonomy in *Feminisms and the Self: The Web of Identity* (London: Routledge, 1995).

12 Susan Brison, "Surviving Sexual Violence," *Journal of Social Philosophy* 24, no. 1 (Spring 1993): 5–22.

13 Patricia Hill Collins, *Black Feminist Thought: Knowledge, Consciousness, and the Politics of Empowerment*

(New York: Routledge, 1991), especially Chs 4 and 5.

14 Minnie Bruce Pratt, "Identity: Skin Blood Heart," in *Yours in Struggle: Three Feminist Perspectives on Anti-Semitism and Racism*, ed. Elly Bulkin, Minnie Bruce Pratt, and Barbara Smith (Brooklyn, New York: Long Haul Press, 1984), pp. 9–63.

15 Sara Ruddick, *Maternal Thinking: Toward a Politics of Peace* (New York: Ballantine, 1989).

16 The chancellor at a university near my own, for example, was recently fired by his university's governing board. The faculty members who supported him thought the problem was, as one of them put it, that the chancellor was "too autonomous, too independent." Faculty supporters described the governing board as wanting a "team player" instead. See Susan C. Thomson and Kim Bell, "Mizzou Chancellor Wants Buyout," *St Louis Post-Dispatch*, June 14, 1996, C7. Note that the figure of a "team player" is a historically masculine metaphor for a cooperative social agent. The differences between women's and men's paradigm images of social cooperation deserve some study.

17 Michael J. Sandel, *Liberalism and the Limits of Justice* (Cambridge: Cambridge University Press, 1982), and Alasdair MacIntyre, *After Virtue*, 2nd edn (Notre Dame, Ind.: University of Notre Dame Press, 1984).

18 Loren E. Lomasky, *Persons, Rights, and the Moral Community* (New York: Oxford University Press, 1987), p. 249. In the now common procedural account of autonomy, a view that I share (see the section on social reconcepualizations), no particular choices are intrinsic to autonomy. An autonomous person might embrace traditional relationships, reject traditional relationships, welcome the Red Guards, or abhor the Red Guards. What matters is how she arrived at her political views and whether those views reflect her own considered convictions. Lomasky construes autonomy as a failing only of those who make political choices he rejects, but this is just as mistaken as assuming that autonomy is a virtue only of those who make what one considers to be the right political choices.

19 Genevieve Lloyd, *The Man of Reason: "Male" and "Female" in Western Philosophy* (Minneapolis: University of Minnesota Press, 1984). See also Lorraine Code, *Rhetorical Spaces: Essays on Gendered Locations* (New York: Routledge, 1995), especially Ch. 10, "Critiques of Pure Reason."

20 Feminist sources include Code, *Rhetorical Spaces*, and Alison M. Jaggar, "Love and Knowledge: Emotion in Feminist Epistemology," in *Gender/Body/Knowledge*, ed. Alison M. Jaggar and Susan R. Bordo (New Brunswick, NJ: Rutgers University Press, 1989), pp. 145–71. Nonfeminist sources include Allan Gibbard, *Wise Choices, Apt Feelings: A Theory of Normative Judgment* (Cambridge, Mass.: Harvard University Press, 1990).

21 A different approach would be to argue that the stereotypic association of women with emotion was always groundless and that women are as able as men to exercise a narrowly cognitive mode of reason. See Louise M. Antony and Charlotte Witt, eds., *A Mind of One's Own: Feminist Essays on Reason and Objectivity* (Boulder, Colo.: Westview Press, 1993), especially the essays by Margaret Atherton and Louise Antony. See the discussion of these essays by Code, *Rhetorical Spaces*, pp. 217–23.

22 See Susan Golombok and Robyn Fivush, *Gender Development* (Cambridge: Cambridge University Press, 1994), pp. 7–8.

23 Ibid., p. 18. A social or relational account of autonomy, such as that presented here, is one that construes social relationships as necessary for autonomy but not sufficient for it. There is nothing about social interconnection as such that entails, causes, or suggests autonomy.

24 Meyers, *Self, Society and Personal Choice*, especially Part 3.

25 This point is, of course, not universal throughout Western cultures. Men of oppressed groups, such as racial minorities, may not have had significantly greater opportunities than the women of their own groups to act and live autonomously.

26 Many feminists have charged the traditional philosophical ideal of autonomy with excessive individualism; see, for example, Lorraine Code, "Second Persons," in *What Can She Know?: Feminist Theory and the Construction of Knowledge* (Ithaca, New York: Cornell University Press, 1991), pp. 76–9.

27 See, for example, Evelyn Fox Keller, *Reflections on Gender and Science* (New Haven, Conn.: Yale University Press, 1985); Nancy Chodorow, *The Reproduction of Mothering: Psychoanalysis and the Sociology of Gender* (Berkeley: University of California Press, 1978); and Jessica Benjamin, *The Bonds of Love: Psychoanalysis, Feminism, and the Problem of Domination* (New York: Pantheon, 1988).

28 Annette Baier, "Cartesian Persons," in *Postures of the Mind: Essays on Mind and Morals* (Minneapolis: University of Minnesota Press, 1985). See also the discussion of this notion in Code, "Second Persons."

29 One prominent philosopher who neglects socialization, and, indeed, social relationships generally, in his account of autonomy is Frankfurt, *Importance of What We Care About*.

30 See the discussion of both of these points by John Christman, "Feminism and Autonomy," in *"Nagging" Questions: Feminist Ethics in Everyday Life*, ed. Dana E. Bushnell (Lanham, Md.: Rowman & Littlefield, 1995), pp. 17–39.

31 Gerald Dworkin provides one example of a procedural account of autonomy; see his *The Theory and*

Practice of Autonomy (Cambridge: Cambridge University Press, 1988), pp. 18, 21–33.

32 See Marina Oshana, "Personal Autonomy and Society," *Journal of Social Philosophy* 29, no. 1 (Spring 1998): 81–102.

33 Feminist theorists who have developed this view include Keller, *Reflections on Gender and Science*; Jennifer Nedelsky, "Reconceiving Autonomy: Sources, Thoughts, and Possibilities," *Yale Journal of Law and Feminism* 1, no. 1 (Spring 1989); 7–36; Meyers, *Self, Society, and Personal Choice*; and Code, "Second Persons." Mainstream theorists who have developed this view include Joseph Raz, *The Morality of Freedom* (Oxford: Clarendon Press, 1986); Dworkin, *Theory and Practice of Autonomy*; and Joel Feinberg, "Autonomy," in *The Inner Citadel*, ed. John Christman (New York: Oxford University Press, 1989), pp. 27–53. For a discussion of the convergence of these two groups around a social conception of autonomy, see Christman, "Feminism and Autonomy," and my "Autonomy and Social Relationships: Rethinking the Feminist Critique," in *Feminists Rethink the Self*, ed. Diana T. Meyers (Boulder, Colo.: Westview Press, 1997), pp. 40–61. Some mainstream philosophers deny that the traditional notion of autonomy, even in its rigorous Kantian formulation, ever really excluded or ignored the importance of interpersonal relationships; see J. B. Schneewind, "The Use of Autonomy in Ethical Theory," in *Reconstructing Individualism: Autonomy, Individuality, and the Self in Western Theory*, ed. Thomas C. Heller, Morton Sosna, and David E. Wellberry (Stanford, Cal.: Stanford University Press, 1986), and Thomas E. Hill, Jr, "The Importance of Autonomy," in *Autonomy and Self-Respect* (Cambridge: Cambridge University Press, 1991).

34 See, for example, Jurgen Habermas, *Moral Consciousness and Communicative Action*, trans. Christian Lenhardt and Shierry Weber Nicholsen (Cambridge, Mass.: MIT Press, 1990), and Joel Anderson, "A Social Conception of Personal Autonomy: Volitional Identity, Strong Evaluation, and Intersubjective Accountability," PhD dissertation, Northwestern University, Evanston, Ill., 1996.

35 See, for example, Sandel, *Liberalism and the Limits of Justice*, p. 19.

36 Richard Rorty, *Contingency, Irony, and Solidarity* (Cambridge: Cambridge University Press, 1989).

37 Gerald Dworkin notes the impossibility of creating our own moral principles. Such a requirement "denies our history.... We... are deeply influenced by parents, siblings, peers, culture, class, climate, schools, accident, genes, and the accumulated history of the species. It makes no more sense to suppose we invent the moral law for ourselves than to suppose that we invent the language we speak for ourselves" (*The Theory and Practice of Autonomy*, p. 36).

38 Ibid., p. 21.

39 If abusive relationships persist for long periods of time, it is usually because the abused partner has, or thinks she has, no other viable options or because she sacrifices her own well-being to that of her abuser. For a survey of why long-time battered women finally seek court orders of protection against abusive male partners, see Karla Fischer and Mary Rose, "When 'Enough is Enough': Battered Women's Decision Making around Court Orders of Protection," *Crime and Delinquency* 41, no. 4 (October 1995): 414–29.

40 I do not endorse this maxim; I merely cite it as an example of the strategies that people use to keep disagreements from disrupting social relationships.

41 See Brison's discussion in "Surviving Sexual Violence," of the difficulties that arose in her relationships with family, friends, and others after she was violently raped.

42 As Dworkin notes, "Those who practice in their daily life a critical reflection on their own value structure will tend to be suspicious of modes of thought that rely on the uncritical acceptance of authority, tradition, and custom" (*The Theory and Practice of Autonomy*, p. 29).

43 For further discussion of this theme, see my *What Are Friends For*? Ch. 9.

44 See Alison MacKinnon, *Love and Freedom: Professional Women and the Reshaping of Personal Life* (Cambridge: Cambridge University Press, 1997), on the hurdles faced by women in Australia at the end of the nineteenth and beginning of the twentieth century who sought higher education and careers outside the home.

45 There are many feminist discussions of problems that women face in social relationships; see, for example, Susan Moller Okin, *Justice, Gender, and the Family* (New York: Basic Books, 1989).

46 See Audrey Lorde, "The Master's Tools Will Never Dismantle the Master's House," *Sister Outsider* (Freedom, Cal.: Crossing Press, 1984), pp. 110–13.

47 On this topic, see the essays in Martha Nussbaum and Jonathan Glover, eds., *Women, Culture and Development: A Study of Human Capabilities* (Oxford: Clarendon Press, 1995).

48 See the essays in *Feminism and Community*, eds. Penny Weiss and Marilyn Friedman (Philadelphia: Temple University Press, 1995).

49 See, for example, Robert E. Goodin, *Protecting the Vulnerable: A Reanalysis of Our Social Responsibilities* (Chicago: University of Chicago Press, 1985); Neera Kapur Badhwar, ed., *Friendship: A Philosophical Reader* (Ithaca, New York: Cornell University Press, 1993); Joan C. Tronto, *Moral Boundaries: A Political Argument for an Ethic of Care* (New York: Routledge, 1994).

50 Should we devalue autonomy for individuals, perhaps recasting it as an ideal for groups only? The notion of group autonomy is extremely

important, especially for oppressed groups; see, for example, Laurence Mordekhai Thomas, *Vessels of Evil: American Slavery and the Holocaust* (Philadelphia: Temple University Press, 1993), pp. 182–89. Group autonomy, however, does not necessarily help individuals when they face oppressive conditions in isolation. It complements but does not replace individual autonomy. In addition, group autonomy promotes its own risk of social disruption in the relationships between groups. The possible advantages, as well as the possible costs, of autonomy's socially disruptive potential simply reappear at a more encompassing level of social integration.

25

Forgetting Yourself

Anita L. Allen

The self is the basic unit of personality and personal identity. It is who and what we are. Philosophers debate competing theories of the self. These theories portray the self as, for example, a "bundle of perceptions" (Chisholm 1994, 97); a rational agent structured and motivated by internalized general norms (Piper 1985, 1988); a homuncular system of effective agents and subagents (Johnston 1988); and a duality of conscious and unconscious motives accessible through psychoanalysis (Erwin 1988). Philosophers also debate the seeming capacities of the self, such as self-knowledge and self-deception. Self-knowledge – what it means to "know thyself" – has been a frequent subject for explorations of mind, language, and epistemology (Cassam 1994), whereas self-deception has been a favorite topic of contemporary moral psychology (McLaughlin and Rorty 1988).

We humans may be able to *know* ourselves and *deceive* ourselves, but, according to an idiomatic English-language expression, we also are able to *forget* ourselves. Though fundamental to persons, selves can be forgotten. Consider this hypothetical instance of forgetting oneself.

> **Case 1**: Jo takes care of her elderly mother, who is in poor health. Jo normally behaves lovingly toward her mother, as she believes she ought. But one day Jo is especially tired and feeling sorry for herself. When her mother makes a request that Jo would ordinarily fill without hesitation or protest, Jo curses, denies the request, and storms away. Afterward, Jo is ashamed and feels fortunate that others did not witness her discourteous behavior.

Jo has "lost her cool." Her outburst is an example of forgetting oneself.

As I shall explain it, to forget yourself is, inadvertently and temporarily, to abandon the manners or morals – the communal norms of decorum or decency – that generally sustain both social approval and self-esteem. Forgetting yourself typically stems from lapses of self-awareness or, as in Case 1, self-control. Often, forgetting yourself is to be in what Gilbert Ryle described as one of those "situations in which a person admits that he did not know at the time what he was doing, although what he was doing was not an automatism but an

Anita L. Allen, "Forgetting Yourself," pp. 104–23 from Diana Tietjens Meyers (ed.), *Feminists Rethink the Self*. Boulder, CO: Westview Press, 1997.

intelligent operation" (1994, 25). A person who forgets himself or herself is not "alive to what he is doing all the time he is doing it" (1994, 27).

Self-deception also involves failing to be wholly alive to what one is up to. When taken literally, forgetting yourself, like deceiving yourself, is a puzzling phenomenon. Self-deception, literally construed, is a matter of fooling the self; it paradoxically entails believing and disbelieving the same propositions at the same time. Forgetting yourself, literally construed, paradoxically entails simultaneously remembering and not remembering your own identity as a person who accepts and adheres to particular norms. If we accept as valid the appealing but controversial conception of the self characterized by Amelie Rorty (McLaughlin and Rorty 1988, 13) as "strongly integrated, capable of critical, truth-oriented reflection, with its various functions in principle accessible to, and corrigible by, one another," both forgetting and deceiving yourself should be impossible. Anyone but one's own self should be forgettable. Anyone but one's own self should be deceivable.

Nevertheless, in hypothetical Case 1, Jo manages to forget herself. A person with Jo's responsibilities might also deceive herself. Imagine the self-deception of sons and daughters like Jo who resent obligations of elder-care but cannot acknowledge resentment concerning the care of their own mothers. Imagine, too, that paradoxes of self-deception and forgetting yourself operate in tandem in such instances: You deceive yourself about the burdens of caring for your mother, refuse to hire a private-duty nurse, allow your frustrations to grow, and eventually forget yourself in a regrettable outburst.

Forgetting yourself has affinities to *akrasia*, also known as "moral backsliding" or "weakness of the will" – a phenomenon Georges Rey (1988) has discussed in connection with self-deception. Like self-deception and forgetting yourself, *akrasia* has a paradoxical quality. Assuming a certain contested conception of the self as rationally motivated and free, how is it possible for a person to know what is right, good, best, or virtuous, but fail to do it? *Akrasia* occurs, if it occurs at all, when a rational person deliberately breaches what he or she knows to be a morally binding behavioral norm. According to may analysis, forgetting yourself also consists of breaching what you know (or at least believe) to be a binding behavioral requirement. But the chief differences between forgetting yourself and *akrasia* are these: First, instances of forgetting yourself can involve nonmoral as well as moral norms; and second, forgetting yourself involves lapses of self-awareness or self-control rather than intentional, deliberate behavior. By contrast, paradigmatic instances of *akrasia* involve strictly moral norms and self-aware, deliberate acts of noncompliance. A moral backslider with the responsibilities of Jo in Case 1 might slip away for an hour each week to satisfy her craving for a certain television program, thereby deliberately violating her admitted obligation to continuously monitor her elderly mother's needs. By definition, then, *akrasia* is a moral breach. (Morality certainly cannot recommend the negligent abandonment of one's helpless charges.) Yet *akrasia* may function to relieve pent-up resentment of the sort that can lead frustrated people to forget themselves.

Philosophers have written volumes about the phenomena of self-knowledge, self-deception, and *akrasia*. The same cannot be said of forgetting yourself. A comprehensive philosophy of the self would include an account of this interesting phenomenon. My purpose is to frame such an account and then to link it to current concerns about awareness of group membership and racial identity. Achieving the liberal ideal of a "color-blind society" may be a practical impossibility. In order for a color-blind society to emerge, people need to be able to put race out of their own minds and keep it out of the minds of succeeding generations of youth. I want to suggest that although it is doubtless possible to put race out of one's mind, many Americans are too racially self-aware and/or race-conscious to do so. Among many African Americans, race-consciousness has become a matter of group pride. For them, forgetting race is "acting white" and acting white is something for which a black should be condemned. To the extent that it breaches an African American subgroup norm against acting white, forgetting race would seem to be explicable as an instance of forgetting yourself.

I do not defend a particular conception of the self, although my analysis may entail some conceptions or rule out others. My account of "forgetting yourself" is consistent with at least one important conception of the self – namely, the conception of the self as governed by rule-like norms. There is considerable appeal to the notion that we are "Kantian" selves "defined by . . . general prescriptive principles [internalized in the normal process of socialization] to which we are usually disposed to conform our emotions, action and habits" (Piper 1985, 182–3). Forgetting ourselves can be seen, from within a "Kantian" framework, as failing to do as we are generally motivated to do – that is, as failing to conform "our emotions, action and habits" to certain socially instilled general prescriptive principles.

1

Forgetting decorum and decency

According to another old-fashioned, idiomatic English-language expression, selves can be forgotten. I can forget myself. You can forget yourself. We can forget ourselves. Even the awkward people described as "self-conscious" and the commanding ones described as "self-possessed" are capable, on occasion, of forgetting themselves.

"Forgetting yourself" is a figure of speech. It is not a literal act. When we "forget ourselves," we have not literally ceased to remember who we are. We know who we are. More precisely, we know as much about ourselves as we ever did. We retain memories of our unique and individual personal identities. We can recall facts about ourselves, such as our names, occupations, ethnicities, and tastes. But when we "forget ourselves," we breach applicable rules, standards, virtues, or other behavioral norms. We fail to comply with norms of social decorum or moral decency applicable to persons with our traits, capacities, roles, and good characters. Fine actors, for example, occasionally forget their lines, and fine citizens occasionally forget to be decent and decorous.

We are social creatures, products of communal forms of life. Communal relationships and values are sometimes said to be constitutive of personal identity, shaping who we are and what we value (Benhabib 1992, 73–4). The social character of the self as dependent upon the material and normative resources of communities does not entail the assumption that people are more automaton than autonomous. To varying degrees, people can and do reflect on the point of conformity to communal conceptions of appropriate and inappropriate affects, attitudes, and conduct.

In many instances, conformity to communal norms of decorum and decency strikes us as something about which we have a choice. And in most instances we choose to go along. Indeed, our decision to conform to well-established or pervasively accepted patterns of behavior often helps to sustain our self-concepts as responsible, cooperative members of society. Thus, the same "good" behavior that wins social approval also earns self-esteem. Capable of what Gilbert Ryle called "higher-order self-dealings" (quoted in Cassam 1994, 39), we adults take on the aspect of "prefect[s] regulating [our] own conduct." We are responsible people who deserve self-esteem and the esteem of others, not because we have blindly adhered to communal norms but, rather, because we have chosen to regulate our conduct in accordance with reasonable social expectations.

Most people behave as they are supposed to, according to social rule and role. Yet whereas many social expectations are hardy enough to survive wintry critique, others wilt under cool scrutiny (Benhabib 1992, 74). In recent decades, the latter has been the fate of the distinctly oppressive social expectations that once confined women and people of color to subservient roles in the national economy of the United States. So, when we say in earnest that someone has forgotten himself or herself, the norms we presuppose may be widely accepted, entrenched communal norms of the sort that the best political, moral, or legal theories would not endorse.

Why we forget ourselves

People typically forget themselves either because they are inattentive (to what they are doing or where they are doing it) or because they are overcome or excited by emotion. Jealousy, anger, lust, and fear can lead individuals to forget themselves. Sometimes it is a drug or alcohol that makes a person less attentive or more subject to their emotions. In fact, people commonly drink to lower their inhibitions. And for the most part, they do so in what mainstream American cultural norms deem appropriate settings and contexts. They drink at home, in bars, and at parties. But I would stress that deliberately ingesting drugs or alcohol so that one can "let down one's hair" is not the same thing as forgetting oneself. Normally, when we are hoping to let down our hair, we are not hoping to forget ourselves. It is one thing to take a drink, hoping it will embolden us to ask a friend to bed; and something else to make a pass, unexpectedly, at our friend's spouse. Only the latter counts as forgetting ourselves. I would also stress, in connection with altered states of consciousness, that although we may joke that a stand-offish, somber person made giddy and gregarious by a drink has forgotten himself, we do not mean it. We are making light of that person's disposition to take the virtue of sobriety to an extreme.

People try not to forget themselves even when they are tired, angry, and intoxicated. For although the consequences of forgetting ourselves can be trivial and amusing, sometimes they are highly shameful and harmful to ourselves and others. The following hypothetical case illustrates an inconsequential, trivial instance of forgetting oneself. In this instance the breach stems from inattention, a lapse of attention brought on by exhaustion and ennui.

> **Case 2**: Pam is a vice president at a major corporation. She is sitting at a table in a windowless conference room filled with staid colleagues who are politely debating proposed strategies for marketing a new product. It is very late in the evening and her mind begins to wander. She begins to think about a pleasant musical she attended the night before. She starts to hum one of its tunes. A close friend sitting nearby gently nudges Pam to restore her attention. Pam then realizes that she had forgotten herself.

Here, forgetting oneself has resulted in a minor breach of social etiquette and professional decorum.

In the United States, people hum aloud in public, but typically in churches or at music lessons, parties, rock concerts, and such. It is not the rule (though also not rare) to hear someone humming while applying for a bank loan or observing the cross-examination of a star witness in court. Sophisticated professionals avoid humming at business meetings. They consider it inappropriate. They know that humming in the midst of a meeting suggests absentmindedness or indifference. Absentminded inattention undermines the confidence of clients, customers, and colleagues. Of course, some successful businesspeople are tolerated as eccentric individualists who are either prone to absentmindedness or consciously unwilling to "play the role." For the latter group, humming during lulls in meetings might be ordinary, self-aware behavior.

A significant feature of Case 2 is that Pam's close friend, rather than another person sitting nearby, nudges her to attention. Forgetting oneself is an asocial moment: The forgetting subject goes private, slipping away from the constraining norms of the public, communal realm. Friends want us to keep our jobs, our "faces," our standing in the community. Good-hearted strangers may want the same thing for us. But there is a limit on acceptable and comfortable paternalistic intrusion by non-intimates. In the realm of mere etiquette and decorum (as in Case 2), perhaps the most polite thing a stranger, mere acquaintance, or co-worker can do when someone forgets himself or herself is to pretend it did not happen. If others convincingly pretend not to have noticed, they spare the forgetting subject the embarrassment of knowing for certain that others witnessed his or her deviance. By contrast, our friends have duties as friends that go beyond polite evasion. They ought not allow us to make fools of ourselves by, for example, violating workplace or other norms. Friends have special permission to reach into our privacy and, with a nudge, a telling glance, or a reprimand, to draw us back into the public arena.

Rebellion and critique

Forgetting oneself is an act of nonconformity, though not an intentional act of rebellion or critique. But, clearly, failing to conform to established norms is sometimes a good thing. Pam (from Case 2) is no rebel against corporate culture, and she is embarrassed by her lapse of decorum. Yet her lapse possibly has a beneficial consequence. It may usefully signal to others that their meeting has gone on too long and should be ended. Similarly, in a society where women are not supposed to talk back to men, beneficial consequences may flow when a normally subservient woman "forgets herself" by telling off her husband or father. Stubbornly conventional cultural insiders would view the woman's behavior as "misbehavior." But letting off steam in response to oppression may have psychological and political advantages that incline outsider or insider culture critics to view inadvertent misbehavior with favor.

A third hypothetical case illustrates a consequential instance of forgetting oneself. In Case 2 the "forgetting" was a matter of inattention; in the following case, as in Case 1, it is a matter of unbridled emotion.

Case 3: Min is a high school teacher. For the third day in a row she is trying to teach history to a group of unruly students who have come to class unprepared. She is angry. In response to a simple question, a volatile student she knows to be suffering from poor self-esteem gives her an especially ill-informed answer. Min blurts out: "Idiot! That's the stupidest thing I've heard all year, and I've heard plenty of stupid things in this class!" The student hurls a pile of textbooks in Min's direction and sobs. Min immediately realizes that her testy words to the vulnerable student were imprudent and wrong.

Min has forgotten herself. And forgetting herself has resulted in a breach of what many might regard as a role-related ethical responsibility. In contemporary American education, name-calling is considered intemperate behavior for teachers. Most teachers do not engage in it at all; but almost anyone can forget himself or herself when sufficiently provoked.

If forgetting ourselves involves innocuous behavior such as humming show tunes at work, it can win us approval as "spontaneous" and "original." But if forgetting ourselves involves injurious behavior such as demoralizing children or the elderly, it can damage our reputations, relationships, and self-esteem. The social realm is constituted such that we forget ourselves only at our peril.

For some, the peril is mortal. In the Jim Crow era, southern blacks who forgot themselves in spontaneous displays of passion in their dealings with whites risked being jailed or lynched. The film version of Alice Walker's *The Color Purple* included a fictional account of a feisty young woman named Sophia who was beaten and jailed for swearing at the white mayor's wife. When dealing with whites, Sophia normally remembered her place, her communal role as a social inferior. But that day, the mayor's scatter-brained wife innocently insulted Sophia in the presence of Sophia's children – and Sophia lost her temper. She forgot herself, and then nearly lost her life.

Social norms of the Old South appear to have made it possible for one and the same behavior to count as moral misdemeanor or serious offense depending upon the race of the offender and victim. My impression is that a white man discovered to have made a spontaneous pass at a white or black woman rarely had cause to fear serious retribution in the hands of black or white society; but a black man discovered to have made a spontaneous pass at a white woman risked death in the hands of an angry white mob. In short, a racist society may construct a particular action as either "forgetting yourself" or "heinous crime" depending upon the race of the offender.

An internal conception

As social beings, our personal identities are intimately linked with our communities of origin and influence, and thus with the behavioral norms they prescribe for us. Individuals internalize (i.e., accept as binding) many of the behavioral norms that they learn from social interactions with others. When individuals conceive of themselves or others as having forgotten themselves, these internalized values are their points of reference. Forgetting oneself, then, entails failing to conform to behavioral norms of the sort we know to be constitutive of individuals situated in communal forms of life.

On what I shall call the "internal" conception of forgetting oneself, to forget oneself is to deviate briefly from an internalized behavioral norm. We can imagine that Pam and her friend from Case 2 have internalized the positive norms of the corporate world as their own. They do not regard humming show tunes as appropriate behavior during business meetings. If in a rare moment of distraction Pam audibly hums, she has acted inappropriately, against the norm. Pam's short-lived deviation from the internally endorsed no-humming norm is an instance of forgetting herself. But now compare Pam to Peter.

Case 4: On his first day with the company as a management trainee, Peter hums to himself during a lull in an important meeting with Pam and others. As it happens, Peter thinks nothing of public humming. He does it anywhere, everywhere, all the time. Peter is unaware that Pam and others regard such behavior as unprofessional. Pam, who is embarrassed for Peter, thinks "That man has forgotten himself."

From an internal perspective, Peter has not forgotten himself at all. He has not internalized the norms of the corporate world. The self that he is values public humming as an appropriate or neutral distraction.

Pam's attribution of "forgetfulness" registers her own values. Indeed, her value judgment has social determinants and is shared by most others in her corporate professional milieu. Her assessment of Peter tells us something about Pam and the social groups to which Pam belongs. Pam is not unlike the adults who say of mannerless children that they have "forgotten themselves," when the children have simply not (yet) grown to accept the norms of the adult world as their own internal social norms. Parents say "Behave yourselves!" and "Don't forget yourselves!" to children to exhort them to use good manners and adhere to social rules. They say these things despite the "truisms of the playroom and schoolroom" (Ryle 1994, 38) that adhering to norms of self-restraint is higher-order behavior and that "[h]igher-order actions are not instinctive" (Ryle 1994, 38). Learning to be a certain sort of disciplined self and learning not to forget that self are components of early childhood education. Sometimes when an adult says "You're forgetting yourself!" to a child displaying socially inappropriate behavior, the truth of the matter is that the child has not yet become a fully socially groomed self. The child cannot forget a self that he or she has not yet become. And like Peter from Case 4, the child cannot breach a norm he or she does not yet recognize as binding. The admonitions of the parent are *ex cathedra*: "Do not forget yourself!" really means "Do not violate communal norms; do as you are supposed to do!"

2

Euphemism, metaphor, and excuse

Aggregated in this section are the key features of my analysis of forgetting yourself, as suggested by the foregoing hypothetical cases. First, the expression "forgetting yourself" functions as a metaphor. It does so because when we say people have forgotten themselves, we fully realize that no such thing has literally occurred. There is no amnesia. It is only *as if* their memories of the socially or morally compliant people – the proper selves – we know they have slipped away.

Forgetting oneself is a *deviation* from a person's ordinary patterns of behavior, which include a tendency to obey social rules of etiquette, morality, and law. People can forget themselves in the internalist sense and violate rules they accept but think are silly; or forget themselves and violate rules they accept and judge to be sound. Whether forgetting oneself will be a source of regret or remorse depends upon the significance one attaches to the patterns or standards of conduct one has breached and their possibly adverse consequences. One might not regret having forgotten oneself and told an amusing off-color joke at a dull family gathering. But one might well regret having forgotten oneself and flown into a violent jealous rage.

Second, "forgetting yourself" functions as euphemism. "She forgot herself" or "He forgot himself" is a distinctly polite way of saying, for example, that a sophisticated person has been vulgar; a sensitive person, insensitive; a kind person, malicious; a calm person, passionate. Speakers normally reserve the "forgetting yourself" expression for situations in which an adult whose behavior, though generally in line, gets out of line, failing to be socially decorous or morally decent.

Third, forgetting oneself is a *brief* and *infrequent* deviation from practice. It is a temporary lapse. Forgetting oneself is not a persistent habit or pattern of ill-mannered or immoral behavior. Forgetting oneself involves short-lived inattention, absentmindedness, and similar lapses of self-awareness; it also entails "losing one's head" to passionate emotion and similar lapses of self-control. The expression "losing oneself" can refer to longer-term lapses of self-awareness. An artist may "lose himself" or "lose herself" in work for hours or even days. Forgetting oneself is not unlike "acting out of character." However, as the phrase is generally understood, people can "act out of character" for a period of time, but they cannot "forget themselves" for more than a few seconds or several minutes. If I join a week-long criminal conspiracy hoping to get money to pay off debts, I act of out character; I do not forget myself.

It seems basic to the concept of forgetting yourself that episodes of inattention (as in Case 2) or unbridled emotion (as in Cases 1 and 3) are infrequent and brief. A typically decorous teacher who experiences several outbursts of anger in one day could aptly report that she repeatedly forgot herself that day. Better yet, she could aptly report that she was not herself that day. But a typically decorous teacher who routinely began breaching rules of decorum and decency day after day would seem to have undergone a change of personality or moral character. Of such a person one might say "He is not himself." Teachers who habitually lash out in anger at their students do not qualify as people who have forgotten themselves. Rather, they are insensitive people with poor self-control. Similarly, it would violate standard conceptual usage to say that people who always swear at the elderly, chew their nails in public, or hum the scores of musicals in meetings have "forgotten themselves."

Fourth, forgetting oneself can be *morally culpable* behavior. Case 3 provides an example. The teacher's behavior in that case is wrong, though perhaps forgivable and excusable, assuming certain familiar facts about the working conditions of the teaching profession. One reason for ascribing moral fault is the recognition that many human beings have the power to cultivate habits and virtues that make forgetting oneself (in the form of, say, absentmindedness and emotionality) less likely. Conversely, inadequate sleep, alcohol consumption, and the use of narcotics – all of which may be quite deliberate and intentional – can lead to lapses of self-control and self-awareness. But the essential point here is that it makes sense for us to hold one another responsible for bad conduct that results from predictable lapses to which we substantially contribute.

Forgetting oneself can have adverse consequences that are either trivial or serious, but *not too serious*. If, for example, the consequences of a person's immoral behavior include very serious physical or emotional injury to others, the expression "forgot himself or herself" no longer comfortably applies. The reason is that saying someone "forgot himself" carries with it the sense that the person has made a mistake of the sort people are entitled to make occasionally. Of course, there is no set list of the kinds of mistakes people are entitled to make. But brutal murder surely should not appear on such a list. Indeed, to describe a vicious murderer as someone who "forgot himself" (as opposed to someone who was temporarily reckless, insane, or enraged) would be to trivialize the infraction in a way that would seem appropriate only in the context of sarcasm or satire.

Finally, the expression "forgetting yourself" serves to excuse or forgive apparently rare or inappropriate conduct. It conveys the message that people who generally do as they are supposed to do are entitled to make a mistake. Every dog is entitled to one bite and every human being is entitled to an occasional social breach. People who forget themselves, then, are not ill-mannered or immoral people, vulgar or bad in essence. If they were, we would describe their misfeasance differently. "Forgetting yourself" presupposes a conception of the self as mannerly or moral. The people who forget themselves are thus understood to fall into the category of corrigible people whom one fully expects to behave well in the future because they have generally done so in the past. We categorize their nonconforming conduct as forgivable, excusable, and rare by attributing it to metaphorical lapses of memory (of their rule-, standard-, or other norm-governed, mannerly, or moral selves) rather than to lapses of virtue. It follows that when a person sincerely declares, "I forgot myself," he or she is imploring others to forgive or excuse what that person regards as atypical, episodic misbehavior.

3

Forgetting race

I want to set aside, for a moment, the concept of "forgetting yourself" and focus briefly on simple, literal forgetting. Forgetting is a kind of cognitive disassociation that occurs all the time. Most of the individual acts and events that constitute our lives are forgotten. Most of the things we happen to remember or try to remember, we eventually forget. And some of the things we forget are subject to later recall. Consider Marcel Proust's *Remembrance of Things Past*, in which the author narrates lush, subtle depictions of the sensory stimuli – tastes, smells, sounds – that lead one to recover pleasant and unpleasant memories of the forgotten past from seeming oblivion.

The capacity to forget is remarkable, as are the range and significance of what we humans are capable of forgetting. We have all heard of people who have forgotten to eat, to pick up their children from school, or to pay for merchandise before leaving a store. Lately, I seem to forget the names of my students once a semester has passed. I frequently forget where I have placed my car keys until I "retrace my steps." I once forgot that I had purchased a bag of ginger-candy of a sort I am wont to crave, until I discovered it in my pantry a week later. I even forgot that I had had a bitter argument with an old friend, until I telephoned him after fifteen years without contact and he (still miffed) reminded me.

Once, I momentarily forgot my race. I forgot that I am an African American in a situation quite like this one.

> **Case 5**: Jan is a university student. She is planning a party. She is discussing possible guests with her close friend, Peg. Peg suggests inviting Bob, who is an African American. Jan likes the idea, but suggests that Bob might feel out of place as the only African American at the party. Puzzled, Peg reminds Jan that *she*, Jan, is also an African American and, therefore, that Bob would not be the only African American at the party. Bemused, Jan realizes that, at least for a moment, she had forgotten her race.

This case, and my own experience, would seem to indicate that race is a forgettable attribute. Yet I would conjecture that forgetting race is an unusual occurrence among African Americans living in the United States. African Americans who escape acute forms of what I call "racial self-consciousness" are still prone to "race-consciousness." These two modes of self-awareness ensure that forgetting race is rare. I would conjecture that even American blacks who are well assimilated into white or multiracial communities are subject to episodes of acute racial self-consciousness and/or race-consciousness.

Racial self-consciousness is awareness of belonging to a putatively inferior racial group, aggravated by feelings of shame and inferiority. I first fell victim to racial self-consciousness back in the 1960s when, at the age of six, I learned that I was a "Negro," called "out of my name" as "nigro," "black," and "nigger."

Race-consciousness, by contrast, is the tendency to select one's race as a subject matter of thought and conversation, but without feelings of personal inferiority. African Americans dwell on race because our dwelling-place is a society with a history of heinous forms of legally enforced racial discrimination and residual racism. Although I seldom talked about race during my childhood and teenage years in mostly racially integrated schools and neighborhoods, I thought about it all the time. Race looms large in black thought, even when it is not a topic of conversation. Conversations among blacks of every social and economic class routinely focus on the causes and consequences of racial disparities in the economic, social, or legal spheres touched by their lives. Indeed, many African Americans develop race-consciousness when they are still very young; and many African American intellectuals possess a highly developed, theoretically sophisticated race-consciousness.

Racialized selves

Not everyone has a significantly racialized identity. But I believe most Americans do. "Race", for present purposes, is a generic name for the familiar categories that we in the United States pervasively employ when identifying individuals and groups for varied public and private purposes. We use racial categories for everything from choosing friends and lovers to allocating employment opportunities.

Our conceptions of race are remarkably functional. They establish social boundaries and set behavioral norms, even though they are complex admixtures of color concepts (White, Black, Red, Yellow, and Brown); quasi-scientific divisions (Caucasian, Negroid, and Mongoloid); and bureaucratic groupings for data collection and census-taking (White, Negro or Black, Asian or Pacific Islander, American Indian, Aleut, and Eskimo). Further complicating matters is the fact that conceptions of race blend a miscellany of popular distinctions, some derogatory, reflecting beliefs about national, continental, or linguistic origins (Irish, German, African American, Korean, Hispanic, Chicano, Haitian, Cuban, Puerto Rican, Multiracial, Eurasian); physical characteristics (cracker, chink); and social or citizenship status (WASP, wetback, dago, nigger). Although our conceptions of race are ambiguous, inconsistent, and, as noted, often derogatory, racial identity becomes an element of personal identity over the course of our lives.

Racial self-consciousness (self-awareness of supposed racial inferiority) is a social pathology. Race-consciousness (awareness of the societal significance of one's race) is not. Indeed, some people regard the *absence* of race-consciousness as pathological, contending that for an African American to lose or fail to acquire race-consciousness is to lose or fail to acquire an appropriate identity. Without such an identity, they argue, the ability to flourish in contemporary American society is seriously impaired. A commonly lodged objection to the adoption of black children by whites is that black children reared mainly among whites will fail to acquire race-consciousness and racial identity.

Similar concerns about the loss of racial awareness and identity are voiced about suburban and affluent black teenagers who associate with white rather than black peers; and about black adults who marry whites or members of other racial groups. Out-marriage by black women seems especially likely to raise these concerns, owing, perhaps, to the assumption that husbands dominate their wives. A white husband, it is assumed, will culturally dominate his black wife and mixed-race children, to the detriment of their identities and to the ultimate detriment of black culture.

It has been many years since the time I forgot my race. But against the background of pervasive concerns about the loss of race-consciousness, identity, and culture, it has been hard to forget that I once forgot.

Forgetting race as forgetting yourself

I presented Case 5, involving the black student who forgets that she is black, as illustrative of ordinary literal forgetting. I suggested that a person can forget that she purchased ginger-candy until reminded and, likewise, that she can forget her race until reminded. But I now want to consider the possibility that forgetting race, as in Case 5, is forgetting yourself.

In some respects, Case 5 is like Case 2, the case of the humming vice president who, in the metaphorical sense elaborated above, "forgot herself." In both cases, a friend brings to another's attention a fact of which the latter was not mindful. In Case 2, a vice president is told that she is humming; in Case 5, a university student is told that she is a member of a certain racial group.

To distinguish the cases, one might begin by pointing out that in Case 2 someone is *informed* for the first time of a fact she did not know, whereas in Case 5 someone is *reminded* of a fact she knew but was not alive to at that moment. Yet the vice president is also, in a sense, reminded of something. She is reminded that she and others believe humming in a business meeting is inappropriate.

Another effort to distinguish the cases might center on the argument that Case 2 involves inadvertent violation of a prescriptive norm (i.e., the no-humming rule), whereas Case 5 involves a mistake of fact and no such violation. For this reason, perhaps Case 5 is best characterized as illustrating an ordinary lapse of memory rather than the phenomenon of "forgetting yourself."

Does speaking to another as if you do not believe you are a member of the race of which you are in fact a member violate a normative prescription? To clarify that the university student in Case 5 was violating a behavioral norm, I want now to look at her behavior, not from the standpoint of general morals and mores but from that of the morals and mores of her African American subgroup. From this perspective Jan is potentially culpable of breaching norms against "acting white." Upon first consideration, it might appear that a black person's ability to forget his or her race is a good thing. Isn't the capacity to forget race, after all, a step toward the color-blind society that the United States Supreme Court has pronounced as our collective, constitutional ideal? If forgetting race is "acting white" and many blacks consider "acting white" bad, so much the worse for blacks' values. They are an impediment to the color-blind society!

I want to suggest that Case 5 is no unambiguously hopeful sign that the color-blind society is on its way or even possible. The norm against "acting white" is indeed problematic for its tendency to stereotype African Americans. But by far the larger problem than that of blacks' expectation that other blacks will not "act white" is the pervasive context of racism and inequality that makes continued segregation attractive.

Community norms

Large communities – nations, states, and cities – generate complex behavioral norms applicable to members of the community. These communal norms generally include "universal" norms that prescribe behavioral standards for everyone in the community and "group-specific" norms that prescribe behavioral standards only for individuals belonging to certain groups within the community. Thus some communal norms may apply only to adults, women, the aristocracy, a religious minority, a race, or a segment of a race. Group-specific communal norms commonly privilege some groups (e.g., Christians in the Third Reich; white males in the Antebellum South) and subordinate others (e.g., Jews in the Third Reich; white women, Indians, and blacks in the Antebellum South).

Some of a community's universal and group-specific norms are fundamental. They structure the relationships on which depend the survival of the community and its various social units – groups, subgroups, families, individuals. People seldom neglect the many norms associated with attributes of personal identity that structure paramount social relations, whether or not they accept those norm as valid. The costs of inattention to the norms that structure and sustain social hierarchies of gender and race can be especially high. For this reason, women and people of color tend to be alive to group-specific norms that safeguard their welfare and peace of mind. Before federal civil rights laws were enacted in the 1960s, prudent southern blacks made a point of being very much alive to their manners and morals when dealing with whites.

Yet periodic inattention to social norms relating to race, gender, and other socially key traits does occur. Recall Alice Walker's Sophia, the black woman who swore at the white mayor's wife, breaching the dominant community's social norms. She was cursed, beaten, and thrown into jail. The story of Sophia makes for powerfully dramatic fiction precisely because it depicts an understandable but atypical hot-headed response to oppressive social subordination.

By contrast, the cost of inattention to the non-fundamental group-specific behavioral norms of a community is generally trivial. No one really cares if a woman spits on the sidewalk, even though public spitting, especially by a woman, is socially disapproved behavior. I have heard the words "She thinks she's a boy!" spoken, with more humor than sanction, in reference to a physically active girl old enough to begin to understand society's behavioral expectations for women. In days past, when gentlewomen and girls failed on occasion to follow the rules of behavior expected of "ladies," such as sitting with the knees pressed together and ankles crossed, they were politely described (without further sanction) as having forgotten themselves. Initiating sexual intimacy could also count as "forgetting yourself" when undertaken by a member of the appropriately modest female sex. Frequent breaches of gender-specific sexual norms were once considered exceedingly risky. Reputedly "promiscuous" women hoping to find "respectable" husbands and providers could easily fail.

Group and subgroup norms

A large community imposes behavioral norms on its members, as do groups within such communities. In fact, groups often generate prescriptive norms applicable to their members. Some of these group-generated norms apply universally to all group members, whereas others apply only to specific subgroups. For example, the African American community has generated norms that apply to all African Americans as well as norms that apply only to African Americans of one sex or the other. Indeed, black women were once expected to assume caretaking roles with respect to orphan grandchildren, nieces, and nephews that black men were not expected to assume.

In addition, as a matter of courtesy, African Americans in traditional neighborhoods in the South were expected to "speak" to other African Americans they met in passing (i.e., to acknowledge them with a polite greeting or nod of the head). Yet they were not expected to behave in this way toward members of other groups, nor did they expect members of other groups to behave in that way toward them. A black person preoccupied in thought, who on that occasion failed to speak, might be viewed as having forgotten herself or himself (although "forgetting" oneself is not, to my knowledge, an expression with much currency in black English or among blacks). The indignant query "Don't you speak?" might also be posed to a person who forgot herself, to shame her into conformity. To cite another example of group-specific norms and their breach, a moral standard still applicable in some segments of the African American community discourages black women from having sex with white men. But a black woman can "forget herself" when passion unexpectedly presents itself.

Americans of all hues share core moral values relating, for example, family responsibility, theism, and other important matters. I do not assume that people of different races have altogether different behavioral standards. The African American custom of greeting others, known as "speaking," doubtless applies with minor variations within other groups and in other regions of the country. Yet members of racial groups have (and are held to) at least some culturally specific standards of decorum and decency that are not shared with members of other groups. In this connection, a grave concern of the 1990s is that young blacks warped by the culture of crack are developing uniquely self-destructive, deviant subgroup norms that could undermine the well-being of vast segments of the African American communities.

Acting white

Inattention can lead one to "forget" that one is a professional in a business meeting. Emotion can lead one to "forget" that one is a caregiver for an elderly relation, or a teacher with responsibility for vulnerable teenagers. There is no limit to the kind of norms that can fall prey to inattention and emotion. However, some classes of norms may be especially resistant to breach when compared to others. Any class of well-internalized norms will be resistant to breach. Yet, quite possibly, well-internalized norms seen as binding but trivial (like some rules of etiquette) are breached more readily than those seen as vital (like rules of law).

We are not so much born with race as born into race as a feature of our social worlds. Yet our racialized social worlds exert such an influence that we seldom entirely escape the pull of constitutive norms. Whether generated by the larger community or by racial subgroups, race-related behavioral norms command such a degree of attention and self-control that noncompliance stemming from brief inattention is especially unusual. In the American context, which has been shaped by a history of colonialism, slavery, legal segregation, and prejudice, we may be particularly unlikely to "forget" the subset of manners and morals that shape the expectations and identities of people of our races. Members of minority groups are highly self-conscious about racial identity and the implications of racial identity for routine transactions with others. Indeed, minority-group members feel they are "different," and that difference colors social experience so pervasively that being inattentive to the racial norms that apply to specific individuals is, for some, barely conceivable.

Jan, the university student in Case 5, forgot her race. Do we fault her, as someone who has wrongfully allowed her African American race to slip out of her mind? Has she forgotten herself – specifically, by failing to be attentive to the norms of her racial group? Jan discussed a party with a white friend. Participating in such a discussion was a form of behavior governed both by community norms and by a set of African American group norms applicable to Jan (like it or not) by virtue of her race.

Among many African Americans, communicating with whites is governed by a whole set of race-specific rules of engagement. Certain affects, topics, and aspects of vocabulary and body language are taboo. One rule dictates against "airing dirty linen" – that is, publicly criticizing other blacks. Another rule dictates against allowing frequent association with white people to cause one to "act white." Jan's behavior – namely, the fact that she thinks and speaks like a white liberal – violates African American social norms against acting white. And behind the norm against thinking and speaking "white" is the notion that to be as psychologically healthy, authentic, and useful as one ought to be, one is obligated to be race-conscious. One is obligated to be alive to being black.

The people condemned most severely for "acting white" are the blacks who are race-conscious but deliberately choose to act white. Acting white means dressing in certain clothes, attending certain events, living in certain neighborhoods, befriending certain people, and so on. Arm-chair psychology suggests that these individuals might act white because they are victims of racial self-awareness searching for self-esteem. Some blacks voice contempt both for light-skinned blacks who "pass" for white and for highly successful blacks who adopt conservative "white" ideologies, such as Supreme Court Justice Clarence Thomas. But fears about losing blacks who "act white" to white society are by no means solely connected either with passing as white or with political conservatism. On the contrary. Parents who value race-consciousness worry about sending their black children to white-dominated public and private schools. Teenagers who value race-consciousness worry about "interracial" dating. And policymakers who value race-consciousness in high culture and politics worry about the survival of historically black colleges, art forms, and civil rights organizations.

Moreover, some people who "act white" are viewed with empathy and concern rather than with contempt. The phenomenon of acting white is a by-product of the civil rights movement. In the present era of integration and affirmative action, which began in the mid-1960s, many blacks have existed in isolation from other blacks, in white-dominated neighborhoods, schools, and workplaces. Many middle-class and affluent young blacks are not thoroughly socialized as blacks. Marked isolation from majority-black communities has permitted some blacks to shed, or even fail to develop, a black identity, racial self-awareness, or race-consciousness. These young blacks act white because they are, in a sense, culturally white.

To know whether Jan's episode of acting white in Case 5 merits contempt or compassion relative to the values and concerns of African Americans, we would have to know more about her. If she is full of self-hate and deliberately acts white to win white approval, she might deserve some of the contempt that would inevitably be heaped upon her by many of her black peers around the nation. But if Jan does not normally "act white" and her doing so on this occasion was inadvertent, her breach of the African American moral rule against acting white could be interpreted with compassion as an excusable instance of "forgetting yourself." Rather than participating in the discussion with her white friend in a way that was mindful of the black person she knows she is, Jan participated (at least for a moment) as if she were white – as if she were a white person of the sort who befriends blacks and cares about their comfort.

Whether Jan forgot her racial identity in the literal or metaphorical sense, her example is troubling. An educated adult black should be race-conscious and, hence, incapable of making an assertion that logically entails that she is white. A lapse like Jan's – and mine – is probably the result of having so closely and frequently associated with whites that one begins unwittingly to imitate the habits of mind and speech of white society, many of which entail that the thinking and speaking subject is white. For six years – all of my four years of college and two of the four years I spent as a graduate student in philosophy – I had little intimate contact with blacks and a great deal of intimate contact with whites. After all, it was the decade of the 1970s, the heyday of affirmative action, and I was bestowed with educational opportunity by elite white institutions. Given the liberal ideal of a color-blind society, it might have been a good thing that I forgot my race, had I not *remembered everyone else's*. Whatever vision of race relations one holds dear – segregationism, nationalism, integrationism, or multiculturalism – one cannot be sanguine about cultural forms that lead people to maintain a racial perspective, yet mistake their own race and its significance.

Alive to our selves

The expression "forgetting yourself" is decidedly old-fashioned. However, the polite concept for which it stands is far from irrelevant to contemporary concerns. As I have shown, the idea of "forgetting oneself" bears an interesting relationship to concerns about group alienation and racial identity.

Overall, the United States is remarkably segregated by race. This is the context in which the group norms against acting white and forgetting race have emerged. Despite a constitutional jurisprudence that nominally promotes a "color-blind" society, most people seem to prefer single-race neighborhoods, schools, churches, and workplaces. At the same time, a special peril of displacement and disapproval flows to members of certain minority racial groups guilty of being dead to their own races.

Yet blacks and other minorities fearing political, economic, and cultural exclusion are not the only ones motivated to remain alive to race. Just about everyone is. Whites are motivated by the fear that inattention could threaten not only their personal safety but also their educational and cultural institutions. I am very drawn to the ideal of a society in which people of differing races enjoy cultural pride but have moved beyond racism, xenophobia, and turf wars (Allen 1996). Yet it is by no means clear as to how this move is to be made, particularly at a time when racial self-consciousness and race-consciousness are so deeply embedded in our behavior and values. The choice facing African Americans today, then, is whether to think about race as black persons or as white persons, rather than not to think about race at all.

African Americans rigidly adhere to race-specific norms (even trivial formalities) *internal* to their racial communities as a means of sustaining communal bases of self-esteem in a seemingly hostile nation. And they rigidly adhere to race-specific norms *external* to their racial communities to avoid conflicts with members of other groups. These behaviors, along with continued racism, xenophobia, and discrimination, have proven to be powerful barriers to meaningful racial integration in the United States.

So many of the public policies debated today – everything from family values, to women's rights, to gay rights, to rights for the disabled, to welfare, to racial justice, to religious and political expression – ultimately relate to the matter of defining selves in opposition to and in light of community and group values. No one wants to be forced out of communion with who and what they believe they really are. Yet with all the current focus on community, social ethics, and personal responsibility, people are more concerned than ever about the downside risks of failing to conform to reasonable social expectations. It seems that everyone wants to be themselves, but no one wants to be without some group basis for sustaining identity and moral self-esteem. Successful navigation of the world thus requires all the attentiveness and emotional control one can muster.

References

Allen, Anita L. 1996. "The Half-Life of Integration." In Stephen Macedo, ed., *Re-Assessing the Sixties*. New York: W. W. Norton.

Benhabib, Seyla. 1992. *Situating the Self: Gender, Community and Postmodernism in Contemporary Ethics* (New York: Routledge).

Cassam, Quassim, ed., 1994. *Self-Knowledge* (Oxford: Oxford University Press).

Chisholm, Roderick. 1994. "On the Observability of the Self." In Quassim Cassam, ed., *Self-Knowledge* (Oxford: Oxford University Press), pp. 94–108.

Erwin, Edward. 1988. "Psychoanalysis and Self-Deception." In Brian McLaughlin and Amelie Okenberg Rorty, eds., *Perspectives on Self-Deception* (Berkeley: University of California Press).

Johnston, Mark. 1988. "Self-Deception and the Nature of Mind." In Brian McLaughlin and Amelie Okenberg Rorty, eds., *Perspectives on Self-Deception* (Berkeley: University of California Press).

McLaughlin, Brian, and Rorty, Amelie Okenberg, eds. 1988. *Perspectives on Self-Deception* (Berkeley: University of California Press).

Piper, Adrian. 1988. "Pseudorationality." In Brian McLaughlin and Amelie Okenberg Rorty, eds., *Perspectives on Self-Deception* (Berkeley: University of California Press).

——. 1985. "Two Conceptions of the Self," *Philosophical Studies* 48: 173–97.

Proust, Marcel. 1961. *Remembrance of Things Past*, trans. C. K. Scott Moncrieff (New York: Random House).

Rey, Georges. 1988. "Toward a Computational Account of *Akrasia* and Self-Deception." In Brian McLaughlin and Amelie Okenberg Rorty, eds., *Perspectives on Self-Deception* (Berkeley: University of California Press).

Rorty, Amelie. 1988. "The Deceptive Self: Liars, Layers, and Lairs." In Brian McLaughlin and Amelie Okenberg Rorty, eds., *Perspectives on Self Deception* (Berkeley: University of California Press).

Ryle, Gilbert. 1994. "Self-Knowledge." In Quassim Cassim, ed., *Self-Knowledge* (Oxford: Oxford University Press), pp. 19–42.

26

Outliving Oneself

Susan Brison

> I died in Auschwitz, but no one knows it.
>
> ***Charlotte Delbo***[1]

Survivors of trauma frequently remark that they are not the same people they were before they were traumatized. As a survivor of the Nazi death camps observes, "One can be alive after Sobibor without having survived Sobibor."[2] Jonathan Shay, a therapist who works with Vietnam veterans, has often heard his patients say, "I died in Vietnam."[3] Migael Scherer expresses a loss commonly experienced by rape survivors when she writes, "I will always miss myself as I was."[4] What are we to make of these cryptic comments?[5] How can one miss oneself? How can one die in Vietnam or fail to survive a death camp and still live to tell one's story? How does a life-threatening event come to be experienced as self-annihilating? And what self is it who remembers having had this experience?

How one answers these questions depends on, among other things, how one defines "trauma" and "the self." In this chapter, I discuss the nature of trauma, show how it affects the self, construed in several ultimately interconnected ways, and then use this analysis to elaborate and support a feminist account of the relational self.[6] On this view the self is both autonomous and socially dependent, vulnerable enough to be undone by violence and yet resilient enough to be reconstructed with the help of empathic others.

My methodology differs from that used in traditional philosophizing about the self, and yields distinctly different results. Philosophers writing about the self have, at least since Locke, puzzled over such questions as whether persons can survive the loss or exchange of their minds, brains, consciousness, memories, characters, and/or bodies.[7] In recent years, increasingly gruesome and high-tech thought experiments involving fusion, fission, freezing, dissolution, reconstitution, and/or teletransportation of an individual have been devised to test our intuitions about who, if anyone, survives which permutations.[8] Given philosophers' preoccupation with personal identity in extreme, life-threatening, and possibly self-annihilating situations, it is odd that they have neglected to consider the accounts of actual trauma victims who report that they are not the same people they were prior to their traumatic transformations.[9] This over-sight may result from the fact that imaginary scenarios, however far-fetched,

Susan Brison, "Outliving Oneself," pp. 38–50, 53–5, 57–66 and 133–8 from *Aftermath: Violence and the Remaking of the Self.* Princeton, NJ: Princeton University Press, 2002.

are at least *conceivable*, whereas the experiences of rape victims, Holocaust survivors, and war veterans are, for most of us, unthinkable. In addition, philosophers are trained to divert their gaze from the messy real world to the neater, more controllable, and more comprehensible realm of pure thought.

As I discussed in the previous chapter, however, feminist theorists writing in the areas of ethics and social, political, and legal philosophy have recently argued for the necessity of focusing on the actual experiences of real people and have made use of first- and third-person narratives in their attempts to do this.[10] Feminist theorists have also stressed the importance of taking context into account, recognizing that we all reason from a "positioned perspective" and that some of us, with "multiple consciousness," reason from a variety of sometimes incompatible perspectives.[11] In addition, feminist theorists have adopted interdisciplinary approaches to subjects, such as personal identity, previously thought to be the exclusive domain of one discipline. I use these feminist methodologies here, incorporating survivor testimonies, situating philosophical questions of the self in the context of actual individuals' lives, acknowledging my own perspective as a survivor, and drawing on the clinical literature on trauma.

Trauma and the Undoing of the Self

There is a much clearer professional consensus among psychologists about what counts as a traumatic event than there is among philosophers concerning the nature of the self.[12] A traumatic event is one in which a person feels utterly helpless in the face of a force that is perceived to be life-threatening.[13] The immediate psychological responses to such trauma include terror, loss of control, and intense fear of annihilation. Long-term effects include the physiological responses of hypervigilance, heightened startle response, sleep disorders, and the more psychological, yet still involuntary, responses of depression, inability to concentrate, lack of interest in activities that used to give life meaning, and a sense of a foreshortened future. A commonly accepted explanation of these symptoms of post-traumatic stress disorder (PTSD) is that, in trauma, the ordinarily adaptive human responses to danger that prepare the body to fight or flee are of no avail. "When neither resistance nor escape is possible," Judith Herman explains, "the human system of self-defense becomes over-whelmed and disorganized. Each component of the ordinary response to danger, having lost its utility, tends to persist in an altered and exaggerated state long after the actual danger is over" (Herman 1992, 34). When the trauma is of human origin and is intentionally inflicted, it not only shatters one's fundamental assumptions about the world and one's safety in it, but it also severs the sustaining connection between the self and the rest of humanity. Victims of human-inflicted trauma are reduced to mere objects by their tormenters: their subjectivity is rendered useless and viewed as worthless. As Herman observes, "The traumatic event thus destroys the belief that one can *be oneself* in relation to others" (Herman 1992, 53). Without this belief, I argue, one can no longer *be oneself* even to oneself, since the self exists fundamentally in relation to others.

How one defines "self" depends in part on what explanatory work one wants the concept of a self to do. Philosophers have invoked this concept in various areas of the discipline in order to account for a wide range of phenomena. The self is, in metaphysics, whatever it is whose persistence accounts for personal identity over time. One metaphysical view of the self holds that it is bodily continuity that accounts for personal identity and the other, that it is continuity of memory, character traits, or other psychological characteristics that makes someone the same person over time. There is also the view, held by poststructuralists, that the self is a narrative, which, properly construed, is a version of the view that psychological continuity constitutes personal identity.[14] In ethics the self is viewed as the locus of autonomous, agency and responsibility and, hence, is the subject of praise or blame. Most traditional accounts of the self, from Descartes' to contemporary theorists', have been individualistic, based on the assumption that one can individuate selves and determine the criteria for their identity over time independent of the social context in which they are situated. In contrast, feminist accounts of the self have focused on the ways in which the self is formed in relation to others and sustained in a social context. On these accounts persons are, in Annette Baier's words, "second persons," that is, "essentially successors, heirs to other persons who formed and cared for them."[15] In addition, the self is viewed as related to and constructed by others in an ongoing way, not only because others continue to shape and define us throughout our lifetimes, but also because our own sense of self is couched in descriptions whose meanings are social phenomena (Scheman 1983).

In what follows, I argue that the study of trauma reveals that the accounts of the embodied self, the self as narrative, and the autonomous self are compatible and complementary, focusing on different aspects of the self. I also argue that the study of trauma provides additional support for the view that each of these aspects of the self is fundamentally relational.

The Embodied Self

Although we recognize other persons most readily by their perceptible, that is, bodily, attributes, philosophers have been loath to identify the self with a body for a host of reasons.[16] A dead body cannot be said to be anyone's self, nor can a living, but permanently comatose, one. We do not typically use a bodily criterion of identity to determine who we ourselves are, and most of us, when imagining Locke's prince, whose soul "enters and informs" the body of a cobbler, would suppose the resulting person to be the prince (Locke 1974, 216). Some philosophers[17] have been concerned to show that the self can survive the death of the body, but perhaps the primary reason philosophers have not identified the self with the body is an ancient bias against our physical nature.[18] Plato praised philosophers for "despising the body and avoiding it," and urged that "[i]f we are ever to have pure knowledge of anything, we must get rid of the body and contemplate things by themselves with the soul by itself."[19] This rejection of the body has been most apparent in the disparaging of the female body, which has been presented as the antithesis to reason. Although, as Sara Ruddick notes, "[t]here is nothing intrinsically masculine about mind and objectivity or anything feminine about passion and physicality,... philosophers have tended to associate, explicitly or metaphorically, passion, affection, and the body with femininity and the mind with masculinity" (1989, 194). How some bodies came to be viewed as "more bodily" than others is a puzzle that Ruddick answers by arguing that the lack of intellectual control over menstruation, pregnancy, labor, and nursing set such female bodily functions against reason, which was viewed as detached, controlled, and impersonal – that is, masculine.

Even Simone de Beauvoir, while arguing that "one is not born, but rather becomes, a woman" (1953, 301), views childbirth and nursing as completely passive, and thus dehumanizing, processes, which keep women mired in immanence. She suggests that "it is not in giving life but in risking life that man is raised above the animal; that is why superiority has been accorded in humanity not to the sex that brings forth but to that which kills" (1953, 72). Although Beauvoir rejects the conclusion that this sex difference justifies male dominance, she nonetheless accepts the premise reducing childbirth to a purely "animal" function.[20]

Beauvoir was the first female philosopher I read and, as a teenager, I shared her disdain for (socially) compulsory marriage and maternity for women in this society. I still share her concerns about constraints on women's reproductive freedom, but I reject her view of pregnancy and motherhood as necessarily passive and tedious processes, even when voluntary. The work of Ruddick and other feminists, who have been redefining motherhood has led me to see the liberatory potential in *chosen* maternity, childbirth, and childrearing. Reading Ruddick's *Maternal Thinking* in 1989, I recognized the ways in which my philosophical training had exacerbated my preexisting tendency to value the cerebral over the corporeal. In pursuing the life of the mind, I had accepted unthinkingly (because unconsciously) its incompatibility with the life of the (gestating and birthing) female body. My reading of Ruddick happened to coincide with a visit to a gynecologist who told me that I might have difficulty conceiving and that if I even suspected I would want to have a child someday I should start trying now.

...My husband (who never felt as compelled to make such a choice) and I started trying to conceive, or, rather, as a friend put it more aptly, stopped trying not to. It was just six months later, however, that I was jumped from behind, beaten, raped, strangled, and left for dead in a ravine. The pleasures of embodiment were suddenly replaced by the pain and terror to which being embodied makes one prey.

I was no longer the same person I had been before the assault, and one of the ways in which I seemed changed was that I had a different relationship with my body. My body was now perceived as an enemy, having betrayed my newfound trust and interest in it, and as a site of increased vulnerability. But rejecting the body and returning to the life of the mind was not an option, since body and mind had become nearly indistinguishable. My mental state (typically, depression) felt physiological, like lead in my veins, while my physical state (frequently, incapacitation by fear and anxiety) was the incarnation of a cognitive and emotional paralysis resulting from shattered assumptions about my safety in the world. The symptoms of PTSD gave the lie to a latent dualism that still informs society's most prevalent attitude to trauma, namely, that victims should buck up, put the past behind them, and get on with their lives. My hypervigilance, heightened startle response, insomnia, and other PTSD symptoms were no more psychological, if that is taken to mean under my conscious control, than were my heartrate and blood pressure.[21]

The intermingling of mind and body is also apparent in traumatic memories that remain in the body, in each of the senses, in the heart that races and skin that crawls whenever something resurrects the only slightly buried terror. As Jonathan Shay writes in his study of combat trauma, "Traumatic memory is not narrative. Rather, it is experience that reoccurs, either as full sensory replay of traumatic events in dreams or flashbacks, with all things seen, heard, smelled, and felt intact, or as disconnected fragments. These fragments may be inexplicable rage, terror, uncontrollable crying, or disconnected body states and sensations" (1994, 172). The main change in the modality as well as in the content of the most salient traumatic memories is that they are more tied to the body than memories are typically considered to be.

...Traumatic flashbacks immobilize the body by rendering the will as useless as it is in a nightmare in which one desperately tries to flee, but remains frozen.

The bodily nature of traumatic memory complicates a standard philosophical quandary concerning which of two criteria of identity – continuous body or continuous memories – should be used to determine personal identity over time. Locke's bodily transfer puzzle in which we are asked to decide who survives "should the soul of a prince... enter and inform the body of a cobbler" (1974, 116) no longer presents us with an either/or choice, depending on which criterion we invoke. If memories are lodged in the body, the Lockean distinction between the memory criterion and that of bodily identity no longer applies.[22]

The study of trauma also replaces the traditional philosophical puzzle about whether the soul can survive the death of the body with the question of whether the self can reconstitute itself after obliteration at the hands of another, after what Cathy Winkler has labeled "social murder" (1991). Winkler describes the way in which, during a rape, the victim is defined out of existence by the attitudes and actions of the rapist, which incapacitate the victim's self. "Without our abilities to think and feel as we choose... our existence becomes like a body on life support," Winkler writes. "During an attack, victims have confronted social death, and grappled with it to save themselves" (1991, 14). The victim's inability to be – and to assert – her self in the context of a rape constitutes at least a temporary social death, one from which a self can be resurrected only with great difficulty and with the help of others.

In the aftermath of trauma, not only is the victim's bodily awareness changed,[23] but she may also attempt to change her body itself in an effort to enhance her control over it. Eating disorders are a common reaction to sexual abuse, as is dressing in ways that disguise one's body. After my own assault, I wished I could add eyes in the back of my head, but I settled for cutting my hair so short that, when viewed from behind, I might be mistaken for a man.

The study of trauma does not lead to the conclusion that the self can be identified with the body, but it does show how the body and one's perception of it are nonetheless essential components of the self. It also reveals the ways in which one's ability to feel at home in the world is as much a physical as an epistemological accomplishment. Jean Améry writes, of the person who is tortured, that from the moment of the first blow he loses "trust in the world," which includes "the irrational and logically unjustifiable belief in absolute causality perhaps, or the likewise blind belief in the validity of the inductive inference." More important, according to Améry, is the loss of the certainty that other persons "will respect my physical, and with it also my metaphysical, being. The boundaries of my body are also the boundaries of my self. My skin surface shields me against the external world. If I am to have trust, I must feel on it only what I *want* to feel. At the first blow, however, this trust in the world breaks down" (1995, 126). Améry goes on to compare torture to rape, an apt comparison, not only because both objectify and traumatize the victim, but also because the pain they inflict reduces the victim to flesh, to the purely physical. This reduction has a particularly anguished quality for female victims of sexual violence who are already viewed as more tied to nature than men and are sometimes treated as mere flesh.[24] It is as if the tormentor says with his blows, "You are nothing but a body, a mere object for my will – here, I'll prove it!"

Those who endure long periods of repeated torture often find ways of dissociating themselves from their bodies, that part of themselves which undergoes the torture. As the research of Herman (1992) and Terr (1994) has shown, child victims of sexual and other physical abuse often utilize this defense against annihilation of the self, and, in extreme cases, even develop multiple personalities that enable one or more "selves" to emerge unscathed from the abuse. Some adult victims of rape report a kind of splitting from their bodies during the assault, as well as a separation from their former selves in the aftermath of the rape.

[...]

What can we conclude from these clinical studies and personal narratives of trauma concerning the relationship of one's self to one's body? Does trauma make one feel more or less tied to one's body? That may depend on one's ability to dissociate. Since I, like most victims of one-time traumatic events, did not dissociate during the assault, I felt (and continue to feel) more tied to my body than before, or, at any rate, more vulnerable to self-annihilation because of it.[25] Those who survived ongoing trauma by dissociating from their bodies may feel that an essential part of themselves was untouched by the trauma, but even they experience, in the aftermath, the physical intrusions of visceral traumatic memories.

These various responses to trauma – dissociation from one's body, separation from the self one was either before or during the trauma – have in common the attempt to distance one's (real) self from the bodily self that is being degraded, and whose survival demands that one do, or at any rate be subjected to, degrading things. But such an attempt is never wholly successful and the survivor's bodily sense of self is permanently altered by an encounter with death that leaves one feeling "marked" for life. The intense awareness of embodiment experienced by trauma survivors is not "the willing or grateful surrender of 'I' to flesh" described by Walker, but more akin to the pain of Kafka's "harrow," cutting the condemned man's "sentence" deeper and deeper into his body until it destroys him.[26]

The Self as Narrative

Locke famously identified the self with a set of continuous memories, a kind of ongoing narrative of one's past that is extended with each new experience (1974). The study of trauma presents a fatal challenge to this view, since memory is so drastically disrupted by traumatic events, unless one is prepared to accept the conclusion that survivors of such events are distinct from their former selves. The literature on trauma does seem to support the view, advocated by Derek Parfit (1986), that the unitary self is an illusion and that we are all composed of a series of successive selves.[27] But how does one remake a self from the scattered shards of disrupted memory? Charlotte Delbo writes of memories being stripped away from the inmates of the death camps, and of the incomprehensibly difficult task of getting them back after the war: "The survivor must undertake to regain his memory, regain what he possessed before: his knowledge, his experience, his childhood memories, his manual dexterity and his intellectual faculties, sensitivity, the capacity to dream, imagine, laugh" (1995, 255).

This passage illustrates a major obstacle to the trauma survivor's reconstructing a self in the sense of a remembered and ongoing narrative about oneself. Not only are one's memories of an earlier life lost, along with the ability to envision a future, but one's basic cognitive and emotional capacities are gone, or radically altered, as well. This epistemological crisis leaves the survivor with virtually no bearings to navigate by. As Améry writes, "Whoever has succumbed to torture can no longer feel at home in the world" (1995, 136). Shattered assumptions about the world and one's safety in it can, to some extent, eventually be pieced back together, but this is a slow and painful process. Although the survivor recognizes, at some level, that these regained assumptions are illusory, she learns that they are necessary illusions, as unshakable, ultimately, as cognitively impenetrable perceptual illusions.[28]

In addition, though, trauma can obliterate one's former emotional repertoire, leaving only a kind of counterfactual, propositional knowledge of emotions. When alerted to the rumors that the camp in which he was incarcerated would be evacuated the next day, Primo Levi felt no emotion, just as for many months he had "no longer felt any pain, joy or fear" except in a conditional manner: "if I still had my former sensitivity, I thought, this would be an extremely moving moment" (1993, 152–3). The inability to feel one's former emotions, even in the aftermath of trauma, leaves the survivor not only numbed, but also without the motivation to carry out the task of constructing an ongoing narrative. [...]

By constructing and telling a narrative of the trauma endured, and with the help of understanding listeners, the survivor begins not only to integrate the traumatic episode into a life with a before and an after, but also to gain control over the occurrence of intrusive memories. When I was hospitalized after my assault I experienced moments of reprieve from vivid and terrifying flashbacks when giving my account of what had happened – to the police, doctors, a psychiatrist, a lawyer, and a prosecutor. Although others apologized for putting me through what seemed to them a retraumatizing ordeal, I responded that it was, even at that early stage, therapeutic to bear witness in the presence of others who heard and believed what I told them. Two and a half years later, when my assailant was brought to trial, I found it healing to give my testimony in public and to have it confirmed by the police, the prosecutor, my lawyer, and, ultimately, the jury, who found my assailant guilty of rape and attempted murder.[29]

How might we account for this process of "mastering the trauma" through repeated telling of one's story? The residue of trauma is a kind of body memory, as Roberta Culbertson notes, "full of fleeting images, the percussion of blows, sounds, and movements of the body – disconnected, cacophonous, the cells suffused with the active power of adrenalin, or coated with the anesthetizing numbness of noradrenalin" (1995, 174). Whereas traumatic memories (especially perceptual and emotional flashbacks) feel as though they are passively endured, narratives are the result of certain obvious choices (e.g., how much to tell to whom, in what order, etc.). This is not to say that the narrator is not subject to the constraints of memory or that the story will ring true however it is told. And the telling itself may be out of control, compulsively repeated. But one can control certain aspects of the narrative and that control, repeatedly exercised, leads to greater control over the memories themselves, making them less intrusive and giving them the kind of meaning that enables them to be integrated into the rest of life.

Not only present listeners, but also one's cultural heritage, can determine to a large extent the way in which an event is remembered are retold, and may even lead one to respond as though one remembered what one did not in fact experience.[30] Yael Tamir, an Israeli philosopher, told me a story illustrating cultural memory, in which she and her husband, neither of whom had been victims or had family members who had been victims of the Holocaust, literally jumped at the sound of a German voice shouting instructions at a train station in Switzerland. The experience triggered such vivid "memories" of the deportation that they grabbed their suitcases and fled the station. [...] The influence of cultural memory on all of us is additional evidence of the deeply relational nature of the narrative self.

The relational nature of the self is also revealed by a further obstacle confronting trauma survivors attempting to reconstruct coherent narratives: the difficulty of regaining one's voice, one's subjectivity, after one has been reduced to silence, to the status of an object, or, worse, made into someone else's speech, an instrument of another's agency. Those entering Nazi concentration camps had the speech of their captors literally inscribed on their bodies. As Levi describes it, the message conveyed by the prisoners' tattoos was "You no longer have a name; this is your new name." It was "a non-verbal message, so that the innocent would feel his sentence written on his flesh" (1989, 119).[31] [...]

As a society, we live with the unbearable by pressuring those who have been traumatized to forget and by rejecting the testimonies of those who are forced by fate to remember. As individuals and as cultures, we impose arbitrary term limits on memory and on recovery from trauma: a century, say, for slavery, fifty years, perhaps, for the Holocaust, a decade or two for Vietnam, several months for mass rape or serial murder. Even a public memorialization can be a forgetting, a way of saying to survivors what someone said after I published my first article on sexual violence: "Now you can put this behind you." But attempting to limit traumatic memories does not make them go away; the signs and symptoms of trauma remain, caused by a source more virulent for being driven underground. [...]

To recover from trauma, according to psychoanalyst Dori Laub, a survivor needs to construct a narrative and tell it to an empathic listener, in order to reexternalize the event. "Bearing witness to a trauma is, in fact, a process that includes the listener" (1992, 70). And to the extent that bearing witness reestablishes the survivor's identity, the empathic other is essential to the continuation of a self. Laub writes of Chaim Guri's film, *The Eighty-First Blow*, which "portrays the image of a man who narrates the story of his sufferings in the camps only to hear his audience say: 'All this cannot be true, it could not have happened. You must have made it up.' This denial by the listener inflicts, according to the film, the ultimately fateful blow, beyond the eighty blows that man, in Jewish tradition, can sustain and survive" (1992, 68).

The Autonomous Self

The view of the self most central to ethics, as well as to social, political, and legal philosophy (at least in the analytic tradition), is one that holds that the self is the locus of autonomous agency, that which freely makes choices and wills actions. This is a self that is considered responsible for its decisions and actions and is an appropriate subject of praise or blame. It is the transformation of the self as autonomous agent that is perhaps most apparent in survivors of trauma. First, the autonomy-undermining symptoms of PTSD reconfigure the survivor's will, rendering involuntary many responses that were once under voluntary control. Intrusive memories are triggered by things reminiscent of the traumatic event and carry a strong, sometimes over-whelming, emotional charge. Not only is one's response to items that would startle anyone heightened, but one has an involuntary startle response to things that formerly provoked no reaction or a subtler, still voluntary one. The loss of control evidenced by these and other PTSD symptoms alters who one is, not only in that it limits what one can do (and can refrain from doing), but also in that it changes what one *wants* to do.

A trauma survivor suffers a loss of control not only over herself, but also over her environment, and this, in turn, can lead to a constriction of the boundaries of her will. If a rape victim is unable to walk outside without the fear of being assaulted again, she quickly loses the desire to go for a walk. If one's self, or one's *true* self, is considered to be identical with one's will, then a survivor cannot be considered to be the same as her pre-trauma self, since what she is able to will post-trauma is so drastically altered. Some reactions that once were under the will's command become involuntary and some desires that once were motivating can no longer be felt, let alone acted upon.

Such loss of control over oneself can explain, to a large extent, what a survivor means in saying, "I am no longer myself." The trauma survivor identifies with her former self not only because that self was more familiar and less damaged, but also because it was more predictable. The fact that, as has been recently discovered, certain drugs, such as Prozac, give PTSD sufferers greater self-control, by making them better able to choose their reactions to things and the timing of their responses, accounts for the common response to such drugs: "they make me more myself" (Kramer 1993). It may also be that after taking Prozac such a person is better able to endorse, or identify with, her new self.[32]

In order to recover, a trauma survivor needs to be able to control herself, control her environment (within reasonable limits), and be reconnected with humanity. Whether the latter two achievements occur depends, to a large extent, on other people. Living with the memory of trauma is living with a kind of disability, and whether one is able to function with a disability depends largely on how one's social and physical environments are set up (Minow 1990). A trauma survivor makes accommodations, figuring out how to live with her limits, but she also realizes that at least some externally imposed limits can be changed. In the year after my assault, when I was terrified to walk alone, I was able to go to talks and other events on campus by having a friend walk with me. I became able to use the locker room in the gym after getting the university to put a lock on a door that led to a dark, isolated passageway, and I was able to park my car at night after lobbying the university to put a light in the parking lot.

These ways of enhancing my autonomy in the aftermath of my assault reinforced my view of autonomy as fundamentally dependent on others. Not only is autonomy compatible with socialization and with caring for and being cared for by others (Meyers 1987, 1989, 1992), but the right sort of interactions with others can be seen to be essential to autonomy. In "Jurisprudence and Gender," Robin West (1988) discusses the tension within feminist theory between, on the one hand, the desire for connection and fear of alienation (in cultural feminism)[33] and, on the other hand, the desire for autonomy and fear of invasion (in radical or "dominance" feminism).[34] Once one acknowledges the relational nature of autonomy, however, this apparent tension can be resolved by noting that the main reason all of us, especially women, have to fear violent intrusions by others is that they severely impair our ability to be connected to humanity in ways we value. It is this loss of connection that trauma survivors mourn, a loss that in turn imperils autonomous selfhood. In order to reestablish that connection in the aftermath of trauma, one must first feel able to protect oneself against invasion. The autonomous self and the relational self are thus shown to be interdependent, even constitutive of one another.

Virginia Held defends a relational account of autonomy in which autonomy does not consist of putting walls around oneself or one's property (as in Isaiah Berlin's phrase for autonomy, "the inner citadel"),[35] but instead, of forming essential relationships with others. Held cites Jennifer Nedelsky, who suggests that "the most promising model, symbol, or metaphor for autonomy is not property, but childrearing. There we have encapsulated the emergence of autonomy through relationship with others.... Interdependence [is] a constant component of autonomy" (Nedelsky 1989, 11).

Trauma survivors are dependent on empathic others who are willing to listen to their narratives. Given that the language in which such narratives are conveyed and are understood is itself a social phenomenon, this aspect of recovery from trauma also underscores the extent to which autonomy is a fundamentally relational notion.[36] [...]

It is not sufficient for mastering the trauma to construct a narrative of it: one must (physically, publicly) say or write (or paint or film) the narrative and others must see or hear it in order for one's survival as an autonomous self to be complete. This reveals the extent to which the self is created and sustained by others and, thus, is able to be destroyed by them. The boundaries of the will are limited, or enlarged, not only by the stories others tell, but also by the extent of their ability and willingness to listen to ours.

In the traditional philosophical literature on personal identity, one is considered to be the same person over time if one can (now) identify with that person in the past or future. One typically identifies with a person in the past if one can remember having that person's experiences and one identifies with a person in the future if one cares in a unique way about that person's future experiences. An interesting result of group therapy with trauma survivors is that they come to have greater compassion for their earlier selves by empathizing with others who experienced similar traumas. They stop blaming themselves by realizing that others who acted or reacted similarly are not blameworthy. Rape survivors, who typically have difficulty getting angry with their assailants, find that in group therapy they are able to get angry on their own behalf by first getting angry on behalf of others (Koss and Harvey 1991).

That survivors gain the ability to reconnect with their former selves by empathizing with others who have experienced similar traumas reveals the extent to which we exist only in connection with others. It also suggests that healing from trauma takes place by a kind of splitting off of the traumatized self which one then is able to empathize with, just as one empathizes with others.[37] The loss of a trauma survivor's former self is typically described by analogy to the loss of a beloved other. And yet, in grieving for another, one often says, "It's as though a part of myself has died." It is not clear whether this circular comparison is a case of language failing us or, on the contrary, its revealing a deep truth about selfhood and connectedness. By finding (some aspects of) one's lost self in another person, one can manage (to a greater or lesser degree) to reconnect with it and to reintegrate one's various selves into a coherent personality.

The fundamentally relational character of the self is also highlighted by the dependence of survivors on others' attitudes toward them in the aftermath of trauma. Victims of rape and other forms of torture often report drastically altered senses of self-worth, resulting from their degrading treatment. That even one person – one's assailant – treated one as worthless can, at least temporarily, undo an entire lifetime of self-esteem (see Roberts 1989, 91). This effect is magnified by prolonged exposure to degradation, in a social and historical context in which the group to which one belongs is despised. Survivors of trauma recover to a greater or lesser extent depending on others' responses to them after the trauma. These aspects of trauma and recovery reveal the deeply social nature of one's sense of self and underscore the limits of the individual's capacity to control her own self-definition.

But what can others do to help a survivor recover from trauma, apart from listening empathically? Kenneth Seeskin argues, in discussing an appropriate response to the Holo-caust, that we who did not experience it cannot hope to understand it and yet to remain silent in the aftermath of it would be immoral. And so, he suggests, we should move beyond theory, beyond an attempt to understand it, to a practice of resistance. As Emil Fackenheim writes, "The truth is that to grasp the Holocaust whole-of-horror is not to comprehend or transcend it, but rather *to say no to it, or resist it*."[38] The "no" of resistance is not the "no" of denial. It is the "no" of acknowledgment of what happened and refusal to let it happen again.

Remaking Oneself

> A child gave me a flower
> one morning
> a flower picked
> for me
> he kissed the flower
> before giving it to me. . . .
> There is no wound that will not heal
> I told myself that day
> and still repeat it from time to time
> but not enough to believe it.
>
> **Charlotte Delbo (1995, 241)**

What is the goal of the survivor? Ultimately, it is not to transcend the trauma, not to solve the dilemmas of survival, but simply to endure. This can be hard enough, when the only way to regain control over one's life seems to be to end it. A few months after my assault, I drove by myself for several hours to visit a friend. Although driving felt like a much safer mode of transportation than walking, I worried throughout the journey, not only about the trajectory of every oncoming vehicle, but also about my car breaking down, leaving me at the mercy of potentially murderous passers-by. I wished I'd had a gun so that I could shoot myself rather than be forced to live through another assault.[39] Later in my recovery, as depression gave way to rage, such suicidal thoughts were quickly quelled by a stubborn refusal to finish my assailant's job for him. I also learned, after martial arts training, that I was capable, morally as well as physically, of killing in self-defense – an option that made the possibility of another life-threatening attack one I could live with. Some rape survivors have remarked on the sense of moral loss they experienced when they realized that they could kill their assailants (and even wanted to!) but I think that this thought can be seen as a salutary character change in those whom society does not encourage to value their own lives enough.[40] And, far from jeopardizing their connections with a community, this newfound ability to defend themselves, and to consider themselves worth fighting for, enables rape survivors to move among others, free of debilitating fears. It gave me the courage to bring a child into the world, in spite of the realization that doing so would, far from making me immortal, make me twice as mortal, by doubling my chances of having my life destroyed by a speeding truck.[41]

But many trauma survivors who endured much worse than I did, and for much longer, found, often years later, that it was impossible to go on. It is not a moral failing to leave a world that has become morally unacceptable. I wonder how some can ask, of battered women, "Why didn't they leave?" while saying, of those driven to suicide by the brutal and inescapable aftermath of trauma, "Why didn't they stay?" Améry wrote, "Whoever was tortured, stays tortured" (1955, 131) and this may explain why he, Levi, Celan, and other Holocaust survivors took their own lives decades after their (physical) torture ended, as if such an explanation were needed.

Those who have survived trauma understand well the pull of that solution to their daily Beckettian dilemma, "I can't go on, I must go on," for on some days the conclusion "I'll go on" cannot be reached by faith or reason.[42] How does one go on with a shattered self, with no guarantee of recovery, believing that one will always "stay tortured" and never "feel at home in the world"? One hopes for a bearable future, in spite of all the inductive evidence to the contrary. After all, the loss of faith in induction following an unpredictable trauma also has a reassuring side: since inferences from the past can no longer be relied upon to predict the future, there's no more reason to think that tomorrow will bring agony than to think that it won't. So one makes a wager, in which nothing is certain and the odds change daily, and sets about willing to believe that life, for all its unfathomable horror, still holds some undiscovered pleasures.[43] And one remakes oneself by finding meaning in a life of caring for and being sustained by others. While I used to have to will myself out of bed each day, I now wake gladly to feed my son whose birth, four years after the assault, gives me reason not to have died. He is the embodiment of my life's new narrative and I am more autonomous by virtue of being so intermingled with him. Having him has also enabled me to rebuild my trust in the world around us. He is so trusting that, before he learned to walk, he would stand with outstretched arms, wobbling, until he fell, stiff-limbed forwards, backwards, certain the universe would catch him. So far, it has, and when I tell myself it always will, the part of me that he's become believes it.

Notes

1 Charlotte Delbo, *Auschwitz and After*, trans. by Rosette C. Lamont (New Haven: Yale University Press, 1995), p. 267 attributes this statement to one of her fellow deportees.

2 Quoted in Lawrence Langer, ed., *Art from the Ashes* (New York: Oxford University Press, 1995), p. 14. The irony of calling the author of this quote a "survivor" is evident, but, it seems to me, linguistically unavoidable.

3 Jonathan Shay, *Achilles in Vietnam: Combat Trauma and the Undoing of Character* (New York: Atheneum, 1994), p. 180. Shay writes, "When a survivor of prolonged trauma loses all sense of meaningful personal narrative, this may result in a contaminated identity. 'I died in Vietnam' may express a current identity as a corpse."

4 Migael Scherer, *Still Loved by the Sun: A Raper Survivor's Journal* (New York: Simon and Schuster, 1992), p. 179.

5 I do not mean to imply that the traumas suffered by these different groups of survivors are the same, or even commensurable. However, researchers such as Judith Herman, in *Trauma and Recovery* (New York: Basic Books, 1992) and Ronnie Janoff-Bulman, in *Shattered Assumptions: Towards a New Psychology of Trauma* (New York: The Free Press, 1992) have persuasively argued that many of those who survive life-threatening traumatic events in which they are reduced to near-complete helplessness later suffer from the symptoms of post-traumatic stress disorder. I would add that they experience a similar disintegration of the self. In this essay, I use the term "victim" as well as the term "survivor" to denote someone who has been victimized by, and yet survived, such a life-threatening trauma. Clearly, many civilians are more traumatized by war (and with greater injustice) than the veterans to whom I refer in this chapter. I mention the latter simply because trauma research on survivors of war has focused on veterans – US veterans in particular – whose trauma symptoms our federal government is obliged to attempt to understand and treat.

6 In defending a feminist account of the relational self, I do not mean to imply that all relational accounts of the self are feminist. Some that are not (necessarily) feminist are those advocated by Hegel, Marx, and contemporary communitarians.

7 John Locke, *An Essay Concerning Human Understanding* (New York: New American Library, 1974/1694), Harold Noonan, *Personal Identity* (New York: Routledge, 1989), and John Perry, *Personal Identity* (Berkeley: University of California Press, 1975) for treatments of personal identity by seventeenth- and eighteenth-century philosophers.

8 See Peter Ungar, *Identity, Consciousness, and Value* (New York: Oxford University Press, 1990), Derek Parfit, *Reasons and Persons* (Oxford: Oxford University Press, 1986), Noonan, ibid., Amelie Oksenberg Rorty, ed., *The Identities of Persons* (Berkeley: University of California Press, 1976), Perry, ibid., for discussions of contemporary theories of personal identity.

9 While most philosophers writing about personal identity have neglected to consider *any* actual transformations of real persons, there are a few notable exceptions. Kathleen Wilkes, *Real People* (New York: Oxford University Press, 1988), p.vii, argues that the "bizarre, entertaining, confusing, and inconclusive thought experiments" so common in philosophical writing about personal identity are not helpful, and, in any case, not needed, "since there are so many actual puzzle-cases which defy the *imagination*, but which we none the less have to accept as facts". She does not discuss trauma, however, and uses third-person scientific accounts of neurological disorders rather than first person narratives in her analysis. Although he does not discuss trauma and the self either, Thomas Nagel examines the effect of commissurotomy on the self in "Brain Bisection and the Unity of Consciousness" in Perry, op. cit.. Three philosophers, however, have in recent writings departed from this tradition of ignoring trauma and have analyzed alleged cases of trauma-induced dissociation and subsequent recovered memories. Ian Hacking, *Rewriting the Soul: Multiple Personality and the Sources of Memory* (Princeton: Princeton University Press, 1995) presents a deeply skeptical treatment of the alleged splitting of the self that occurs during severe child abuse, while Naomi Scheman considers the multiple personalities constructed by severely abused children to be "a comprehensible, perhaps even rational, response to an intolerable situation, a way of maintaining some degree of agency in the face of profoundly soul-destroying attacks on one's ability to construct a sense of self" in "Though This be Method, Yet there is Madness in It," in *A Mind of One's Own*, Antony and Witt, eds, (Boulder: Westview Press, 1993), p. 164. Diana T. Meyers, in "The Family Romance" in Meyers, ed., *Feminist Social Thought* (New York: Routledge, 1997), pp. 440–57, mediates between these two views with an account focusing, not on whether the incest trope that "figures" such recovered memories is historically accurate, but, rather, on whether such a figuration is useful to the alleged victims.

10 For discussions of the usefulness of such narratives, see Susan Brison, "The Theoretical Importance of

Practice," *Nomos* 37 (1995), pp. 216–38 and "On the Personal as Philosophical," *APA Newsletter* 95 (1995), pp. 37–40.

11 See Deborah K. King, "Multiple Jeopardy, Multiple Consciousness: The Context of a Black Feminist Ideology," *Signs* 14 (1988), pp. 42–72, Maria Lugones, "Playfulness, 'World'-Traveling, and Loving Perception," *Hypatia* 2 (1987), pp. 3–19, and Mari Matsuda, "When the First Quail Calls: Multiple Consciousness as Jurisprudential Method," *Women's Rights Law Reporter* 11 (1989), pp. 7–10.

12 This is not (merely) because philosophers are a more disputatious lot, but rather because psychologists need at least the appearance of clarity and agreement in order to categorize illnesses, make diagnoses, carry out research, fill out insurance claim forms, and so on.

13 This paraphrases Judith Herman's description of traumatic events (op. cit., p. 33). This description and the following discussion of trauma are distilled from Herman's book as well as from Ronnie Janoff-Bulman, "Characterological versus Behavioral Self Blame: Inquiries in to Depression and Rape," *Journal of Personality and Social Psychology* 37 (1979), pp. 1798–809, and Shay, op. cit..

14 While some poststructuralists hold that the self is a fiction, not all do, and this is not, in any case, implied by the view that it is a narrative. I think the clinical studies and narrative accounts of trauma discussed below show that the self is not a fiction, if that is taken to mean that it is freely constructed by some narrator. No one, not even Stephen King, would voluntarily construct a self so tormented by trauma and its aftermath.

15 Annette Baier, Postures of the Mind (Minneapolis: University of Minnesota Press, 1985), p. 84. For other discussions of the relational self, see Alison Jaggar, *Feminist Politics and Human Nature* (Totowa: Rowman & Allenheld, 1983), and Diana Meyers, *Subjection and Subjectivity* (New York: Routledge, 1994). Virginia Held, *Feminist Morality* (Chicago: University of Chicago Press, 1993), pp. 57–64 gives an excellent survey of feminist views of the relational self in so far as they bear on moral theory.

16 An exception is Bernard Williams, "The Self and the Future," *Philosophical Review* 79 (1970), pp. 161–80, who presents a thought experiment that prompts the intuition that in at least some cases of so-called body transfer, we would identify with the surviving individual who has our body, and not the one who has our memory and other psychological characteristics.

17 Most famously, Descartes in his *Meditations* (1984).

18 In refreshing contrast to this disciplinary bias is the philosophical writing on embodiment by Iris Young, *Throwing Like a Girl and Other Essays in Feminist Philosophy and Social Theory* (Indianapolis: Indiana University Press, 1990).

19 Plato, *Phaedo*, II.65c–67d.

20 Two critiques of Beauvoir's position on maternity and childbirth are presented in Sara Ruddick, *Maternal Thinking* (Boston: Beacon Press, 1989), pp. 192–3, 275 n. 11 and Catriona Mackenzie, "A Certain Lack of Symmetry: de Beauvoior on Autonomous Agency and Women's Embodiment," in Evans, ed., *Texts in Culture: Simone de Beauvoir, "The Second Sex"* (Manchester: Manchester University Press, 1996).

21 That fear, anxiety, and so on are psychological, and hence controllable, responses to trauma is an assumption underlying the view, held by many liberals, that victims of hate speech should simply toughen their emotional hides to avoid being affected adversely by it. This view presupposes a mind-body split more thoroughgoing than that defended by Descartes.

22 If memories do not reside solely in the mind or in the body, but rather are a function of the way in which consciousness "inhabits" a body, then not only Locke's thought experiment, but also Sydney Shoemaker's (in Perry, op. cit., pp. 119–34), and Bernard Williams' (op. cit.) appear to be incoherent as described.

23 And, in the case of the extreme trauma endured by Holocaust survivors, their bodies themselves were drastically changed, by starvation, disease, and torture.

24 An especially striking literary illustration of this is the scene in *Studs Lonigan* in which the narrator says of the woman Weary Reilly is about to rape, "She was his meat" (James T. Farrell, *Studs Lonigan*, Book II [New York: Vanguard, 1935], 396). I thank Blanche Gelfant for drawing my attention to this passage.

25 See Lenore Terr, *Unchained Memories* (New York: HarperCollins, 1994) for an account of different responses to one-time and ongoing traumas.

26 Kafka, Franz, "In the Penal Colony," in *The Penal Colony: Stories and Short Pieces*, trans. Willa and Edwin Muir (New York: Schocken, 1948), 191–227.

27 Parfit would not, however, agree with the relational account of the self I am defending here. In her comments on a draft of this chapter, Susan Dwyer wondered "how many people who have not suffered trauma have a clear sense of what it was like to be them at some earlier point in their lives." She guessed "not many," and suggested that this "explains a number of rituals we engage in, taking photographs of significant events, keeping a diary, marking anniversaries, valuing family (i.e., people who were there, too, who can tell you about your former self)."

28 Bruno Bettelheim, *Surviving and Other Essays* (New York: Knopf, 1979) discusses the "personality-disintegrating" effects of being in a German concentration camp (p. 25). "Being subjected to living in an extreme situation somehow contaminates permanently the old life and the old personality. This suggests that a personality which did not

protect the individual against landing in an extreme situation seems so deficient to the person that he feels in need of widespread restructuring" (pp. 123–4). In spite of this conviction, trauma survivors are forced to reacquire at least some of their earlier illusions if life is to continue to be livable.

29 Of course, not many rape survivors are fortunate enough to have such an experience with the criminal justice system, given the low rates of reporting, prosecuting, and conviction of rapists. I also had the advantage of having my assailant tried in a French court, in which the adversarial system is not practiced, so I was not cross-examined by the defense lawyer. In addition, since the facts of the case were not in dispute and my assailant's only defense was an (ultimately unsuccessful) insanity plea, no one in the courtroom questioned my narrative of what happened.

30 I am not suggesting that for this reason the memories of trauma survivors are less reliable than others' memories. In the subsequent story, Yael Tamir did not have a false memory of actually having lived through the Holocaust. Rather, the cultural climate in which she was raised led her to respond instinctively to certain things (a shouting German voice at a train station) in ways characteristic of those who had actually been deported. In any case, since all narrative memory involves reconstruction, trauma survivors' narratives are no less likely to be accurate than anyone else's. (I thank Susan Dwyer for encouraging me to make this last point more explicit.)

31 Primo Levi, *The Drowned and the Saved* (New York: Random House, 1989), p. 119 writes that "[a]t a distance of forty years, my tattoo has become a part of my body," which no longer taints his sense of self.

32 For an example of an endorsement account of autonomy, see Harry Frankfurt, *The Importance of What We Care About* (New York: Cambridge University Press, 1988), chs 5 and 12.

33 Two of the most prominent proponents of what West calls "cultural feminism" (and others have Called "difference feminism") are Carol Gilligan, *In a Different Voice* (Cambridge: Harvard University Press, 1982) and Ruddick, op. cit.

34 The best-known advocate of "radical" or "dominance" feminism is Catharine MacKinnon, *Feminism Unmodified* (Cambridge: Harvard University Press, 1987).

35 The militaristic nature of this image is brought out by an update of this notion mentioned to me by Diana Meyers: autonomy as "the inner missile silo"!

36 In addition, not simply what we are able to express, but also what we are able to feel, can be seen to be a function of one's social relations. See Naomi Scheman, "Individualism and the Objects of Psychology," in Harding and Hintikka, eds. *Discovering Reality* (Boston: D. Reidel, 1983), pp. 225–44.

37 This is one of the positive aspects of a kind of multiple consciousness. Cf. Scheman, ibid., Lugones, op.cit., Matsuda, op.cit., and King, op.cit.

38 Seeskin (1988, 120), quoting Emil Fackenheim, *To Mend the World* (New York: Schocken, 1982), 239.

39 When I later mentioned this to my therapist, she replied, reasonably enough, "Why not shoot the assailant instead?" But for me that thought was not yet thinkable.

40 I should make a distinction here between the ability to kill in self-defense and the desire to kill as a form of revenge. While I think it is morally permissible to possess and to employ the former, acting on the latter is to be morally condemned.

41 The idea that a child makes one twice as mortal comes from Barbara Kingsolver. A character in her story "Covered Bridges" says, "Having a child wouldn't make you immortal. It would make you twice as mortal. It's just one more life you could possibly lose, besides your own. Two more eyes to be put out, and ten more toes to get caught under the mower." Barbara Kingsolver, *Homeland and Other Stories* (New York: Harper & Row, 1989), 59–60.

42 Samuel Beckett, *Three Novels* (New York: Grove, 1965), p. 414. What Beckett actually writes is "you must go on, I can't go on, I'll go on," translating his original ending to *L'Innommable* (Paris: Minuit, 1953), 213: "*il faut continuer, je ne peux pas continuer, je vais continuer.*" I'm grateful to Thomas Trezise for pointing out this passage.

43 For a discussion of Pascal's wager, see Blaise Pascal, *Pensées*, trans. W. F. Trotter (New York: Dutton, 1958) and for William James' discussion of "the will to believe," see James, *The Will to Believe* (New York: Longmans, Green, 1986).

Part VII

What Would Liberation Be?

Introduction to Part VII

Feminism is fundamentally a freedom movement, and as such, feminists have long debated visions of liberation. Equality, in some sense of the term, has always been a large part of the feminist vision, and this distinguishes feminism from, say, movements for religious freedom. Feminism demands the end of sexist oppression, but what does such a state of affairs look like? What would free and equal women and men be like? How does society need to change for this to come about? What can we demand of society or of individuals in order to achieve the vision of liberation that we prefer? As in many other areas of feminist thought, two dominant threads can be discerned. The equality feminists, most of whom are liberals, argue that women and men must have substantive equality for liberation, and that when this comes about there will be an end to gender, where gender is defined as the hierarchical domination of females by males through normative social roles. The difference feminists, a group that includes both cultural feminists and radical feminists, argue that there cannot be substantive equality between males and females, but rather argue for the equal evaluation of femininity and masculinity. Theorists differ on what counts as substantive equality, of course. In the view of some liberals, substantive equality will require girls and boys to receive the same upbringing and laws to favor social arrangements that do not discriminate by gender. Others will argue that it is enough to offer options and allow girls and boys, men and women to sort themselves among these as they prefer. The problem with this course of action from the perspective of the liberal is that women's and men's preferences have been formed (or rather, deformed) under conditions of women's oppression, and they are likely to be reproduced in any future in which there are gender roles of any kind. Some argue that there is no way at this point to know whether women and men can have substantive equality, or whether they would want it. As Catharine MacKinnon puts it, "Take your foot off our necks, then we will hear in what tongue women speak." If we are radically uncertain about the proper vision of liberation, then one course of action would be to focus on the process, allowing the end to sort itself out as we approach it. Feminist progress would then involve increasing women's freedom, and perhaps men's freedom as well, without staking a bet on what differences would continue to exist between men and women.

In this part we include four chapters that consider the end or goal of feminist activism and the path for achieving it. We begin with Simone de Beauvoir's conclusion to *The Second Sex*. Although Beauvoir was a socialist, we count her among the equality feminists because she argues for the end of discrimination in education and employment along the lines of gender. Her essay begins with a harsh judgment of women of her day; they are stuck in immanence, that is, concerned about the mundane, the merely survival oriented, and the trivial rather than the transcendent projects of humanity. She had argued throughout her book that this is not the result of natural inferiority, but rather that women have been taught inferiority, and that different social circumstances will allow women to be the equals of men in the human projects that really matter: art, literature, science, philosophy, and the like. Implicitly Beauvoir rejects the traditionally female childbearing, nurturing, and domestic projects, although she admits that these can be performed in more or less transcendent ways. The first step toward liberation, Beauvoir argues, is to increase women's economic status. Moral and psychological advance will follow from this for both men and women. Women will give up their dependence and accept responsibility for their existence when they are capable to surviving independently, and men will give up their domineering and superior attitude and gain a new freedom as well. Beauvoir thinks that sexuality will preserve a differentiation between men and women, but that this difference will not be a bar to their equality because it does not significantly affect other areas of life.

Catharine MacKinnon holds that the social ideology of "difference" between the sexes, which often produces distinctions between them in reality, cannot be permitted to rationalize inequality of the sexes. MacKinnon, a law professor as well as a political philosopher, discusses two approaches to equality, akin to our equality vs difference feminism, and rejects them in favor of her "dominance" approach. One approach, which she labels the "difference" approach argues that women and men should be treated the same in the law, except where there are clear differences between the sexes, such as with pregnancy. The other approach follows Carol Gilligan's view that women have a unique moral perspective that ought to be valued highly and protected by society and the law. MacKinnon argues that both kinds of feminists are mistaken to seek equality only where the sexes can be considered the same, because under conditions of male dominance, women will often not be, or be seen to be, the same as men, and seeing them as different, and compensating that difference, will also be a socially coded form of imposing inferiority, even when it seems to be an improvement. Instead we should seek to eliminate the dominance that men as a group exercise over women as a group. That is, she argues that we need not take a position on the origin or value of sexual difference, but rather we must simply demand that whether or not there is difference there is no justification for social dominance of one gender by the other. Any inequality in social power between men and women should be seen as suspect and in need of legal rectification.

Susan Moller Okin offers a practical way for society to end the social dominance of men over women in "Toward a Humanist Justice," namely for men and women to share all unpaid childcare and domestic responsibilities evenly. This would, she believes, bring about the end of gender. In Okin's view the family is the main site of gender injustice; it is where women are exploited and abused, where men dominate and exploit, and where children learn to reproduce the unjust gender relations of their parents. Gender just is this hierarchical relation between men and women that is structured and reproduced by family life. Okin clearly believes that androgyny is both good and possible, but she admits that in the short term, many women would be even worse off were society to restructure in favor of androgyny now. Wives who have specialized in domestic labor, for example, will be at a disadvantage in the marketplace. An immediate corrective would be to demand that spouses share all paid income equally in case one spouse performs more of the unpaid labor, and to ensure that upon divorce, the resulting households have approximately the same standard of living.

In the final chapter of the book, "Feminism, Utopianism, and the Role of the Ideal in Political Philosophy," Drucilla Cornell considers charges that feminism is too utopian, and defends her ideal of liberation against these charges. Cornell's vision of liberation is the freedom of what she calls the "imaginary domain," which is the "freedom to create ourselves as sexed beings, as feeling and reasoning persons."[1] Cornell thinks that our sexual freedom is at the very heart of freedom and our emotional and intellectual capacities. Freedom, rather than equality, is for her the primary demand of feminism. One form of the utopian charge is that feminism resembles the utopian cum totalitarian projects of the twentieth century, as the term "feminazi" suggests. On this view, feminism demands that everyone conform to certain standards of sexual desire and behavior. Cornell responds that her ideal of freedom cannot be accused of totalitarian tendencies, since what she proposes is that everyone have the license to express themselves sexually as they will, provided that their expression allows others the same freedom. Another form of the utopian charge is that the ideal cannot be brought about in practice. Cornell defends herself against this charge by arguing that the ideal of the imaginary domain simply expresses the desires implicit in actions of feminists and gay rights activists to be able to express their sexuality freely. Furthermore, she argues that what is possible cannot be known in advance of social transformation, and thus feminism must take freedom as the ideal rather than some substantive notion of equality.

Note

1 Drucilla Cornell, *At the Heart of Freedom*, Princeton, NJ: Princeton University Press, 1998, p. ix.

27

Conclusion from *The Second Sex*

Simone de Beauvoir

Conclusion

No, woman is not our brother; through indolence and depravity we have made of her a being apart, unknown, having no weapon other than her sex, which not only means constant strife but is moreover an unfair weapon of the eternal little slave's mistrust – adoring or hating, but never our frank companion, a being set apart as if in *esprit de corps* and freemasonry."

Many men would still subscribe to these words of Laforgue; many think that there will always be "strife and dispute," as Montaigne put it, and that fraternity will never be possible. The fact is that today neither men nor women are satisfied with each other. But the question is to know whether there is an original curse that condemns them to rend each other or whether the conflicts in which they are opposed merely mark a transitional moment in human history.

Simone de Beauvoir, "Conclusion," pp. 716–32 from *The Second Sex*, translated and edited by H. M. Parshley. New York: Alfred A. Knopf, 1953. © 1952 and renewed 1980 by Alfred. A. Knopf, a division of Random House, Inc. Used by permission of Alfred A. Knopf, a division of Random House, Inc. and The Random House Group Ltd.

We have seen that in spite of legends no physiological destiny imposes an eternal hostility upon Male and Female as such; even the famous praying mantis devours her male only for want of other food and for the good of the species: it is to this, the species, that all individuals are subordinated, from the top to the bottom of the scale of animal life. Moreover, humanity is something more than a mere species: it is a historical development; it is to be defined by the manner in which it ideals with its natural, fixed characteristics, its *facticité*. Indeed, even with the most extreme bad faith in the world, it is impossible to demonstrate the existence of a rivalry between the human male and female of a truly physiological nature. Further, their hostility may be allocated rather to that intermediate terrain between biology and psychology: psychoanalysis. Woman, we are told, envies man his penis and wishes to castrate him; but the childish desire for the penis is important in the life of the adult woman only if she feels her femininity as a mutilation; and then it is as a symbol of all the privileges of manhood that she wishes to appropriate the male organ. We may readily agree that her dream of castration has this symbolic significance: she wishes, it is thought, to deprive the male of his transcendence.

But her desire, as we have seen, is much more ambiguous: she wishes, in a contradictory fashion, to *have* this transcendence, which is to suppose that she at once respects it and denies it, that she intends at once to throw herself into it and keep it within herself. This is to say that the drama does not unfold on a sexual level; further, sexuality has never seemed to us to define a destiny, to furnish in itself the key to human behavior, but to express the totality of a situation that it only helps to define. The battle of the sexes is not immediately implied in the anatomy of man and woman. The truth is that when one evokes it, one takes for granted that in the timeless realm of Ideas a battle is being waged between those vague essences the Eternal Feminine and the Eternal Masculine; and one neglects the fact that this titanic combat assumes on earth two totally different forms, corresponding with two different moments of history.

The woman who is shut up in immanence endeavors to hold man in that prison also; thus the prison will be confused with the world, and woman will no longer suffer from being confined there: mother, wife, sweetheart are the jailers. Society, being codified by man, decrees that woman is inferior: she can do away with this inferiority only by destroying the male's superiority. She sets about mutilating, dominating man, she contradicts him, she denies his truth and his values. But in doing this she is only defending herself; it was neither a changeless essence nor a mistaken choice that doomed her to immanence, to inferiority. They were imposed upon her. All oppression creates a state of war. And this is no exception. The existent who is regarded as inessential cannot fail to demand the re-establishment of her sovereignty.

Today the combat takes a different shape; instead of wishing to put man in a prison, woman endeavors to escape from one; she no longer seeks to drag him into the realms of immanence but to emerge, herself, into the light of transcendence. Now the attitude of the males creates a new conflict: it is with a bad grace that the man lets her go. He is very well pleased to remain the sovereign subject, the absolute superior, the essential being; he refuses to accept his companion as an equal in any concrete way. She replies to his lack of confidence in her by assuming an aggressive attitude. It is no longer a question of a war between individuals each shut up in his or her sphere: a caste claiming its rights goes over the top and it is resisted by the privileged caste. Here two transcendences are face to face; instead of displaying mutual recognition, each free being wishes to dominate the other.

This difference of attitude is manifest on the sexual plane as on the spiritual plane. The "feminine" woman in making herself prey tries to reduce man, also, to her carnal passivity; she occupies herself in catching him in her trap, in enchaining him by means of the desire she arouses in him in submissively making herself a thing. The emancipated woman, on the contrary, wants to be active, a taker, and refuses the passivity man means to impose on her. Thus Elise and her emulators deny the values of the activities of virile type; they put the flesh above the spirit, contingence above liberty, their routine wisdom above creative audacity. But the "modern" woman accepts masculine values: she prides herself on thinking, taking action, working, creating, on the same terms as men; instead of seeking to disparage them, she declares herself their equal.

In so far as she expresses herself in definite action, this claim is legitimate, and male insolence must then bear the blame. But in men's defense it must be said that women are wont to confuse the issue. A Mabel Dodge Luhan intended to subjugate D. H. Lawrence by her feminine charms so as to dominate him spiritually thereafter; many women, in order to show by their successes their equivalence to men, try to secure male support by sexual means; they play on both sides, demanding old-fashioned respect and modern esteem, banking on their old magic and their new rights. It is understandable that a man becomes irritated and puts himself on the defensive; but he is also double-dealing when he requires woman to play the game fairly while he denies them the indispensable trump cards through distrust and hostility. Indeed, the struggle cannot be clearly drawn between them, since woman is opaque in her very being; she stands before man not as a subject but as an object paradoxically endued with subjectivity; she takes herself simultaneously as *self* and as *other*, a contradiction that entails baffling consequences. When she makes weapons at once of her weakness and of her strength, it is not a matter of designing calculation: she seeks salvation spontaneously in the way that has been imposed on her, that of passivity, at the same time when she is actively demanding her sovereignty; and no doubt this procedure is unfair tactics, but it is dictated to her by the ambiguous situation assigned her. Man, however, becomes indignant when he treats her as a free and independent being and then realizes that she is still a trap for him; if he gratifies and satisfies her in her posture as prey, he finds her claims to autonomy irritating; whatever he does, he feels tricked and she feels wronged.

The quarrel will go on as long as men and women fail to recognize each other as peers; that is to say, as long as femininity is perpetuated as such. Which sex is the more eager to maintain it? Woman, who is being emancipated from it, wishes none the less to retain its privileges; and man, in that case, wants her to assume its limitations. "It is easier to accuse one sex than to excuse the other," says Montaigne. It is vain to apportion praise and blame. The truth is that if the vicious circle is so hard to break, it is because the two sexes are each the victim at once of the other and of itself. Between two adversaries confronting each other in their pure liberty, an agreement could be easily reached: the more so as the war profits neither. But the complexity of the whole affair derives from the fact that each camp is giving aid and comfort to the enemy; woman is pursuing a dream of submission, man a dream of identification. Want of authenticity does not pay: each blames the other for the unhappiness he or she has incurred in yielding to the temptations of the easy way; what man and woman loathe in each other is the shattering frustration of each one's own bad faith and baseness.

We have seen why men enslaved women in the first place; the devaluation of femininity has been a necessary step in human evolution, but it might have led to collaboration between the two sexes; oppression is to be explained by the tendency of the existent to flee from himself by means of identification with the other, whom he oppresses to that end. In each individual man that tendency exists today; and the vast majority yield to it. The husband wants to find himself in his wife, the lover in his mistress, in the form of a stone image; he is seeking in her the myth of his virility, of his sovereignty, of his immediate reality. "My husband never goes to the movies," says his wife, and the dubious masculine opinion is graved in the marble of eternity. But he is himself the slave of his double: what an effort to build up an image in which he is always in danger! In spite of everything his success in this depends upon the capricious freedom of women: he must constantly try to keep this propitious to him. Man is concerned with the effort to appear male, important, superior; he pretends so as to get pretense in return; he, too, is aggressive, uneasy; he feels hostility for women because he is afraid of them, he is afraid of them because he is afraid of the personage, the image, with which he identifies himself. What time and strength he squanders in liquidating, sublimating, transferring complexes, in talking about women, in seducing them, in fearing them! He would be liberated himself in their liberation. But this is precisely what he dreads. And so he obstinately persists in the mystifications intended to keep woman in her chains.

That she is being tricked, many men have realized. "What a misfortune to be a woman! And yet the misfortune, when one is a woman, is at bottom not to comprehend that it is one," says Kirkegaard.[1] For a long time there have been efforts to disguise this misfortune. For example, guardianship has been done away with: women have been given "protectors," and if they are invested with the rights of the old-time guardians, it is in woman's own interest. To forbid her working, to keep her at home, is to defend her against herself and to assure her happiness. We have seen what poetic veils are thrown over her monotonous burdens of housekeeping and maternity: in exchange for her liberty she has received the false treasures of her "femininity." Balzac illustrates this maneuver very well in counseling man to treat her as a slave while persuading her that she is a queen. Less cynical, many men try to convince themselves that she is really privileged. There are American sociologists who seriously teach today the theory of "low-class gain." In France, also, it has often been proclaimed – although in a less scientific manner – that the workers are very fortunate in not being obliged to "keep up appearances" and still more so the bums who can dress in rags and sleep on the side-walks, pleasures forbidden to the Count de Beaumont and the Wendels. Like the carefree wretches gaily scratching at their vermin, like the merry Negroes laughing under the lash and those joyous Tunisian Arabs burying their starved children with a smile, woman enjoys that incomparable privilege: irresponsibility. Free from troublesome burdens and cares, she obviously has "the better part." But it is disturbing that with an obstinate perversity – connected no doubt with original sin – down through the centuries and in all countries, the people who have the better part are always crying to their benefactors: "It is too much! I will be satisfied with yours!" But the munificent capitalists, the generous colonists, the superb males, stick to their guns: "Keep the better part, hold on to it!"

It must be admitted that the males find in woman more complicity than the oppressor usually finds in the oppressed. And in bad faith they take authorization from this to declare that she has *desired* the destiny they have imposed on her. We have seen that all the main features of her training combine to bar her from the roads of revolt and adventure. Society in general – beginning with her respected parents – lies to her by praising the lofty values of love, devotion, the gift of herself, and then concealing from her the fact that neither lover nor husband nor yet her children will be inclined to accept the burdensome charge of all that. She cheerfully believes these lies because they invite her to follow the easy slope: in this others commit their worst crime against her; throughout her life from childhood on, they damage and corrupt her by designating as her true vocation this submission, which is the temptation of every existent in the anxiety of liberty. If a child is taught idleness by being amused all day long and never being led to study, or shown its usefulness, it will hardly be said, when he grows up, that he chose to be incapable and ignorant; yet this is how woman is brought up, without ever being impressed with the necessity of taking charge of her own existence. So she readily lets herself come to count on the protection, love, assistance, and supervision of others, she lets herself be fascinated with the hope of self-realization without *doing* anything. She does wrong in yielding to the temptation; but man is in no position to blame her, since he has led her into the temptation. When conflict arises between them, each will hold the other responsible for the situation; she will reproach him with having made her what she is: "No one taught me to reason or to earn my own living"; he will reproach her with having accepted the consequences: "You don't know anything, you are an incompetent," and so on. Each sex thinks it can justify itself by taking the offensive; but the wrongs done by one do not make the other innocent.

The innumerable conflicts that set men and women against one another come from the fact that neither is prepared to assume all the consequences of this situation which the one has offered and the other accepted. The doubtful concept of "equality in inequality," which the one uses to mask his despotism and the other to mask her cowardice, does not stand the test of experience: in their exchanges, woman appeals to the theoretical equality she has been guaranteed, and man the concrete inequality that exists. The result is that in every association an endless debate goes on concerning the ambiguous meaning of the words *give* and *take*: she complains of giving her all, he protests that she takes his all. Woman has to learn that exchanges – it is a fundamental law of political economy – are based on the value the merchandise offered has for the buyer, and not for the seller: she has been deceived in being persuaded that her worth is priceless. The truth is that for man she is an amusement, a pleasure, company, an inessential boon; he is for her the meaning, the justification of her existence. The exchange, therefore, is not of two items of equal value.

This inequality will be especially brought out in the fact that the time they spend together – which fallaciously seems to be the same time – does not have the same value for both partners. During the evening the lover spends with his mistress he could be doing something of advantage to his career, seeing friends, cultivating business relationships, seeking recreation; for a man normally integrated in society, time is a positive value: money, reputation, pleasure. For the idle, bored woman, on the contrary, it is a burden she wishes to get rid of; when she succeeds in killing time, it is a benefit to her: the man's presence is pure profit. In a liaison what most clearly interests the man, in many cases, is the sexual benefit he gets from it: if need be, he can be content to spend no more time with his mistress than is required for the sexual act; but – with exceptions – what she, on her part, wants is to kill all the excess time she has on her hands; and – like the storekeeper who will not sell potatoes unless the customer will take turnips also – she will not yield her body unless her lover will take hours of conversation and "going out" into the bargain. A balance is reached if, on the whole, the cost does not seem too high to the man, and this depends, of course, on the strength of his desire and the importance he gives to what is to be sacrificed. But if the woman demands – offers – too much time, she becomes wholly intrusive, like the river overflowing its banks, and the man will prefer to have nothing rather than too much. Then she reduces her demands; but very often the balance is reached at the cost of a double tension: she feels that the man has "had" her at a bargain, and he thinks her price is too high. This analysis, of course, is put in somewhat humorous terms; but – except for those affairs of jealous and exclusive passion in which the man wants total possession of the woman – this conflict constantly appears in cases of affection, desire, and even love. He always has "other things to do" with his time; whereas she has time to burn; and he considers much of the time she gives him not as a gift but as a burden.

As a rule he consents to assume the burden because he knows very well that he is on the privileged side, he has a bad conscience; and if he is of reasonable good will he tries to compensate for the inequality by being generous. He prides himself on his compassion, however, and at the first clash he treats the woman as ungrateful and thinks, with some irritation: "I'm too good to her." She feels she is behaving like a beggar when she is convinced of the high value of her gifts, and that humiliates her.

Here we find the explanation of the cruelty that woman often shows she is capable of practicing; she has a good conscience because she is on the unprivileged side; she feels she is under no obligation to deal gently with the favored caste, and her only thought is to defend herself. She will even be very happy if she has occasion to show her resentment to a lover who has not been able to satisfy all her demands: since he does not give her enough, she take savage delight in taking back everything from him. At this point the wounded lover suddenly discovers the value *in toto* of a liaison each moment of which he held more or less in contempt: he is ready to promise her everything, even though he will feel exploited again when he has to make good. He accuses his mistress of blackmailing him: she calls him stingy; both feel wronged.

Once again it is useless to apportion blame and excuses: justice can never be done in the midst of injustice. A colonial administrator has no possibility of acting rightly toward the natives, nor a general toward his soldiers; the only solution is to be neither colonist nor military chief; but a man could not prevent himself from being a man. So there he is, culpable in spite of himself and laboring under the effects of a fault he did not himself commit; and here she is, victim and shrew in spite of herself. Sometimes he rebels and becomes cruel, but then he makes himself an accomplice of the injustice, and the fault becomes really his. Sometimes he lets himself be annihilated, devoured, by his demanding victim; but in that case he feels duped. Often he stops at a compromise that at once belittles him and leaves him ill at ease. A well-disposed man will be more tortured by the situation than the woman herself: in a sense it is always better to be on the side of the vanquished; but if she is well-disposed also, incapable of self-sufficiency, reluctant to crush the man with the weight of her destiny, she struggles in hopeless confusion.

In daily life we meet with an abundance of these cases which are incapable of satisfactory solution because they are determined by unsatisfactory conditions. A man who is compelled to go on materially and morally supporting a woman whom he no longer loves feels he is victimized; but if he abandons without resources the woman who has pledged her whole life to him, she will be quite as unjustly victimized. The evil originates not in the perversity of individuals – and bad faith first appears when each blames the other – it originates rather in a situation against which all individual action is powerless. Women are "clinging," they are a dead weight, and they suffer for it; the point is that their situation is like that of a parasite sucking out the living strength of another organism. Let them be provided with living strength of their own, let them have the means to attack the world and wrest from it their own subsistence, and their dependence will be abolished – that of man also. There is no doubt that both men and women will profit greatly from the new situation.

A world where men and women would be equal is easy to visualize, for that precisely is what the Soviet Revolution *promised*: women raised and trained exactly like men were to work under the same conditions[2] and for the same wages. Erotic liberty was to be recognized by custom, but the sexual act was not to be considered a "service" to be paid for; woman was to be *obliged* to provide herself with other ways of earning a living; marriage was to be based on a free agreement that the spouses could break at will; maternity was to be voluntary, which meant that contraception and abortion were to be authorized and that, on the other hand, all mothers and their children were to have exactly the same rights, in or out of marriage; pregnancy leaves were to be paid for by the State, which would assume charge of the children, signifying not that they would be *taken away* from their parents, but that they would not be *abandoned* to them.

But is it enough to change laws, institutions, customs, public opinion, and the whole social context, for men and women to become truly equal? "Women will always be women," say the skeptics. Other seers prophesy that in casting off their femininity they will not succeed in changing themselves into men and they will become monsters. This would be to admit that the woman of today is a creation of nature; it must be repeated once more that in human society nothing is natural and that woman, like much else, is a product elaborated by civilization. The intervention of others in her destiny is fundamental: if this action took a different direction, it would produce a quite different result. Woman is determined not by her hormones or by mysterious instincts, but by the manner in which her body and her relation to the world are modified through the action of others than herself. The abyss that separates the adolescent boy and girl has been deliberately opened out between them since earliest childhood; later on, woman could not be other than what she *was made*, and that past was bound to shadow her for life. If we appreciate its influence, we see clearly that her destiny is not predetermined for all eternity.

We must not believe, certainly, that a change in woman's economic condition alone is enough to transform her, though this factor has been and remains the basic factor in her evolution; but until it has brought about the moral, social, cultural, and other consequences that it promises and requires, the new woman cannot appear. At this moment they have been realized nowhere, in Russia no more than in France or the United States; and this explains why the woman of today is torn between the past and the future. She appears most often as a "true woman" disguised as a man, and she feels herself as ill at ease in her flesh as in her masculine garb. She must shed her old skin and cut her own new clothes. This she could do only through a social evolution. No single educator could fashion a *female human being* today who would be the exact homologue of the *male human being*; if she is raised like a boy, the young girl feels she is an oddity and thereby she is given a new kind of sex specification. Stendhal understood this when he said: "The forest must be planted all at once." But if we imagine, on the contrary, a society in which the equality of the sexes would be concretely realized, this equality would find new expression in each individual.

If the little girl were brought up from the first with the same demands and rewards, the same severity and the same freedom, as her brothers, taking part in the same studies, the same games, promised the same future, surrounded with women and men who seemed to her undoubted equals, the meanings of the castration complex and of the oedipus complex would be profoundly modified. Assuming on the same basis as the father the material and moral responsibility of the couple, the mother would enjoy the same lasting prestige; the child would perceive around her an androgynous world and not a masculine world. Were she emotionally more attracted to her father – which is not even sure – her love for him would be tinged with a will to emulation and not a feeling of powerlessness; she would not be oriented toward passivity. Authorized to test her powers in work and sports, competing actively with the boys, she would not find the absence of the penis – compensated by the promise of a child – enough to give rise to an inferiority complex; correlatively, the boy would not have a superiority complex if it were not instilled into him and if he looked up to women with as much respect as to men.[3] The little girl would not seek sterile compensation in narcissism and dreaming, she would not take her fate for granted; she would be interested in what she was *doing*, she would throw herself without reserve into undertakings.

I have already pointed out how much easier the transformation of puberty would be if she looked beyond it, like the boys, toward a free adult future: menstruation horrifies her only because it is an abrupt descent into femininity. She would also take her young eroticism in much more tranquil fashion if she did not feel a frightened disgust for her destiny as a whole; coherent sexual information would do much to help her over this crisis. And thanks to coeducational schooling, the august mystery of Man would have no occasion to enter her mind: it would be eliminated by everyday familiarity and open rivalry.

Objections raised against this system always imply respect for sexual taboos; but the effort to inhibit all sex curiosity and pleasure in the child is quite useless; one succeeds only in creating repressions, obsessions, neuroses. The excessive sentimentality, homosexual fervors, and platonic crushes of adolescent girls, with all their train of silliness and frivolity, are much more injurious than a little childish sex play and a few definite sex experiences. It would be beneficial above all for the young girl not to be influenced against taking charge herself of her own existence, for then she would not seek a demigod in the male – merely a comrade, a friend, a partner. Eroticism and love would take on the nature of free transcendence and not that of resignation; she could experience them as a relation between equals. There is no intention, of course, to remove by a stroke of the pen all the difficulties that the child has to overcome in changing into an adult; the most intelligent, the most tolerant education could not relieve the child of experiencing things for herself; what would be asked is that obstacles should not be piled gratuitously in her path. Progress is already shown by the fact that "vicious" little girls are no longer cauterized with a red-hot iron. Psychoanalysis has given parents some instruction, but the conditions under which, at the present time, the sexual training and initiation of woman are accomplished are so deplorable that none of the objections advanced against the idea of a radical change could be considered valid. It is not a question of abolishing in woman the contingencies and miseries of the human condition, but of giving her the means for transcending them.

Woman is the victim of no mysterious fatality; the peculiarities that identify her as specifically a woman get their importance from the significance placed upon them. They can be surmounted, in the future, when they are regarded in new perspectives. Thus, as we have seen, through her erotic experience woman feels – and often detests – the domination of the male; but this is no reason to conclude that her ovaries condemn her to live forever on her knees. Virile aggressiveness seems like a lordly privilege only within a system that in its entirety conspires to affirm masculine sovereignty; and woman *feels* herself profoundly passive in the sexual act only because she already *thinks* of herself as such. Many modern women who lay claim to their dignity as human beings still envisage their erotic life from the standpoint of a tradition of slavery: since it seems to them humiliating to lie beneath the man, to be penetrated by him, they grow tense in frigidity. But if the reality were different, the meaning expressed symbolically in amorous gestures and postures would be different, too: a woman who pays and dominates her lover can, for example, take pride in her superb idleness and consider that she is enslaving the male who is actively exerting himself. And here and now there are many sexually well-balanced couples whose notions of victory and defeat are giving place to the idea of an exchange.

As a matter of fact, man, like woman, is flesh, therefore passive, the plaything of his hormones and of the species, the restless prey of his desires. And she, like him, in the midst of the carnal fever, is a consenting, a voluntary gift, an activity; they live out in their several fashions the strange ambiguity of existence made body. In those combats where they think they confront one another, it is really against the self that each one struggles, projecting into the partner that part of the self which is repudiated; instead of living out the ambiguities of their situation, each tries to make the other bear the abjection and tries to reserve the honor for the self. If, however, both should assume the ambiguity with a clear-sighted modesty, correlative of an authentic pride, they would see each other as equals and would live out their erotic drama in amity. The fact that we are human beings is infinitely more important than all the peculiarities that distinguish human beings from one another; it is never the given that confers superiorities: "virtue," as the ancients called it, is defined at the level of "that which depends on us." In both sexes is played out the same drama of the flesh and the spirit, of finitude and transcendence; both are gnawed away by time and laid in wait for by death, they have the same essential need for one another; and they can gain from their liberty the same glory. If they were to taste it, they would no longer be tempted to dispute fallacious privileges, and fraternity between them could then come into existence.

I shall be told that all this is utopian fancy, because woman cannot be "made over" unless society has first made her really the equal of man. Conservatives have never failed in such circumstances to refer to that vicious circle; history, however, does not revolve. If a caste is kept in a state of inferiority, no doubt it remains inferior; but liberty can break the circle. Let the Negroes vote and they become worthy of having the vote; let woman be given responsibilities and she is able to assume them. The fact is that oppressors cannot be expected to make a move of gratuitous generosity; but at one time the revolt of the oppressed, at another time even the very evolution of the privileged caste itself, creates new situations; thus men have been led, in their own interest, to give partial emancipation to women: it remains only for women to continue their ascent, and the successes they are obtaining are an encouragement for them to do so. It seems almost certain that sooner or later they will arrive at complete economic and social equality, which will bring about an inner metamorphosis.

However this may be, there will be some to object that if such a world is possible it is not desirable. When woman is "the same" as her male, life will lose its salt and spice. This argument, also, has lost its novelty: those interested in perpetuating present conditions are always in tears about the marvelous past that is about to disappear, without having so much as a smile for the young future. It is quite true that doing away with the slave trade meant death to the great plantations, magnificent with azaleas and camellias, it meant ruin to the whole refined Southern civilization. The attics of time have received its rare old laces along with the clear pure voices of the Sistine *castrati*,[4] and there is a certain "feminine charm" that is also on the way to the same dusty repository. I agree that he would be a barbarian indeed who failed to appreciate exquisite flowers, rare lace, the crystal-clear voice of the eunuch, and feminine charm.

When the "charming woman" shows herself in all her splendor, she is a much more exalting object than the "idiotic paintings, overdoors, scenery, showman's garish signs, popular chromos," that excited Rimbaud; adorned with the most modern artifices, beautified according to the newest techniques, she comes down from the remoteness of the ages, from Thebes, from Crete, from Chichén-Itzá; and she is also the totem set up deep in the African jungle; she is a helicopter and she is a bird; and there is this, the greatest wonder of all: under her tinted hair the forest murmur becomes a thought, and words issue from her breasts. Men stretch forth avid hands toward the marvel, but when they grasp it, it is gone; the wife, the mistress, speak like everybody else through their mouths: their words are worth just what they are worth; their breasts also. Does such a fugitive miracle – and one so rare – justify us in perpetuating a situation that is baneful for both sexes? One can appreciate the beauty of flowers, the charm of women, and appreciate them at their true value; if these treasures cost blood or misery, they must be sacrificed.

But in truth this sacrifice seems to men a peculiarly heavy one; few of them really wish in their hearts for woman to succeed in making it; those among them who hold woman in contempt see in the sacrifice nothing for them to gain, those who cherish her see too much that they would lose. And it is true that the evolution now in progress threatens more than feminine charm alone: in beginning to exist for herself, woman will relinquish the function as double and mediator to which she owes her privileged place in the masculine universe; to man, caught between the silence of nature and the demanding presence of other free beings, a creature who is at once his like and a passive thing seems a great treasure. The guise in which he conceives his companion may be mythical, but the experiences for which she is the source or the pretext are none the less real: there are hardly any more precious, more intimate, more ardent. There is no denying that feminine dependence, inferiority, woe, given women their special character; assuredly woman's autonomy, if it spares men many troubles, will also deny them many conveniences; assuredly there are certain forms of the sexual adventure which will be lost in the world of tomorrow. But this does not mean that love, happiness, poetry, dream, will be banished from it.

Let us not forget that our lack of imagination always depopulates the future; for us it is only an abstraction; each one of us secretly deplores the absence there of the one who was himself. But the humanity of tomorrow will be living in its flesh and in its conscious liberty; that time will be its present and it will in turn prefer it. New relations of flesh and sentiment of which we have no conception will arise between the sexes; already, indeed, there have appeared between men and women friendships, rivalries, complicities, comradeships – chaste or sensual – which past centuries could not have conceived. To mention one point, nothing could seem to me more debatable than the opinion that dooms the new world to uniformity and hence to boredom. I fail to see that this present world is free from boredom or that liberty ever creates uniformity.

To begin with, there will always be certain differences between man and woman; her eroticism, and therefore her sexual world, have a special form of their own and therefore cannot fail to engender a sensuality, a sensitivity, of a special nature. This means that her relations to her own body, to that of the male, to the child, will never be identical with those the male bears to his own body, to that of the female, and to the child; those who make much of "equality in difference" could not with good grace refuse to grant me the possible existence of differences in equality. Then again, it is institutions that create uniformity. Young and pretty, the slaves of the harem are always the same in the sultan's embrace; Christianity gave eroticism its savor of sin and legend when it endowed the human female with a soul; if society restores her sovereign individuality to woman, it will not thereby destroy the power of love's embrace to move the heart.

It is nonsense to assert that revelry, vice, ecstasy, passion, would become impossible if man and woman were equal in concrete matters; the contradictions that put the flesh in opposition to the spirit, the instant to time, the swoon of immanence to the challenge of transcendence, the absolute of pleasure to the nothingness of forgetting, will never be resolved; in sexuality will always be materialized the tension, the anguish, the joy, the frustration, and the triumph of existence. To emancipate woman is to refuse to confine her to the relations she bears to man, not to deny them to her; let her have her independent existence and she will continue none the less to exist for him *also*: mutually recognizing each other as subject, each will yet remain for the other an *other*. The reciprocity of their relations will not do away with the miracles – desire, possession, love, dream, adventure – worked by the division of human beings into two separate categories; and the words that move us – giving, conquering, uniting – will not lose their meaning. On the contrary, when we abolish the slavery of half of humanity, together with the whole system of hypocrisy that it implies, then the "division" of humanity will reveal its genuine significance and the human couple will find its true form. "The direct, natural, necessary relation of human creatures is the *relation of man to woman*," Marx has said.[5] "The nature of this relation determines to what point man himself is to be considered as a *generic being*, as mankind; the relation of man to woman is the most natural relation of human being to human being. By it is shown, therefore, to what point the *natural* behavior of man has become *human* or to what point the *human* being has become his *natural* being, to what point his *human nature* has become his *nature*."

The case could not be better stated. It is for man to establish the reign of liberty in the midst of the world of the given. To gain the supreme victory, it is necessary, for one thing, that by and through their natural differentiation men and women unequivocally affirm their brotherhood.

Notes

1 *In Vino Veritas*. He says further: "Politeness is pleasing – essentially – to woman, and the fact that she accepts it without hesitation is explained by nature's care for the weaker, for the unfavored being, and for one to whom an illusion means more than a material compensation. But this illusion, precisely, is fatal to her. . . . To feel oneself freed from distress thanks to something imaginary, to be the dupe of something imaginary, is that not a still deeper mockery? . . . Woman is very far from being *verwahrlost* (neglected), but in another sense she is, since she can never free herself from the illusion that nature has used to console her."

2 That certain too laborious occupations were to be closed to women is not in contradiction to this project. Even among men there is an increasing effort to obtain adaptation to profession; their varying physical and mental capacities limit their possibilities of choice; what is asked is that, in any case, no line of sex or caste be drawn.

3 I knew a little boy of eight who lived with his mother, aunt, and grandmother, all independent and active women, and his weak old half-crippled grandfather. He had a crushing inferiority complex in regard to the feminine sex, although he made efforts to combat it. At school he scorned comrades and teachers because they were miserable males.

4 Eunuchs were long used in the male choirs of the Sistine Chapel in Rome, until the practice was forbidden by Pope Leo XIII in 1880. The operation of castration caused the boy's soprano voice to be retained into adulthood, and it was performed for this purpose. – Translator.

5 *Philosophical Works*, vol. VI (Marx's italics).

28

Difference and Dominance: On Sex Discrimination

Catharine A. MacKinnon

What is a gender question a question of? What is an inequality question a question of? These two questions underlie applications of the equality principle to issues of gender, but they are seldom explicitly asked. I think it speaks to the way gender has structured thought and perception that mainstream legal and moral theory tacitly gives the same answer to them both: these are questions of sameness and difference. The mainstream doctrine of the law of sex discrimination that results is, in my view, largely responsible for the fact that sex equality law has been so utterly ineffective at getting women what we need and are socially prevented from having on the basis of a condition of birth: a chance at productive lives of reasonable physical security, self-expression, individuation, and minimal respect and dignity. Here I expose the sameness/difference theory of sex equality, briefly show how it dominates sex discrimination law and policy and underlies its discontents, and propose an alternative that might do something.

Catharine A. MacKinnon, "Difference and Dominance: On Sex Discrimination," pp. 32–45 and 240–5 (notes) from *Feminism Unmodified: Discourses on Life and Law*. Cambridge, MA: Harvard University Press, 1987.

According to the approach to sex equality that has dominated politics, law, and social perception, equality is an equivalence, not a distinction, and sex is a distinction. The legal mandate of equal treatment – which is both a systemic norm and a specific legal doctrine – becomes a matter of treating likes alike and unlikes unlike; and the sexes are defined as such by their mutual unlikeness. Put another way, gender is socially constructed as difference epistemologically; sex discrimination law bounds gender equality by difference doctrinally. A built-in tension exists between this concept of equality, which presupposes sameness, and this concept of sex, which presupposes difference. Sex equality thus becomes a contradiction in terms, something of an oxymoron, which may suggest why we are having such a difficult time getting it.

Upon further scrutiny, two alternate paths to equality for women emerge within this dominant approach, paths that roughly follow the lines of this tension. The leading one is: be the same as men. This path is termed gender neutrality doctrinally and the single standard philosophically. It is testimony to how substance gets itself up as form in law that this rule is considered formal equality. Because this approach mirrors the ideology of the social world, it is considered abstract, meaning transparent of substance; also for this reason it is considered not only to be *the* standard, but *a* standard at all. It is so far the leading rule that the words "equal to" are code for, equivalent to, the words "the same as" – referent for both unspecified.

To women who want equality yet find that you are different, the doctrine provides an alternate route: be different from men. This equal recognition of difference is termed the special benefit rule or special protection rule legally, the double standard philosophically. It is in rather bad odor. Like pregnancy, which always calls it up, it is something of a doctrinal embarrassment. Considered an exception to true equality and not really a rule of law at all, this is the one place where the law of sex discrimination admits it is recognizing something substantive. Together with the Bona Fide Occupational Qualification (BFOQ), the unique physical characteristic exception under ERA policy, compensatory legislation, and sex-conscious relief in particular litigation, affirmative action is thought to live here.[1]

The philosophy underlying the difference approach is that sex *is* a difference, a division, a distinction, beneath which lies a stratum of human commonality, sameness. The moral thrust of the sameness branch of the doctrine is to make normative rules conform to this empirical reality by granting women access to what men have access to: to the extent that women are no different from men, we deserve what they have. The differences branch, which is generally seen as patronizing but necessary to avoid absurdity, exists to value or compensate women for what we are or have become distinctively as women (by which is meant, unlike men) under existing conditions.

My concern is not with which of these paths to sex equality is preferable in the long run or more appropriate to any particular issue, although most discourse on sex discrimination revolves about these questions as if that were all there is. My point is logically prior: to treat issues of sex equality as issues of sameness and difference *is to take a particular approach*. I call this the difference approach because it is obsessed with the sex difference. The main theme in the fugue is "we're the same, we're the same, we're the same." The counterpoint theme (in a higher register) is "but we're different, but we're different, but we're different." Its underlying story is: on the first day, difference was; on the second day, a division was created upon it; on the third day, irrational instances of dominance arose. Division may be rational or irrational. Dominance either seems or is justified. Difference *is*.

There is a politics to this. Concealed is the substantive way in which man has become the measure of all things. Under the sameness standard, women are measured according to our correspondence with man, our equality judged by our proximity to his measure. Under the difference standard, we are measured according to our lack of correspondence with him, our womanhood judged by our distance from his measure. Gender neutrality is thus simply the male standard, and the special protection rule is simply the female standard, but do not be deceived: masculinity, or maleness, is the referent for both. Think about it like those anatomy models in medical school. A male body is the human body; all those extra things women have are studied in ob/gyn. It truly is a situation in which more is less. Approaching sex discrimination in this way – as if sex questions are difference questions and equality questions are sameness questions – provides two ways for the law to hold women to a male standard and call that sex equality.

Having been very hard on the difference answer to sex equality questions, I should say that it takes up a very important problem: how to get women access to everything we have been excluded from, while also valuing everything that women are or have been allowed to become or have developed as a consequence of our struggle either not to be excluded from most of life's pursuits or to be taken seriously under the terms that have been permitted to be our terms. It negotiates what we have managed in relation to men. Legally articulated as the need to conform normative standards to existing reality, the strongest doctrinal expression of its sameness idea would prohibit taking gender into account in any way.

Its guiding impulse is: we're as good as you. Anything you can do, we can do. Just get out of the way. I have to confess a sincere affection for this approach. It has gotten women some access to employment[2] and education,[3] the public pursuits, including academic,[4] professional,[5] and blue-collar work;[6] the military;[7] and more than nominal access to athletics.[8] It has moved to change the dead ends that were all we were seen as good for and has altered what passed for women's lack of physical training, which was really serious training in passivity and enforced weakness. It makes you want to cry sometimes to know that it has had to be a mission for many women just to be permitted to do the work of this society, to have the dignity of doing jobs a lot of other people don't even want to do.

The issue of including women in the military draft[9] has presented the sameness answer to the sex equality question in all its simple dignity and complex equivocality. As a citizen, I should have to risk being killed just like you. The consequences of my resistance to this risk should count like yours. The undercurrent is: what's the matter, don't you want me to learn to kill... just like you? Sometimes I see this as a dialogue between women in the afterlife. The feminist says to the soldier, "we fought for your equality." The soldier says to the feminist, "oh, no, *we* fought for *your* equality."

Feminists have this nasty habit of counting bodies and refusing not to notice their gender. As applied, the sameness standard has mostly gotten men the benefit of those few things women have historically had – for all the good they did us. Almost every sex discrimination case that has been won at the Supreme Court level has been brought by a man.[10] Under the rule of gender neutrality, the law of custody and divorce has been transformed, giving men an equal chance at custody of children and at alimony.[11] Men often look like better "parents" under gender-neutral rules like level of income and presence of nuclear family, because men make more money and (as they say) initiate the building of family units.[12] In effect, they get preferred because society advantages them before they get into court, and law is prohibited from taking that preference into account because that would mean taking gender into account. The group realities that make women more in need of alimony are not permitted to matter, because only individual factors, gender-neutrally considered, may matter. So the fact that women will live their lives, as individuals, as members of the group women, with women's chances in a sex-discriminatory society, may not count, or else it is sex discrimination. The equality principle in this guise mobilizes the idea that the way to get things for women is to get them for men. Men have gotten them. Have women? We still have not got equal pay,[13] or equal work,[14] far less equal pay for equal work,[15] and we are close to losing separate enclaves like women's schools through this approach.[16]

Here is why. In reality, which this approach is not long on because it is liberal idealism talking to itself, virtually every quality that distinguishes men from women is already affirmatively compensated in this society. Men's physiology defines most sports,[17] their needs define auto and health insurance coverage, their socially designed biographies define workplace expectations and successful career patterns, their perspectives and concerns define quality in scholarship, their experiences and obsessions define merit, their objectification of life defines art, their military service defines citizenship, their presence defines family, their inability to get along with each other – their wars and rulerships – defines history, their image defines god, and their genitals define sex. For each of their differences from women, what amounts to an affirmative action plan is in effect, otherwise known as the structure and values of American society. But whenever women are, by this standard, "different" from men and insist on not having it held against us, whenever a difference is used to keep us second class and we refuse to smile about it, equality law has a paradigm trauma and it's crisis time for the doctrine.

What this doctrine has apparently meant by sex inequality is not what happens to us. The law of sex discrimination that has resulted seems to be looking only for those ways women are kept down that have *not* wrapped themselves up as a difference – whether original, imposed, or imagined. Start with original: what to do about the fact that women actually have an ability men still lack, gestating children in utero. Pregnancy therefore is a difference. Difference doctrine says it is sex discrimination to give women what we need, because only women need it. It is not sex discrimination not to give women what we need because then only women will not get what we need.[18] Move into imposed: what to do about the fact that most women are segregated into low-paying jobs where there are no men. Suspecting that the structure of the marketplace will be entirely subverted if comparable worth is put into effect, difference doctrine says that because there is no man to set a standard from which women's treatment is a deviation, there is no sex discrimination here, only sex difference. Never mind that there is no man to compare with because no man would do that job if he had a choice, and of course he has because he is a man, so he won't.[19]

Now move into the so-called subtle reaches of the imposed category, the de facto area. Most jobs in fact require that the person, gender neutral, who is qualified for them will be someone who is not the primary caretaker of a preschool child.[20] Pointing out that this raises a concern of sex in a society in which women are expected to care for the children is taken as day one of taking gender into account in the structuring of jobs. To do that would violate the rule against not noticing situated differences based on gender, so it never emerges that day one of taking gender into account was the day the job was structured with the expectation that its occupant would have no child care responsibilities. Imaginary sex differences – such as between male and female applicants to administer estates or between males aging and dying and females aging and dying[21] – I will concede, the doctrine can handle.

I will also concede that there are many differences between women and men. I mean, can you imagine elevating one half of a population and denigrating the other half and producing a population in which everyone is the same? What the sameness standard fails to notice is that men's differences from women are equal to women's differences from men. There is an *equality* there. Yet the sexes are not socially equal. The difference approach misses the fact that hierarchy of power produces real as well as fantasied differences, differences that are also inequalities. What is missing in the difference approach is what Aristotle missed in his empiricist notion that equality means treating likes alike and unlikes unlike, and nobody has questioned it since. Why should you have to be the same as a man to get what a man gets simply because he is one? Why does maleness provide an original entitlement, not questioned on the basis of *its* gender, so that it is women – women who want to make a case of unequal treatment in a world men have made in their image (this is really the part Aristotle missed) – who have to show in effect that they are men in every relevant respect, unfortunately mistaken for women on the basis of an accident of birth?

The women that gender neutrality benefits, and there are some, show the suppositions of this approach in highest relief. They are mostly women who have been able to construct a biography that somewhat approximates the male norm, at least on paper. They are the qualified, the least of sex discrimination's victims. When they are denied a man's chance, it looks the most like sex bias. The more unequal society gets, the fewer such women are permitted to exist. Therefore, the more unequal society gets, the *less* likely the difference doctrine is to be able to do anything about it, because unequal power creates both the appearance and the reality of sex differences along the same lines as it creates its sex inequalities.

The special benefits side of the difference approach has not compensated for the differential of being second class. The special benefits rule is the only place in mainstream equality doctrine where you get to identify as a woman and not have that mean giving up all claim to equal treatment – but it comes close. Under its double standard, women who stand to inherit something when their husbands die have gotten the exclusion of a small percentage of the inheritance tax, to the tune of Justice Douglas waxing eloquent about the difficulties of all women's economic situation.[22] If we're going to be stigmatized as different, it would be nice if the compensation would fit the disparity. Women have also gotten three more years than men get before we have to be advanced or kicked out of the military hierarchy, as compensation for being precluded from combat, the usual way to advance.[23] Women have also gotten excluded from contact jobs in male-only prisons because we might get raped, the Court taking the viewpoint of the reasonable rapist on women's employment opportunities.[24] We also get protected out of jobs because of our fertility. The reason is that the job has health hazards, and somebody who might be a real person some day and therefore could sue – that is, a fetus – might be hurt if women, who apparently are not real persons and therefore can't sue either for the hazard to our health or for the lost employment opportunity, are given jobs that subject our bodies to possible harm.[25] Excluding women is always an option if equality feels in tension with the pursuit itself. They never seem to think of excluding men. Take combat.[26] Somehow it takes the glory out of the foxhole, the buddiness out of the trenches, to imagine us out there. You get the feeling they might rather end the draft, they might even rather not fight wars at all than have to do it with us.

The double standard of these rules doesn't give women the dignity of the single standard; it also does not (as the differences standard does) suppress the gender of its referent, which is, of course, the female gender. I must also confess some affection for this standard. The work of Carol Gilligan on gender differences in moral reasoning[27] gives it a lot of dignity, more than it has ever had, more, frankly, than I thought it ever could have. But she achieves for moral reasoning what the special protection rule achieves in law: the affirmative rather than the negative valuation of that which has accurately distinguished women from men, by making it seem as though those attributes, with their consequences, really are somehow ours, rather than what male supremacy has attributed to us for its own use. For women to affirm difference, when difference means dominance, as it does with gender, means to affirm the qualities and characteristics of powerlessness.

Women have done good things, and it is a good thing to affirm them. I think quilts are art. I think women have a history. I think we create culture. I also know that we have not only been excluded from making what has been considered art; our artifacts have been excluded from setting the standards by which art is art. Women have a history all right, but it is a history both of what was and of what was not allowed to be. So I am critical of affirming what we have been, which necessarily is what we have been permitted, as if it is women's, ours, possessive. As if equality, in spite of everything, already ineluctably exists.

I am getting hard on this and am about to get harder on it. I do not think that the way women reason morally is morality "in a different voice."[28] I think it is morality in a higher register, in the feminine voice. Women value care because men have valued us according to the care we give them, and we could probably use some. Women think in relational terms because our existence is defined in relation to men. Further, when you are powerless, you don't just speak differently. A lot, you don't speak. Your speech is not just differently articulated, it is silenced. Eliminated, gone. You aren't just deprived of a language with which to articulate your distinctiveness, although you are; you are deprived of a life out of which articulation might come. Not being heard is not just a function of lack of recognition, not just that no one knows how to listen to you, although it is that; it is also silence of the deep kind, the silence of being prevented from having anything to say. Sometimes it is permanent. All I am saying is that the damage of sexism is real, and reifying that into differences is an insult to our possibilities.

So long as these issues are framed this way, demands for equality will always appear to be asking to have it both ways: the same when we are the same, different when we are different. But this is the way men have it: equal and different too. They have it the same as women when they are the same and want it, and different from women when they are different and want to be, which usually they do. Equal and different too would only be parity.[29] But under male supremacy, while being told we get it both ways, both the specialness of the pedestal and an even chance at the race, the ability to be a woman and a person, too, few women get much benefit of either.

There is an alternative approach, one that threads its way through existing law and expresses, I think, the reason equality law exists in the first place. It provides a second answer, a dissident answer in law and philosophy, to both the equality question and the gender question. In this approach, an equality question is a question of the distribution of power. Gender is also a question of power, specifically of male supremacy and female subordination. The question of equality, from the standpoint of what it is going to take to get it, is at root a question of hierarchy, which – as power succeeds in constructing social perception and social reality – derivatively becomes a categorical distinction, a difference. Here, on the first day that matters, dominance was achieved, probably by force. By the second day, division along the same lines had to be relatively firmly in place. On the third day, if not sooner, differences were demarcated, together with social systems to exaggerate them in perception and in fact, *because* the systematically differential delivery of benefits and deprivations required making no mistake about who was who. Comparatively speaking, man has been resting ever since. Gender might not even code as difference, might not mean distinction epistemologically, were it not for its consequences for social power.

I call this the dominance approach, and it is the ground I have been standing on in criticizing mainstream law. The goal of this dissident approach is not to make legal categories trace and trap the way things are. It is not to make rules that fit reality. It is critical of reality. Its task is not to formulate abstract standards that will produce determinate outcomes in particular cases. Its project is more substantive, more jurisprudential than formulaic, which is why it is difficult for the mainstream discourse to dignify it as an approach to doctrine or to imagine it as a rule of law at all. It proposes to expose that which women have had little choice but to be confined to, in order to change it.

The dominance approach centers on the most sex-differential abuses of women as a gender, abuses that sex equality law in its difference garb could not confront. It is based on a reality about which little of a systematic nature was known before 1970, a reality that calls for a new conception of the problem of sex inequality. This new information includes not only the extent and intractability of sex segregation into poverty, which has been known before, but the range of issues termed violence against women, which has not been. It combines women's material desperation, through being relegated to categories of jobs that pay nil, with the massive amount of rape and attempted rape – 44 percent of all women – about which virtually nothing is done;[30] the sexual assault of children – 38 percent of girls and 10 percent of boys – which is apparently endemic to the patriarchal family;[31] the battery of women that is systematic in one quarter to one third of our homes;[32] prostitution, women's fundamental economic condition, what we do when all else fails, and for many women in this country, all else fails often;[33] and pornography, an industry that traffics in female flesh, making sex inequality into sex to the tune of eight billion dollars a year in profits largely to organized crime.[34]

These experiences have been silenced out of the difference definition of sex equality largely because they happen almost exclusively to women. Understand: for this reason, they are considered *not* to raise sex equality issues. Because this treatment is done almost uniquely to women, it is implicitly treated as a difference, the sex difference, when in fact it is the socially situated subjection of women. The whole point of women's social relegation to inferiority as a gender is that for the most part these things aren't done to men. Men are not paid half of what women are paid for doing the same work on the basis of their equal difference. Everything they touch does not turn valueless because they touched it. When they are hit, a person has been assaulted. When they are sexually violated, it is not simply tolerated or found entertaining or defended as the necessary structure of the family, the price of civilization, or a constitutional right.

Does this differential describe the sex difference? Maybe so. It does describe the systematic relegation of an entire group of people to a condition of inferiority and attribute it to their nature. If this differential were biological, maybe biological intervention would have to be considered. If it were evolutionary, perhaps men would have to evolve differently. Because I think it is political, I think its politics construct the deep structure of society. Men who do not rape women have nothing wrong with their hormones. Men who are made sick by pornography and do not eroticize their revulsion are not underevolved. This social status in which we can be used and abused and trivialized and humiliated and bought and sold and passed around and patted on the head and put in place and told to smile so that we look as though we're enjoying it all is not what some of us have in mind as sex equality.

This second approach – which is not abstract, which is at odds with socially imposed reality and therefore does not look like a standard according to the standard for standards – became the implicit model for racial justice applied by the courts during the sixties. It has since eroded with the erosion of judicial commitment to racial equality. It was based on the realization that the condition of Blacks in particular was not fundamentally a matter of rational or irrational differentiation on the basis of race but was fundamentally a matter of white supremacy, under which racial differences became invidious as a consequence.[35] To consider gender in this way, observe again that men are as different from women as women are from men, but socially the sexes are not equally powerful. To be on the top of a hierarchy is certainly different from being on the bottom, but that is an obfuscatingly neutralized way of putting it, as a hierarchy is a great deal more than that. If gender were merely a question of difference, sex inequality would be a problem of mere sexism, of mistaken differentiation, of inaccurate categorization of individuals. This is what the difference approach thinks it is and is therefore sensitive to. But if gender is an inequality first, constructed as a socially relevant differentiation in order to keep that inequality in place, then sex inequality questions are questions of systematic dominance, of male supremacy, which is not at all abstract and is anything but a mistake.

If differentiation into classifications, in itself, is discrimination, as it is in difference doctrine, the use of law to change group-based social inequalities becomes problematic, even contradictory. This is because the group whose situation is to be changed must necessarily be legally identified and delineated, yet to do so is considered in fundamental tension with the guarantee against legally sanctioned inequality. If differentiation is discrimination, affirmative action, and any legal change in social inequality, is discrimination – but the existing social differentiations which constitute the inequality are not? This is only to say that, in the view that equates differentiation with discrimination, changing an unequal status quo is discrimination, but allowing it to exist is not.

Looking at the difference approach and the dominance approach from each other's point of view clarifies some otherwise confusing tensions in sex equality debates. From the point of view of the dominance approach, it becomes clear that the difference approach adopts the point of view of male supremacy on the status of the sexes. Simply by treating the status quo as "the standard," it invisibly and uncritically accepts the arrangements under male supremacy. In this sense, the difference approach is masculinist, although it can be expressed in a female voice. The dominance approach, in that it sees the inequalities of the social world from the standpoint of the subordination of women to men, is feminist.

If you look through the lens of the difference approach at the world as the dominance approach imagines it – that is, if you try to see real inequality through a lens that has difficulty seeing an inequality as an inequality if it also appears as a difference – you see demands for change in the distribution of power as demands for special protection. This is because the only tools that the difference paradigm offers to comprehend disparity equate the recognition of a gender line with an admission of lack of entitlement to equality under law. Since equality questions are primarily confronted in this approach as matters of empirical fit[36] – that is, as matters of accurately shaping legal rules (implicitly modeled on the standard men set) to the way the world is (also implicitly modeled on the standard men set) – any existing differences must be negated to merit equal treatment. For ethnicity as well as for gender, it is basic to mainstream discrimination doctrine to preclude any true diversity among equals or true equality within diversity.

To the difference approach, it further follows that any attempt to change the way the world actually is looks like a moral question requiring a separate judgment of how things ought to be. This approach imagines asking the following disinterested question that can be answered neutrally as to groups: against the weight of empirical difference, should we treat some as the equals of others, even when they may not be entitled to it because they are not up to standard? Because this construction of the problem is part of what the dominance approach unmasks, it does not arise with the dominance approach, which therefore does not see its own foundations as moral. If sex inequalities are approached as matters of imposed status, which are in need of change if a legal mandate of equality means anything at all, the question whether women should be treated unequally means simply whether women should be treated as less. When it is exposed as a naked power question, there is no separable question of what ought to be. The only real question is what is and is not a gender question. Once no amount of difference justifies treating women as subhuman, eliminating that is what equality law is for. In this shift of paradigms, equality propositions become no longer propositions of good and evil, but of power and powerlessness, no more disinterested in their origins or neutral in their arrival at conclusions than are the problems they address.

There came a time in Black people's movement for equality in this country when slavery stopped being a question of how it could be justified and became a question of how it could be ended. Racial disparities surely existed, or racism would have been harmless, but at that point – a point not yet reached for issues of sex – no amount of group difference mattered anymore. This is the same point at which a group's characteristics, including empirical attributes, become constitutive of the fully human, rather than being defined as exceptions to or as distinct from the fully human. To one-sidedly measure one group's differences against a standard set by the other incarnates partial standards. The moment when one's particular qualities become part of the standard by which humanity is measured is a millenial moment.

To summarize the argument: seeing sex equality questions as matters of reasonable or unreasonable classification is part of the way male dominance is expressed in law. If you follow my shift in perspective from gender as difference to gender as dominance, gender changes from a distinction that is presumptively valid to a detriment that is presumptively suspect. The difference approach tries to map reality; the dominance approach tries to challenge and change it. In the dominance approach, sex discrimination stops being a question of morality and starts being a question of politics.

You can tell if sameness is your standard for equality if my critique of hierarchy looks like a request for special protection in disguise. It's not. It envisions a change that would make possible a simple equal chance for the first time. To define the reality of sex as difference and the warrant of equality as sameness is wrong on both counts. Sex, in nature, is not a bipolarity; it is a continuum. In society it is made into a bipolarity. Once this is done, to require that one be the same as those who set the standard – those which one is already socially defined as different from – simply means that sex equality is conceptually designed never to be achieved. Those who most need equal treatment will be the least similar, socially, to those whose situation sets the standard as against which one's entitlement to be equally treated is measured. Doctrinally speaking, the deepest problems of sex inequality will not find women "similarly situated"[37] to men. Far less will practices of sex inequality require that acts be intentionally discriminatory.[38] All that is required is that the status quo be maintained. As a strategy for maintaining social power first structure reality unequally, then require that entitlement to alter it be grounded on a lack of distinction in situation; first structure perception so that different equals inferior, then require that discrimination be activated by evil minds who *know* they are treating equals as less.

I say, give women equal power in social life. Let what we say matter, then we will discourse on questions of morality. Take your foot off our necks, then we will hear in what tongue women speak. So long as sex equality is limited by sex difference, whether you like it or don't like it, whether you value it or seek to negate it, whether you stake it out as a grounds for feminism or occupy it as the terrain of misogyny, women will be born, degraded, and die. We would settle for that equal protection of the laws under which one would be born, live, and die, in a country where protection is not a dirty word and equality is not a special privilege.

Notes

1 The Bona Fide Occupational Qualification (BFOQ) exception to Title VII of the Civil Rights Act of 1964, 42 U.S.C. § 2000 e-(2)(e), permits sex to be a job qualification when it is a valid one. The leading interpretation of the proposed federal Equal Rights Amendment would, pursuing a similar analytic structure, permit a "unique physical characteristic" exception to its otherwise absolute embargo on taking sex into account. Barbara Brown, Thomas I. Emerson, Gail Falk, and Ann E. Freedman, "The Equal Rights Amendment: A Constitutional Basis for Equal Rights for Women," 80 *Yale Law Journal* 893 (1971).

2 Title VII of the Civil Rights Act of 1964, 42 U.S.C. § 2000 e; Phillips v. Martin-Marietta, 400 US 542 (1971). Frontiero v. Richardson, 411 US 484 (1974) is the high-water mark of this approach. *See also* City of Los Angeles v. Manhart, 435 US 702 (1978); Newport News Shipbuilding and Dry Dock Co. v. EEOC, 462 US 669 (1983).

3 Title IX of the Education Amendments of 1972, 20 U.S.C.§1681; Cannon v. University of Chicago, 441 US 677 (1981); Mississippi University for Women v. Hogan, 458 US 718 (1982); *see also* De La Cruz v. Tormey, 582 F.2d 45 (9th Cir. 1978).

4 My impression is that women appear to lose most academic sex discrimination cases that go to trial, although I know of no systematic or statistical study on the subject. One case that won eventually, elevating the standard of proof in the process, is Sweeney v. Board of Trustees of Keene State College, 439 US 29 (1979). The ruling for the plaintiff was affirmed on remand, 604 F.2d 106 (1st Cir. 1979).

5 Hishon v. King & Spalding, 467 US 69 (1984).

6 See, for example, Vanguard Justice v. Hughes, 471 F. Supp. 670 (D. Md. 1979); Meyer v. Missouri State Highway Commission, 567 F.2d 804, 891 (8th Cir. 1977); Payne v. Travenol Laboratories Inc., 416 F. Supp. 248 (N.D. Mass. 1976). *See also* Dothard v. Rawlinson, 433 US 321 (1977) (height and weight requirements invalidated for prison guard contact positions because of disparate impact on sex).

7 Frontiero v. Richardson, 411 US 484 (1974); Schlesinger v. Ballard, 419 US 498 (1975).

8 This situation is relatively complex. *See* Gomes v. R.I. Interscholastic League, 469 F. Supp. 659 (D. R.I. 1979); Brenden v. Independent School District, 477 F.2d 1292 (8th Cir. 1973); O'Connor v. Board of Education of School District No. 23, 645 F.2d 578 (7th Cir. 1981); Cape v. Tennessee Secondary School Athletic Association, 424 F. Supp. 732 (E.D. Tenn. 1976), *rev'd*, 563 F.2d 793 (6th Cir. 1977); Yellow Springs Exempted Village School District Board of Education v. Ohio High School Athletic Association, 443 F. Supp. 753 (S.D. Ohio 1978); Aiken v. Lieuallen, 593 P.2d 1243 (Or. App. 1979).

9 Rostker v. Goldberg, 453 US 57 (1981). *See also* Lori S. Kornblum, "Women Warriors in a Men's World: The Combat Exclusion," 2 *Law & Inequality: A Journal of Theory and Practice* 353 (1984).

10 David Cole, "Strategies of Difference: Litigating for Women's Rights in a Man's World," 2 *Law & Inequality: A Journal of Theory and Practice* 34 note 4 (1984) (collecting cases).

11 Devine v. Devine, 398 So. 2d 686 (Ala. Sup. Ct. 1981); Danielson v. Board of Higher Education, 358 F. Supp. 22 (S.D.N.Y. 1972); Weinberger v. Wiesenfeld, 420 US 636 (1975); Stanley v. Illinois, 405 US 645 (1971); Caban v. Mohammed, 441 US 380 (1979); Orr v. Orr, 440 US 268 (1979).

12 Lenore Weitzman, "The Economics of Divorce: Social and Economic Consequences of Property, Alimony and Child Support Awards," 28 *U.C.L.A. Law Review* 1118, 1251 (1982), documents a decline in women's standard of living of 73 percent and an increase in men's of 42 percent within a year after divorce.

13 Equal Pay Act, 29 U.S.C. § 206(d)(1) (1976) guarantees pay equality, as does case law, *but cf.* data on pay gaps, "Introduction," note 2.

14 Examples include Christenson v. State of Iowa, 563 F.2d 353 (8th Cir. 1977); Gerlach v. Michigan Bell Tel. Co., 501 F. Supp. 1300 (E.D. Mich. 1980); Odomes v. Nucare, Inc., 653 F.2d 246 (6th Cir. 1981) (female nurse's aide denied Title VII remedy because her job duties were not substantially similar to those of better-paid male orderly); Power v. Barry County, Michigan, 539 F. Supp. 721 (W.D. Mich. 1982); Spaulding v. University of Washington, 740 F.2d 686 (9th Cir. 1984).

15 County of Washington v. Gunther, 452 US 161 (1981) permits a comparable worth-type challenge where pay inequality can be proven to be a correlate of intentional job segregation. *See also* Lemons v. City and County of Denver, 17 FEP Cases 910 (D. Colo. 1978), *aff'd*, 620 F.2d 228 (10th Cir. 1977), *cert. denied*, 449 US 888 (1980); AFSCME v. State of Washington, 770 F.2d 1401 (9th Cir. 1985). *See generally* Carol Jean Pint, "Value, Work and Women," 1 *Law & Inequality: A Journal of Theory and Practice* 159 (1983).

16 Combine the result in Bob Jones University v. United States, 461 US 547 (1983) with Mississippi University for Women v. Hogan, 458 US 718 (1982), and the tax-exempt status of women-only schools is clearly threatened.

17 A particularly pungent example comes from a case in which the plaintiff sought to compete in boxing matches with men, since there were no matches sponsored by the defendant among women. A major reason that preventing the woman from competing was found not to violate her equality rights was that the "safety rules and precautions [were] developed, designed, and tested in the context of all-male competition." Lafler v. Athletic Board of Control, 536 F. Supp. 104, 107 (W.D. Mich. 1982). As the court put it: "In this case, the real differences between the male and female anatomy are relevant in considering whether men and women may be treated differently with regard to their participating in boxing. The plaintiff *admits* that she wears a protective covering for her breasts while boxing. Such a protective covering . . . would violate Rule Six, Article 9 of the Amateur Boxing Federation rules currently in effect. The same rule *requires* contestants to wear a protective cup, a rule obviously designed for the unique anatomical characteristics of men." Ibid., at 106 (emphasis added). The rule is based on the male anatomy, therefore not a justification for the discrimination but an example of it. This is not considered in the opinion, nor does the judge discuss whether women might benefit from genital protection, and men from chest guards, as in some other sports.

18 This is a reference to the issues raised by several recent cases which consider whether states' attempts to compensate pregnancy leaves and to secure jobs on return constitute sex discrimination. California Federal Savings and Loan Assn. v. Guerra, 758 F.2d 390 (9th Cir. 1985), *cert. granted* 54 U.S.L.W. 3460 (US Jan. 13, 1986); *see also* Miller-Wohl v. Commissioner of Labor, 515 F. Supp. 1264 (D. Montana 1981), *vacated and dismissed*, 685 F.2d 1088 (9th Cir. 1982). The position argued in "Difference and Dominance" here suggests that if these benefits are prohibited under Title VII, Title VII is unconstitutional under the equal protection clause.

This argument was not made directly in either case. The American Civil Liberties Union argued that the provisions requiring pregnancy to be compensated in employment, without comparable coverage for men, violated Title VII's prohibition on pregnancy-based classifications and on sex. Montana had made it illegal for an employer to "terminate a woman's employment because of her pregnancy" or to "refuse to grant to the employee a reasonable leave of absence for such pregnancy." Montana Maternity Leave Act § 49-2-310(1) and (2).

According to the ACLU, this provision "grants pregnant workers certain employment rights not enjoyed by other workers . . . Legislation designed to benefit women has . . . perpetuated destructive stereotypes about their proper roles and operated to deny them rights and benefits enjoyed by men. The [Montana provision] deters employers from hiring women who are or may become pregnant, causes resentment and hostility in the workplace, and penalizes men." Brief of American Civil Liberties Union, *et al. amicus curiae*, Montana Supreme Court No. 84-172, at 7. The National Organization for Women argued that the California provision, which requires employers to give pregnant workers unpaid disability leave with job security for up to four months, would violate Title VII should Title VII be interpreted to permit it. Brief of National Organization for Women, *et al.*, United States Court of Appeals for the Ninth Circuit, 685 F.2d 1088 (9th Cir. 1982).

When Congress passed the Pregnancy Discrimination Act, amending Title VII, 42 U.S.C. § 2000 e(k), it defined "because of sex" or "on the basis of sex" to include "because of or on the basis of pregnancy, childbirth, or related medical conditions; and women affected by pregnancy, childbirth, or related medical conditions shall be treated the same for all employment-related purposes." In so doing, Congress arguably decided that one did not have to be the same as a man to be treated without discrimination, since it guaranteed freedom from discriminatory treatment on the basis of a condition that is not the same for men as it is for women. It even used the word "women" in the statute.

Further, Congress made this decision expressly to overrule the Supreme Court decision in General Electric v. Gilbert, 429 US 125 (1976), which had held that failure to cover pregnancy as a disability was not sex discrimination because the line between pregnant and nonpregnant was not the line between women and men. In rejecting this logic, as the Court found it did expressly in Newport News Shipbuilding and Dry Dock Co. v. EEOC, 462 US 669, 678 (1983), Congress rejected the implicit measuring of women's entitlement to equality by a male standard. Nor need all women be the same, that is, pregnant or potentially so, to have pregnancy-based discrimination be sex-based discrimination.

Upholding the California pregnancy leave and job security law, the Ninth Circuit opinion did not require sameness for equality to be delivered: "The PDA does not require states to ignore pregnancy. It requires that women be treated equally . . . [E]quality under the PDA must be measured in employment opportunity, not necessarily in amounts of money expended – or in amounts of days of disability leave expended. Equality . . . compares coverage to actual need, not coverage to hypothetical identical needs." California Federal v. Guerra, 758 F.2d 390 (9th Cir. 1985) (Ferguson, J.). "We are not the first court to announce the goal of Title VII is equality of employment opportunity, not necessarily sameness of treatment." Ibid., at 396 note 7.

19 Most women work at jobs mostly women do, and most of those jobs are paid less than jobs that mostly men do. See, for example, Pint, note 15 above, at 162–3 nn.19, 20 (collecting studies). To the point that men may not meet the male standard themselves, one court found that a union did not fairly represent its women in the following terms: "As to the yard and driver jobs, defendants suggest not only enormous intellectual requirements, but that the physical demands of those jobs are so great as to be beyond the capacity of any female. Again, it is noted that plaintiffs' capacity to perform those jobs was never tested, despite innumerable requests therefor. It is also noted that defendants have never suggested *which* of the innumerable qualifications they list for these jobs (for the first time) the plaintiffs might fail to meet. The court, however, will accept without listing here the extraordinary catalogue of feats which defendants argue must be performed in the yard, and as a driver. That well may be. However, one learns from this record that one cannot be too weak, too sick, too old and infirm, or too ignorant to perform these jobs, *so long as one is a man*. The plaintiffs appear to the layperson's eye to be far more physically fit than many of the drivers who moved into the yard, over the years, according to the testimony of defense witnesses . . . In short, they were all at least as fit as the men with serious physical deficits and disabilities who held yard jobs." Jones v. Cassens Transport, 617 F. Supp. 869, 892 (1985) (emphasis in original).

20 Phillips v. Martin-Marietta, 400 US 542 (1971).

21 Reed v. Reed, 404 US 71 (1971) held that a statute barring women from administering estates is sex discrimination. If few women were taught to read and write, as used to be the case, the gender difference would not be imaginary in this case, yet the social situation would be even more sex discriminatory than it is now. Compare City of Los Angeles v. Manhart, 434 US 815 (1978), which held that requiring women to make larger contributions to their retirement plan was sex discrimination, in spite of the allegedly proven sex difference that women on the average outlive men.

22 Kahn v. Shevin, 416 US 351, 353 (1974).

23 Schlesinger v. Ballard, 419 US 498 (1975).

24 Dothard v. Rawlinson, 433 US 321 (1977); *see also* Michael M. v. Sonoma County Superior Court, 450 US 464 (1981).

25 Doerr v. B. F. Goodrich, 484 F. Supp. 320 (N. D. Ohio 1979). Wendy Webster Williams, "Firing the Woman to Protect the Fetus: The Reconciliation of

Fetal Protection with Employment Opportunity Goals Under Title VII," 69 *Georgetown Law Journal* 641 (1981). *See also* Hayes v. Shelby Memorial Hospital, 546 F. Supp. 259 (N. D. Ala. 1982); Wright v. Olin Corp., 697 F.2d 1172 (4th Cir. 1982).

26 Congress requires the Air Force (10 U.S.C. § 8549 [1983]) and the Navy (10 U.S.C. § 6015 [1983]) to exclude women from combat, with some exceptions. Owens v. Brown, 455 F. Supp. 291 (D.D.C. 1978), had previously invalidated the prior Navy combat exclusion because it prohibited women from filling jobs they could perform and inhibited Navy's discretion to assign women on combat ships. The Army excludes women from combat based upon its own policies under congressional authorization to determine assignment (10 U.S.C. § 3012 [e] [1983]).

27 Carol Gilligan, *In a Different Voice* (1982).

28 Ibid.

29 I argued this in Appendix A of my *Sexual Harassment of Working Women: A Case of Sex Discrimination* (1979). That book ends with "Women want to be equal and different, too." I could have added "Men are." As a standard, this would have reduced women's aspirations for equality to some corresponding version of men's actualities. But as an observation, it would have been true.

30 Diana Russell and Nancy Howell, "The Prevalence of Rape in the United States Revisited," 8 *Signs: Journal of Women in Culture and Society* 689 (1983) (44 percent of women in 930 households were victims of rape or attempted rape at some time in their lives).

31 Diana Russell, "The Incidence and Prevalence of Intrafamilial and Extrafamilial Sexual Abuse of Female Children," *7 Child Abuse & Neglect: The International Journal* 133 (1983).

32 R. Emerson Dobash and Russell Dobash, *Violence against Wives: A Case against the Patriarchy* (1979); Bruno v. Codd, 90 Misc. 2d 1047, 396 N.Y.S. 2d 974 (Sup. Ct. 1977), *rev'd*, 64 A.D. 2d 582, 407 N.Y.S. 2d 165 (1st Dep't 1978), *aff'd* 47 N.Y. 2d 582, 393 N.E. 2d 976, 419 N.Y.S.2d 901 (1979).

33 Kathleen Barry, *Female Sexual Slavery* (1979); Moira K. Griffin, "Wives, Hookers and the Law: The Case for Decriminalizing Prostitution," 10 *Student Lawyer* 18 (1982); Report of Jean Fernand-Laurent, Special Rapporteur on the Suppression of the Traffic in Persons and the Exploitation of the Prostitution of Others (a United Nations report), in *International Feminism: Networking against Female Sexual Slavery* 130 (Kathleen Barry, Charlotte Bunch, and Shirley Castley eds.) (Report of the Global Feminist Workshop to Organize against Traffic in Women, Rotterdam, Netherlands, Apr. 6–15, 1983 [1984]).

34 Galloway and Thornton, "Crackdown on Pornography – A No-Win Battle," *US News and World Report*, June 4, 1984, at 84. *See also* "The Place of Pornography," *Harper's*, November 1984, at 31 (citing $7 billion per year).

35 Loving v. Virginia, 388 US 1 (1967), first used the term "white supremacy" in invalidating an anti-miscegenation law as a violation of equal protection. The law equally forbade whites and blacks to intermarry. Although going nowhere near as far, courts in the athletics area have sometimes seen that "same" does not necessarily mean "equal" nor does "equal" require "same." In a context of sex inequality like that which has prevailed in athletic opportunity, allowing boys to compete on girls' teams may diminish overall sex equality. "Each position occupied by a male reduces the female participation and increases the overall disparity of athletic opportunity which generally exists." Petrie v. Illinois High School Association, 394 N.E. 2d 855, 865 (III. 1979). "We conclude that to furnish exactly the same athletic opportunities to boys as to girls would be most difficult and would be detrimental to the compelling governmental interest of equalizing general athletic opportunities between the sexes." Ibid.

36 The scholars Tussman and tenBroek first used the term "fit" to characterize the necessary relation between a valid equality rule and the world to which it refers. J. Tussman and J. tenBroek, "The Equal Protection of the Laws," 37 *California Law Review* 341 (1949).

37 Royster Guano Co. v. Virginia, 253 US 412, 415 (1920): "[A classification] must be reasonable, not arbitrary, and must rest upon some ground of difference having a fair and substantial relation to the object of the legislation, so that all persons similarly circumstanced shall be treated alike." Reed v. Reed, 404 US 71, 76 (1971): "Regardless of their sex, persons within any one of the enumerated classes . . . are similarly situated . . . By providing dissimilar treatment for men and women who are thus similarly situated, the challenged section violates the Equal Protection Clause."

38 Washington v. Davis, 426 US 229 (1976) and Personnel Administrator of Massachusetts v. Feeney, 442 US 256 (1979) require that intentional discrimination be shown for discrimination to be shown.

29

Toward a Humanist Justice

Susan Moller Okin

The family is the linchpin of gender, reproducing it from one generation to the next. As we have seen, family life as typically practiced in our society is not just, either to women or to children. Moreover, it is not conducive to the rearing of citizens with a strong sense of justice. In spite of all the rhetoric about equality between the sexes, the traditional or quasi-traditional division of family labor still prevails. Women are made vulnerable by constructing their lives around the expectation that they will be primary parents; they become more vulnerable within marriages in which they fulfill this expectation, whether or not they also work for wages; and they are most vulnerable in the event of separation or divorce, when they usually take over responsibility for children without adequate support from their ex-husbands. Since approximately half of all marriages end in divorce, about half of our children are likely to experience its dislocations, often made far more traumatic by the socioeconomic consequences of both gender-structured marriage and divorce settlements that fail to take account of it. I have suggested that, for very important reasons, the family *needs* to be a just institution, and have shown that contemporary theories of justice neglect women and ignore gender. How can we address this injustice?

Susan Moller Okin, "Toward a Humanist Justice," pp. 170–86 and 209–10 (notes) from *Justice, Gender, and the Family*. New York: Basic Books, 1989.

This is a complex question. It is particularly so because we place great value on our freedom to live different kinds of lives, there is no current consensus on many aspects of gender, and we have good reason to suspect that many of our beliefs about sexual difference and appropriate sex roles are heavily influenced by the very fact that we grew up in a gender-structured society. All of us have been affected, in our very psychological structures, by the fact of gender in our personal pasts, just as our society has been deeply affected by its strong influence in our collective past. Because of the lack of shared meanings about gender, it constitutes a particularly hard case for those who care deeply about both personal freedom and social justice. The way we divide the labor and responsibilities in our personal lives seems to be one of those things that people should be free to work out for themselves, but because of its vast repercussions it belongs clearly within the scope of things that must be governed by principles of justice. Which is to say, in the language of political and moral theory, that it belongs both to the sphere of "the good" and to that of "the right."

I shall argue here that any just and fair solution to the urgent problem of women's and children's vulnerability must encourage and facilitate the equal sharing by men and women of paid and unpaid work, of productive and reproductive labor. We must work toward a future in which all will be likely to choose this mode of life. A just future would be one without gender. In its social structures and practices, one's sex would have no more relevance than one's eye color or the length of one's toes. No assumptions would be made about "male" and "female" roles; childbearing would be so conceptually separated from child rearing and other family responsibilities that it would be a cause for surprise, and no little concern, if men and women were not equally responsible for domestic life or if children were to spend much more time with one parent than the other. It would be a future in which men and women participated in more or less equal numbers in every sphere of life, from infant care to different kinds of paid work to high-level politics. Thus it would no longer be the case that having no experience of raising children would be the practical prerequisite for attaining positions of the greatest social influence. Decisions about abortion and rape, about divorce settlements and sexual harassment, or about any other crucial social issues would not be made, as they often are now, by legislatures and benches of judges overwhelmingly populated by men whose power is in large part due to their advantaged position in the gender structure. If we are to be at all true to our democratic ideals, moving away from gender is essential. Obviously, the attainment of such a social world requires major changes in a multitude of institutions and social settings outside the home, as well as within it.

Such changes will not happen overnight. Moreover, any present solution to the vulnerability of women and children that is just and respects individual freedom must take into account that most people currently live in ways that are greatly affected by gender, and most still favor many aspects of current, gendered practices. Sociological studies confirm what most of us already infer from our own personal and professional acquaintances: there are no currently shared meanings in this country about the extent to which differences between the sexes are innate or environmental, about the appropriate roles of men and women, and about which family forms and divisions of labor are most beneficial for partners, parents, and children.[1] There are those, at one extreme, for whom the different roles of the two sexes, especially as parents, are deeply held tenets of religious belief. At the other end of the spectrum are those of us for whom the sooner all social differentiation between the sexes vanishes, the better it will be for all of us. And there are a thousand varieties of view in between. Public policies must respect people's views and choices. But they must do so only insofar as it can be ensured that these choices do not result, as they now do, in the vulnerability of women and children. Special protections must be built into our laws and public policies to ensure that, for those who choose it, the division of labor between the sexes does not result in injustice. In the face of these difficulties – balancing freedom and the effects of past choices against the needs of justice – I do not pretend to have arrived at any complete or fully satisfactory answers. But I shall attempt in this final chapter to suggest some social reforms, including changes in public policies and reforms of family law, that may help us work toward a solution to the injustices of gender.

Marriage has become an increasingly peculiar contract, a complex and ambiguous combination of anachronism and present-day reality. There is no longer the kind of agreement that once prevailed about what is expected of the parties to a marriage. Clearly, at least in the United States, it is no longer reasonable to assume that marriage will last a lifetime, since only half of current marriages are expected to. And yet, in spite of the increasing legal equality of men and women and the highly publicized figures about married women's increased participation in the labor force, many couples continue to adhere to more or less traditional patterns of role differentiation. As a recent article put it, women are "out of the house but not out of the kitchen."[2] Consequently, often working part-time or taking time out from wage work to care for family members, especially children, most wives are in a very different position from their husbands in their ability to be economically self-supporting. This is reflected, as we have seen, in power differentials between the sexes within the family. It means also, in the increasingly common event of divorce, usually by mutual agreement, that it is the mother who in 90 percent of cases will have physical custody of the children. But whereas the greater need for money goes one way, the bulk of the earning power almost always goes the other. This is one of the most important causes of the feminization of poverty, which is affecting the life chances of ever larger numbers of children as well as their mothers. The division of labor within families has always adversely affected women, by making them economically dependent on men. Because of the increasing instability of marriage, its effects on children have now reached crisis proportions.

Some who are critical of the present structure and practices of marriage have suggested that men and women simply be made free to make their own agreements about family life, contracting with each other, much as business contracts are made.[3] But this takes insufficient account of the history of gender in our culture and our own psychologies, of the present substantive inequalities between the sexes, and, most important, of the well-being of the children who result from the relationship. As has long been recognized in the realm of labor relations, justice is by no means always enhanced by the maximization of freedom of contract, if the individuals involved are in unequal positions to start with. Some have even suggested that it is consistent with justice to leave spouses to work out their own divorce settlement.[4] By this time, however, the two people ending a marriage are likely to be far *more* unequal. Such a practice would be even more catastrophic for most women and children than is the present system. Wives in any but the rare cases in which they as individuals have remained their husbands' socioeconomic equals could hardly be expected to reach a just solution if left "free" to "bargain" the terms of financial support or child custody. What would they have to bargain *with*?

There are many directions that public policy can and should take in order to make relations between men and women more just. In discussing these, I shall look back to some of the contemporary ways of thinking about justice that I find most convincing. I draw particularly on Rawls's idea of the original position and Walzer's conception of the complex equality found in separate spheres of justice, between which I find no inconsistency. I also keep in mind critical legal theorists' critique of contract, and the related idea, suggested earlier, that rights to privacy that are to be valuable to all of us can be enjoyed only insofar as the sphere of life in which we enjoy them ensures the equality of its adult members and protects children. Let us begin by asking what kind of arrangements persons in a Rawlsian original position would agree to regarding marriage, parental and other domestic responsibilities, and divorce. What kinds of policies would they agree to for other aspects of social life, such as the workplace and schools, that affect men, women, and children and relations among them? And let us consider whether these arrangements would satisfy Walzer's separate spheres test – that inequalities in one sphere of life not be allowed to overflow into another. Will they foster equality within the sphere of family life? For the protection of the privacy of a domestic sphere in which inequality exists is the protection of the right of the strong to exploit and abuse the weak.

Let us first try to imagine ourselves, as far as possible, in the original position, knowing neither what our sex nor any other of our personal characteristics will be once the veil of ignorance is lifted.[5] Neither do we know our place in society or our particular conception of the good life. Particularly relevant in this context, of course, is our lack of knowledge of our beliefs about the characteristics of men and women and our related convictions about the appropriate division of labor between the sexes. Thus the positions we represent must include a wide variety of beliefs on these matters. We may, once the veil of ignorance is lifted, find ourselves feminist men or feminist women whose conception of the good life includes the minimization of social differentiation between the sexes. Or we may find ourselves traditionalist men or women, whose conception of the good life, for religious or other reasons, is bound up in an adherence to the conventional division of labor between the sexes. The challenge is to arrive at and apply principles of justice having to do with the family and the division of labor between the sexes that can satisfy these vastly disparate points of view and the many that fall between.

There are some traditionalist positions so extreme that they ought not be admitted for consideration, since they violate such fundamentals as equal basic liberty and self-respect. We need not, and should not, that is to say, admit for consideration views based on the notion that women are inherently inferior beings whose function is to fulfill the needs of men. Such a view is no more admissible in the construction of just institutions for a modern pluralist society than is the view, however deeply held, that some are naturally slaves and others naturally and justifiably their masters. We need not, therefore, consider approaches to marriage that view it as an inherently and desirably hierarchical structure of dominance and subordination. Even if it were conceivable that a person who did not know whether he or she would turn out to be a man or a woman in the society being planned would subscribe to such views, they are not admissible. Even if there were no other reasons to refuse to admit such views, they must be excluded for the sake of children, for everyone in the original position has a high personal stake in the quality of childhood. Marriages of dominance and submission are bad for children as well as for their mothers, and the socioeconomic outcome of divorce after such a marriage is very likely to damage their lives and seriously restrict their opportunities.

With this proviso, what social structures and public policies regarding relations between the sexes, and the family in particular, could we agree on in the original position? I think we would arrive at a basic model that would absolutely minimize gender. I shall first give an account of some of what this would consist in. We would also, however, build in carefully protective institutions for those who wished to follow gender-structured modes of life. These too I shall try to spell out in some detail.

Moving Away from Gender

First, public policies and laws should generally assume no social differentiation of the sexes. Shared parental responsibility for child care would be both assumed and facilitated. Few people outside of feminist circles seem willing to acknowledge that society does not have to choose between a system of female parenting that renders women and children seriously vulnerable and a system of total reliance on day care provided outside the home. While high-quality day care, subsidized so as to be equally available to all children, certainly constitutes an important part of the response that society should make in order to provide justice for women and children, it is only one part.[6] If we start out with the reasonable assumption that women and men are equally parents of their children, and have equal responsibility for both the unpaid effort that goes into caring for them and their economic support, then we must rethink the demands of work life throughout the period in which a worker of either sex is a parent of a small child. We can no longer cling to the by now largely mythical assumption that every worker has "someone else" at home to raise "his" children.

The facilitation and encouragement of equally shared parenting would require substantial changes.[7] It would mean major changes in the workplace, all of which could be provided on an entirely (and not falsely) gender-neutral basis. Employers must be required by law not only completely to eradicate sex discrimination, including sexual harassment. They should also be required to make positive provision for the fact that most workers, for differing lengths of time in their working lives, are also parents, and are sometimes required to nurture other family members, such as their own aging parents. Because children are borne by women but can (and, I contend, should) be raised by both parents equally, policies relating to pregnancy and birth should be quite distinct from those relating to parenting. Pregnancy and childbirth, to whatever varying extent they require leave from work, should be regarded as temporarily disabling conditions like any others, and employers should be mandated to provide leave for all such conditions.[8] Of course, pregnancy and childbirth are far *more* than simply "disabling conditions," but they should be treated as such for leave purposes, in part because their disabling effects vary from one woman to another. It seems unfair to mandate, say, eight or more weeks of leave for a condition that disables many women for less time and some for much longer, while *not* mandating leave for illnesses or other disabling conditions. Surely a society as rich as ours can afford to do both.

Parental leave during the postbirth months must be available to mothers and fathers on the same terms, to facilitate shared parenting; they might take sequential leaves or each might take half-time leave. All workers should have the right, without prejudice to their jobs, seniority, benefits, and so on, to work less than full-time during the first year of a child's life, and to work flexible or somewhat reduced hours at least until the child reaches the age of seven. Correspondingly greater flexibility of hours must be provided for the parents of a child with any health problem or disabling condition. The professions whose greatest demands (such as tenure in academia or the partnership hurdle in law) coincide with the peak period of child rearing must restructure their demands or provide considerable flexibility for those of their workers who are also participating parents. Large-scale employers should also be required to provide high-quality on-site day care for children from infancy up to school age. And to ensure equal quality of day care for all young children, *direct government subsidies* (not tax credits, which benefit the better-off) should make up the difference between the cost of high-quality day care and what less well paid parents could reasonably be expected to pay.

There are a number of things that schools, too, must do to promote the minimization of gender. As Amy Gutmann has recently noted, in their present authority structures (84 percent of elementary school teachers are female, while 99 percent of school superintendents are male), "schools do not simply reflect, they perpetuate the social reality of gender preferences when they educate children in a system in which men rule women and women rule children." She argues that, since such sex stereotyping is "a formidable obstacle" to children's rational deliberation about the lives they wish to lead, sex should be regarded as a relevant qualification in the hiring of both teachers and administrators, until these proportions have become much more equal.[9]

An equally important role of our schools must be to ensure in the course of children's education that they become fully aware of the politics of gender. This does not only mean ensuring that women's experience and women's writing are included in the curriculum, although this in itself is undoubtedly important.[10] Its political significance has become obvious from the amount of protest that it has provoked. Children need also to be taught about the present inequalities, ambiguities, and uncertainties of marriage, the facts of workplace discrimination and segregation, and the likely consequences of making life choices based on assumptions about gender. They should be discouraged from thinking about their futures as *determined* by the sex to which they happen to belong. For many children, of course, personal experience has already "brought home" the devastating effects of the traditional division of labor between the sexes. But they do not necessarily come away from this experience with positive ideas about how to structure their own future family lives differently. As Anita Shreve has recently suggested, "the old home-economics courses that used to teach girls how to cook and sew might give way to the new home economics: teaching girls *and boys* how to combine working and parenting."[11] Finally, schools should be required to provide high-quality after-school programs, where children can play safely, do their homework, or participate in creative activities.

The implementation of all these policies would significantly help parents to share the earning and the domestic responsibilities of their families, and children to grow up prepared for a future in which the significance of sex difference is greatly diminished. Men could participate equally in the nurturance of their children, from infancy and throughout childhood, with predictably great effects on themselves, their wives or partners, and their children. And women need not become vulnerable through economic dependence. In addition, such arrangements would alleviate the qualms many people have about the long hours that some children spend in day care. If one parent of a preschooler worked, for example, from eight to four o'clock and the other from ten to six o'clock, a preschool child would be at day care for only six hours (including nap time), and with each one or both of her or his parents the rest of the day. If each parent were able to work a six-hour day, or a four-day week, still less day care would be needed. Moreover, on-site provision of day care would enable mothers to continue to nurse, if they chose, beyond the time of their parental leave.[12]

The situation of single parents and their children is more complicated, but it seems that it too, for a number of reasons, would be much improved in a society in which sex difference was accorded an absolute minimum of social significance. Let us begin by looking at the situation of never-married mothers and their children. First, the occurrence of pregnancy among single teenagers, which is almost entirely unintended, would presumably be reduced if girls grew up more assertive and self-protective, and with less tendency to perceive their futures primarily in terms of motherhood. It could also be significantly reduced by the wide availability of sex education and contraception.[13] Second, the added weight of responsibility given to fatherhood in a gender-free society would surely give young men more incentive than they now have not to incur the results of careless sexual behavior until they were ready to take on the responsibilities of being parents. David Ellwood has outlined a policy for establishing the paternity of all children of single mothers at the time of birth, and for enforcing the requirement that their fathers contribute to their support throughout childhood, with provision for governmental backup support in cases where the father is unable to pay. These proposals seem eminently fair and sensible, although the minimum levels of support suggested ($1500 to $2000 per year) are inadequate, especially since the mother is presumed to be either taking care of the child herself or paying for day care (which often costs far more than this) while she works.[14]

Third, never-married mothers would benefit greatly from a work structure that took parenthood seriously into account, as well as from the subsidization of high-quality day care. Women who grew up with the expectation that their work lives would be as important a part of their futures as the work lives of men would be less likely to enter dead-ended, low-skilled occupations, and would be better able to cope economically with parenthood without marriage.

Most single parenthood results, however, not from single mothers giving birth, but from marital separation and divorce. And this too would be significantly altered in a society not structured along the lines of gender. Even if rates of divorce were to remain unchanged (which is impossible to predict), it seems inconceivable that separated and divorced fathers who had shared equally in the nurturance of their children from the outset would be as likely to neglect them, by not seeing them or not contributing to their support, as many do today. It seems reasonable to expect that children after divorce would still have two actively involved parents, and two working adults economically responsible for them. Because these parents had shared equally the paid work and the family work, their incomes would be much more equal than those of most divorcing parents today. Even if they were quite equal, however, the parent without physical custody should be required to contribute to the child's support, *to the point where the standards of living of the two households were the same*. This would be very different from the situation of many children of divorced parents today, dependent for both their nurturance and their economic support solely on mothers whose wage work has been interrupted by primary parenting.

It is impossible to predict all the effects of moving toward a society without gender. Major current injustices to women and children would end. Men would experience both the joys and the responsibilities of far closer and more sustained contact with their children than many have today. Many immensely influential spheres of life – notably politics and the professional occupations – would for the first time be populated more or less equally by men and women, most of whom were also actively participating parents. This would be in great contrast to today, when most of those who rise to influential positions are either men who, if fathers, have minimal contact with their children, or women who have either forgone motherhood altogether or hired others as full-time caretakers for their children because of the demands of their careers. These are the people who make policy at the highest levels – policies not only *about* families and their welfare and about the education of children, but about the foreign policies, the wars and the weapons that will determine the future or the lack of future for all these families and children. Yet they are almost all people who gain the influence they do in part by never having had the day-to-day experience of nurturing a child. This is probably the most significant aspect of our gendered division of labor, though the least possible to grasp. The effects of changing it could be momentous.

Protecting the Vulnerable

The pluralism of beliefs and modes of life is fundamental to our society, and the genderless society I have just outlined would certainly not be agreed upon by all as desirable. Thus when we think about constructing relations between the sexes that could be agreed upon in the original position, and are therefore just from all points of view, we must also design institutions and practices acceptable to those with more traditional beliefs about the characteristics of men and women, and the appropriate division of labor between them. It is essential, if men and women are to be allowed to so divide their labor, as they must be if we are to respect the current pluralism of beliefs, that society protect the vulnerable. Without such protection, the marriage contract seriously exacerbates the initial inequalities of those who entered into it, and too many women and children live perilously close to economic disaster and serious social dislocation; too many also live with violence or the continual threat of it. It should be noted here that the rights and obligations that the law would need to promote and mandate in order to protect the vulnerable need not – and should not – be designated in accordance with sex, but in terms of different functions or roles performed. There are only a minute percentage of "househusbands" in this country, and a very small number of men whose work lives take second priority after their wives'. But they can quite readily be protected by the same institutional structures that can protect traditional and quasi-traditional wives, so long as these are designed without reference to sex.

Gender-structured marriage, then, needs to be regarded as a currently necessary institution (because still chosen by some) but one that is socially problematic. It should be subjected to a number of legal requirements, at least when there are children.[15] Most important, there is no need for the division of labor between the sexes to involve the economic dependence, either complete or partial, of one partner on the other. Such dependence can be avoided if both partners have *equal legal entitlement* to all earnings coming into the household. The clearest and simplest way of doing this would be to have employers make out wage checks equally divided between the earner and the partner who provides all or most of his or her unpaid domestic services. In many cases, of course, this would not change the way couples actually manage their finances; it would simply codify what they already agree on – that the household income is rightly shared, because in a real sense jointly earned. Such couples recognize the fact that the wage-earning spouse is no more supporting the homemaking and child-rearing spouse than the latter is supporting the former; the form of support each offers the family is simply different. Such couples might well take both checks, deposit them in a joint account, and really share the income, just as they now do with the earnings that come into the household.

In the case of some couples, however, altering the entitlement of spouses to the earned income of the household as I have suggested *would* make a significant difference. It would make a difference in cases where the earning or higher-earning partner now directly exploits this power, by refusing to make significant spending decisions jointly, by failing to share the income, or by psychologically or physically abusing the nonearning or low-earning partner, reinforced by the notion that she (almost always the wife) has little option but to put up with such abuse or to take herself and her children into a state of destitution. It would make a difference, too, in cases where the higher-earning partner indirectly exploits this earning power in order to perpetuate the existing division of labor in the family. In such instances considerable changes in the balance of power would be likely to result from the legal and societal recognition that the partner who does most of the domestic work of the family contributes to its well-being just as much, and therefore rightly *earns* just as much, as the partner who does most of the workplace work.

What I am suggesting is *not* that the wage-working partner pay the homemaking partner for services rendered. I do not mean to introduce the cash nexus into a personal relationship where it is inappropriate. I have simply suggested that since both partners in a traditional or quasi-traditional marriage work, there is no reason why only one of them should get paid, or why one should be paid far more than the other. The equal splitting of wages would constitute public recognition of the fact that the currently unpaid labor of families is just as important as the paid labor. If we do *not* believe this, then we should insist on the complete and equal sharing of both paid and unpaid labor, as occurs in the genderless model of marriage and parenting described earlier. It is only if we *do* believe it that society can justly allow couples to distribute the two types of labor so unevenly. But in such cases, given the enormous significance our society attaches to money and earnings, we should insist that the earnings be recognized as equally earned by the two persons. To call on Walzer's language, we should do this in order to help prevent the inequality of family members in the sphere of wage work to invade their domestic sphere.

It is also important to point out that this proposal does not constitute unwarranted invasion of privacy or any more state intervention into the life of families than currently exists. It would involve only the same kind of invasion of privacy as is now required by such things as registration of marriages and births, and the filing of tax returns declaring numbers and names of dependents. And it *seems* like intervention in families only because it would alter the existing relations of power within them. If a person's capacity to fulfill the terms of his or her work is dependent on having a spouse at home who raises the children and in other ways sustains that worker's day-to-day life, then it is no more interventionist to pay both equally for their contributions than only to pay one.

The same fundamental principle should apply to separation and divorce, to the extent that the division of labor has been practiced within a marriage. Under current divorce laws, as we have seen, the terms of exit from marriage are disadvantageous for almost all women in traditional or quasi-traditional marriages. Regardless of the consensus that existed about the division of the family labor, these women lose most of the income that has supported them *and* the social status that attached to them because of their husband's income and employment, often at the same time as suddenly becoming single parents, and prospective wage workers for the first time in many years. This combination of prospects would seem to be enough to put most traditional wives off the idea of divorcing even if they had good cause to do so. In addition, since divorce in the great majority of states no longer requires the consent of both spouses, it seems likely that wives for whom divorce would spell economic and social catastrophe would be inhibited in voicing their dissatisfactions or needs within marriage. The terms of exit are very likely to affect the use and the power of voice in the ongoing relationship. At worst, these women may be rendered virtually defenseless in the face of physical or psychological abuse. This is not a system of marriage and divorce that could possibly be agreed to by persons in an original position in which they did not know whether they were to be male or female, traditionalist or not. It is a fraudulent contract, presented as beneficial to all but in fact to the benefit only of the more powerful.

For all these reasons, it seems essential that the terms of divorce be redrawn so as to reflect the gendered or nongendered character of the marriage that is ending, to a far greater extent than they do now.[16] The legal system of a society that allows couples to divide the labor of families in a traditional or quasi-traditional manner *must* take responsibility for the vulnerable position in which marital breakdown places the partner who has completely or partially lost the capacity to be economically self-supporting. When such a marriage ends, it seems wholly reasonable to expect a person whose career has been largely unencumbered by domestic responsibilities to support financially the partner who undertook these responsibilities. This support, in the form of combined alimony and child support, should be far more substantial than the token levels often ordered by the courts now. *Both postdivorce households should enjoy the same standard of living.* Alimony should not end after a few years, as the (patronizingly named) "rehabilitative alimony" of today does; it should continue for at least as long as the traditional division of labor in the marriage did and, in the case of short-term marriages that produced children, until the youngest child enters first grade and the custodial parent has a real chance of making his or her own living. After that point, child support should continue at a level that enables the children to enjoy a standard of living equal to that of the noncustodial parent. There can be no reason consistent with principles of justice that some should suffer economically vastly more than others from the breakup of a relationship whose asymmetric division of labor was mutually agreed on.

I have suggested two basic models of family rights and responsibilities, both of which are currently needed because this is a time of great transition for men and women and great disagreement about gender. Families in which roles and responsibilities are equally shared regardless of sex are far more in accord with principles of justice than are typical families today. So are families in which those who undertake more traditional domestic roles are protected from the risks they presently incur. In either case, justice as a whole will benefit from the changes. Of the two, however, I claim that the genderless family is more just, in the three important respects that I spelled out at the beginning of this book: it is more just to women; it is more conducive to equal opportunity both for women and for children of both sexes; and it creates a more favorable environment for the rearing of citizens of a just society. Thus, while protecting those whom gender now makes vulnerable, we must also put our best efforts into promoting the elimination of gender.

The increased justice to women that would result from moving away from gender is readily apparent. Standards for just social institutions could no longer take for granted and exclude from considerations of justice much of what women now do, since men would share in it equally. Such central components of justice as what counts as productive labor, and what count as needs and deserts, would be greatly affected by this change. Standards of justice would become *humanist*, as they have never been before. One of the most important effects of this would be to change radically the situation of women as citizens. With egalitarian families, and with institutions such as workplaces and schools designed to accommodate the needs of parents and children, rather than being based as they now are on the traditional assumption that "someone else" is at home, mothers would not be virtually excluded from positions of influence in politics and the workplace. They would be represented at every level in approximately equal numbers with men.

In a genderless society, children too would benefit. They would not suffer in the ways that they do now because of the injustices done to women. It is undeniable that the family in which each of us grows up has a deeply formative influence on us – on the kind of persons we want to be as well as the kind of persons we are.[17] This is one of the reasons why one *cannot* reasonably leave the family out of "the basic structure of society," to which the principles of justice are to apply. Equality of opportunity to become what we want to be would be enhanced in two important ways by the development of families without gender and by the public policies necessary to support their development. First, the growing gap between the economic well-being of children in single-parent and those in two-parent families would be reduced. Children in single-parent families would benefit significantly if fathers were held equally responsible for supporting their children, whether married to their mothers or not; if more mothers had sustained labor force attachment; if high-quality day care were subsidized; and if the workplace were designed to accommodate parenting. These children would be far less likely to spend their formative years in conditions of poverty, with one parent struggling to fulfill the functions of two. Their life chances would be significantly enhanced.

Second, children of both sexes in gender-free families would have (as some already have) much more opportunity for self-development free from sex-role expectations and sex-typed personalities than most do now. Girls and boys who grow up in highly traditional families, in which sex difference is regarded as a determinant of everything from roles, responsibilities, and privileges to acceptable dress, speech, and modes of behavior, clearly have far less freedom to develop into whatever kind of person they want to be than do those who are raised without such constraints. It is too early for us to know a lot about the developmental outcomes and life choices of children who are equally parented by mothers and fathers, since the practice is still so recent and so rare. Persuasive theories such as Chodorow's, however, would lead us to expect much less differentiation between the sexes to result from truly shared parenting. Even now, in most cases without men's equal fathering, both the daughters and the sons of wage-working mothers have been found to have a more positive view of women and less rigid views of sex roles; the daughters (like their mothers) tend to have greater self-esteem and a more positive view of themselves as workers, and the sons, to expect equality and shared roles in their own future marriages.[18] We might well expect that with mothers in the labor force *and* with fathers as equal parents, children's attitudes and psychologies will become even less correlated with their sex. In a very crucial sense, their opportunities to become the persons they want to be will be enlarged.

Finally, it seems undeniable that the enhancement of justice that accompanies the disappearance of gender will make the family a much better place for children to develop a sense of justice. We can no longer deny the importance of the fact that families are where we first learn, by example and by how we are treated, not only how people do relate to each other but also how they *should*. How would families not built on gender be better schools of moral development? First, the example of co-equal parents with shared roles, combining love with justice, would provide a far better example of human relations for children than the domination and dependence that often occur in traditional marriage. The fairness of the distribution of labor, the equal respect, and the *inter*dependence of his or her parents would surely be a powerful first example to a child in a family with equally shared roles. Second, as I have argued, having a sense of justice requires that we be able to empathize, to abstract from our own situation and to think about moral and political issues from the points of view of others. We cannot come to either just principles or just specific decisions by thinking, as it were, as if we were nobody, or thinking from nowhere; we must, therefore, learn to think from the point of view of others, including others who are different from ourselves.

To the extent that gender is de-emphasized in our nurturing practices, this capacity would seem to be enhanced, for two reasons. First, if female primary parenting leads, as it seems to, to less distinct ego boundaries and greater capacity for empathy in female children, and to a greater tendency to self-definition and abstraction in males, then might we not expect to find the two capacities better combined in children of both sexes who are reared by parents of both sexes? Second, the experience of *being* nurturers, throughout a significant portion of our lives, also seems likely to result in an increase in empathy, and in the combination of personal moral capacities, fusing feelings with reason, that just citizens need.[19]

For those whose response to what I have argued here is the practical objection that it is unrealistic and will cost too much, I have some answers and some questions. Some of what I have suggested would not cost anything, in terms of public spending, though it would redistribute the costs and other responsibilities of rearing children more evenly between men and women. Some policies I have endorsed, such as adequate public support for children whose fathers cannot contribute, may cost more than present policies, but may not, depending on how well they work.[20] Some, such as subsidized high-quality day care, would be expensive in themselves, but also might soon be offset by other savings, since they would enable those who would otherwise be full-time child carers to be at least part-time workers.

All in all, it seems highly unlikely that the *long-term* costs of such programs – even if we count only monetary costs, not costs in human terms – would outweigh the long-term benefits. In many cases, the cycle of poverty could be broken – and children enabled to escape from, or to avoid falling into, it – through a much better early start in life.[21] But even if my suggestions would cost, and cost a lot, we have to ask: How much do we care about the injustices of gender? How much do we care that women who have spent the better part of their lives nurturing others can be discarded like used goods? How ashamed are we that one-quarter of our children, in one of the richest countries in the world, live in poverty? How much do we care that those who raise children, *because* of this choice, have restricted opportunities to develop the rest of their potential, and very little influence on society's values and direction? How much do we care that the family, our most intimate social grouping, is often a school of day-to-day injustice? How much do we *want* the just families that will produce the kind of citizens we need if we are ever to achieve a just society?

Notes

1 See Susan Moller Okin, *Gender, Justice, and the Family*, Basic Books, 1989, Ch. 3, pp. 67–8.

2 "Women: Out of the House But Not Out of the Kitchen," *New York Times*, February 24, 1988, pp. AI, C10.

3 See, for example, Marjorie Maguire Schultz, "Contractual Ordering of Marriage: A New Model for State Policy," *California Law Review* 70, no. 2 (1982); Lenore Weitzman, *The Marriage Contract: Spouses, Lovers, and the Law* (New York: The Free Press, 1981), parts 3–4.

4 See, for example, David L. Kirp, Mark G. Yudof, and Marlene Strong Franks, *Gender Justice* (Chicago: University of Chicago Press, 1986), pp. 183–5. Robert H. Mnookin takes an only slightly less laissez-faire approach, in "Divorce Bargaining: The Limits on Private Ordering," *University of Michigan Journal of Law Reform* 18, no. 4 (1985).

5 I say "so far as possible" because given the deep effects of gender on our psychologies, it is probably more difficult for us, having grown up in a gender-structured society, to imagine not knowing our sex than anything else about ourselves. Nevertheless, this should not prevent us from trying.

6 It seems reasonable to conclude that the effects of day care on children are probably just as variable as the effects of parenting – that is to say, very widely variable depending on the quality of the day care and of the parenting. There is no doubt that good out-of-home day care is expensive – approximately $100 per full-time week in 1987, even though child-care workers are now paid only about two-thirds as much per hour as other comparably educated women workers (Victor Fuchs, *Women's Quest for Economic Equality* [Cambridge: Harvard University Press, 1988], pp. 137–8). However, it is undoubtedly easier to control its quality than that of informal "family day care." In my view, based in part on my experience of the excellent day-care center that our children attended for a total of seven years, good-quality day care must have small-scale "home rooms" and a high staff-to-child ratio, and should pay staff better than most centers now do. For balanced studies of the effects of day care on a poor population, see Sally Provence, Audrey Naylor, and June Patterson, *The Challenge of Daycare* (New Haven: Yale University Press, 1977); and, most recently, Lisbeth B. Schorr (with Daniel Schorr), *Within Our Reach – Breaking the Cycle of Disadvantage* (New York: Anchor Press, Doubleday, 1988), Ch. 8.

7 Much of what I suggest here is not new; it has formed part of the feminist agenda for several decades, and I first made some of the suggestions I develop here in the concluding chapter of *Women in Western Political Thought* (Princeton: Princeton University Press, 1979). Three recent books that address some of the policies discussed here are Fuchs, *Women's Quest*, Ch. 7; Philip Green, *Retrieving Democracy: In Search of Civic Equality* (Totowa, NJ: Rowman and Allanheld, 1985), pp. 96–108; and Anita Shreve, *Remaking Motherhood: How Working Mothers Are Shaping Our Children's Future* (New York: Fawcett Columbine, 1987), pp. 173–8. In Fuchs's chapter he carefully analyzes the potential economic and social effects of alternative policies to improve women's economic status, and concludes that "child-centered policies" such as parental leave and subsidized day care are likely to have more of a positive impact on women's economic position than "labor market policies" such as antidiscrimination, comparable pay for comparable worth, and affirmative action have had and are likely to have. Some potentially very

effective policies, such as on-site day care and flexible and/or reduced working hours for parents of young or "special needs" children, seem to fall within both of his categories.

8 The dilemma faced by feminists in the recent California case *Guerra v. California Federal Savings and Loan Association*, 107 S. Ct. 683 (1987) was due to the fact that state law mandated leave for pregnancy and birth that it did *not* mandate for other disabling conditions. Thus to defend the law seemed to open up the dangers of discrimination that the earlier protection of women in the workplace had resulted in. (For a discussion of this general issue of equality versus difference, see, for example, Wendy W. Williams, "The Equality Crisis: Some Reflections on Culture, Courts, and Feminism," *Women's Rights Law Reporter* 7, no. 3 [1982].) The Supreme Court upheld the California law on the grounds that it treated workers equally in terms of their rights to become parents.

9 Amy Gutmann, *Democratic Education* (Princeton: Princeton University Press, 1987), pp. 112–15; quotation from pp. 113–14. See also Elisabeth Hansot and David Tyack, "Gender in American Public Schools: Thinking Institutionally," *Signs* 13, no. 4 (1988).

10 A classic text on this subject is Dale Spender, ed., *Men's Studies Modified: The Impact of Feminism on the Academic Disciplines* (Oxford: Pergamon Press, 1981).

11 Shreve, *Remaking Motherhood*, p. 237.

12 Although 51 percent of infants are breast-fed at birth, only 14 percent are entirely breast-fed at six weeks of age. Cited from P. Leach, *Babyhood* (New York: Alfred A. Knopf, 1983), by Sylvia Ann Hewlett in *A Lesser Life: The Myth of Women's Liberation in America* (New York: Morrow, 1986), p. 409, *n*34. Given this fact, it seems quite unjustified to argue that lactation *dictates* that mothers be the primary parents, even during infancy.

13 In Sweden, where the liberalization of abortion in the mid-1970s was accompanied by much expanded birth-control education and information and reduced-cost contraceptives, the rates of both teenage abortion and teenage birth decreased significantly. The Swedish teenage birth-rate was by 1982 less than half what it had been in the 1970s. Mary Ann Glendon, *Abortion and Divorce in Western Law* (Cambridge: Harvard University Press, 1987), p. 23 and *n*65. Chapter 3 of Schorr's *Within Our Reach* gives an excellent account of programs in the United States that have proven effective in reducing early and unplanned pregnancies. Noting the strong correlation between emotional and economic deprivation and early pregnancy, she emphasizes the importance, if teenagers are to have the incentive not to become pregnant, of their believing that they have a real stake in their own futures, and developing the aspirations and self-assertiveness that go along with this. As Victor Fuchs points out, approximately two-thirds of unmarried women who give birth are twenty or older (*Women's Quest*, p. 68). However, these women are somewhat more likely to have work skills and experience, and it seems likely that many live in informal "common law marriage" heterosexual or lesbian partnerships, rather than being *in fact* single parents.

14 David Ellwood, *Poor Support: Poverty in the American Family* (New York: Basic Books, 1988), pp. 163–74. He estimates that full-time day care for each child can be bought for $3000 per year, and half-time for $1000. He acknowledges that these estimated costs are "modest." I think they are unrealistic, unless the care is being provided by a relative or close friend. Ellwood reports that, as of 1985, only 18 percent of never-married fathers were ordered to pay child support, and only 11 percent actually paid any (p. 158).

15 Mary Ann Glendon has set out a "children first" approach to divorce (Glendon, *Abortion and Divorce*, pp. 94ff.); here I extend the same idea to ongoing marriage, where the arrival of a child is most often the point at which the wife becomes economically dependent.

I see no reason why what I propose here should be restricted to couples who are legally married. It should apply equally to "common law" relationships that produce children, and in which a division of labor is practiced.

16 My suggestions for protecting traditional and quasi-traditional wives in the event of divorce are similar to those of Lenore Weitzman in *The Divorce Revolution: The Unexpected Social and Economic Consequences for Women and Children in America* (New York: The Free Press, 1985), Ch. 11, and Mary Ann Glendon in *Abortion and Divorce*, Ch. 2. Although they would usually in practice protect traditional wives, the laws should be gender-neutral so that they would equally protect divorcing men who had undertaken the primary functions of parenting and homemaking.

17 Here I paraphrase Rawls's wording in explaining why the basic structure of society is basic. "The Basic Structure as Subject," *American Philosophical Quarterly* 14, no. 2 (1977): 160.

18 Shreve, *Remaking Motherhood*, Chs. 3–7.

19 See, for example, Sara Ruddick, "Maternal Thinking," *Feminist Studies* 6, no. 2 (1980); Diane Ehrensaft, "When Women and Men Mother," in *Mothering: Essays in Feminist Theory*, ed. Joyce Trebilcot (Totowa, NJ: Rowman and Allanheld, 1984); Judith Kegan Gardiner, "Self Psychology as Feminist Theory," *Signs* 12, no. 4 (1987), esp. 778–80.

20 David Ellwood estimates that "if most absent fathers contributed the given percentages, the program would actually save money" (*Poor Support*, p. 169).

21 Schorr's *Within Our Reach* documents the ways in which the cycle of disadvantage can be effectively broken, even for those in the poorest circumstances.

30

Feminism, Utopianism, and the Role of the Ideal in Political Philosophy

Drucilla Cornell

The Charge Against Feminism

That feminism frightens some people, challenging many established religious, traditional kinships, and cultural norms, is only too evident. That these challenges produce anxiety is hardly surprising. But the root charge against feminism – that we are totalitarians, hence "feminazis" – is deeply disturbing ethically. There are no feminist death squads, let alone concentration camps, so that the effect of the term is to trivialize the human devastation Nazism left in its wake. Yet despite the glaring inappropriateness of the comparison, the term continues to have a certain credibility in our public culture, the charge implying that if they could, feminists would forcibly impose their own vision of a sexually egalitarian society, stomping on people's basic freedoms and intimate associations.

Drucilla Cornell, "Feminism, Utopianism, and the Role of the Ideal in Political Philosophy," pp. 174–86 and 229–32 (notes) from *At the Heart of Freedom: Feminism, Sex, and Equality*. Princeton, NJ: Princeton University Press, 1998.

Is the Imaginary Domain a Bad Utopian Ideal?

In other words, feminists are "bad utopians" in that their blueprint for a good society is wholly out of touch with what is possible for actual human beings to live out in their daily home, work, or public lives. Perfectionists, feminists would reshape our natures no matter what it took, so as to transform us into creatures without gender or sex. Given the "perfectionist" experiments associated with socialist states in the twentieth century, it is hardly surprising that many people would be wary of another. More broadly speaking, the charge against utopianism is meant to indicate that the writer is simply out of touch with reality rather than armed to change it.

But can a charge of bad utopianism be made to stick against the ideal of the imaginary domain, either in the sense that it is out of touch with reality or is the ideological arm of the feminist police? I think not. Thomas Nagel has argued that the problem of utopianism almost inevitably arises in political philosophy because it "presents an ideal of collective life, and it tries to show people one by one that they should want to live under it."[1] As he points out, if political philosophy is to accomplish both tasks, the psychology of what reasonable people can be expected to accept has to be part of the justification of any ideal of political life.[2] Since a mere appeal to the badness of people cannot in and of itself be given moral weight as an argument against change without completely undercutting the ideal function of political philosophy, the key is what *reasonable* people can be expected to accept. As Nagel recognizes, this is most particularly the case because people change, indeed become ethically better or worse depending on their political, economic, and social circumstances. Thus it is that people will be able to change enough to accept a political ideal, and this changing can be part of what it means to include psychological motivation in the justification of the ideal itself.

The question then becomes: Can we expect reasonable people to accept the ideal of the imaginary domain? Currently, the basic idea of reasonableness in political liberalism is that each of us accords each other the recognition that each is to be treated as a free and equal person before both the law and within the other basic institutions of our society. The heat generated by the dispute over "family values" and the attacks on feminazis show that the vast majority of heterosexuals feel very strongly about their right to orient themselves to their own sexuality and establish intimate associations in their own way. They stress over and over again how important their families are to them, how important it is to them that they be the ones to give meaning to the place of love and sex in life, not some outside political or moral authority. The one real exception to this desire to be free of outside political and moral authority is the fathers' movement, which has based its argument in part on men's incapacity to be reasonable. Arguing with heterosexual men won't help, so the story goes, since they can't hear the reasons through the roar of their hormones. I will only note here my acceptance of the Kantian ethical presupposition that all human beings, including straight white men, have the capacity for reasonableness.

The question then becomes, is it reasonable for people to deny to others what they insist upon as a matter of right for themselves? The answer to that is of course no. It cannot be reasonable to degrade those who have chosen a sexuality and family life that does not match some norm that others hold dear by treating them as something less than free and equal persons. Thus, if lesbian couples are not allowed to be parents, they are clearly being compelled to live out lives in ways not of their own choosing.

Here again, the value of an interpretative approach to the discontinuity thesis is seen to allow us to distinguish between those who want to impose their view of what appropriate sex is on everyone else and those who argue that as sexuate beings all of us have to be accorded treatment as free and equal persons. I need to stress this point. The discontinuity thesis demands that we separate our own individual concepts of the good from what we can impose on all of us as a matter of right, given our equal standing as persons. To read the imaginary domain as an endorsement of one kind of sexual life or intimate association misses the philosophical basis on which it is defended. The separation of the right from the good is crucial for the recognition of our equal personhood precisely because our own deeply held convictions about what is good for us sexually may push us in the direction of thinking that our way is the only way. A lesbian couple taking on parenting does not in any way interfere with a heterosexual couple's right to parenthood; rather, both couples should have the right to set up their intimate lives in the way they imagine is best for them.

Some heterosexuals have argued that the open existence of gays and lesbians violates their "right" to live out their lives as they see fit – a life free of the presence of gays and lesbians. But what in fact they are claiming is the right to control access to public space in accordance with what they define as "good" sexuality.[3] In a politically liberal society, such discrimination would violate the rights of others to be treated as free and equal persons. Moreover, the presence of openly gay and lesbian persons in no way denies equal personhood to anyone, nor does it create hierarchical gradations of sexual difference that mark some as persons less worthy of happiness. We are all to be left with the right to orient ourselves sexually and make our families as we see fit.

To argue that the privileging of one form of sexuality or family is inconsistent with equal treatment of persons seeks only to end the *privilege* of heterosexual families, not that form of family.[4] To confuse the two positions is to fail to see that political recognition of the right in matters of the heart demands discontinuity between what any one of us thinks is good sexually for us or for other people, including our children, from what can be imposed by the laws and basic institutions of society. The right of each adult person to self-representation of his or her sexuate being is what is reasonably to be expected in a politically liberal culture because without it, public recognition of each one of us as a free person would be seriously undermined if not altogether denied. Here we should note that the imaginary domain is neither out of touch with the ideals of a politically liberal culture nor does it explicitly endorse, or worse yet enforce, any nontraditional, non-heterosexual relationship as the "good" relationship.

In our society, some ways of seeing the world and relationships are simply not available to people deeply divided by race and class and, indeed, by our engendering into two sexes. But the experience of valuing the freedom to orient oneself sexually and live openly with loved ones is actually widely shared. Of course, homophobic denial blocks awareness of how horrific it is for a lesbian mother to lose custody of her children simply because she lives openly with her lover. Still, we can appeal to what all humans share in our struggle to have others recognize that the importance of love, sex, and family is no less important just because one is not heterosexual. That these values are widely shared affords a strong basis for our further argument against having the state interfere in the sexual lives of *any* consenting adults, of whom very few would want to have the state in their bedroom.

I do not mean to trivialize the power of denial or underestimate the role of unconscious fantasies underpinning the so-called judgments people often make condemning the sex lives of others. It is indeed difficult to reflect on one's sex or on one's sexual desires, which draw us into the deepest recesses of our unconscious fantasy life. Sex and desire are common denominators, and by valuing them for themselves, people can see the freedom that should be given to all others in the name of the fundamental public values of a politically liberal culture.[5]

In the last fifty years families in the United States have changed drastically. A lesbian baby boom would have been unimaginable in the 1950s. The ideal of the imaginary domain gives form to what is actually happening. People are claiming the space, both psychic and public, for a self-representation of their sexuate being. One aspect of Stonewall was the absolute refusal on the part of gay men and lesbians to concede that just being gay made someone an outlaw.[6] To give symbolic form to what is being claimed in actuality is part of the role of *ideals* in political philosophy.

The Desirability of Stabilization

To demand the imaginary domain as a matter of right is to seek stabilization of the political recognition of the moral status of gays, lesbians, women, and other forms of sexuate being that are being dreamed up around the world. For some activists and theorists, the demand for stabilization inherent in the concept of right makes all "rights talk" suspect.[7] Better to do without stabilization, to give up fighting for the right, in the name of keeping all possibilities for struggle open. For example, the labor movement in this country long disputed the question of whether or not it was desirable for unions to seek legal recognition.[8] The argument is that laws can always be used against those who advocate them, and rights are only so much paper unless there is someone or some movement to demand their enforcement.

While appreciating the valid political worry about the double edged sword of the role of enunciated rights in limiting what can be open to political contest, I do not believe it is applicable here. It is helpful to frame this distinction in the terms of temporality. Insofar as they are lasting, enunciated rights fix a desirable present into the future, thus closing out future possibilities for liberation and potentially reinforcing existing power structures they were meant to challenge. But in the end, what is stabilized is the right of the person to claim herself as her own design. Rather than freezing the present, it asserts the right to future possibilities. This protection of the future inherent in the definition of the ideal can help free our political struggle from the burden of past identities, both singular and collective, as the only truth of who we are. Of course this freedom will be sought within the symbolic material that shapes the imaginary domain, symbolic material that consists of representational forms, unconscious fantasies, and prohibitions through which we have been gendered. Our right to our imaginary domain does not disavow the material constraints of how we are sexed, but is a right to imagine, represent, and symbolize the meaning of the material constituents of sex and gender as we lead our lives as sexuate beings. So defined, the ideal does not endorse any theory of the truth of women's identity. Thus, it cannot easily be charged with reinforcing what it seeks to challenge – women's identity as the unequal sex.

Of course, the demand for this right is deeply destabilizing in societies, including our own, in light of what has not been granted, which is why many Western feminists have historically been ambivalent about the political possibilities in a demand for equal rights.[9] But to demand rights provides a rallying call precisely because it can give form to political struggle and, at least in the West, can tie feminism to some of the most fundamental concepts of social order in modern Western democracy.[10] As I have argued throughout this book, a person's right to the self-representation of her sexuate being is a conclusion logically drawn from the politically liberal understanding of what the recognition of us all as free and equal persons means; moreover, it is inconsistent with privileging any one form of the family as good and so to be imposed upon us all by the state or by the basic institutions of society.

What is Legitimate Stability in Kantian Political Philosophy?

No doubt the institutionalization of this right would be destabilizing to those who have been brought up to expect that women and gays and lesbians would not and should not have it. But this kind of destabilization cannot morally count against change since it turns on the expectation that some of us, because of our sexuate being, will continue to be graded down, treated as less than free and equal persons. As Rawls has argued, only a just society can claim any legitimate basis for stability, and as we have seen, the principles of a just society can be generated only through a representational device that postulates all persons as free and equal.

The demand that women be evaluated as free and equal persons is thus a condition for legitimate stability. No use of the imaginary domain is utopian in the sense that Nagel describes: "A project of transformation is often condemned as utopian if it will not lead to a result which is stable in this sense – a result which generates its own support by calling forth new possibilities of mutual respect and recognition of moral equality through adherence to co-operative institutions."[11] If women were recognized as free and equal persons, our current form of social organization would clearly be shaken up. People would undoubtedly be called upon to change, since certain social forms could no longer be assumed as just in the normal course of things – for example, that men would have wives who did most of the child care. Of course, men could still be free to try to set up their lives in this way, and nothing would prevent women from seeking out and valuing a traditional family life. But it would be foolish to say that the changes would not be far reaching, since patriarchal social, political, and cultural forms have been a mainstay of what we think of as civilization.

But the changes demanded by the political recognition of the ideal of the imaginary domain would not controvert anyone's freedom. What kinds of psychic and ethical changes would actually take place would be left to us. Moreover, these kinds of changes would take time. More important, no one would be legally, let alone violently, forced to change. Supposedly, the fear of feminism has been that it forces people into one sexual model because that is the only way to end male domination. But the imaginary domain insists, on the contrary, that as a matter of right we should not impose any model of sexual life but rather that people should be allowed to craft their own. To give people this freedom does not mean that they have to use it in any particular way. The ideal of the imaginary domain narrowly tailored in the name of the freedom it seeks to protect sharply parts ways with feminist projects of transformation that try to give content to what sex can mean by enforcing legal definitions of either femininity or masculinity, so as to end male domination.[12] The degradation prohibition that I defend does allow for certain forms of sexual conduct to be legally regulated, but only to the extent that they controvert the recognition of all of us as free and equal persons.[13]

The Imaginary Domain and Gender Identification

When the imaginary domain is politically defended as a matter of right, there is no appeal to a moral condemnation of the value of gender identification or of any particular form of family. If we stayed with Kant's moral philosophy alone, the value of gender identification would be called sharply into question. Christine Korsgaard has made this argument powerfully:

> According to an old quip, Christianity has not been tried and found too difficult, but rather has been found too difficult and so not tried. Despite some currently popular claims about the bankruptcy of the

> Enlightenment, I believe that this is true of Enlightenment ideals. Communitarians, champions of the family, and the promoters of ethnic and gender-identification may suppose that they have somehow discovered that the ideal of the sovereign individual is inadequate for human flourishing. But the truth is that many of them have balked when they realized how different a world that respects the ideal would have to be from the one we live in now. The centrality of gender is one of the things that would have to go.[14]

I agree with Korsgaard that if we solely remain with the Kantian ideal of freedom, it would demand that little or no value be given to gender identity; but we have learned much about the complexity of sex since Kant's time, so that we cannot dismiss easily the complexity of sexual difference.

The political and ethical justification of the imaginary domain and an understanding of what sexual freedom can be for gendered beings are tempered by the recognition of psychoanalytic insight. Thus we are conscious of the moorings of our own symbolic order, of the meanings of masculinity and femininity, and of how the deep desires human beings have are shaped by the intertwinement of real and fantasied relationships from which we can never fully extricate ourselves. This recognition of the complexity of sex and gender identifications, although in no way an argument against the Kantian ideal of freedom, does demand its reformulation. People cannot and should not be legally forced to confront, let alone revalue, identifications that have made them who they are. But people *can* be given the psychic and moral space for the exploration of new possibilities and for the chance to rework the fabric of the web of meanings out of which the self is spun. This then is what the imaginary domain offers as a legal and political ideal.

On the other hand, a full-blown feminist ethical justification for the imaginary domain clearly implies doubt as to the *value* of rigid gender identification. Judith Butler has written "of the cost of articulating a coherent identity position by producing, excluding, and repudiating a domain of abjected specters that threaten the arbitrarily closed domain of subject positions."[15]

The imaginary domain as both a psychic and a moral space for recovery of "new" and "old" identifications demands that we not be subjected, as a matter of law, to an "arbitrarily closed domain of subject positions."[16] Toni Morrison captures the effect of this closed domain in her novel *Sula* when she writes, "Nobody knew my rose of the world but me.... I had too much glory. They don't want glory like *that* in nobody's heart."[17] The ethic that one not only can, but should, represent a range of identifications is what opens up the space for a woman with glory in her heart.

Is it utopian to argue that we can and should keep space open for the representations of "new" and "old" identifications through which we reimagine and reshape who we are? Some schools of psychoanalysis would clearly say yes, since they insist that the basic repression upon which civilization is founded is the symbolization of the relationship to the mother. According to one version of the Freudian story, human beings become adults by turning toward the father, both for an actual relationship and as the master image of the ideal human being. But what is repressed is still always "there," and the debate among psychoanalysts is what can be made with the "thereness" that is there. Again, some schools of psychoanalysis warn us off this project as dangerous to psychic and political "health."[18]

But whose health? And at what cost? The cost to us is that, as women, we are denied a symbolizable relationship with the Mother and to the feminine. We are left with a dearth of symbolizations of the feminine and of sexual difference, not the least because these images are presented to us with racial stereotypes already in the picture. The feminine escapes us because its meanings cannot be pinned down, except for the elusive ideal of the desirable Woman ever present in the media. But these ideals project an object of desire, not a person who can reimagine herself through reidentification while keeping the meaning of who she is in motion. Heterosexual white men, seemingly privileged ones, have an established ideal that is held out for them to meet – thus, they do not seem to be buried under a slew of contradictory images of what it means to be "sexy" – but what does their privilege amount to? The little boy can identify with masculine cultures through his likeness to the Father – both have the penis – but only by subjecting himself to the codes of masculinity.[19] The psychic organization of the masculine subject is guaranteed a fixed position in the realm of phallic reference. But the price paid for this position is that all other forms of identification, particularly with the feminine other, must be abjected. For almost every man, the fantasy that he has the phallus is always belied by his relations with actual men in the hierarchical world of work. Thus, he can always lose what gives him identity by being pushed out of the boys' club, by being exposed as a "sissy" and one who "can't cut it."

Of course, the story of civilization and its discontents is highly speculative and has been sharply challenged for so being.[20] But it has become part of our shared cultural knowledge and, indeed, even our sense of reality, that gender identity cannot be challenged because it psychoanalytically grounds the possibility of adulthood. The Kantian argument defended in this book is that no matter how seemingly rooted in social reality gender identification might be now, this reality cannot be used to exclude women from the moral community of persons. As a moral and political matter, women must be left free.

A deontological theory can seem utopian because it insists on the separation between right and reality. But it is just this separation that makes a broad deontology so powerful in feminist theory. First, it shifts the grounds on which critics can challenge feminism as unrealistic: on the level of right, it does not matter whether or not "in reality" women have ever been free or not. Second, it foregrounds the centrality of freedom in feminist politics because it does not begin its argument for equality through an appeal to our likeness to men but to our political recognition as free persons who must be given the moral and psychic space to represent how women see themselves as sexuate beings. The role of the imaginary domain, as of any ideal, is to represent the separation of right from reality, and to maintain the critical edge that delimits the conflation of the two.

Feminism also challenges the idea that rigid gender identity is so firmly rooted in reality that we cannot imagine new ways of being "sexed" that are less costly to both men and women.[21] A good definition of *utopian* is that what is possible cannot be known in advance of social transformation. This is the sense of *utopian* I have consistently defended[22] because of the pride of place given to the imagination, including its function as fundamental to reason.

Let us not forget that Rawls's hypothetical experiment in imagination allows him to represent the rationality of the principles of justice. I agree completely with Rawls that we need representational devices in political philosophy;[23] and indeed, that the imaginary domain should be understood to help us represent what the original position demands in terms of the equivalent evaluation of sexual difference. My only disagreement with Rawls, at least the Rawls of *A Theory of Justice*, is that the form of justice, including the principles of justice, cannot and should not be figured once and for all.[24]

As with the principles of justice, so with ourselves. How we know who we are and how we have been formed sexually is part of a complex process through which we formulate a self with a personal story. Because who we could become in a society in which women were fully recognized as free and equal persons is not yet possible for us to experience, the process of reimagining ourselves does not have an end point.

Utopianism has always been tied to the imagination, to visions of what is truly new. A world in which we could all share in life's glories would be one radically different from our own society. Yet what is possible always changes as we change with the transformations we try to realize. Is it then utopian to think that we could share in life's glories? Is it a mere fantasy, or is the presence of the dream *itself* not proof enough that it might be possible? At last it is up to us to turn yesterday's utopia into a new sense of reality.

Notes

1 Thomas Nagel, *Equality and Partiality* (New York: Oxford University Press, 1991), p. 21.

2 For Nagel this intertwinement of the ideal with the persuasive functions of political philosophy is what distinguishes it from other branches of knowledge such as scientific truth. Ibid., p. 23.

3 See Judith Stacey, *In the Name of the Family: Rethinking Family Values in the Postmodern Age* (Boston: Beacon Press, 1996), Ch. 5 for an overview of the debates surrounding gay and lesbian families.

4 See Andrew J. Cherlin, *The Changing American Family and Public Policy* (Washington, D.C.: Urban Institute Press, 1988), for an account of the ways in which heterosexual families are privileged by state policy.

5 Maggie Gallagher, *The Abolition of Marriage: How We Destroy Lasting Love* (Washington, D.C.: Regnery Publishing, 1996).

6 See John D'Emilio, "A New Beginning: The Birth of Gay Liberation," in *Sexual Politics, Sexual Communities: The Making of a Homosexual Minority*

in the United States, 1940–1970 (Chicago: University of Chicago Press, 1983), Ch. 12.

7 For a very sophisticated and illuminating genealogy of rights and their limits, see Wendy Brown, *States of Injury: Power and Freedom in Late Modernity* (Princeton: Princeton University Press, 1995), p. 97.

8 See Thomas Geoghegan, *Which Side Are You On? Trying to Be for Labor When It's Flat on Its Back* (New York: Farrar, Straus and Giroux, 1991).

9 Joan Wallach Scott, *Only Paradoxes to Offer: French Feminists and the Rights of Man* (Cambridge: Harvard University Press, 1996).

10 Ibid., for discussion of paradoxes that are inherent in this rallying call.

11 Nagel, *Equality and Partiality*.

12 See Drucilla Cornell, *The Imaginary Domain: Abortion, Pornography, and Sexual Harassment* (New York: Routledge, 1995).

13 For my discussion of the degradation prohibition and of sexual harassment more generally, see Ch. 4 in *The Imaginary Domain*.

14 Christine M. Korsgaard, "A Note on the Value of Gender-Identification," in *Women, Culture, and Development: A Study of Human Capabilities*, ed. Martha Nussbaum and Jonathan Glover (Oxford: Clarendon Press, 1995) p. 402.

15 Judith Butler, *The Psychic Life of Power: Theories in Subjection* (Stanford, Calif.: Stanford University Press, 1997) p. 49.

16 Ibid.

17 Toni Morrison, *Sula* (New York: Knopf, 1973), epigraph.

18 See *Feminine Sexuality: Jacques Lacan and the école freudienne*, ed. Juliet Mitchell and Jacqueline Rose, trans. Jacqueline Rose (New York: W. W. Norton, 1985).

19 See Cornell, "What Is Ethical Feminism?" in *Feminist Contentions: A Philosophical Exchange* (New York: Routledge, 1995), for a longer discussion of this basically Lacanian theory of sexual difference.

20 Sigmund Freud, *Civilization and Its Discontents*, ed. and trans. James Strachey (New York: W. W. Norton, 1962).

21 For my understanding of how it is possible for us to live "beyond accommodation," see *Beyond Accommodation: Ethical Feminism and the Deconstruction of Law* (New York: Routledge, 1991).

22 This interpretation of the ethical service provided by an analysis of the limits of theoretical reason obviously breaks with the idea of utopianism associated with socialist experiments. Marx himself was a bitter foe of utopianism, seeking to displace dreams and fantasies of an ideal society with rigorous scientific analysis of the inherent contradictions of capitalism. Still, in the twentieth century, socialism came to be identified with utopianism in the sense that communist parties sought to impose that truth of the good by force, if necessary, if this good conflicted with the economic and political aspirations of the persons living in those societies. What I have defended as the moment of utopianism inherent in deconstruction counters the conflation of possibility and reality because theoretical reason is limited and thus kept from grasping the truth of what can be actualized. I argue that the impossibility of knowing what is possible is what keeps open social transformations and new realities that cannot yet be thought, because they are inconceivable within the constraints of our current symbolic order (See Drucilla Cornell, *The Philosophy of the Limit* [New York: Routledge, 1992]).

Socialism as actualized in the five-year plans of the Soviet Union was often reduced to a utilitarian calculus in which the political and economic good was forcibly imposed. Such plans necessarily implied that the good could be theoretically calculated in advance. The irony of the scientific socialism is that it ignored the category of novelty in the name of certain truth. My argument has been, on the contrary, that what is truly new, and what the utopian aspirations are to achieve it, should not be trivialized as unrealistic, because the truth of what is possible cannot be theoretically derived from reality.

23 The ethical desirability for representational devices in political philosophy has been challenged by Heideggerians. I am well aware that many Heideggerians would not phrase the objection in that way since, for Heidegger, the ethical is also challenged as an ontic and thus not a philosophical category. "Ethically desirable" is not a Heideggerian phrase.

Of course, it is impossible to be fair in an endnote to the richness of the Heideggerian suspicion of representation. Still, I feel compelled at least to note the objection since it remains a serious challenge to all forms of Kantian political philosophy and, indeed, to the idea of political philosophy itself. In crude summary, Heidegger challenged Western philosophy for the reduction of Being to its representations, a reduction inseparable from the domination of technological reason (*The Question Concerning Technology and Other Essays*, trans. William Lovitt [New York: Harper and Row, 1977]). Political philosophy, so the argument goes, no matter how it attempts to distinguish instrumental rationality from reason, will be implicated in the eclipse of Being and the perpetuation of teleological theory since it seeks to implement the representation of political possibility that still stands in for what cannot be adequately represented.

Of course many Heideggerians understand that "representation" is inevitable, but hold strongly only that hypothetical experiments in the imagination cannot escape capture by teleological reason. (See John D. Caputo, *Radical Hermeneutics: Repetition, Deconstruction, and the Hermeneutic Project* [Bloomington:

Indiana University Press, 1987], Chs 9 and 10; and Reiner Schurmann, *Heidegger on Being and Acting: From Principles to Anarchy* [Bloomington: Indiana University Press, 1987].) The rejection of political philosophy as *necessary* "perceptual teleology" is of course not the only rereading of Heidegger. (See "Political Philosophy Today" and "Ontology of Freedom: Heidegger and Political Philosophy," in Fred R. Dallmayr, *Polis and Praxis: Exercises in Contemporary Political Theory* [Cambridge: MIT Press, 1984]).

If theoretical knowledge is claimed from these experiments in the imagination so that knowledge of political philosophy is determined by them, then I would agree that these experiments have lost their "experimental" character and have indeed become a "perceptual teleology." In this sense, Rawls's statements in *A Theory of Justice* that the hypothetical experiment in the imagination could determine the principles of justice would be a "perceptual teleology." In his later works, Rawls's insistence on the humility of philosophy imposed by political liberalism seems a significant step away from a perceptual teleology (See "The Law of Peoples" *Critical Theory* [Autumn 1993]).

My own position, again in crude summary, is that just because we are stuck with representations of ourselves and our world, we are ethically called upon to reimagine, to give form to political principles. The metaphor of the imaginary domain is obviously one example of such an effort to reimagine the legal form society should give to persons as sexuate beings.

24 Rawls may no longer hold that position in *Political Liberalism* (New York: Columbia University Press, 1993).

Index